The First Book
—Rita Dove

Open it.
Go ahead, it won't bite.
Well . . . maybe a little.

More a nip, like. A tingle.
It's pleasurable, really.

You see, it keeps on opening.
You may fall in.

Sure, it's hard to get started;
remember learning to use

knife and fork? Dig in:
You'll never reach bottom.

It's not like it's the end of the world—
just the world as you think

you know it.

Rita Dove served as Poet Laureate of the United States and Consultant to the Library of Congress from 1993 to 1995 and is currently Poet Laureate of the Commonwealth of Virginia. She has received numerous literary and academic honors, among them the 1987 Pulitzer Prize in Poetry and, most recently, the 2003 Emily Couric Leadership Award, the 2001 Duke Ellington Lifetime Achievement Award, the 1997 Sara Lee Frontrunner Award, the 1997 Barnes & Noble Writers for Writers Award, the 1996 Heinz Award in the Arts and Humanities, and the 1996 National Humanities Medal.

LANGUAGE ARTS WORKSHOP

PURPOSEFUL READING AND WRITING INSTRUCTION

Nancy Frey
San Diego State University

Douglas B. Fisher
San Diego State University

PEARSON

Merrill
Prentice Hall

Upper Saddle River, New Jersey
Columbus, Ohio

Library of Congress Cataloging-in-Publication Data

Frey, Nancy
  Language arts workshop : purposeful reading and writing instruction / Nancy Frey, Douglas B. Fisher.
    p.cm.
  Includes bibliographical references and index.
  ISBN 0–13–111732–7
  1. Language arts—Correlation with content subjects. 2. Literacy instruction. 3. Interdisciplinary approach in education.
I. Fisher, Douglas—II. Title.

  LB1631.F73 2005
  428'.43—dc22   2004027552

Vice President and Executive Publisher: Jeffery W. Johnston
Senior Editor: Linda Ashe Montgomery
Senior Development Editor: Hope Madden
Senior Production Editor: Mary M. Irvin
Senior Editorial Assistant: Laura Weaver
Design Coordinator: Diane C. Lorenzo
Photo Coordinator: Maria B. Vonada
Production Coordination and Text Design: Thistle Hill Publishing Services, LLC
Cover Designer: Bryan Huber
Cover Image: Anthony Magnacca/Merrill
Production Manager: Pamela D. Bennett
Director of Marketing: Ann Castel Davis
Marketing Manager: Darcy Betts Prybella
Marketing Coordinator: Brian Mounts

This book was set in Garamond by Carlisle Communications, Ltd. It was printed and bound by R. R. Donnelley and Sons Company, Inc. The cover was printed by Coral Graphic Services, Inc.

Photo Credits: Anne Vega/Merrill, 3, 205, 329; Scott Cunningham/Merrill, 33, 119, 153, 365; Anthony Magnacca/Merrill, 69, 271; David Mager/Pearson Learning Photo Studio, 237; Linda Peterson/Merrill, 303.

Pearson Education Ltd.
Pearson Education Singapore Pte. Ltd.
Pearson Eduation Canada, Ltd.
Pearson Education—Japan

Pearson Education Australia Pty. Limited
Pearson Education North Asia Ltd.
Pearson Education de Mexico, S.A. de C.V.
Pearson Education Malaysia Pte. Ltd.

10 9 8 7 6 5 4 3 2 1
ISBN: 0–13–111732–7

For Aida Allen, teacher extraordinaire,
for sharing your skills with us and your students in every grade, K–5.

Preface

The language arts workshop provides teachers with an exciting and effective way to organize and integrate reading and writing instruction across the language arts. *Language Arts Workshop: Purposeful Reading and Writing Instruction* proposes a practical and research-based framework in which both reading and writing workshops are addressed and integrated.

The text is practical and overflowing with strategies illustrated with examples from real classrooms and real teachers. The language arts workshop provides readers a clear vision of this approach in practice and a step-by-step framework for implementation.

The information you'll find in these chapters

- Grounds the language arts workshop approach with a clear theoretical foundation
- Provides a well-organized workshop framework
- Incorporates the gradual release of responsibility model
- Directs teachers to strategies for working with the whole class, in small groups, in learning centers, and with individual students
- Addresses areas of need for literacy and language arts development, including oral language, spelling, vocabulary, word study, fluency, and comprehension
- Incorporates authentic children's literature
- Links assessment to instruction
- Allows teachers to tailor instruction to meet individual student needs

The instructional strategies outlined in this book have been implemented in schools across the country. As in an apprenticeship, novice students learn a craft under the guidance of a skilled and knowledgeable teacher-guide. Students first observe a new skill or strategy being modeled, then practice it with guidance. As the learner becomes more confident, he or she collaborates with other students to refine understanding. Finally, the learner is able to utilize the skills or strategies independently. The responsibilities of both the teacher and the student shift as learning occurs.

PHILOSOPHY

Effective teaching stems from understanding how children learn, understanding what instructional strategies work to improve outcomes, and knowing how to organize instruction so children can learn. By combining reading and writing workshop with a focus on the processes required to develop literacy, this book prepares you to meet curricular objectives, time constraints, and, most importantly, the needs of each student in your classroom.

As you read and study the ideas in this text, you'll learn to successfully integrate the teaching of all major language arts skills and strategies through a workshop approach. Consistent with the gradual release of responsibility model, an integrated reading and writing workshop allows you to tailor instruction to meet specific student needs and answers the question, "How can I most effectively organize my literacy program?"

ORGANIZATION

This intuitively organized volume uses a predictable structure to build from the text's foundational knowledge to the components of the language arts workshop. The format will reinforce the concepts being covered, model the language arts workshop, and provide specific skills and strategies for classroom implementation.

Part 1: You, Your Students, and Your Texts

In the *Introduction* and Chapter 1, *Principles of the Language Arts Workshop*, you'll be guided through foundational information, learning why this approach works and seeing it played out in classrooms as you gain a fundamental understanding of this approach to literacy instruction.

Part 2: Components of the Language Arts Workshop

Concise and compelling chapters illustrate the four components: Shared Reading and Writing, Guided Reading and Writing, Collaborative Reading and Writing, and Independent Reading and Writing. You'll learn how to address each, and how they fit together. Practical and authentic examples of the gradual release of responsibility in each of the literacy processes model the approach in whole group, small group, and independent learning environments. You'll see how you can match this instructional approach to meet specific student needs. The application springs from the clearly stated research base and is always illustrated with classroom examples to model the effective and engaging use of the language arts workshop.

To develop a deep understanding of the language arts workshop and how it can truly benefit your students, the chapters

- Cover each component's characteristics
- Provide guidelines for each approach
- Discuss planning
- Detail the materials you'll need
- Discuss grouping
- Outline the criteria you'll need to consider for each approach
- Discuss assessment
- Cover skills

- Develop strategies
- Provide practical tips

Part 3: Approaches to Teaching in the Language Arts Workshop

These chapters specifically address areas of need for language arts and literacy development. You'll find chapters on Oral Language, Spelling and Word Study, Vocabulary Development, Fluency, Comprehension, and Assessment. In each case, the research on the literacy process is presented, followed by examples for developing the components of each process within the language arts workshop framework. You'll see samples illustrating whole group, small group, collaborative and cooperative learning centers, and individual student experiences to complete the picture of this balanced, engaging, and successful way to approach language arts teaching with your class.

SPECIAL FEATURES

A number of features in this text will help you deepen your understanding of the language arts workshop.

Organization and Reflection

Chapters begin and end with features that will pique your curiosity, guide your reading, and prompt you to reflect on what you've learned.

- *Questions to Consider* begin each chapter to help ready you for each chapter's content.
- *Key Vocabulary* prepares you for the terms to come and provides a handy reference for studying.
- *Big Ideas* at the beginning and end of each chapter provide an excellent overview and summary of chapter concepts.
- *Check Your Understanding* features at the end of every chapter help you verify your comprehension of chapter topics.

Classroom Experience

- *A Look Inside* vignettes precede chapter content, providing a glimpse into authentic classroom teaching and successful language arts workshops.
- *Spotlight on Instruction* features are peppered throughout chapters, bringing you into the classrooms that have experienced real success with the language arts workshop and illustrating specific chapter concepts as they are played out with students.

Application

- *Teacher Tips* located throughout chapters offer concrete ideas for implementing the language arts workshop in your own classroom.
- *Classroom Connections* end each chapter with applications you can use to implement chapter concepts to gain a broader understanding of chapter topics and to put what you've learned into practice.

Accountability

- *Evidence Based* icons are sprinkled throughout chapters to draw your attention to skills and strategies supported by scientific research.

FROM THE UNIVERSITY TO YOUR OWN CLASSROOM

This book has been created to provide not only a solid foundation for you in your methods courses but also to serve as a resource for you in your own classroom. Each chapter contains specific skills and strategies related to the workshop approach. You can also utilize these tools created specifically for classroom implementation:

- *Appendixes* Three appendixes provide you with a wealth of recommended children's book titles, grouped for your convenience by grade level and by genre. With these lists, you will be off and running as you plan your students' reading experiences.

- *Compendium of Assessments* This invaluable resource of more than 30 assessment tools, forms, and rubrics will illustrate the important assessment concepts discussed throughout the chapters and provide you a bank of imperative information-gathering devices for your own classroom.

- *CD-ROM* This free media, packaged with each text, provides a database of thousands of excellent children's literature titles right at your fingertips. Search the database for appropriate books by grade level, genre, author, or illustrator. You can even verify which awards each title has won, to guarantee the quality of each title.

SUPPLEMENTS

Companion Website This robust online support system available at www.prenhall.com/frey offers many rich and meaningful ways to deepen and expand the information presented to you in the text.

- IRA/NCTE Standards Integration, delivered through chapter correlations as well as adaptable lessons that can be saved to your hard drive or disk, provides you with lessons to take into your own classroom that align with both national and state standards.

- Self-Assessments help you gauge your understanding of text concepts.

- Web Links provide useful connections to all standards and many other invaluable online literacy sources.

Electronic Instructor's Manual This useful tool for instructors, available with an instructor's access code online at the Prentice Hall catalog at www.prenhall.com (search by title under Language Arts Workshop and click on Instructor Resources), provides rich instructional support, including:

- A test bank of multiple-choice and essay tests

- PowerPoints specifically designed for each chapter

- Chapter-by-chapter materials, including chapter objectives, suggested readings, discussion questions, and in-class activities

ACKNOWLEDGMENTS

We have had the opportunity to learn alongside a number of skilled teachers as they have increased their students' literacy learning. We thank all of the teachers who invited us into their classrooms and shared detailed information about their practices. We are honored to be among so many highly skilled and qualified teachers!

This book would not have been completed without the support, assistance, and encouragement of several key individuals in the City Heights Educational Collaborative. Maureen Begley, Kelly Moore, Sheryl Segal, and Elizabeth Soriano—the literacy resource teachers at Rosa Parks Elementary in San Diego—have been with us every step of the way. Their deep understanding of literacy instruction for diverse learners, combined with their willingness to share their ideas, has resulted in significant achievement gains for students, the creation of an amazing learning community, and an opportunity for us to continue to explore quality, evidenced-based literacy instruction. Dr. Ian Pumpian's vision of schools in which all students are respected and valued learners has been a constant force in our writing.

Our ideas have also been influenced by our teachers and mentors. We owe a huge debt and a great thank you to the people at San Diego State University who have taught us so much about language, literacy, and thinking, especially Dr. Diane Lapp, Dr. James Flood, Dr. Nancy Farnan, and Dr. Leif Fearn. Each of these scholars has shaped our thinking about instruction and what it means to be literate in today's world.

Our understandings of children's literature and teaching with books has been extended through our interactions with Dr. Helen Foster James. We are also lucky to have the opportunity to work with and learn from some excellent librarians, especially Rose Pope at Rosa Parks Elementary, Margo Denton at Monroe Clark Middle School, and Dennis Donley at Hoover High School.

And finally, our editors Linda Montgomery and Hope Madden's belief in this project and their skill in guiding us from concept through production have resulted in this book that you are reading.

We would also like to acknowledge the reviewers whose thoughtful feedback made this a better book. We thank them all: Mary Pippitt Cervantes, California State University, Hayward; Patricia DeMay, University of West Alabama; Alan Frager, Miami University; Carol J. Fuhler, Iowa State University; Carolyn Jaynes, California State University, Sacramento; Margot Kinberg, National University; Maria J. Meyerson, University of Las Vegas, Nevada; Laurie Elish-Piper, Northern Illinois University; and Debra Price, Sam Houston State University.

Nancy Frey

Douglas Fisher

Contents

PART 2
COMPONENTS OF THE LANGUAGE ARTS WORKSHOP

Introduction to the Language Arts Workshop

While this introduction is not intended to fully explain all the "whys" and "hows" of language arts instruction, we hope it will provide an overview of an exciting and effective means for organizing literacy instruction in your classroom.

Perhaps the best way to experience the language arts workshop is to first view it through the eyes of a teacher and student. Aida Allen, a fifth grade teacher in San Diego, California, uses the language arts workshop to organize literacy instruction for her 32 students. Her students all speak Spanish as a first language and have become biliterate in both English and Spanish. Figure I.1 illustrates how she and Tino, one of her students, spend a morning in the language arts workshop.

A LOOK INSIDE THE LANGUAGE ARTS WORKSHOP

Throughout the text, you'll find glimpses into the language arts workshop. To highlight the structure of the lesson, the first look inside, shown in Figure I.1, is presented as a table.

THE ROLES OF TEACHERS AND LEARNERS

Do you recall when you first learned to ride a bicycle? You probably had an opportunity to watch others ride a bike, and they may have even shared some good ideas with you about how to ride without falling. Soon, you were ready to try it, although it was helpful to have someone running behind you as he or she held the back of the bicycle seat. As you gained your balance, you began riding with other children who also shared their ideas about riding. Finally, you could ride independently because you had mastered all the skills and strategies for competent bicycle riding. It's likely you even developed a few tricks of your own.

In the language arts workshop, the teacher orchestrates a set of experiences designed to give each learner opportunities to read and write using a model not unlike the adult who helped you to learn to ride a bike. Students first observe a new skill or strategy being modeled then practice it with guidance. As the learner becomes more confident, he or she collaborates with other students to refine understanding. Finally, the learner is able to utilize the skills or strategies independently and may even create new ways beyond the ones originally taught. Like the workshop day demonstrated by Ms. Allen and Tino, the responsibilities of both the teacher and the student shift as learning occurs (see Figure I.2).

Figure I.1   Language Arts Workshop in Action

	What Ms. Allen Does	*What Tino Does*
9:00–9:20 AM FOCUS LESSON	Ms. Allen welcomes the students and introduces a **focus lesson** on character analysis using an excerpt from *The Most Beautiful Place in the World* (Cameron, 1993). This reading tells the story of Juan, a young boy who is abandoned by his parents. She displays the reading on the overhead so that all the students can view it. Ms. Allen tells her students that the purpose of the lesson is to discover how the author lets the reader know about the attributes of the characters. She models her own comprehension for the students as she reads it using a Think Aloud strategy and makes notes on a graphic organizer. Next, students work in pairs to highlight other clues in the passage. Ms. Allen instructs her students to look for similar devices during their literature circle readings and distributes another copy of the graphic organizer to use.	Tino has his own copy of the reading and follows the text while Ms. Allen reads aloud. Using a copy of the graphic organizer, he and his partner Maggie makes similar notes about the characters of Juan, Mama, and the man his mother will marry.
9:20–9:40 AM GUIDED AND COLLABORATIVE LEARNING	Ms. Allen meets with a group of students for **guided reading.** Today they are reading an expository article about the orphan trains that relocated 100,000 children from New York City to the American west between 1854–1929. She has determined the level of the reading using the Fry Readability Scale (Fry, 2002) to match the text difficulty to the instructional level of these students.	Tino meets with his literature circle group during **collaborative learning.** He and his classmates are reading *Hatchet* (Paulsen, 1999), a story of a 13-year-old boy who survives a plane crash in a remote part of Alaska. Tino and his group discuss clues the author has supplied in chapter 2 about Brian's character and his ability to survive hardship. They use the graphic organizer Ms. Allen introduced during the focus lesson to write notes. The group agrees to read chapters 3 and 4 before their next meeting.
9:40–10:00 AM GUIDED AND COLLABORATIVE LEARNING	Ms. Allen meets with a small group of students, including Tino, for guided reading instruction. Because this group reads more complicated text, she has selected an expository reading on the development of child labor laws during the 19th century. Ms. Allen showed them photographs of children at work (www.historyplace.com/unitedstates/childlabor/) and guided them through a reading from the social studies textbook on child labor.	Tino meets with Ms. Allen and four other students to participate in a guided reading lesson.
10:00–10:25 AM INDEPENDENT READING WITH CONFERRING	Ms. Allen meets individually with a total of five students to **confer** with them about their readings. Each student brings their reading log and the current book they are reading. She asks them to read a favorite passage and makes notes about their oral reading. Next, she discusses the story and clarifies vocabulary. Each meeting lasts about five minutes.	Tino uses his **independent reading** time to finish chapters 3 and 4 of *Hatchet* and writes observational notes on stickies about Brian's character. Because he is the vocabulary enricher for the group this week, he records tricky or unusual words in his notebook to look up later.
10:25–10:50 AM INDEPENDENT WRITING WITH CONFERRING	Ms. Allen meets with five students to discuss their writing. Tino is one of the students and brings his writer's notebook to the **conference.** He asks to see the photographs of child laborers Ms. Allen showed during guided reading. Ms. Allen and Tino make a plan for Tino to create a story based on one of the photographs.	Tino meets with Ms. Allen to plan his next piece. After conferring with Ms. Allen, he returns to his desk to begin writing.
10:50–11:00 AM SHARE AND CLOSURE	Ms. Allen invites the class to discuss important characters they read about in their literature circle groups. Elizabeth, a student currently reading *Bud, Not Buddy* (Curtis, 2000) with her literature circle, shares Bud's character traits with the class.	Tino participates in the share session.

Figure 1.2   Language Arts Workshop Diagram

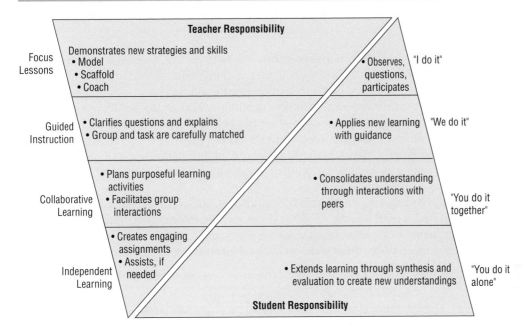

LANGUAGE ARTS WORKSHOP: PURPOSEFUL READING AND WRITING INSTRUCTION

Each word in this text's title was carefully chosen. Attention to each word will provide you with some context for our thinking about teaching students to read and write.

"Language Arts"   What does the phrase **language arts** mean to you? To us, the term describes the various processes that humans use to communicate and understand the world. We use listening, speaking, reading, writing, and viewing to make meaning. We know that these are not discrete or isolated skills, but rather they are connected in profound ways. In school, the language arts are defined as "curriculum areas particulary concerned with the development and improvement" of these communicative processes (Harris & Hodges, 1995, p. 133).

"Workshop"   The next word we selected in the title is **workshop.** To us, a workshop is a place where people produce things; a place where people come together to create. Workshops mean that people work together and that there are different skills used and needed by different people. In schools, workshop is also a philosophy and means for organizing instructional time. Reading and writing workshops are designed to provide time for students to respond to texts they have read and write about their ideas (Atwell, 1987; Calkins, 1986). We view the workshop model as a context for students to learn and perfect their craft. However, this does not mean that students work on whatever they want, whenever they want. Instead, we view workshop as a time for students to move toward independence through a series of learning events that allow them to assume more responsibility for literacy tasks through increasing competency. This echoes the tradition of the workshop as a place for apprenticeship, where novices learn a craft under the guidance of a skilled and knowledgeable guide.

"Purposeful"

We also selected the term **purposeful.** We believe that language arts instruction should be purposeful, that teachers matter, and that what they do matters most. You will be a powerful force in the classroom and it will be up to you to see that students learn to read and write. Unlike breathing, children do not learn to read and write on their own. They need you, their teacher, to facilitate, coach, and foster their development and understanding. Students do not learn to read and write, or enjoy reading and writing, simply because they are told to. Establishing a purpose for reading and writing is critical for student engagement, motivation, and achievement (Smith, 2000; Wilhelm, 2001).

We all read and write for different purposes, including for pleasure and enjoyment, to find something out, to share some specific information, to identify a central idea or theme, or to understand what we think and know. We also know that effective teachers consider three dimensions in their instruction:

1. *Task control*—decisions about the task, how students will be involved in the task, and how it will be assessed
2. *Authenticity*—decisions about the choice of tasks as they relate to meaningful and relevant learning in students' lives
3. *Teacher's role*—when, where, and to what extent the teacher will participate in each task (Pearson & Fielding, 1991, p. 847)

"Reading and Writing"

We also use the terms **reading and writing** to remind ourselves that students cannot simply learn to communicate orally. Too many of our students fail to learn to read and write while they are in school. In fact, 21–23% of adults in the United States are classified at Level 1 in literacy (on a 5-point scale), meaning that they cannot perform basic literacy tasks like locating an intersection on a map or entering background information on a social security card application form (Reder, 1998). An additional 28% of Americans were classified at Level 2, meaning they could not correctly determine the gross pay on a paycheck (Reder, 1998). This translates to 90 million American adults who lack functional literacy skills. In addition, an unspecified but growing number of young adults are alliterate, meaning that they can read but choose not to (Beers, 1996).

"Instruction"

Instruction is the last word in the title of this text. Instruction is the act of teaching and is designed to bridge the gap between what students already know and what they need to know. The impact of effective instruction delivered by a knowledgeable teacher cannot be overstated. A series of studies linking student achievement to teacher effectiveness was conducted in the 1990s. They found that on standardized testing measures, students in classrooms with the most effective teachers gained an average of 53 percentage points in an academic year, compared to an average of 14 percentage points for those in classrooms with the least effective teachers (Sanders & Horn, 1994; Wright,

Figure I.3 Progress in Student Achievement by Teacher Effectiveness

Teacher Effectiveness	*Student Progress for One Academic Year*
Most effective	53 percentile points
Average effectiveness	34 percentile points
Least effective	14 percentile points

Horn, & Sanders, 1997). See Figure I.3 for an illustration of these values.

So what is effective instruction? Marzano, Pickering, and Pollock (2001) identified three factors that influence effective instruction:

- The instructional strategies used
- The management strategies used
- The design of the curriculum used by the teacher

In other words, sheer personality alone doesn't do it. Effective teaching stems from understanding how children learn, understanding which instructional strategies work to improve outcomes, and knowing how to organize instruction so children can learn. It is this ability to design and implement thoughtful curricula that sequences instruction and provides students with the substance of what they need to learn. The language arts workshop offers a format for sequencing reading and writing instruction. This is accomplished through a series of instructional arrangements that allow students to move through a series of learning activities arranged in a format that provides opportunities to apply all the language arts. Therefore, *Language Arts Workshop: Purposeful Reading and Writing Instruction* focuses on the methods for organizing instruction and assessment in order for students to develop as readers and writers throughout their elementary and middle school years.

References

Atwell, N. (1987). *In the middle: Writing, reading, and learning with adolescents.* Portsmouth, NH: Heinemann.

Beers, G. K. (1996). No time, no interest, no way! The three voices of aliteracy. Part I. *School Library Journal, 42*(2), 30–33.

Calkins, L. M. (1986). *The art of teaching writing.* Portsmouth, NH: Heinemann.

Harris, T. L., & Hodges, R. E. (Eds.). (1995). *The literacy dictionary: The vocabulary of reading and writing.* Newark, DE: International Reading Association.

Marzano, R. J., Pickering, D. J., & Pollock, J. E. (2001). *Classroom instruction that works: Research-based strategies for increasing student achievement.* Alexandria, VA: Association for Supervision and Curriculum Development.

Pearson, P. D., & Fielding, L. (1991). Comprehension instruction. In R. Barr, M. L. Kamil, P. Mosenthal, & P. D. Pearson (Eds.), *Handbook of Reading Research* (Vol. II, pp. 815–860). Mahwah, NJ: Erlbaum.

Reder, S. (1998). *State of literacy in America: Estimates at the local, state, national levels.* Washington, DC: National Institute for Literacy.

Sanders, W. L., & Horn, S. P. (1994). The Tennessee value-added assessment system (TVAAS): Mixed model methodology in educational assessment. *Journal of Personnel Evaluation in Education, 8,* 299–311.

Smith, M. C. (2000). The real-world reading practices of adults. *Journal of Literacy Research, 32,* 25–52.

Wilhelm, J. (2001). *Improving comprehension with think about strategies: Modeling what good readers do.* New York: Scholastic.

Wright, S. P., Horn, S. P., & Sanders, W. L. (1997). Teacher and classroom context effects on student achievement: Implications for teacher evaluation. *Journal of Personnel Evaluation in Education, 11,* 57–67.

LANGUAGE ARTS WORKSHOP

Principles of the Language Arts Workshop

BIG IDEAS ABOUT THE LANGUAGE ARTS WORKSHOP

The language arts workshop represents a way of organizing meaningful instruction so that students can benefit from a balanced approach to literacy. Students in the language arts workshop read and write every day and spend time working with their teacher, collaborating with peers, and working independently. The theoretical underpinnings of the language arts workshop are grounded in research and represent current thinking about effective instruction for students with diverse learning needs, including English language learners, students with disabilities, and students who read at, above, or below grade level.

Questions to Consider

When you have finished reading this chapter, you should be able to answer these questions:

- How do students learn?
- How does reading develop over time?
- How does writing develop over time?
- How do we support students with unique learning needs?
- How should students be grouped for instruction?
- What are the components of effective literacy instruction?
- What is the format of the language arts workshop?
- What materials are used in the language arts workshop?

Key Vocabulary

Zone of Proximal Development

Comprehensible input

Gradual release of responsibility

Developmental phases of reading

Cueing systems

Reading comprehension strategies

Developmental phases of writing

Accommodations

Modifications

Flexible grouping

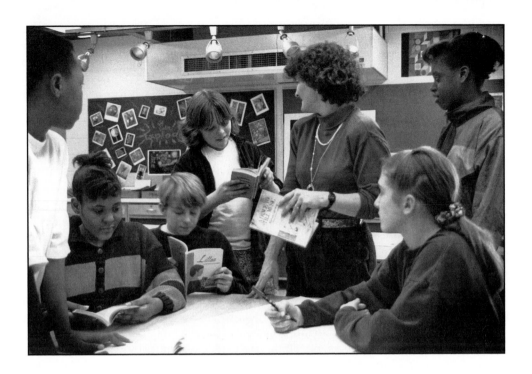

A LOOK INSIDE

See www.nieonline
.com

On her way to class, Ms. Nguyen picks up 10 copies of the local newspaper that were delivered as part of her Newspapers in Education program. She will use these newspapers as an important part of today's language arts workshop at one of the collaborative learning centers as part of her focus on helping students understand text structures. As we enter Ms. Nguyen's fourth grade classroom, we note the range of texts around the room. In one corner, she has a classroom library. The library is organized to facilitate students finding books. On the south wall of the classroom library, books are organized by difficulty. Each shelf has a code that students use to determine if the book is at their independent reading level. On the west wall of the classroom library, books are organized by type, or genre. Students can quickly select from the shelves of poetry, biography, science fiction, and so on. Beyond the library is a bank of four computers. Ms. Nguyen knows that her students like to read from the Internet and are especially interested in *anime,* a sort of animation that originated in Japan, which uses vibrant colors and action-packed plots.

Beyond the computer area is a listening station that contains a tape recorder, six earphones, and a number of books-on-tape. There are also three magazine racks that contain current issues of *Ranger Rick, National Geographic Kids, Music Alive!, Sports*

Illustrated for Kids, Discovery Girls Magazine, Weekly Reader, Time for Kids, and *Cricket.* In addition, there are books all over the classroom. There are informational books about fish located near the fish tank, "how to" books located in the fix-it corner, and books about all kinds of sports in the cupboard with the sports equipment.

In other words, Ms. Nguyen has books and other reading materials all over her classroom. It took her several years to collect all of these books and she is proud of the variety her students can access. As Ms. Nguyen notes, "I had to know what to look for—I had to know the genres (types of books) that my students need to and want to read." We agree with her. Classrooms have to be more than a collection of books found at a garage sale. With knowledge about what to look for, teachers can create classrooms that engage students with texts of all types.

Ms. Nguyen begins her language arts workshop with a focus lesson using an article from the newspaper on a local water reclamation project in their community. After the focus lesson, five students join her for guided instruction, this time using the article to compose letters to their city council representative. Other children use the research materials in the classroom, including a web page she bookmarked, several magazines with feature articles on the water crisis in the western U.S., and an informational brochure from the local water agency to develop interview questions for a guest speaker who will visit next week. The guest speaker, a local farmer who uses environmentally sound irrigation practices, will answer questions about water use. Later in the morning, all the students independently read the picture book, *A Drop of Water: A Book of Science and Wonder* (Wick, 1997) and write a description of the water cycle in their science journals. Ms. Nguyen is pleased with the flexibility the language arts workshop affords her to combine social studies content on state history with earth science content. "And the best part is that we're accomplishing our reading and writing goals, too!" she remarks.

HOW DO STUDENTS LEARN?

As you can imagine, there is no shortage of ideas, theories, and anecdotes to answer this question. Our thinking has been influenced by a number of significant principles including a developmental view to literacy, the Zone of Proximal Development, the gradual release of responsibility model of instruction, and the importance of meaningful experiences. These principles help us to answer the question of how students learn.

Developmental View of Literacy

Perspectives on learning have moved far from the predominant theories of behaviorism and psychoanalysis of the early 20th century. The influence of the developmental work of Vygotsky, Piaget, Montessori and others have shaped our approach to learning and the educational systems that support it. Clay (2003) asks:

> How do developmental theories influence teachers' assumptions about children? These explanations, particularly in language and cognitive areas, have created for teachers vocabulary and knowledge structures that allow them to think beyond what the child does to what may be occurring in children's heads. (p. 49)

A developmental perspective of learning means that the teacher understands that a child's response is not merely "correct" or "incorrect" but rather a reflection of what the child understands at that moment. Therefore, the teacher's role is not simply to evaluate what is correct or incorrect but instead to recognize that the children's responses are an opportunity to hypothesize how they are using their knowledge to arrive at an answer. This requires the classroom teacher to understand how children learn as they grow, especially how they develop literacy knowledge. Closely related to a developmental perspective is the concept that a learner can perform skills beyond his or her independent level when assisted by a teacher or more capable peer. This higher level of performance is referred to as the Zone of Proximal Development (ZPD) (Vygotsky, 1978).

Zone of Proximal Development

Lev Vygotsky, a 20th century Russian psychologist, defined the ZPD as:

> the distance between the actual developmental level as determined by independent problem solving and the level of potential development as determined through problem solving under adult guidance or in collaboration with a more capable peer. (p. 86)

This means that learning takes place not at the student's independent level, but rather at the level the student can reach with assistance from another. Undoubtedly, this is how you learned to drive. You didn't simply put yourself behind the wheel one day and begin driving. Instead, someone who knew how to drive (possibly someone who had recently learned how to drive) sat in the passenger seat and coached you. With proper coaching, you were able to perform a complex skill at a level that exceeded what you could have accomplished alone. You were functioning in your ZPD during that time. Likewise, students can learn a skill or strategy when they receive coaching from a teacher or peer. The concept of the Zone of Proximal Development has been translated into a way of organizing literacy instruction in the classroom, called the gradual release of responsibility model (Pearson & Fielding, 1991).

Gradual Release of Responsibility Model

The Gradual Release of Responsibility Model is a widely used model of instruction that begins with explicit instruction of a skill or strategy then moves to guided instruction as students try it on for themselves as shown in Figure 1.1. Students gradually assume more responsibility for using the skill or strategy as they work with one another as well as independently. The language arts workshop is predicated on a gradual release of responsibility as the teacher moves from modeling to guiding learners in a skill or strategy, providing coaching as they become more proficient, and eventually turning over the task to them as they work independently. In the language arts workshop, the teacher initially controls the reading and writing through direct instruction in focus lessons. Students assume more control in the guided instruction segment of the workshop. Skills first introduced and refined in these phases of the workshop are practiced with peers during collaborative learning and become part of the student's repertoire of skills in the independent phase of the workshop.

As powerful as this model of instruction is, it will not be successful without connections to the lives of learners. Meaningful experiences enhance learning acquisition because the student can apply the new knowledge to the situation.

Figure 1.1   The Gradual Release of Responsibility Model in the Language Arts Workshop

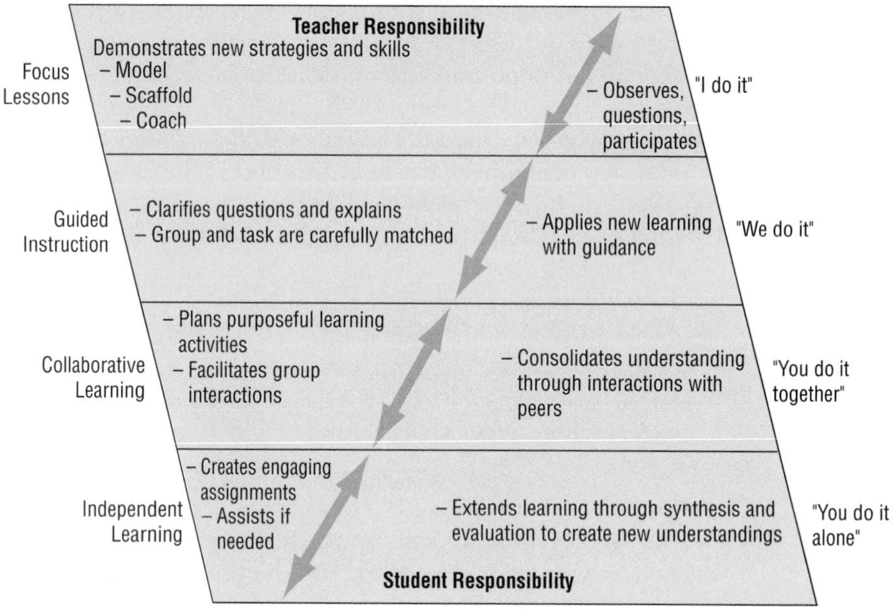

Meaningful Experiences

A basic premise of learning is that when experiences are meaningful to the learner, the ability to learn increases. For example, your ability to learn the concepts in this textbook is directly related to the relevancy of learning about language arts instruction in your life. If you were studying to be an engineer, your ability to learn these principles would be somewhat diminished because the content is not as useful in an engineering degree program. In the same regard, student learning is driven by the questions formulated by the learner (Harste, 1993). Furthermore, learning is social in nature and springs from the interactions we have with others (Halliday, 1975). Therefore, an important role of the teacher is to foster questions among students and create meaningful experiences that allow them to interact with one another. In the language arts workshop, skills and strategies introduced during the focus lesson are practiced and extended through guided, collaborative, and independent learning.

Each of these components of the language arts workshop are explained in subsequent chapters.

Because literacy learning is developmental in nature, sound instruction follows the same path through a gradual release model. As well, the acquisition of reading occurs in phases. How are the details of reading acquisition related to instructional practice?

HOW DOES READING DEVELOP OVER TIME?

As children learn to read, they move through a series of phases of development. Classroom instruction must be responsive to these phases of development in order for students to acquire the skills necessary to read and the strategies necessary to understand what they are reading. In early literacy development, these strategies used by the reader are referred to as cueing systems. The strategies of meaning, an early cueing system, become more sophisticated over time and come to be known collectively as comprehension strategies. In order to capitalize on cueing and comprehension systems, it is important to understand the phases of reading.

Phases of Reading

Anyone who has spent time with children knows that the expectations for a six-year-old differ from those for a twelve-year-old. This is because these two children differ from one another physically, emotionally, and socially. As well, we view literacy learning through the lens of developmental phases. These phases are not rigid and stage-bound, for little in human development (except perhaps puberty) is marked by an irreversible advancement from one condition to another. Instead, we look at phases of literacy development as markers of progression that many learners pass through. Not every learner will exhibit all the behaviors, nor will they be solely in one phase at a given time. Typical phases of reading can be described as the following:

- *Emergent readers* are experimenting with reading. During this phase they are learning that print carries a message, how books work, and are beginning to recognize letters and words.
- *Early readers* are reading simple texts and have a larger bank of words they can read and write. They utilize a variety of basic strategies to figure out known and unknown words.
- *Transitional readers* are reading a variety of texts and understand that each has its own unique text structure. When seeking information, they consult more than one source. They are also becoming more aware of the strategies they are using.
- *Self-extending readers* read a wide range of texts and apply critical literacy skills to analyze the authenticity and value of the information. They continue to acquire increasingly more sophisticated literacy skills through extensive reading and discussion.

Cueing systems are what we use to read.

All readers in every phase of reading utilize a number of clues to figure out the print on the page. These clues are collectively called cueing systems.

Cueing Systems

Emergent and early readers rely on a set of **cueing systems** in order to read a text (Goodman & Goodman, 1994). These can be thought of as clues the reader extracts from their knowledge of how print works to determine what the squiggly black lines on the page represent. Over time, these cues become more consolidated and their reading becomes more fluent. Fluency refers to a reader's ability to read smoothly, accurately, and with appropriate expression.

Detailed discussion of using cueing systems in instruction can be found in chapter 2.

- *Graphophonic cues* are those associated with the relationship between the symbols (letters) and their sounds. As learners develop these sound/symbol relationships, they recognize the patterns in clusters of letters (e.g., *pan, man,* and *fan*).
- *Syntactic cues* are governed by the grammatical rules of the language. This does not mean that the reader can name the rule, but rather that they recognize that words occur in a particular order.

- *Semantic cues* are connected to the meaning of the words. A reader using semantic cues reads, "The house was small and blue" not "The horse was small and blue."
- *Pragmatic cues* are related to the social use of language in a culture. For instance, it is the ability to recognize that *Mother, Mom, Mommy,* and *Ma* are names for the same person.

Students learn to activate these cueing systems through reading connected text. Connected text refers to a series of words and sentences linked in a meaningful way, as opposed to isolated words. Readers are not encouraged to use one cueing system at a time, but rather to utilize multiple cueing systems as they read. When students read connected text, they apply comprehension strategies to support their understanding.

Comprehension Strategies

Comprehension strategies are taught to students of all developmental levels to be used as tools to support their own understanding of the text (Harvey & Goudvis, 1999; Keene & Zimmerman, 1997). Indeed, comprehension instruction has been identified as an essential teaching practice by the National Reading Panel (National Institute of Child Health and Human Development, 2000). Like tools in a toolbox, the key to the usefulness of these strategies is in the proper application of a strategy to suit a purpose. These include:

The National Reading Panel report can be found at www.nationalreadingpanel.org

- *Questioning strategies* to predict and anticipate what might occur next in the text, solve problems, and clarify their understanding.
- *Summarizing strategies* to identify important information and provide an accurate recount.
- *Inferencing strategies* to "read between the lines" in order to identify clues in the text.
- *Self-monitoring strategies* to determine when the reader understands what they have read and notice when they have not.
- *Connection strategies* to integrate what a reader has experienced and has learned with the information being read.
- *Analysis strategies* to identify literary devices, determine author's purpose, and evaluate texts.

As with cueing strategies, we believe there is a danger in teaching comprehension strategies in isolation of one another. Pinnell and Fountas (2003) remind us that

> [t]hese strategies are not linear in that first you engage one then another. In fact, reducing complex systems to a list . . . probably oversimplifies reading. *Teaching strategies one at a time and telling students to consciously employ them, one at a time,* may actually interfere with deep comprehension and make reading a meaningless exercise. (pp. 7–8)

Explicit information on metacognition and instruction of comprehension strategies can be found in chapter 10.

Comprehension strategies are a key element in the effort to develop students' ability to attend to their own learning. This awareness of how one learns is referred to as metacognition.

The development of reading over time goes hand in hand with the development of writing. As students learn to read the printed word, they also learn to represent words and ideas on the page. Like reading, writing follows a developmental progression.

HOW DOES WRITING DEVELOP OVER TIME?

The development of a writer begins even before a child can compose in a manner that is understood by others. By the age of two or three, many toddlers are scribbling messages on paper and then "reading" their message to a delighted adult. Young children also visually represent ideas and concepts through drawing, an important literacy skill. Students entering kindergarten often exhibit these very early writing skills. As with reading, they move through a series of phases, frequently displaying traits in more than one phase at a time.

Phases of Writing

- *Emergent writers* are learning how print works, especially in seeing the permanence of writing. They can recount events in sequence, such as giving directions or telling a story, and are using known letters and words in their writing.
- *Early writers* possess a larger bank of known letters and words and are able to use them more quickly in their writing, although the writing is sometimes constrained by the limits of their written vocabulary. An early writer's work is characterized by conventions of storytelling, especially formulaic writing such as "once upon a time."
- *Transitional writers* apply more sophisticated text structures to their work and can utilize structures used by other authors to create original text, such as writing haikus. Their sentences are more complex and they are beginning to use transitional phrases.
- *Self-extending writers* write for a variety of purposes and audiences. Their word choices are sophisticated and flexible and they engage in all aspects of editing to refine their work.

At every phase of writing development, the act of writing must be promoted. Students need opportunities to write and receive instruction on the aspects of writing. Like cueing systems in reading, these aspects of writing instruction foster acquisition of skills and strategies necessary for writing. These include conventions of language, reading experiences, and instruction in the craft of writing.

Aspects of Writing Instruction

It probably won't surprise you to hear that writing is an incredibly complex skill that requires a sophisticated set of instructional techniques. Anyone who has faced a blank page without a clue as how to begin knows this. The challenge, of course, is that the act of writing leads the writer in directions they may not have expected. Writer Anne Lamott says that "very few writers know what they are doing until they've done it" (1995, p. 22). And she was talking about professional writers!

In the language arts workshop, our goal is to get students writing frequently and fluently using a growing repertoire of skills regarding the *conventions* of the language such as spelling, punctuation, and word choice. These skills are developed through intentional instruction. We also know that writers need exposure to other good writers through *reading experiences* with rich narrative and expository text. Finally, they need time to experiment with the *craft* of writing by creating original texts of many genres, including poetry, response to literature, technical writing, and persuasive essays. Good writing doesn't occur only because of instruction on conventions. Good writing does not occur only through reading good literature. Good writing does not occur only through writing a lot using lots of different formats. It occurs when all of these things are interwoven—conventions, reading experiences, and experimenting with craft. Thus, the language arts workshop features time when conventions are taught, time for rich reading experiences, and time for experimentation with craft.

Although learners move through developmental phases of reading and writing acquisition, no student will move neatly and conveniently from one phase to the next. This is especially true of students with diverse learning needs in our classrooms, including English language learners and students with disabilities. These learners require more specialized approaches to instruction that support growth in reading and writing.

HOW DO WE SUPPORT STUDENTS WITH UNIQUE LEARNING NEEDS?

English language learners and students with disabilities represent an important part of the American school population. Their presence in our classrooms and communities is to be celebrated as part of the rich fabric of life in our country.

English Language Learners

In the 2001–2002 school year, more than 3,700,000 children (7.9% of the school population) in K–12 schools in the United States received services and supports as English language learners (Hoffman, 2003). These classroom supports include attention to comprehensible input and English language development methods to support language acquisition.

Comprehensible input. Stated simply, comprehensible input is any spoken message you can

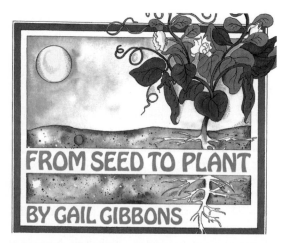

understand. For example, an English language learner's comprehensible input is enhanced when the spoken message being heard is predictable and easy to understand. Using gestures and real objects (referred to as realia), is effective because they enhance comprehensible input, allowing the learner to use the information conveyed nonverbally to match to the spoken words. The input hypothesis ($i + 1$) is a theory of how second and subsequent languages are learned and is closely related to the theory of the Zone of Proximal Development (Krashen, 1985). As with ZPD, Krashen proposes that language is learned when the message is just beyond the threshold of competence, but not so difficult as to be not understood at all. For example, a teacher can read aloud the picture book *From Seed to Plant* (Gibbons, 1993) after examining seeds at several stages of development. While

From Seed to Plant, written and illustrated by Gail Gibbons. Used with the permission of Holiday House.

some students may not have known vocabulary words like *seed, stem,* and *leaf* independently, they can now understand and use them because of the additional support of the pictures and plants.

English language development methods. English language development (ELD) is an overarching term used to describe a constellation of instructional approaches to ensure that students acquire English while also learning content. In other words, teachers must ensure that they have language goals infused into every activity or lesson in which students are engaged. There are a number of specific ELD methods, such as language brokers in which students who speak the same language but who have different proficiencies in English work together (Herrell & Jordan, 2003). There are also a host of strategies that are more generic but that work wonders for English learners, such as interactive read alouds (Fisher, Flood, Lapp, & Frey, 2004).

The language arts workshop is an excellent place for English language learners to develop both content knowledge and literacy skills. As we have noted, the format of the workshop provides time for whole class, small group, and independent work. This format allows the teacher to differentiate instruction and ensure that students learning English benefit from these methods. Students with disabilities may also need curricular supports to achieve their full potential in the general education classroom.

> English learners need to be taught English, not simply *in* English.

Students with Disabilities

It is likely that students with physical, cognitive and behavioral support needs will be part of your classroom and thus your language arts workshop. A conservative estimate indicates that there were over 6,300,000 students with disabilities, representing 13.3% of the K–12 population, in U.S. schools during the 2001–2002 year (Hoffman, 2003). Federal legislation such as the Individuals with Disabilities Act (IDEA, 1997) require that these students with disabilities access the core academic curriculum in the regular classroom with their peers without disabilities (Fisher & Frey, 2003). More importantly than simple compliance with Federal regulations, there is evidence that students without disabilities benefit academically, socially, and personally from their interactions with students with disabilities (Snell & Janney, 2000; Staub & Peck, 1994–1995).

> Providing support for students with disabilities in regular classes is called inclusive education.

Our experience and published research suggests that students with disabilities can be effectively and meaningfully educated in the regular classroom when appropriate supports and services are provided (Fisher & Frey, 2001; Hunt, Soto, Maier, & Doering, 2003; Waldron & McLeskey, 1998). The evidence to date suggests that students with disabilities need access to personal supports, curriculum supports, behavioral supports and technology supports (Buswell, Schaffner, & Seyler, 1999). You will likely have access to a special education teacher and possibly a paraprofessional to assist you in educating students with disabilities in your classroom (Thousand, Villa, & Nevin, 2002).

> PEAK Parent Center, www.peakparent.org, provides parents and teachers with current information.

These personal supports will be complemented by accommodations and modifications that are provided to you by the special education support team. Instructional materials may need to be altered, or an in-class activity may be changed to promote participation by the student with a disability. Projects, homework, and assessments may also be changed to ensure learning is meaningful. The decision to provide accommodations and modifications is made by the Individual Education Plan (IEP) team, of which the general education teacher is a member.

- *Accommodations* increase a student's access to the existing curriculum by altering how the student receives information or demonstrates mastery. Accommodations do not significantly alter what is being learned, only how it is being learned. For example, accommodations in the language arts workshop include books on tape, enlarged print, or extended time to complete an assignment.

- *Modifications* are more significant changes to the curriculum itself. Most commonly, the student is responsible for mastering specific aspects of the curriculum and the difficulty is reduced.

For more information on teaching in an inclusive classroom, see *Creating an Inclusive School* by Richard Villa and Jacqueline Thousand in the reference list.

Because accommodations and modifications cannot be evaluated out of the context in which they are being used, the IEP team must determine when the amount of changes is significant enough to constitute a modified curriculum. In that light, we have provided a list of accommodations and modifications that can be applied in the language arts workshop in Figure 1.2.

With these types of support, the language arts workshop is a superior place for students with disabilities to learn to read and write. As Kluth and Darmody-Latham (2003) note, the regular classroom with its focus on quality literacy instruction is an appropriate, appealing, and challenging place for students with disabilities to learn. Ryndak, Morrison, and Sommerstein (1999) clearly demonstrated the benefits of providing both quality inclusive education and quality literacy instruction to students with disabilities. We hope your classroom is a place in which all students, including those with disabilities, receive excellent instruction as they learn to read and write.

For more information on creating a classroom community, see Mara Sapon-Shevin's book *Because We Can Change the World* in the reference list.

In every language arts workshop classroom there are students with diverse learning needs, including English language learners and students with disabilities. As you may have noticed, we have strong feelings about the education of all students. We want all students to feel welcome and respected in school. This requires a concerted effort on the part of the teacher to create a sense of community in the classroom. Students need to be grouped for various instructional purposes, but making those grouping decisions can be challenging without a system for making such decisions.

HOW SHOULD STUDENTS BE GROUPED FOR INSTRUCTION?

One of the structures sometimes used in elementary and middle school classrooms has a harmful effect on the classroom community: permanent ability grouping. This practice not only disrupts the sense of community that students enjoy, it also has a negative impact on student achievement, particularly among students who struggle to achieve (Broussard & Joseph, 1998; Mallery & Mallery, 1999). Students who experience permanent ability groups report less satisfaction with school and believe that they are failures (Boaler, William, & Brown, 2000). Slavin and Braddock (1993) further suggest that permanent ability grouping is not only academically and socially harmful, but that it undermines the democratic values of the United States.

In contrast with permanent ability grouping, the language arts workshop relies on a number of grouping patterns within its structure (Flood, Lapp, Flood, & Nagel, 1992; Lapp, Flood, Goss, 2000). These patterns include whole class, small group guided learning, cooperative and collaborative groups, partner interactions, and

Figure 1.2   Sample Accommodations and Modifications

Ideas for Use with Instructional Materials

Tape focus lessons

Allow film or video and supplements
   in place of text

Offer a personal dry erase board

Use print enlarger or light box to illuminate text

Use adapted computer hardware or software

Dictate to a partner who writes it out
   or types it on the computer

Organize pictures instead of words
   into categories

Provide visual aids to stimulate ideas for writing

Allow the use of computers for writing

Tape the assignment to the desk

Provide a clipboard that can be clamped to the
   desk or wheelchair tray to secure papers

Use materials on the student's reading level

Use complementary software or adapted
   computer hardware

Ideas for Use with In-Class Activities

Break down new skills into small steps

Underline or highlight important words
   and phrases

Pick key words from book to read on
   each page

Turns pages in book while others read

Rewrite text or use easy to read versions

Have student complete sentences supplied by
   the teacher orally or in writing

Assign a peer buddy for activity

Engage students in read, write, pair, share
   activities

Ideas for Use with Projects and Homework

Assign smaller quantities of work

Allow more time for completion

Encourage oral contributions

Provide concept maps

Provide sample sentences for students to use
   .as a model

Assign homework partners

Substitute projects for written assignments

Ideas for Use with Assessments

Underline or highlight text directions

Reduce the number of questions by selecting
   representative items

Permit oral responses to tests using a
   tape recorder

Put choices for answers on index cards

Use the sentence or paragraph as a unit of
   composition rather than an essay

Use photographs in oral presentations to the
   class

Re-word test questions in easier terms

Source: Fisher, D., Frey, N., & Sax, C. (2004). *Inclusive elementary schools: Recipes for success* (2nd ed.). Colorado Springs, CO: Peak Parent Center. Used with permission.

individualized instruction. Navan (2002) noted that flexible grouping benefits all students, including those with exceptionally high ability.

Flexible Grouping   Teachers in the language arts workshop group students in at least three ways:

- *Teacher-selected groups*. At some points during the day or week, the teacher selects which students will work in specific groups. This is most common in the guided instruction portion of the workshop because this is a time to focus on developing specific skills among a group of students. Because this grouping is formed out of data-specific needs at a given point in time, the

More information on
assessments can be
found in chapter 11.

members of these groups should change regularly. These changes are made based on sound assessment information.

- *Student-selected groups*. At other times, students select the members of their groups. This occurs most often when there are projects that need to be completed outside of the school day. Allowing students to select the members of their groups ensures that students have complementary schedules to accomplish learning tasks.

- *Random groups*. At still other times, groups are formed randomly. This ensures that every student in the class has a chance to interact with every other student in the class. These heterogeneous groups are used in collaborative learning centers when the teacher wants to ensure that the groups are mixed by ability, skills, background knowledge, fluency, and interests. There are a number of ways to form random groups, including drawing names from a hat, using playing cards in which all the 3s, 4s, 5s (and so on) form groups, or counting off by numbers.

Teacher Tip

The language arts workshop format ensures that the harmful effects of ability group do not occur in your classroom. Importantly, the language arts workshop format also allows for you to meet with groups of students to address specific needs. One way to assess your classroom to determine if the groups have become permanent and need to be changed is to sit at the guided reading or writing table and call the name of a student. If several other students in the room put down their pencils in anticipation of joining the group, it is likely time to make a change. Again, remember to make the changes based on the best assessment information that you have carefully gathered.

These grouping strategies ensure students will receive instruction with a variety of peers as they move through the shared, guided, collaborative, and independent phases of the language arts workshop. However, the content of what is taught in the workshop must be evidence-based, implemented within an effective literacy program, and part of a balanced curriculum. Collectively, these form a framework for effective practice.

WHAT ARE THE COMPONENTS OF EFFECTIVE LITERACY TEACHING?

In 2000, a team of researchers, educators, and parents reported their findings in a review of thousands of research studies conducted since 1966. Their goal was to identify the necessary instructional components key to learning to read. This group, the National Reading Panel (NRP), named five strategies as evidence-based, meaning that a significant number of studies supported their use in effective literacy teaching.

**Evidence-Based
Instruction**

The components of effective literacy instruction include developing an awareness of the sounds of the language (called *phonemic awareness*) and the relationship between letters and the sounds they represent (*phonics*). In addition, the NRP identified *fluency development* and *vocabulary development* as essential components of comprehension. Finally, intentional instruction in *comprehension* strategies must occur from the beginning of a child's entry into school. These five essential compo-

Evidence Based

Figure 1.3   Five Essential Components of Reading

Reading with children and helping them practice specific reading components can dramatically improve their ability to read. Scientific research shows that there are five essential components of reading that children must be taught in order to learn to read. Adults can help children learn to be good readers by systematically practicing these five components:

- Recognizing and using individual sounds to create words, or **phonemic awareness**. Children need to be taught to hear sounds in words and that words are made up of the smallest parts of sound, or phonemes.

- Understanding the relationships between written letters and spoken sounds, or **phonics**. Children need to be taught the sounds individual printed letters and groups of letters make. Knowing the relationships between letters and sounds helps children to recognize familiar words accurately and automatically, and "decode" new words.

- Developing the ability to read a text accurately and quickly, or **reading fluency**. Children must learn to read words rapidly and accurately in order to understand what is read. When fluent readers read silently, they recognize words automatically. When fluent readers read aloud, they read effortlessly and with expression. Readers who are weak in fluency read slowly, word by word, focusing on decoding words instead of comprehending meaning.

- Learning the meaning and pronunciation of words, or **vocabulary development**. Children need to actively build and expand their knowledge of written and spoken words, what they mean and how they are used.

- Acquiring strategies to understand, remember and communicate what is read, or **reading comprehension strategies**. Children need to be taught comprehension strategies, or the steps good readers use to make sure they understand text. Students who are in control of their own reading comprehension become purposeful, active readers.

Source: U.S. Department of Education, Office of Intergovernmental and Interagency Affairs, Educational Partnerships and Family Involvement Unit, *Reading Tips for Parents,* Washington, D.C., 2003.

nents of reading appear in Figure 1.3. Based on the findings of the NRP, The U.S. Department of Education published indicators of effective literacy programs (2003).

Effective Literacy Programs

The indicators for effective programs are not narrow and prescriptive, but rather can be accomplished using a number of different scheduling structures. As stated in the list in Figure 1.4, the emphasis should be on sustained periods of instruction, including time each day when students read silently and aloud. There is a focus on assessment for the purpose of informing instructional decisions. In addition, skills and strategies at the letter, word, and text level are taught, and all of this is accomplished through connections between reading and writing. Therefore, evidence-based instruction in an effective literacy program must drive the language arts workshop.

The Language Arts Workshop

Another look at our table of contents reveals that we will systematically address each of these components. These components of effective reading programs are imbedded into the language arts workshop.

- *Assessment occurs throughout the academic year and the results are used to inform instruction.* Time each week is set aside to assess student literacy progress.

- *A meaningful amount of time is dedicated to literacy instruction.* The language arts workshop is designed to be implemented in 2-hour blocks each day.

> **Figure 1.4**   Components of a Quality Reading Program
>
> - Every teacher is excited about reading and promotes the value and fun of reading to students.
> - All students are carefully evaluated, beginning in Kindergarten, to see what they know and what they need to become good readers.
> - Reading instruction and practice lasts 90 minutes or more a day in first, second and third grades and 60 minutes a day in Kindergarten.
> - All students in first, second and third grades who are behind in reading get special instruction and practice. These students receive, throughout the day, a total of 60 extra minutes of instruction.
> - Before or after-school help is given to all students beyond first grade who need extra instruction or who need to review skills. Summer school is available for students who are behind at the end of the year.
> - Reading instruction and practice includes work on letters, sounds and blending sounds. Students learn to blend letters and sounds to form new words.
> - Learning new words and their meaning is an important part of instruction.
> - Students have daily spelling practice and weekly spelling tests.
> - The connection between reading and writing is taught on a daily basis. Students write daily. Papers are corrected and returned to the students. By the end of second grade, students write final copies of corrected papers. Corrected papers are sent home for parents to see.
> - All students have a chance to read both silently and aloud in school each day and at home every night.
> - Every classroom has a library of books that children want to read. This includes easy books and books that are more difficult.
> - The School library is used often and has many books. Students may check books out during the summer and over holidays.
>
> **Source**: U.S. Department of Education, Office of Intergovernmental and Interagency Affairs, Educational Partnerships and Family Involvement Unit, *Reading Tips for Parents,* Washington, D.C., 2003.

- *Instruction is balanced between part-to-whole and whole-to-part approaches.* The language arts workshop features instruction in letters and words, reading connected text, purposeful writing, and oral language development.

- *There is a reading-writing connection.* Development of reading and writing proficiency occurs when students have rich reading experiences and opportunities for purposeful writing. The language arts workshop provides both.

- *Reading and writing occur daily.* In the language arts workshop, these events occur with the teacher, with peers, and independently.

Ultimately, the language arts workshop is intended to work within a balanced curriculum across the day. This curriculum includes science, mathematics, and social studies content, as well as the visual and performing arts. Because the language arts workshop enhances these other curricular areas, it is essential that content area reading and writing are incorporated into these literacy experiences. It is possible to accomplish these goals of instruction because the format of the workshop provides a flexible structure.

WHAT IS THE FORMAT OF THE LANGUAGE ARTS WORKSHOP?

The language arts workshop is meant to form the basis for a meaningful literacy program. Within the workshop, students participate in a model of instruction that allows them to use literacy skills and strategies on a daily basis. In addition, students read and write every day, collaborate with peers, and work independently. The teacher meets with students as a whole group, in small groups, and individually. While not every student meets with the teacher every day, these meetings occur several times a week. In most districts, a 2-hour block of time is devoted to literacy instruction. Therefore, the following section describes how time is used across a 120-minute time period. The language arts workshop diagram in Figure 1.5 first describes these instructional phases.

Time Organization

More information on focus lessons can be found in chapter 2.

Chapter 3 discusses guided phase.

Collaborative learning is the focus of chapter 4.

Independent reading information is located in chapter 5.

These important topics are discussed in chapters 5 and 11, respectively.

The first 20 minutes is devoted to the **focus lesson** and consists of a shared reading or writing experience with an identified purpose that will be practiced again during the workshop. Next, the teacher meets with two small groups of students for 20 minutes for **guided instruction** in reading or writing. Students in these groups have been selected based on similar needs or interests. While the teacher meets for guided instruction, the rest of the class is engaged in **collaborative learning.** Collaborative learning may occur in pairs or in slightly larger groups, but all students are working with at least one other person. After two rotations, students work for 25 minutes on **independent reading.** While students read independently, the teacher meets with individual students to **confer** and **assess** reading. Next, students work on their **independent writing** for another 25 minutes while the teacher again **confers** and **assesses,** this time for writing. Figure 1.6 represents how time is organized in a two-hour block of time.

Of course, not all instruction necessary for effective practice can be offered in one session of the language arts workshop. This requires a perspective across the week to see how instruction unfolds.

Language arts workshop across a week. The language arts workshop is not meant to be a rigid structure that follows the same pattern day after day. As you review the sample weekly schedule, you will notice that on some days the teacher is collecting assessment information, while at other times he or she meets with individual students to confer about reading and writing. In addition, while guided instruction occurs each day, it is not always with the same students. It is critical to plan time for reteaching concepts students may not have mastered the first time. In our experience, well-intentioned teachers do not ever get to reteaching because they do not set aside time to do so. In the language arts workshop, time for reteaching is planned each week. If you don't need to reteach anyone during a particular week, you can move on with your curriculum. Figure 1.7 features a sample weekly schedule for the language arts workshop.

Flexibility in the language arts workshop. A note about sample schedules—they are only intended to give a broad guide to the structure of the workshop. We believe that the best teaching is responsive teaching. Good teachers watch their students closely to see how the lesson is going. When teachable moments occur, when a student asks a profound question, when a puzzled look on a child's face suggests he is confused,

Figure 1.5   Language Arts Workshop Diagram

	What Ms. Allen Does	**What Tino Does**
9:00–9:20 AM **FOCUS LESSON**	Ms. Allen welcomes the students and introduces **a focus lesson** on character analysis using an excerpt from *The Most Beautiful Place in the World* (Cameron, 1993). This reading tells the story of Juan, a young boy who is abandoned by his parents. She displays the reading on the overhead so that all the students can view it. Ms. Allen tells her students that the purpose of the lesson is to discover how the author lets the reader know about the attributes of the characters. She models her own comprehension for the students as she reads it using a Think Aloud strategy and makes notes on a graphic organizer. Next, students work in pairs to highlight other clues in the passage. Ms. Allen instructs her students to look for similar devices during their literature circle readings and distributes another copy of the graphic organizer to use.	Tino has his own copy of the reading and follows the text while Ms. Allen reads aloud. Using a copy of the graphic organizer, he and his partner Maggie makes similar notes about the characters of Juan, Mama, and the man his mother will marry.
9:20–9:40 AM **GUIDED AND COLLABORATIVE LEARNING**	Ms. Allen meets with a group of students for **guided reading.** Today they are reading an expository article about the orphan trains that relocated 100,000 children from New York City to the American west between 1854–1929. She has determined the level of the reading using the Fry Readability Scale (Fry, 2002) to match the text difficulty to the instructional level of these students.	Tino meets with his literature circle group during **collaborative learning.** He and his classmates are reading *Hatchet* (Paulsen, 1999), a story of a 13-year-old boy who survives a plane crash in a remote part of Alaska. Tino and his group discuss clues the author has supplied in chapter 2 about Brian's character and his ability to survive hardship. They use the graphic organizer Ms. Allen introduced during the focus lesson to write notes. The group agrees to read chapters 3 and 4 before their next meeting.
9:40–10:00 AM **GUIDED AND COLLABORATIVE LEARNING**	Ms. Allen meets with a small group of students, including Tino, for guided reading instruction. Because this group reads more complicated text, she has selected an expository reading on the development of child labor laws during the 19th century. Ms. Allen showed them photographs of children at work (www.historyplace.com/ unitedstates/childlabor/) and guided them through a reading from the social studies textbook on child labor.	Tino meets with Ms. Allen and four other students to participate in a guided reading lesson.

Figure 1.5	Language Arts Workshop Diagram *(continued)*

	What Ms. Allen Does	*What Tino Does*
10:00–10:25 AM **INDEPENDENT** **READING WITH** **CONFERRING**	Ms. Allen meets individually with a total of five students to **confer** with them about their readings. Each student brings their reading log and the current book they are reading. She asks them to read a favorite passage and makes notes about their oral reading. Next, she discusses the story and clarifies vocabulary. Each meeting lasts about five minutes.	Tino uses his **independent reading** time to finish chapters 3 and 4 of *Hatchet* and writes observational notes on stickies about Brian's character. Because he is the vocabulary enricher for the group this week, he records tricky or unusual words in his notebook to look up later.
10:25–10:50 AM **INDEPENDENT** **WRITING WITH** **CONFERRING**	Ms. Allen meets with five students to discuss their writing. Tino is one of the students and brings his writer's notebook to the **conference.** He asks to see the photographs of child laborers Ms. Allen showed during guided reading. Ms. Allen and Tino make a plan for Tino to create a story based on one of the photographs.	Tino meets with Ms. Allen to plan his next piece. After conferring with Ms. Allen, he returns to his desk to begin writing.
10:50–11:00 AM **SHARE AND** **CLOSURE**	Ms. Allen invites the class to discuss important characters they read about in their literature circle groups. Elizabeth, a student currently reading *Bud, Not Buddy* (Curtis, 2000) with her literature circle, shares Bud's character traits with the class.	Tino participates in the share session.

good teachers follow the child. This undoubtedly messes up the carefully crafted schedule. So be it. After all, who's the schedule for? If something has to give on a particular day in order to accommodate these important events, be flexible about it. Don't let the occasional deviations from the schedule discourage you.

It is equally important to remember that expected lapses in schedules do not mean there should be no schedule at all. Children thrive on knowing what to expect, and teachers find they accomplish far more when a thoughtful schedule is planned and implemented.

Teaching Content in the Language Arts Workshop

When you read the description of Ms. Allen's and Tino's day, you may have been surprised to see social studies content being taught. Because literacy development is essential to learning content, it only makes sense that content areas are incorporated into the workshop as well as taught at other points in the day. There is simply too much content knowledge to ever be effectively taught in the brief amount of time typically devoted to these subjects.

We are cautious about the uneven use of informational texts in literacy instruction at the elementary and middle school levels. Students typically have far more extensive experience with reading stories than with reading nonfiction and this impacts both their background knowledge and their understanding of how to read these texts. A survey of several basal reading series for second-, fourth-, and sixth-grade students revealed that only 16%–22% of the readings were informational

Figure 1.6   The Language Arts Workshop in a Two-Hour Block

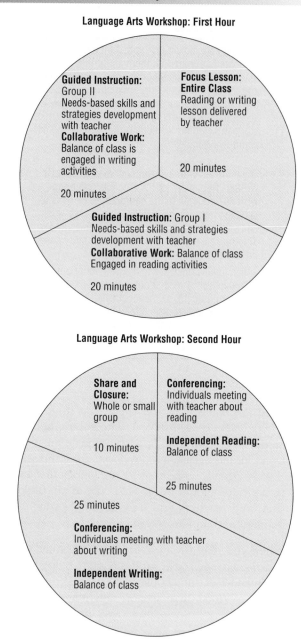

Language Arts Workshop: First Hour

Guided Instruction:
Group II
Needs-based skills and
strategies development
with teacher
Collaborative Work:
Balance of class is
engaged in writing
activities

20 minutes

Focus Lesson:
Entire Class
Reading or writing
lesson delivered
by teacher

20 minutes

Guided Instruction: Group I
Needs-based skills and strategies
development with teacher
Collaborative Work: Balance of class
Engaged in reading activities

20 minutes

Language Arts Workshop: Second Hour

**Share and
Closure:**
Whole or small
group

10 minutes

Conferencing:
Individuals meeting
with teacher about
reading

Independent Reading:
Balance of class

25 minutes

25 minutes

Conferencing:
Individuals meeting with teacher
about writing

Independent Writing:
Balance of class

in nature (Moss & Newton, 2002). Similarly, Duke (2000) reported that in some schools, first graders averaged just 3.6 minutes per day with informational text. Students simply must have frequent opportunities to read and write informational text within the language arts workshop if they are to master the many content standards before them.

Figure 1.7   Sample Weekly Schedule for the Language Arts Workshop

	Monday	Tuesday	Wednesday	Thursday	Friday
Focus Lesson: 20 minutes	Reading	Writing	Reading	Writing	Reading
Guided Lesson 1: 20 minutes OR **Collaborative Work 1:** 20 minutes	**Guided Reading:** Group I **Collaborative Reading:** Literature Circle (Group 2) Centers (Groups 3 and 4)	**Guided Writing:** Group 3 **Collaborative Writing:** Groups 1, 2, and 4	**Guided Reading:** Group 3 **Collaborative Reading:** Literature Circle (Group 4) Centers (Groups 1 and 2)	**Guided Writing:** Group 1 **Collaborative Writing:** Groups 2, 3, and 4	**Guided Reading:** Meet with students who will benefit from reteaching **Collaborative Reading:** Rest of class
Guided Lesson 2: 20 minutes OR **Collaborative Work 2:** 20 minutes	**Guided Reading:** Group 2 **Collaborative Reading:** Literature Circle (Groups 3 and 4) Centers (Group 1)	**Guided Writing:** Group 4 **Collaborative Writing:** Groups 1, 2, and 3	**Guided Reading:** Group 4 **Collaborative Reading:** Literature Circles (Groups 1 and 2) Centers (Group 3)	**Guided Writing:** Group 2 **Collaborative Writing:** Groups 1, 3, and 4	**Guided Writing:** Meet with students who will benefit from reteaching **Collaborative Writing:** Rest of class
Independent Reading with Conferring: 25 minutes	**Assess** individual students in reading	**Confer** with 5 students on reading	**Assess** individual students in reading	**Confer** with 5 students on reading	**Sustained Silent Reading:** Entire class
Independent Writing with Conferring: 25 minutes	**Assess** individual students in writing	**Confer** with 5 students on writing	**Assess** individual students in writing	**Confer** with 5 students on writing	**Author's Chair/ Literacy Lounge**
Share and Closure: 10 minutes	Oral language development	Oral language development	Oral language development	Oral language development	Oral language development

While the language arts workshop can be implemented anywhere within a balanced curriculum, it is helpful to view it embedded in the school day and week. Figure 1.8 contains a sample schedule of how the language arts workshop fits into the week.

WHAT ARE THE MATERIALS USED IN THE LANGUAGE ARTS WORKSHOP?

As you can imagine, there are a wide range of texts that you can use in the language arts workshop. You will likely have a basal reader in your classroom. **Basal readers** are student textbooks designed to teach reading in a sequential, skill-oriented way. These texts are useful in the language arts workshop because they provide you and your students with easy access to a wide range of texts organized in a thoughtful manner to address the standards at your grade level. You will likely supplement the basal with trade books, newspapers, on-line readings, graphic novels, poems, songs,

Figure 1.8   LAW in a Balanced Curriculum

Sample Weekly Schedule for the Entire Day

Time	Monday	Tuesday	Wednesday	Thursday	Friday
8:00–8:15 AM	Morning Meeting	Morning Meeting	Morning Meeting	Morning Meeting	Morning Meeting
8:15–8:30 AM	Sustained Silent Reading	Sustained Silent Reading	Sustained Silent Reading	Sustained Silent Reading	Sustained Silent Reading
8:30–9:00 AM	Word Study	Word Study	Word Study	Word Study	Word Study
9:00–11:00 AM	Language Arts Workshop	Language Arts Workshop	Language Arts Workshop	Language Arts Workshop	Language Arts Workshop
11:00–11:30 AM	Visual and Performing Arts	Music	Physical Education	Library	Physical Education
11:30 AM–12:15 PM	Lunch and Recess	Lunch and Recess	Lunch and Recess	Lunch and Recess	Lunch and Recess
12:15–1:15 PM	Mathematics	Mathematics	Mathematics	Mathematics	Mathematics
1:15–2:15 PM	Science	Social Studies	Science	Social Studies	Science
2:15–2:30 PM	Afternoon Meeting	Afternoon Meeting	Afternoon Meeting	Afternoon Meeting	Afternoon Meeting

and many other readings. Regardless of the sources you use, there are things that every teacher needs to know about texts.

Classroom Texts   The primary types of texts in classrooms are textbooks, guided reading books, and trade books. Together, these comprise the main materials used by teachers to deliver daily reading instruction.

Textbooks. We use this term to refer to a large group of materials purchased by schools for teachers to use in their classrooms. Textbooks are produced by commercial publishers exclusively for the school market and are designed to provide teachers with material that is gauged to the students' reading and interest levels. Commercial reading programs may be formatted as a collection of readings at a single level, called a **basal.** Larger texts containing hundreds of readings, called **anthologies,** are used with older readers. The readings consist mostly of poems, short stories, and excerpts of longer books written by well-known authors. The readability of the text is wider in an anthology and the readings are chosen by the teacher based on the needs of the students. Basal readers and anthologies come with a number of support materials for use by the teacher. The primary support material is the **teacher's edition,** which contains all of the material in the student edition, as well as suggestions for teaching the content, assessing student learning, and making accommodations for students who need more support. Additional support materials for teachers may include assessment guides, blackline masters to be reproduced as worksheets, and multimedia components such as CD-ROMs and audiotapes. Supplementary materials are produced for students as well. Some commercial reading programs come with student workbooks to practice skills and additional readings related to the stories in the basal or anthology.

Guided reading books. Another type of commercial reading program popular in many school districts is **guided reading** books. These materials are packaged as individual titles rather than one large book. Typical guided reading programs offer six copies of each title (enough for a small reading group), with several titles available for each reading level. These books are small in size and have a paper binding so that young students can easily handle them. Guided reading books are more commonly used in the early grades (K–3) and are not typically accompanied by a teacher's edition.

Decodable texts. **Decodable texts** are often used with young students or students who struggle with reading. The words in decodable books are restricted to spelling patterns that the reader can decode given his or her existing sound-letter knowledge (Brown, 1999–2000). A text is typically considered to be decodable if at least 80% of the words can be sounded out by the reader. For example, the following sentence is highly decodable because it relies on a restricted spelling pattern:

A fat cat sat on a mat.

More information about sight words is presented in chapter 7.

Some high-frequency sight words are used as well. Sight words are those words that are taught to be recognized immediately rather than sounded out. In the previous decodable sentence, *a* and *on* are considered to be sight words. One concern about decodable books is that many are not authentic pieces of literature, instead having been created solely to teach reading. To balance the use of decodable books in guided and independent instruction, teachers suggest that read aloud selections be made from quality, authentic literature (Watson, 1997).

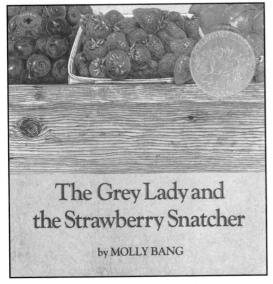

From *The Grey Lady and the Strawberry Snatcher* by Molly Bang, © 1996 by Simon & Schuster. Used by permission of Simon & Schuster.

Trade books. Books produced for the public market are called **trade books.** These are the titles typically found in bookstores and libraries around the country. Trade books have assumed a more prominent role in reading instruction because the quality of the literature is viewed as being higher than the stories produced for reading instruction. The type of literature available in trade books is sometimes referred to as authentic literature because it is read by children outside of school. Trade books are available to schools in text sets, multiple copies that can be read simultaneously by a group of students and their teacher for discussion.

Picture books. In addition to these traditional classroom texts, it is common to find picture books in classrooms. **Picture books** are books in which a majority of the page is an illustration and the text is more limited in length. The finest picture books combine "two distinct forms of creative expression, words and pictures . . . [to] create conditions of dependence and interdependence"

(Cullinan & Person, 2001, p. 624). Working together, they tell a story that uses both visual and textual elements to engage readers. For example, *A Bad Case of the Stripes* (Shannon, 1998) is an example of a book that uses both pictures and words in a large format to tell the story of a girl who gives up something she likes (in this case, lima beans) so that she can fit in socially with her classmates. She immediately contracts a strange malady that causes her skin to take on patterns and hues in her environment, much like a chameleon. While this book could be considered "fantasy" as people do not become striped with color due to a lack of lima beans, most teachers will call it a picture book to describe the format of the book. Many states and districts have lists of suggested trade books and picture books by grade level. We have included a sample list of quality literature by grade level in appendix 1.

Texts That Expand Student Understanding

Teachers use commercial reading programs and trade and picture books for reading instruction. However, effective teachers know that students benefit from exposure to other types of text that expand their understanding of reading and of the world around them. These include wordless books, newspapers, digital sources, and graphic novels and anime.

Wordless books. Wordless books, as their name suggests, contain little or no written text. Instead, the illustrations propel the story. In years past these books had been associated only with toddlers, but this form has been expanded to tell sophisticated stories as well. The book *Middle Passage: White Sails, Black Cargo* (Feelings, 1995) is aimed at a middle school audience and movingly portrays the plight of Africans stolen from their homes and sold as slaves in America. Teachers also use wordless books with struggling readers of all ages as the text does not give away an intended audience or reading level. Wordless books are popular with students as well as they like to write their own words for the book. For example, the Caldecott winner *Tuesday* (Wiesner, 1991) pictorially describes a night in which it rains frogs. This wordless book allows young writers to compose imaginative original text. A sample of wordless books can be viewed in Figure 1.9.

Figure 1.9 Wordless Books

Bang, M. (1984). *The grey lady and the strawberry snatcher.* New York: Simon & Schuster.
Banyai, I. (1995). *Zoom.* New York: Viking.
Briggs, R. (1978). *The snowman.* New York: Random House.
DePaola, T. (1978). *Pancakes for breakfast.* New York: Harcourt Brace Jovanovich.
Hoban, T. (1990). *Shadows and reflections.* New York: Greenwillow.
Feelings, T. (1995). *Middle passage: White ships, black cargo.* New York: Dial.
Jenkins, S. (1995). *Looking down.* New York: Houghton.
Mayer, M. (1967). *A boy, a dog, and a frog.* New York: Dial.
Rohmann, E. (1994). *Time flies.* New York: Crown.
Weitzman, J. P. (1998). *You can't take a balloon into the Metropolitan Museum.* New York: Dial.
Wiesner, D. (1991). *Tuesday.* New York: Clarion.
Wiesner, D. (1999). *Sector 7.* New York: Clarion.

Newspapers. Newspapers in the classroom offer current local, national, and international information at a relatively low cost. Because multiple copies can be easily obtained, the newspaper can be useful for collaborative small group work among students. The contents of the newspaper offer a wealth of materials for teaching reading and writing. For example, editorial cartoons can be analyzed, and maps that accompany news articles can be used to teach about geography. Even the youngest readers can cut apart comic strips and reassemble them to practice sequencing in stories. Many local papers participate in the Newspapers in Education program, a partnership of newspapers that distribute classroom sets of newspapers at no cost. Related websites contain lesson plans and teaching ideas for using the newspaper to teach reading and content skills. Here are a few tips for using the newspaper in your classroom from the Fredericksburg (VA) Free-Lance Star (www.fredericksburg.com/flshome/):

> Information about Newspapers in Education can be found at www.nieonline.com.

- *Teach young students how to handle the newspaper.* Many children have little or no experience handling the newspaper. Take the time to teach them how to fold and organize.

- *Provide instruction on the organizational structure of the paper.* Show students how each section is labeled by a letter of the alphabet, and each page in the section is numbered.

- *Introduce one section of the newspaper at a time.* This prevents learners from becoming overwhelmed with the volume of information in the paper.

- *Teach the vocabulary of the newspaper.* Newspapers have their own unique vocabulary. *Headline, caption, byline, column,* and *editorial* may be unfamiliar concepts to your students. Teach them how to use the vocabulary accurately to identify parts of the paper.

- *Allow for free reading time.* One of the pleasures of newspaper reading is the ability to choose topics of interest. Provide free reading time to allow students an opportunity to explore the wealth of information offered.

Digital sources. To say that technology is changing rapidly is certainly an understatement. Consider the circumstances of students graduating from high school in 2004 (Leu, Kinzer, Coiro, & Cammack, 2004):

> Many graduates started their school career with literacies of paper, pencil, and book technologies but will have finished having encountered the literacies demanded by a wide variety of information and communication technologies (ICT): Web logs (blogs) . . . World Wide Web browsers, Web editors, e-mail . . . instant messaging . . . listservs, bulletin boards, avatars, virtual worlds, and many others. These students experienced new literacies at the end of their schooling unimagined at the beginning. (p. 1571)

The challenge in classrooms is to offer students access to technology that is becoming available to classrooms at an ever-increasing rate. This challenge is not new—teachers have faced this throughout the history of education. What is more recent is the phenomenon of student knowledge of technology outstripping that of the teacher. How many of us have seen a teacher appeal to a student to help with a truculent piece of technology? While the pace of technology development shows no signs of slowing, we as teachers must consider how students will use these texts in our classrooms. National standards of technology have been developed to inform use in K–12 classrooms and can be viewed in their entirety at http://cnets.iste.org/currstands/cstands-netss.html.

In particular, the standard on using technology research tools is meaningful in our discussion about texts. This refers to a student's ability to locate and evaluate information found on the Internet and in other digital forms, including CD-ROM and DVD-R. Teachers can facilitate development of these skills by ensuring that some reading material is always available in digital form. For example, websites can be bookmarked on the classroom computer for use during independent reading and digital source software can be installed to provide students with up-to-date information on a variety of topics.

Graphic novels and anime. Wade and Moje describe this category of readings as "unacknowledged and unsanctioned texts" because they are rarely used by the teacher in the classroom (2000, p. 621). However, these texts play an important role in the lives of students because they are the ones chosen by them to read outside of school. This is particularly true for older and reluctant readers. Comic books, professional wrestling magazines, even some kinds of trade novels are often deemed by the teacher as being unworthy of attention. (Dav Pilkey's *Captain Underpants* series is criticized by some teachers for its mildly naughty humor.)

Graphic novels and *anime* have recently drawn the attention of researchers interested in engaging reluctant readers (Chandler-Olcott & Mahar, 2003; Frey & Fisher, 2004). Graphic novels look much like comic books but are usually longer and contain a single story, rather than employing the serial format common to comic books. These books are derived from a Japanese literary form called *manga* and have seen a surge in popularity among adolescent readers in the last decade. The art most commonly used in graphic novels is *anime*, a style associated with Japanese animation featuring characters with large heads and oversized eyes. Although many graphic novels focus on superheroes, a growing number examine broader topics. Indeed, the adult graphic novel *Maus: A Survivor's Tale* (Speigelman, 1990) won a Pulitzer Prize in 1992 and the movie *Road to Perdition* was developed from a graphic novel by the same name (Collins, 2002). Like any text, graphic novels should be carefully screened before placing in the classroom. We have compiled a list of graphic novels in Figure 1.10 that may be of interest for your students.

Criteria for Selecting Books for the Language Arts Workshop

An important part of the language arts workshop is a classroom library full of high quality narrative and informational texts. These books become the materials you will use in focus lessons, guided instruction, collaborative learning, and the independent phase of the workshop. The books you select should:

- Provide students examples of quality writing
- Grant students access to excellent illustrations
- Offer a range of reading levels
- Allow them to see themselves—their religion, ethnicity, language, and culture

Figure 1.10 Graphic Novels

Bey, E. (1997). *Still I rise: A cartoon history of African Americans.* New York: W. W. Norton.

Giardino, V. & Johnson, J. [trans.]. (1997). *A Jew in communist Prague: Adolescence.* New York: NBM.

Golnick, L. (2002). *The cartoon history of the universe.* New York: Doubleday.

Kochalka, J. (2003). *Peanut butter and Jeremy.* Gainesville, FL: Alternative Comics.

Medley, L. (2000). *Castle waiting.* Portland, OR: Lucky Roads.

Morrison, T., & Morrison, S. (2003). *Who's got game? The ant or the grasshopper?* New York: Scribner.

Morrison, T., & Morrison, S. (2003). *Who's got game? The lion or the mouse?* New York: Scribner.

Morrison, T., & Morrison, S. (2004). *Who's got game? Poppy or the snake?* New York: Scribner.

Speigelman, A., & Mouly, F. (2000). *Little lit: Folklore and fairy tale funnies.* New York: HarperCollins.

Speigelman, A., & Mouly, F. (2001). *Little lit: Strange stories for strange kids.* New York: HarperCollins.

Speigelman, A., & Mouly, F. (2003). *Little lit: It was a dark and silly night.* New York: HarperCollins.

Winnick, J. (2000). *The adventures of Barry Weins, boy genius.* New York: Henry Holt.

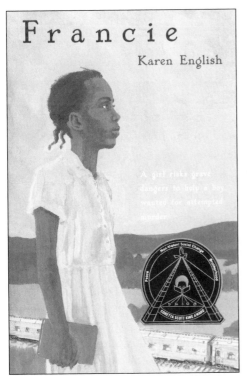

Jacket art © 1999 by Tim Hall from FRANCIE by Karen English. Used with the permission of Farrar, Straus and Giroux.

- Permit them to interact through reading with people who have different experiences and beliefs
- Depict a variety of family structures
- Offer a balance of gender in terms of characters and what the characters do
- Interrupt gender, racial, or ability stereotypes

One of the ways to find quality books is to review titles that have received national recognition. For example, the American Library Association awards the Newbery (for writing) and the Caldecott (for illustration) each year to the best children's books. In addition, the Orbus Pictus is awarded for outstanding nonfiction written for children. The Correta Scott King award and the Tomas Rivera award are also excellent sources of books. These books can easily be located via an Internet search for the award or on an online bookstore.

Each state also awards a series of "young reader medals" for books that are particularly popular with students in the state. The state reading association or library association will have a list of these awards by year.

In addition, the International Reading Association created the "children's choices" and "teacher choices" awards for both young children and adolescents. These books can be found on the International Reading Association webpage at www.reading.org.

BIG IDEAS ABOUT THE LANGUAGE ARTS WORKSHOP

The language arts workshop is established upon principles of learning, especially the Zones of Proximal Development and the gradual release of responsibility model of instruction. A developmental approach to reading and writing is utilized in the workshop to foster literacy acquisition. This focus on the individual learner makes language arts workshop ideal for students with language or learning needs. The diversity of the classroom requires flexible grouping strategies to ensure students participate in a wide array of learning tasks. In addition, the language arts workshop features evidence-based components of literacy instruction. Finally, students learn through the organizational structures of the workshop that allow them to learn in a variety of ways, and with a variety of materials.

INTEGRATING THE STANDARDS

Create lesson plans that meet your state's standards by visiting our Companion Website at www.prenhall.com/frey. There you'll find lessons created to meet the NCTE/IRA Standards. Adapt them to meet the standards of your own state through links to your state's standards, and keep them in the online portfolio. You can collect lesson plans for each chapter in an online portfolio, providing you with invaluable tools to meet your state's standards when you head into your own classroom.

CHECK YOUR UNDERSTANDING

1. How do students learn?
2. How does reading develop over time?
3. How does writing develop over time?
4. How do we support students with unique learning needs?
5. How should students be grouped for instruction?
6. What are the components of effective literacy instruction?
7. What is the format of the language arts workshop?
8. What materials are used in the language arts workshop?

CLASSROOM CONNECTIONS

1. Meet with your classroom teacher to discuss literacy instruction. What does he or she consider to be the important aspects of literacy development?
2. You will be exposed to many excellent resources and ideas in your classroom. Set up a file system to organize these ideas for later use in your own practice.
3. Keep a disposable flash camera in your desk at school and take photographs (with permission) of ideas you want to remember, including bulletin boards, language charts, and classroom layout.
4. Meet with your teacher to discuss the schedule for the class. Make a detailed schedule for yourself and ask for a copy of the school's calendar as well.

References

Boaler, J., William, D., & Brown, M. (2000). Students' experiences of ability grouping—disaffection, polarisation and the construction of failure. *British Educational Research Journal, 26,* 631–648.

Broussard, C. A., & Joseph, A. L. (1998). Tracking: A form of educational neglect? *Social Work in Education, 20,* 110–120.

Brown, K. J. (1999–2000). What kind of text—for whom and when? Textual scaffolding for beginning readers. *The Reading Teacher, 53,* 292–307.

Buswell, B. E., Schaffner, C. B., & Seyler, A. B. (Eds.). (1999). *Opening doors: Connecting students to curriculum, classmates, and learning* (2nd ed.). Colorado Springs, CO: Peak Parent Center.

Chandler-Olcott, K., & Mahar, D. (2003). Adolescents' "anime"-inspired "fanfictions": An exploration of multiliteracies. *Journal of Adolescent & Adult Literacy, 46,* 556–566.

Clay, M. M. (2003). Child development. In J. Flood, D. Lapp, J. R. Squire, & J. M. Jensen (Eds.), *Handbook of research in teaching the English language arts* (2nd ed., pp. 46–52). Mahwah, NJ: Erlbaum.

Cullinan, B. E., & Person, D. G. (2001). *The continuum encyclopedia of children's literature.* New York: Continuum.

Duke, N. K. (2000). 3.6 minutes per day: The scarcity of informational texts in first grade. *Reading Research Quarterly, 35,* 202–224.

Fisher, D., Flood, J., Lapp, D., & Frey, N. (2004). Interactive read alouds: Is there a common set of implementation practices. *The Reading Teacher, 58,* 8–17.

Fisher, D., & Frey, N. (2001). Access to the core curriculum: Critical ingredients for student success. *Remedial and Special Education, 22,* 48–57.

Fisher, D., & Frey, N. (Eds.). (2003). *Inclusive urban schools.* Baltimore: Paul H. Brookes.

Flood, J., Lapp, D., Flood, S., & Nagel, G. (1992). Am I allowed to group? Using flexible patterns for effective instruction. *The Reading Teacher, 45,* 608–616.

Frey, N., & Fisher, D. (2004). Using graphic novels, anime, and the Internet in an urban high school. *The English Journal, 93*(3), 19–25.

Goodman, Y. M., & Goodman, K. S. (1994). To err is human: Learning about language processes by analyzing miscues. In R. B. Ruddell, M. R. Ruddell, & H. Singer (Eds.), *Theoretical models and processes of reading* (4th ed., pp. 104–123). Newark, DE: International Reading Association.

Halliday, M. A. K. (1975). *Learning how to mean: Explorations in the development of language.* London: Edward Arnold.

Harste, J. C. (1994). Literacy as curricular conversations about knowledge, inquiry, and morality. In R. B. Ruddell, M. R. Ruddell, & H. Singer (Eds.), *Theoretical models and processes of reading* (4th ed., pp. 1220–1242). Newark, DE: International Reading Association.

Harvey, S., & Goudvis, A. (1999). *Strategies that work: Teaching comprehension to enhance understanding.* York, ME: Stenhouse.

Herrell, A., & Jordan, M. (2003). *Fifty strategies for teaching English language learners* (2nd ed.). Upper Saddle River, NJ: Merrill/Prentice Hall.

Hoffman, L. M. (2003). *Overview of public elementary and secondary schools and districts: School year 2001–2002.* Washington, DC: National Center for Educational Statistics.

Hunt, P., Soto, G., Maier, J., & Doering, K. (2003). Collaborative teaming to support students at risk and students with severe disabilities in general education classrooms. *Exceptional Children, 69,* 315–332.

Keene, E. O., & Zimmermann, S. (1997). *Mosaic of thought: Teaching comprehension in a reader's workshop.* Portsmouth, NH: Heinemann.

Kluth, P., & Darmody-Latham, J. (2003). Beyond sight words: Literacy opportunities for students with autism. *The Reading Teacher, 56,* 532–535.

Krashen, S. D. (1985). *The input hypothesis: Issues and implications.* New York: Longman.

Lamott, A. (1995). *Bird by bird: Some instructions on writing and life.* New York: Anchor Doubleday.

Lapp, D., Flood, J., & Goss, K. (2000). Desks don't move—students do: In effective classroom environments. *The Reading Teacher, 54,* 31–36.

Leu, D. J., Jr., Kinzer, C. K., Coiro, J. L., & Cammack, D. W. (2004). Toward a theory of new literacies emerging from the internet and other information and communication technologies. In R. B. Ruddell & N. J. Unrau (Eds.), *Theoretical models and processes of reading* (5th ed., pp. 1570–1613). Newark, DE: International Reading Association.

Mallery, J. L., & Mallery, J. G. (1999). The American legacy of ability grouping: Tracking reconsidered. *Multicultural Education, 7,* 13–15.

Moss, B., & Newton, E. (2002). An examination of the informational text genre in basal readers. *Reading Psychology, 23,* 1–13.

National Institute of Child Health and Human Development. (2000). *Report of the National Reading Panel. Teaching children to read: An evidence-based assessment of the scientific research literature on reading and its implications for reading instruction* (NIH Publication No. 00–4769). Washington, DC: U.S. Government Printing Office.

Navan, J. L. (2002). Enhancing the achievement of "all" learners means high ability students too. *Middle School Journal, 34*(2), 45–49.

Pearson, P. D., & Fielding, L. (1991). Comprehension instruction. In R. Barr, M. L. Kamil, P. Mosenthal, & P. D. Pearson (Eds.), *Handbook of reading research* (Vol. II, pp. 815–860). Mahwah, NJ: Erlbaum.

Pinnell, G. S., & Fountas, I. C. (2003). Teaching comprehension. *The California Reader, 36*(4), 7–14.

Ryndak, D. L., Morrison, A. P., & Sommerstein, L. (1999). Literacy before and after inclusion in general education settings: A case study. *Journal of the Association for Persons with Severe Handicaps, 24,* 5–22.

Sapon-Shevin, M. (1998). *Because we can change the world: A practical guide to building cooperative, inclusive classroom communities.* Boston: Pearson Allyn & Bacon.

Slavin, R. E., & Braddock, J. H. III (1993). Ability grouping: On the wrong track. *College Board Review, 168,* 11–17.

Snell, M. E., & Janney, R. (2000). *Social relationships and peer support.* Baltimore: Paul H. Brookes.

Staub, D., & Peck, C. A. (1994–1995). What are the outcomes for nondisabled students? *Educational Leadership, 52*(4), 36–40.

Thousand, J. S., Villa, R. A., & Nevin, A. I. (Eds.). (2002). *Creativity and collaborative learning: The practical guide to empowering students, teachers, and families* (2nd ed.). Baltimore: Paul H. Brookes.

Villa, R. A., & Thousand, J. S. (Eds.) (1995). *Creating an inclusive school.* Alexandria, VA: Association for Supervision and Curriculum Development.

Vygotsky, L. S. (1978). *Mind in society.* Edited by M. Cole, V. John-Steiner, S. Scribner, & E. Soberman. Cambridge, MA: Harvard University Press.

Wade, S. E., & Moje, E. B. (2000). The role of text in classroom learning. In M. L. Kamil, P. B. Mosenthal, P. D. Pearson, & R. Barr (Eds.), *Handbook of reading research* (Vol. III, pp. 609–628). Mahwah, NJ: Erlbaum.

Waldron, N. L., & McLeskey, J. (1998). The effects of an inclusive school program on students with mild and severe learning disabilities. *Exceptional Children, 64,* 395–405.

Watson, D. (1997). Beyond decodable texts—Supportive and workable literature. *Language Arts, 74,* 635–643.

Children's Literature Cited

Collins, M. A. (2002). *Road to perdition.* New York: Pocket.

Feelings, T. (1995). *Middle passage: White sails, black cargo.* New York: Dial.

Gibbons, G. (1993). *From seed to plant.* New York: Holiday House.

Pilkey, D. (1997). *The adventures of Captain Underpants: An epic novel.* New York: Blue Sky.

Shannon, D. (1998). *A bad case of the stripes.* New York: Scholastic.

Speigelman, A. (1990). *Maus: A survivor's tale.* New York: Pantheon.

Wick, W. (1997). *A drop of water: A book of science and wonder.* New York: Scholastic.

Wiesner, D. (1991). *Tuesday.* New York: Clarion.

CHAPTER

Focus Lessons

Shared Reading and Shared Writing in the Language Arts Workshop

BIG IDEAS ABOUT FOCUS LESSONS

Part 2 of this book provides details and examples of each of the components of the workshop, including focus lessons, guided instruction, collaborative learning, and independent learning. It is important to note that literacy develops along a continuum. And, as Farnan, Flood, and Lapp (1994) point out, "there is no point on the continuum that denotes too much literacy or, for that matter, not enough. There are no good or bad places to be, only places informed by children's previous knowledge and construction of literacy concepts" (p. 136).

This chapter discusses the introductory portion of the language arts workshop—the focus lesson. These lessons are brief in nature (up to 20 minutes) and are designed to highlight a key skill or strategy for teaching and learning: The focus lesson prepares students to practice using the skill or strategy during the remainder of the workshop. The research-based practices of shared reading and shared writing form the heart of the focus lesson. In this chapter we will provide detailed scenarios and accompanying lesson plans to illustrate the usefulness of shared reading and shared writing focus lessons in the language arts workshop.

Questions to Consider

When you have completed this chapter, you should be able to answer these questions:

- What is a focus lesson?
- What is the role of active teaching in the language arts workshop?
- In what ways can shared reading and shared writing be used to teach essential literacy skills?

Key Vocabulary

Active teaching

Modeling

Scaffolding

Coaching

Focus lessons

Shared reading

Sound/Letter Correspondence

Concepts of Print

Informational text

Comprehension Strategies

Think aloud

Shared writing

Language Experience Approach

Interactive writing

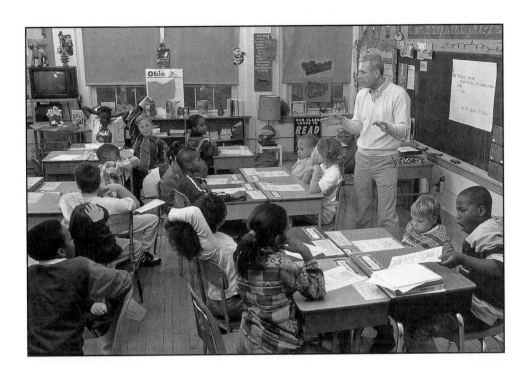

A LOOK INSIDE

Regie Routman calls these "innovations on stories" (1988, p. 68).

Interactive writing is a form of shared writing where the students take turns writing the message on chart paper.

The 20 students in Ms. Thayer's first-grade class are eager to begin the lesson on this crisp October day. An oversized copy of the book *The Meanies* (Cowley, 1998) is on an easel and the children are comfortably seated on a large rug. Another easel holds a large chart paper tablet and an assortment of markers. Ms. Thayer has used this book in her shared reading and shared writing focus lessons all week. Today they will be rewriting the text using the patterns of language established by Cowley. Using interactive writing instruction, Ms. Thayer and her students begin to write a new story called *The Kind Ones*. After discussing how kind ones might behave, they agree on the composition of the first page of their new class book:

What do kind ones do?
They hold the door for others,
They hold the door for others,
They hold the door for others,
That's what kind ones do.

Ms. Thayer invites individual students to come up to the chart to add words while rehearsing the message, figuring out the encoding strategies needed to correctly spell the words, and checking the original text to ensure they are maintaining the language patterns of the book. At the end of this focus lesson, students will write their own pages for inclusion in the class book. Six-year-old Julian is heard to remark, "I love writing books! Do you think Joy Cowley gets help like this, too?"

FOCUS LESSONS IN THE LANGUAGE ARTS WORKSHOP

The ancient link between lectures and reading is probably due to the practice of reading aloud to an audience because books were scarce and few could read.

When people hear the word "teach," most immediately picture a person standing in front of a classroom lecturing and writing on a chalkboard. Would it surprise you to know that the word "lecture" comes from the Latin *lectus* meaning "the act of reading"? In the elementary classroom, teachers don't really lecture, but rather they provide direct instruction. Good and Brophy call this **active teaching** and define it as "demonstrating skills, explaining concepts and assignments, conducting participatory activities, and reviewing" (2003, p. 368).

Active Teaching

Direct instruction refers to the explicit modeling of a skill or concept and serves as the backbone of a teacher's practice.

In education, this is called the gradual release of responsibility model.

No one would consider handing an unfamiliar tool to a child and simply letting them discover on their own how to use it; this could result in needless damage and injury. Instead, the child is shown how to use it and given useful information about the tool and its purpose. Only then would they be given a chance to use it themselves, and then it would be with the proper materials and supervision. This analogy holds true for active teaching as well. The teacher shows students a new skill or strategy, offers precautions to avoid common mistakes, and provides necessary background information. All the while, the teacher is asking questions to monitor understanding. If students are confused, the teacher provides clarification. Only then do the learners try the new skills or strategies for themselves.

Active teaching occurs when a teacher knowledgeable in content, developmental phases of literacy, and learning theory consolidates these elements to create engaging instruction. This instruction follows a sequence that involves first providing students with information, then demonstrating through modeling. Next, student understanding is clarified through scaffolding, and additional support is provided through coaching between peers. The purpose of this sequence of instruction is to move beyond the "telling phase" of giving information to further enhance learning through practices that prepare students to apply the information on their own.

- *Modeling* is the practice of demonstrating how a skill or strategy is used for the purpose of teaching and reinforcing information. In literacy instruction this is commonly accomplished through reading or writing a piece of text. The use of modeling has been identified as an effective means of instruction because it gives learners an opportunity to observe a more knowledgeable person using a skill or strategy (Bandura, 1986).
- *Scaffolding* involves bridging the gap between what students can do and what they need to do through a series of prompts, questions, and tasks (Bruner, 1975). Scaffolding allows for feedback as students answer questions, giving the teacher the opportunity to clarify understanding and reteach. In some cases, the teacher may need to model again.

- *Coaching* occurs when students work with a partner to complete a short task that requires applying the information. Through their interaction with one another or with the teacher, students further develop an understanding of what is being taught. Both scaffolding and coaching are closely related to Vygotsky's (1978) theory of the Zone of Proximal Development because the intended outcome is to increase competency through the support of a teacher or peer.

This sequence of instruction can be described as an "I do it, we do it, you do it" pattern (Frey, 2004). In the first phase, the teacher demonstrates how something is done ("I do it"). Next, the task is attempted with the teacher leading students through the process ("We do it"). Finally, students try it for themselves with a partner ("You do it"). It should be noted that while this pattern may appear to be sequenced in a strict order, in reality effective teachers continually cycle through these steps as needed (Rosenshine & Meister, 1992). Keep in mind that in any given group of learners, some students may need additional examples and prompts.

In the language arts workshop, modeling, scaffolding and coaching are featured in every lesson taught. The focus lesson, which occurs at the beginning of every language arts workshop, is constructed around these principles of active teaching.

The Focus Lesson While the overall format of the language arts workshop allows structured time for students to try their hand at working through new strategies and skills, they must be first taught how to use them. We refer to this portion of the language arts workshop as the **focus lesson** (Cohle & Towle, 2001). This instructional event begins with the teacher stating the purpose of the lesson. A number of studies have found that when the teacher states objectives and provides feedback, student learning increases (Marzano, 1998; Marzano, Pickering, & Pollock, 2001). This is followed by modeling through demonstration—stopping to emphasize the parts that offer examples of the stated purpose. Next, the teacher scaffolds instruction by asking questions and delivering prompts to foster discussion and to check for understanding. In addition, students coach one another using the skill or strategy highlighted in the focus lesson. During the entire focus lesson, the teacher observes students to determine who might need further instruction. Finally, the teacher reviews the lesson and explains how the class will practice this strategy or skill during the next phase of the workshop, the activity time. A planning template for developing a focus lesson appears in Figure 2.1.

The remainder of this chapter will examine the use of the components of the focus lesson through the lens of shared reading and shared writing instruction. We will explain the purpose and research base for these practices, and discuss the practical considerations of implementing shared reading and shared writing focus lessons in the language arts workshop. We will use this focus lesson template to present real classroom scenarios of teachers in the language arts workshop.

SHARED READING IN THE LANGUAGE ARTS WORKSHOP

The language arts workshop begins with the focus lesson, a concise example of direct instruction through active teaching. Every focus lesson has three major components—modeling, scaffolding, and coaching. When focus lessons are presented systematically, students have an opportunity to first see, then practice, the literacy skills they are acquiring.

Figure 2.1   Planning Tool for Focus Lessons

Assessed Need: I have noticed that the students in my classroom need to work on:
Standards:
Text I will use to demonstrate the strategy I plan to teach is:
Materials needed for this lesson are:
Purpose of the lesson is:
SEQUENCE OF FOCUS LESSON *MODEL* *Parts to emphasize* *SCAFFOLD* *Questions to ask* *COACH* *Students practice with partners* *ASSESS* *These are the students who need extra support*
Independent Practice *Students will practice using the strategy during activity time*
Source: Adapted from Leah Allen.

Shared reading focus lessons in the language arts workshop are an effective tool for instructing students. All students have access to the text, which may be in a big book format, a piece of text displayed on a screen using an overhead projector, or on copies of the reading for every student. These lessons are designed to maximize participation among all students in the class because they are consistent with a gradual release of responsibility model (Pearson & Fielding, 1991).

What Is Shared Reading?

Shared reading is an instructional procedure that utilizes text that can be viewed by both the teacher and the student at the same time, often consisting of material that is slightly above what the children can read independently (Holdaway, 1979).

The responsibility for reading the text is "shared" because the students follow the print silently while the teacher reads aloud. During subsequent re-readings, students read aloud as well.

For younger students in kindergarten through second grade, an oversized version of a picture book measuring approximately 24 inches or more in width is commonly used. The primary advantage of using a big book is that the large print and illustrations are visible to the students. Likewise, pocket charts and teacher-made language charts are also used because they are easily seen. Teachers of older students often display the shared reading text on an overhead projector, or provide each child with a photocopy of the text. In other cases, a reading from the basal or a textbook is used as the basis for the focus lesson.

Characteristics of shared reading lessons. Shared reading is recognizable in the way it is delivered by the teacher. In the language arts workshop, a shared reading event is likely to be short and lively, and the text may be read more than once to reinforce the skills or strategies being taught. As students become comfortable, they are encouraged to read along with the teacher. Rog (2001) describes five characteristics for shared reading:

- Large print
- Brief, engaging lessons that encourage student participation
- Suitable for mixed ability groups
- Repeated readings to reinforce concepts
- Emphasis on skills at the letter, word, sentence, and text levels

Taken together, a well-constructed shared reading focus lesson serves as an effective method for introducing key strategies and skills through active teaching. Shared reading allows the teacher to instruct through modeling by demonstrating how a skill or strategy is applied to a reading. After modeling, the teacher asks questions to foster discussion and provides prompts to scaffold student understanding as they read text that is initially new to them. Students interact to coach each other as they apply the new skill or strategy.

Effectiveness of shared reading. Shared reading is an effective instructional procedure for developing young readers' ability to figure out words because students learn to apply their knowledge of word order to predict a word (Manning, Manning, Long, & Kamii, 1993). For example, after reading the nursery rhyme "Jack and Jill" several times during a shared reading focus lesson, emergent readers can correctly read the words of the poem because they have become familiar with the order of the words. Shared reading has been documented to be effective for fostering reading acquisition for emergent and early readers (Reutzel & Cooter, 1990) and especially with struggling readers (Sacks & Mergendoller, 1997) because they are able to practice and rehearse graphophonic, syntactic, and semantic cueing systems to read meaningful text. These results extend to older students as well. Rashotte, McPhee and Torgensen (2001) reported that shared reading was a component of an effective program for increasing reading fluency of older struggling readers. The National Reading Panel identified shared reading as an effective instructional tool for providing students with opportunities to engage in repeated readings of a passage for the purposes of increasing comprehension and fluency (NRP, 2000).

Margin notes:

Remember, in shared reading, the teacher—a fluent reader—reads aloud.

Evidence Based

Cueing systems are used by young readers to decode and understand print.

Of course, it is essential to remember that the act of shared reading does not create readers—it is what the teacher does inside the shared reading event that makes the difference. Like all aspects of teaching, a successful shared reading focus lesson requires careful planning. Effective teachers craft their lessons based on the needs of the students, then identify materials that furnish the necessary features for the teaching purpose. Finally, they create a sequence of instruction that includes modeling through demonstration, scaffolding through questions and prompts, and coaching through peer interactions. In this way, students acquire important skills and strategies needed for accurate, efficient, and meaningful reading.

TEACHING SKILLS AND STRATEGIES THROUGH SHARED READING FOCUS LESSONS

Shared reading as an instructional tool can provide teachers with a vehicle to teach essential literacy skills and strategies through meaningful text. For emergent readers, these may include sound/letter correspondence (Adams, 1995) and concepts about print like punctuation, word boundaries, and directionality (Clay, 2000). For older readers, important skills such as using text features (Herber, 1978) and comprehension strategies (Keene & Zimmermann, 1997) can be modeled through shared reading instruction. Let's look more closely at how each of these essential literacy skills can be taught through a shared reading focus lesson in a language arts workshop. We will follow each discussion of a reading skill or strategy with a classroom scenario and accompanying lesson plan.

Sound/Symbol Correspondence

The mastery of the sounds and symbols of the language is fundamental for early reading acquisition and therefore is an important feature of primary classroom instruction. The symbols of written language are the letters of the alphabet. **Sound/symbol relationships** describe the association between the sound of a letter or combination of letters and the letters that represent that sound. These sound/symbol relationships are frequently described as the "building blocks of language," yet a challenge is how to teach these in ways that transfer to the practical use of language, namely, reading and writing. Many researchers and teachers advocate the use of meaningful text (e.g., books, poems, and songs) as part of a process for teaching how these building blocks are used to construct written language. These materials are used in combination with systematic, explicit instruction of a purposeful sequence of letters and sounds (Armbruster, Lehr, & Osborn, 2001; Eldredge, Reutzel, & Hollingsworth, 1996). In this way, young readers have occasion to employ their growing knowledge of the building blocks of language within the context of engaging reading material.

Student interest is an important element in engagement and learning.

Mrs. Moore frequently uses poems and song lyrics to teach her first-grade students about word families. Word families (also called rimes) are groups of rhyming words that end with the same vowels and consonants. For example, *thing, bring,* and *spring* are all part of the *–ing* word family. In addition, her students are learning to use a variety of onsets to decode words and create new ones. The onset consists of the first consonant letters up to the first vowel. In the word *spring, spr-* is the onset and *-ing* is the rime. She has selected a poem featuring the *–ing* word family to use as the basis of her focus lesson on sound/symbol correspondence.

Spotlight on Instruction

Teaching Sound/Letter Correspondence in First Grade

Mrs. Moore used the rhyme "Groundhog" on a language chart to teach her students about the /ing/ word family. The text on her chart reads,

Silly little thing,
Does your shadow bring
Something that tells me
When we will have spring?

She begins by activating background knowledge about Groundhog Day (February 2). Mrs. Moore has previously read aloud *It's Groundhog Day!* (Kroll, 1995) and *Gregory's Shadow* (2002). In science they have previously created shadows on surfaces and have viewed photographs of shadows to make predictions about what objects were used to create each one. Mrs. Moore has selected this rime because her previous assessments demonstrate that the emergent readers in her class are beginning to attend to the final letters in words.

Mrs. Moore first reads the poem aloud to students while using a pointer under each word so they can track the sentences. She then reads it again and invites students to join in. After the second reading, they discuss the meaning of the poem and answer the question posed by the poem. On the third reading she says, "I hear words that rhyme in this poem. The rhyming words sound like /ing/. I'm going to read it again to listen closely for the words I say that sound like /ing/". This time she reads the poem slowly and pauses to

MODELING.   emphasize the rhyming words *thing, bring, something,* and *spring.*

She then asks students to place pieces of colored transparent highlighting tape over the -*ing* portion of the rhyming words to further draw their attention to this letter combination. When Jamie needs help finding the correct letter combination in *something,* she asks him to say the word aloud to hear the

SCAFFOLDING.   sounds. This prompt helps Jamie correctly highlight the letters. After discussing the spelling and sounds of the rime, she asks the students to think of other words that have the same ending sound. She uses alphabet letter cards to prompt their understanding. For example, when she pairs a large card with the letter /s/ on it with another bearing the letters /ing/, her students are able to quickly respond, "Sing!"

COACHING.   Finally, she asks her students to turn to their partner and tell one another words from the poem that are in the -*ing* word family and then write them in their Word Families journal. She moves around to listen to their partner talk, making anecdotal notes about individual students she has identified for as-

See chapter 7 on word study and spelling for ways to construct and use word family journals.   sessment purposes. Importantly, she is also using this time to determine whether they are ready to apply what they have learned during the remainder of the language arts workshop. After this focus lesson is over, they will use smaller versions of the same letter cards to construct new words from the -*ing* word family, then add them to the list begun in the word family journal. A completed lesson plan can be seen in Figure 2.2.

Figure 2.2   Lesson Plan for Groundhog Day Poem

Assessed Need: I have noticed that the students in my classroom need to work on: **/ing/ word family**
Standards: **McREL LA Std.5.1.5: Uses basic elements of phonetic analysis to decode unknown words**
Text I will use to demonstrate the strategy I plan to teach is: **Language chart poem - "The Groundhog"**
Materials needed for this lesson are: **Language chart, /ing/ sentence strip, large letter cards d,k,p,r,s,w to make new words, identical small letter cards for students** **Colored highlighting tape**
Purpose of the lesson is: **Locate /ing/ words in poem** **Develop new words using consonants**
SEQUENCE OF FOCUS LESSON **Activate background knowledge by asking about Groundhog Day and shadows experiment** *MODEL* read aloud twice and invite students to read along *Parts to emphasize* **Put tape over /ing/ in thing** **Discuss vocabulary** *SCAFFOLD* ask students to place highlighting tape over /ing/ words **Prompt as needed by repeating word slowly, chunking word to focus on /ing/** *Questions to ask* **What do we know about Groundhog Day?** **What new words can we make for our new word family? - use letter cards to support their answers** *COACH* *Students practice with partners* **Tell your neighbor the words in the poem that end with /ing/** **Write words in Word Family journal** *ASSESS* *These are the students who need extra support* **Collect notes on Jose, Eileen, and Mark**
Independent Practice *Students will practice using the strategy during activity time* **Students will use letter cards to make words from the /ing/ family and write them into their Word Families journal on the /ing/ page.**

Concepts About Print

Like sound/symbol relationships, emergent readers must also learn how text works on a page and how it carries its message. Referred to as **concepts about print** (Clay, 1985), this group of skills encompasses the following:

- Book handling—Able to locate the front and back cover, title, author and illustrator's names, and turn each page from beginning to end

- Locating the message—Understands that the print, not the picture, carries the message
- Directionality—Knows that print is read from left to right and top to bottom
- Return Sweep—Understands that at the end of each line, the print resumes at the far left on the next line below
- One-to-one correspondence—Matches print words to spoken words by pointing
- First and last—Can locate the first and last letters of a word, and the first and last letters of a sentence
- Punctuation—Knows that punctuation marks (period, question mark, exclamation mark, and comma) have different meanings

These concepts about print are critical for young readers and are taught throughout the day so that young readers have many opportunities to see them being used. An

Spotlight on Instruction

Teaching Concepts About Print in Kindergarten

MODELING.

The 20 kindergarten students in Ms. Lee's class have assembled on the rug around her rocking chair. To her left is an easel with a big book version of *Baby Gets Dressed* (Cowley, 1989). This predictable text contains a simple two-word pattern on each page depicting a toddler being dressed after her bath. Predictable text relies on a pattern to assist emergent readers in anticipating the words on the page. She begins by holding the book upside down and backwards. As the children giggle and protest, she asks them what's wrong. Moishe calls out, "You're holding it wrong!" Miss Lee then asks him to come up to place the book correctly on the easel. She then identifies the front and back covers of the book and locates the names of the author and illustrator. To activate background knowledge and support their comprehension, she asks the students questions about the picture of the baby on the front cover. Several children make personal connections regarding their younger brothers and sisters, and Miss Lee tells them the main idea of the story—helping a young child get dressed.

MODELING.

SCAFFOLDING.

COACHING.

See chapter 3 on guided reading in the language arts workshop.

In addition to book handling skills, Miss Lee knows that these emergent readers need practice with one-to-one matching of spoken words to print. After reading the entire book to the children so they will be familiar with the pattern, she begins the story again, placing highlighter tape over each word that represents an article of clothing. She then reads the book using a wooden pointer to move carefully under each word as she reads it. She begins the story a fourth time, inviting students to come up to the easel to read and point with her. Since the wooden pointer is too cumbersome for small hands, she has a number of small items for them to use, including rubber witch fingers (available around Halloween in most novelty shops) and chopsticks dipped on one end with glitter glue. She provides physical and gestural prompts when needed to support each student's effort, deliberately choosing children who she anticipates will need extra help. Meanwhile, she has the rest of the students clap once as each word is read. Although subtle, the physical movement and sound generated by each student serves as a cue to one another. After this focus lesson, students will practice one-to-one matching by using smaller versions of the same book during their guided reading lesson. A completed version of this lesson is featured in Figure 2.3.

effective time for modeling these concepts is through the shared reading focus lesson in the language arts workshop. Big books are especially useful for this because the size of the entire book allows for easy viewing and lots of chances to point and touch.

The goals of Ms. Lee's focus lesson on concepts about print are to practice book handling skills and one-to-one matching of words on the page with her kindergarten students. She has selected a big book to demonstrate these skills and will also use the opportunity to review vocabulary to ensure students understand the story.

Figure 2.3 Lesson Plan for One-to-One Matching

Assessed Need: I have noticed that the students in my classroom need to work on: **Book handling skills - locating front and back cover, title, and author/illustrator** **One-to-one matching - spoken words and print**
Standards: **McREL LA Std. 5.1.2: Understands how print is organized** **McREL LA Std. 5.1.4: Uses meaning cues to understand a story**
Text I will use to demonstrate the strategy I plan to teach is: **Baby Gets Dressed by Joy Cowley**
Materials needed for this lesson are: **Big book, highlighter tape, pointers for students**
Purpose of the lesson is: **To practice previously taught book handling skills and matching** **To discuss sequence of story as baby gets dressed (pants, shirt, petticoat, dress)**
SEQUENCE OF FOCUS LESSON **Review book handling skills by placing big book on easel upside down and backwards** *MODEL* **Locate front and back cover, title, and author and illustrator names** *Parts to emphasize* **What is the baby doing?** **Read once for meaning and highlight clothing words** **Read again using pointer to demonstrate one-to-one matching** *SCAFFOLD* **Students demonstrate 1:1 correspondence using pointers, give physical assistance as needed** *Questions to ask* **What will happen after baby gets out of the bathtub?** *COACH* *Students practice with partners* **Students clap once as each word is read** *ASSESS* *These are the students who need extra support* **Have Monique, Abel, Sarah, and Bart demonstrate matching, with physical assistance as needed**
Independent Practice *Students will practice using the strategy during activity time* **Guided reading groups**

Using Informational Texts

As students begin to use more complex reading materials, their need for additional strategies increases as well. While students are more comfortable using narrative texts, especially stories and chapter books, they are often less adept at using **informational** reading materials like textbooks, reference materials, and nonfiction books. Informational text contains "ideas, facts, and principles related to the physical, biological, or social world" (Fountas & Pinnell, 2001, p. 399). This unfamiliarity may in part be due to the relative lack of exposure to informational texts in elementary and middle school. A recent study of basal readers revealed that no more than 20% of these materials was devoted to informational text, meaning that students had less opportunity in their reading program to receive instruction in how to understand it (Moss & Newton, 2002). Another study found an overall lack of use of informational texts in first-grade classrooms, as low as 3.6 minutes per day (Duke, 2000). Lack of instruction using informational texts may explain why even on-grade level readers in middle school score a full year level lower on comprehension of informational texts when compared to their narrative reading levels (Langer, 1985).

A distinguishing characteristic of informational text is the use of **text features.** These are the structural items used by the author to convey the content. These features serve as markers for the reader to better understand the text. For instance, in this book you are using a number of text features to understand this chapter, including the headings and subheadings, bulleted items, diagrams, and photographs. These structures support and expand a reader's comprehension of the concepts in the reading.

Mr. Ronaldo's eighth-grade class has been studying the lives of Native Americans as part of their social studies course. Because he understands the connection between literacy and content area learning, he uses the structure of the language arts workshop to support the development of readers in his class. He has designed a central question to organize the unit (Fisher & Frey, 2001)—how were Native Americans affected by the territorial expansion of the United States? In two weeks, assigned groups of students will be performing an original play depicting how specific tribes were affected. Since incorporating information from a wide variety of source materials is necessary to successfully complete this project, Mr. Ronaldo will teach a focus lesson on using maps and a reading from the social studies textbook to extrapolate information about each tribe.

Spotlight on Instruction

Teaching Text Features in Eighth Grade

Mr. Ronaldo introduces the lesson by distributing photocopies of three maps of North America and asks students to open their social studies textbooks to a reading on the lives of Native Americans. The first map illustrates where Native American tribes were located before the arrival of Columbus, while the second shows the location of major tribes in 1880. The third map diagrams how tribes in each region lived, whether through intensive farming, hunting and gathering, or a combination of both. The written text and captions state the main idea from these three maps—the forced movement of tribes had many negative effects, due in part to relocation to areas of the country that did not support their way of life.

(continued)

MODELING.

Mr. Ronaldo displays the first two of the three maps on the overhead and draws the students' attention to the maps titles and subheadings. "When I read a map, I look to the title for specific information about the purpose of the map. I always read it first before trying to interpret the map," he instructs.

SCAFFOLDING.

By now, the students understand that the maps are separated in time by nearly 400 years. He then asks them to locate one tribe, the Cherokee, and compare and contrast where the tribe was located on the two maps. As the class watches, he marks their original location in the western Carolinas and their territory in Oklahoma on the 1880 map. "Doesn't that make you wonder why they moved? Let's take a look at the article I've given you. Maps tell us a lot but we need more information to understand." Mr. Ronaldo is creating a task that will answer some of the questions he has spurred in the minds of his students about the startling change in Native American territories.

As he places the textbook passage on the overhead, he reminds them to use the headings to quickly locate the section they need. "You don't want to read the whole thing!" he tells them. "Scan the article first for title headings that signal you about the contents. This helps you locate the information you want as rapidly as possible."

Jenn raises her hand and asks, "Is it under eastern tribes or western tribes, Mr. R.? There are two major headings on this page."

MODELING.

"You're right, Jenn! Good readers make a prediction and scan down the text to see if they can locate the keyword 'Cherokee'. If you don't find it in your first choice, go to your second." He demonstrates this strategy on his transparency copy of their textbook, moving his hand back and forth across the page to simulate his eye movement. When he locates the word, 'Cherokee' under the western tribes heading, he highlights it with an overhead marker so students can locate it in their textbook copy. He then reads the passage aloud while the students follow along. The main idea of the reading is that the Cherokees faced many hardships during their forced relocation to Oklahoma, called the Trail of Tears. But the reading also goes on to describe the continuing challenges faced by the tribe after their arrival.

MODELING.

"The last part of that reading mentioned the declining quality of life after their arrival in Oklahoma. That makes me realize that I don't really know much about what the tribes did to survive. I know I've got a third map I haven't used yet. I'm going to go back to it to find more information." With that, Mr. Ronaldo displays the third map, entitled "How Native Americans Lived" and draws their attention to the area on the eastern seaboard marked in orange, as well as the western region signified in red. "When I see a color-coded map, it signals me to look for the map legend to understand the code." After consulting the map legend, he and the class discuss the importance of the change in the way of life for the Cherokee, who were forced to

COACHING.

give up their farming culture and turn to hunting and gathering in their new territory. Finally, he directs their attention back to the passage on the Cherokee and confirms that the maps and the written text support his conclusion. "Each of your groups has a tribe you're studying. Repeat this same procedure using your own tribe and discuss it with your group." With that, he listens in to the conversations in each group and clears up confusion about use and interpretation of the written and visually represented information. Later, they will incorporate the information they have extrapolated from the three maps and the reading into the play they are writing during activity time. A completed version of this lesson is featured in Figure 2.4.

Comprehension Strategies

The ability to comprehend the text is the ultimate measure of reading ability. For this reason, **comprehension instruction** permeates the language arts workshop. Keene (2002) describes a proficient reader's comprehension strategies:

- Activates relevant prior knowledge before, during, and after reading text
- Determines the most important ideas and themes in a text
- Asks questions of him- or herself, the authors, and the texts
- Creates visual and other sensory images from text during and after reading
- Draws inferences from text
- Synthesizes what he or she has read
- Uses a variety of fix-up strategies to repair comprehension when it breaks down (pp. 84–85)

Figure 2.4 Lesson Plan for Native American Reading

Assessed Need: I have noticed that the students in my classroom need to work on: **Use a variety of maps and written information to gather, apply, and extend their knowledge about their assigned tribe**
Standards: **McREL LA Std 4.III.4: Uses a variety of resource materials to gather information for research topics**
Text I will use to demonstrate the strategy I plan to teach is: **Maps and reading about where and how Native Americans lived (social studies textbook pp. 178-185)**
Materials needed for this lesson are: **Overheads of maps and reading, student photocopies of maps**
Purpose of the lesson is: **Model the use of three resources (2 maps, article) to gather pertinent information**
SEQUENCE OF FOCUS LESSON *MODEL* **Use a think-aloud strategy to model what I do as a reader to locate information from maps and text** *Parts to emphasize* **Discuss map features, including headings and legends** **Use headings in reading to scan for information** *SCAFFOLD* **Have students locate Cherokee on all three maps** *Questions to ask* **What do the maps tell us about the changes in the quality of life for the Cherokee?** *COACH* **Assist small groups as they discuss information related to their tribe** *Students practice with partners* **Students work with their group partners to locate similar information about their tribe** *ASSESS* *These are the students who need extra support* **Check with Iroquois group - make sure they know that their tribe is portrayed on second map as Huron and Ojibwe, as well as Iroquois (make sure they can connect this to their Six Nations research)**
Independent Practice *Students will practice using the strategy during activity time* **Continue working on play and incorporate this new information**

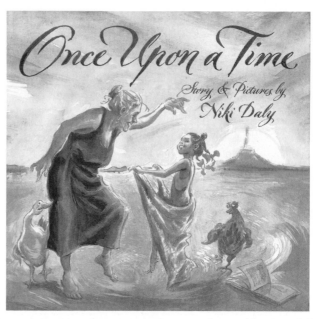

This encouraging story conveys the power and magic of a good book and the joy of having a good friend to share it with.

ONCE UPON A TIME © 2003 by Niki Daly. Used with the permission of Farrar, Straus and Giroux.

You may not be consciously aware of the comprehension strategies you are using right now as you read this text, but if you understand this paragraph then you are likely using some of these strategies. These comprehension strategies are activated by the reader in the form of questions he or she mentally composes before, during, and after reading. These self-generated questions allow the reader to continually evaluate, compare and contrast information, make connections to personal experiences, formulate images of characters and settings, and predict what the author will discuss next.

However, novice readers are not as adept at applying these self-questioning strategies to support and clarify their understanding of the text. Indeed, many readers, particularly struggling ones, are unaware that good readers engage in self-questioning while reading. Therefore, instruction of self-questioning strategies to support comprehension must go beyond merely telling. Instead, it must be explicitly modeled by the teacher and consciously practiced by the students so that they recognize the usefulness of the strategy beyond the text they are currently reading. An excellent method for modeling comprehension strategies during focus lessons is the **think aloud** (Davey, 1983). A think aloud models the questions fluent readers mentally ask when they read. The teacher models these processes during the focus lesson by making statements and self-questioning in a manner that gives students insight into how the teacher is processing the text.

Ms. Carver uses a think aloud strategy to model self-questioning during the reading of a passage from *Number the Stars* (Lowry, 1989). The goal of her lesson is to teach her fourth grade students how to use self-questioning to support their own understanding as they read. She alternates between the written text and the think aloud, with her think aloud comments appearing in italics.

See chapter 10 for a complete discussion on comprehension instruction.

Spotlight on Instruction

Teaching Comprehension Strategies in Fourth Grade

Ms. Carver asks her students to get out their copies of *Number the Stars* while she places a transparency of the same pages on the overhead projector. "Boys and girls," she begins, "today we're going to use a strategy to help us understand something when we read. Good readers think about questions and ideas related to the story as they read. I'm going to tell you the questions and ideas I think about when I am reading. I'll give you a chance to try it with your reading partner." After leading a discussion of the plot so far, she begins to read while students follow silently in their books (emphasis added).

"Your names?" the officer barked.

"Annemarie Johansen. And this is my sister—"

"Quiet! Let her speak for herself. Your name?" He was glaring at Ellen. *"Barked" and "glaring" are words the author is using to help me imagine this Nazi officer's anger.*

Ellen swallowed. "Lise," she said, and cleared her throat. "Lise Johansen." *I know why she's lying. She doesn't want them to know she's Jewish. I'll bet the Johansens will also lie for Ellen.*

The officer stared at them grimly. "Now," Mama said in a strong voice, "you have seen that we are not hiding anything. May my children go back to bed?" *I was right. That's just what Mrs. Johansen did.*

The officer ignored her. Suddenly he grabbed a handful of Ellen's hair. Ellen winced. *Why would he pull Ellen's hair?*

MODELING.

He laughed scornfully. "You have a blond child sleeping in the other room. And you have this blond daughter" he gestured toward Annemarie with his head. "Where did you get the dark-haired one?" *Oh, no! What will the Johansens say? Now I understand why the title of this chapter is "Who Is the Dark-Haired One?"* (Lowry, 1989, pp. 46–47).

After discussing the content of the passage, she leads a discussion about the think aloud. "What are the ways I helped myself to understand what was happening in the story?" she asks. Jerome offers, "You made predictions about what would happen next." Delia adds, "You asked questions, like when the Nazi pulled Ellen's hair." While students respond, Ms. Carver records their ideas on chart paper. When finished, the list reads:

- Make predictions and confirmations
- Ask questions
- Make connections to the title
- Visualize

SCAFFOLDING.

COACHING.

She asks students to listen to the next portion of the story and make suggestions about predictive statements and questions. She pauses after every few sentences to prompt suggestions and writes their ideas on a second piece of chart paper. They continue to practice as a class using the next few pages of text. After several cycles of modeling and scaffolding, she asks students to work in pairs to read a page from the book to one another using think aloud statements to support comprehension. Ms. Carver's full lesson plan can be found in Figure 2.5.

Figure 2.5   Lesson Plan for Comprehension Skills Reading

Assessed Need: I have noticed that the students in my classroom need to work on: **Questioning the text to support their own comprehension**
Standards: **McREL LA Std. II.3. Makes, confirms, and revises simple predictions about what will be found in a text (e.g., uses prior knowledge and ideas presented in text, illustrations, titles, topic sentences, key words, and foreshadowing clues)**
Text I will use to demonstrate the strategy I plan to teach is: **Number the Stars (Lowry, 1989), pp. 46-49**
Materials needed for this lesson are: **Overhead transparencies of text, overhead marker**
Purpose of the lesson is: **Create questions and statements that relate to the reading**
SEQUENCE OF FOCUS LESSON *MODEL* **read pp. 45-46, model think aloud strategy of comprehension strategies** *Parts to emphasize* **Use visualization, prediction, confirming, and questioning** *SCAFFOLD* **Chart student responses, use their answers to guide think alouds for next passage** *Questions to ask* **How did I help myself as a reader when I read the passage?** *COACH* **Partner-read pp. 48-49 to conclude chapter** *Students practice with partners* **Students make statements, predictions, and ask questions as they read to one another** *ASSESS* **Collect observational notes of student evidence of this strategy** *These are the students who need extra support* **Be sure to observe Maria and Bethany - they struggled with yesterday's lesson and may need some reteaching during guided reading group**
Independent Practice *Students will practice using the strategy during activity time* **Students read chapter 6 during independent reading and note examples in their reading log of their use of self-questioning**

The teachers in the four lessons you have read about in this section used a variety of practical ideas to make their shared reading focus lesson run more smoothly. While simple, these practical tips help ensure your lesson will accomplish your goals.

PRACTICAL TIPS FOR SUCCESSFUL SHARED READING FOCUS LESSONS

Since shared reading is constructed around visual access to the text, the right materials are an important consideration. The print must be of a sufficient size so that all the students can see it. As discussed earlier, this may be a big book, a textbook, teacher created language chart, or a copy of the reading on an overhead transparency.

Big Books

Teachers in kindergarten through second grade most frequently use big books for shared reading focus lessons. These books have several advantages, including visibility due to their large size and the availability of child-sized versions of the same text for follow-up use with individual students. Maximize the usefulness of your big books by taking these ideas into consideration.

- *Display.* Increase visibility and ease of handling by using an easel with a tray designed for this purpose. This keeps your hands free and provides a place to store materials. If students sit on the carpet, be sure the height is suitable.
- *Direct attention.* Young readers are not always adept at looking where you want them to look and can thereby miss your teaching point. Use items that direct your students' attention such as highlighting tape and pointers. These materials can be used by students as well to locate letters, words, or other text features.
- *Storage.* Big books are large and can pose a storage problem. Meanwhile, you want to make these books available for students to reread when working in collaborative groups. You can remove the shelves from a bookcase to create a storage space that will accommodate oversized books.

Charts

Charts are a popular choice for teachers in a language arts workshop because they can reproduce virtually anything at very little cost or time. Large tablets of lined chart paper (usually 24″ × 36″) are part of the basic supplies of elementary classrooms. Poems and song texts are especially easy to replicate on charts because they are typically brief in nature. Here are some hints for creating charts for shared reading focus lessons.

- *Keep text brief.* Choose text that is no more than 100 words or so in length. Too many words crowded on a language chart make it difficult for young readers to track.
- *Write for visibility.* Use large block letters in cool colors to maximize visibility. Consider the colors you're using as well. Cool colors like blue, green, and black can be seen at a greater distance; yellow, orange and red should be confined to highlighting only. Emergent and early readers will benefit from charts written with two alternating colors per line (for instance, the first line is blue, the second is green, the third is blue) to support their tracking. Remember that you're modeling handwriting as well as reading strategies. Use three lines to form letters in a simple block style and skip a line between each row of text.
- *Make it permanent.* Laminate charts you want to use more than once. Although this is not necessary for every chart you construct, it is a great way to extend the life of the ones you'll use again the next year. Another advantage to lamination is that you can write on them with dry-erase markers and clean them later.

- *Store for reuse.* Organize charts so students can use them. Charts that have been previously taught during focus lessons become independent reading materials later. To preserve charts, use a sentence strip folded in half with a small hole (about 2 inches) cut in the center. Slide a clothes hanger through the hole in the sentence chart, then staple to the top of the language chart. A diagram of this system can be found in Figure 2.6.

Charts can then be coded according to genre, subject, or skill using stickers. For example, readings about the seasons have a sticker of a snowflake in the corner of the sentence strip, while those used during the science unit on plants bear a sticker of a flower. All the charts can then be hung on a chart stand for easy access.

Readings on Overheads

Older students read more complex text that needs to be displayed in a different manner. Most commonly, teachers reproduce a passage from a book or article on an overhead transparency. As with big books and charts, their effective use requires their own unique materials.

- *Enlarge.* Use the "enlarge" feature on the copier machine to make the text more legible. Font sizes used in books are rarely large enough to be seen on an overhead projector.

- *Direct attention.* Students benefit from methods for directing their attention on the proper section of the text. Washable overhead markers can be used for underlining and highlighting. A colored transparency can be cut into strips to highlight entire sections of text.

- *Reveal.* Chunk the text to shorten the length of passages by using a sheet of paper to block part of the transparency. Remember that you can place the sheet of paper *under* the transparency so you can still see the words. This will help you make smooth transitions to the next paragraph.

Whether using big books, charts, or overhead transparencies, the purpose is to display meaningful text to use as a tool for teaching skills and strategies. Therefore, the materials must be displayed and used in ways that enhance your instruction.

SHARED WRITING IN THE LANGUAGE ARTS WORKSHOP

Shared writing is an approach to instruction that provides the teacher and students with an opportunity to co-create text. As with shared reading, the gradual release of responsibility model is used to promote writing acquisition. We use shared writing as a way to describe writing experiences that teachers and students engage in jointly to create original text.

What Is Shared Writing?

Shared writing (McKenzie, 1985) is an instructional activity that relies on the joint attention of the teacher and the students, and often serves as an umbrella term for several group writing practices, including **Language Experience Approach (LEA)** (Ashton-Warner, 1965) and **interactive writing** (McCarrier, Pinnell, & Fountas,

Figure 2.6   Constructing a Chart for Shared Reading

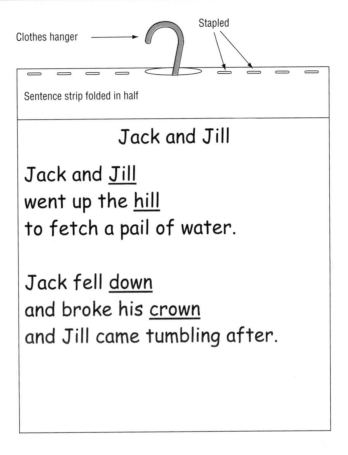

2000). The teacher may take direct dictation from students, writing verbatim what is said (LEA) or guide the composition of the message before scribing it on a large chart for all to see (shared writing). At other times, students may take turns writing the letters themselves (interactive writing). Although Language Experience Approach (LEA) and interactive writing differ on some key points, they have characteristics held in common.

Characteristics of shared writing lessons. A shared writing lesson utilizes the same active teaching model used in shared reading focus lessons. Writing is modeled through demonstration and scaffolded through questions and prompts. Student and teacher interaction is important for coaching as students apply what was taught in the focus lesson to their own writing. Features of shared writing lessons include:

- Text is co-created by teacher and students through rich conversation
- Language used is natural to the child

- Text is created for a purpose
- Writing occurs in full view of the students
- Text is used again for reading

An important advantage of using shared writing is that it provides a forum for discussing any and all aspects of writing, including letter formation, layout and spacing on the page, word choice, and content. The extent to which these are featured in a lesson is determined by student need. Shared writing has been found to be an effective instructional approach for teaching students how to compose and evaluate their writing.

Evidence Based

What is the effectiveness of shared writing? Shared writing consists of two processes—the discussion that takes place in composing the message, and the procedures for recording that message on paper. The conversations that are essential to these mutual composition processes are equally as important as the written product itself because both oral language development and writing skills are the focus of the lessons. The development of speaking and listening skills are inexorably bound in the acquisition of reading and writing (Burns, Griffin, & Snow, 1999). The authors of the New Standards Project identified three standards of oral language development (National Center on Education and the Economy, 2001):

- Habits
- Kinds of talk and resulting genres
- Language use and conventions (p. 11)

Shared writing experiences directly access the second goal, "Kinds of Talk and Resulting Genres" because they require children to converse in four key ways (NCEE, 2001):

- Narrative talk
- Explaining and seeking information
- Getting things done
- Producing and responding to performances (p. 23)

In addition to the development of oral language skills, young writers are able to witness *how* the message gets from their minds to the paper. Cunningham, Moore, Cunningham, and Moore note that "[a]s children watch the teacher record their ideas, they notice the left-to-right, top-to-bottom, and other print conventions used in writing. They also hear print jargon being used by the teacher. . . " (2004, p. 43). Further, the learning extends beyond print conventions for older students as they observe how writers wrestle with word choice and syntax for accuracy and eloquence (Fisher & Frey, 2003).

Jane Hansen (2001), a researcher of writing development in children, points out that another benefit of these shared writing experiences is that students begin to *evaluate* writing. Despite the allure to reduce all acts of writing to a linear recipe of brainstorming, drafting, editing, revising, and publishing, real writers engage in several of these processes simultaneously, often writing a few words or sentences, pausing to check for spelling or content, changing a word, continuing for a few more sentences, thinking of an idea to use later, then rereading the entire paragraph again. Fearn and Farnan (2001) refer to this as an interactive writing process because there may be more than one process occurring at the same time. This ability to engage in multiple processes simultaneously is predicated on the notion that evaluation is taking place. It is analogous to the cueing systems used by readers. Real readers do not decode, then look at the syntax, then check for their semantic understanding. Instead, they consolidate these cueing systems by evaluating what they need to understand the message. Likewise, when students engage in shared writing, they see the teacher model continuous evaluation of the writing product. The development of good writers, like good readers, focuses on increasing their agility at being able to engage in simultaneous processes efficiently and accurately. Skilled teachers can address key skills and strategies around composition and evaluation through shared writing focus lessons.

TEACHING SKILLS AND STRATEGIES THROUGH SHARED WRITING FOCUS LESSONS

Teachers commonly use two major types of instructional methods in shared writing focus lessons. The first is Language Experience Approach, with its emphasis on using the students' natural language as a basis for text development. The second is interactive writing, which requires students to collaboratively write the text itself under the direction of the teacher.

Language Experience Approach

Language Experience Approach (LEA) uses a child's language to create original text for reading (Ashton-Warner, 1965; Stauffer, 1970). Originally used with preschoolers, LEA was built on the notion that text using the child's language patterns would be easier to read. In most LEA lessons, the teacher writes down exactly what the child says. Teachers may be tempted to correct errors in grammar and syntax, but remember that the point is to create text they can then read back. When the language is familiar, the likelihood of being able to do so successfully is increased. The use of LEA has expanded to include older students, especially struggling writers and English language learners (Fisher & Frey, 2003). Shared experience is essential for LEA, as the students need to have a common bank of knowledge to participate. This means that the teacher must first attend to creating experiences for students to discuss.

Creating experiences. An operative word in LEA is "experience" and this is key to successful LEA lessons. Some students may not have experienced a particular event and thus are unable to offer language about the topic. Imagine, for instance, how difficult it would be for you to discuss an American Fourth of July if you had never seen or celebrated the holiday. Therefore, teachers often create a shared experience with the class in order to use the event later in an LEA lesson. Field trips and school activities are ideally suited for this because all the students have attended and can then return to the

This is based on the popular book by Judith Viorst, *Alexander and the Terrible, Horrible, No Good, Very Bad Day.*

classroom to talk about it. Some of these events lead to unexpected conversations. When one of the authors took her class on a disastrous field trip that included a severe thunderstorm, a leaking bus roof, and a driver who lost the keys, the shared experience became a class book entitled "The Terrible, Horrible, No Good, Very Bad Field Trip"!

Creating text. As stated earlier, the purpose of an LEA lesson is to capture the natural language of children. This is accomplished through establishing a purpose for the writing and initiating a conversation to fulfill the stated purpose. Sometimes referred to as "authentic writing," the goal is to create a purpose for the writing that is viewed as meaningful for the students, not just the teacher. Many students respond to a purpose associated with the permanence of the written product. For example, daily class news and bound books are both popular choices.

Daily class news is constructed to report on the events that occur within the classroom community. While these events may appear mundane to the outsider, they are often of great interest to the students. Topics can range from the lunch menu to classroom visitors and academic activities. The importance of composing the daily class news has less to do with the topic than the composing and writing experience itself. A few things to remember for effective daily class news writing:

- Do it every day
- Date each entry
- Make sure the students can clearly see what is being written as it is being written
- Reread the entry several times with the class
- Make it easily available for future reading

Class books serve another purpose for LEA lessons. These can be small or large in size and contain the original written text composed with the students. Remember that LEA relies on preserving the language of the students, so resist the urge to edit. Like the daily class news, they should be written so that all students can see the print being developed on the page. Photographs or illustrations may be added later to the text, or not, depending on the goals of the lesson. The emphasis is not on turning out elaborately bound and laminated works of art. Many of these class books are simply a stapled sheaf of papers. The real value of these class books is that the students generate text they can practice reading because it is in their natural language.

Mr. Matsumoto, a third-grade teacher, uses a language experience approach in the language arts workshop to create a class book on family biographies. The 25 students in Mr. Matsumoto's classroom have been working on a family biography project for the last two weeks. They have read other family biographies like excerpts from *Little House on the Prairie* (Wilder, 1973) and *Cheaper by the Dozen* (Gilbreth & Carey, 2002). They have constructed family trees and a family timeline. Their next assignment will be to interview one adult member of their family to create an essay about this person's life. These essays will eventually be assembled into a class book. Mr. Matsumoto knows that his students will need a structure to the interview if they are to assemble useful notes. He has decided to use a Language Experience Approach focus lesson in order to draft possible questions for use in their interview protocol.

—— 𝓮𝓸✦𝓼𝓸 ——

Spotlight on Instruction

Teaching with Language Experience Approach in Third Grade

MODELING.

Mr. Matsumoto introduces the lesson by explaining that an interview protocol is a method used by writers to remember to ask important questions and take good notes. "A good idea for taking notes is to leave spaces between the questions so that when they give you an answer, you can write it down easily," he says. Mr. Matsumoto then tells the class that he is going to interview Ms. Jefferson, the teacher next door, while they watch. He then shows them the interview protocol he previously constructed on chart paper. It contains three questions:

1. How old are you?
2. What is your favorite thing about teaching third grade?
3. Do you remember when you first met me?

Ms. Jefferson arrives and takes a seat in front of the class. Mr. Matsumoto begins by asking her how old she is, and she tells him politely that it is none of his business. Mr. Matsumoto writes this down and asks the second question about teaching third grade. She replies that eight-year-olds ask interesting questions that make her think about the world in new ways. Again, Mr. Matsumoto writes this down on the chart paper while the students watch. He then asks her his final question and she gives a one-word response: "Yes." Again, he scribes her answer and thanks her for her time.

SCAFFOLDING.

Having created a shared experience, he is now ready to turn the discussion over to them. "I have two things I'd like for you to think about. Do these questions give me the information I want? How can I improve them?" What ensues is a lively discussion about the appropriateness of the first question. Jordan volunteers, "My dad told me it's not nice to ask ladies how old they are." Mr. Matsumoto then remarks that some men as well as women don't like to answer that question.

The class agreed that the second question was a good one and thought that it should be kept because Ms. Jefferson's answer was an interesting one. They also agreed that the third question was a problem because he only got a one-word answer from Ms. Jefferson. Linnette suggested that they change the question to read, "What do you remember about the first time we met?" and Mr. Matsumoto adds that to the list.

COACHING.

He then invites them to suggest other questions for use in an interview protocol. After scribing five of them, he instructs the students to work in partners to develop two more questions. While the pairs work together, he checks for understanding. Several minutes later, he signals an end to the partner work and writes down their suggestions on the growing list, even when a grammatical or semantic error is present. When he's finished, he tells the class, "Now we've got a long list of possible questions. You don't want to use them all, and some of them won't work in your interview. What I'd like you to do during activity time is select eight to ten questions for your interview protocol. You can rewrite and reword them in any way." With that, these third graders get to work on developing an interview instrument for their biographical essay. Mr. Matsumoto's lesson plan can be found in Figure 2.7.

Of course, LEA lessons should be viewed as only one method of shared writing instruction. While there are benefits to using this approach, it alone cannot provide all the opportunities for detailed instruction in writing. Students need to move smoothly to the composition of original text that produces writing consistent with

Figure 2.7　Language Experience Approach Lesson Plan

Assessed Need: I have noticed that the students in my classroom need to work on: **Asking questions that yield the information they are seeking**
Standards: **McREL LA Std. 4.II.7: Uses strategies to gather and record information**
Text I will use to demonstrate the strategy I plan to teach is: **Create questions to be used as an interview protocol for the family biography project**
Materials needed for this lesson are: **Chart paper** **markers**
Purpose of the lesson is: **Draft possible questions for them to refine during activity time**
SEQUENCE OF FOCUS LESSON *MODEL* *Parts to emphasize* **Establish purpose: generating interview questions for an interview protocol** **Model interview questions with Mrs. Jefferson:** **How old are you?** **What's your favorite part about teaching third grade?** **Do you remember the first time you met me?** *SCAFFOLD* *Questions to ask* **Do these questions get the information I want?** **How can I improve them?** **What other questions should we add to the protocol?** *COACH* *Students practice with partners* **Develop two other questions together for possible use in the interview protocol** **Write their questions on chart for selection and editing during activity time** *ASSESS* *These are the students who need extra support* **Visit each pair to check for understanding**
Independent Practice *Students will practice using the strategy during activity time* **Students will select questions from class list to edit for use in their interview protocol**

the conventions of the English language. Interactive writing instruction is a highly effective means for accomplishing this goal.

Interactive Writing

Interactive writing is a collaborative form of writing between students and teacher. Unlike LEA, the teacher "shares the pen" with the students, allowing them to write the message for all to see (McKenzie, 1985). Another important difference is that interactive writing messages are accurate in both spelling and content. Like LEA, it is often based on a shared experience and written on large chart paper. Lyons and Pinnell (2001) identify five key elements of interactive writing instruction:

- Planning
- Deciding the precise text
- How print works
- Word solving
- Reading and writing connections (p. 125)

Furthermore, these processes are not strictly linear, but rather are revisited in order to make them increasingly simultaneous in the minds of young writers. This is consistent with Fearn and Farnan's (2001) observations about the interactive writing processes because it requires continuous evaluation of the writing on the part of the students and teacher. An example of an interactive writing product can be found in Figure 2.8. Let's look at each of these key elements more closely to see how they are used in the classroom.

Planning. The first step of the interactive writing lesson is to establish a purpose for the text. Whether it is a response to literature ("What was our favorite part of the story we just read?"), directions for growing a flower, or a class letter for Back to School night, the reason for writing must be clearly recognized. This is accomplished through talk led by the teacher, who guides students through an initial gathering of ideas. Like LEA, this may come from a shared experience, like a book, class science experiment, or upcoming event.

Deciding the precise text. All writing consists of formulating ideas that are then narrowed to a specific string of words intended to convey those ideas. Therefore, after ideas have been generated it is necessary to begin to refine the message. McCarrier, Pinnell, and Fountas refer to this as "negotiation . . . through an active discussion and guided planning" (2000, p. 85).

A skillful teacher understands that all the students must feel a connection to the message, not just the more verbal and assertive members of the class. As such, you may need to consider a variety of ways to include all students in the composition process. Some teachers draw popsicle sticks with student names written on them in order to ensure they are calling on all the children. Another effective method is to invite students to "turn to a partner" to talk about a key point before discussing it in a large group. An advantage of this technique is that all the children have an opportunity to share their thoughts with another person, as well as listen to another.

Partner conversations also increase the amount of time students listen and speak, thus improving their oral language skills.

Figure 2.8 Interactive Writing Sample

This is our writing.

Word choice is also part of the discussion at this point in the lesson. A major goal of interactive writing is to arrive at a jointly composed message that is semantically and syntactically correct. Therefore, anomalies in vocabulary and grammar must be discussed. The goal is not to simply tell, but to scaffold their understanding through the use of prompts so they can correct errors themselves. For example, a grammatical error might be addressed by asking the students to say it both ways aloud to decide which version sounds better. Once consensus is reached and a precise text has been orally composed, the class is now ready to commit the message to the page.

How print works. Young writers may have difficulty with the layout of the text on the page, in particular the space needed for each word and between each word. Directionality, both left to right and top to bottom, must be considered as well. Older writers are also learning about punctuation, indenting, and capitalization. These are sometimes called **print conventions** because they are governed by the rules of the language. The teacher first leads students in a rehearsal of the agreed message so that students can more easily recall the exact wording. They may also count the words to formulate a prediction about how much space they will need. Finally, the rehearsal should also include the pauses and inflections that will indicate the punctuation necessary. In order to assist young writers with spacing issues, provide young writers with a wooden clothespin to hold a space between words. This reinforces the essential concept that space, as well as the letters themselves, carries meaning.

Teacher Tip

Word solving. In the typical interactive writing lesson, each word of the message is analyzed so that students can spell it correctly. A sight word may appear on a **word wall** and can be copied. A word wall is an area of the classroom where sight words are taught and displayed alphabetically for easy use by students. Students decode other words using their current knowledge of the way letters and sounds work. The key is for the teacher to have an understanding of what the students currently know in order to scaffold instruction. Sounds that are unknown to the students should be given by the teacher so as not to consume valuable instructional time devoted to concepts that are too difficult for them. For example, the /ph/ sound in "phone" is not likely to be known by kindergarteners in October; the teacher is wiser to write this portion of the word himself and instead invite the students to listen to the final consonant in the word. The /n/ phoneme is in their current repertoire and should be written by a student.

The teacher leads the students through the process of decoding each word, then invites a student to come up to the language chart to write the agreed letter. The teacher may gently prompt the student as to where to begin writing the letter, coaching them as they write with a black magic marker. All the students then repeat the letter until the entire word has been written. As each word is written, the message thus far is reread to make sure that the agreed text is being composed and to identify the next word.

As noted earlier, the goal of interactive writing instruction is to create a correct message, however, students are also likely to make errors. Interactive writing instruction is done with a black magic marker and cannot (and should not) be erased. Erasures can be distracting and upsetting to young writers. Instead, 1″ wide white correction tape is used to cover the error. The child then writes the letter correctly on top of the tape. In this way, the error is dealt with quickly, the student gets another opportunity to practice it correctly, and the flow of the message is not disrupted.

Reading and writing connections. Reading and writing, like listening and speaking, are closely linked as receptive and expressive forms of literacy. Types, or genres, of writing should be explicitly introduced to students. Genres of writing include poetry, lists, stories, and letters. When composing and constructing original text in interactive writing, be sure to include a variety of writing genres within the lessons. Natural reading and writing connections occur when students write an innovation of a story or when they create a sign for the classroom. For example, the opening scenario for this chapter was an innovation lesson.

Interactive Writing Instruction Work for Older Students

While it is true that interactive writing instruction was initially designed for emergent writers, teachers of older students have found success using this technique in their classes. Increasingly, interactive writing is viewed as part of a gradual release of responsibility model for writing with adolescents (Fisher & Frey, 2003). Struggling writers and English language learners can profit from focus lessons on specific aspects of writing, such as composition, punctuation, and word choice.

Ms. Harper, a seventh grade teacher, is using interactive writing to connect a book the class recently read to their mathematical studies. The 32 students in this class have been reading *How Much Is a Million?* in their mathematics class for the past two days (Schwartz, 1993). The facts illustrated in the book have amazed the students. For instance, a goldfish bowl large enough to hold one million goldfish could also hold a whale. Ms. Harper will be using an interactive writing experience for students to formulate a similar algebraic problem and then explain how they will solve it. She is particularly interested in focusing on their use of accurate technical vocabulary in describing how they will solve the problem. The mathematical problem they design will become a partner project in their pre-algebra class later in the day. The students will utilize the language chart they have created to guide their mathematics work.

Spotlight on Instruction

Teaching with Interactive Writing in Seventh Grade

Ms. Harper begins by explaining the purpose of the lesson and the importance of creating a mathematical investigation plan that will guide their work. She rereads some of *How Much Is a Million?* and invites discussion about other things they would like to know about.

She asks, "I've learned so much from this book about what a million of something might look like. What are some examples of things here in the school that we could multiply to a million?"

Several students offer their suggestions and Ms. Harper keeps track of them on a small note pad so she doesn't forget their ideas. They discuss the merits of investigating a million rulers, erasers, books, tennis balls, and lunch tickets. The teacher continues to ask questions in order to prompt further conversation about the possibilities and challenges of each. Over the course of several minutes, the class has gradually come to consensus that they will use tennis balls.

"Let's turn that into a algebra question," she says, reminding them of their task of creating an investigation plan. After some negotiation, they agree that the precise text will read, "How much space is needed to hold one million tennis balls?" She has them repeat the question several times so they will remember the

(continued)

MODEL.

SCAFFOLD.

SCAFFOLD.

COACH.

exact wording of their guiding question. When Denny misspells *million,* she uses the white correction tape to cover it and directs his attention to the algebra word wall for the correct spelling. "Remember to use the word wall when you get stuck. It's there to help you."

"Now we need to create a plan," she reminds them. "We can't count a million tennis balls. Could this shoebox help?"

Now the class buzzes with the possibility. "Before we talk about it, turn to your partner and talk with him or her about how the shoebox might help solve our mathematical dilemma." After giving them a minute or so to talk, she brings the class discussion back to her again. "Let's hear those good ideas."

Several students offer their thoughts about filling the shoebox with tennis balls, then figuring out how many boxes they would need to hold 1,000,000 of them. Eventually, she brings the conversation back to the investigation plan. "Let's write this up as a plan. What exactly will we need to do in order to solve this problem? Let's be sure to use the correct vocabulary so our computations will be accurate."

Guided by Ms. Harper, the students first formulate the exact wording of the investigation plan, prompting them as needed on word choice, spelling, and punctuation. She continues to invite students up to the front of the class to write each word of the plan (see Figure 2.9).

Later they will complete their investigation with their partners and bring their results to the next class meeting to see if they need to revise their plan. Meanwhile, Ms. Harper has given her students an opportunity to write about their mathematical thinking, a skill frequently tested on state assessments. Her complete lesson plan is featured in Figure 2.10.

Figure 2.9   Language Chart for Interactive Writing Lesson

How much room is needed to store

one million tennis balls?

To solve this problem, we will measure a shoebox to find the volume in square inches (length × width × height = V).

Then we will fill the shoebox with tennis balls and count.
(T = # of tennis balls in the box).

Next we will calculate how many shoeboxes are needed to store 1,000,000 tennis balls.
1,000,000 ÷ T = B (# of boxes)

We will calculate the volume of space needed to store B boxes. V × B = space needed in square inches.

We will bring our calculations to our next math class to discuss conversions.

Figure 2.10 Lesson Plan for Interactive Writing

Assessed Need: I have noticed that the students in my classroom need to work on: **Engaging in critical thinking in reading and mathematics**
Standards: **McREL LA.4.III.6. Organizes information and ideas from multiple sources in systematic ways (e.g., time lines, outlines, notes, graphic representations)**
Text I will use to demonstrate the strategy I plan to teach is: **How Much Is a Million? by David M. Schwartz** **Interactive writing**
Materials needed for this lesson are: **Chart paper, markers, pointer, correction tape**
Purpose of the lesson is: **Create a mathematics investigation plan based on How Much Is a Million?**
SEQUENCE OF FOCUS LESSON *MODEL* *Parts to emphasize* **Set purpose – create a mathematics investigation plan** **Reread excerpts of How Much Is a Million?** **Lead discussion about possible ideas** *SCAFFOLD* *Questions to ask* **What questions motivated the author to write this book?** **What are we curious about?** **How will we find the answer to the question we ask?** *COACH* *Students practice with partners* **Invite students to discuss in partners during interactive writing lesson** **Use mathematics word wall for vocabulary** **Introduce shoebox as a means for solving the problem** *ASSESS* *These are the students who need extra support* **Carolyn and Leo will use shoe boxes with the dimensions already marked on them**
Independent Practice *Students will practice using the strategy during activity time* **Students will work in pairs to solve the problem using shoe boxes to multiply the results**

Teachers using shared writing techniques like Language Experience Approach and interactive writing, design lessons that foster conversation and discussion about a shared experience. As with shared reading, we have several practical recommendations for making your shared writing focus lessons successful.

PRACTICAL TIPS FOR SUCCESSFUL SHARED WRITING FOCUS LESSONS

The shared writing focus lesson results in a piece of original text co-produced by teacher and students. The development of this text requires materials for creating the chart or class book. In addition, students utilize a variety of support materials to write the letters and words necessary for the message.

Charts and Class Books

Most original texts created through shared writing are produced on chart paper. Materials needed for language charts include lined or unlined chart tablet paper and magic markers. Daily class news reports are usually brief in length (1–3 sentences) and don't require a full sheet of chart paper, so look for chart paper in alternative sizes such as 12″ × 18″. Class books are best written on loose white construction paper and then stapled together later as pages. An easel supports the chart and provides the writer with a sturdy surface to write upon. Of course, shared writing lessons that are not intended to result in a permanent product can be composed on a dry erase board or overhead transparency.

Lined or unlined paper? Some educators recommend using unlined chart paper during shared writing experiences with emergent writers so that it does not distract them from creating letters on the page. You can make this determination by observing your students to see whether they are ready for lined paper.

Pencils or markers? An advantage to using a magic marker is that it can be seen clearly by all students in the room. When a pencil is used, if an error is made on the chart during interactive writing, students may attempt to erase the error, sometimes wearing a hole in the page. An error made with a marker cannot be erased, but it can easily be corrected with white correction tape. This tape is available from most teaching supply stores in a variety of widths.

Support Materials

Students utilize support materials in the classroom to correctly compose a shared writing message. A small whiteboard or Magna Doodle® is an excellent tool for the teacher to use to model the formation of a letter. Because any portion of the surface can be wiped clean with a single sweep, the Magna Doodle is ideal to demonstrate how the substitution of a letter creates a series of words in a word family. In addition, students use print materials in the classroom to compose.

Print resource materials. Access to print resource materials is important for students as they solve words and sentences. These materials should be easily viewed by all and used frequently by the teacher. Examples of these print resource materials include alphabet cards and word walls featuring sight words. It's common for teachers to hang alphabet cards above the blackboard. However, students sitting on the floor or at their desks have difficulty seeing the letters. Consider displaying the cards just below the chalk or marker tray so that they are at the students' eye level. Emergent writers often learn to recognize the names of their classmates early in the school year. Therefore, keep a name chart of class names nearby for students to use in the class compositions.

BIG IDEAS IN SHARED READING AND SHARED WRITING

Shared reading is an instructional practice that utilizes enlarged text to allow students to participate in meaningful reading with the support of the teacher. The teacher

Figure 2.11   Key Elements of Shared Reading and Shared Writing

Active Teaching Practice	Purpose	What the Teacher Does	What the Students Do
Shared reading (Holdaway, 1979)	Focus on comprehension and decoding strategies using connected text	• Reads aloud to students • Focuses on teaching points using the text	• Follow along while teacher reads • Join in reading aloud familiar text
Language Experience Approach (Ashton-Warner, 1965)	Show how speech is represented as print	• Takes dictation of student-constructed message	• Tell a story or message for the teacher to scribe
Shared Writing (McKenzie, 1985)	Focus on meaning of message	• Negotiates message through discussion • Teacher scribes agreed message	• Negotiates message through discussion
Interactive writing (McCarrier, Pinnell, & Fountas, 2000)	Focus on meaning of message and conventions of print	• Negotiates meaning through discussion • Guides the writing of the message	• Negotiates meaning through discussion • Writes message with teacher guidance

demonstrates the strategies used by successful readers while students "share" the task by engaging in reading along. Students then reread with the teacher in order to practice the skill or strategy being taught. Short texts may be read in their entirety by the teacher before rereading with the students; longer readings may be chunked into smaller sections (e.g., paragraphs), with the cycle of teacher modeling and shared reading being repeated several times.

Shared writing is a term that is used to describe collaborative writing experiences between teacher and students. Teachers using the Language Experience Approach (LEA) (Ashton-Warner, 1965) transcribe natural student language into the printed word so that students can begin to learn that print carries a message. Grammatical errors may be left intact because they are early attempts by students to formulate messages. Interactive writing (McCarrier, Pinnell, & Fountas, 2000) differs in that the students do the writing and the accuracy of the message is refined before it is written. Both emphasize the importance of oral language development within the lesson, not just the final written product. A summary of the key elements of shared reading and shared writing can be found in Figure 2.11.

 INTEGRATING THE STANDARDS

Create lesson plans that meet your state's standards by visiting our Companion Website at www.prenhall.com/frey. There you'll find lessons created to meet the NCTE/IRA Standards. Adapt them to meet the standards of your own state through links to your state's standards, and keep them in the online portfolio. You can collect lesson plans for each chapter in an online portfolio, providing you with invaluable tools to meet your state's standards when you head into your own classroom.

CHECK YOUR UNDERSTANDING_____

This chapter discussed shared reading and shared writing practices in the language arts workshop. Take a few minutes to check your understanding of the content of this chapter.

1. What is a focus lesson?
2. What is the role of active teaching in the language arts workshop?
3. In what ways can shared reading and shared writing be used to teach essential literacy skills?

CLASSROOM CONNECTIONS_____

1. Talk with your teacher about the literacy skills that he or she is currently emphasizing. Why are these important? How are they connected to the state standards?
2. Select a literacy skill being taught in your classroom and design a focus lesson using the planning tool in Figure 2.1.
3. Set up a resource file for storing good ideas you are seeing in your classroom. Label one *Shared Reading* and the other *Shared Writing*. Add materials and lesson plans for future use.

References

Adams, M. (1995). *Beginning to read: Thinking and learning about print.* Cambridge, MA: MIT Press.

Armbruster, B. B., Lehr, F., & Osborn, M. (2001). *Put reading first: The research building blocks for teaching children to read.* Jessup, MD: Partnership for Reading.

Ashton-Warner, S. (1965). *Teacher.* New York: Simon & Schuster.

Bandura, A. (1986). *Psychological modeling: Conflicting theories.* Chicago: Aldine-Atherton.

Bruner, J. (1975). The ontogenesis of speech acts. *Journal of Child Language, 2,* 1–40.

Burns, M., Griffin, P., & Snow, C. (1999). *Starting out right: A guide to promoting children's reading success.* Washington, DC: National Academy Press.

Clay, M. M. (1985). *The early detection of reading difficulties* (3rd ed.). Portsmouth, NH: Heinemann.

Clay, M. M. (2000). *Concepts about print: What have children learned about the way we print language?* Portsmouth, NH: Heinemann.

Cohle, D. M., & Towle, W. (2001). *Connecting reading and writing in the intermediate classroom: A workshop approach.* Newark, DE: International Reading Association.

Cunningham, P. M., Moore, S. A., Cunningham, J. W., & Moore, D. W. (2004). *Reading and writing in elementary classrooms: Research-based K–4 instruction* (5th ed.). Boston: Pearson Education.

Davey, B. (1983). Think-aloud: Modelling the cognitive processes of reading comprehension. *Journal of Reading, 27,* 44–47.

Duke, N. K. (2000). 3.6 minutes per day: The scarcity of informational texts in first grade. *Reading Research Quarterly, 35,* 202–224.

Eldredge, J. L., Reutzel, D. R., & Hollingsworth, P. M. (1996). Comparing the effectiveness of two oral reading practices: Round-robin reading and the shared book experience. *Journal of Literacy Research, 28,* 201–225.

Fearn, L., & Farnan, N. (2001). *Interactions: Teaching writing and the language arts.* Boston: Houghton Mifflin.

Fisher, D., & Frey, N. (2001). *Responsive curriculum design in secondary schools: Meeting the diverse needs of students.* Latham, MD: Scarecrow.

Fisher, D., & Frey, N. (2003). Writing instruction for struggling adolescent readers: A gradual release model. *Journal of Adolescent and Adult Literacy, 46,* 396–405.

Frey, N. (2004). *The effective teacher's guide: 50 ways for engaging students in learning.* San Diego, CA: APD Publications.

Fountas, I. C., & Pinnell, G. S. (2001). *Guiding readers and writers grades 3–6: Teaching comprehension, genre, and content literacy.* Portsmouth, NH: Heinemann.

Good, T. L., & Brophy, J. E. (2003). *Looking in classrooms* (9th ed.). Boston: Allyn & Bacon.

Hansen, J. (2001). *When writers read* (2nd ed.). Portsmouth, NH: Heinemann.

Herber, H. L. (1978). *Teaching reading in content areas* (2nd ed.). Upper Saddle River, NJ: Prentice Hall.

Holdaway, D. (1979). *The foundations of literacy.* Portsmouth, NH: Heinemann.

Keene, E. O. (2002). From good to memorable: Characteristics of highly effective comprehension teaching. In C. C. Block, L. B. Gambrell, & M. Pressley (Eds.), *Improving comprehension instruction: Rethinking research, theory, and classroom practice* (pp. 80–105).

Keene, E. O., & Zimmermann, S. (1997). *Mosaic of thought: Teaching comprehension in a reader's workshop.* Portsmouth, NH: Heinemann.

Langer, J. A. (1985). Children's sense a genre: A study of performance on parallel reading and writing. *Written Communication, 2,* 157–187.

Lyons, C. A., & Pinnell, G. S. (2001). *Systems for change in literacy education: A guide to professional development.* Portsmouth, NH: Heinemann.

Manning, M., Manning, G., Long, R., & Kamii, C. (1993). Preschoolers' conjectures about segments of a written sentence. *Journal of Research in Childhood Education, 8*(1), 5–11.

Marzano, R. J. (1998). *A theory-based meta-analysis of research on instruction.* Aurora, CO: McREL.

Marzano, R. J., Pickering, D. J., & Pollock, J. E. (2001). *Classroom instruction that works: - Research-based strategies for increasing students achievement.* Alexandria, VA: Association for Supervision and Curriculum Development.

McCarrier, A., Pinnell, G. S., & Fountas, I. C. (2000). *Interactive writing: How language and literacy come together, K–2.* Portsmouth, NH: Heinemann.

McKenzie, M. G. (1985). *Shared writing: Apprenticeship in writing in language matters.* London: Centre for Language in Primary Education.

Moss, B., & Newton, E. (2002). An examination of the informational text genre in basal readers. *Reading Psychology, 23*(1), 1–13.

National Center on Education and the Economy. (2001). *Speaking and listening for preschool through third grade.* Washington, DC: Author.

National Reading Panel (2000). *Teaching children to read: An evidence-based assessment of the scientific research literature on reading and its implications for reading instruction*

(Report of the subgroups). Washington, DC: National Institute for Child Health and Human Development.

Pearson, P. D., & Fielding, L. (1991). Comprehension instruction. In R. Barr, M. L. Kamil, P. Mosenthal, & P. D. Pearson (Eds.), *Handbook of reading research* (Vol. III, pp. 815–860). Mahwah, NJ: Erlbaum.

Rashotte, C. A., MacPhee, K., & Torgensen, J. K. (2001). The effectiveness of a group reading instruction program with poor readers in multiple grades. *Learning Disabilities Quarterly, 24,* 119–134.

Reutzel, D. R., & Cooter, R. B. (1990). Whole language: Comparative effects on first-grade reading achievement: *Journal of Educational Research, 83,* 252–257.

Rog, L. J. (2001). *Early literacy instruction in kindergarten.* Newark, DE: International Reading Association.

Rosenshine, B. & Meister, C. (1992). The use of scaffolds for teaching higher-level cognitive strategies. *Educational Leadership, 49*(7), 26–33.

Routman, R. (1988). *Transitions: From literature to literacy.* Portsmouth, NH: Heinemann.

Sacks, C. H., & Mergendoller, J. R. (1997). The relationship between teachers' theoretical orientation toward reading and student outcomes in kindergarten children with different initial reading abilities. *American Educational Research Journal, 34,* 721–739.

Stauffer, R. G. (1970). *The language experience approach to the teaching of reading.* New York: Harper & Row.

Vygotsky, L. S. (1978). *Mind in society: The development of higher psychological processes.* Cambridge, MA: Harvard University Press.

Literature Cited

Cowley, J. (1989). *Baby gets dressed.* New York: Wright Group/McGraw-Hill.

Cowley, J. (1998). *The meanies.* New York: Wright Group/McGraw-Hill.

Freeman, D. (2002). *Gregory's shadow.* New York: Puffin.

Gilbreth, F. B., Jr., & Carey, E. G. (2002). *Cheaper by the dozen.* New York: Perennial.

Kroll, S. (1995). *It's Groundhog Day!* New York: Scholastic.

Lowry, L. (1989). *Number the stars.* New York: Laurel Leaf.

Schwartz, D. M. (1993). *How much is a million?* New York: Harper Trophy.

Wilder, L. I. (1973). *Little house on the prairie.* New York: Harper Trophy.

3

Guided Reading and Writing in the Language Arts Workshop

BIG IDEAS IN GUIDED INSTRUCTION

Guided reading is an instructional approach for teaching small groups of students who have been grouped because of similar strengths and areas of need. These lessons are 20–30 minutes in length and are notable for the use of text that is carefully matched to the learners. The focus of guided reading lessons for emergent and early readers centers on the use of cueing systems to decode and understand the printed word. Transitional and self-extending readers benefit from lessons on cognitive cues, especially comprehension strategies.

Like guided reading, guided writing is also implemented with small groups of students with similar writing strengths and areas of need. These lessons may focus on the craft of writing or on the processes that lead to the development of clear and concise original text. In all cases, the teacher provides direct instruction on one or more elements to develop and refine student skills.

Questions to Consider

When you have completed this chapter, you should be able to answer these questions:

- In what ways do teachers make decisions about grouping in guided instruction?
- What is the structure of a guided reading lesson?
- What are the cueing systems in reading?
- How are questions and prompts used in guided instruction?
- What is guided writing?
- What is process writing?
- What is a balanced approach to writing?
- How are essential skills and strategies taught through guided writing?

Key Vocabulary

Guided instruction

Homogeneous grouping

Heterogeneous grouping

Guided reading

Picture walk

Round robin reading

Choral reading

Independent level

Instructional level

Frustration level

Guided writing

Writing processes

Writing models

Generative writing

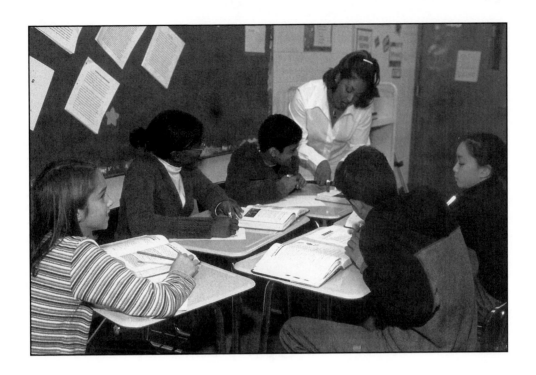

A LOOK INSIDE

Ms. Alexander is seated at a kidney-shaped table with five fourth-graders. She has called this small group in order to deliver teacher-directed guided reading instruction. Today she has selected a passage from *Boy: Tales of a Childhood* by Roald Dahl (1984) as a means for teaching comprehension strategies related to character development. In the previous lesson, they read Dahl's recount of a boyhood prank when he and his friends planted a dead mouse in a candy jar of an unpleasant shop owner.

Ms. Alexander begins by charting responses from students on the character traits of seven-year-old Dahl revealed in the story thus far. Ariane notes that Dahl likes adventure because "his favorite thing to do is race his bicycle."

Kim adds, "We know he loves candy, too, because he wrote a whole chapter about a candy store."

Sasha chimes in, "He's kind of mean, too, because he put that dead mouse in the candy jar." The group agrees with this, although Kim admits that it is also funny.

"Those are great observations," says Ms. Alexander. "You've noticed that this author tells us about himself by describing actions, rather than just telling us 'I like adventure' or 'I am kind of mean.' Good readers infer character traits by looking at what the character says and does, not just by relying on the author to do our thinking for us. Now, let's find out what happened at the candy store after Roald put the dead mouse in the candy jar. Be sure to pay attention to how the actions tell us about the character."

Next, Ms. Alexander asks the students to open their books to the next chapter. After she reminds them to "whisper read" in soft voices and avoid choral reading, she asks them to begin when they are ready. As they read quietly, she moves around the table to listen to the reading of individual students, taking anecdotal notes as she goes. The students read about the boys' discovery the next day that the shop is closed, and a broken jar of candy lays on the floor of the shop. Roald's friend convinces him that the shop owner has been frightened to death. When the boys arrive at school, they are made to line up on the playground, a signal that something is wrong.

Ms. Alexander listens to Ariane read the passage about Roald's relief when he sees the shop owner with the headmaster, then his attempt to go unnoticed in line as the angry woman seeks to identify the boys. Ms. Alexander stops Ariane and says, "What is Roald feeling?"

Ariane flashes a smile and replies, "He's feeling guilty!"

"How do you know that?" probes Ms. Alexander.

"He's looking at his shoes! Whenever I do something wrong in class, I look down at the floor so you won't see me. I mean . . . " Ariane stammers.

"It's OK," smiles Ms. Alexander, "I know what you mean!"

GUIDED INSTRUCTION IN THE LANGUAGE ARTS WORKSHOP

As noted in the previous chapter, active teaching involves demonstration, explanation, questioning, and clarification (Good & Brophy, 2003). This begins with shared reading and shared writing lessons that allow the teacher to demonstrate skills and strategies to the whole class. However, this instruction alone does not provide students with all the experiences they need to integrate these practices into their repertoire of literacy behaviors. Most are likely to need designated time with a teacher and a small group of peers. This time is referred to as **guided instruction** because it serves as a bridge between teacher modeling and student independence. We are reminded of Anita Archer's description of a sequence of effective teaching (personal communication, February 2003):

- **I** do it
- **We** do it
- **You** do it

Using this framework, shared reading and writing is the "I do it" part, while guided reading and writing is the "We do it" portion of the sequence. Independent work makes up the third component of Archer's framework. In the language arts workshop, the teacher designs lessons that flow from modeled lesson to guided instruction to independent practice so that students can assume more control over their reading and writing. This is consistent with the gradual release of responsibility model (Pearson & Fielding, 1991).

See chapter 1 in this book for a review of this model.

The daily and weekly schedules featured in the introduction of this book provide a template for organizing time in the language arts workshop. As you can see, guided instruction occurs during the largest portion of the first hour of the language arts workshop. After the shared reading or shared writing lesson has been conducted at the beginning of the workshop, most students work for the next 40 minutes on collaborative reading and writing activities with peers. Meanwhile, the teacher is delivering guided instruction to small groups of students. Teachers make decisions about how students are grouped using guidelines that promote effective guided learning.

Guidelines for Guided Instructional Groups

As discussed in chapter 1, grouping decisions play an important role in the language arts workshop. Throughout the workshop experience, students have opportunities to work with one another in student-selected and teacher-selected groups. During guided instruction, the teacher constructs small groups based on strengths and needs, interests, or other factors related to the task or to social development. These groups change frequently to maximize interactions between and among students.

Small groups. The purpose of holding guided instructional groups to no more than six students is so that the teacher can provide more direct contact time with each learner. When group sizes grow beyond this number, management demands may take precedence over instruction. In addition, the small size of the group allows the teacher to observe each student up close in the act of learning. Insight into a child's problem solving skills can inform future instruction because the teacher gains an understanding of what students do when they get to a "tricky part" of the text.

Although the group should not exceed six, it is acceptable for it to be as small as one student. This is especially true when working with students who struggle to read and write. While it may be tempting to place all the lowest achieving students in one group, it is likely that they require more individualized instruction than their grade level peers because their skill profiles are more idiosyncratic. In our experience, normally progressing readers and writers tend to have a great deal in common with one another, while those who struggle tend to be unique in their patterns of strength and areas of need.

Students have similar literacy strengths and needs. Most commonly, teachers form guided instructional groups based on similar literacy strengths and needs, called a **homogeneous** group. This is done for two reasons—practicality and peer support. It is practical because the teaching day simply does not have enough minutes in it to allow for individual instruction for each student. Small group structures also capitalize on the power of peer influence on learning. Stated another way, students benefit from the questions and insights of their peers in a teacher-directed group (Cazden, 1988).

Determining what literacy strengths and needs a child possesses is determined through assessment, particularly those assessments created and conducted by the teacher (Frey & Hiebert, 2003). These assessments may be completed during guided instruction or at other times in the instructional day, particularly during conferencing in the language arts workshop. In addition to the traditional means of assessing student literacy (i.e., reading level, phonics knowledge, comprehension), the teacher may also decide to group according to other factors related to student interest or for reasons related to social development. Flood, Lapp, Flood, and Nagel (1992) suggest considering these dimensions of grouping:

See chapter 5 for a detailed look at conferencing with students.

- *Skills development.* Are there students who could benefit from instruction concerning a specific skill?

- *Interest.* Is this a topic of particular interest to specific students in the class?
- *Work habits.* Are there students who could benefit from time spent with classmates with more effective work habits?
- *Prior knowledge of content.* Do some students possess a high level of knowledge about a topic?
- *Prior knowledge of strategies.* Are there some students who could benefit from instruction about the use of a particular reading or writing strategy?
- *Social development.* Are there students who could benefit socially from spending time with certain classmates?

While some of these factors such as skills development, interest, and prior knowledge of content or strategies suggest a homogeneous grouping pattern, others result in a heterogeneous grouping pattern. A **heterogeneous** group is one that is mixed in ability according to one or more factors. For example, a group formed based on work habits or for social development is likely to be heterogeneous in nature in order to capitalize on the relative strengths of members of the group. These factors are summarized in Figure 3.1.

Grouping patterns change frequently. We have stated that students are grouped based on a number of considerations, especially student strengths and needs. It is also vital to remember that these grouping patterns should not be static. In other words, the reading or writing group a child belongs to in September should not be comprised of the same classmates in May. It is essential for students to benefit from numerous opportunities to learn with one another; flexible grouping patterns ensure this happens. It is equally critical that students see themselves as contributors to the learning of others; flexible grouping patterns ensure this happens as well.

A common criticism of guided instruction groups is that students identify too closely with a particular peer group, especially those perceived as struggling readers and writers. There are a variety of negative effects associated with being in the "low reading group," including low self-esteem and failure to progress (Juel, 1990).

Figure 3.1 Considerations for Grouping

Considerations for Grouping During Guided Instruction	
Grouping Pattern	**Instructional Purpose**
Skills development	Teach a specific skill
Interest	Topic is engaging to a particular group of students
Work habits	Access peer supports within the group
Prior knowledge of content	Group will benefit from direct instruction on the topic
Prior knowledge of strategies	Group will benefit from direct instruction on the use of a strategy
Social development	Students are grouped to foster positive social relationships and social skills

Source: Adapted from Flood, J., Lapp, D., Flood, S., & Nagel, G. (1992). Am I allowed to group? Using flexible patterns for effective instruction. *The Reading Teacher, 45,* p. 610. Copyright © 1992 by the International Reading Association.

It is important that reading groups are reconstituted frequently so that no student feels they are permanently assigned to a low-achieving guided reading or writing group. That means that groups should be remixed every four to six weeks. We use an unwritten rule that if other students stand up when the first one is called, it's time to change groups!

Of course, careful consideration about how students are grouped is only one part of guided instruction. In the language arts workshop, these groups are formed in order to implement two powerful forms of teaching—guided reading and guided writing. The latter half of this chapter is devoted to a detailed examination of guided writing instruction. Next, we will explain what guided reading instruction is and how it can be used in your classroom.

GUIDED READING INSTRUCTION IN THE LANGUAGE ARTS WORKSHOP

Guided reading books are usually small paperback readers containing only one story, whereas basals are collections of many stories.

Guided reading instruction has long been a hallmark of the effective literacy teacher's classroom. While it has been called various names throughout the previous century, including high/middle/low ability reading groups (Gray, 1925), Directed Reading Activity (Betts, 1946), or three-to-five groups (Marita, 1965), the central concept has been to teach small groups of children to read using texts matched to their skills. It has evolved over the last decade into a practice called **guided reading** (Antonacci, 2000; Cunningham & Allington, 2003; Fountas & Pinnell, 1996).

What Is Guided Reading?

In guided reading, small groups of students with similar learning needs are grouped together for a short time to receive specific instruction from the teacher using text that is carefully matched to their current skills. These materials may include leveled guided reading books, basals, or texts the teacher has gathered. The purpose of guided reading is to deliver customized lessons based on recent assessment information. These assessments may be collected during the guided reading lesson or at other times during the language arts workshop.

Effectiveness of Guided Reading

Evidence Based

The effectiveness of guided reading as an instructional strategy for developing readers is grounded in an approach to literacy that emphasizes the role of the learner in the process. For much of the 20th century, the role of the reading teacher was viewed as a dispenser of information to children who needed to be prepared to read before beginning to read. This so-called "readiness model" dominated reading instruction and it was commonly believed that children should not be taught to read until they reached 6.5 years of age (Smith, 2002). This prevailing readiness model was challenged in 1971 by Frank Smith, who stated that "reading was not something one was taught, but rather something one learned to do . . . one learned to read from reading" (Pearson, 2002, p. 433). Therefore, "the function of teachers is not so much to teach reading as to help children read" (Smith, quoted in Pearson, 2002, p. 433).

The teacher and the student work together to apply strategies and skills to decode and comprehend the text. This format has been shown to be effective for struggling readers (Short, Kane, & Peeling, 2000). It has proven useful for building fluency (Stahl & Kuhn, 2002), comprehension (Dymock, 1998), and to move students to independent, silent reading (Worthy & Broaddus, 2001–2002). Guided reading offers an effective method for instruction using informational materials (Villaume & Brabham, 2001). These findings are echoed by the National Reading Panel, who reported that guided oral reading "had a significant and positive effect on word recognition, fluency, and comprehension across a range of grade levels" (NRP, 2000, p. 12). The structure of the guided reading lesson is designed to build these reading skills through careful reading of meaningful texts.

What Is the Structure of a Guided Reading Lesson Plan?

Like all good instruction, planning is a critical part of an effective guided reading lesson. Good teachers know better than to be lulled into a false sense of security about teaching a book simply because it appears to have simple text. Knowing the text and your students well increases the likelihood that learning will occur. Give yourself and your students every benefit by preparing carefully for the guided reading lesson. A lesson planning form appears in Figure 3.2.

Figure 3.2 Guided Reading Lesson Plan

Guided Reading Lesson Plan

Students _____   Classroom Teacher _____
_____   Date _____

Familiar Book: Result of Observation:	Level:
New Book: Targeted skills for this lesson: Standards:	Level:

Book Introduction:

Word Work:	Writing:

Student Reading:

Questions:

Guided reading lessons are typically between 20 and 30 minutes in length, depending on the needs and stamina of the students. Stamina is a legitimate consideration for guided reading because this intensive instructional time may be the most cognitively demanding period of the day for students. Because the group is small and instructionally similar, the pacing of these lessons is quicker than other times of the day. Early and emergent readers in particular may tire during the first weeks of guided reading instruction.

Although guided reading lessons do not need to follow a rigid sequence of instruction, several components are generally recognized and recommended. Figure 3.3 below gives a suggested time sequence for a 20-minute and 30-minute lesson, although these times should be adjusted to meet the needs of your students. Let's look more closely at each of these components.

The familiar text. The guided reading lesson begins with a reading the students have seen before. For emergent and early readers, this is likely to be the book they read during their previous lesson. Transitional and self-extending readers are often reading longer texts that are not finished in one lesson. Therefore, they reread a portion from the last lesson, often the passages preceding the end of the previous stopping point. There are two reasons for doing this. First, engaging in repeated readings of the same text builds fluency, the ability to read smoothly, accurately, and with expression (Askew, 1993). Fluency is linked closely with a reader's ability to comprehend (Samuels, 1979). Second, rereading aids in recall and the ability to incorporate new information, both important when reentering a partially read text (Millis & King, 2001).

> See chapter 9 for more information about fluency.

At the opening of the guided reading lesson, the teacher invites students to revisit the familiar reading for five minutes or so. This is an ideal time for the teacher to collect assessment information about individual students. These assessment procedures may include anecdotal notes or running records. After students have "warmed up," the teacher transitions the group to a new book introduction.

> More information about these assessments can be found in chapter 11.

Text introduction. The text introduction is a time for teacher-directed instruction. Think of the introduction as the time when your guided reading plan is the most detailed. This is your opportunity to activate prior knowledge, preview the text, and provide direct instruction about the specific strategies or skills to be highlighted in this lesson.

Figure 3.3 Suggested Times for Guided Reading Lessons

	20-Minute Guided Reading Lesson	30-Minute Guided Reading Lesson
Familiar reading	3 minutes	5 minutes
Book introduction	5 minutes	5 minutes
Word Work	5 minutes*	3 minutes
Writing	5 minutes*	3 minutes
Student Reading	5 minutes	10 minutes
Questioning	2 minutes	4 minutes

*In 20-minute lessons, choose either word work or writing as an element of the lesson.

When using books with illustrations, the format of the introduction is referred to as a **picture walk.** The purpose of a picture walk is not to tell children everything that will happen in the story. Rather, an effective picture walk prepares students for the language they will encounter in the book while giving them a sense of the theme or plot of the story. It also invites them to consider what they already know about the topic and what personal experiences they have had that are alike and different from those portrayed in the book. A well-crafted picture walk leaves readers with a few questions that can only be answered by reading the book (Holdaway, 1979). In our own practice, we rarely show children the last picture in the book so that they will have a purpose for discovering how the book ends. The written text itself is not the focus during the picture walk, although specific words or phrases may be highlighted by the teacher because they are a part of the skills being taught in the lesson. Remember that the picture walk is not a pop quiz—do not pepper students with questions about the book and its illustrations. Recognize that this is a chance for you to introduce vocabulary, themes or main ideas, and a purpose for reading. Figure 3.4 is a checklist of items to consider in completing an effective picture walk.

Texts read by transitional and self-extending readers may not contain pictures or illustrations. The introduction moves from being a picture walk to a discussion of what is known about the topic and how it connects to the personal experiences of the students. There is still room for sharing the theme and plot of a narrative text, or the main ideas of an informational one. Again, be careful not to disclose too much, but rather give students a taste of what to anticipate. Much like the previews for the

Figure 3.4   Considerations for Picture Walks in Guided Reading

Teacher's Role	Examples of Questions and Prompts
Examine the Cover	What do you see on the cover? Use vocabulary from the story to describe the scene. Based on this picture, what do you think the book will be about? This picture reminds me of _____. Has that happened to you?
State the theme	This book is about _____. The characters in this story learn about _____.
View illustrations	Point out important details in the pictures. State the names of the characters. Ask for personal connections. Ask questions about prior knowledge. (Remember when we learned about _____?)
Practice unfamiliar language	When _____ happens, the main character says, _____. Let's all say that together. Invite students to locate new vocabulary words on the page.
Pose a question to be answered by reading	What will _____ do to solve his problem? How do _____? I wonder how _____?

newest Hollywood blockbuster, this introduction should prepare students for the big ideas while leaving them with questions that can only be answered by reading.

Like the language arts workshop itself, text introductions can be viewed as a gradual release model. Emergent readers need extensive support through the picture walk, but this support is gradually faded as the students' strategies for increasingly independent reading become more refined. Marie Clay described this as a gradient of teacher involvement as the teacher moves from more direct instruction in the book introduction for young readers to asking a few thought-provoking questions to whet the appetite of older readers (1991b). Figure 3.5 contains a chart for book introductions at each phase of reading development.

Word work. This element may come before or after students read independently; however, there should be a time for working with words during the guided reading lesson. Teachers will often position this element before student reading in order to introduce vocabulary or word study skills necessary for more accurate reading.

Word study and vocabulary development are discussed at length in chapters 7 and 8.

For emergent and early readers, word work may focus on phonics instruction and sight word development. For transitional and self-extending readers, word work may focus on spelling, word meanings, words with multiple meanings, or word families. Regardless, the teacher selects the focus words before students begin the lesson. While chapters 7 and 8 will expand on this, it is important to note now that young readers benefit most when they receive word recognition instruction that includes these practices:

- Making and breaking words
- Manipulating letters to form new words
- Locating these words in printed text
- Learning the meaning of the words (Juel & Minden-Cupp, 1999–2000)

Figure 3.5 Book Introduction Checklist

Element	Emergent	Early	Transitional	Self-Extending
Cover	√	√		
Title	√	√	√	√
End papers reviews			√	√
Illustrations	√ (All)	√ (Some)		
Plot	√	√	√	
Theme or main idea	√	√	√	√
Vocabulary *locate on page*	√			
Vocabulary *definitional*	√	√	√	√

Because reading and writing are so closely linked, consider incorporating writing into every guided reading lesson.

Evidence Based

Writing. Like word work, this element may occur before or after student reading. The writing portion during guided reading is brief, so any extended writing should be completed in the collaborative or independent phases of the language arts workshop so as not to consume instructional time intended for reading. Organization and management of materials is critical during guided reading. In order to minimize lost instructional time due to a transition to writing, use a guided reading student journal. This may take the form of a notebook or a packet of blank pages stapled together with a construction paper cover. The use of a journal eliminates the need for locating paper. A partial list of possible writing ideas to use before or after the reading appears below in Figure 3.6.

Student reading. Everything in the guided reading lesson thus far has been designed to lead to this element of the lesson—student reading of the text. For transitional and self-extending readers, this is accomplished through silent reading. The teacher may designate stop points in the text so the group can discuss the reading and clarify misunderstandings. Not surprisingly, this is not realistic with emergent readers who do not read silently, or early readers who are just beginning to do so. Therefore, it can be a temptation to have each child either take turns publicly reading a portion of the text or allowing all of them to read in unison. This practice, called **round robin reading,** is an ineffective and potentially detrimental approach to reading instruction. In their book *Good-bye Round Robin,* Optiz and Rasinski (1998) summarize the research on the negative implications of this practice:

- *It does not reflect authentic reading.* Rarely is reading aloud a part of anyone's daily life.
- *It reinforces ineffective reading behaviors.* Students must follow along, even when another student is reading inaccurately.
- *It causes subvocalization.* While reading along students subvocalize all the words, leading to slower rates.
- *It creates behavior problems.* Some read ahead to get ready for their part; others misbehave because they don't want to read.
- *It discourages self-correction.* Others correct the reader before he or she is given a chance to figure it out.

Figure 3.6   Writing Ideas to Use Before or After Reading

Before reading	*After reading*
• Copy the words introduced during word work portion of the lesson.	• Write a sentence that summarizes the book.
• Write vocabulary words for the story and include a definition in the student's own words.	• Discuss your recommendation for or against the book.
• Write a sentence predicting what will occur in the book.	• Answer the prediction question created before the reading.
• Write a question the book may answer.	• Predict what might happen next in a sequel to the story.
	• Note the important facts in the text.
	• Discuss whether the events were real, imaginary, or a mixture of both.

- *Instructional time is lost.* Reading aloud is slower than silent reading.

- *It creates anxiety in some students.* Children who do not read well worry that they will be humiliated in front of their peers. (pp. 7–8)

See chapter 9 for information on reader's theater.

Another practice, called **choral reading,** refers to the practice of having students read in unison. Choral reading can be an effective tool for building fluency through repeated readings, especially reader's theater. It is also an appropriate strategy for dramatic performances such as the recitation of a poem. Its usefulness is limited in guided reading however, because the purpose here is to provide more individualized support for students. There may be brief passages that lend themselves to choral reading, particularly alliterative sentences or rhyming passages that beg to be heard aloud. Having said that, the student reading portion of the guided reading lesson should be devoted to the individual.

So how can you encourage individual reading that does not devolve into round robin reading? Teach younger students how to "whisper read" using very soft voices. As they read, get up from your chair and listen in over the shoulders of each child. If you hear the whisper reading beginning to take on a choral tone, stop a student to ask a question. This changes his timing in relation to the other students. Another effective strategy is to use an "inside-outside" arrangement. Before beginning to read, ask students to alternate their chairs so that some face toward the table and others face away. This creates some quiet space for each reader by reducing the distraction of hearing someone else reading.

Questioning. The subject of questioning is critical to the guided reading process because it lies at the heart of instruction. Once students have finished the reading for the lesson, pose literal and inferential questions to them. Retelling is a query at the literal level and is closely associated with comprehension. Invite students to retell and encourage them to use their books to support their retelling. Good readers return to the text as needed and this should be considered an acceptable classroom practice. For instance, asking how the Big Bad Wolf disguised himself in *Little Red Riding Hood* is an example of a literal question (Ransom, 2001). In addition, ask questions that require students to infer meaning about the text, such as questions that ask about the main idea, or about the author's purpose for writing the book. An example of an inferential question for the same book is inquiring about why the wolf chose to disguise himself as an old woman and not a young man. Questioning after the reading should also invite readers to make connections to themselves and to other books they have read. These may include questions that probe their reactions and opinions of the text. Asking a reader about his or her thoughts concerning talking to strangers encourages connections between the story and personal experience. Although every question you may

From *Alexander and the Terrible, Horrible, No Good, Very Bad Day and Other Stories and Poems* by Judith Viorst, illustrated by Ray Cruz, © 1987 by Simon & Schuster. Used by permission of Simon & Schuster.

ask cannot be anticipated in advance, it is useful to prepare a few literal and inferential questions to begin meaningful discussion of what they have read.

You are now acquainted with the structure used in a guided reading lesson plan. However, an effective guided reading lesson is more than just a series of instructional elements strung together. A hallmark of guided instruction is the scaffolding that occurs when a teacher asks questions and gives prompts to help students use strategies to solve a problem. In guided reading, the teacher scaffolds instruction using statements based on cueing systems. We'll take a detailed look at cueing systems, then examine how teachers use these cueing systems to create questions for guided reading instruction.

Using Cueing Systems in Guided Reading

Guided reading with emergent and early readers centers on the cueing systems recognized as essential to meaningful reading (Goodman & Goodman, 1994). These cueing systems are consolidated by fluent readers in order to decode and comprehend the meaning of the written message on the page. You'll recall from chapter 1 that these cueing systems, as shown in Figure 3.7, are:

- *Graphophonic*—Able to combine letters with the sounds they represent
- *Syntactic*—Understands the grammatical structures in the language
- *Semantic*—Knows the meaning of the words
- *Pragmatic*—Knows the social world

Graphophonics. In the early years, the graphophonics cueing system is built through the many sound, letter, and word-related activities of school. Look at the Latin root words of that term—*graph* means to write or draw, and *phon* means sound or voice. Therefore, graphophonics refers to the relationship between letters, clusters, and words and the sounds they represent. The instructional activities for teaching graphophonics include phonemic awareness and phonics tasks related to sound/letter correspondence. In addition, word walls and word sorts are used to increase student knowledge of graphophonics. A word wall is a large display of words arranged in alphabetical order used for reading and writing instruction.

Review chapter 2 for a discussion of these skills.

See chapter 7 for a detailed look at this instruction.

Figure 3.7   Cueing Systems in Reading

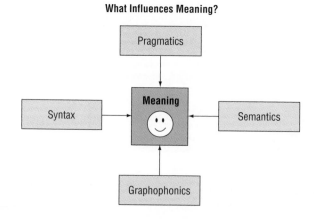

What Influences Meaning?

Syntactic. The syntactic cueing system is developed through an increasing understanding of the grammatical rules of the language. By this we are not referring to the ability to recite grammar rules, but rather the internal mechanisms that readers recognize when a sentence is syntactically correct and when it is not. For example, look at this sentence:

> The meegials were deeply concerned about the impeding squibnet of the casslets.

Now answer these questions:

- Who was worried?
- What event were they worried about?
- Who was the object of their worrying?

If you answered:

- The meegials
- A squibnet that would occur soon
- The casslets

See chapter 6 for more information on oral language development.

then you have syntactical knowledge of the English language, despite the fact that the sentence contained nonsense words. Syntactical knowledge is taught in a number of ways, especially exposure to written language through shared and guided reading, and oral language development through teacher and student talk.

Semantic. Syntactical knowledge without semantic knowledge is limiting, however. In order to fully understand the previous example, you would need to be familiar with the vocabulary as well. If you were told that *meegials* are small, peaceful creatures that live on a distant planet, and *casslets* are a fierce, warring tribe from a nearby land, the meaning of the sentence would take further shape. If you also understand that a *squibnet* is a declaration of war, you can now more fully appreciate the troubles faced by the *meegials*. Semantic knowledge is developed through vocabulary instruction, especially word analysis, synonyms (words that are alike in meaning), and antonyms (words that are opposite in meaning).

You used word analysis skills when you considered the Latin root words in the term *graphophonics*.

Pragmatic. Finally, the pragmatic cueing system is developed through knowledge of how language is used by people. It can include recognizing when something is meant to be funny, or solemn, or provocative. Pragmatics also relate to an understanding of the voice of a character in a story. For example, consider this sentence:

> The small child exclaimed, "By jove, I'm surprised to discover I'll be having crunchy peanut butter on my sandwich today!"

It was your pragmatic knowledge that raised a red flag on this sentence construction because we know that small children do not speak this way. Compare it to this more pragmatically correct sentence:

> The small child whined, "But I don't *like* that kind of peanut butter!"

It's likely that you were able to visualize this scene because it is consistent with your understanding of the language and behaviors of young children. The pragmatic cueing system, like the syntactic one, is expanded through shared and guided reading experiences and rich oral language development.

These four cueing systems form the basis for teaching guided reading. The teacher's role is to provide support to the reader through prompts and questions. Our colleague Patricia Kelly (personal communication) reminds us that "the trick is to say the right thing in order for the reader to do the work." Teaching is not telling, and the key to guided reading instruction is to respond to a student's oral reading error through a question or prompt that causes the student to arrive at a correct response—a fundamental principle of scaffolding. Guided reading instruction is scaffolded through questions and prompts based on the cueing systems.

Scaffolding Using Questions and Prompts

Questioning and prompting are the key tools for teaching during guided reading because they serve to scaffold a child's understanding of the strategies needed to understand the text. During guided instruction, the well-chosen question helps the student get to the solution in ways that merely telling does not. While there is a place for giving a child the answer, it is not the same as teaching because the student may not be able to access the same information again independently.

> Giving the answer is appropriate when it is too frustrating for the student or is well beyond their current skill level.

Being able to ask the right question is predicated on an understanding of the processes and strategies the student can utilize to arrive at the correct answer. These questions and prompts are only useful when they activate the correct problem solving strategies needed by the student. The questions and prompts used for emergent and early readers focus on the cueing systems.

> Prompts are statements made by the teacher to trigger a mode of thinking in the student.

Questions and prompts using cueing systems. Young readers use cueing systems to make sense of the print on the page. Over time, the reader consolidates these cueing systems, resulting in more fluent reading. Therefore, a goal of guided reading instruction for these readers is to help them develop and activate these cueing systems through prompts and questions. These range from questions like "Does that look right?" (graphophonics) to "Make your voice sound like a question" (pragmatics). The prompts and questions in the following chart are inspired by the work of many researchers on the reading development of children in emergent and early strategies of reading (Clay, 1993, 2001; Fountas & Pinnell, 1996; Routman, 1988). Examples of these types of prompts and questions can be found in Figure 3.8. We suggest copying this chart and placing it inside a plastic sleeve for use at your guided reading table.

> These cognitive cues are discussed more extensively in chapter 10.

Questions and prompts that foster comprehension. In addition to activating cueing systems, teachers ask questions that foster a deeper understanding of the text a child is reading. The intent of these questions and prompts is to promote reading comprehension through the use of cognitive cues, more commonly called strategies. These comprehension strategies include predicting, monitoring, cross-checking, and applying fix-up strategies. Questions to activate these comprehension strategies are organized into before, during, and after reading the text. These questions are intended to increase comprehension of the reading through direct instruction of effective reading behaviors.

- *Before reading* questions and prompts should focus on activating students' prior knowledge and making predictions about what they expect to find in

Figure 3.8   Prompt Chart for Guided Reading

Prompt Chart for Guided Reading Instruction for Emergent and Early Readers

Graphophonic	*Syntax*	*Semantics*	*Pragmatics*
Does it look right?	Does it sound right?	Does it make sense?	Does that seem true to you?
Get your mouth ready to make the first sound.	Were the words in the right order?	Is that the word you expected to see there?	Make it sound like talking.
Cover the _____ to make the sound.	Try that again and listen for it to sound right.	Look at the picture to see if it makes sense.	Make your voice sound like _____ (a question, surprise, etc.).
Does that word look like another one you know?	Can you change the words for it to sound right?	What do you expect will happen next in the story? Check to see if you're right.	What do you expect it will say next? Check to see if you're right.
Did you see that word before on this page?			

the text. Background knowledge may include personal experiences, previous readings on the same topic, or familiarity with the author. Questions asked by the teacher should direct students' attention to making predictions based on prior knowledge and observations about the title, cover, and any illustrations or diagrams in the book. When students approach an unfamiliar text by first considering what they know about a topic and anticipating what they expect to encounter, they are practicing effective behaviors of good readers.

- *During reading* it is important to stop at critical parts in the text to ask questions to check for understanding. Many teachers mark these stopping places in advance with a sticky note containing the questions they want to ask. Questions asked during the reading invite students to consider what they know thus far, to check the predictions they made before the reading, and to anticipate what will happen next. By stopping occasionally throughout the reading to ask and answer questions, students are encouraged to monitor their understanding of the text.

- *After reading* questions often center on recalling and retelling the important points in the reading. These are valid queries and give the teacher insight into the students' literal comprehension of the text. However, students also need to hear and answer inferential comprehension questions in order to become more adept at reading "between the lines" to understand what else the author means. A chart of possible questions to ask before, during, and after reading appears in Figure 3.9.

The questions and prompts used during guided reading instruction scaffold a reader's understanding about how the print on the page is understood. In addition, questions and prompts foster the use of strategies essential to comprehension of the

Figure 3.9   Questioning Chart for Before, During, and After Guided Reading Instruction

Before	During	After
Based on the title, what do you expect this book to be about?	What do you know about _____ so far?	What surprised you?
What do you already know about _____?	What do you expect will happen next?	What do you believe the author wants us to know?
Have you read other works by this author?	What words have confused you?	Does this remind you of other books you have read?
	What is the problem so far?	Are there any connections with your own life?
	Have you ever experienced something like this?	If a person wants to find out more about this subject, what could they read?

text. This brings us to the next key element of the guided reading lesson—choosing an appropriate text.

Matching Materials with Students

Perhaps no other element of guided instruction is as vital as the careful matching of materials to students. In guided reading and writing instruction, materials are identified based on students' current performance. The goal is to select materials that are neither too difficult nor too easy for the students—a phenomenon sometimes called the Goldilocks Rule (Ohlhausen & Jepsen, 1992). Worthy, Broaddus, and Ivey call this "books that fit" (2001, p. 66). In guided reading, students are assessed on their ability to read and comprehend text accurately using assessment procedures such as running records and Informal Reading Inventories. A portion of chapter 11 is devoted to implementing and interpreting these assessment instruments.

The most common formula for selecting these texts consists of three levels of student performance. The first, the **independent level,** is considered to be text read accurately at a rate of 95% or higher, with a comprehension level of 90%–100% as measured by questions. Students who read a text with 89% or less accuracy and less than 75% comprehension are considered to be at their **frustration level** because the number of errors interferes too greatly with meaning. Text read accurately at a rate of 90%–94% and a comprehension rate of 75%–89% is called a child's **instructional level.** Teachers use instructional level text in guided reading instruction because it provides the students with enough challenges to focus their attention on their problem-solving skills without being so difficult that all meaning is lost. Figure 3.10 contains a chart summarizing these levels.

These levels are relative to the skills of the reader and vary depending upon those skills. In addition to relative difficulty as it relates to the individual, books used for guided reading instruction are leveled according to the complexity of the text. Lists are created to inform teachers who are choosing texts for use in their guided reading groups. These lists, or text gradients, are widely used by teachers to organize instructional groups. Text gradients are either described using a leveling system or a readability formula.

Leveling Systems

Most books designed for guided reading instruction have been leveled by the publisher, although leveling systems are not uniform. Some of the most popular leveling systems are Fountas and Pinnell (1999), Weaver (2000), and Clay (1991a).

Figure 3.10   Matching Guided Reading Materials to Student Skill Levels

If a student reads with an accuracy rate of. . .	And a comprehension rate of. . .	This text is at his or her. . .	And is suitable for. . .
95%–100%	90%–100%	Independent level	Independent reading
90%–94%	75%–89%	Instructional level	Guided reading
89% or less	75% or less	Frustration level	Read alouds or shared reading

Figure 3.11   Comparison of Print Formats

> # The boy ran fast.
> ### The boy ran fast!
> *The boy ran fast!*

For a listing of leveled books, see www.hubbardscupboard.org/guided_reading.html

Although closely related, they do vary somewhat. These and other leveling systems consider several factors in assigning a difficulty level.

Format of the book. This encompasses a number of factors, including size of font, placement of the print on the page, and amount of punctuation. For example, compare the ease of reading for the sentences in Figure 3.11.

The second sentence is considered slightly more difficult because of its font type and size (notice the difference in how the letter /a/ is written) as well as the use of an exclamation point at the end. The third, although containing the same words, is more difficult still because of the use of a cursive font style.

Content and vocabulary. Because readers utilize their background knowledge to understand what they read, content and vocabulary affect difficulty. A book that otherwise appears easy will rate a higher level of difficulty if the subject matter is likely to be new to students. For this reason, informational text is often assigned a higher book level than a comparable narrative piece.

Text structure. The availability of pictures that closely match the written text will be rated as easier than those with less specific illustrations. Expository text with diagrams, photographs, headings, and captions lower the difficulty level because the reader has multiple sources of information to utilize.

Length and complexity of sentences. Generally speaking, more complex sentences contain more words and bigger words (more syllables). These longer sentences contain more ideas as well and are equated with more difficult text.

Publishers of guided reading materials provide these leveled systems to assist teachers in choosing appropriate text that matches the instructional needs of a reader. However, many other reading materials do not come with information as to the difficulty. Readability formulas are useful for calculating the relative difficulty of nearly any text.

Figure 3.12 Fry Readability Graph

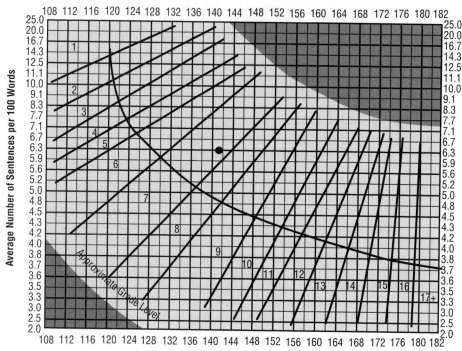

Sources: Fry, Edward B. (1968, April). A readability formula that saves time. *Journal of Reading, 11*(7), 513–516. Fry, Edward B. (1977, December). Fry's Readability Graph: Clarifications, validity, and extension to level 17. *Journal of Reading, 21*(3), 242–252.

Readability Formulas

Readability formulas have been utilized extensively as a means to replace outdated grade level formulas for rating text difficulty. An advantage to these readability formulas is that teachers can easily compute them using any reading material.

Fry readability formula. Designed by Ed Fry (2002), a readability rating can be calculated using the graph in Figure 3.12. Simply select three 100-word passages from the book, preferably one each from the beginning, middle, and end. Next, count the number of sentences in each passage and syllables in each passage. After doing this for each passage, average each of the two factors (number of syllables and number of sentences) then plot it on the graph. This will yield an approximate grade level.

Electronic readability sources. Another easily accessible tool for determining readability formulas can be found on your computer. Most word processing software has a feature for determining text difficulty. Simply type in a passage from a book you would like to assess for readability then run the calculation. For example, the Microsoft® Word program can compute a Flesch Reading Ease Score, a 100-point scale. On this scale, the higher the score the easier it is to read. Your computer can also report a Flesch-Kincaid Grade Level Score to approximate difficulty.

To run both these calculations on Word, go to "Tools" on the toolbar and select Spelling and Grammar. After running the spell check for the document, click on Options and check "Show readability formulas." After clicking OK, the program will report both scores. The Flesch Reading Ease Score for this section was a moderately difficult 51.4 and the Flesch-Kincaid Grade Level Score was 9.7.

As you can see from this data, readability formulas do not factor other elements that can influence difficulty, such as content. For example, a Flesch-Kincaid Grade Level analysis on a passage from *Cat's Cradle* by Kurt Vonnegut (1998), a decidedly adult satire of a world on the brink of an apocalypse, revealed a level score of 2.3 because it contained short, clipped dialogue. While this is not a typical result, it does highlight some shortcomings to relying on readability formulas alone without considering the content and the reader.

So far in this chapter, we've discussed the purposes of guided reading and the organization of a guided reading lesson. In addition, we have examined the two most powerful tools used by teachers in guided reading instruction—scaffolding through questions and prompts, and careful selection of text. Now let's go inside two classrooms to watch how teachers use guided reading in their language arts workshops.

TEACHING SKILLS AND STRATEGIES THROUGH GUIDED READING LESSONS

Guided reading instruction is used to provide readers with an opportunity to read text at their instructional level under the guidance of a teacher who can scaffold his or her use of strategies to read new text. With emergent and early readers, the focus is on using cueing systems to understand the print on the page.

Guided Reading Instruction with Younger Readers

Guiding reading instruction with beginning readers is challenging because it is easy to give in to the temptation to tell a student a word or phrase they have misread. The ability to deliver the right question or prompt that correctly elicits a child's use of a strategy takes years to develop. In this first-grade classroom, we'll see Mr. Michaels teaching three readers about reading with expression.

─── ❧❀❧ ───

Spotlight on Instruction

Teaching Fluency and Expression in First Grade

FLUENCY.

See chapter 11 for more information about running records.

Mr. Michaels calls Catrina, Tony, and Maggie to the guided reading table. These first graders read *Fire, Fire* (Randall, 1994) two days earlier and will start the lesson by revisiting this familiar book. Mr. Michaels asks his students to read the book quietly to themselves while he listens in. Today he will be collecting a running record on Tony to monitor his progress.

After they have each finished the familiar book, Mr. Michaels shows them the new book they will be reading today, *Baby Bear's Present* (Randall, 1994). He begins by asking them to remember a time when they went to the store but did not get what they wanted. All of the students quickly relate to this experience, so he connects those memories to the plot of this story. As he discusses some of the illustrations, he points out the expressions on Baby Bear's face as his father insists he get a toy train rather than the toy car he really wants. He even has the children repeat some of Baby Bear's dialogue to get a sense of the flow of the language.

After introducing the story, he turns his attention to the long- and short-a words used in the story. Using 3 × 5 cards he made for the lesson, Mr. Michaels practices these words with the group members

(continued)

WORD WORK.

.

COACHING.

MODELING

WRITING.

and then invites them to sort the words by vowel sound under cards labeled *train* and *car*. Next, he moves into the student reading portion of the lesson. Again, all three students are asked to whisper-read while Mr. Michaels listens in to each of them. When Catrina stumbles on the word *father*, he says, "Something wasn't quite right. What can you do to help yourself?" Catrina replies, "Get my mouth ready," but she also glances quickly at the illustration. This time, she solves the word correctly and continues. He then turns his attention to Tony, listening to the part of the story when Baby Bear tells his father what he wants. "Make it sound like talking," Mr. Michaels reminds Tony. Next, he listens in to Maggie's slow reading pace. "Can you read this part more quickly?" he asks. When Maggie's second attempt is not much better, Mr. Michaels says, "Listen to the way I say it. Then you try." This time, Maggie reads with increased fluency.

Mr. Michaels knows that oral language development is important during guided reading, so when they have finished he asks Maggie and Catrina to retell the story to one another while he serves as Tony's partner. Mr. Michaels is able to make some quick notes on an oral language checklist he is using. Satisfied that they have understood the text, he finishes the lesson by inviting them to write a sentence about the story in their journal.

This lesson is typical for guided reading lessons in the first grade. These early readers are well on their way to consolidating their cueing systems and are gaining more information from the written word than from illustrations. A copy of his lesson plan can be found in Figure 3.13.

Figure 3.13 Guided Reading Lesson Plan for *Baby Bear Goes Fishing*

Guided Reading Lesson Plan

Students **Tony, Catrina, Maggie**　　　　　Classroom Teacher **Mr. Michaels**

　　　　　　　　　　　　　　　　　　　Date **December 12**

Familiar Book: **Fire, Fire (Randall, 1994)**　　　　**Level: 8** Result of Observation: **Running record—98% ACC—Tony**
New Book: **Baby Bear's Present (Randall, 1994)**　　**Level: 1.6** Targeted skills for this lesson: **Fluency and expression, using short- and long-a sounds in words** Standards: **McREL LA Std. 8.1.4. Uses different voice level, phrasing, and intonation for different situations** **McREL LA Std. 5.1.3. Uses basic elements of phonetic analysis (e.g., common letter/sound relationships, beginning and ending consonants, vowel sounds)**
Book Introduction: **Ask students when they have had the experience of going to the store but not getting what they want. What did they do to solve it? Picture walk using some of the pictures and discuss Baby Bear's problem when his father wants to buy him a toy he doesn't want. How will he solve it?**

Word Work: **Word sort of short- and long-a sounds in book—sort words by sounds, especially /ai/**	Writing: **Students will write a sentence describing the story in their journals**

Student Reading: **Students whisper-read while I listen in (pay attention to Tony's reading—look out for choral reading. Reinforce expressive voices for dialogue.**
Questions: **Have students retell the story by talking with partner—I pair with Tony to gauge comprehension.** **How did Baby Bear solve his problem?** **How would the story be different if Baby Bear had gotten the toy?**

Figure 3.14 Guided Reading Lesson Plan for *They Fought for Freedom*

Guided Reading Lesson Plan

Students **Anahi, Artemio,**   Classroom Teacher **Ms. Allen**

Bianca, Lupita, Jorge, Leo   Date **October 9**

Familiar Book: Level: **5.5**
Result of observation: **Artemio—subvocalizes, no errors—reads slowly**

New Book: **They Fought For Freedom (Feldman, 1999)**   Level: **5.5**
Targeted skills for this lesson:
Identify how each child made heroic choices during the Civil Rights Movement
Standards: **McRel LA Std. 7.II.5 Summarizes and paraphrases information in texts (e.g., includes the main idea and significant supporting details of a reading selection)**

Book Introduction: **Review photographs in book—when did this take place?**
Setting: **Locate locations on map of U.S.**
Theme: **individuals can make a difference, even if they are children, when they stand up for what they believe**
Question: **How did 6 children make choices to stand up for their rights?**

Word Work: **Discuss freedom, Civil Rights Movement, heroic** **Enter words in journal and write definitions in own words**	Writing: **Make notes on graphic organizer on each child profiled in the text**

Student Reading: **Student read silently—stop at bottom of pg. 5 to discuss, then continue reading to pg. 8**
Model use of graphic organizer for information on Gwendolyn Patton
Finish Ernest Green during collaborative writing

Questions: **How was Gwendolyn Patton heroic?**
Do you think her actions helped the Civil Rights Movement? Why or why not?

Guided Reading Instruction with Older Readers The purpose for guided reading with older students shifts to a greater emphasis on comprehension strategies across longer pieces of text. This next lesson provides us with a view of a group of fifth graders who are working on summarizing and paraphrasing information using an informational reading. The lesson plan appears in Figure 3.14.

Spotlight on Instruction

Teaching Summarizing and Paraphrasing in Fifth Grade

Five students in Ms. Allen's fifth-grade class, all English language learners, approach the reading table. Guided reading has been occurring routinely for weeks and they bring their guided reading journals with them. Ms. Allen distrubutes the guided reading books she will be using for the next two lessons—*They Fought for Freedom: Children in the Civil Rights Movement* (Feldman, 1999). This 16-page expository text is part of the school's fifth-grade social studies collection and covers content related to the social studies standards. She has chosen a short article on Rosa Parks to use as her familiar book warm-up. Ms. Allen tells the students

(continued)

Integration of content area topics in reading instruction is an effective teaching tool for English learners.

Fluency building.

ACTIVATING PRIOR KNOWLEDGE.

PREVIEWING CONTENT.

WORD WORK.

WRITING.

LITERAL COMPREHENSION.

INFERENTIAL COMPREHENSION.

to read silently for a few minutes to review the content and motions for Leo to whisper-read so she can listen. She writes some anecdotal notes about Leo's performance in her guided reading notebook and then invites them to turn their attention to the new book.

Because the book offers so many photographs, she asks the students to review them and make a prediction about when the events took place. Anahi immediately remarks that one photograph "looks like the kids in the movie *Grease*," and Bianca accurately predicts that the pictures were taken in the 1950s and 1960s. Robert locates both Rosa Parks and Martin Luther King, Jr., in two other photographs. Ms. Allen uses a map of the United States to pinpoint several locations in the south and then points to the title of the book. She informs the students that the book is about six children who chose to act in heroic ways and discusses the theme of "individuals making a difference."

Before reading the book, Ms. Allen knows that a few vocabulary words need to be reviewed. She has selected *freedom*, *Civil Rights movement*, and *heroic* to discuss. As the students enter these words into their journals, she asks them about each word, building on their prior knowledge. She even points out the *–ic* suffix on *heroic* and connects it to other words on the word wall, including *fantastic* and *athletic*. She then distributes the graphic organizer they will be using to take notes on each of the children profiled in the book. See Figure 3.15 for a copy of her graphic organizer.

Ms. Allen turns the reading over to them, instructing her students to read silently until they reach the bottom of the first profile on Gwendolyn Patton. After checking for understanding, she asks them to read silently to the end of the second profile. As they read she moves around the table, listening to the whisper-reading of Bianca and Robert. As each finishes, they begin to make notes on the graphic organizer. With a few minutes left in the lesson, she asks them to turn to a partner to tell one another about Gwendolyn's heroism. She partners with Anahi to hear her response. Finally, she asks whether they thought Gwendolyn's actions helped the Civil Rights movement. Bianca answers in the affirmative, explaining that having a child sent away from a lunch counter would cause lots of people to be upset and talk about it.

As the timer is about to ring, Miss Allen asks the students to use the book to complete the information on Ernest Green, the second profile they read today. She reminds them that when they return for guiding reading in a few days they will finish the book and the graphic organizer. Anahi's completed graphic organizer appears in Figure 3.16.

Figure 3.15 Graphic Organizer for *They Fought for Freedom*

Gwendolyn Patton	Ernest Green	Claudette Colvin
Age:	Age:	Age:
Year:	Year:	Year:
Heroic Act:	Heroic Act:	Heroic Act:
	How did these six children stand up for their rights?	
Audrey Fay Hendricks	Larry Russell	Sheyann Webb
Age:	Age:	Age:
Year:	Year:	Year:
Heroic Act:	Heroic Act:	Heroic Act:

Figure 3.16 Anahi's Completed Graphic Organizer

Graphic organizer for *They Fought for Freedom*.

Gwendolyn Patton	Ernest Green	Claudette Calvin
Age: 9	Age: 17	Age: 10
Year: 1950 and 1960	Year: 1957	Year: 1955
Heroic Act: Spilt in a counter.	Heroic Act: He was the fist African American to go to all white school.	Heroic Act: She refused to give up her siet to a white person on the bus.

How did these six children stand up for their rights?

Audrey Fay Hendricks	Larry Russell	Sheyann Webb
Age: 9	Age: 13–17	Age: 8
Year: 1963	Year: 1963	Year: 1965
Heroic Act: She was in a protest march and got arrested for 7 days.	Heroic Act: he marched in the Children Crusade and got arrested for ten days.	Heroic Act: She was the youngest marcher in "Bloody Sunday."

PRACTICAL TIPS FOR SUCCESSFUL GUIDED READING LESSONS: MATERIALS

As with all instructional preparation, guided reading is enhanced by the use of specific materials to support student learning. Many of these materials are useful for both emergent/early readers as well as transitional/self-extending readers. Others are more specific for a particular developmental level. We've created a list of practical tips to enhance your guided reading instruction.

Tools for Guided Reading

Guided reading instruction requires specific tools for making lessons run smoothly. The basic materials to support guided reading instruction include:

- *Leveled texts for each reader.* Sharing texts is not recommended because students read at different paces and are encouraged to look back over previous pages to confirm information.
- *Chart paper and markers.* The teacher will often use these to record ideas and organize information for all students to see.
- *Writing instruments for students.* Because the connection between reading and writing is so strong, guided reading lessons often include a writing activity.
- *3 × 5 note cards.* These small cards are versatile and inexpensive. Young readers can use them to isolate words on the page, while older students can

use them to take notes. The teacher can easily create vocabulary or sight word cards for use by the group.

- *Notebook for teacher observations.* Guided instruction is an opportunity to watch students up close as they work through unfamiliar text. We recommend a binder with a section for each student. The teacher can then record anecdotal records to review later.

- *Assessment tools.* Keep blank copies of running records and observation checklists handy for easy use. Copies of these can be found at the end of this book in the compendium on assessments.

While these tools are useful in nearly all guided reading lessons, younger readers will benefit from instruction that includes some specialized materials.

Additional Materials for Emergent and Early Readers

Because instruction for beginning readers focuses on cueing systems, it is helpful to have these items on hand to model how print works. We keep these materials close by our reading table when working with young readers:

- *Magnetic letters.* These inexpensive materials are useful for quickly displaying words and manipulating the letter arrangements to reinforce teaching points.

- *Magna Doodle.* This "dustless chalkboard" has been around since 1974 and has become a classroom favorite for primary grade teachers. Students enjoy writing and erasing, and the teacher can model words on it. The "magic" slide bar can be used to erase letters at the beginning and end of words, nicely emphasizing the difference between words like *cat*, *scat*, and *cats*

To find out how Magna Doodles and lots of other things work, check out www.howstuffworks. com.

- *White boards and markers.* Use these for student responses. They can practice writing words you've targeted for instruction. The ones available in catalogs can get expensive when you want one for every child. Ask your local home improvement store to cut 8″ × 10″ squares of fiberglass shower board—the surface wipes clean when dry-erase markers are used.

- *Sentence strips.* Like 3 × 5 note cards, these are inexpensive and useful. Write a sentence with students, then cut the sentences apart, word by word, for students to reassemble. This is a great way to build knowledge of syntax.

Older readers are often reading longer books and can benefit from tools that enhance their ability to remember information across several lessons. These materials are excellent for use in classrooms with transitional and self-extending readers.

Additional Materials for Transitional and Self-Extending Readers

Students reading at the transitional and self-extending developmental levels need tools to take notes, record their thoughts and responses, and clarify their understanding of unfamiliar words using reference materials.

- *Sticky notes.* Encourage students to monitor their comprehension by encouraging them to use sticky notes while reading. Depending on your instructional purpose, they can record unfamiliar vocabulary, make notes about the use of literary devices, or jot down reactions, questions, or connections.

Figure 3.17 Materials Checklist for Guided Reading

General Materials for Guided Reading
❏ Leveled text for each reader
❏ Chart paper and markers for language charts
❏ Writing implements for students
❏ 3 × 5 notecards
❏ Notebook for teacher observation notes
❏ Assessment tools
Materials for Emergent and Early Readers
❏ Magnetic letters
❏ Magna Doodle*
❏ White boards and markers
❏ Sentence strips
❏ **Materials for Transitional and Self-Extending Readers**
❏ Sticky notes
❏ Journals
❏ Reference materials (dictionary, thesaurus, atlas)

*Magna Doodle is a registered trademark of Fisher-Price.

- *Journals.* As with younger students, the connection between reading and writing is powerful. Use student journals to take notes on vocabulary and respond to reflective questions.
- *Reference materials.* Guided reading is a time to instruct on how to clarify the unknown through the use of reference materials. Have a dictionary and thesaurus nearby to locate unknown words. Don't overlook the importance of maps to locate the setting of narrative and informational texts. We've included a checklist of these materials in Figure 3.17.

GUIDED WRITING IN THE LANGUAGE ARTS WORKSHOP

Like guided reading, **guided writing** is a time when the teacher meets with small groups of students to provide direct instruction. The purpose is to develop student writing proficiency so that they are able to communicate effectively for a variety of purposes. During guided writing, the teacher offers specific instruction through active teaching on a skill or strategy related to the craft and conventions of writing. Students then compose orally at first to give them an opportunity to explore language use and receive feedback from others. Students use the skill or strategy while the teacher scaffolds and coaches through questioning and prompts related to both oral and written composition.

Effectiveness of Guided Writing

There is far less research on the various aspects of writing instruction when compared to reading research. Many of the studies on writing have a reading component and are not solely focused on writing. This is not the weakness it may first appear to be—after all, reading and writing are closely connected and skills in one influence performance in the other (Dyson, 1994). Some researchers have looked at the guided instruction in writing and have found promising results. For example, struggling readers and writers in a third-grade classroom who participated in guided writing along with other aspects of literacy instruction improved both their writing and reading scores significantly over the course of the year (Short, Kane, & Peeling, 2000). Similar benefits have been established with at-risk adolescents who received guided informational and expository writing instruction (Fisher & Frey, 2003; Sweeney, Ehrhardt, Gardner, Jones, Greenfield, & Fribley, 1999). Similarly, a study of fifth-grade students with learning disabilities found that not only did their writing performance improve with guided writing in the writing workshop, but also their motivation and confidence to write (Furr, 2003). In all of these studies, improvement was attributed to the guided instruction on aspects of writing. This direct instruction of writing skills and strategies is somewhat different from the writing workshop model found in many classrooms.

Evidence Based

Much has been written about the writing workshop model as a means for promoting the writing process (Calkins, 1986; Fletcher & Portalupi, 2001). These traditional workshop models emphasize **process writing** as a means for improving student proficiency. The language arts workshop differs somewhat from these models in its emphasis on a gradual release of responsibility model of writing instruction. This difference between models lies in the focus on direct instruction of writing. In order to understand these differences, let's look first at the process of writing.

What Is Process Writing?

The term "process writing" refers to the stages a writer moves through to bring a piece from ideas to a final product. This philosophy was widely influenced by the work of Janet Emig, who used a case study approach to researching the processes used by eight high school seniors as they wrote (Emig, 1971). She discovered that these writers reported that they moved through a specific set of steps to bring their writing to a finished stage. These and other studies radically altered the way school writing was viewed. "Before, the thinking was about *what* people wrote; after, the thinking was about *how* people wrote" (Fearn & Farnan, 2001, p. 182). Graves (1975) extended this area of study by applying a similar research approach to the work of seven-year-olds. These processes of writing were formally identified by Calkins (1986) and others as a series of phases:

- *Prewriting*—Formulating ideas that may or may not be utilized in a later writing piece; sometimes referred to as *brainstorming*
- *Drafting*—The first commitment of these ideas to paper
- *Revising*—Revisiting the draft to add, delete, or change what has been written
- *Editing*—The written piece is approaching its final form and is ready for corrections and feedback on content from the teacher or peers
- *Publishing*—The final form of the piece is ready to share with others

This description of the writing process has been helpful for teachers in identifying the many demands on the writer in bringing a piece to its final form. The vocabulary of the writing process can be useful to young writers as well, especially in building their understanding of the tasks involved in bringing a writing project to a satisfactory end product. The traditional definition of a writing workshop encompasses this stance to writing. In these classrooms, students work independently then collaborate at other times with the teacher or peers to refine and polish their writing.

However, we have also seen the writing process become the curriculum itself, replacing both genres of writing and the necessary explicit instruction needed for students to improve their writing. In some classrooms, even very young children may work on a piece for weeks before it is declared finished. In others, we have witnessed continual attempts at improving a piece of writing that in all likelihood should have been abandoned. A further complication is due to the fact that each writer applies a unique combination of these processes within their own writing. It is possible that too much time has been dedicated to independent writing at the expense of writing instruction. In the language arts workshop, we advocate a balanced approach to writing.

> Genres of writing include summaries, reports of information, persuasive writing, and technical documents.

Balanced Approach to Writing Instruction

One of the challenges to writing instruction of any kind is that reducing the complex processes a writer uses to few key words and phrases can result in an oversimplified and misleading formula. Like the complex behaviors associated with reading, the systems utilized by the writer consolidate into an increasingly elegant and fluid process. Writers rarely begin by brainstorming then move directly to drafting, followed by revisions, and so on. In reality, they engage in one or more of these processes at a given time. It is important to note that researchers on the writing process do not suggest that it is stage-bound; in fact, they often apply the word *recursive* to describe the cycles a writer moves through as they draft, revise, edit, revise again, and so on (Calkins, 1986). However, this view may be limiting as well.

Consider your own writing practices. It is likely that you brainstorm, revise, and edit within nearly every sentence, jumping back to tweak a noun phrase, correct a spelling error, or add another idea. You probably don't restrict yourself to doing these things only when you have reached the end of the piece. Fearn and Farnan (2001) describe this as an iterative model of writing because it encompasses the many moves a writer makes to get the words down on the page. In the language arts workshop, guided writing instruction is dedicated to teaching young writers the skills necessary to make decisions using the *processes* of writing.

Using the Processes of Writing in Guided Writing

The ability to make these moves in an agile fashion requires explicit instruction on how it is done, complete with lots of modeling and coaching. This is followed by opportunities to work with others and independently to gain an increasing sense of confidence. The time when this direct instruction occurs is during guided writing in the language arts workshop. By finding the middle ground in instruction through borrowing the best of process writing with the best of product writing, students benefit from a balanced approach to writing.

During guided writing, the craft and conventions of writing are taught using writing models. Frames for writing are used to serve as a skeleton for original writing. In addition, the work of other writers is used to explore how authors use their writing to convey a message. Other guided writing lessons focus on conventions of sentence construction. This basic unit of writing serves as the linchpin for all original writing. Throughout lessons on craft and conventions, students use aspects of the processes of writing (brainstorming, drafting, editing, revising, and publishing) to polish their original text. In this model, the processes of writing are imbedded into instruction, rather than serving as the organizational structure for

Figure 3.18 Guided Writing Lesson Plan

Students:
Purpose of lesson:
Standards:
Materials needed:
SEQUENCE OF LESSON: *MODEL* *SCAFFOLD* *COACH*
ASSESS
NOTES

instruction. Therefore, skills and strategies are taught in every guided writing lesson so that students can apply them in their own writing.

TEACHING SKILLS AND STRATEGIES THROUGH GUIDED WRITING LESSONS

Like guided reading, guided writing lessons are between twenty and thirty minutes long, depending on the developmental levels of the students and the purpose for the lesson. These lessons have a format similar to the shared writing lesson plan. Most of the lesson is familiar to you and includes modeling, scaffolding, and coaching, all regarded as effective instructional practices. Each lesson ends with assessment as well because you must be clear about the product you want to see. A guided writing planning form is featured in Figure 3.18.

Although guided writing lessons can and should focus on the needs of the learners as they make progress in their curriculum, we like two particular types of lessons for use in guided writing, writing models and generative writing (Fisher & Frey, 2003).

Writing Models Instruction

Writing models use existing writing to provide a ready-made scaffold for student writing. By utilizing partially constructed texts, young writers can use this as a pattern while still creating an original product. The use of existing text to improve writing skills is well known among professional writers like Ann Lamott and Stephen King, who point to their experiences with this technique as an important formative stage of their development. Avi (2003), the prolific Newbery Award-winning children's author, describes his writing strategy when he was an adolescent:

> I would choose a writer, be it Shakespeare or Hemingway, and read until my head was stuffed with their work. Then I'd try to copy their styles. Never having been

taught a style, never pushed to find one voice, I wrote in *many* styles, many voices—which I believe explains my wide range of styles about which folks often puzzle. It is *not* experimentation. It's simply that I always ask myself this question: *Here is a story. What is the best way to tell it?* (p. 9)

Author studies. Writing as an integral component of an author study makes excellent reading-writing connections. Author studies are thematic units of instruction focused on one author's works. Students read these works and analyze for writer's craft and style, content themes, and text-to-text connections. Hansen reminds us "when writers read, they evaluate" (2001, p. 7). Guided writing models provide students with an opportunity to evaluate and in the process build their identity as a writer. Ideas for guided writing author studies include:

- Write a story about the school in the style of Dr. Seuss
- Weave five poems together to tell a story, such as *Love That Dog* (Creech, 2003)
- Create a class book version of Gary Paulsen's (1998) *My Life in Dog Years*, featuring a biographical or autobiographical chapter written by each member of the class

Writing frames. These are closely related to author studies but utilize sentence stems to be completed by the student. The sentence stems are linked conceptually and the finished product reads as a cohesive text. By supplying some of the words while leaving enough blank to allow the writer to influence the texture of the piece, frames encourage students who lack the stamina for sustained writing to experience a sense of completion.

A popular example of the writing frame is the "I Am. . ." poem. This writing frame is notable for its flexibility across age levels and reading materials (Fisher & Frey, 2003).

1. I am (special characteristics or nouns about you)
2. I wonder (something you are curious about)
3. I hear (an imaginary sound)
4. I want (a desire of yours)
5. I am (repeat first line of poem)
6. I pretend (something you pretend to do)
7. I feel (an imaginary feeling)
8. I touch (an imaginary touch)
9. I worry (something that truly bothers you)
10. I cry (something that makes you very sad)
11. I am (repeat first line of the poem)
12. I understand (something you know is true)
13. I say (something you believe in)
14. I dream (something you dream about)
15. I try (something you make an effort about)
16. I hope (something you actually hope for)
17. I am (repeat the first line of the poem)

Figure 3.19 Student "I Am . . ." Poem from *Parrot in the Oven*

I Am Poem

_____

I am _____

I wonder _____

I hear _____

I want _____

I am _____

I pretend _____

I feel _____

I touch _____

I worry _____

I cry _____

I am _____

I understand _____

I say _____

I dream _____

I try _____

I hope _____

I am _____

The "I Am. . . ." poem can also be used to assume the voice of a fictional or real-life character. The poem gives students an opportunity to explore what it is they know about the character. Tran, an eighth-grade student, was reading the book *Parrot in the Oven: Mi Vida* (Martinez, 1998) with his literature circle. During guided writing, Tran created the "I Am. . . ." poem (shown in Figure 3.19) in the voice of the gun used by the protagonist's father to frighten the family.

It is easy to view the "I Am. . . ." poem as a device for fostering responses to literature, especially as they apply to describing insights about a character in a piece of narrative text. Consider the array of uses for expository writing connected to content area learning. The sentence stems can be altered to elicit factual knowledge about a topic. Imagine students completing this version of the "I Am. . . ." poem on

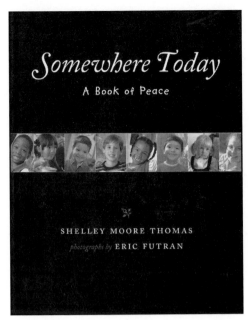

SOMEWHERE TODAY: A BOOK OF PEACE by
Shelley Moore Thomas, illustrated by Eric Futran.
Text © 1998 by Shelley Moore Thomas.
Photographs © 1998 by Eric Futran. Cover
reprinted by permission of Albert Whitman &
Company.

Excerpted from Make Someone Smile and 40 More Ways to
Be a Peaceful Person by Judy Lalli, M. S. © 1996. Used with
permission from Free Spirit Publishing Inc., Minneapolis, MN;
1-866-703-7322; www.freespirit.com. All rights reserved.

topics as diverse as pumpkin seeds, the Lincoln Monument, molecules, or the ancient city of Rome.

Patterned books. An interesting amalgam of author studies and "I Am. . ." poems is the use of patterned books in writing. Using the predictable text of a patterned story, students write a new version of the book. This is especially useful for emergent and early writers. For example, the Eric Carle story *The Very Hungry Caterpillar* (1983) features repetitive text chronicling the week-long eating adventures of a caterpillar. Young writers can adapt this story using some of the author's words by writing a version called *The Very Hungry Alligator.* Routman (1988) refers to this type of instructional activity as a writing innovation. They are particularly valuable for developing oral language, reading, and writing skills.

Older readers can utilize patterned books in their writing as well. For example, the book *Somewhere Today: A Book About Peace* (Thomas, 1998) offers a predictable pattern—each sentence starts with the phrase "Somewhere today" and provides readers with an idea that may contribute to peace. For example, one page says, "Somewhere today someone is being a friend instead of fighting" (p. 16). Students can be invited to write their own "somewhere today" sentences during guided writing instruction and create a companion book to the one Thomas wrote.

In addition to these patterned books, others offer lists for students to extend. Two examples include *Make Someone Smile: And 40 More Ways to Be a Peaceful Person* (Lalli, 1996) and *39 Uses for a Friend* (Ziefert, 2001). Again, the language development that occurs through oral composition is invaluable to young writers.

Paragraph frames. Similar to the "I Am. . ." poem, paragraph frames provide a series of sentence stems intended to scaffold the writer's original writing while furnishing an organizational structure. Paragraph frames are not intended as a fill-in-the-blank writing exercise. Instead, they should be introduced after rich oral development of ideas and concepts. This preliminary stage of oral composition assists writers in organizing their own thoughts about a topic. After the discussion, the paragraph frame is introduced and the students are instructed to add original sentences within or after it. This is more sophisticated than traditional story starters, which begin with a sentence stem like, "It

Figure 3.20 Sample Paragraph Frames

Creative Writing
They came for me! I wasn't doing anything and then . . . They said, " . . . " But I . . . And then . . .

Biographical/Autobiographical
I was thinking about my life. When I was young . . . But today . . . The best thing about my life is . . . I am lucky because . . .

Report of Information
Memorial Day is more than a day off. Memorial Day gave me time to think about . . . I also remembered . . . I know that . . . I miss . . . But . . . I wonder what other people thought about on Memorial Day. I think . . .

was a dark and stormy night . . . " because they provide more structure for the writer. A paragraph frame might look like this:

> _____ is an important part of my life. When I think about . . . I like to share . . . I could teach you . . .

Notice that the frame establishes a direction for the writer without being prescriptive. Furthermore, the writer does not need to use these sentences in sequence, but can add their own original writing within the frame. As noted before, they also allow the writer to extend the topic further. These frames can be easily created to reflect expository writing as well. For example:

> Hurricanes are violent storms that form over the warm water of the world's oceans. Characteristics of hurricanes . . . These storms are measured . . . Warning systems . . . The primary dangers of hurricanes are . . .

Other sample paragraph frames appear in Figure 3.20.

RAFT (Role, Audience, Format, Topic). Another writing model that can be used for both narrative and expository writing is RAFT (Santa & Havens, 1995). RAFT stands for Role, Audience, Format, and Topic and is used by young writers to construct a cohesive piece of writing that acknowledges voice, reader, purpose, and content. In guided writing, this frame provides the teacher with a structure for teaching these essential elements while students engage in meaningful writing. A simple RAFT for first graders might look like this:

- *Role*—Goldilocks
- *Audience*—The Three Bears
- *Format*—A letter
- *Topic*—I am sorry I went into your house

In order to successfully complete this RAFT, students must understand the story, the characteristics of a letter, and the social language of apologies. This RAFT writing frame works equally well for expository writing. Consider this example for sixth-grade students after viewing an interactive website on volcanoes:

Visit the Annenberg/ CPB website at http://www.learner. org/exhibits/ volcanoes/entry.html

- *Role*—Volcanologist
- *Audience*—Newspaper readers in Tacoma, Washington
- *Format*—Letter to the editor
- *Topic*—Threat of eruption from Mt. Rainier

Increase the variability of these writing frames by altering one or more elements within the guided writing group. In this way, students can write and then read each other's perspectives. These variable writing frames can be anchored in a common text. We have found that picture books are especially useful because the brief nature of the anchor text lessens the amount of time students need to search out information. Examples of variable RAFT writing frames appear in Figure 3.21 below.

Let's watch as a third-grade teacher uses RAFT to teach letter writing.

Figure 3.21   Variable RAFT Writing Frames

Thank You, Mr. Falker **(Polacco, 1998)**	*Thank You, Mr. Falker* **(Polacco, 1998)**	*Thank You, Mr. Falker* **(Polacco, 1998)**
R—self **A**—a teacher who changed your life **F**—persuasive essay **T**—why was this person instrumental in your life?	**R**—self **A**—self **F**—autobiographical incident **T**—feeling "dumb"	**R**—Mr. Falker **A**—himself **F**—teacher's journal **T**—first impressions of Trisha
My Dream of Martin Luther King **(Ringgold, 1998)**	*My Dream of Martin Luther King* **(Ringgold, 1998)**	*My Dream of Martin Luther King* **(Ringgold, 1998)**
R—self **A**—author **F**—graduation speech **T**—dreams for this world	**R**—children of Dr. King **A**—their father **F**—letter **T**—you have been a role model to us	**R**—Rosa Parks **A**—judge **F**—persuasive letter **T**—why I should be allowed to sit anywhere on the bus
For the Love of the Game: Michael Jordan and Me **(Greenfield, 1999)**	*For the Love of the Game: Michael Jordan and Me* **(Greenfield, 1999)**	*For the Love of the Game: Michael Jordan and Me* **(Greenfield, 1999)**
R—self **A**—parents **F**—poem **T**—my goals and dreams	**R**—self **A**—Michael Jordan **F**—list of questions **T**—overcoming obstacles	**R**—Michael Jordan **A**—you **F**—autobiographical paragraph **T**—obstacles overcome

Source: Developed by Justin Philips.

Figure 3.22   RAFT Writing Lesson Plan

Students: **Luis, Madeline, Bianca, Mark, Kristen, Ann**
Purpose of lesson: **Write a three-paragraph letter using Smoky Night (Bunting, 1999). Heading, greeting, 1st paragraph—introduction, 2nd paragraph—invitation, 3rd—closing, and signature**
Materials needed: **6 copies of Smoky Night, friendly letter checklist, peer editing rubric**
Standards: **McREL LA Writing 2.11.2: Uses paragraph form in writing (e.g., indents the first word of a paragraph, uses topic sentences, recognizes a paragraph as a group of sentences about one main idea, uses an introductory and concluding paragraph, writes several related paragraphs)**
SEQUENCE OF LESSON: *MODEL*   Introduce RAFT for this lesson: R—Daniel   A—Mrs. Kim   F—friendly letter   T—let's meet to talk about our cats   Use checklist to evaluate sample letter on language chart.   *SCAFFOLD*   Make text available for students. Use checklist and rubric to review elements of a friendly letter.   *COACH*   Provide support for students in spelling, content, and conventions as needed. Remind them to use checklist
ASSESS   Students will use checklist to self-assess.
NOTES   Next lesson: Peer editing of letters

Spotlight on Instruction

RAFT Guided Writing in Third Grade

The Caldecott Medal is awarded annually for outstanding illustration in children's literature. Learn more about the Caldecott at www.ala.org

Luis, Madeline, Bianca, Mark, Kristen, and Ann approach the guided writing table and settle into their seats while their teacher, Mr. Pham, distributes copies of a picture book they had read during their shared reading focus lesson. The book, *Smoky Night,* (Bunting, 1999) is a Caldecott-winning story of a conflict between Daniel's cat and his neighbor Mrs. Kim's cat. The backdrop is the Los Angeles riots and the book ends with the pet owners reconsidering the importance of living together peacefully. Mr. Pham's lesson plan can be seen in Figure 3.22.

Mr. Pham introduces the RAFT the students will be using in their writing.

- *Role*—Daniel
- *Audience*—Mrs. Kim

(continued)

Mr. Pham creates rubrics on the Rubistar website, available at www.rubistar.4teachers.org.

- *Format*—Friendly letter
- *Topic*—Let's meet to talk about our cats

He also distributes a rubric they have been using for the last few weeks in creating friendly letters, as well as a checklist they'll be using during today's lesson. The rubric can be viewed in Figure 3.23. "We'll use these today to write a friendly letter from Daniel to Mrs. Kim. Let's imagine what he might say to her to encourage her to meet him." The group eagerly begins listing ideas for him to record. Madeline suggests that Daniel would need to be very kind and say "please and thank you a lot." Mark adds that maybe it would be easier to invite Mrs. Kim's cat as well because "she would probably come if it was for the cats."

MODELING AND SCAFFOLDING.

He then distributes a checklist of elements in a friendly letter and displays a language chart he created with another group. The checklist can be viewed in Figure 3.24. Using the checklist, the students evaluate the letter on the language chart for the necessary elements.

After reminding the students to use the book to check for details to use in the letter, the students begin writing in their notebooks. Mr. Pham observes his students as they write, making notes about their individual progress. He prompts when needed, helping Ann when she is stuck on how to begin and asking Luis about the lack of details in his second paragraph when he notes that there is no information about where or when to meet. As each of them finishes, they reread their letters with him and check off the elements. The guided writing lesson is drawing to a close, so he reminds them to bring the rubric the next time when they will read the letters written by members of their group. The text of Bianca's letter appears in Figure 3.25.

Figure 3.23 Writing Rubric for Friendly Letter

Student Name: _____

Category	4	3	2	1
Greeting and Closing	No mistakes	1–2 mistakes	3 or more mistakes	No greeting or closing
Format	Has all the elements of a friendly letter.	Has almost all the elements of a friendly letter.	Has several of the elements of a friendly letter.	Has few of the elements of a friendly letter.
Ideas	It was easy to figure out what the letter was about.	It was mostly easy to figure out what the letter was about.	Had to read it more than once to figure out what the letter was about.	It was hard to figure out what the letter was about.
Grammar and Spelling (Conventions)	No spelling or grammar mistakes.	1–2 mistakes in grammar or spelling.	3–4 mistakes in grammar or spelling.	More than 4 mistakes in grammar or spelling.
Capitalization and Punctuation	No mistakes in capitalization and punctuation.	1–2 errors in capitalization and punctuation.	3–4 errors in capitalization and punctuation.	More than 4 errors in capitalization and punctuation.

Figure 3.24 Checklist for Elements of a Friendly Letter

My friendly letter contains:

☐ heading with the letter writer's address

☐ date of the letter

☐ greeting with the person's name

☐ first paragraph states purpose of the letter

☐ second paragraph is an invitation

☐ third paragraph offers a thank you

☐ closing

☐ signature

Figure 3.25 Bianca's RAFT Letter

Mrs. Kim
2334 Oak Street
Los Angeles, CA 99009

Dear Mrs. Kim,

Will you and your cat come to my house for milk and cookies?
We can talk about the riots. Our neighborhood is hurt now. I
will have milk for our cats to share. We can share, too.

Yours truly,

Daniel

Generative Writing

In addition to writing models, we use **generative writing** during guided writing instruction. Teacher-directed small group instruction offers a valuable opportunity to provide carefully designed lessons that lead students through an organized process for writing with clarity and originality. However, this does not mean that writing should be reduced to isolated skills at the expense of purpose, voice, content, and conventions. We know that problems can occur when a student is full of ideas but does not possess the means to get the message down on paper. Likewise, the student who has mastered the conventions but has difficulty with generating ideas is equally at risk. Through generative writing instruction, teachers provide students with strategies for creating cohesive writing while engaged in authentic tasks. Dorn and Soffos (2001) describe a continuum of difficulty when completing generative writing:

- *Adding* words to a text is easier to do.
- *Deleting* words from a text is harder to do; deleting lines or phrases is even more difficult.
- *Substituting* words for other words is still more difficult because it requires writers to know multiple meanings for words.
- *Rearranging* sentences and paragraphs is the most difficult skill (pp. 6–7).

Three forms of generative writing are generative sentences, sentence combining, and GIST summary writing. These instructional strategies operate at the sentence, paragraph, and text levels.

Generative sentences. Generative sentences can be described as initially brief pieces of text that are systematically expanded under the guidance of the teacher. It is based on Fearn and Farnan's (2001) work with Given Word Sentences and is extended through additional scaffolding and coaching. A series of prompts are offered to move students from one idea formulated at the letter or word level, then more fully realized as a piece of connected text. These prompts are usually paced with a timer to keep the lesson moving and to increase fluency at both the written and creative levels (Fearn, 1976; Guilford, 1968).

A generative sentence session begins at the letter level and involves position within the word. For example, students are instructed to write a word that contains the letter *c* in the second position. After they have written them, they share words like *active, icicle, occur,* and *across.* (This may prompt an interesting discussion on why these words all begin with vowels.) Once they have written a word, they now use it in a sentence. The following sentences were created using the focus words:

- Being *active* is good for your health.
- The *icicle* fell off the roof.
- An accident can *occur* when people are careless.
- I sailed *across* the lake.

In a matter of minutes, students have moved from considering letters and spelling to factoring content and grammar in order to create a sentence that meets the criteria of the English language. Notice how the writer of the third sentence had to figure out where *occur* could fit into the sentence. Stated another way, in a short time the teacher provided a series of tasks that required the writers to consolidate all their cueing systems to develop original sentences. It is this consolidation of the visual, structural, and contextual processes that is essential to developing fluent writers.

The activity can be extended to the paragraph level. The sentence the students created now becomes the topic sentence for a paragraph. The challenge is to link a series of ideas together to produce a coherent piece of connected text. In a matter of minutes, students have moved across a continuum of writing skills without ever isolating any of those skills at the expense of meaningful writing.

The number of steps used to get to the paragraph level depends on the developmental level of the writers. Emergent and early writers need letter prompts focused at the beginning and end of words. Transitional and self-extending writers may not need the letter prompt at all. A variation of the generative sentence instructional strategy is to begin at the word level. This is especially effective for content area learning because the teacher chooses the focus word. For example, students can be given the word *pilgrim* to construct into accurate sentences. These sentences then serve as a topic sentence for a more detailed informational paragraph that provides the teacher with information about students' content knowledge as well as writing skills. To add complexity, the teacher can provide writers with a specific place in the sentence that the word must be used. For example, during a fifth-grade lesson on the U.S. Constitution, the teacher might ask students to create sentences that are at least eight words long, with the last word being *Constitution*. Alternatively, a teacher may ask a group of students to create a sentence with the word *they're* in the third position of the sentence. This allows the teacher to assess grammar knowledge as well as word meanings.

Teacher Tip

Sentence combining. Students learn to write by building words into sentences that represent ideas. They also learn to write through taking away what is not necessary. This taking away process is critical for good editing. A hallmark of effective writing is the way sentences "hang together" to support the reader's understanding of the message the writer is attempting to convey. An effective technique for teaching about the nuances involved in transforming adequate sentences into those that resonate is sentence combining (Mellon, 1968).

Sentence combining provides students with an opportunity to utilize syntactic knowledge to create more sophisticated sentences. In a typical activity, students work with a passage of syntactically correct but choppy sentences and rework them to create sentences that preserve the original meaning while increasing the flow of the language.

Syntax is the grammar and structure of a language.

For example, Ms. Sandoval used a reading from an Internet website entitled "The History of Basketball" (www.all-sports-posters.com/historyofbasketball.html) to teach sentence combining with a group of fifth-grade students. She selected key sentences from the reading and rewrote them to make them less complex. She then distributed copies of the sentences along with scissors for each of the students in her guided writing group and instructed them to cut out each of the 11 sentence strips. She then challenged them to rewrite the story so that it contained no more than seven sentences. Together they performed "sentence surgery," cutting unnecessary words out of the disjointed statements. Using the sentence strips as manipulatives, they moved them around on the table until satisfied that they had created a smoother sounding document.

Frederico wrote the new passage using strategies of sentence combining. His passage contains six sentences.

> Basketball has stood the test of time because the rules have barely changed since it was invented. The game was invented by Dr. James Naismith, who was the physical education teacher for a high school. In 1891, the athletic director told him to invent an indoor game to play in the winter because the kids were getting rowdy. Dr. Naismith invented a game in 14 days with 13 basic rules. The first game was played with a soccer ball and peach baskets. Dr. Naismith would be considered a genius today, like Bill Gates, but he never made a profit from his invention.

It is important to keep in mind what sentence combining can and cannot do. Strong (2001) cautions that the effectiveness of sentence combining is diminished in the absence of other components of writing instruction. However, like spoken language, a complex weaving of skills must take place in order to result in a meaningful written message. Syntax is an important part of the fabric of language and these syntactic lessons should be used as one part of a balanced writing program.

Herrell (2000) has used this summary writing strategy with great success with English language learners.

GIST summary writing. A third form of generative writing instruction is Generating Interaction between Schema and Text or GIST (Cunningham, 1982). The purpose of GIST is to introduce a systematic way for students to write summaries of informational text. Summary writing is a type of writing tested widely on state assessments and is characterized by the ability to write clear, concise, and accurate sentences while paraphrasing content. The ability to write summaries also appears to be linked to reading comprehension (Nelson, 1992).

Students using the GIST strategy read a piece of informational text that has been segmented into shorter passages by the teacher. This is accomplished by either marking the reading or by writing a list of "stop points" on the board. Students read the entire text first, then reread it. This time, they pause at each stop point to create an original sentence that summarizes the portion they have just read. Because they are limited to only one sentence for each passage, they must carefully craft each line to contain all the important information. Oral composition is useful at this stage because students can revise and refine their sentences before committing them to paper. When completed, students reread their summary sentences one more time to confirm that the paragraph they have created contains the "gist" of the message. Let's take a look at a GIST guided writing lesson taught to a small group of seventh graders.

Figure 3.26   Guided Writing Lesson Plan for *Phineas Gage*

Students: **Karanne, Lupe, Le, Jessica, Marco, Edgar**
Purpose of lesson: Introduce GIST summary writing strategy
Standards: McREL LA Writing 2.III.2: Uses paragraph form in writing (e.g., arranges sentences in sequential order, uses supporting and follow-up sentences, establishes coherence within and among paragraphs)
Materials needed: Copies of GIST text from *Phineas Gage* (Fleischman, 2002)
SEQUENCE OF LESSON: *MODEL* Introduce GIST strategy and point out stop points marked on text. Because this text has been used during shared reading, discuss the main ideas of the reading. Have students read the first passage silently then model writing a summary sentence on the language chart. Use Think Aloud to model writing decisions. Repeat procedure for second passage. *SCAFFOLD* Questions to ask: What are the characteristics of a summary? What is the difference between main ideas and supporting details? How can sentences be expanded to contain multiple related ideas? *COACH* Students read remaining passages and write summary sentences. When completed, students reread sequence of summary sentences and make changes so paragraph reads smoothly.
ASSESS Take anecdotal notes on Edgar's progress.
NOTES Instruct students to place summaries in their literature circle notebooks for use when reading *Phineas Gage*.

Spotlight on Instruction

GIST Guided Writing in Seventh Grade

Three boys and two girls reluctantly approach the guided writing table, suspiciously eyeing the realistic-looking plastic brain placed in the middle. They had been studying functions of the brain in their science class, so Ms. Oum decided to infuse this content into her language arts workshop. This same group was scheduled to begin reading *Phineas Gage: A Gruesome But True Story About Brain Science* the following week (Fleischman, 2002). She grouped them for this lesson based on the complexity of the activity and used this guided writing lesson as a way to pre-teach some of the text. Her lesson plan can be seen in Figure 3.26. Ms. Oum distributes a copy of a passage from the beginning of *Phineas Gage*. Earlier during shared

(continued)

reading they had read a longer passage about the plight of Phineas, who survived an accident in which a large iron bar passed through his head, leaving him with brain damage that affected his personality. His alarming change in behavior after the injury led scientists to understand for the first time that specific regions of the brain govern personality and behavior. She would now incorporate part of this text into a guided writing lesson. The students immediately notice that their photocopies of the passage had lines marked "STOP" appearing several times throughout the reading. A portion of the text she handed out appears in Figure 3.27.

"We'll be using a technique called GIST to write a summary of the reading. Writing a summary is important for comprehension. It's also a kind of writing you're often asked to do in school. Certain careers also require summary writing—a police officer writes reports, for instance." Ms. Oum continues, "I've marked this reading in several places. At each stop point, we're going to write one summary sentence containing the important information in that section of the passage. When we're finished, we'll have a string of sentences to form a summary paragraph." She reminds them that summary writing should never be done during the first reading, but only after the entire text has been read.

After they all read the first segment silently, she composes a summary sentence using a think aloud strategy by stating her decisions as a writer verbally. She discusses how she uses a dependent clause to construct a complex sentence containing multiple ideas. She also points out that his age, height, and town were probably not important details in a summary. She writes this sentence on a language chart:

Phineas Gage, a railroad worker in Vermont, is about to have a terrible accident.

She repeats the process for the next segment, this time composing the summary sentence with the assistance of the students. They agree on the following:

He will survive for eleven years after the accident and others will learn about how the brain works, but he will never be the same.

<table>
<tr><td>Writing conventions include capitalization, punctuation, and spelling.</td></tr>
</table>

Satisfied that they have the hang of it, she turns the writing over to them. After adding the first two sentences to their journals, they continue reading and writing several more summary sentences. Ms. Oum observes Edgar as he writes, pausing to ask him questions about word choice and writing conventions when he gets stuck.

As each student finishes, she invites them to reread their summary sentences as a single piece of text, making necessary edits as they go. When completed, Karanne's GIST summary reads:

Phineas Gage, a railroad worker in Vermont, is about to have a terrible accident. He will survive for eleven years after the accident and others will learn about how the brain works, but he will never be the same. Everyone wonders whether Gage was lucky or unlucky to survive. Phineas had the dangerous job of blasting rock to build the railroad. An important tool for his railroad work was the tamping rod, a 3'7", 13.5-pound iron bar used to set explosives.

Karanne and the others will finish the reading and complete the task during independent writing. When completed, they will have an accurate summary of the event that left Phineas with a hole in his head.

Figure 3.27   Passage from *Phineas Gage*

The most unlucky/lucky moment in the life of Phineas Gage is only a minute or two away. It's almost four-thirty in the afternoon on September 13, 1848. Phineas is the foreman of a track construction gang that is in the process of blasting a railroad right-of-way through Cavendish, Vermont. Phineas is twenty-six years old, unmarried, and five feet, six inches tall, short for our time but about average for his. He is good with his hands and good with his men, "possessing an iron will as well as an iron frame," according to his doctor. In a moment, Phineas will have a horrible accident.   STOP

It will kill him, but it will take another eleven years, six months, and nineteen days to do so. In the short run, Phineas will make a full recovery, or so it will seem to those who didn't know him before. Old friends and family will know the truth. Phineas will never be his old self again. His "character" will change. Long after the accident, his doctor will make him world famous, but fame will do him little good. Yet for many others—psychologists, medical researchers, doctors, and especially those who suffer brain injuries—Phineas Gage will become someone worth knowing.   STOP

That's why we know so much about Phineas. It's been 150 years since his accident, yet we are still learning more about him. There's also a lot about Phineas we don't know and probably never will. The biggest question is the simplest one and the hardest one to answer: Was Phineas lucky or unlucky? Once you hear his story, you can decide for yourself. But right now, Phineas is working on the railroad and his time has nearly come.   STOP

Building a railroad in 1848 is muscle work. There are no bulldozers or power shovels to open a way through Vermont's Green Mountains for the Rutledge & Burlington Railroad. Phineas's men work with picks, shovels, and rock drills. Phineas's special skill is blasting. With well-placed charges of black gunpowder, he shatters rock. To set those charges, he carries a special tool of the blasting trade, his "tamping iron." Some people confuse a tamping iron with a crowbar, but they are different tools for different jobs.   STOP

A tamping iron is for the delicate job of setting explosives. Phineas had his tamping iron made to order by a neighborhood blacksmith. It's a tamping iron rod that is three feet, seven inches long and weights thirteen and a half pounds. It looks like an iron spear. At the base, it's fat and round, an inch and three quarters in diameter. The fat end is for tamping—packing down— loose powder. The other end comes to a sharp, narrow point and is for poking holes through the gunpowder to set the fuse. Phineas's tamping iron is very smooth to the touch, smooth from the blacksmith's forge as well as constant use.   STOP

Source: Fleischman, J. (2002). *Phineas Gage: A gruesome but true story about brain science* (pp. 1–2). Boston: Houghton Mifflin. Used with permission.

PRACTICAL TIPS ABOUT GUIDED WRITING: WRITING BEHAVIORS

Just as there are differences in the growth of readers, so there are with writers. Children can be regarded as emergent, early, transitional, or self-extending writers. It is important to recognize the writing behaviors evident at each stage of development in order to plan instruction.

Emergent Writers

These writers are just beginning to gain control of print and how it works. They are still learning that print carries messages, and that they can create a new idea and then represent it on paper for others to appreciate. The youngest of writers can generate text that retells a sequence of events in a story or in their personal lives, although the language used is likely to be fairly simple, with few complex sentences containing more than one or two ideas. Their writing contains letters and words they know, and their name is likely to be prominently featured in their texts.

Early Writers

Story grammar consists of character, setting, plot, and problem/solution, and so on.

Early writers are able to more rapidly recall letters, and therefore can scribe their message more quickly. However, they are prone to formulaic writing that incorporates the limited number of words they can spell. (Any first grade teacher can testify to the plethora of student-generated sentences that begin with "I like _____".) These early writers are engaging in editing, as evidenced by the increase in eraser marks and crossed-out words. They can generate their own ideas for writing topics and are applying some elements of story grammar to their own writing. Late in this phase, they will begin writing multi-paragraph texts, although the ideas forwarded at the beginning of the piece may get lost along the way.

Transitional Writers

Students in this phase of development are actively incorporating varied approaches in their original writing. For example, they create titles for their pieces, "grabber" sentences to gain the reader's attention, and use descriptive vocabulary to evoke a response from the reader. Indeed, it is this recognition of the role of the audience that is a hallmark of the writer in this phase of development. They are beginning to apply rudimentary structures to longer texts, such as listing directions for completing a task or writing a biography that contains the type of information expected in this literary form. Because their vocabulary has grown along with their language sophistication, there are more complex sentences containing multiple idea units. They can utilize transition phrases and conjunctions to build these longer sentences. Their stamina has increased as well. Both mean sentence length and overall length of the text has increased. An important indicator of a transitional writer is his or her ability to sustain an idea or concept over the course of multiple paragraphs.

Self-Extending Writers

Metacognition is the ability to understand and act upon one's own learning and thinking.

These sophisticated writers understand they are engaged in a complex process that is influenced by their application of specific strategies. This metacognitive awareness serves them well in being able to analyze their own writing as well as the writing of others. Self-extending writers are expanding their repertoire of writing genres and can write narratives, technical documents, responses to literature, and biographies/autobiographies. Importantly, they understand that each of these genres is governed by specific rules; the skills used to create a science lab report differ from writing a poem. Their control of the language, especially as it applies to vocabulary and multiple meanings, makes it easier for them to engage in a full editing process. These characteristics can be seen in Figure 3.28.

BIG IDEAS ABOUT GUIDED READING AND GUIDED WRITING

Guided reading is the instructional practice of teaching a small group of students who are reading at a similar level. Each child has his or her own copy of a text that has been carefully matched to the instructional purpose of the lesson. The lesson begins with a familiar text to build fluency then progresses through a book introduction. Students may work with words or write either before or after they read. The teacher uses questions and prompts to activate cueing systems and comprehension strategies and listens carefully as each child reads.

Figure 3.28   Developmental Writing Characteristics

Emergent Writers	Early Writers
• Learning how print works • See the permanence of writing • Retell events in sequence • Simple sentence construction • Known words prominently used	• Rapid recall of letters and known words • Will use formulaic writing • Writing constrained by limited known words • Story grammar evident • Longer texts, although ideas may not be consistent
Transitional Writers	**Self-Extending Writers**
• Apply text structures in their original writing • Recognize audience • Longer texts with sustained ideas • More complex sentences • Use of transition phrases and conjunctions	• Purposeful direction to audience • Sees writing as an extension of the writer • Writes to multiple genres • Word choice is sophisticated and flexible • Engages in all aspects of editing

The purpose of guided writing is to provide students with direct instruction of necessary skills and strategies needed for effective writing. Writers follow a developmental progression similar to reading acquisition and at all phases of development are motivated by engaging and authentic writing tasks. Two types of guided writing instruction are writing models and generative writing. Writing models are used to give students a variety of experiences with aspects of good writing, especially language use and meaning making. These models provide a scaffold for writers to attach their original writing. Generative writing focuses on intentional instruction of the skills and strategies needed for effective writing. These are also imbedded in meaningful writing tasks and the writing that originates in guided writing lessons may be extended to other parts of the language arts workshop.

 INTEGRATING THE STANDARDS

Create lesson plans that meet your state's standards by visiting our Companion Website at www.prenhall.com/frey. There you'll find lessons created to meet the NCTE/IRA Standards. Adapt them to meet the standards of your own state through links to your state's standards, and keep them in the online portfolio. You can collect lesson plans for each chapter in an online portfolio, providing you with invaluable tools to meet your state's standards when you head into your own classroom.

CHECK YOUR UNDERSTANDING

This chapter focused on guided reading and guided writing practices within the language arts workshop. Take a few minutes to check your understanding of the content of this chapter.

1. In what ways do teachers make decisions about grouping in guided instruction?

2. What is the structure of a guided reading lesson?

3. What are the cueing systems in reading?

4. How are questions and prompts used in guided instruction?

5. What is guided writing?

6. What is process writing?

7. What is a balanced approach to writing?

8. How are essential skills and strategies taught through guided writing?

CLASSROOM CONNECTIONS

1. Discuss with your teacher how grouping decisions are made in the classroom. What does he or she feel are the advantages and disadvantages to grouping?

2. Use the planning tool in Figure 3.18 to develop and implement a writing skill or strategy being taught in your classroom.

3. Arrange with your teacher and supervisor to visit other classrooms at your school. Add files labeled *Guided Reading and Guided Writing* to collect materials and lesson plans.

References

Antonacci, P. A. (2000). Reading in the zone of proximal development: Mediating literacy development in beginner readers through guided reading. *Reading Horizons, 41*(1), 19–33.

Askew, B. J. (1993). The effect of multiple readings on the behaviors of children and teachers in an early intervention program. *Reading and Writing Quarterly: Overcoming Learning Difficulties, 9,* 307–315.

Avi. (2003). A sense of story. *Voices from the Middle, 11*(1), 8–14.

Betts, E. A. (1946). *Foundations of reading instruction.* New York: American Book Company.

Calkins, L. M. (1986). *The art of teaching writing.* Portsmouth, NH: Heinemann.

Cazden, C. B. (1988). *Classroom discourse: The language of teaching and learning.* Portsmouth, NH: Heinemann.

Clay, M. M. (1991a). *Becoming literate: The construction of inner control.* Portsmouth, NH: Heinemann.

Clay, M. M. (1991b). Introducing a new storybook to young readers. *The Reading Teacher, 45,* 264–273.

Clay, M. M. (1993). *Reading recovery: A guidebook for teachers in training.* Portsmouth, NH: Heinemann.

Clay, M. M. (2001). *Change over time in children's literacy development.* Portsmouth, NH: Heinemann.

Cunningham, J. (1982). Generating interactions between schema and text. In J. A. Niles & L. A. Harris (Eds.), *New inquiries in reading research and instruction* (pp. 42–47). Washington, DC: National Reading Conference.

Cunningham, P. M., & Allington, R. L. (2003). *Classrooms that work: They can all read and write* (3rd ed.). Boston: Allyn & Bacon.

Dorn, L. J., & Soffos, C. (2001). *Scaffolding young writers: A writers' workshop approach.* Portland, ME: Stenhouse.

Dymock, S. J. (1998). A comparison study of the effects of text structure training, reading practice, and guided reading on reading comprehension. *National Reading Conference Yearbook, 47,* 90–102.

Dyson, A. H. (1994). Viewpoints: The word and the world—Reconceptualizing written language development or, do rainbows mean a lot to little girls? In R. B. Ruddell, M. R. Ruddell, & H. Singer (Eds.), *Theoretical models and processes of reading* (4th ed., pp. 297–322). Newark, DE: International Reading Association.

Emig, J. (1971). *The composing processes of twelfth graders.* Urbana, IL: National Council of Teachers of English.

Fearn, L. (1976). Individual development: A process model in creativity. *Journal of Creative Behavior, 10*(1), 55–64.

Fearn, L., & Farnan, N. (2001). *Interactions: Teaching writing and the language arts.* Boston: Houghton Mifflin.

Fisher, D., & Frey, N. (2003). Writing instruction for struggling adolescent readers: A gradual release model. *Journal of Adolescent and Adult Literacy, 46,* 396–405.

Fletcher, R., & Portalupi, J. (2001). *Writing workshop: The essential guide.* Portsmouth, NH: Heinemann.

Flood, J., Lapp, D., Flood, S., & Nagel, G. (1992). Am I allowed to group? Using flexible patterns for effective instruction. *The Reading Teacher, 45,* 608–616.

Fountas, I. C., & Pinnell, G. S. (1996). *Guided reading: Good first teaching for all students.* Portsmouth, NH: Heinemann.

Fountas, I. C., & Pinnell, G. S. (1999). *Matching books and readers: Using leveled books to guide reading.* Portsmouth, NH: Heinemann.

Frey, N., & Hiebert, E. H. (2003). Teacher-based assessment of literacy learning. In J. Flood, D. Lapp, J. R. Squire, & J. Jensen (Eds.), *Handbook of research on teaching the English language arts* (2nd ed., pp. 608–618). Mahwah, NJ: Lawrence Erlbaum.

Fry, E. (2002). Readability versus leveling. *The Reading Teacher, 56,* 286–291.

Furr, D. (2003). Struggling readers get hooked on writing. *The Reading Teacher, 56,* 518–525.

Good, T. L., & Brophy, J. E. (2003). *Looking in classrooms* (9th ed.). Boston: Allyn & Bacon.

Goodman, Y. M., & Goodman, K. S. (1994). To err is human: Learning about language processes by analyzing miscues. In R. R. Ruddell, M. R. Ruddell, & H. Singer (Eds.), *Theoretical models and processes of reading* (4th ed., pp. 104–123). Newark, DE: International Reading Association.

Graves, D. H. (1975). An examination of the writing processes of seven-year-old children. *Research in the Teaching of English, 9*(3), 227–241.

Gray, W. S. (1925). Reading activities in school and society. In G. M. Whipple (Ed.), *The twenty-fourth yearbook of the National Society for the Study of Education, Part I* (pp. 1–18). Bloomington, IL: Public School Publishing.

Guilford, J. P. (1968). *Intelligence, creativity, and their educational implications.* San Diego: R. R. Knapp.

Hansen, J. (2001). *When writers read* (2nd ed.). Portsmouth, NH: Heinemann.

Herrell, A. L. (2000). *Fifty strategies for teaching English language learners.* Upper Saddle River, NJ: Merrill/Prentice-Hall.

History of basketball: Hoops. (n.d.). Retrieved March 3, 2003 from www.all-sports-posters.com/historyofbasketball.html.

Holdaway, D. (1979). *The foundations of literacy.* Sydney, Australia: Ashton Scholastic.

Juel, C. (1990). Effects of reading group assignment on reading development in first and second grade. *Journal of Reading Behavior, 22,* 233–254.

Juel, C., & Minden-Cupp, C. (1999–2000). One down and 80,000 to go: Word recognition instruction in the primary grades. *The Reading Teacher, 53,* 332–335.

Marita, S. M. (1965). *A comparative study of beginning reading achievement under three classroom organizational patterns—modified individualized, three-to-five groups, and whole-class language-experience* (Report No. CRP-2659). Milwaukee, WI: Marquette University. (ERIC Document Reproduction Service No. ED003477).

Mellon, J. C. (1968). *Transformational sentence-combining: A method for enhancing the development of syntactic fluency in English composition: Final report.* Cambridge, MA: Harvard University.

Millis, K. K., & King, A. (2001). Rereading strategically: The influences of comprehension ability and a prior reading on the memory for expository text. *Reading Psychology, 22*(1), 41–65.

National Reading Panel. (2000). *Report of the National Reading Panel: Teaching children to read: An evidence-based assessment of the scientific research literature on reading and its implications for reading instruction.* Washington, DC: National Institute of Child Health and Human Development.

Nelson, J. R. (1992). The effects of teaching a summary skills strategy to students identified as learning disabled on their comprehension of science text. *Education and Treatment of Children, 15,* 228–243.

Ohlhausen, M. M., & Jepsen, M. (1992). Lessons from Goldilocks: "Somebody's been choosing my books but I can make my own choices now!" *The New Advocate, 5,* 31–46.

Optiz, M. F., & Rasinski, T. V. (1998). *Good-bye round robin: 25 effective oral reading strategies.* Portsmouth, NH: Heinemann.

Pearson, P. D. (2002). American reading instruction since 1967. In N. B. Smith's *American reading instruction* (Special ed., pp. 419–486). Newark, DE: International Reading Association.

Pearson, P. D., & Fielding, L. (1991). Comprehension instruction. In R. Barr, M. L. Kamil, P. Mosenthal, & P. D. Pearson (Eds.), *Handbook of reading research (Vol. II),* (pp. 815–860). Mahwah, NJ: Erlbaum.

Routman, R. (1988). *Transitions from literature to literacy.* Portsmouth, NH: Heinemann.

Samuels, S. J. (1979). The method of repeated readings. *The Reading Teacher, 32,* 403–408.

Santa, C., & Havens, L. (1995). *Creating independence through student-owned strategies: Project CRISS.* Dubuque, IA: Kendall-Hunt.

Short, R. A., Kane, M., & Peeling, T. (2000). Retooling the reading lesson: Matching the right tools to the job. *The Reading Teacher, 54,* 284–295.

Smith, N. B. (2002). *American reading instruction* (Special ed.). Newark, DE: International Reading Association.

Stahl, S. A., & Kuhn, M. R. (2002). Making it sound like language: Developing fluency. *The Reading Teacher, 55,* 582–584.

Strong, W. J. (2001). *Coaching writing: The power of guided practice.* Portsmouth, NH: Heinemann.

Sweeney, W. J., Ehrhardt, A. M., Gardner, R. III, Jones, L., Greenfield, R., & Fribley, S. (1999). Using guided notes with academically at-risk high school students during a remedial summer social studies class. *Psychology in the Schools, 36,* 305–318.

Villaume, S. K., & Brabham, E. G. (2001). Guided reading: Who is in the driver's seat? *The Reading Teacher, 55*, 260–263.

Vonnegut, K., Jr. (1963). *Cats cradle*. New York: Delacorte.

Weaver, B. M. (2000). *Leveling books K–6: Matching readers to text*. Newark, DE: International Reading Association.

Worthy, J., & Broaddus, K. (2001–2002). Fluency beyond the primary grades: From group performance to silent, independent reading. *The Reading Teacher, 55*, 334–343.

Worthy, J., Broaddus, K., & Ivey, G. (2001). *Pathways to independence: Reading, writing, and learning in grades 3–8*. New York: Guilford.

Children's Literature Cited

Bunting, E. (1999). *Smoky night*. San Diego: Harcourt.

Carle, E. (1983). *The very hungry caterpillar*. New York: Putnam.

Creech, S. (2003). *Love that dog*. New York: HarperTrophy.

Feldman, E. B. (1999). *They fought for freedom: Children in the civil rights movement*. New York: McGraw-Hill School Division.

Fleischman, J. (2002). *Phineas Gage: A gruesome but true story about brain science*. New York: Houghton Mifflin.

Greenfield E. (1999). *For the love of the game: Michael Jordan and me*. New York: HarperCollins

Lalli, J. (1996). *Make someone smile: And 40 more ways to be a peaceful person*. Minneapolis, MN: Free Spirit.

Martinez, V. (1998). *Parrot in the oven: Mi vida*. New York: HarperTrophy.

Paulsen, G. (1998). *My life in dog years*. New York: Delacorte.

Polacco, P. (1998). *Thank you, Mr. Falker*. New York: Philomel.

Randall, B. (1994). *Fire, fire*. Orlando, FL: Rigby.

Randall, B. (1994). *Baby bear's present*. Orlando, FL: Rigby.

Ransom, C. (2001). *Little red riding hood*. New York: McGraw Hill.

Ringgold, F. (1998). *My dream of Martin Luther King*. New York: Dragonfly.

Thomas, S. M. (2002). *Somewhere today: A book about peace*. New York: Albert Whitman.

Ziefert, H. (2001). *39 uses for a friend*. New York: Putnam.

CHAPTER

Collaborative Learning in the Language Arts Workshop

BIG IDEAS ABOUT COLLABORATIVE LEARNING

Collaborative learning helps students extend their comprehension and writing strategies through peer learning. These opportunities allow students to work within their zones of proximal development as they assist and coach one another. The reading and writing strategies used during the collaborative learning phase of the language arts workshop are taught first during focus lessons and guided instruction. Collaborative learning serves as a bridge to independent reading and writing.

Questions to Consider

When you have finished reading this chapter, you should be able to answer these questions:

- What learning theories are associated with collaborative learning?
- What are the key elements of collaborative learning?
- What is collaborative reading?
- What is collaborative writing?
- How can students be taught to respond to peer writing?

Key Vocabulary

Collaborative learning

Cooperative learning

Literacy learning centers

Group and individual accountability

Collaborative reading

Reciprocal teaching

Collaborative writing

Progressive writing

Student-generated language charts

Paired writing

Partner reading

Echo reading

Collaborative Strategic Reading

Literature circles

Group writing

Peer response to writing

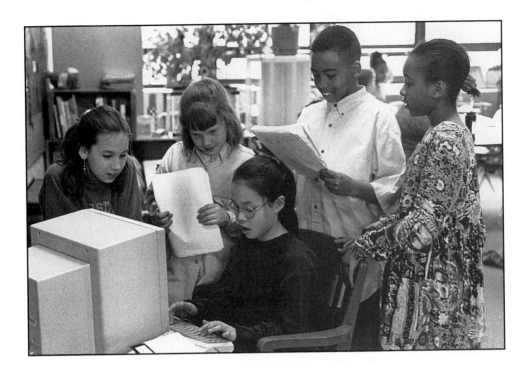

⁓⊰❦⊱⁓

A LOOK INSIDE

Notes about the roles used in literature circles are discussed below.

Four sixth-grade students are deeply involved in a discussion about the book they are reading in their literature circle, *The Music of Dolphins* (Hesse, 1996). The story centers on a young girl who has been raised in warm Caribbean waters by a school of dolphins. Named Mila by her rescuers, she is brought to a facility to be studied by scientists who are interested in the language development of feral children. However, Mila hopes to escape this bewildering environment and return to the only family she has ever known.

David, the Discussion Director, opens the conversation. "In chapter 53, Mila begs Doctor Beck to let her go back to the ocean, but the doctor says she can't because she will go to prison. What did all of you think about that?"

"I think Mila said it best on page 163—'I look at her. I am already in prison.' Mila feels trapped, like she's suffocating," offers Stephanie, the Passage Master.

Marisol, the Illustrator, holds up her notebook for everyone to see. "That sentence meant a lot to me, too. I drew a picture of a girl in a cage at the zoo. I was remembering her conversation with her friend Justin, when he asked her if she got tired of people coming to look at her all the time."

The Discussion Director asks another question when the group gets quiet. "Reynaldo, you're the Connector. Do you have an idea to add?" At this, Reynaldo responds. "Well, I wrote this in my notebook. 'Mila feels like she's just a thing, not a person, and that nobody except for Justin even tries to see her as anything more than a dolphin girl. It feels that way in school sometimes, when everyone is checking everyone else out and deciding whether they're cool or not. It's like no one even bothers to look past your clothes or hair or where you live.'"

These students are participating in a collaborative learning format called literature circles (Daniels, 1994). Students are assigned these roles for each literature circle meeting to discuss the book they have chosen to read. In between meetings, they read independently and make notes in their notebooks to be used in the next discussion. Each meeting is directed entirely by the students themselves who determine the direction of the conversation, the assignment of roles, and the next reading task.

> Providing students with notebooks is a good way to encourage their note-taking.

❧❦☙

COLLABORATIVE LEARNING IN THE LANGUAGE ARTS WORKSHOP

A critical linchpin in the language arts workshop is **collaborative learning**. We use the term *collaborative learning* in reference to work done with peers. These peer-assisted learning opportunities furnish students with a means of applying the skills and strategies they have learned during focus lessons and guided instruction. Collaborative learning also serves as a bridge to independent work, a goal of all instruction. The roots of collaborative learning can be found in the learning theories of Vygotsky.

Learning Theories in Peer Learning

> This contrasts with the belief that our behavior is innate or formed before we are born.

Perhaps the most influential theorist on the role of peer-assisted learning is Lev Vygotsky, who stated that all learning is the product of sociocultural phenomena, mediated by interactions with others (Berk & Winsler, 1995). The learner's view of the world is shaped by these social interactions. Therefore, collaboration with peers becomes a necessary part of the learning process of a child. Indeed, Vygotsky identified both the teacher and peers as important agents in the learning process (Crain, 2000).

Vygotsky's Zones of Proximal Development. You will recall from our discussion in chapter 1 that the ZPD is defined by the tasks a learner can successfully complete with minimal assistance from another (Crain, 2000). Students who assist one another in completing a task that might otherwise be too difficult for either to complete alone are considered to be working within their zone of proximal development. Typically, one peer is identified as being more knowledgeable about the task; in group situations, this role is often shared by several students. Many of us have found ourselves working in a group where the problem is solved through the discussion among all members. So it is with peer learning.

In addition to solving the task at hand, another goal of this type of learning is to foster mastery of skills and strategies that can be used independently in the future. This learning occurs when these "external and social activities are gradually internalized by the child . . . creat[ing] internal dialogues that form the processes of mental regulation" (Wood, 1998, p. 98). Stated differently, the language used by two students to figure out a task together eventually becomes part of the internal problem-solving processes used independently by each child.

Bandura's observational learning. Vygotsky's social learning theory as it relates to the role of peers was further extended through the work of Albert Bandura. His contribution to the knowledge base was the theory of observational learning. Bandura documented the learning of young children acquiring complex skills such as weaving through their observation of a more knowledgeable model (Bandura, 1965). He argued that when children are given the opportunity to watch another perform a task, they are more likely to duplicate the same task successfully. Bandura (1965) identified a pattern of observational learning that includes:

- *Attention* to the task
- *Retention* (remembering) of what has been observed
- *Reproduction* of the task
- *Motivation* in the learning environment to repeat the task (or not)

Bandura's theories of learning combined the roles of cognition with the behavioral aspects of the environment. He recognized that there must be both a supportive environment in which to learn and an opportunity to observe others performing the task. These elements of peer-assisted learning—performing tasks together that are challenging but not frustrating within a motivating learning environment—has been further explored in numerous studies on the effectiveness of this instructional approach.

Effectiveness of Peer Learning

The power of peer-to-peer learning has been well documented in the research on effective instruction. Much of the research has been focused on **cooperative learning,** a type of collaborative learning structure. Cooperative and collaborative learning are closely related, although in cooperative learning there is both individual and shared accountability for the outcomes of the task. As you will see when we discuss collaborative learning, some activities are constructed this way, while others rely only on accountability for the individual student.

The key to both cooperative and collaborative learning is the nature of the task—it should require more than one person to complete.

Cooperative learning is an instructional arrangement that allows two to six students the opportunity to work together on a shared task in order to jointly construct their knowledge and understanding of the content (Johnson & Johnson, 1999). This instructional arrangement is featured in most elementary and middle school teachers' classroom practices, although many also report that they struggle with how to support the peer interactions within the groups (Tomlinson, Moon, & Callahan, 1997).

Evidence Based

The effectiveness of cooperative learning has been impressive. Not surprisingly, many of the positive results are social. Studies have demonstrated positive effects on the interactions between students in middle school (Gillies, 2003). Middle school students also reported that they favored this type of learning over working independently (Mueller & Fleming, 2001). Elementary students in classrooms that utilized cooperative learning techniques were found to have higher levels of motivation and a more positive perception of school (Battistich & Solomon, 1993).

These positive results are not confined to social development. For example, cooperative learning opportunities have resulted in improved writing for struggling adolescent writers (Hallenbeck, 2002) and increased reading comprehension skills for elementary students (Battistich & Solomon, 1993). Importantly, these techniques have been found to be particularly effective in promoting academic achievement for English language learners (Gersten & Baker, 2000), students identified as gifted (Coleman & Gallagher, 1995) and students with disabilities (Stevens & Slavin, 1995). A key advantage to cooperative learning is that students are grouped heterogeneously, allowing learners of mixed ability levels to support each other's learning. This learning arrangement has been shown to be effective for learners of all ability levels (Slavin, 1991).

Knowing the evidence supporting an instructional strategy is important for every teacher; knowing how to implement it is another. Reflective teachers consider these factors when designing and implementing collaborative learning:

- How will the students be grouped?
- What are the goals of the group?
- Where do the groups fit into my instructional sequence?
- What accountability measures will be used?

In the next section we will discuss keys to successful collaborative learning in the language arts workshop.

Key Elements for Collaborative Learning

Heterogeneous grouping means that students with diverse learning profiles learn together. This contrasts with *homogeneous* grouping in which students with similar abilities or experiences learn together.

Although there is a strong research base on the effectiveness of peer-assisted learning in cooperative and collaborative groups, it is widely recognized that peer-assisted learning is challenging to implement (Antil, Jenkins, Wayne, & Vadasy, 1998). Like all good instruction, collaborative learning requires careful planning to be successful for teachers and students. We have included a planning guide in Figure 4.1 for you to use as you consider key elements, including grouping, goal setting, the instructional sequence, and the accountability measures to be used.

Before we explore each of these considerations, let's discuss the organizational structure. The optimal time for students to work collaboratively is during **literacy learning centers.** Literacy learning centers in the language arts workshop are offered after focus lessons and during guided instruction. While the teacher is providing guided reading or writing instruction to small, homogeneous groups of students, others are working together in heterogeneous groups. Students move in and out of literacy learning centers using the Center Activity Rotation System (CARS) (Lapp, Flood, & Goss, 2000). These literacy learning centers may be organized around collaborative reading and writing experiences like those discussed later in this chapter, or on aspects of literacy development like oral language, fluency, comprehension, word study, spelling, vocabulary, genres, and technology. The success of these literacy learning centers is dependent on each child's ability to work with others. As you can see from Figure 4.2, the majority of students are engaged in heterogeneous small group literacy learning centers while the teacher meets with a specifically selected group of students for guided reading or writing instruction. As we discussed in chapter 3, these guided instructional lessons can last between 20 and 30 minutes, so the teacher can meet with several groups per day.

Each of these aspects of literacy are featured in part 3 of this book.

Grouping. One of the first decisions a teacher must consider when using collaborative learning is how to pair or group students. Should the groups be comprised of students working at a similar level (homogeneous grouping) or of differing levels (heterogeneous)? Effective teachers tell us that when they are making grouping decisions

See chapter 1 for more information on grouping practices.

Figure 4.1   Planning Checklist for Collaborative Learning

Planning for Collaborative Learning Groups

Task: _____   Dates: _____to_____

How will the students be grouped?
❑ Homogeneously
❑ Heterogeneously

What are my goals for the group?
Social

Academic

Where do the groups fit into my instructional sequence?
Focus lesson preceding group work:

What accountability measures will be used?
Group accountability

Individual accountability

Chapter 3.

Evidence Based

they consider how the group might receive help when faced with a difficult task. In teacher-directed groups such as guided reading and guided writing, the teacher is available to provide help. However, in collaborative learning the students are working apart from the teacher and help from an adult is not as easily obtained. Therefore, the help must emerge from within the group. This help is more likely to occur in mixed-ability pairs or groups. This advice is supported by student feedback as well. In a study of grouping preferences of more than 500 elementary schoolchildren, Elbaum, Schumm, and Vaughn (1997) reported that students preferred mixed-ability groups (especially pairs) to homogeneous groups. On a related note, Bennett and Cass (1989) found that ratios were important to heterogeneous groups. They noted that the optimal group was composed of two lower-performing and one higher-performing student. In groups where the ratio was reversed (two higher-performing students to one lower-performing one), the lone struggling student was often left out of the activities. It is interesting to note that the higher-achieving students performed equally well in both circumstances (Bennett & Cass, 1989).

Because of a particular task demand, the teacher may decide to group homogeneously. For example, a particular activity may be well beyond the skills of a particular group of students. After all, if the task is truly too difficult, these students are likely to be left out of the learning process completely while others in the group complete the task. In any case, remember to regroup frequently so that all students have the opportunity to work with one another.

Figure 4.2 Center Activity Rotation System

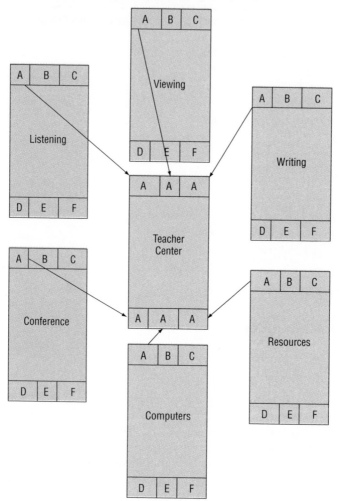

Source: Chart from Lapp, D., Flood, J., & Goss, K. (2000, September). Teaching Ideas: Desks don't move—Students do: In effective classroom environments. *The Reading Teacher, 54*(1), 31–36. Reprinted with permission of Diane Lapp and the International Reading Association.

Goal setting. Successful collaborative learning pairs or groups understand what their goals are for the task. Groups need specific directions concerning the task. For example, if they are working together to compose a poem, provide them with a rubric describing the features of the poem and the characteristics of the final product, especially the due date and quality indicators like spelling and neatness. Younger children can benefit from task cards that describe each step in detail. Many students benefit from timelines as well. Multi-step tasks can be broken down into units of time to give the pair or group another way of monitoring their progress. See Figure 4.3 for an example of a timeline used in a third-grade class during the language arts workshop.

Figure 4.3	Timeline for Collaborative Reading

Group Members: _____   _____

Date: _____

You will be conducting a scavenger hunt using the book *Looking At Insects*
by David Glover. Be sure to watch your time!

Time	Task	Answers
5"	Locate the Table of Contents, Glossary, and Index. Write their page numbers. ➡	
5"	What is the heaviest insect in the world? Use the Table of Contents to help you.	
10"	What are the body parts all insects have? Find the diagram that will help you.	
5"	What is nectar? Use the glossary to help you.	
5" Partner #1 - Draw and label your favorite insect in the box below.		5" Partner #2 - Draw and label your favorite insect in the box below.

Sequencing instruction. When collaborative learning occurs in the language arts workshop, it is likely to influence its effectiveness. Students should not be working on tasks before an adequate amount of active teaching through modeling, scaffolding and coaching has occurred. In the language arts workshop, this happens primarily during shared reading and shared writing focus lessons. Only after the skill or strategy has been modeled should students move to working in pairs or groups. This sequence of instruction has been shown to be more effective than grouping homogeneously first for explicit instruction (Mason & Good, 1993).

Chapter 2.

Active teaching of the whole group first, followed by small group work.

Accountability. A common criticism of collaborative or cooperative learning is that the distribution of labor may be uneven. However, this can only occur when there is a flawed accountability system in place. Authorities on this type of instructional arrangement recommend both **group** and **individual accountability** measures. This means that students earn two grades—one for the group product and one for their individual contribution. For example, in the collaborative reading task shown in Figure 4.3, both partners are asked to draw and label their favorite insect. Individual accountability can also come in the form of student feedback (Johnson, Johnson, Holubec, & Roy, 1984). This may be done on a weekly basis or may be task-specific (i.e., completion of a literature circle discussion). Figure 4.4 shows a group feedback

Figure 4.4 Group Feedback Sheet

How did your group work together during partner reading? Group members: _____ _____			
	Always	Sometimes	Not Yet
We listen carefully to the other person's reading.			
We help each other when we're stuck on a word.			
We encourage each other by saying nice things.			
We make sure the other person is ready before we begin.			

sheet for a partner reading assignment. Using a group self-assessment is especially useful for students in primary grades.

Self-assessments are useful as well when developing collaborative learning skills in the classroom. Students in intermediate and middle school grades are developmentally more capable of distinguishing between the work of the group and their own role in influencing group dynamics. They can complete an individual feedback sheet that gives them an opportunity to reflect on their contributions as well as invite them to set goals for future collaborative partnerships. These are completed and turned in with the written work. A combination of goal-setting and opportunities for self-evaluation have been shown to improve academic achievement (Schunk, 1998). An example of an individual feedback sheet for older students appears in Figure 4.5. An individual self-assessment for younger students appears in Figure 4.6.

A Helping Curriculum

Before examining each specific instructional model in detail, it is important to recognize the life skills that are developed through the use of collaborative learning. While these life skills are valuable, they may be challenging for some students, especially younger ones. Some students may have difficulty working with others, particularly when it involves the give and take of collaborative learning. Lack of experience with peers, temperament, and differences in communication skills can all contribute to negative experiences in the group. We believe that all children need to learn a "helping curriculum" necessary for successful human interactions (Sapon-Shevin, 1998). In particular, all students should have many opportunities to do each of the following:

- Ask for help
- Offer help
- Accept help
- Decline help

Figure 4.5 Individual Self-Assessment for Older Students

Name: _____   Date: _____

Name of Project/Assignment: _____

Evaluate your contributions to the collaborative task you completed. Read each statement and circle the number in the column on the right that represents *your* role best.

1 = Never
2 = Rarely
3 = Sometimes
4 = Usually
5 = Always

I contributed ideas to the discussion.	1	2	3	4	5
I listened to the ideas of others.	1	2	3	4	5
I asked questions.	1	2	3	4	5
I located resources when needed.	1	2	3	4	5
I completed my tasks on time.	1	2	3	4	5
I did my fair share of the work.	1	2	3	4	5

My best contribution to this task was _____.

The next time I work in a group, I will improve on _____.

Based on my assessment, I would give myself a grade of _____.

Figure 4.6 Self-Assessment for Younger Students

Name: _____   Date: _____

Type of Work I Did: _____

Partners' Names: _____

How do I rate my work?

	Always	Sometimes	Not Yet
I asked questions.			
I listened when others talked.			
I did a fair share of the work.			
I used ideas from other people, not just my own.			
I was prepared to work.			

Consider, for instance, what is needed to complete each. The first skill, asking for help, has been explored in depth by psychologists. Nelson-LeGall (1981) and others break down this complex task into five components:

- Become aware of the need for help
- Decide to seek help
- Identify potential helper(s)
- Use strategies to elicit help
- Evaluate help-seeking episode (Alevin, Stahl, Schworm, Fischer, & Wallace, 2003, p. 281)

Offering help necessitates another set of skills. For example, the student must recognize the verbal and non-verbal cues of others who may need assistance. Once offered, there must be a tacit agreement reached between the two that help offered will be graciously accepted. If the person being offered the help wants to persist on their own for a while longer, then that child needs to be able to politely decline the offer.

Each of these requires a sophisticated level of cognitive and language skills in order to complete the sequence successfully. Some young children are able to complete this sequence with high levels of competence; many others cannot. Therefore, collaborative learning in the language arts workshop requires explicit teaching of the helping curriculum in addition to the academic strategies needed for meaningful interactions. Like all other teaching, these helping skills are taught through explicit instruction, modeling, and guided practice.

By establishing learning conditions favorable to collaborative learning, the peer-led portion of the language arts workshop will run more smoothly and result in rewarding exchanges between students. Keep in mind that these skills should be taught first through focus lessons and guided instruction. As students become more proficient at the helping curriculum and self-assessment, they will be prepared to apply them to collaborative learning situations. In the next section, we will describe how these skills are developed and extended through a variety of collaborative reading instructional strategies.

> Teachers use tools like the ones featured in this chapter to support the cognitive, language, and social demands of collaborative learning.

COLLABORATIVE LEARNING IN READING

After focus lessons and guided instruction, students need to spend time practicing what they have learned. A skill or strategy may be modeled during the focus lesson then taught more explicitly during guided reading. However, during these phases of the workshop the teacher is providing high levels of support. Many learners may not be ready to walk away from the guided reading table fully able to use the skill or strategy independently. Collaborative reading serves as a bridge to independence because students work in pairs or groups to refine their mastery of the task.

> What Is Collaborative Reading?

Collaborative reading provides students with opportunities to make meaning of a text with their peers. When students read and discuss texts together, they apply comprehension strategies and support the understanding of others. We use collaborative reading as an umbrella term to describe a number of peer reading activities, including partner reading, collaborative strategic reading, literature circles, and reciprocal teaching. While each of these peer reading arrangements possesses unique features, there are common elements. First, students work in pairs or groups of no more than six. Second, the work they do is outside the immediate supervision of the teacher. Instead, they guide their own discussions and make decisions about how the task will be completed. A third element common to these collaborative reading practices is that students work with text to deepen their understanding of the content and the processes they use to comprehend. One of the most popular collaborative reading activities used in classrooms is partner reading.

Partner Reading— "Knee to Knee"

Of all the collaborative reading strategies that will be discussed in this chapter, **partner reading** is perhaps the one best suited for younger students and those who have had little experience with peer learning. This instructional format is used to complete a reading task developed by the teacher. Students work in pairs to read and discuss a common text together. This is sometimes called "knee to knee" reading (Calkins, 2000). When working in pairs, students may ask each other questions, make predictions, or clear up confusion. In the language arts workshop, partner reading follows a focus lesson or guided reading lesson on a particular text or strategy.

For example, after participating in a focus lesson on tracking two characters' dialogue using markers like "he said" and "she replied," second-grade students Brittany and Adriana work together to identify which character is speaking in a passage from the book *Junie B. Jones and the Stupid Smelly Bus* (Park, 1992). They first use two different highlighting markers to distinguish the speech of each character, then read it aloud together by assuming the role of one of the characters. Next, they switch roles and read to one another again.

Partner reading strategies like the one described above improve reading fluency through repeated reading. Fluency is a reader's ability to read smoothly, accurately, and with expression. These fluency skills are essential to comprehend the text being read. A challenge to building fluency is that it is most effectively accomplished through repeated readings of the same passage. However, this may not be perceived as motivating and interesting to many students, especially those who protest, "I already read that part!" Partner reading can give students a reason to read a text more than once because they have someone to read to and with.

Many other strategies for building fluency can be found in chapter 9.

A related partner reading strategy is called **echo reading.** First one student reads a paragraph aloud, then the other repeats the paragraph. Poetry and picture books with rhyming sentences are particularly suitable for echo reading because the students can experience the rhythms and cadence of lively prose. Young readers enjoy echo reading books like *Five Little Monkeys Jumping on the Bed* and its familiar refrain "when the doctor said, 'No more monkeys jumping on the bed!'" (Christelow, 1989). Older students can use echo reading to practice poetry and song texts. Fifth graders in Ms. Allen's class used echo reading to learn the lyrics to a song they selected for their school Parent Night performance.

Evidence Based

The interactions between students doing partner reading can take a turn for the worse if not monitored and supported. MacGillivray and Hawes conducted a study of the negotiated roles of students during partner reading (1994). They identified four possible role sets:

- *Coworkers*. Children shared the workload equally and assisted each other.
- *Fellow artists*. Students performed for each other.

- *Teacher/student.* One child models and instructs while the other follows.

- *Boss/employee.* One child did all the work while the other supervised.

Clearly, the last role set is not productive. Students benefit from guidelines for effective partner reading. Look again at Figure 4.6 for a self-assessment for young partner readers.

Partner reading is a relatively easy instructional arrangement to implement and is particularly suitable for use at the beginning of the school year, for younger or less experienced students, and when the focus of the task is on practice. Larger groups of students can engage in a more structured practice called Collaborative Strategic Reading.

Collaborative Strategic Reading

Informational text is sometimes referred to as expository text.

Collaborative Strategic Reading (CSR) is a technique used by small groups of heterogeneously grouped students to read and comprehend text (Klinger & Vaughn, 1998). Typically used in groups of five, it is well suited for use with informational text, although narrative can be utilized as well. A text is divided into smaller sections so that the group stops from time to time to discuss what they know so far and what is confusing or unclear. The strength of this approach is in the utilization of cooperative learning principles to practice comprehension strategies. The group uses four strategies to understand the text:

- Preview

- Click and Clunk

- Get the Gist

- Wrap Up

Each of these strategies is taught and practiced as a whole group until students are able to utilize them without teacher support. A study of CSR in fourth-grade classrooms suggests that students who had been carefully taught each of the strategies focused the majority of their talk (65%) on the content of the reading, and another 25% on the procedural aspects of CSR (Klinger, Vaughn, & Schumm, 1998). By comparison, only 2% of their talk was off-task.

Before the reading: Preview. This step is performed before the reading. Students discuss what they already know about the topic of the reading and make predictions about what may be learned in the reading. By creating prediction questions, students can begin to anticipate the information they may encounter during the reading.

During the reading: Click and Clunk. "Clicks" is the term used by the researchers to describe smooth reading that makes sense to the student, much like the hum of a well-oiled machine. On the other hand, "clunks" describe the times when a reader encounters an unfamiliar word or concept. Together, clicks and clunks represent self-monitoring behaviors used by fluent readers. The clunks signal the readers that fix-up strategies are needed. After noticing that a problem has occurred, the reader can:

- *Reread* the sentence or paragraph.

- *Read ahead* until the end of the sentence or paragraph.

- *Analyze* the word for familiar affixes or root words.

- *Ask* someone else what it means.

During CSR, students read a passage from the text then discuss their clunks. Using their collective knowledge, they clarify each other's understanding of the word or concept in question.

During the reading: Get the Gist. At the end of each section of the passage, students summarize the main ideas and important facts. Like prediction and self-monitoring, summarizing is a comprehension behavior used by more fluent readers (Brown & Day, 1983). Both Click and Clunk and Get the Gist are repeated several times until the entire reading has been completed.

After the reading: Wrap Up. Once the group has finished with the reading, they revisit the predictions made before the reading to check for accuracy. They also generate questions and answers that focus on the main ideas and important facts.

Students are assigned roles for CSR so that the discussion will flow more smoothly (Klinger & Vaughn, 1998). These roles include:

- *Leader* who makes sure the strategies are used and seeks help from the teacher when needed
- *Clunk expert* who leads discussion on how to figure out unknown words or concepts
- *Announcer* who makes sure everyone has a chance to participate
- *Reporter* who shares the group's work during the share portion of the language arts workshop
- *Timer* who monitors the time so the group can complete the task during collaborative learning

A student task sheet for CSR can be viewed in Figure 4.7. These task sheets aid students in performing their roles.

Figure 4.7 Student Task Sheet for Collaborative Strategic Reading

When?	What?	Sounds Like?
Before the reading	Preview	What do we know about this topic? What do we expect to find out in this reading?
During the reading	Click and Clunk	What can I do to fix this clunk? **Reread** the sentence or paragraph. **Read ahead** until the end of the sentence or paragraph. **Analyze** the word for familiar affixes or root words. **Ask** your partner what it means.
During the reading	Get the Gist	What do we know so far? What is the main idea? What are the important facts?
After the reading	Wrap Up	What did we learn?

Source: Adapted from Klinger, J. K., & Vaughn, S. (1998). Using collaborative strategic reading. *TEACHING Exceptional Children, 30*(6), 32–37. Used with permission.

Spotlight on Instruction

Collaborative Strategic Reading in Fourth Grade

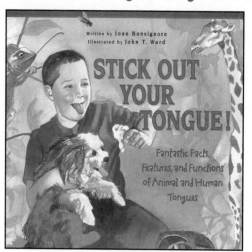

Stick Out Your Tongue! Fantastic Facts, Features and Functions of Animal and Human Tongues. Used with permission from Peachtree Publishers.

A group of fourth-grade students used Collaborative Strategic Reading with the picture book *Stick Out Your Tongue!* (Bonsignore, 2001). The teacher had introduced the book during shared reading and now they were working in their small groups to finish the book.

Ting, the leader of the group, asked everyone to read the page then called on Kimberly, the Clunk Expert, to start the discussion about difficult vocabulary. "Did anyone have a clunk—a tricky word?"

"I had a bunch of them," said Marvin. Alicia, the Announcer, reminded him to pick one so that everyone would have a turn. "I pick this word then," said Marvin, pointing to 'proboscis.' "I don't even know how to say it!"

Kimberly followed. "I had trouble with that one, too. Let's look at the list to see how we can figure it out. Let's reread the sentence." After all of them finished rereading, Marvin exclaimed, "There it is! It's 'a mouthpart that extends out and forms a long, thin tube.' It's right here in the picture." He points to the illustration of a moth using his proboscis to suck nectar from the center of a daisy.

"The illustrator even drew a picture of a boy drinking from a straw to remind us of how it works," offered Wilfredo. The leader continued the conversation and the group discussed *blossom* (Marvin knew this word), *nectar* (they made a connection to *nectarine* and decided it was something sweet) and *Madagascar* (they used context clues to determine that it was a place, then consulted an atlas to pinpoint its location).

Wilfredo, the Timer, reminded the group that they needed to "get the gist" if they were going to finish this passage. After discussing the main idea of the passage, they each wrote a sentence in their journal, as shown in Figure 4.8.

After reading three more pages of the book together, the group had developed several summary sentences. During the share portion of the language arts workshop, reporters for each group read their sentences and discussed the reading.

Figure 4.8 Student Sentence for CSR

> # Moths and butterflies use a proboscis to suck nectar from flowers.

Literature Circles The emphasis of Collaborative Strategic Reading is on self-monitoring to recognize when a word or sentence doesn't make sense and then employ problem-solving strategies to make the meaning clear. As students become increasingly fluent readers, they are ready to delve deeper in their discussions. **Literature circles** provide students with an opportunity to explore their understanding of a text while building comprehension in a collaborative learning arrangement (Daniels, 2002a).

Like CSR, literature circles "are small, temporary discussion groups who have chosen to read the same story, poem, article, or book . . . Each member prepares to take specific responsibilities in the upcoming discussion, and everyone comes to the group with the notes needed to help perform that job" (Daniels, 1994, p. 13). The opening scenario for this chapter was an example of a literature circle. These collaborative reading groups are usually heterogeneous and change with each new text.

A variation of literature circles is book club (Raphael, Pardo, Highfield, & McMahon, 1997). Like literature circles, book clubs are student-led small groups who discuss a common text. There is more emphasis placed on journal writing and the reader's reactions to the story, and roles in book clubs are not assigned.

Roles in literature circles. Several formats are available for teachers to use, depending on the text and needs of the students. Like all collaborative learning formats, these roles must be taught systematically to the entire group before students are asked to take on these tasks independently. Younger readers and those new to literature circles enjoy these roles (Daniels, 2002a):

- *Discussion Director* who creates questions to begin the conversation
- *Passage Picker* who selects interesting parts of the story to read aloud to the group
- *Artful Artist* who draws a picture to represent an important character, idea, problem, or setting
- *Connector* who makes connections between events or characters in the book and personal experiences, other books, or events in the world

Some groups are larger and require additional jobs. Optional jobs include:

- *Word Finder* who selects unusual or difficult vocabulary for discussion
- *Character Captain* who describes attributes of important characters in the book

Older students are ready for more sophisticated roles. In addition to the Discussion Director and Connector, other roles are transformed or added (Daniels, 2002a):

- *Literary Luminary* who chooses passages for discussion and formulates theories on their importance in the story
- *Illustrator* who creates a sketch, graph, flow chart, or diagram to portray a topic for discussion
- *Summarizer* who composes a statement that captures the main idea of the reading
- *Vocabulary Enricher* who locates important words and provides a definition for the group
- *Researcher* who investigates background information that is key to understanding the reading

Students use these roles in order to practice comprehension tools that eventually become part of their independent repertoire of reading strategies. Over time, as students become more proficient, these roles are faded out in favor of more natural dialogue. Indeed, if used too long, roles may constrain rich conversation because students feel restricted to discussing only their tasks rather than consolidating all these comprehension strategies (Daniels, 2002b). For this reason, it is recommended that role sheets be used for only a few weeks, until students become comfortable with the way these comprehension strategies are used. As role sheets are phased out, students begin using sticky notes or journals to capture their ideas for the next discussion.

After introducing literature circle roles to her fifth graders, Ms. Allen began structuring tasks so that each student would use these comprehension strategies together. During a shared reading, they listened to and discussed a popular song entitled, *Where Is the Love?* by the Black Eyed Peas featuring Justin Timberlake. Students then moved into their literature circles to analyze the lyrics with their peers. Each student made notes using several comprehension strategies. Martha's notes appear in Figure 4.9.

Ms. Allen subscribes to a teaching music magazine called *Music Alive* (www.musicalive.com), which provides a CD and teaching ideas each month.

Figure 4.9   Martha's Discussion Notes for "Where Is the Love?"

Summarizer: What is the main idea of this song? Give two examples.

The main idea in the song is the people think of the bad things instead of the good things

Examples
1. People try to stop terrorism.
2. But people don't understand.

Vocabulary Enricher: What are three special or important words in the song? What do they mean to you?

1. preach: many people say things to people but they don't do it.

2. Love: many people don't understand this song and it is all about love.

Passage Picker: Choose a line from the song that is important to you. Why?

1. People killing: people dying
2. Where is love
3. Why are the pieces of love that don't belong
4.

Connector: Make a *text-to-text* or *text-to-world* connection.

This song reminds me of September 11. This was a very special song.

From ESPERANZA RISING by Pam Muñoz Ryan.
Copyright © 1999 by Pam Muñoz Ryan. Reprinted by
permission of Scholastic Inc.

Selecting texts in literature circles. In most literature circle arrangements, students choose the book or article they would like to read. This practice is consistent with the research on engagement indicating that student choice in academic tasks is a powerful motivator (Deci & Ryan, 1980). Many teachers begin by introducing the reading options for the literature circle with a book talk. An effective book talk for students includes:

- Title and author
- Background information of interest to students
- A description of the genre (narrative, expository, poetry, etc.)
- Reading an excerpt aloud to pique student interest

Once all the titles have been introduced and discussed, students mark their selections on a preference sheet by indicating their first, second, and third choices. The teacher then constructs collaborative groups organized by student choice. Of course, the teacher may use other information to influence membership decisions, including social structures, text difficulty, and academic need. An example of a preference sheet used in a sixth-grade class appears in Figure 4.10.

Figure 4.10 Student Preference Sheet for Literature Circle

Name: _____   Date: _____

Period: _____

Our theme for the next literature circle is "Tough Times: Girls Confronting Adversity." Please rank order the book you would like to read. Consider what you learned in the book talk today, including your interest in the topic and the author.

_____ A Step from Heaven (An, 2001)
_____ Out of the Dust (Hesse, 1999)
_____ Lyddie (Patterson, 1994)
_____ Riding Freedom (Ryan, 1998)
_____ Esperanza Rising (Ryan, 2000)

Please write the title of the book you read in your last literature circle, "Tough Times: Boys Confronting Adversity."

_____

Text genres in literature circles. While literature circles are most closely associated with narrative texts, other genres, including expository texts, poetry, and memoirs can also be used. Literature circles are less appropriate for dense informational texts like textbooks and reference materials such as encyclopedia entries. Daniels (2002a) recommends that expository texts with narrative features are more useful for literature circles. These include:

- Biographies
- Memoirs
- Travelogues/adventures
- Historical accounts
- Historical novels

When using expository texts like those noted above, changes in roles are required. A discussion sheet for the sixth-grade literature circle entitled "A Picture's Worth 1000 Words" featured biographies of famous artists. The discussion sheet in Figure 4.11 features roles reflecting the use of expository texts and its emphasis on extracting factual material.

Literature circles are an effective collaborative learning tool for narrative and poetic texts, as well as some types of expository texts that contain narrative elements. Another effective structure for collaborative reading is called reciprocal teaching.

Figure 4.11   Discussion Notes for "A Picture's Worth 1000 Words" Literature Circle

Name: _____   Date: _____

Period: _____   Title: _____

Group Members:_____
_____

Please have notes prepared in advance of your literature circle meetings. Use these questions to guide your notemaking.

Discussion: *What questions are you thinking about at the end of this reading? What are you wondering about? What is confusing or unclear?*

Golden Lines: *What sections of the text caught your attention? This could be something surprising, weird, or well said. Make a note of the page number and beginning words so you can read it to your group. Be sure to write why you chose it.*

Connections: *What personal events were you reminded of in this reading? Are there other books you have read that connect with this story? How?*

Illustration: Make a simple picture or diagram that represents this reading to you. Remember that what's important is not your artistic ability—it's your ideas.

Reciprocal Teaching

The shift to informational texts increases rapidly during the elementary and middle grades as students shift from reading stories to reading for information. With narrative texts, good readers look to clues in the text itself to make meaning of the story being told—these literary elements like foreshadowing, dialogue, and character development signal the reader for what is to come. However, expository texts require more background knowledge to understand and use different text structures like cause and effect or compare/contrast (Lorch, 1989). Therefore, a different type of collaborative reading arrangement is needed to practice comprehension strategies for informational texts.

Reciprocal teaching is used in student-directed groups of four (Palincsar & Brown, 1986). The text is segmented into smaller chunks, allowing students to check their understanding periodically throughout the reading. This is accomplished using a structured discussion format and is performed several times until the reading is complete. The teacher may create the stopping points for discussion in advance, or the group may decide how best to break up the text. At each stopping point, students use four kinds of comprehension strategies to understand the text:

- *Questioning* the text by asking literal and inferential questions of one another
- *Clarifying* understanding through discussion of how confusion might be cleared up (for example, using a dictionary, checking the glossary, asking the teacher)
- *Summarizing* the main ideas of the passage
- *Predicting* what the author will discuss next, based on what is known so far

Like CSR and literature circles, the strength of this approach is in the consolidation of comprehension practices used during the reading process. These four steps do not need to be performed in a fixed order, but rather can be discussed in the order the group decides.

Evidence Based

Research on reciprocal teaching. The use of this instructional strategy is widespread in schools, thus a considerable number of studies have been conducted on the effects. It has been found to be motivating for students considered to be at-risk (Carter, 1997) and struggling readers (Alfassi, 1998). Rosenshine and Meister (1994) reviewed 16 separate studies on reciprocal teaching and found the strategy to be effective in a wide range of classroom settings. In particular, they noted that reciprocal teaching improved standardized testing results in reading comprehension.

Introducing reciprocal teaching. Like other collaborative reading strategies, the techniques used in reciprocal teaching must first be taught so that students are comfortable using them in collaborative groups. In the language arts workshop, each role is modeled during shared reading until all four have been introduced. As with literature circles, specific roles are used until students are ready to use all the strategies together in a group meeting.

Question stems. Many teachers use question stems to support student dialogue within the group. Because the text is not read in advance, but rather is chunked, read, and discussed in the same sitting, question stems can be useful when group members are at a loss for what to say next. Sample question stems can be seen in Figure 4.12.

Figure 4.12   Question Stems for Reciprocal Teaching

Prediction

We look and listen for clues that will tell us what may happen next or what we will learn from the text.

Good predictions are based on . . .
- what we already know
- what we understand from the text
- what pictures, charts, or graphs tell us

I think . . .
I predict . . .
I bet . . .
I wonder . . .

Question

We test ourselves about what we just read by asking ourselves questions.
We see if we really understand and can identify what is important.
We ask different kinds of questions:
- Factual questions:
    Who, what, when, where?
- Interpretive questions:
    How, why?
- Beyond the text questions:
    I wonder if . . .
    I'm curious about . . .

Clarify

We clear up confusion and find the meaning of unfamiliar words, sentences, ideas, or concepts.
This is confusing to me . . .
I need to reread, slow down, look at the graphs or illustrations, or break the word apart.
When I began reading this, I thought . . .
Then, when I read this part, I realized . . .
It didn't make sense until I . . .

Summarize

We restate the main ideas, events, or points.
A good summary includes . . .
- key people, items, or places
- key words and synonyms
- key ideas and concepts

The main point is . . .
If I put the ideas together, I now understand that . . .

The most important thing I read was . . .

Source: Fisher, D., & Frey, N. (2003). *Improving adolescent literacy: Strategies at work.* Upper Saddle River, NJ: Merrill/Prentice Hall.

Figure 4.13	Discussion Sheet for Reciprocal Teaching

Reading: _____ Period: _____ Date: _____

> **Prediction:**
>
>
>

> **Question:**
>
>
>

> **Clarification:**
>
>
>

> **Summary Statement:**
>
>
>

Was the prediction confirmed: YES   NO

Details:

Source: Fisher, D., & Frey, N. (2003). *Improving adolescent literacy: Strategies at work.* Upper Saddle River, NJ: Merrill/Prentice Hall.

Spotlight on Instruction

Reciprocal Teaching in Eighth Grade

In an eighth-grade language arts workshop, four students gather around a table to discuss their latest reading. They have been reading *Roll of Thunder, Hear My Cry* (Taylor, 1983) and have raised many questions regarding race. Their teacher, Mr. Hansen, selected a brief reading on facts about race for his students to read during collaborative learning. Entitled "Ten Things Everyone Should Know About Race," the one-page expository text presents facts in a list format. Leah, Charles, Francisco, and Zena have used reciprocal teaching a number of times and quickly begin chunking the text. They also utilize the discussion notes framework given to them by Mr. Hansen to remind them of the comprehension strategies they need to use. The discussion notes can be found in Figure 4.13, while the text they read is in Figure 4.14.

"It seems to me that it makes sense to read a couple of items at a time. They probably have a lot to do with each other," says Zena. The others agree and draw lines under the third, sixth, and tenth items then read the title and opening statement silently.

(continued)

QUESTIONING.

CLARIFYING.

PREDICTING.

SUMMARIZING.

"The writer for this website really made our job easy!" remarks Francisco. "The questions are all right there for us. So there's my prediction—the list will answer the questions at the beginning of this reading. Let's read the first set of facts."

After reading the first statement about race as a modern concept, the conversation picks up. Leah offered, "I'm really surprised that the word 'race' didn't exist before 1500. How can that be?"

"I guess it's because of what it says in the third fact—'human subspecies don't exist.' I never thought of it exactly that way before, but it's not like we can be divided up like the plants we're studying about in science," says Charles.

"I wonder why it got changed around all of a sudden," speculates Francisco. "What happened to make people think about race?"

"We've still got to summarize," Zena reminds the group. "How about this? 'Race is an idea that started in 1500, even though there's no genetic reason for it.' How does that sound?"

"That's good—write it down on the list for us. Let's read the next three so we can get finished," Leah says.

The group continues until the text is finished. By the end, they have created some summary sentences that will be used when Mr. Hansen leads the entire class in a discussion of the article.

Matching Collaborative Reading Techniques with Students

The collaborative reading techniques introduced in this chapter are designed to foster conversation about the meaning of a text and the strategies good readers use to understand them. These discussions occur between and among peers who work alongside one another to comprehend the reading. While these collaborative reading techniques share a common element of peer-directed discussion about a text, the sophistication of the demands on the participants varies. To ensure success in your classroom, we advise taking your students' developmental levels into account when identifying appropriate collaborative reading structures. Figure 4.15 shows a chart detailing how collaborative reading can be expanded through the grade levels. This chart should be advisory only—the success of a strategy in an individual classroom is far more complex. We have seen wonderful reciprocal teaching events occur in primary classrooms using simplified language and would never dissuade a teacher from trying these techniques in his or her classroom.

COLLABORATIVE LEARNING IN WRITING

Collaborative writing involves students working together to decide on the meaning and composition of a message. This involves oral language skills like negotiation and compromise, as well as writing skills such as co-editing and co-revising. Collaborative writing in the language arts workshop can take several directions. It can be a small group creative writing exercise like progressive writing or group writing. As well, collaborative learning time can be used as an opportunity for peer editing.

What Is Collaborative Writing?

In **collaborative writing,** pairs or groups of students co-construct original writing. Unlike other acts of writing, this involves a host of skills, including sharing ideas, listening to the ideas of others, and formulating ways to incorporate the two. Depending on the task, there may be times when students are working in face-to-face interactions, while at other times they are writing alone to fulfill the agreements reached among the co-writers. At still other times, collaborative writers may work in editing partnerships, giving feedback on individually generated writing assignments. Students not experienced at co-writing may benefit from first experiencing some "shoulder to shoulder" writing

Figure 4.14   Eighth-Grade Reading for Reciprocal Teaching

RACE - The Power of an Illusion
Ten Things Everyone Should Know About Race

Our eyes tell us that people look different. No one has trouble distinguishing a Czech from a Chinese, but what do those differences mean? Are they biological? Has race always been with us? How does race affect people today? There's less — and more — to race than meets the eye:

1. **Race is a modern idea.** Ancient societies, like the Greeks, did not divide people according to physical distinctions, but according to religion, status, class, even language. The English language didn't even have the word 'race' until it turns up in 1508 in a poem by William Dunbar referring to a line of kings.

2. **Race has no genetic basis.** Not one characteristic, trait or even one gene distinguishes all the members of one so-called race from all the members of another so-called race.

3. **Human subspecies don't exist.** Unlike many animals, modern humans simply haven't been around long enough or isolated enough to evolve into separate subspecies or races. Despite surface appearances, we are one of the most similar of all species.

4. **Skin color really is only skin deep.** Most traits are inherited independently from one another. The genes influencing skin color have nothing to do with the genes influencing hair form, eye shape, blood type, musical talent, athletic ability or forms of intelligence. Knowing someone's skin color doesn't necessarily tell you anything else about him or her.

5. **Most variation is within, not between, "races."** Of the small amount of total human variation, 85% exists within any local population, be they Italians, Kurds, Koreans or Cherokees. About 94% can be found within any continent. That means two random Koreans may be as genetically different as a Korean and an Italian.

6. **Slavery predates race.** Throughout much of human history, societies have enslaved others, often as a result of conquest or war, even debt, but not because of physical characteristics or a belief in natural inferiority. Due to a unique set of historical circumstances, ours was the first slave system where all the slaves shared similar physical characteristics.

7. **Race and freedom evolved together.** The U.S. was founded on the radical new principle that "All men are created equal." But our early economy was based largely on slavery. How could this anomaly be rationalized? The new idea of race helped explain why some people could be denied the rights and freedoms that others took for granted.

8. **Race justified social inequalities as natural.** As the race idea evolved, white superiority became "common sense" in America. It justified not only slavery but also the extermination of Indians, exclusion of Asian immigrants, and the taking of Mexican lands by a nation that professed a belief in democracy. Racial practices were institutionalized within American government, laws, and society.

9. **Race isn't biological, but racism is still real.** Race is a powerful social idea that gives people different access to opportunities and resources. Our government and social institutions have created advantages that disproportionately channel wealth, power, and resources to white people. This affects everyone, whether we are aware of it or not.

10. **Colorblindness will not end racism.** Pretending race doesn't exist is not the same as creating equality. Race is more than stereotypes and individual prejudice. To combat racism, we need to identify and remedy social policies and institutional practices that advantage some groups at the expense of others.

Source: Copyright © California Newsreel from the video series, *Race — The Power of an Illusion*, available from www.newsreel.org.

Figure 4.15   A Grade Level Continuum of Collaborative Reading Techniques

	Partner Reading	Collaborative Strategic Reading	Literature Circles	Reciprocal Teaching
K	📖			
1	📖			
2	📖	📖		
3	📖	📖	📖	
4	📖	📖	📖	📖
5	📖	📖	📖	📖
6	📖	📖	📖	📖
7	📖	📖	📖	📖
8	📖	📖	📖	📖

experiences that are individually generated, but in the company of other writers. One of the easiest of these "shoulder to shoulder" writing activities is progressive writing.

Progressive Writing

Progressive writing is accomplished in a small group of three or more students. It is timed (usually 2-minute intervals) and begins with a writing prompt furnished in advance by the teacher. At the end of 2 minutes, each writer passes their paper to the person sitting next to them. They read the paper they have received then add new writing to extend the story or ideas. This cycle of writing and reading new papers is repeated until everyone has had an opportunity to write a portion of each story.

Progressive writing is a non-threatening way to introduce true collaborative writing. While the stories are developed linearly, each writer must incorporate the ideas of others into his or her writing in order to make the story work. Although somewhat basic in nature, this type of collaborative writing is used among adult writers as well. For example, the young adult novel *P.S. Longer Letter Later* (Danziger & Martin, 1998) was composed by two authors who each assumed the voice of an adolescent and mailed letters back and forth to one another.

There are a number of progressive writing groups online, including ones sponsored by the Tag Your It Society (www.tagyourit.org).

Student-Generated Language Charts

Although not strictly a writing activity, **student-generated language charts** can serve as an intermediate writing activity that inspires young writers to discuss a text they have read and then arrive at an agreed message. A student-generated language chart begins with the discussion of a book or text already read by the students, perhaps during a shared or guided reading lesson. The common text becomes the focal point of the discussion. The teacher develops a chart in advance of the discussion with sentence stems or questions already written (Roser, Hoffman, Labbo, & Farest, 1992). The pair or group of students then discusses responses to each prompt, arriving at a consensus. For example, a student-generated language chart for a group of first-grade students focused on the story *Don't Let the Pigeon Drive the Bus!* (Willems, 2003). They had heard this story several times during an earlier read aloud and were now ready to discuss it. The teacher wrote these prompts on the chart:

- The pigeon is . . .
- This story reminds us of when . . .
- We think the author wrote this story because . . .
- We would recommend this story to . . .

Students discussed each of these sentence stems and co-composed their responses, then took turns recording the answers on behalf of the group. This activity gave them experience at listening to others and considering new ideas. Later, they shared their responses with the rest of the class.

Student-generated language charts are useful for engaging young writers in conversation about a story. The prompts can focus on aspects of reading and writing, including story grammar elements such as character, plot, and setting (Roser, Hoffman, Labbo, & Farest, 1992). In addition, they provide students with an opportunity to talk about a collaboratively generated message.

Paired Writing

Paired writing involves two students of differing ability levels working together to develop a piece of original text (Topping, 1995). The higher-ability student serves as the helper to the writer (Sutherland & Topping, 2001). In paired writing, the pen is controlled by the writer, with the helper serving as a coach and guide. In particular, the helper assists with idea generation through questioning, and problem-solving conventions of writing such as spelling and punctuation. The helper's main role is to serve as a motivator and keep the writing moving. These roles are reciprocal as well—writer and helper are free to change roles at any time during the session. The evidence on the effectiveness of paired reading suggests that there is a positive effect on the writing of both students (Sutherland & Topping, 2001). A flowchart of the process of paired writing appears in Figure 4.16.

Group Writing

From an early age, students should be encouraged to write together. **Group writing** allows children, working in groups of three to five, to jointly compose a piece of writing. In kindergarten and first-grade, children should have opportunities to choose who they will write with, as they are likely to be more productive with friends (Cunningham & Allington, 2003). Older students can be assigned to writing groups or work with groups of their own choosing. In all cases, students should be encouraged to first compose the story orally, talking through the details. They can then write the story together and share it with others. Students in all grades often enjoy illustrating the piece as well.

One method for developing group writing is to establish a collaborative book project. The topic of the book can involve personal stories united in a theme, or be tied to a content area such as social studies. Leal (2003), a second-grade teacher, described a book-authoring project on the history of the community. She invited guest speakers to discuss their recollections of the town and watched films and read stories about the history of the region. The first chapter of the book was composed during a series of shared writing lessons and chapter titles were developed for the rest of the book. Students were assigned to one of five groups, each focusing on one chapter. The groups spent several weeks drafting, editing, and revising their chapters, as well as reading the chapters of other groups. By the end, the class had authored a detailed account of aspects of life in the community (Leal, 2003).

Figure 4.16   Paired Reading Role Chart

Steps of Paired Writing	Role of the Writer	Role of the Helper
Brainstorming	Answer questions	Ask questions: who, what, when, where, why, and how Take notes
Drafting	Writer says a sentence	Read notes Help with spelling (tell, copy, write it for them)
Reading	Listens	Read draft aloud
Editing	Makes editing marks on draft	Looks at edits, adds those that are missing
Revision	Makes a new copy using edited draft	

Class-authored books featuring group writing can be developed on a myriad of topics, such as informational writing related to a science unit ("Volcanoes Around the World") or a narrative piece ("Scary Stories from Room 107"). Whatever the topic, the focus should be on the development of a collaborative writing piece that uses the craft and conventions being taught in shared and guided writing.

Peer Response to Writing

During the language arts workshop, students are preparing longer writing pieces. Many of these have been initiated during a focus lesson, then refined during guided writing sessions. Eventually, the student writer needs to find out what a reader understands. This is consistent with the practices of professional writers, who seek the feedback of an editor to refine their work. **Peer response** is another aspect of collaborative writing processes. Unlike the other writing activities we have profiled in this section, peer response does not involve the creation of original text. Instead, students come together as fellow writers to read each other's work and give constructive feedback. However, we offer several caveats to the use of peer response in the language arts workshop:

- The writer determines when they are in need of peer feedback
- Not all writing needs peer feedback
- Teachers, not students, should offer feedback on the details of the piece
- Students should provide feedback that is focused on a reader's needs and writer's strategies

We advocate authentic writing that is not bound by an artificially constructed schedule of writing "phases". This can deteriorate into a series of meaningless deadlines a student struggles to meet in order to satisfy a grading requirement. This means that the writer decides when he or she is ready for peer feedback. Few things are more dispiriting than receiving criticism about a piece the writer knows is not ready. This can serve to discourage the writer and prevent him or her from seeking such feedback in the future.

Figure 4.17   Types of Peer Responses

Type of Response	Definition	Example
Global praise	Intended to make the writer feel good about his or her work.	"Great paper."
Personal response	Focuses on involvement of the writer as a person, not as a writer.	"Did this really happen to you?"
Text playback	Focuses on ideas or organization of the text.	"I think you wrote an excellent conclusion."
Sentence edits	Focuses on one or more sentences or grammar.	"Run-on sentence."
Word edits	Focuses on the use of words or spelling.	"You used this phrase too many times. Maybe you should try another."
Reader's needs	Focuses on needs or the reactions of the reader.	"This part is confusing to the reader."
Writer's strategies	Focuses on facilitating the writer's work by discussing the techniques that were used or could be used.	"In the fourth paragraph you get to the 'meat' of the experience. What if you didn't tell this in chronological order?"

Source: Adapted from Simmons, J. (2003). Responders are taught, not born. *Journal of Adolescent & Adult Literacy, 46,* 686. Copyright © 2003 by the International Reading Association.

In Figure 4.17, Simmons (2003) describes several types of peer responses that students offer to one another during peer editing.

Some of these peer responses are less helpful than others. In particular, global praise does little to provide the writer with any feedback that might be useful. As well, feedback that only focuses on word- and sentence-level editing mirrors what the teacher often does and may not be welcome by fellow students. Rather, peer editing should focus primarily on reader needs and writer strategies. The purpose of seeking peer responses is not to have the work evaluated, but instead to hear what a reader might understand or be confused about (Simmons, 2003).

Teaching effective peer responses. As we have stated before, the skills students need in collaborative learning should first be taught and modeled by the teacher. One of the most effective techniques is to share the teacher's writing in order to give students an opportunity to offer specific praise, retell the story as they understand it, ask questions about confusing parts, and offer suggestions related to the writing. These are detailed in Figure 4.18.

Once the responses have been taught, students can use a simple peer response form to give back to the writer. It is helpful for writers to receive comments in writing so they have an idea of what to do next. It should also be said that the teacher should review these peer comments in order to monitor whether students are offering helpful feedback. An example of a peer response form is in Figure 4.19.

Figure 4.18   Techniques to Teach Peer Responses

Technique	What the teacher does	What students do
Share your writing	Share a piece of writing and ask for responses	Offer comments on the teacher's writing
Clarify evaluation versus response	Model the difference between evaluative statements and helpful responses	Understand that response is personable and helpful
Model specific praise	Show how you tell a writer what you like as a reader	Learn that "cheerleading" is too general to be helpful
Model understanding	Restate the meaning of the piece	Learn that reflecting back the piece to the writer is helpful
Model questions	Create questions about what you don't understand	Learn that questions help the writer clarify his or her purpose
Model suggestions	Clarify writing techniques	Appreciate that a responder leaves a writer knowing what to do next
Comment review	Read the comments of peers to writers	Get teacher feedback on comments

Source: Adapted from Simmons, J. (2003). Responders are taught, not born. *Journal of Adolescent & Adult Literacy, 46*, 690. Copyright © 2003 by the International Reading Association.

Figure 4.19   Peer Response Feedback Form

Peer Response for Writing

Reader: _____   Writer: _____

Title: _____   Date: _____

What are the best things about this writing?

Retell the main ideas of the story using your own words:

What questions do you have for the writer so you can understand the story better?

What suggestions do you have for the writer to make the piece stronger? (Be specific).

Figure 4.20   Peer Response Poster in Third-Grade Classroom

  How Fellow Writers Talk

1. Tell your fellow writer what you liked best.

2. Retell the story or main ideas in your own words.

3. Ask questions about the parts you don't understand.

4. Give your fellow writer your good ideas about making it even better.

5. Thank the writer for sharing his or her writing with you.

Figure 4.21   Peer Response Poster in Third-Grade Classroom

 How Fellow Writers Listen

1. Listen to the ideas your fellow writer offers.

2. Ask questions about ideas you don't understand.

3. Thank your fellow writer for reading your writing.

4. Use the ideas you like in your next draft.

Spotlight on Instruction

Peer Response in Third Grade

Jesse and Ray settle into two small rocking chairs below a sign that reads "Writers At Work." Jesse asked Ray earlier to read a report he had written about spiders. After reading it and filling out a peer response form, Ray was ready to talk with his friend about the piece. He looked at the posters hung nearby to help students with their conversations. (See Figures 4.20 and 4.21 for a look at these posters.)

"I liked reading about spiders because I like spiders, too," began Ray. "It was interesting, and I liked the part about the wolf spider best. I was surprised that some of them can kill a toad!"

SPECIFIC PRAISE.   "I liked that part, too!" said Jesse, warming to the topic.

(continued)

RETELLING.

Ray continued, "I think the main ideas you wrote about were that spiders are good because they eat bad insects and they are mostly not poisonous. Then you told about weird spiders like wolf spiders, black widows, and funnel web spiders."

Jesse responded, "That's right. That's what my report's about. I want to draw pictures of them, too."

MAKING SUGGESTIONS.

"Here's my question about your spider report. Do any of these spiders live here? I would like to know if they live here," Ray offered.

"The funnel web spider doesn't live here," said Jesse, sounding a little disappointed. "It only lives in Australia. It's a deadly spider, too. Australia has all the cool stuff. They have box jellyfish, too. That's the most poisonous jellyfish in the world."

"I can help you draw the pictures if you want. There's a good spider book in the library."

As students become more cognizant of how they write, they can begin participating in peer editing. Editing at the word and sentence level is less likely to be useful to the writer and can become evaluative. These are best left to the teacher. Instead, students should be taught how to offer feedback that is focused on reader needs and writer strategies.

BIG IDEAS IN COLLABORATIVE READING AND WRITING

Collaborative reading involves student partners who work together to make meaning of a common text. Some are done in pairs, as with partner reading. Others involve larger groups of students, such as with literature circles. Collaborative Strategic Reading or reciprocal teaching can be used by a group to read informational text. Both involve the assignment of roles for each group member. The roles are intended to mirror the comprehension strategies used by good readers.

The success of collaborative reading instructional strategies is influenced by two factors—selection of a developmentally appropriate technique that suits the strengths and skills of the children, and the extent to which students have been prepared to utilize the technique. Although many factors influence what is appropriate, including the composition and size of the class, previous experience, and language skills, a suggested timeline for collaborative reading strategies begins with partner reading for primary grades. In the late primary or early intermediate grades, collaborative strategic reading can be introduced. Students in intermediate grades are ready for book clubs and literature circles, and those in late intermediate and middle school grades will respond well to reciprocal teaching.

Progressive writing, student-generated language charts, paired writing, and group writing are collaborative writing strategies useful in the language arts workshop. Group writing experiences build a student's experience at discussing writing and making decisions with others about the content of a story. Students like doing these writing activities because they can work alongside each other. Collaborative writing also offers an opportunity to solicit peer responses. However, students need to be taught how to offer feedback in ways that are helpful.

 ## INTEGRATING THE STANDARDS

Create lesson plans that meet your state's standards by visiting our Companion Website at www.prenhall.com/frey. There you'll find lessons created to meet the NCTE/IRA Standards. Adapt them to meet the standards of your own state through links to your state's standards, and keep them in the online portfolio. You can collect lesson plans for each chapter in an online portfolio, providing you with invaluable tools to meet your state's standards when you head into your own classroom.

CHECK YOUR UNDERSTANDING

This chapter focused on collaborative reading and writing practices in the language arts workshop. Now that you have read this chapter, check your understanding of the main ideas discussed.

1. What are the learning theories associated with collaborative learning?
2. What are the key elements of collaborative learning?
3. What is collaborative reading?
4. What is collaborative writing?
5. How can students be taught to respond to peer writing?

CLASSROOM CONNECTIONS

1. Meet with your teacher to learn how he or she uses collaborative learning in the classroom. What are the advantages? What are the biggest challenges?
2. Design a book scavenger hunt for your students using a format similar to the one in Figure 4.3. What do you notice about your students and their ability to work with one another?
3. Take photographs in your classroom of the posters and signs your teacher uses to manage students and their collaborative learning activities. Photographs are useful when you set up your own classroom.

References

Alfassi, M. (1998). Reading for meaning: The efficacy of reciprocal teaching in fostering reading comprehension in high school students in remedial reading classes. *American Educational Research Journal, 35,* 309–332.

Alevin, V., Stahl, E., Schworm, S., Fischer, F., Wallace, R. (2003). Help seeking and help design in interactive learning environments. *Review of Educational Research, 73,* 277–317.

Antil, L., Jenkins, J., Wayne, S., & Vadasy, P. (1998). Cooperative learning: Prevalence, conceptualizations, and the relation between research and practice. *American Educational Research Journal, 35,* 419–454.

Bandura, A. (1965). Vicarious processes: A case of no-trial learning. In L. Berkowitz (Ed.), *Advances in experimental social psychology* (Vol. II). New York: Academic Press.

Battistich, V., & Solomon, D. (1993). Interaction processes and student outcomes in cooperative learning groups. *Elementary School Journal, 94,* 19–32.

Bennett, N., & Cass, A. (1989). The effects of group composition on group interactive processes and pupil understanding. *British Educational Research Journal, 15*(1), 19–32.

Berk, L., & Winsler, A. (1995). *Scaffolding children's learning: Vygotsky and early childhood education.* Washington, DC: National Association for the Education of Young Children.

Brown, A. L., & Day, J. D. (1983). Macrorules for summarizing texts: The development of expertise. *Journal of Verbal Learning and Verbal Behavior, 22,* 1–14.

Calkins, L. M. (2000). *The art of teaching reading* (2nd ed.). Portsmouth, NH: Heinemann.

Carter, C. J. (1997). Why reciprocal teaching? *Educational Leadership, 54*(6), 64–68.

Coleman, M. R., & Gallagher, J. J. (1995). The successful blending of gifted education with middle schools and cooperative learning: Two studies. *Journal for the Education of the Gifted, 18*, 362–384.

Crain, W. (2000). *Theories of development: Concepts and applications* (4th ed.). Upper Saddle River, NJ: Prentice Hall.

Cunningham, P. M., & Allington, R. L. (2003). *Classrooms that work: They can all read and write* (3rd ed.). Boston: Pearson.

Daniels, H. (1994). *Literature circles: Voice and choice in student-centered classrooms.* York, ME: Stenhouse.

Daniels, H. (2002a). *Literature circles: Voice and choice in book clubs and reading groups* (2nd ed.). York, ME: Stenhouse.

Daniels, H. (2002b). Rethinking role sheets. *Voices from the Middle, 10*(2), 44–45.

Deci, E. L., & Ryan, R. M. (1985). *Intrinsic motivation and self-determination in human behavior.* New York: Plenum.

Elbaum, B., Schumm, J. S., & Vaughn, S. (1997). Urban middle-elementary students' perceptions of grouping formats for reading instruction. *Elementary School Journal, 97*, 475–500.

Gersten, R., & Baker, S. (2000). What we know about effective instructional practices for English-language learners. *Exceptional Children, 66*, 454–470.

Gillies, R. M. (2003). The behaviors, interactions, and perceptions of junior high school students during small-group learning. *Journal of Educational Psychology, 95*, 137–147.

Hallenbeck, M. J. (2002). Taking charge: Adolescents with learning disabilities assume responsibility for their own writing. *Learning Disability Quarterly, 25*, 227–246.

Johnson, D. W., & Johnson, R. T. (1999). Making cooperative learning work. *Theory Into Practice, 38*(2), 67–73.

Johnson, D., Johnson, R., Holubec, E. J., & Roy, P. (1984). *Circles of learning: Cooperation in the classroom.* Alexandria, VA: Association for Supervision and Curriculum Development.

Klinger, J. K., & Vaughn, S. (1998). Using collaborative strategic reading. *TEACHING Exceptional Children, 30*(6), 32–37.

Klinger, J. K., Vaughn, S., & Schumm, J. S. (1998). Collaborative strategic reading during social studies in heterogeneous fourth-grade classrooms. *Elementary School Journal, 99*, 3–20.

Lapp, D., Flood, J., & Goss, K. (2000). Desks don't move—students do: In effective classroom environments. *The Reading Teacher, 54*, 31–36.

Leal, D. J. (2003). Digging up the past, building the future: Using book authoring to discover and showcase a community's history. *The Reading Teacher, 57*, 56–60.

Lorch, R. F., Jr. (1989). Text signaling devices and their effects on reading and memory processes. *Educational Psychology Review, 1*, 209–234.

MacGillivray, L., & Hawes, S. (1994). "I don't know what I'm doing—they all start with B": First graders negotiate peer reading interactions. *The Reading Teacher, 48*, 210–217.

Mason, D. A., & Good, T. L. (1993). Effects of two-group and whole-class teaching on regrouped elementary students' mathematics achievement. *American Educational Research Journal, 30*, 328–360.

Mueller, A., & Fleming, T. (2001). Cooperative learning: Listening to how children work at school. *Journal of Educational Research, 94*, 259–265.

Nelson-LaGall, S. (1981). Help-seeking: An understudied problem-solving skill in children. *Journal of Genetic Psychology, 148*, 53–62.

Palincsar, A. S., & Brown, A. L. (1986). Interactive teaching to promote independent learning from text. *The Reading Teacher, 39,* 771–777.

Raphael, T. E., Pardo, L. S., Highfield, K., & McMahon, S. I. (1997). *Book club: A literature-based curriculum.* Littleton, MA: Small Planet.

Rosenshine, B., & Meister, C. (1994). Reciprocal teaching: A review of the research. *Review of Educational Research, 64,* 479–530.

Roser, N. L., Hoffman, J. V., Labbo, L. D., & Farest, C. (1992). Language charts: A record of story time talk. *Language Arts, 69,* 44–52.

Sapon-Shevin, M. (1998). *Because we can change the world: A practical guide to building cooperative, inclusive classroom communities.* Boston: Allyn & Bacon.

Schunk, D. H. (1998). Goal and self-evaluative influences during children's cognitive skill learning. *American Educational Research Journal, 33,* 359–382.

Simmons, J. (2003). Responders are taught, not born. *Journal of Adolescent & Adult Literacy, 46,* 684–693.

Slavin, R. E. (1991). Synthesis of research on cooperative learning. *Educational Leadership 48*(5), 71–82.

Stevens, R. J., & Slavin, R. E. (1995). Effects of a cooperative learning approach in reading and writing on academically handicapped and nonhandicapped students. *Elementary School Journal, 95,* 241–262.

Sutherland, J. A., & Topping, K. J. (1999). Collaborative creative writing in eight year olds: Comparing cross-ability fixed-role and same-ability reciprocal-role pairing. *Journal of Research in Reading, 22,* 154–179.

Topping, K. J. (1995). *Paired reading, spelling and writing: The handbook for teachers and parents.* New York: Cassell.

Tomlinson, C. A., Moon, T. R., & Callahan, C. M. (1997). Use of cooperative learning at the middle level: Insights from a national survey. *Research in Middle Level Education Quarterly, 20*(4), 37–55.

Wood, D. (1998). *How children think and learn* (2nd ed.). Oxford, UK: Blackwell.

Children's Literature Cited

An, N. (2001). *A step from heaven.* Asheville, NC: Front Street.

Bonsignore, J. (2001). *Stick out your tongue! Fantastic facts, features, and functions of animal and human tongues.* Atlanta, GA: Peachtree.

Christelow, E. (1989). *Five little monkeys jumping on the bed.* New York: Scott, Foresman.

Danziger, P., & Martin, A. M. (1998). *P. S. longer letter later.* New York: Scholastic.

Glover, D. (1998). *Looking at insects.* Barrington, IL: Rigby.

Hesse, K. (1996). *The music of dolphins.* New York: Scholastic.

Hesse, K. (1999). *Out of the dust.* New York: Scholastic.

Park, B. (1992). *Junie B. Jones and the stupid smelly bus.* New York: Random House.

Patterson, K. (1994). *Lyddie.* New York: Puffin.

Ryan, P. M. (1996). *Riding freedom.* New York: Scholastic.

Ryan, P. M. (2000). *Esperanza rising.* New York: Scholastic.

Taylor, M. D. (1983). *Roll of thunder, hear my cry.* New York: Bantam.

Willems, M. (2003). *Don't let the pigeon drive the bus!* New York: Hyperion.

Independent Reading, Writing, and Conferring in the Language Arts Workshop

BIG IDEAS ABOUT INDEPENDENT LEARNING

In the language arts workshop, independent learning provides a time for students to apply skills and strategies practiced during focus lessons, guided instruction, and collaborative learning to their reading and writing. This is not to say that independent learning is done silently and alone, but rather that every student has an opportunity to utilize skills and strategies in their own work. The teacher is an active presence during independent learning, often meeting with individual learners to discuss his or her work.

Questions to Consider

When you have completed this chapter, you should be able to answer these questions:

- What are the goals of independent learning?
- What is the Silent Sustained Reading?
- What is independent reading?
- What is the purpose of independent writing?
- How do teachers confer with students about reading and writing?

Key Vocabulary

Independent work

Conferring

Self-regulation

Competence

Setting goals

Achieving goals

Procedural instruction

Literary instruction

Strategic instruction

Silent Sustained Reading (SSR)

Reader response theory

Efferent

Aesthetic

Independent writing

Emergent writers

Early writers

Transitional writers

Self-extending writers

Author's chair

Publishing

Conferences

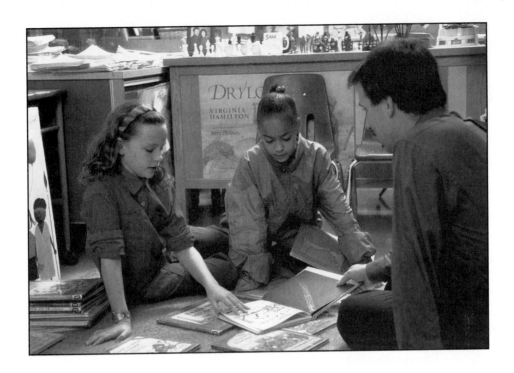

A LOOK INSIDE

Although it is independent reading time in Mrs. Garcia's fourth-grade class, it is far from silent. Several children are clustered in a comfortable corner of the room where rocking chairs and braided rugs offer an inviting space to get lost in a book. Trisha and Leon are looking through a basket in the classroom library labeled "Gold Rush Books" while Kaleem, Sonje, and Melissa are already reading. The pages of their books sprout sticky notes with handwritten notations.

While most of the students are settling into their independent reading, Mrs. Garcia is seated at a small table in another corner of the room. To her left are a binder labeled "Student Reading Conferences" and a stack of observation forms like the one in Figure 5.1. Patrice, a girl with braids and a quick smile, is discussing her book with her teacher.

"Tell me about the book you're reading, Patrice. What has happened so far?" asks Mrs. Garcia.

"It's really good! I'm reading *Seeds of Hope* (Gregory, 2001) and it's about a girl named Susanna who is traveling on a ship to get to Oregon. Her mom died on the ship and her dad lost all their money. Now they're going to go to California because they heard about gold," offers Patrice. This novel, told in diary form, has been a popular choice among many of the boys and girls in the class during the last few weeks.

Figure 5.1   Reading Conference Form

Student Reading Conference

Name: _____   **Date:** _____

Title and Author: _____

Retelling (check all that apply)

❏ discusses important events
opinion

❏ offers salient details

❏ uses text to support retelling

Notes:

❏ states opinion ☐ provides support for

❏ needs prompts to expand answers

Making Connections (check all that apply)

❏ text to self _____

❏ text to text _____

❏ text to world _____

Notes:

Oral Reading Fluency

❏ reads accurately

❏ fluently, in long phrases

❏ choppy, in short phrases

Notes:

❏ word by word

❏ with expression

❏ flat and without expression

Goals for Next Meeting

After asking a few more questions to confirm Patrice's comprehension, Mrs. Garcia asks her to read a passage that was meaningful to her. Patrice chose the journal entry when Susanna's father told her they would be going to California instead of Oregon. While Patrice reads, Mrs. Garcia makes notes about Patrice's reading fluency and her use of expression. Mrs. Garcia then asks Patrice about connections she had made during the reading. Patrice turned to the section of the book about when Susanna's father told her he was going to be a gold miner, not a doctor. "I was thinking about another book I read this year called *Riding Freedom* (Ryan, 1999). Susanna reminds me of Charley in *Riding Freedom* because she has to learn how to rely on herself when her parents aren't there for her anymore."

> This is called a text-to-text connection.

As their reading conference draws to an end, Mrs. Garcia and Patrice develop a goal for Patrice to look for connections to history since they are studying the California Gold Rush in social studies. With that, Patrice leaves the table with her book in hand. Looking back over her shoulder, she remarks, "I'll let you know what happens next!"

From RIDING FREEDOM by Pam Muñoz Ryan. Copyright © 1996 by Pam Muñoz Ryan. Reprinted by permission of Scholastic Inc.

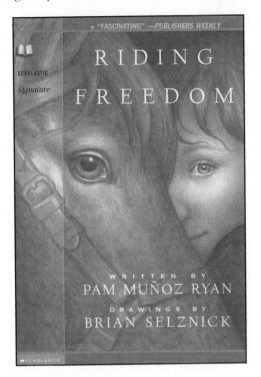

FOSTERING INDEPENDENCE IN THE LANGUAGE ARTS WORKSHOP

A guiding principle of the language arts workshop is that students should achieve a level of independence in utilizing literacy strategies that makes it possible for them to express their own thoughts and ideas, and to understand the thoughts and ideas of others. Marie Clay refers to this as "the high demand from the first days of school for children to read and write texts according to their competencies but always as independently as possible" (2001, p. 48). After all, as educators our intent is to develop a set of skills in each learner that ultimately can be utilized outside the presence of the teacher. The ability of each student to engage in **independent work,** like all aspects of learning, is fostered through explicit instruction.

> Independence in reading and writing is the goal of the language arts workshop.

An important advantage of developing independent learners is that the teacher can then use his or her time to support the efforts of individual students. Within every class there exist some students who need more specialized teacher supports; as well, every student, regardless of achievement level, needs personal contact with the teacher. As busy classroom teachers know, this can only happen on a consistent basis when all the students know how to work independently. A powerful practice for making contact with each student is known as **conferring.** Teachers confer with students through rich conversations about their reading and writing practices.

This chapter focuses on the roles of students and teachers in the independent phase of the language arts workshop. While students work independently to practice the literacy skills and strategies they have been taught during focus lessons, guided instruction, and collaborative learning, teachers are conferring to engage individual learners in important conversations about their learning.

What Are the Goals of Independent Learning?

It seems as if the practice of students working quietly and independently at individual tasks is as old a concept as school itself. Many of us have memories of toiling away at worksheets while the teacher walked up and down the aisles. Rarely were any words exchanged, other than asking questions about a particular aspect of the assignment. When completed, these were turned in to be graded. Rarely did we understand how any of these worksheets connected to our learning. The goal for children instead seemed to be in completing the workbook or pile of dittos.

There are several difficulties associated with this model of independent work. For one, the work completed independently may focus on many repetitions of the same isolated skills, leading to disengagement and boredom (Anderson, Brubaker, Alleman-Brooks, & Duffy, 1985). This is especially true for struggling readers who will sometimes focus on getting the assignment done rather than on the learning intended in its design (Anderson et al., 1985). For example, envision the child who completes a spelling assignment of writing each word ten times by instead writing each letter in a vertical column of ten until the entire word is completed. After completing the list, the student is no closer to remembering how to spell the word than when he or she began. When we talk about independent learning in the language arts workshop, we are not referring to activities like worksheets intended to keep students quiet and occupied. We are also not talking about a "laundry list of activities. . . dioramas, shadow boxes, word jumbles, word searches, and so on" (Harvey & Goudvis, 2000, p. 38). Instead, the independent phase of the workshop is a time for students to practice the new skills and strategies they are learning. Therefore, the goals of independent learning for our students include developing self-regulation skills, increasing competence, and learning to set goals for themselves.

Writing words in a list is an ineffective spelling strategy. For effective spelling instruction, see chapter 7.

Self-regulation. At its best, when independent learning is used as an important part of the gradual release of responsibility, students derive many benefits, both academic and personal (Pearson & Fielding, 1991). For example, in their study of third graders, Stright and Supplee (2002) found that students were more likely to ask for help and monitor their progress during these times, although they were also likely to be more disorganized. Recall that asking for help is seen as a positive in classrooms (Nelson-Le Gall & Glor-Scheib, 1985). Independent work also provides students with opportunities to manage their time, monitor their progress, and solve problems. Good and Brophy (2003) call this **self-regulation** and consider it to be an essential component of the curriculum:

The gradual release of responsibility is an instructional approach that moves from modeling, to guided instruction, to independent practice.

Seeking help is part of the helping curriculum described in chapter 4.

Evidence Based

> Students cannot learn self-regulation and self-control if the teacher does all of the alerting, accountability, and so on. They need to be taught to manage time (we have fifteen minutes to finish a task) and to define their own work and procedures (what is the critical problem—how else might the problem be approached?). This appropriate management necessitates that rules and structures—the scaffolding—be progressively altered to encourage more responsibility for self-control. (p. 137)

When students have daily opportunities to engage in meaningful independent learning, they not only practice literacy skills and strategies, they also develop the ability to regulate and monitor their pace of work and problem-solving skills. At other phases in the language arts workshop, a student's pacing and problem-solving is still shared with the teacher and peers. The independent learning phase is the time students can try to practice these work skills.

Competence. In addition to self-regulation, independent learning gives students a chance to develop a sense of **competence.** Competence is a learner's perception of his or her abilities and an understanding of the effort needed to accomplish a task. While many speak of the importance of self-esteem in the learning process, it is competence that really contributes to a learner's self-esteem (Fearn & Farnan, 2001; White, 1957). It is through a sense of competence that self-esteem is built. In turn, this increases motivation, because we are motivated to do those things we know we do well. When students have the opportunity to explore their own competence through independent learning, they grow in their self-perception of their competence, including (Good & Brophy, 2003):

- *An internal locus of control.* Students learn that effort comes from within and that the quality of the work they do is influenced by their level of effort (Stipek & Weisz, 1981).

- *Attribution to internal, controllable causes.* Students learn that their level of success is a combination of ability and effort, not factors like bad luck (Whitley & Frieze, 1985).

- *An incremental concept of ability.* Students learn that their own learning is developed through activity and is not a fixed and static construct (Dweck, 1999).

Goal setting. A final positive aspect of independent work is that it allows students to gain experience at **setting** and **achieving goals.** Alexander and Jetton (2000, p. 297) describe students as possessing one or more goal orientations that serve to propel or inhibit their learning. These goal orientations are:

- *Performance goals.* Students who view learning through this lens are interested in teacher recognition and good grades. The extrinsic rewards of the task become the goal for completing the work (Dweck & Leggett, 1988).

- *Mastery goals.* Students with this orientation are interested in the content of the task and the opportunity to expand their own knowledge base (Nicholls, 1989).

- *Work-avoidant goals.* Some students are primarily interested in completing the task with the least amount of effort necessary (Meece & Holt, 1993).

Consider how each of these goals relate to your learning.

All students are motivated by a combination of these goals to varying degrees. However, it is important to recognize that all of these exist and that the second, for mastery, should be the most highly developed of all. Therefore, during the independent phase of the language arts workshop, students experience many opportunities to set goals and monitor their progress toward them. In addition, teachers coach students in this process during conferring.

Conferring will be discussed in detail later in this chapter.

What Does Independent Learning Look Like in the Language Arts Workshop?

The independent phase of the language arts workshop comprises the majority of time, up to 40%. During the independent phase, students engage in independent reading and writing while the teacher delivers individual support and meets with students to discuss their literacy practices (conferring). The purpose of the independent phase is for students to practice what they have been learning. Like the collaborative learning phase, students need to be instructed as how to best spend their time extending their own learning through reading and writing.

See the introduction for more information about structuring the workshop time.

The success of independent reading and writing relates directly to the extent that students have been instructed in the "how's and why's" of their tasks. Atwell describes three kinds of instruction that need to occur for students to be successful in the workshop—**procedural, literary,** and **strategic** (1987). A chart of these types of lesson topics appears in Figure 5.2.

Figure 5.2   Focus Lesson Topics for Independent Reading and Writing

Procedural
• Retrieving and replacing materials
• Monitoring the noise level in the class
• Good places in the class to read and write
• Using computers during independent reading and writing
• Using a reading log
• Choosing and abandoning books
• Using a writing journal
• Making notes during reading
• Turning in work
• Asking for help and giving help

Literary
• Story grammar (character, setting, plot, problem/solution)
• Literary devices (simile, metaphor, tone, voice, alliteration, idioms, analogies, foreshadowing, point of view, theme, parallel episodes)
• Plot lines (beginning, conflict, rising action, climax, denouement)
• Types of narrative structures (novels, novellas, poems)
• Types of expository structures (essays, technical, research reports)
• Genres of reading and writing
• Use of dialogue and quotations
• How illustrations are used in picture books
• Main idea and details
• Facts and opinions

Skills and Strategies
• Making predictions
• Drawing inferences
• Figuring out unknown words
• Writing a summary
• Using a graphic organizer with a text
• Visualizing
• Making connections (text to self, text to text, text to world)
• Developing questions
• Self-monitoring comprehension
• Using transition words
• Utilizing conventions
• Notemaking

Procedural instruction. These lessons focus on the management of independent reading and writing time. For example, students need to know how to retrieve and replace books and materials, how to monitor the noise level in the room, and how to get help from the teacher or another peer. These and other procedures ensure that the room runs smoothly during independent time.

Literary instruction. As students move through the emergent and early phases of reading, they learn about the literary devices used in books. This **story grammar** includes characters, setting, problem and solution. The use of simple frameworks like story grammar assist young readers in comprehending the narrative texts they are reading. Older students need to recognize other literary devices used by authors such as simile and metaphor, dialogue and exposition. Students working in this phase of the language arts workshop practice identifying, interpreting, and using the literary devices they have learned about during their focus lessons.

Strategic instruction. In addition to learning about the techniques and frameworks used by good writers to develop engaging text, students also need to develop a metacognitive awareness of what good readers do to support their understanding of a reading. In particular, good readers:

- Enhance their understanding
- Acquire and use their knowledge
- Monitor their understanding
- Develop insight (Harvey & Goudvis, 2000, p. 8)

Likewise, good writers purposefully engage in a number of complex behaviors. Good writers:

- Adhere to the conventions of the language
- Utilize organizational devices
- Employ transitions to enhance the reader's understanding
- Craft sentences and paragraphs that accurately reflect the writer's intentions (Fearn & Farnan, 2001)

In order for students to utilize these tools, they must receive instruction in them and then have many opportunities to practice them. We cannot state this concept too many times—the independent phase of the language arts workshop is not a time for students to engage in "activities" that keep their hands busy and their minds idle. The independent phase is dedicated time to practice, make mistakes, try again, and ultimately master the skills and strategies taught during the shared, guided, and collaborative phases of the workshop.

INDEPENDENT READING IN THE LANGUAGE ARTS WORKSHOP

Independent reading is an especially positive and enjoyable part of the language arts workshop because students have dedicated time to read and try on the strategies they have been learning as a group. Within the independent reading time are two distinctly different reading opportunities. Both of these should be available to students at different times during the week. Each possesses unique goals and purposes. One is independent reading connected to focus lessons and guided instruction. The other is **Sustained Silent Reading (SSR).**

What Is the Effectiveness of Independent Reading and SSR?

The effectiveness of SSR and independent reading are rooted in two concepts—increasing **reading volume** and developing positive reading attitudes.

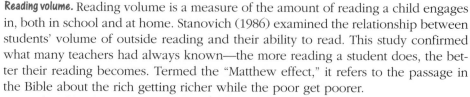

Evidence Based

Reading volume. Reading volume is a measure of the amount of reading a child engages in, both in school and at home. Stanovich (1986) examined the relationship between students' volume of outside reading and their ability to read. This study confirmed what many teachers had always known—the more reading a student does, the better their reading becomes. Termed the "Matthew effect," it refers to the passage in the Bible about the rich getting richer while the poor get poorer.

A related study compared students' standardized test scores in reading and the amount of outside reading they did. Like the earlier study, the results indicated that there was a strong correlation between reading volume and achievement (Anderson, Wilson, & Fielding, 1988). A table of the results can be seen in Figure 5.3. These and similar studies spurred the interest in creating time during the school day when students could read for an extended period of time.

Positive reading attitudes. In addition to the connection between reading and achievement, other studies have demonstrated the importance of positive reading attitudes. Concern over this topic is well-founded because student attitudes toward reading decline through the elementary years, especially among boys (Kush & Watkins, 1996). A large-scale study based on national testing results suggested that students who had positive attitudes toward reading (described as "engaged readers") outperformed older, disengaged readers (Campbell, Voelkl, & Donahue, 1997). An analysis of

Figure 5.3   Relationship Between Achievement and Outside Reading

Percentile Rank	Minutes of reading per day (books)	Words read per year
98	65.0	4,358,000
90	21.1	1,823,000
80	14.2	1,146,000
70	9.6	622,000
60	6.5	432,000
50	4.6	282,000
40	3.2	200,000
30	1.8	106,000
20	0.7	21,000
10	0.1	8,000
2	0.0	0

Source: Adapted from Anderson, R. C., Wilson, P. T., & Fielding, L. G. (1988). Growth in reading and how children spend their time outside of school. *Reading Research Quarterly, 23,* 285–303. Copyright © 1988 by the International Reading Association.

fourth graders' results on the same test revealed that engaged readers from low-income backgrounds outperformed disengaged readers from higher socioeconomic backgrounds (Guthrie, Schafer, & Huang, 2001). These positive attitudes toward reading are developed through:

- Setting learning goals
- Texts that relate to a student's personal experiences
- Support from the teacher on making choices
- Texts with interesting topics
- Instruction in reading strategies
- Opportunities to collaborate with other students
- A positive environment that is not driven by extrinsic rewards
- Evaluation that provides feedback on progress, rather than tests of knowledge
- Personal connections to the teacher
- Cohesive instruction (Guthrie & Wigfield, 2000)

What about the National Reading Panel (NRP) report? Much has been written about the absence of independent reading in the National Reading Panel's report on effective reading instruction. Some have interpreted this to mean that the absence of independent reading in the report is an indication that it should not be used. However, the NRP report states that the studies they reviewed on independent reading were correlation, not causation studies. In other words, the studies examined showed a relationship between good readers and increased time spent reading. However, the studies were not designed to show that independent reading *caused* a rise in achievement. The NRP (2000) went on to explain that they could not recommend independent reading as the only means of reading instruction:

> You can read the National Reading Panel report at www.nationalreadingpanel.org

> It should be made clear that these findings do not negate the positive influence that independent silent reading may have on reading fluency, nor do the findings negate the possibility that wide independent reading significantly influences vocabulary development and reading comprehension. Rather, there are simply not sufficient data from well-designed studies capable of testing questions of causation to substantiate causal claims. The available data do suggest that independent silent reading is not an effective practice when used as the *only* type of reading instruction to develop fluency and other reading skills, particularly with students who have not yet developed critical alphabetic and word reading skills. (p. 13, emphasis added)

We agree that independent reading should not serve as the only means of reading instruction, for the same reason that independent writing cannot serve as the only method for teaching writing. Remember that this book is about purposeful instruction that occurs in a thoughtful manner through focus lessons, guided instruction, and collaborative learning. In this regard, independent reading should be viewed as the time when students increase their reading volume while practicing the skills and strategies taught throughout the language arts workshop. As you will see, these principles of reading volume and motivation are present in Sustained Silent Reading and independent reading, although to differing degrees. First, we will take an in-depth look at SSR, then discuss independent reading.

What Is Sustained Silent Reading?

SSR is time during the day when students have an opportunity to choose books to read for pleasure (McCracken, 1971). No other activities occur during SSR and all students in the class engage in silent reading simultaneously. In addition, the teacher reads for pleasure as well, providing a model of adult reading for the students. These opportunities for reading are called by many names, including Drop Everything and Read (DEAR), Silent Sustained Reading (SSR), Be Excited About Reading (BEAR), Sustained Quiet Reading Time (SQUIRT), and Uninterrupted Sustained Silent Reading (USSR).

What Are the Differences Between SSR and Independent Reading?

There are some differences between SSR and independent reading, although both of them have their place in the language arts workshop. In particular, they differ in their purposes, book selection and access, accountability, and roles of the student and teacher. A summary of these differences can be seen in Figure 5.4.

Goals and purpose. The primary goals of SSR are to develop students' positive attitudes toward reading, especially as a recreational activity, and increase reading volume.

Figure 5.4 Overview of SSR and Independent Reading

	Sustained Silent Reading	Independent Reading
Goals and Purpose	• Reading for pleasure	• Building mastery through practice
Book selection	• Student choice	• Teacher choice and student choice
Book access	• Wide range of genres and levels	• Level and genre chosen to meet individual needs
Accountability	• No records kept	• Logs and reflections are essential
What are students doing?	• Reading quietly	• Reading and writing reflections • Conferring with teacher
What is the teacher doing?	• Brief book talk • Reading quietly	• Conferring with students • Observing • Assessing
Follow-up activity	• Students can volunteer to briefly talk about a book; this is not always a part of an SSR session	• Students spend 20 minutes discussing their reading. The discussion is related to the purpose set at the beginning of the session

On the other hand, the goal of independent reading is to provide time for practice of skills and strategies taught in the workshop.

Book selection. In SSR, the student makes the ultimate decision about what he or she will read. The teacher provides guidance and information about choosing books that are a "good fit," but a child is not discouraged from reading a particular book. In independent reading, the teacher has more influence over what will be read because the text should connect to a particular strategy or skill being taught. In addition, the teacher may consider a student's independent reading level, background knowledge, and interest in selecting a text.

Book access. During independent reading, a narrow range of texts are made available because the purpose is to practice utilizing a skill or strategy. In SSR, students have access to and read a wide range of materials, including nontraditional texts like comic books, magazines, and web-based information.

Accountability. During independent reading, students spend some of their time completing reading logs, graphic organizers, and writing reflections about the reading. In SSR, non-accountability is the hallmark. Students simply read.

Student's role. As stated above, students in SSR read until the end of the time allotted, then transition to the next activity. During independent reading, students may be reading, writing about their reading, or conferring with the teacher about their reading.

Teacher's role. During SSR, the teacher reads to provide an adult model of recreational reading. At times, the teacher may also introduce a new book to students. Linda Gambrell (1989) calls these "blessed books" because the teacher's interest in the book elevates it to a new status in the class. During independent reading, the teacher is conferring with students, assessing and observing while students read.

Follow-up activities. In SSR, students may be invited to share a book they are reading. However, this is never a requirement and students are free to volunteer or not. In independent reading, a sharing phase is included at the end of each reading period. These share sessions are based on the assignment given before independent reading begins. The sharing phase is scheduled for approximately 10–20 minutes.

Information about ways to encourage sharing are presented later in this chapter.

Factors for SSR Success

Janice Pilgreen (2000), a teacher who has designed, implemented, and studied an SSR program that eventually became a schoolwide program, describes eight factors she considers to be essential (2000).

Factor one: Access. Students need a large range and volume of reading materials to choose from. These choices should include books representing many genres, including picture books, chapter books, narrative stories, biographies and autobiographies, realistic and science fiction, and informational texts on a wide variety of topics. In addition, nontraditional texts like magazines, newspapers, graphic novels, and comic books should be available. A list of graphic novels appropriate for school

Figure 5.5 Graphic Novels

Bey, E. (1997). *Still I rise: A cartoon history of African Americans.* New York: W. W. Norton.

Giardino, V. & Johnson, J. [trans.]. (1997). *A Jew in communist Prague: Adolescence.* New York: NBM.

Golnick, L. (2002). *The cartoon history of the universe.* New York: Doubleday.

Kochalka, J. (2003). *Peanut butter and Jeremy.* Alternative Comics.

Medley, L. (2000). *Castle waiting.* Portland, OR: Lucky Roads.

Morrison, T., & Morrison, S. (2003). *Who's got game? The ant or the grasshopper?* New York: Scribner.

Morrison, T., & Morrison, S. (2003). *Who's got game? The lion or the mouse?* New York: Scribner.

Morrison, T., & Morrison, S. (2004). *Who's got game? Poppy or the snake?* New York: Scribner.

Speigelman, A., & Mouly, F. (2000). *Little lit: Folklore and fairy tale funnies.* New York: HarperCollins.

Speigelman, A., & Mouly, F. (2001). *Little lit: Strange stories for strange kids.* New York: HarperCollins.

Speigelman, A., & Mouly, F. (2003). *Little lit: It was a dark and silly night.* New York: HarperCollins.

Winnick, J. (2000). *The adventures of Barry Weins, boy genius.* New York: Henry Holt.

is provided in Figure 5.5. If computers are present, interesting web pages can be bookmarked in advance by the teacher. In order to boost access, texts should represent a wide range of reading levels and some books should be available on tape for students to enjoy.

Factor two: Appeal. Appeal is closely related to access and specifically addresses the notion of what is developmentally appropriate for students. Pilgreen defines appeal as "reading materials [that] are sufficiently interesting and provocative enough for students to want to read them" (2000, p. 9). This is especially important for intermediate and middle school students, whose interest in reading often begins to wane during these years (Kush & Watkins, 1996). As well, the topics of some narrative and expository books may be less desirable for use as a whole class reading; however, these topics are often precisely what students want to read about. Books about difficult subjects can be made available during SSR in order to engage and educate without turning it into an academic exercise. Although some topics may be uncomfortable for teachers to discuss in their classrooms, it is important that students see themselves and realistic portrayals of their lives in the books they read (Leland & Harste, 1999). There are a wide range of sensitively written materials available about topics such as death, divorce, nontraditional families, sexuality, substance abuse, and family violence. Many of these books remain children's favorites despite their limited use in classrooms. A good source for finding favorite books of young people is the Children's Choice List, published every year by the International Reading Association and available at http://www.reading.org. For notable adolescent books, consult the National Council of Teachers of English for the Young Adult Choices, voted on each year by teenagers across the country, at http://www.ncte.org.

Factor three: Conducive environment. Students in SSR don't just read at their desks—they read everywhere. A comfortable corner with pillows and chairs, like the one featured

Figure 5.6 Reading Corner

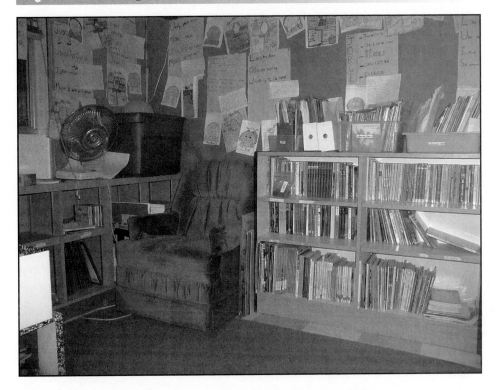

Figure 5.7 Student Expectations for SSR

> ### *Student Expectations During SSR*
>
> 📖 Read for the entire SSR period.
> 📖 Read anything (except textbooks and assigned material).
> 📖 Respectfully share your thoughts and opinions about what you're reading. We all learn from each other.
> 📖 Be respectful of others. This means reading quietly.
> 📖 You may sit or recline wherever you like as long as it does not disturb others.
> 📖 Please don't ask to leave the room at this time—it disturbs others and shortens your opportunity to read for pleasure.

in Figure 5.6, appeals to some students. These cozy places encourage students to curl up with a good book.

Of course, there aren't enough corners to accommodate every child in the classroom. Most students will choose to read at their desks or at tables around the classroom. However, every student needs a classroom that is quiet and has a minimim of interruptions. Some teachers hang a sign on the outside of their door that announces, "Sshh! We're Reading." Others post rules and expectations designed specifically for SSR. Figures 5.7 and 5.8 show two posters used in a seventh-grade classroom.

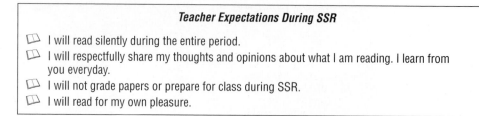

Figure 5.8 Teacher Expectations for SSR

> ### Teacher Expectations During SSR
>
> 📖 I will read silently during the entire period.
> 📖 I will respectfully share my thoughts and opinions about what I am reading. I learn from you everyday.
> 📖 I will not grade papers or prepare for class during SSR.
> 📖 I will read for my own pleasure.

Factor four: Encouragement. Encouragement does not come in the form of extrinsic rewards like points or grades but from opportunities to talk about books with peers and teachers. In most successful SSR programs, teachers and students conduct brief book talks to tell others about books they recommend. In schoolwide SSR efforts, encouragement is also noted in public promotions of reading. For example, at Monroe Clark Middle School in San Diego, the school launched a year-long campaign based on the popular "Got Milk?" advertisements by the National Dairy Council. They called theirs "Got Book?" and created posters of teachers and administrators posing with their favorite reading material.

Public relations campaigns can help remind students of the importance of reading.

Factor five: Staff training. Like all effective instructional practices, SSR efforts are often supported by staff development. Teachers who are introducing SSR to their classrooms can plan procedures, rules, and book rotations between classes. These collegial conversations are also useful for solving problems that may arise and will ensure a smoothly running SSR program.

Factor six: Non-accountability. Although we discussed this earlier, it bears repeating. A key feature of Silent Sustained Reading is that students are not completing logs, writing reflections and book reports, and otherwise doing schoolwork. During the entire SSR session, students read quietly and get lost in their books.

Factor seven: Follow-up activities. During SSR time, follow-up activities are not projects related to the books students are reading. Instead, students can volunteer to discuss their reading, but are not compelled to do so. These conversations typically last three to five minutes and may be partner conversations, small group conversations, or whole class dialogues.

Factor eight: Distributed time to read. SSR programs occur at regularly scheduled intervals, several times a week. In some cases they may happen daily, although this is likely to occur outside of the language arts workshop, after lunch for example. When students anticipate SSR on a regular basis, they fall into the habit of engaging in recreational reading.

Remember, SSR is about developing reading habits.

The look and feel of SSR is influenced by the developmental levels of the class. In kindergarten and first grade, SSR is rarely silent and is sustained for only brief periods of time—perhaps ten minutes or so. Younger children are likely to want more, not less, time to discuss their books after SSR. Let's take a look now at SSR in a sixth-grade classroom during the language arts workshop.

Spotlight on Instruction

Sustained Silent Reading in Sixth Grade

BOOK TALK.

Mr. McCarthy signals the class that the collaborative learning portion of the workshop is nearing an end. "Three minutes until SSR!" his voice booms. Students working in literacy centers wind up their activities and begin to put away their materials. Others rummage through the contents of their backpacks to find their reading materials. Magazines and paperbacks emerge and students eye the most coveted spots in the classroom. However, they are familiar with the routine and wait for Mr. McCarthy to call names. "It looks like Marcella, Marco, Edgar, Jude, and Kathleen have first dibs on the reading corner today," he announces. (This teacher draws names from a set of cards for the reading corner in order to eliminate squabbles.) As the five move to the beanbag chairs and floor pillows, Mr. McCarthy continues. "I wanted to do a book talk today because I just read this great book over the weekend. It's called *Zulu Dog* (Ferreira, 2002) and it's about a boy named Vusi, who lives in South Africa, and a dog he saves from a leopard attack. One of the things I liked about this book was the way the author wrote about when Vusi finds that the burrow where the dog had been living was attacked. Listen to this:

> When his father has gone, Vusi falls to the ground at the entrance by the burrow. The boy stretches his hand down the hole and feels nothing but sand. He wants to cry, but he refuses to give up hope. He pushes his shoulder as far as it will go, trying to reach deeper, imagining his arm is an elastic band as he stretches, stretches, stretches. His fingers scrabble furiously in the dirt at the bottom of the hole, hoping for the touch of warm puppy fur. Nothing. (p. 23)

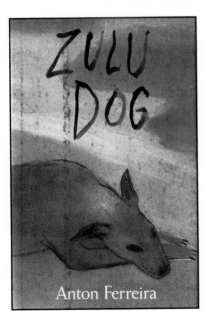

Jacket art © 2002 by Vivienne Flesher from ZULU DOG by Anton Ferreira. Used with the permission of Farrar, Straus and Giroux.

"That's the part that really got me. Anyway, if you like the sound of this book, it'll be over here in the classroom library." Many pairs of eyes follow Mr. McCarthy as he places the book on a shelf. He then pauses to start a CD of instrumental music, a signal that SSR is ready to begin. "You folks know what to do—read quietly, read what you're interested in, and remember, get lost—in a book!" He sets the timer for 20 minutes.

While Mr. McCarthy reads a novel, other students are reading a wide variety of texts. Angela is reading *The Skin I'm In* (Flake, 1998), a novel about an African-American girl with darker skin who struggles to fit into her peer group. Kimberley is reading the inside cover of *Zulu Dog,* and Marco and Edgar, who have been watching the wildfires in California all week, are poring over the illustrations in a large book called *Disaster! Catastrophes That Shook the World* (Bonson & Platt, 1997). Given the current news, they are particularly intrigued by the diagrams of the Great Fire of London. Molly is seated at the computer and is reading an online version of a newspaper from the city she used to live in. After 20 minutes, the timer sounds and students reluctantly close books and shut down computers. Even Mr. McCarthy tries to read one more sentence as he closes his book. "Does anyone want to talk about what they're reading? Any recommendations?" asks the teacher.

Marco and Edgar, who had been enthusiastic about their disaster book, volunteer to give a book talk. "We're reading this cool book about disasters like the *Titanic* and the Black Death," says Marco. "Yeah, today we were looking at the drawings about the Great Fire of London," continues Edgar. "Would you recommend the book? Why?" reminds Mr. McCarthy. "Oh, yeah, the best part about it is the drawings. There's all

(continued)

these little facts in there and you really have to hunt for them," Marco says. "Like how people started killing foreigners while the fire was still going on because they wanted to blame someone. That's just messed up."

After finishing their colorful endorsement of the book, Edgar, Marco, and the rest of the class continue on with their instructional day. In the meantime, Mr. McCarthy has accomplished several important goals for SSR—building positive attitudes toward reading by emphasizing student choice, a supportive environment, access to appealing books, and an atmosphere of encouragement. All in all, a great way to spend 20 minutes.

What Is Independent Reading?

Like SSR, independent reading is built on a foundation of increasing reading volume and positive attitudes toward reading. However, this instructional approach differs in important ways from SSR. Independent reading is part of the gradual release of responsibility as students practice the skills and strategies they have been learning during the shared, guided, and collaborative aspects of the language arts workshop. Lucy Calkins calls this "the most important part of the reading workshop" (2001, p. 68). The teacher is actively engaging with students about their reading. At times, the teacher may be circulating and assisting to provide individual instruction, while at other times he or she is conferring with students about their literacy practices. After the independent reading phase, students participate in a share session to discuss their use of strategies during the reading.

Book Selection

Independent reading level is considered to be 95% or above in accuracy and 90% on comprehension.

Since the independent phase of the workshop is intended to connect to the focus lesson, the teacher is the one who is primarily responsible for selecting the texts to be read. Students also have a voice in choosing books that are of interest to them. Depending on the students' developmental reading levels, books may be selected in one of several ways. However, all books should be at their independent reading level.

Emergent and early readers. These students are reading small books with a limited number of words. Therefore, young children may need access to five or ten of these books at a time. We suggest using guided reading books the students have already mastered. This way, the teacher can be sure that the students know how to read these books. When a child has successfully mastered a book, have them add it to their collection of independent reading books.

These are not the only books students should have access to. The picture books in the classroom library can be grouped in advance in baskets labeled for independent reading. Since emergent and early readers are only beginning to read, the picture books they read should include predictable books like *Polar Bear, Polar Bear, What Do You See?* (Martin & Carle, 2003) and alphabet books like *The City ABC Book* (Milich, 2001). Be sure to set aside specific times for children to "shop" for books so that their independent reading time is not consumed by browsing.

Early readers are ready to use other methods for choosing books. One easy technique is the "five finger method." Students choose a book and turn to a page in the middle. They use the fingers on one hand to keep track of the number of unknown words they encounter on the page. If they have used all five fingers by the end of the page, the book is too difficult.

Transitional and self-extending readers. Students at this stage of development are reading chapter books so the number of books they need in their possession at a given time

Cover from *The City ABC Book* by Zoran Milich is used by permission of Kids Can Press Ltd., Toronto. Cover photographs © 2001 Zoran Milich.

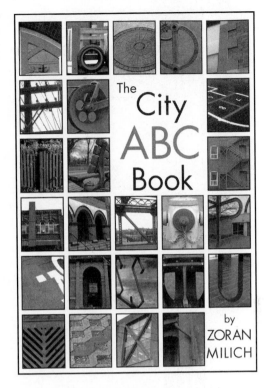

is reduced to two at most. Some teachers use conferring time to help a reader select a new book for independent reading, and this is particularly advisable for transitional readers. Self-extending readers are more likely to be able to select books on their own, although conversations during conferring can reveal difficulties individuals may be experiencing in selecting the "just right" book. Some teachers use Mondays as a "browsing day" to select new books for independent reading.

Organizing Materials

As you can imagine, materials organization can make or break independent reading. If students spend half of the allotted time looking for books, locating sticky notes, and searching for their reading log, the amount of time spent reading is seriously diminished. Many teachers keep a book basket in the center of each table for independent reading. These baskets can usually hold the materials needed for several children. The materials in the basket include:

- A ziplock bag labeled with the child's name to hold independent reading books
- A reading log, also labeled with the child's name
- Bookmarks
- Pencils and pens
- Comment cards (see Figure 5.13)
- Sticky notes
- A reflection journal for each student

Figure 5.9   Ms. Allen's Book Basket

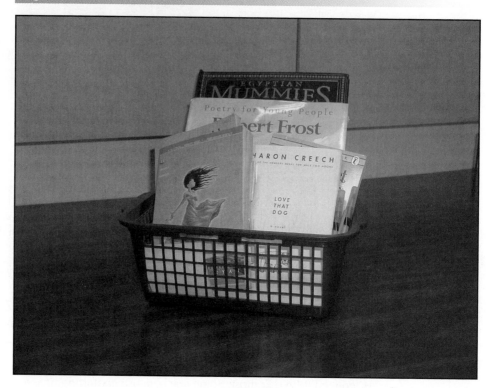

Using baskets like these ensures that, as independent reading begins, all students can readily access their materials and get down to the business of reading. The teacher can also easily check reading logs, journals, and book titles. A photograph of a book basket in Ms. Allen's class appears in Figure 5.9.

What About Students Who Can't Read Independently?

See chapter 4 for more examples of collaborative reading.

Keep in mind that independent reading does not always have to be a solo activity. Some students, due to social, academic, or language differences, may benefit from collaborative reading. Collaborative reading can include partner reading, echo reading, and choral reading with a peer. With emergent and early readers, these partnerships may be the norm on most days, with less truly "independent" reading occurring. For transitional and self-extending readers, collaborative reading may be used to support a student who has trouble reading or when two students want to engage with the same text, as was the case when Marco and Edgar were reading about disasters.

Electronic media can also be utilized during independent reading to provide extra support for students who need it. Books on tape are durable and low cost, particularly when the tapes are made at school. Enlist the aid of parent volunteers, high school students looking for community service hours, or even other students in the class to create tapes of popular books. One teacher we know records his own tapes and includes added instructions like, "Wave to me when we get to the bottom of this

Figure 5.10   Reading Log Template

Title of book	Author	Start date	Finish date	Genre

Students Respond During Independent Reading

page" or "Oh, that's a great word, you better write that down in your journal" as a method for monitoring attention and comprehension.

A goal of independent reading is to provide students with an opportunity to write about thoughts, ideas, and connections. These written responses are usually brief in nature and can be structured using a variety of tools to organize their thoughts. We have included several samples of these tools at the end of this chapter to provide you with samples of reading logs and comment cards for a range of grade levels.

Reading logs. Nearly all teachers want students to keep track of the books they have read during independent reading, and nearly all students need a way to organize that information. Reading logs are best kept simple, as you want to avoid student responses which are primarily clerical. A simple reading log appears in Figure 5.10. Students can easily reproduce this in a spiral notebook kept for independent reading.

Emergent and early readers need a simpler format for keeping track of their reading. The example in Figure 5.11 is more appropriate for students who are still mastering writing. This reading log can be stored on a clipboard for ease of writing.

During book talks and other discussions, many students hear about titles they would like to read in the future. Encourage students to keep a list of books they are interested in. The list in Figure 5.12 will help them when they are ready to select a new book for independent reading.

Comment cards. Students use these simple note-taking frameworks to jot down thoughts and ideas related to the strategies and skills they are practicing. These can

| Figure 5.11 | Reading Log for Younger Readers |

Name _____

Title	Author	Did you like it?
		☺ ☺ ☹
		☺ ☺ ☹
		☺ ☺ ☹
		☺ ☺ ☹
		☺ ☺ ☹
		☺ ☺ ☹
		☺ ☺ ☹
		☺ ☺ ☹

be duplicated and placed in the book baskets so they are easily accessible. A sample comment card appears in Figure 5.13. For example, when Ms. Allen taught about foreshadowing in her focus lesson, she asked her fifth graders to look for evidence of foreshadowing during independent reading. Jeremy reviewed the previous chapters he had already read and wrote several notes on his comment card about *Frindle* (Clements, 1996) (see Figure 5.14).

From *Frindle* by Andrew Clements, cover illustration by Brian Selznick, © 1996 by Simon & Schuster. Used by permission of Simon & Schuster.

Sticky notes. As students become more adept at making notes as they are reading, they can move from comment cards to sticky notes. These small notes can be positioned to "underline" important passages students encounter. A challenge of using sticky notes is teaching students how to use them with an economy of words. Learners who have been accustomed to writing on 8½″ × 11″ sheets of paper may attempt to crowd too many words onto these small notes. Like all new strategies, students should be instructed on how to use the notes through focus lessons. It is useful for them to have a bank of simple notations available to abbreviate thoughts while still preserving meaning. A bookmark of reader's notations appears in Figure 5.15 and can be duplicated on sturdy tag paper for durability. Teachers can cut colored transparency sheets (available at most office supply stories) to simulate sticky notes, then write on them using the reader's notations during shared readings displayed on the overhead projector.

Reflection journals. Independent readers not only read for meaning, they also reflect on and discuss their readings with others. In order to support their discussions, students need to make notes and write down their thoughts and observations. The purpose for reading should be es-

Figure 5.12   Book Interest List

Title	Author	What it's about	Where I heard about it

Figure 5.13   Comment Cards

Comment Card	*Comment Card*	*Comment Card*
During today's reading, I am looking for:	During today's reading, I am looking for:	During today's reading, I am looking for:
I found examples on:	**I found examples on:**	**I found examples on:**
Pg. _____	Pg. _____	Pg. _____
Pg. _____	Pg. _____	Pg. _____
Pg. _____	Pg. _____	Pg. _____
Pg. _____	Pg. _____	Pg. _____

tablished at the beginning of the independent phase of the language arts workshop, with appropriate instruction about what to look for in the reading. Many teachers find that instructing students to begin each session on a new page (complete with date, title, and page numbers) is helpful for keeping students organized. The content of these reflection journals is used during class discussions; these journals are also read by the

Figure 5.14   Jeremy's Comment Card

Comment Card
During today's reading, I am looking for:
foreshadowing
I found examples on:
Pg.___1___   Was Nick a trouble-maker?   Hard to say.
Pg.___8___   Mrs. Granger didn't just enjoy the dictionary. She *loved* the dictionary— almost worshipped it.
Pg.___12___   It was still a week before school and Nick already felt like fifth grade was going to be a very long year.
Pg.___

Figure 5.15   Reader's Notations

Reader's Notations Use these marks to make your notations easier to write and read!	
Π	connection, leads to
√	cause and effect
re	in reference to
i.e.	that is
e.g.	for example
=	equal; is
≈	approximately equal
≠	not equal; not
←pg. #	connects to another page
Def.?	unknown word to look up
W/	with
W/O	without
&	and

teacher. These response journal entries can contain myriad topics, but generally can be categorized into one of three broad areas: *looking for evidence, writing about reading,* and *personal responses.* Students can divide their response journals into these categories and write responses based on the purpose for the lesson.

Looking for evidence. These response journal entries focus on the author's craft and how language is used to convey meaning. Topics suitable for the evidence portion of the journal include vocabulary, analyzing text, and the ways language and its conventions are used. A partial list of topics for this type of response can be found in Figure 5.16.

Writing about reading. When students write about reading, they focus on the strategies they use as readers to support their own comprehension. These strategies include visualization, inferencing, making personal, textual, and historical connections, and synthesizing information. A suggested list of topics for writing about reading appears in Figure 5.17.

These comprehension strategies will be examined more closely in chapter 10.

Personal responses. Readers make meaning at the word level through understanding the vocabulary, and at the sentence and paragraph level by understanding how ideas are crafted by the author to tell a story or forward a position on a topic. Readers also

Figure 5.16   Looking for Evidence Response Journal Topics

🔍	***Looking for Evidence***
Vocabulary	• Unfamiliar words • Predicting word meanings • Using resources to locate new words
Analyzing text	• Story grammar (character, setting, plot, problem/solution) • Literary devices (simile, metaphor, tone, voice, alliteration, idioms, analogies, foreshadowing, point of view, theme, parallel episodes) • Plot lines (beginning, conflict, rising action, climax, denouement) • Types of narrative structures (novels, novellas, poems) • Types of expository structures (essays, technical, research reports) • Genres of reading and writing • Use of dialogue and quotations • How illustrations are used in picture books • Main idea and details • Facts and opinions
Language and conventions	• Word choice • Punctuation • Using text features (table of contents, glossary, index, captions, diagrams) • Non-fiction conventions

make meaning through their own personal response to the text. As they read, they consider their own personal experiences to make judgments about the text—"This reminds me of the time . . . " They activate their background knowledge to determine the veracity of the text—"Could this happen?" Finally, they analyze the text for its usefulness to them—"Is this interesting to me?" The words on the page do not simply lie there waiting to be consumed without analysis by the reader. Instead, there is a transaction between the text and the reader that makes each relationship unique. This is why, for example, one person can love a book while another considers it a complete waste of time. Those transactions form the basis for **reader response theory** (Rosenblatt, 1938/1995).

Reader response theory suggests that reading experiences can be described as a balance between **efferent** (information-seeking) and **aesthetic** (emotional) responses. It is important to note that one is not more valued than another, but rather that each reading experience can be represented on a continuum of these two responses. For example, a reader's response to Robert Frost's poem "Stopping By Woods on a Snowy Evening" may be primarily aesthetic as the reader enjoys how Frost crafts his words and meter. However, there is still likely to be an efferent component as the reader constructs understanding about the woods. At the other extreme, a reader's response to the book *How Animals Shed Their Skin* (Tatham, 2002) may be primarily efferent as they look for information about leopard frogs. Even then, there is likely to be an aesthetic response as well when they view the weird and wonderful animals in the photographs. Although these terms are not necessary to teach students (we shudder at the thought of a second grader offering, "I would

Figure 5.17	Writing About Reading Response Journal Topics

	Writing About Reading
Predictions	• Developing questions • Activating background knowledge • Writing and checking predictions • Determining author's purpose
Connections	• Text-to-self • Text-to-text • Text-to-world • Text-to-history
Inferences	• Looking for clues • Interpreting illustrations • Interpreting titles • Analyzing dialogue • Considering background knowledge
Visualization	• Looking for sensory words • Sketch-to-stretch (drawing) • Wordless picture books • Analyzing diagrams
Synthesis	• Determining author's message • Big ideas • Changing your opinion based on new information • Summarizing content • Compare and contrast two ideas

like to make an aesthetic response to *Madeline*") it is important that students have many opportunities to explore their personal responses about the material they are reading. This insight builds their metacognitive skills as they become conscious of their learning and serves as a critical component in self-monitoring comprehension.

Personal responses in journals can also serve as the seed for ideas to be further explored in independent writing. When teachers meet with students to confer, they read journal entries together to discuss writing that can be expanded into more polished pieces (Calkins, 2001). These personal responses can be organized around personal connections, developing opinions, and extensions. A partial list of topics that tap into a reader's transaction with a text can be found in Figure 5.18.

Students Share Their Reflections   The end of independent reading is signaled by the share session (Hagerty, 1992). This is time devoted to discussing the work students did during their reading. These sessions can be done collaboratively in small groups or as a whole class. Share sessions typically last 10 to 20 minutes to allow students to move beyond superficial comments to richer observations about the text, their use of strategies, and their personal responses. For children in grades K–2, share sessions are typically shorter in duration and conducted as a whole group.

Figure 5.18   Personal Response Topics

	Personal Responses
Personal connections	• Illustrate the story • This reminds me of . . . • A time in my life • Author study
Developing opinions	• What do you think about the book? • Book review • Favorite character • Favorite part • Believability • Authenticity • Accuracy • Author bias • Literary critiques
Extensions	• What do you want to know next? • What do you think happens after the book ends? • What information was left out of the book?

Oral language development is the focus of chapter 6.

Time to share offers numerous benefits for readers. First, it is useful for oral language development at both the social and content levels. For English language learners, it is an occasion to engage in academic language. Share sessions also provide opportunities for students to hone listening skills, particularly when they are encouraged to make connections to peers' comments, rather than directing their conversations to the teacher. Share sessions are critical for students to clarify their understanding of a text or strategy, ask questions, and formulate opinions. Hagerty explains that share sessions offer benefits for students and teachers:

Benefits for students:

- Validates their ideas
- Gives them an opportunity to express what they've learned
- Encourages positive feeback from others
- Provides them with an avenue for connecting their prior knowledge and experience with the text
- Gives them an opportunity to go beyond the literal retell level to a more in-depth analysis

Benefits for teachers:

- Provides a systematic way to observe and evaluate student interaction
- Gives an authentic setting for assessment
- Helps the teacher become aware of strategies individual students use as readers

- Provides an integration for all components of literacy (reading, writing, speaking, and listening)
- Strengthens community (Hagerty, 1992, p. 32)

As students become more adept at large group shares, they can begin sharing in small groups. As with all aspects of the language arts workshop, it should never be assumed that students know *how* to participate in rich discussions. Therefore, these should be explicitly taught so that students can begin to take on these discourse skills for themselves.

For young children, this instruction can be conducted through a focus lesson on what good discussions look like, sound like, and feel like. A language chart like the one in Figure 5.19 can be developed and then posted to refer to when the discussion gets off track.

> These skills are also useful when students work in literature circles.

Role of the Teacher in Share Sessions

The teacher is the facilitator of the discussions that occur after independent reading. This means that teachers need to have a few questions prepared in advance in order to move the conversation. These questions should be directly related to the focus lesson and independent reading. For example, a third-grade teacher's focus lesson centered on how the author used vivid language in *Harvesting Hope: The Story of Cesar Chavez* (Krull, 2003). During independent reading, students continued to read the picture book and made notes on their comment cards when they found evidence of vivid language. When independent reading was finished, the teacher invited discussion about examples of vivid language in the book. Students offered their observations and furnished evidence using the notes on their comment cards. Meanwhile, the teacher charted their responses on a language chart. By preparing questions in advance, the teacher ensures that the arc of the lesson that began with the shared reading is seen through to completion after the independent reading.

Questions can be used more creatively as well. "Secret questions" can be written on index cards and given to individual students in order to seed the conversation (Calkins, 1994). If some students rarely participate in share sessions, the teacher can

Figure 5.19   Language Chart for Share Sessions

What Are Good Share Sessions?		
Looks like	**Sounds like**	**Feels like**
• Heads are nodding • People are interested • People are leaning forward • There is eye contact • People are taking turns	• One person is speaking • A "busy buzz" • Questions and answers • Appropriate disagreement • People reading and learning	• I am important • What I have to say is important • What I think matters • I can help others figure things out

Source: Adapted from Vogt, MaryEllen. (1996). Creating a response-centered curriculum with literature discussion groups. In L. B. Gambrell & J. F. Almasi (Eds.), *Lively discussions! Fostering engaged reading* (pp. 181–193). Newark, DE: International Reading Association. Reprinted with permission of MaryEllen Vogt and the International Reading Association.

prepare several "talking passes" to distribute in advance. By doing this, students who receive the card know they will be guaranteed an opportunity to talk (Hagerty, 1992). Let's take a look now at a share session in a first-grade classroom.

Figure 5.20	Sequence Stories for First Grade

First Grade Sequence Stories for Independent Reading
Carle, E. (1995). *The very hungry caterpillar.* New York: Penguin.
Cristolow, E. (1998). *Five little monkeys jumping on the bed.* New York: Houghton Mifflin.
Keats, E. J. (1999). *Over in the meadow.* New York: Puffin.
Numeroff, L. J. (2002). *If you take a mouse to school.* New York: HarperCollins.
Van Rynbach, I. (Illus.). (1995). *Five little pumpkins.* Honesdale, PA: Boyds Mill Press.
Wood, A. (1984). *The napping house.* San Diego: Harcourt Brace.

Spotlight on Instruction

Independent Reading and Share in First Grade

It is early October and the six-year-olds in Mr. Targas's first-grade classroom have been reading sequence stories to understand how an author can tell a tale that builds on the action. During the focus lesson, Mr. Targas used *Joseph Had a Little Overcoat* (Tayback, 1999) to chart the sequence of events that occurred as Joseph's coat became more worn and was converted into a jacket, vest, tie, patch, and button. During collaborative reading, students worked in small groups to create similar charts for *There Was an Old Lady Who Swallowed a Fly* (Tayback, 1997).

The children in this class are still learning about independent reading. During the past few weeks, they have had other focus lessons on responding to books and creating alternative versions of the stories they have read. Now Mr. Targas is easing students into independent reading by creating a lesson that is likely to be completed successfully by every student in the class. This teacher understands that when students are learning a new strategy, the complexity of the content should be reduced so that they can concentrate their efforts on the task itself.

After multiple experiences with sequenced texts, students were ready to read and discuss other texts during independent reading. Mr. Targas created a book box of similar stories for students to select. Because he has a wide range of independent reading levels in his class he made certain to select books that would be useful for all students. His list of books can be seen in Figure 5.20.

During independent reading students selected titles from the box to create their own sequence chart. After reading the book the first time, they completed a page of notes in their reading journals using a format similar to the one seen in Figure 5.21. While students worked, Mr. Targas met with individual students to confer about their work and offered support for others who needed clarification about their reading. After 30 minutes, he signaled the class using a rain stick he keeps for such occasions. Mr. Targas believes that the gentle sound of the rain stick is better suited for transitions from quiet work periods like independent reading and writing.

Teacher Tip

When students have finished reading and responding, they begin the share phase of the language arts workshop. Earlier, while students read, Mr. Targas distributed four "share passes" to students so they would

(continued)

be guaranteed a time to talk (see Figure 5.22). The students use these passes when they choose. "Remember to use your journals because that's where you have some of your good ideas written down. We're going to start by talking about the books you read. We paid attention to the sequences in our stories today, so let's start there. Who would like to begin?"

Over the next 10 minutes, the class discusses the plots of the stories and the sequences used. Stephanie remarks that her book, *The Napping House* (Wood, 1984), reminded her of the time the ceiling fan fell down in the living room one night and woke everyone in the house. Although making this kind of connection was not part of the independent reading assignment, Mr. Targas knows that the notes students gather are only a starting point, and he is pleased to support discussion that takes a different direction.

Figure 5.21   Reading Journal Format for Sequence Stories

Title of book: _____   **Author:** _____

This book was about

The best part of this book was

One way the author could change this book is

Here's what happened in the story (use pictures and words)

1	2	3
4	5	6

Figure 5.22   Share Pass for a First-Grade Classroom

Share Pass
It's your turn to share your ideas with us today.
We can't wait!

INDEPENDENT WRITING IN THE LANGUAGE ARTS WORKSHOP

Independent writing is a time for students to apply the skills and strategies learned during focus lessons, guided instruction, and collaborative learning.

What Is Independent Writing?

Like independent reading, this phase of the language arts workshop is intended to give students a chance to write and discuss their writing with others. **Independent writing** is a time when students "just write" but it should always be with a purpose. Perhaps a good way to explain the features of independent writing is to first discuss what it is *not*.

Independent writing is not. . .

- Writing to prompts
- Reader responses to books
- Everyone writing the same thing at the same time

Independent writing is. . .

- A chance to find out how other authors compose
- Practice under the guidance of a teacher
- The work of every writer

Characteristics of Writing Genres

Students are taught the characteristics of writing genres so they can use these elements in their own writing. Skillful use of these elements allows the writer to convey ideas in a way that is understood by the intended audience. Figure 5.23 contains a summary of common features of several genres.

Summary. Summaries are a brief restatement of a text's main ideas. Summaries should not contain extended quotes or borrow the author's original words. Summaries should be much shorter than the original, by at least 60% if not more. Additionally, summaries should identify the original source and demonstrate a student's understanding of a text's subject matter. Students are often taught to write summaries using a strategy called GIST, or Generating Interaction between Schemata and Text (Cunningham, 1982). Instruction using the GIST strategy teaches students to chunk the text into sections then write a single summary sentence to capture the "gist" of the passage. The sentences are assembled in order to create a summary of the original text.

Chapter 10 contains an example of GIST for teaching summary writing.

Report of information. A factual report conveys information or observations, often generically referred to as an essay. The purpose of this type of writing is to inform, not to persuade or react, and is commonly used in science and social studies contexts. Students must learn not to interject themselves or their opinions into this type of writing and instead use credible sources to support the facts they present. Typically, a report of information has a common structure that includes an opening paragraph that explains to readers what they will find in the paper, the body of the paper organized to lead readers through the information, and a conclusion in which information is summarized. In other words, the report of information provides a forum for writers to report the information they have analyzed, summarize conclusions they have drawn from the information, consider alternatives to the information presented, and make a series of recommendations based on the information. Reports

Figure 5.23   Features of Common Writing Genres

Genre	Features	What students need to be able to do
Summary	Brief restatement of a text's main ideas	• Use original language • Do not exceed 60% of length of text
Report of information	Factual report containing information or observations	• Use multiple sources • Refrain from expressing opinions • Use an introduction, body, and conclusion
Response to literature	Interpret a reading based on personal connections, literary devices used by the author	• Make judgments and support claims • Make connections to self, other texts, and the world
Autobiography or biography	Factual account of their lives or the lives of others	• Document sources • Anticipate the reader's questions
Technical	Instructions, memos, e-mails, minutes of meetings	• Identify sequence accurately • Consider pertinent variables • Use correct format for document
Persuasive	Seeks to convince a reader about the validity of a position or action	• Define a position • Offer supporting evidence • Address concerns of the reader

Content area instruction means social studies, science, math, art, etc.

of information can be taught in the language arts workshop and during content area instruction. Regardless of when the report of information is taught, it should be modeled, and students should be provided examples of good essays.

Response to literature. From the time children enter school, effective teachers encourage them to respond to what they have read. At the earliest stages of reading, teachers ask their students what they liked or did not like about a particular story. To learn how to respond to literature, students need opportunities to talk about books and share their ideas with others. Written responses to literature are a natural extension of these discussions about a book and provide students with an opportunity to consider and react to a reading. Of course they need to use appropriate literary terms as well as understand how to discuss and critique literature.

Chapter 6 provides a number of oral language development activities for responding to literature.

Young readers also need their teachers to model responses to literature. As Rosenblatt (1995) and Probst (2003) note, understanding one's response to literature is ultimately a transaction between the reader and the text. This theory suggests that meaning is not found in the text alone, but in the interaction that occurs between the reader and the reading. Thus, the reader's experiences, background knowledge, and opinions flavor the meaning derived from the words on the page. For example, it is likely that a child's response to *The Wall* (Bunting, 1990), a picture book about a family's visit to the Vietnam Memorial in Washington, DC, is likely to be different from other classmates if her own family lost a relative in the war.

It is the teacher, Rosenblatt (1938/1995) maintains, that influences how students learn to interact and transact with literature. As Martinez and Roser (1991) state

Research suggests the powerful effect of the teachers' modeling of response to literature on the subsequent responses of young children. There is evidence that responders (expert and naïve) in the same setting tend to react in the same ways toward text. The teacher who conjectures, connects, appreciates, muses, challenges and questions aloud shows the child how the mature responder interacts with text. By modeling these responses both during and after the reading of stories, the teacher encourages children's active participation. (p. 652)

Teachers accomplish this in a number of ways in the language arts workshop. For example, you'll note the use of a "think aloud" strategy in chapter 10. When teachers share their thinking with students, especially thinking in real time as they read, students begin to grasp the various ways in which they can respond to texts. Further, teachers use a writing prompt called RAFT (Santa & Havens, 1995) to focus students on different perspectives in writing their responses. RAFT is an acronym for Role, Audience, Format, and Topic. As you will see in chapter 10, RAFTs are used to teach students to write for different audiences and to write from different perspectives in different forms.

As students get older and are more skilled writers, they will be asked to produce papers in which they analyze a piece of literature or a poem. Typically their writing is guided by a series of questions, such as:

Information on RAFTs also appears in chapter 4.

- What happened in the story?
- What point do you think the author is making in the story?
- Do you think the story mirrors real life?

To respond to these types of questions, students need experience writing these responses, talking about literature, and receiving feedback. Of course, all of these things can happen in the language arts workshop!

Biography and autobiography. Students are also expected to write factual accounts of their lives and the lives of others. In our experience, students particularly like this genre. They enjoy reading about others and take pleasure in writing about themselves and people they find interesting.

The key to writing good biographies and autobiographies is in questioning. Teaching students to create quality questions up front will ensure that they have interesting things to write about. In addition, they need to collect enough information to tell a good story about the person. They should learn to document their sources and use descriptive language to capture the readers' interest.

As Fearn and Farnan (2001) note, learning to write biographies and autobiographies can start with students constructing autobiographical incidents. Using this approach, students do not write complete biographies, but instead collect a series of feelings, events, memories, or other interesting things that happen to them. Fearn and Farnan advocate that students record these autobiographical incidents several times per week. We suggest that these events be recorded during independent time in the language arts workshop. Periodically, students can be asked to re-read their collected incidents and write a themed paper that analyzes some events for a longer text. These can be discussed and edited during collaborative learning time and students can receive feedback during guided instruction or conferences.

Technical. Another type of writing students are expected to do is generically known as technical writing. Once the sole responsibility of colleges, teachers today are expected to provide students instruction in this genre. Technical writing ranges from technical reports and manuals to e-mail and memos. The challenge in technical writing is to express complex ideas simply. This could involve students writing the process for making a peanut butter and jelly sandwich or instructions for using a software program on a computer. Regardless, the goal is that the reader understands the instructions or information and can complete the associated tasks.

Fearn and Farnan (2001) suggest that technical writing begin with short, simple, and clear sentences. They note that students can rewrite sentences in which the directions are unclear as they develop their sense of technical writing. We suggest that students have regular assignments in which they use technical writing. For example, students can write memos to one another to inform or persuade; they can write the instructions for learning centers that are used during collaborative learning; they can write instruction manuals for things in the classroom; and they can write business letters after field trips, to thank donors, and to request materials or books.

Persuasive. In persuasive writing, students must try to convince others to agree with the facts as they present them, share values that are outlined, accept specific arguments and conclusions, or adopt a way of thinking. This type of writing is often regarded as the most difficult for students to master. They must commit to a line of reasoning and not introduce new topics within the paper. In addition, they need to demonstrate clear thinking through convincing arguments, and support those statements with ample, credible evidence. At the end of the piece, they must summarize their logic and thinking in a conclusion.

The language arts workshop structure is useful for teaching students to write in this genre. During focus lessons, you can introduce the format and style by sharing the persuasive writing of others. During guided instruction, you can question students about their facts and the ways in which they have shared their ideas. During collaborative learning, students can provide their peers with feedback on their writing. Finally, during independent learning, students can revise their papers and complete the tasks.

Purpose of Independent Writing

While independent writing is notable for what it is not, the purposes of creating this dedicated time are very clear. These purposes can be organized in three categories.

Learning effective writing habits. Students who learn effective habits of writing will increase the efficiency and quality of their writing. Young writers need experience at how to organize materials, how to utilize reference materials to support content, and the skills needed to get the ideas down on paper.

Kinds of writing and resulting genres. Good writers know how to move from ideas to words, sentences, and paragraphs. The less adept writer will be frustrated with his or her inability to transmit ideas to the reader. The craft of writing includes word choice, perspective, and matching techniques to genres.

Conventions and language usage. Selecting the correct genre of writing to fit a purpose goes hand in hand with the conventions associated with clear writing. Good writers use punctuation, spelling, and grammatical structures to ensure that readers understand their message.

See chapter 1 for more information on writing processes.

The process of writing. Good writers understand that there is a process to writing and that their awareness of the process can facilitate writing. While we do not advocate for a strictly sequential approach to writing that moves students through a lockstep system, it is useful for students to learn that some general techniques are commonly used by writers.

- *Prewriting* is formulating ideas that may or may not be utilized in a later writing piece; sometimes referred to as *brainstorming*.
- *Drafting* is the first commitment of these ideas to paper.
- *Revising* is revisiting the draft to add, delete, or change what has been written.
- *Editing* is done as the written piece is approaching its final form. The draft is ready for corrections and feedback on content from the teacher or peers.
- *Publishing* is sharing the final form of the piece with others.

If these purposes sound familiar, they should. In chapter 2 we identified purposes of language as a communication tool and described three elements of oral language development: habits, kinds of talk and resulting genres, and language use and conventions (National Center on Education and the Economy, 2001). Like speaking, writing is a form of communication and these elements are useful in describing effective writing practices.

Teaching the Elements of Independent Writing

Like independent reading, these elements are first taught during focus lessons and guided instruction. Students continue to practice them during collaborative writing experiences with peers. The independent writing phase is a time to consolidate these elements to produce cohesive writing. All of the elements (habits, genre, conventions, and process) are utilized by the writer as they create thoughtful pieces.

Developmental Writing

The types of writing students engage in are influenced by developmental levels and purposes for writing. These developmental levels can be described as **emergent, early, transitional,** and **self-extending.** Certain types of independent writing activities are associated with these developmental phases. An overview of these phases and types of writing can be found in Figure 5.24.

See chapter 7 on spelling for more discussion on emergent writing.

Emergent writers. Students who are in the emergent stage of writing are experimenting with the concept that print carries a message. These students are combining both experimental knowledge of spelling and a growing understanding of how language works. The work of emergent writers is likely to be heavily reliant on drawings as well as writing. Emergent writers are encouraged to write for social communication, to explain what they know about a topic, and to retell their experiences. In the language arts workshop, emergent readers spend their time writing:

- Messages to other classmates (e.g., notes to be placed in the class mailbox)
- Lists (e.g., ingredients for a peanut butter and jelly sandwich)

✏	Behaviors	Types of writing for these writers
Emergent	• Print carries a message • Uses writing and drawing • Invented spelling • 1:1 correspondence between spoken and printed words simple messages of 1 or 2 sentences	• Messages to other classmates • Lists • Labels and signs • News about themselves • Retelling an event that happened in school
Early	• Spelling with beginning/ending sounds, some vowels • Strings sentences together • Beginnings and endings of stories • Simple dictionaries used	• Selects topics of their own choosing • Brief original stories and story innovations • Short texts about informational topics • Letters, invitations, and postcards • Notes to family, self • Personal accounts • Poems • Scripts • Explanations • Summaries • Recipes
Transitional	• Uses most spelling and punctuation conventionally • Multi-paragraph pieces are more cohesive • Distinguishes between features of genres • Compound sentences • Expanded word choice • Uses reference materials	• Writing in multiple genres • Author studies to examine the craft of writing • Dialogue • Rules and procedures for a variety of activities to practice technical writing • Persuasive pieces to support a position • Business letters • Informational reports • Essays • Compare/contrast
Self-extending	• Flexibly operates between genres • Seeks peer and teacher feedback and integrates it into their writing • Recognizes value of using wide variety of sources • Punctuation, word usage, and grammatical structures are accurate and innovative • Writer's individual voice and style is apparent • Utilizes writing as a means for clarifying their own thinking	• Research papers • Adopting author styles • Poems • Plays • Newspapers • Technical reports • Desktop publishing • Persuasive essays • Letters to the editor • Memoirs • Developing WebQuests

- News about themselves (e.g., their birthday party)
- Retelling an event that happened in school (e.g., watching the caterpillars in the class science center spin a cocoon)

Early writers. Students who have moved to the early phase of writing (typically sometime during first or second grade) are using many more of the conventions of writing, especially spelling and simple punctuation. Their writing is likely to be more discernable to other readers and will often contain strings of sentences that are being crafted into paragraphs.

These writers are recognizable by their new levels of independence as well. Early writers are selecting their own topics, engaging in some self-editing, and beginning to experiment with more writing genres, especially story telling ones. They are beginning to consult outside sources of information to include in their writing, especially expository texts, simple dictionaries, and word walls. In addition to the types of writing listed for emergent writers in the language arts workshop, early writers spend their time:

> Early writers will often begin all their stories with "Once upon a time . . ."

- Selecting topics of their own choosing
- Writing brief original stories and story innovations (e.g., projecting themselves into fairy tales)
- Creating short texts about informational topics (e.g., "My Book About Lizards")

Transitional writers. Students in the transitional phase of writing are engaged in using a wide range of genres in their writing. They can write short informational reports using academic vocabulary, create multi-paragraph essays on personal experiences, and construct original poems. Their writing can be recognized by more regular spelling and grammatical structures, and use of compound sentences. Although this phase, like the others, is not strictly bound by grade level, many transitional writers emerge between grades 3–5. These transitional writers are more cognizant of the processes associated with writing and are revising more of their work based on feedback from peers and the teacher, although this is more likely to be at the sentence and paragraph level rather than the document level. They are becoming more sophisticated in their use of multiple sources of information to support their own writing. Transitional writers in the language arts workshop spend their time:

- Writing in multiple genres (e.g., poetry, informational reports, narratives)
- Engaging in author studies to examine the craft of writing (e.g., Lemony Snicket author study on the use of irony)
- Writing rules and procedures for a variety of activities to practice technical writing (e.g., directions for how to travel from school to the student's home)
- Persuasive pieces to support a position (e.g., why I should have a pet)

Some transitional writers have difficulty in moving away from formulaic writing. Although we do not require that students respond to prompts during independent writing, we have found that some students benefit from using a new structure to extend their writing. One simple structure for transitional writers is the Writer's Digest structure (www.writersdigest.com). The student begins by writing a 5 word sentence to introduce the piece. Next, the writer uses each word in the sentence as the beginning word in five consecutive paragraphs of a story. For example, the sentence "Cats make the best pets" leads the first paragraph. The second paragraph begins with "make" while the third paragraph starts with "the." This pattern can be repeated as many times as needed to tell the tale; we are not suggesting that all stories contain five paragraphs.

Self-extending writers. Students in this phase of writing are notable for their ability to select the appropriate genre to match the task. They are learning to organize their ideas for longer pieces so that the plot moves well (narrative) or the information is described in a logical manner (expository). Increasingly complex sentences are seen in the writing and word choice becomes more precise. Self-extending writers work toward two ideals: conciseness and precision. Their ability to edit is more sophisticated and they are more likely to reread their writing and retool sentences or sections to more clearly support subsequent text. Self-extending writers in the language arts workshop:

- Operate flexibly between genres (i.e., they can develop multiple forms of writing during the same day)
- Seek peer and teacher feedback and integrate it into their writing
- Recognize the value of using a wide variety of sources to develop their writing and seek original sources, not just those provided by the teacher
- Use accurate and innovative punctuation, word usage, and grammatical structures
- Demonstrate an individual voice and style
- Utilize writing as a means for clarifying their own thinking

Organizing Materials

The availability of certain materials in the classroom can assist students in their independent writing. These materials range from writing implements and supplies to resource materials. Figure 5.25 contains a list of materials useful for independent writing. Because many of these items are redundant (paper, writing implements), we have listed items to add to your classroom as students develop as writers.

What About Students Who Can't Write Independently?

Review chapter 1 for a discussion of accommodations and modifications.

Visit aacintervention.com for more information about innovative technology for classroom use.

Due to language, cognitive, or physical differences, a student may not be able to write independently in the same way as the other students in the class. When faced with this challenge, some teachers mistakenly exclude the student from the activity, rather than making accommodations or modifications to the task that would allow the student to participate. Remember that accommodations are changes to *how* the student demonstrates mastery, while modifications are changes to *what* they master. Alternatives to traditional independent writing can include:

- Composing into a tape recorder
- Using voice recognition software like Write OutLoud (www.donjohston.com)
- Using translation software
- Composing with picture symbol systems like Boardmaker (www.mayer-johnson.com)

Figure 5.25 Materials for Independent Writing

✎ Materials for Independent Writing ✎		
Emergent	Paper (lined and unlined) Markers Pens Pencils Envelopes, "stamps" Wordless books	Rubber letter stamps Stamp pad Name chart Mailbox Word wall of sight words ABC books
Early	Easy dictionaries Word wall of high-frequency words Easy readers Editing checklist Trade books	Folders Correction tape Scissors Rulers Scratch paper Stapler and remover
Transitional	Dictionaries Thesauri Rhyming dictionaries Word wall of common misspellings	Editing checklist Maps Software with grammer and spelling checks
Self-extending	Vocabulary word wall Bookmarked web sites Reference materials	Editing checklist Style manuals

- Organizing ideas with Kidspiration software (www.inspiration.com)
- Using a personal dictionary with thematic or high-frequency words

Students Share Their Independent Writing

See chapter 4 for tips about using peer feedback in your classroom.

The share portion of independent writing differs from independent reading in that this segment (10–20 minutes) is used primarily for peer feedback. However, there are times when a writer may be ready for a public reading of a completed work. This is sometimes referred to as the **author's chair.** Other pieces may be bound into a more permanent form, called **publishing.** In both cases, the writer has an opportunity to share his or her writing with members of the class. Lucy Calkins calls this "the beginning of a writerly life" (1994, p. 261).

Author's chair. For some types of writing, a public performance of the finished product represents the natural culmination of the writing experience or task. Many teachers set aside a day, perhaps once a month, when writers can share their completed works with the class. Some teachers make a ceremony out of it, right down to the use of a specially labeled chair. Younger writers are often eager to share their writing; older students may be more reluctant. When one of the authors was teaching poetry writing to fourth graders, many of the students were self-conscious about standing in front of the class. This problem was solved by introducing the practice of "Beat Poetry." Young poets donned dark sunglasses and a beret to affect the look of a 1950's beat poet. After reading their work, the audience would respond by snapping fingers and saying, "Cool, daddio!" Before long, the students had relaxed and could perform without the accoutrements.

Middle school students may be even less likely to stand in front of the class to read their writing. The purpose of author's chair is to engage the writer in the act of sharing his or her work; it makes little difference whether it is an audience of 1 or 35. Knowing that her students open up more in small groups, a teacher we know holds "Literacy Lounge" one Friday a month. She arranges the tables in the room in small groups and covers them with a tablecloth and centerpiece. Hot chocolate and shortbread cookies are served while writers meet in groups of four to discuss their writing. By making the setting pleasant and non-threatening, this teacher lowers students' affective filters while promoting exchange of ideas within her class (Krashen, 1982).

Teacher Tip

The affective filter is influenced by self-confidence and anxiety and can interfere with learning.

Publishing. In addition to sharing finished work in the author's chair, some pieces may be suitable for publication in a more permanent form. These are then made avail-

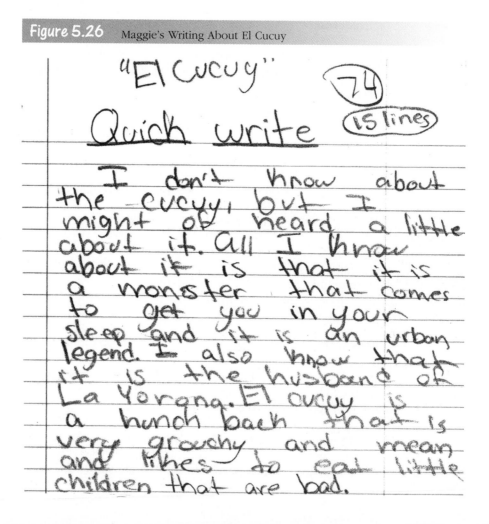

Figure 5.26   Maggie's Writing About El Cucuy

"El Cucuy"

Quick write   74   15 lines

I don't know about the cucuy, but I might of heard a little about it. All I know about it is that it is a monster that comes to get you in your sleep and it is an urban legend. I also know that it is the husband of La Yorona. El cucuy is a hunch back that is very grouchy and mean and likes to eat little children that are bad.

able in the classroom and can be read by other students and visitors. Here are some ideas for publishing works in your classroom.

- *Elements of a finished work.* These may include a cover, dedication page, table of contents, about the author page, and index.
- *Word processing.* Once the work is finished, some students like the look of computer print for their book. If appropriate, the student can also illustrate these pages.
- *Bound copies.* Many schools have binding machines for making sturdy books for publishing.
- *Class books and anthologies.* Works of poetry, recipes, and other short pieces based on similar themes can be gathered together to create a class book.
- *Web-based publishing.* There are a number of companies that will reproduce a book for classroom use. The finished product is on glossy paper with a hardback cover.

Spotlight on Instruction

Independent Writing in Fifth Grade

Ms. Allen promotes the use of independent writing throughout the day. Her goal is to have students engaged in writing as a means to clarify their understanding about a topic, as a tool for personal expression, and to support dialogue between students. At times, independent writing is a brief event meant to tap into each student's prior knowledge about a topic. For example, Ms. Allen posted this question on the board one morning: *"Who is el Cucuy?"* The students in this fifth-grade biliteracy class are fluent in both Spanish and English so she expected that some, but not all, would recognize the name of the Mexican folklore figure. Maggie was unsure about El Cucuy but seemed to tap into forgotten knowledge as she progressed in her writing. She also made a connection to La Llorona, another scary folktale character (see Figure 5.26).

Romel made a much more personal connection to this question and elaborated on personal experience as he recalled the stories his mother told him when he was younger (see Figure 5.27).

Later, during a read aloud focused on the genre of folktales and legends, Ms. Allen read the book *El Cucuy* (Hayes, 2003) in both English and Spanish and students discussed how this story related to other folktales around the world, especially the Bogeyman, who hides under the bed and snatches disobedient children who refuse to go to sleep.

At other times, Ms. Allen uses independent writing as a means for promoting dialogue between students. During one of these times,

El Cucuy: A Bogeyman Cuento in English and Spanish, by Joe Hayes, illustrated by Honorio Robledo. Published by Cinco Puntos Press, www.cincopuntos.com

(continued)

Mariah composed a brief essay about her vision of her future. She discussed her desire to become a nature photographer and used this writing in a small group peer editing session with another classmate in Figure 5.28.

In independent writing, some pieces continue to be developed and eventually evolve into other written text. Mariah's writing about photography evolved into a portion of an autobiographical essay. She later shared this with other classmates in the Author's Chair (see Figure 5.29).

Ms. Allen recognizes that independent writing is done for a variety of purposes. Writers in her language arts workshop write to clarify their understanding, to discuss ideas with classmates, and in some cases to develop more sophisticated pieces. At all times, they use a process of writing that is interactive and dynamic.

Figure 5.27 Romel's Writing About El Cucuy

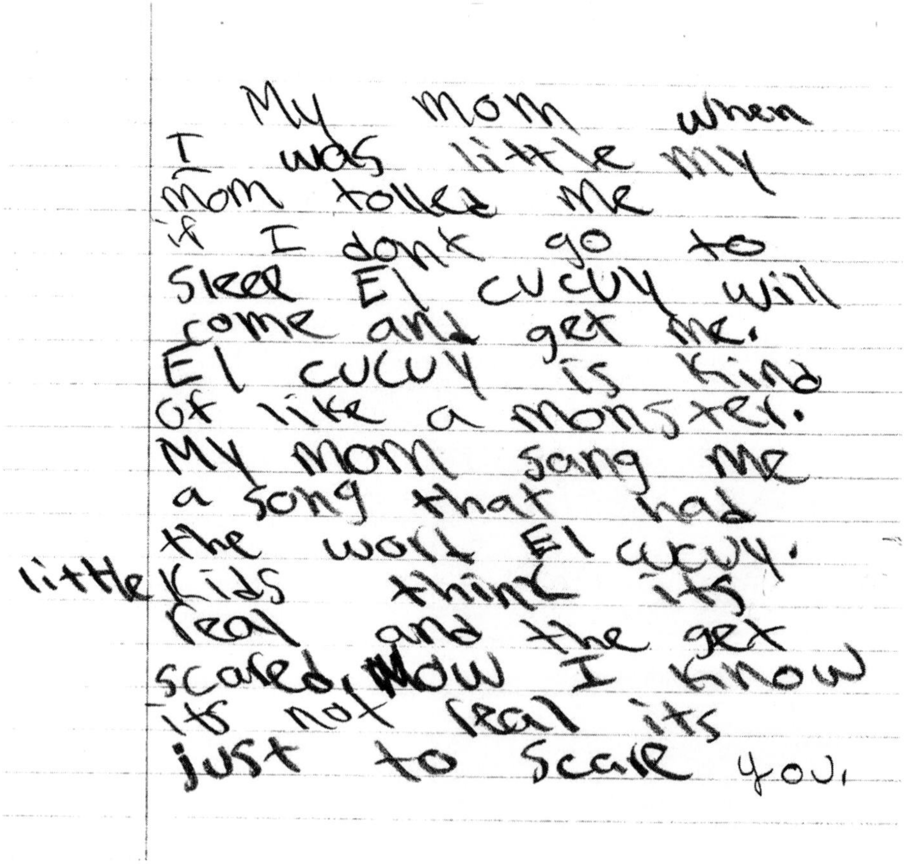
My mom when
I was little my
mom tolled me
if I dont go to
sleep El cucuy will
come and get me.
El cucuy is kind
of like a monster.
My mom sang me
a song that had
the worl El cucuy.
little kids think its
real and the get
scared. Now I know
its not real its
just to scare you.

Figure 5.28   Mariah's Writing About Photography

<u>4th</u>   Mariah

Daily Writing

The way I picture myself when I grow up is I want to be a photographer that takes pictures of nature! A, I'm a fan of photography because its all in the past, or sometimes at the museums I see pictures of old dinasour bones.

Nature is mostly what I want to take pictures of. Valcanoes are cool. Maybe, when I'm older, I can travel to Hawaii and take pictures of valcanoes over there.

Figure 5.29   Excerpt from Mariah's Autobiographical Essay

Mariah

Hi, my name is Mariah I'm 10 years old I was born on may 1993. I am the first child of my parents Alma and Louis Fox. I enjoy fruits and vegetables exept onions and radish. All of my friends love to play with ma and think I am very pretty . I broke a kids nose once when I was 4 years old, to find out what happened to me next keep on reading!, or else.

When I was in preschool there was these three boys who always followed me around. so one day this boy named Christian was teazing me and I ignored him, so he took my headband right off my head and ran. of course I was mad ran after him. once I caught up to him I grabbed the headband and socked him right in the nose , and broke it.

A photographer is what I want to be. Photographers seem like they are very peaceful people. photographers also get to travel and get to relax and take pictures of nature. The first thing that comes to my mind when I see myself older is my hand about to push the button on a camera, facing a mountain. I want to be a photographer because thats just what I want to be, plus it sounds like fun and thats what I am.

CONFERRING IN THE LANGUAGE ARTS WORKSHOP

Because students are reading or writing independently, the teacher can use some of this time to meet individually with students. This conversation is called conferring and provides the teacher with an excellent assessment opportunity.

What Is Conferring?

Conferring is a time when the teacher meets with individual students to discuss their independent reading and writing. These meetings, or **conferences,** allow the teacher to gauge the progress of each student, clarify information, and provide feedback for next steps in students' reading and writing. In addition, teachers keep records of these conversations for later reflection about individual student progress. These conferences are brief in nature (5 minutes or so) because lengthier instruction should be reserved for the guided instruction portion of the language arts workshop. Teachers usually average between three and five student conferences per independent reading/writing session.

Effective conferences, whether they are for reading or writing, contain four elements. Because each conference event is short, these happen very quickly. When conferring, the student and teacher use the child's work as evidence. The teacher focuses on only one or two points during a single session. A helpful sequence for a conference is as follows:

- *Inquiry.* The teacher begins by conversing with the student about his or her work. The goal is to assess the student on one literacy focus topic per session.
- *Decisions.* Based on the evidence culled from the opening conversation, the teacher rapidly makes a decision about what should be taught next.
- *Instruction.* The teacher provides a minute or two of procedural, literary, or strategic instruction to help the student move to the next level of independent work.
- *Recordkeeping.* The teacher makes anecdotal notes about the main points of the conference.

These notes will be consulted again later for further instructional and evaluative decisions. It is not uncommon for teachers to customize their conferring forms to meet the unique needs of their classrooms. A basic format for a conference appears in Figures 5.30 and 5.31. The first (Figure 5.30) is an overview form so the teacher can glance at it to ensure all students are conferring on a regular basis. The second (Figure 5.31) is to record the details of an individual conference.

Some teachers hold conferences at a desk designated for this use; others move about the classroom with a notebook in hand, conferring at the student's desk. There are advantages and disadvantages to each approach. On the one hand, the teacher's desk offers a quieter location and an easier way to manage recordkeeping. However, it does keep the teacher stationary and less able to manage behavior in the classroom.

Teacher Tip

Figure 5.30   Overview Form for Conferences

		Class Record for Conferences			
Name	**Date**	**Type of conference**	**Topic discussed**	**Next meeting**	**Purpose of next meeting**

Types of Conferences:
RC—reading conference
WC—writing conference
O—other (specify)

Figure 5.31   Individual Conference Form

Reading/Writing Conference Record Form

Name: _____   Type of Conference: _____

Teacher: _____

Date	Inquiry	Decisions	Instruction	Recordkeeping

Roaming conferences allow for on-the-spot behavior management but can be more difficult to organize papers. In either case, we suggest a binder for conferring.

Organizing teacher materials. It is helpful to divide a three-ring binder into sections for each child to use during conferring. Doing so allows the teacher to keep the following information in each student's section:

- Current assessment information, including informal reading inventories or running records
- A record of conferences
- Reading log of book titles
- Blank paper
- Sticky notes for reminders about following up

Asking effective questions. The challenge of an effective conference is to ask questions that are specific enough to yield useful information without making the question so narrow that the student is constricted in his or her response. Questions should be open-ended to allow for student response while leading the student toward an eventual goal or objective.

More information on questioning can be found in chapter 10 on comprehension.

What Comprises a Reading Conference?

The goal of a reading conference is to engage a student in a conversation about the book he or she is reading. The purpose of the conference is determined by the teacher and student together because the conversation should be a give and take of questions and ideas. However, there are several suggested topics a reading conference may focus on. In any case, the student and teacher should use both the book and reading journal during the conversation. The scenario at the beginning of this chapter is a reading conference. Useful topics for a reading conference include:

- Listen to the student read aloud
- Discuss something in the story
- Ask the student if there is something he or she didn't understand
- Refer to the focus lesson taught that day
- Discuss the content of the book
- Discuss the writer's craft
- Review the student's list of books read (Figure 5.10) or his list of reading interests (Figure 5.12)
- Together set goals
- Discuss recent journal entries (Fountas & Pinnell, 2001, p. 139)

Spotlight on Instruction

Writing Conference in Fifth Grade

The students in Ms. Allen's class have been developing an autobiographical essay during independent writing. She is conducting a writing conference with Artemio about the status of his essay. She begins by having him read a favorite part. His draft can be seen in Figure 5.32. He reads, "In 10 years I could see myself being in 12th grade. I could see myself being a 12th grader because I'm smart, I'm intelegent, and a nice guy. I could also see myself been a Driving Intrudctror. I hope I have an excellent life."

Invite writers to read aloud from their writing.

Although Artemio has made a few spelling and grammatical errors, Ms. Allen does not begin with that topic. She makes a few notes about these details, then asks him, "What do you want help with today?" Artemio replies that he had read his essay to another classmate who told him she was confused by the second paragraph. "I'm not sure how to fix it, though," he offers. "How about if I read it to you and you can just listen to see what it's missing?" says the teacher. She then reads the paragraph while Artemio listens. "Is that what you meant to tell the reader?" she asks.

Take anecdotal notes.

Ask what kind of assistance the writer needs.

"Well, I was trying to tell them about when my grandma and grandpa had another wedding because they had been married for like 50 years. We all went to the wedding and it was fun. It seems kind of confusing, though," replies Artemio.

The teacher and student then spend the next few minutes creating a list of details he wants to include about the wedding. "When a writer has to share a series of ideas, they write a list so they don't forget anything," Ms. Allen replies. When Artemio leaves the conference, he will rewrite this paragraph. Once completed, he will ask Angelica, his peer editor, to see if the message is clearer.

Show the writer how to do something.

Help the writer set a goal.

"I'll see you soon, Artie," says the teacher as she sends him off to his desk. "I can't wait to hear what happened at that wedding!"

Figure 5.32   Artemio's Autobiographical Essay

Artemio

Autobiography

"Hi!" My name is Artemio! I'm a funny guy! You can call me Arty. In my house they call me JR. I was born on May 29, 1993. My hobby is to play soccer. I was born on San Diego. My favorite food is pizza. I had been with Mrs. Allen two years. Sometimes in my house I'm doldrum I'm going to share something that has changed my life.

When I was seven my grama and my grampa were married I'll never forget because thats along time ago and their were my whole family. I love my family I'll never forget because my family was togethe and I didn't worry because we didn't have any problem.

In ten years I could see myself being in 12th grade. I could see myself been a 12th grader because I'm smart, I'm intelegent, and a nice guy. I also could see myself been a Driving Intructor. I hope I have an excelent life.

What Comprises a Writing Conference? The goals of a writing conference, as stated above, are to find out more about the writer, help them decide what they will do next, teach a strategy that will help them accomplish this, and record anecdotal notes for later reflection. Fountas and Pinnell describe eight possible things a teacher can do during a writing conference:

- Listen to the student read the writing aloud
- Find out what kinds of help the writer wants
- Talk with students about specific aspects of his or her writing
- Find the "gems" in a student's writing and show them
- Reinforce the writer's strengths
- Show the writer how to do something
- Review the writer's notebook or completed draft
- Set writing goals (2001, p. 79)

BIG IDEAS ABOUT INDEPENDENT READING AND WRITING AND CONFERRING

Independent reading is time during the language arts workshop when students get to practice using the strategies they have been using during other parts of the instructional day. One type of independent reading is Silent Sustained Reading (SSR). The main purpose of SSR is to increase reading volume through dedicated time for reading books of the student's choice. Choice is a hallmark of SSR and is considered an important factor in developing positive motivation and attitude toward reading. The teacher also reads and models joy of reading.

During other times, independent reading takes on more structure through teacher direction. A focus lesson introduces the purpose and may include procedural, literary, or strategic lessons. Typically, students read a book that has been selected by the teacher because it features opportunities for the reader to utilize the strategies they have been learning. Students may respond in a reading log or journal and then use these notes to participate in a share session with other students.

Independent writing is a time when students are provided an opportunity to apply the skills they have been learning to create original texts. Students write for a variety of purposes and have a voice in the choice of topics and in making editing decisions. The type of writing a student engages in is influenced by the developmental level of the student and the purpose for writing. Emergent writers need many opportunities to write to themselves and their classmates both through text and pictures. Early writers are eager to practice their growing knowledge of the ways words work and how stories are created. Transitional writers use multiple sources of information to influence their writing and utilize techniques for writing to improve the message. Self-extending writers are flexible in their ability to create many genres of text. They use writing as a tool for clarifying their own understanding of a concept or idea.

Teachers and students confer about independent reading and writing. The goal of these conferences is to engage the student in an individual conversation about their work. A useful sequence for teachers to utilize during a conference is to first inquire, then make decisions about the immediate needs of the student. Next, provide brief instruction about the procedural, literacy, or strategic skill to be taught. Be sure to note important details of the conference for next time and end the session with a goal that the student can accomplish.

INTEGRATING THE STANDARDS

Create lesson plans that meet your state's standards by visiting our Companion Website at www.prenhall.com/frey. There you'll find lessons created to meet the NCTE/IRA Standards. Adapt them to meet the standards of your own state through links to your state's standards, and keep them in the online portfolio. You can collect lesson plans for each chapter in an online portfolio, providing you with invaluable tools to meet your state's standards when you head into your own classroom.

CHECK YOUR UNDERSTANDING

1. What are the goals of independent learning?
2. What is the Silent Sustained Reading?
3. What is independent reading?
4. What is the purpose of independent writing?
5. How do teachers confer with students about reading and writing?

CLASSROOM CONNECTIONS

1. With your teacher, discuss how independent work is used in the classroom. What does your teacher feel are the necessary skills students need to be taught in order to work independently?
2. With permission from your teacher, establish an SSR program in your classroom. Develop a schedule for SSR, rules and procedures, and a series of focus lessons to teach your students how to successfully engage in SSR.
3. Develop a folder of professional materials for each of the following: Independent Reading, Independent Writing, and Conferring. Ask your teacher for copies of good tools he or she uses for these instructional strategies. File these copies for your own future classroom practice.

References

Alexander, P. A., & Jetton, T. L. (2000). Learning from text: A multidimensional and developmental perspective. In M. L. Kamil, P. B. Mosenthal, P. D. Pearson, & R. Barr (Eds.), *Handbook of reading research* (Vol. III, pp. 285–310). Mahwah, NJ: Erlbaum.

Anderson, L., Brubaker, N., Alleman-Brooks, J., & Duffy, G. (1985). A qualitative study of seatwork in first-grade classrooms. *Elementary School Journal, 86,* 123–140.

Anderson, R. C., Wilson, P. T., & Fielding, L. G. (1988). Growth in reading and how children spend their time outside school. *Reading Research Quarterly, 23,* 285–303.

Atwell, N. (1987). *In the middle: Writing, reading, and learning with adolescents.* Upper Montclair, NJ: Boynton/Cook.

Calkins, L. M. (1994). *The art of teaching writing: New edition.* Portsmouth, NH: Heinemann.

Calkins, L. M. (2001). *The art of teaching reading.* New York: Longman.

Campbell, Jay R., Voelkl, K. E., & Donahue, P. L. (1997). *NAEP 1996 trends in academic progress.* (Report No. NCES-97-986). Princeton, NJ: National Assessment of Educational Progress. (ERIC Document Reproduction Service No. ED411327)

Clay, M. M. (2001). *Change over time in children's literacy development.* Portsmouth, NH: Heinemann.

Cunningham, J. (1982). Generating interactions between schemata and text. In J. A. Niles & L. A. Harris (Eds.), *New inquiries in reading research and instruction* (pp. 42–47). Washington, DC: National Reading Conference.

Dweck, C. S. (1999). *Self-theories: Their role in motivation, personality, and development.* Philadelphia, PA: Psychology Press.

Dweck, C. S., & Leggett, E. L. (1988). A social-cognitive approach to motivation and personality. *Psychological Review, 95,* 256–273.

Fearn, L., & Farnan, N. (2001). *Interactions: Teaching writing and the language arts.* Boston: Houghton Mifflin.

Gambrell, L. B. (1989). The importance of being a reading mentor, model, and motivator. *The California Reader, 23,* 9–11.

Good, T. L., & Brophy, J. E. (2003). *Looking in classrooms* (9th ed.). Boston: Allyn & Bacon.

Guthrie, J. T., & Schafer, W. D., & Huang, C. (2001). Benefits of opportunity to read and balanced instruction on the NAEP. *Journal of Educational Research, 94,* 145–162.

Guthrie, J. T., & Wigfield, A. (2000). Engagement and motivation in reading. In M. L. Kamil, P. B. Mosenthal, P. D. Pearson, & R. Barr (Eds.), *Handbook of reading research* (Vol. III, pp. 403–424). Mahwah, NJ: Erlbaum.

Hagerty, P. (1992). *Readers' workshop: Real reading.* New York: Scholastic.

Harvey, S., & Goudvis, S. (2000). *Strategies that work: Teaching comprehension to enhance understanding.* York, ME: Stenhouse.

Krashen, S. D. (1982). *Principles and practice in second language acquisition.* New York: Pergamon.

Kush, J. C., & Watkins, M. W. (1996). Long-term stability of children's attitudes toward reading. *Journal of Educational Research, 89,* 315–319.

Leland, C., & Harste, J. (1999). Is this appropriate for children? Books that bring realistic social issues into the classroom. *Practically Primary, 4*(3), 4–6.

Martinez, M. G., & Roser, N. L. (1991). Children's responses to literature. In J. Flood, J. M. Jensen, D. Lapp, & J. R. Squire (Eds.), *Handbook of research on teaching the English language arts* (pp. 643–654). New York: Macmillan.

McCracken, R. A. (1971). Initiating sustained silent reading. *Journal of Reading, 14,* 521–524, 582–583.

Meece, J. L., & Holt, K. (1993). A pattern analysis of students' achievement goals. *Journal of Educational Psychology, 85,* 582–590.

National Center on Education and the Economy. (2001). *Speaking and listening for preschool through third grade.* Pittsburgh, PA: Author.

National Reading Panel. (2000). *Teaching children to read: An evidence-based assessment of the scientific research literature on reading and its implications for reading instruction.* Washington, DC: National Institute of Child Health and Human Development.

Nelson-Le Gall, S., & Glor-Scheib, S. (1985). Help seeking in elementary classrooms: An observational study. *Contemporary Educational Psychology, 10,* 58–71.

Nicholls, J. G. (1989). *The competitive ethos and democratic education.* Cambridge, MA: Harvard University Press.

Pearson, P. D., & Fielding, L. (1991). Comprehension instruction. In R. Barr, M. L. Kamil, P. Mosenthal, & P. D. Pearson (Eds.), *Handbook of reading research* (Vol. II, pp. 815–860). Mahwah, NJ: Erlbaum.

Pilgreen, J. L. (2000). *The SSR handbook: How to organize and manage a sustained silent reading program.* Portsmouth, NH: Boynton/Cook.

Probst, R. E. (2003). Response to literature. In J. Flood, D. Lapp, J. R. Squire, & J. M. Jensen (Eds.), *Handbook of research on teaching the English language arts* (2nd ed.) (pp. 814–824). Mahwah: NJ: Lawrence Erlbaum Associates.

Rosenblatt, L. M. (1938/1995). *Literature as exploration.* New York: Modern Language Association.

Santa, C., & Havens, L. (1995). *Creating independence through student-owned strategies: Project CRISS.* Dubuque, IA: Kendall-Hunt.

Stanovich, K. E. (1986). Matthew effects in reading: Some consequences of individual differences in the acquisition of literacy. *Reading Research Quarterly, 21,* 360–407.

Stipek, D., & Weisz, J. (1981). Perceived personal control and academic achievement. *Review of Educational Research, 51,* 101–137.

Stright, A. D., & Supplee, L. H. (2002). Children's self-regulatory behaviors during teacher-directed, seat-work, and small-group instructional contexts, *Journal of Educational Research, 95,* 235–246.

Vogt, M. E. (1996). Creating a response-centered curriculum with literature discussion groups. In L. B. Gambrell & J. F. Almasi (Eds.), *Lively discussions! Fostering engaged reading.* Newark, DE: International Reading Association.

White, R. (1957). Adler and the future of ego psychology. *Journal of Individual Psychology, 13,* 112–124.

Whitley, B. E., & Frieze, I. H. (1985). Children's causal attributions for success and failure in achievement settings: A meta-analysis. *Journal of Educational Psychology, 77,* 608–616.

Children's Literature Cited

Bemelmans, L. (1939). *Madeline.* New York: Penguin.

Bonson, R., & Platt, R. (1997). *Disaster! Catastrophes that shook the world.* New York: DK Publishing.

Bunting, E. (1990). *The Wall.* New York: Clarion.

Clements, A. (1996). *Frindle.* New York: Aladdin.

Ferreira, A. (2002). *Zulu dog.* New York: Frances Foster.

Flake, S. G. (1998). *The skin I'm in.* New York: Hyperion.

Frost, R. (1957). Stopping by woods on a snowy evening. In H. Ferris (Ed.), *Favorite poems: Old and new* (p. 67). New York: Doubleday.

Gregory, K. (2001). *Seeds of hope: The gold rush diary of Susanna Fairchild (Dear America).* New York: Scholastic.

Hayes, J. (2003). *El cucuy: A bogeyman cuenio in English and Spanish.* El Paso, TX: Cinco Puntos Press.

Krull K. (2003). *Harvesting hope: The story of Cesor Chavez.* San Diego, CA: Harcourt.

Martin, B., Jr., & Carle, E. (2003). *Panda bear, panda bear, what do you see?* New York: Henry Holt.

Milich, Z. (2001). *The city ABC book.* Tonawanda, NY: Kids Can Press.

Ryan, P. M. (1999). *Riding freedom*. New York: Scholastic.

Snicket, L. (2001). *A box of unfortunate events: The trouble begins*. New York: HarperCollins.

Tatham, B. (2002). *How animals shed their skin*. New York: Franklin Watts.

Tayback, S. (1997). *There was an old lady who swallowed a fly*. New York: Viking.

Tayback, S. (1999). *Joseph had a little overcoat*. New York: Viking.

Wood, A. (1984). *The napping house*. San Diego, CA: Harcourt Brace.

6

Speaking and Listening in the Language Arts Workshop

BIG IDEAS ABOUT SPEAKING AND LISTENING

There is significant evidence that oral language is an important component of the language arts workshop and the overall development of literacy for students (Pinnell & Jaggar, 2003). Fearn and Farnan (2001) maintain that the only way to teach children to read and write is through interactions between the language arts. The New Standards Project said it even more clearly, namely that "Speaking and listening are to reading and writing what walking is to running" (National Center on Education and the Economy, 2001, p. i).

Questions to Consider

When you have finished reading this chapter, you should be able to answer these questions:

- What are the relationships between speaking, listening, reading, and writing?
- What interaction skills do students use?
- What are effective questioning habits?
- What is accountable talk?

Key Vocabulary

Language registers

Classroom discourse

Initiate-Respond-Evaluate (I-R-E)

Oral language

Accountable talk

Think-Pair-Share

Read-Write-Pair-Share

Storytelling

Shared writing

K-W-L

Oral cloze

Discussion web

ReQuest

Intertextuality

Jigsaw

Table topics

Oral composition

Group retelling

Tableau

Author's chair

Extemporaneous speaking

———— ❧ ————

A LOOK INSIDE

More information on
discussion webs is
presented later in this
chapter.

"The secret is to give them something to talk about. There's nothing adolescents like
better than a good controversy" says eighth-grade teacher Mr. Alvarez. He values the
role of oral language development in developing critical thinking skills for use in
reading and writing. He begins by distributing a discussion web to foster meaningful conversation (Alvermann, 1991). This graphic organizer features a question in the
center of the page: "Is the fast food industry responsible for the super-sizing of Americans?" Although some are eager to answer immediately, he reminds them to first
write responses supporting both a "yes" and "no" position in the columns labeled
on the discussion web. As they write he leans in to quietly assist Carmelita with
spelling a word she is stuck on, then prompts Andrew to be sure to add items to the
"no" side of his web.

After a few minutes, Mr. Alvarez opens the question for discussion. Greg offers
that Americans are getting fatter and Carmelita concurs, citing a news report she
heard on television a few nights earlier. Elizabeth takes a different tact, explaining
that in her opinion, people are responsible for their own health and no one is making them eat more food. Luz mentions a news story she heard on the radio about a
man suing McDonald's because he was overweight. "It sounds like we have some

pretty strong opinions but need more facts. Let's take a look at this reading for some more information," instructs Mr. Alvarez. With that, he offers a reading outlining some of the issues surrounding this controversy. "I want you to read it for the purpose of collecting information both in support of the fast food industry's position as well as nutritionists'. When you notice an issue, jot it down on your discussion web."

As students read, Mr. Alvarez moves quietly around the table, occasionally asking a student to read aloud quietly so he can listen to them. He observes students making notes on the reading and the discussion web and watches for signs of completion. "Now we've got some more facts! Let's try to answer that question again. Is the fast food industry responsible for the super-sizing of Americans?" asks Mr. Alvarez.

A lively debate ensues as students alternately condemn and defend the fast food industry, citing facts from the reading. Mr. Alvarez returns to the discussion web one last time. "Please take a few minutes to review your notes. In the third section, add any points you heard during the discussion that you did not include originally." After the students have completed this task, he has one final set of instructions for them. "You've got the basis for a persuasive essay. Please use your notes to write one in support of either side of the issue. Remember to acknowledge the other position in your writing. I've also got some additional materials for you to consult. One excellent source is this book, *Fast Food Nation* (Schlosser, 2002). It will be in the independent reading section of the classroom if you'd like to choose it." With that, these learners return to their desks, possessing the tools to write a compelling essay. Mr. Alvarez smiles to himself as he hears the debates continuing even as the students begin to write. "Like I said, there's nothing they like better than a good controversy!"

Mr. Alvarez's students use the notation bookmark featured in chapter 5.

ORAL LANGUAGE DEVELOPMENT IN THE LANGUAGE ARTS WORKSHOP

What does it mean to communicate? Typical dictionary definitions suggest that communication is a process by which information is exchanged between individuals through a common system of symbols, signs, or behavior. Thus, communication is a broader term that encompasses nonverbal systems, speaking, reading, listening, and writing. In addition, communication can occur in ways we do not typically consider. For example, insects "communicate" with pheromones. Animals communicate by urinating on objects to mark their territory. Humans, on the other hand, do not need to rely on these unconventional means! Instead, they speak and listen. We've adopted the speaking and listening definitions forwarded by Cooper and Morreale (2003a), namely:

> *Speaking* is the uniquely human act or process of sharing and exchanging information, ideas, and emotions using oral language. Whether in daily information interactions or in more formal settings, communicators are required to organize coherent messages, deliver them clearly, and adapt them to their listeners.

> *Listening* is the process of receiving, constructing meaning from, and responding to spoken and/or nonverbal messages. People call on different listening skills depending on whether their goal is to comprehend information, critique and evaluate a message, show empathy for the feelings expressed by others, or

appreciate a performance. Taken together, the communication skills of speaking and listening, called **oral language**, form the basis for thinking (p. x).

What Is the Relationship of Oral Language to Thinking?

Creative thinking is gasoline while critical thinking is steering wheel. Both are needed to accomplish the goal.

Both creative and critical thinking are essential in learning and extending understanding. Creative thinking is often measured as the ability to generate original responses, such as in a brainstorming activity (Guilford, 1959). Critical thinking can be thought of as the ability to evaluate those ideas to determine which are worth developing, then formulating and implementing a plan to do so (Paul, Binker, Jensen, & Kreklau, 1990).

Humans have been using their voices much longer than their pens to engage in creative and critical thinking. In fact, the first writing system, Sumerian cuneiforms, was not developed until around 4000 B.C.E. (Ouaknin,1999). In comparison, we know that humans have been communicating orally for at least 50,000 years (Ong, 1989). Before then, recording systems of one kind or another, such as notches on a stick or pictures on a cave wall, were the only forms of "writing" that existed. Instead, oral traditions served humans well in conveying information that kept other members of the tribe alive, healthy, and safe.

> Indeed, language is so overwhelmingly oral that of all the many thousands of languages—possibly tens of thousands—spoken in the course of human history only around 106 have ever been committed to a degree sufficient to have produced literature, and most have never been written at all. Of the some 3000 languages spoken that exist today only some 78 have a literature. (p. 7)

Therefore, we do not see speaking and listening as merely foundational to reading and writing. Rather, we see speaking and listening as intricately connected with reading and writing (Pinnell & Jaggar, 2003). Another way to think about these literacy processes is input versus output: listening and reading are receptive skills while speaking and writing are expressive skills. They are so closely related that they must be taught together in the language arts workshop. As Fisher noted with her first-grade students, "if we can talk about it, we can write about it; if we can write about it, we can read about it" (2003, p. 6).

What Are the Relationships Between Speaking, Listening, Reading, and Writing?

Evidence Based

A significant body of research has been developed to support the notion of interrelatedness among and between literacy processes (speaking, listening, reading, and writing). For example, Burgess (2002) noted the relationship between oral language development and subsequent growth in phonological sensitivity, a predictor of reading ability. Similarly, Cooper, Roth, Speece, and Schatschneider (2002), report that oral language development positively contributes to progress of early reading through specific influence on development of phonological awareness. Although it seems obvious to state, it is important to note that poor listening skills are associated with lower academic achievement (Ross, 1964) and low levels of reading comprehension (Devine, 1978). Further, increasing oral language skills are associated with improved reading and writing achievement (Harste & Short, 1988).

How Does Oral Language Develop?

As with reading and writing, language follows a developmental path. A series of developmental phases describe the progression of children as they learn to use language in increasingly sophisticated ways. You may recall from our discussion in chapter 1 that the term *phase* connotes that children may exhibit the features of one phase while still using features from previous phases and developing features from future phases. This phase concept differs from typical stage models in which students must complete a stage to move to the next. You'll note that as young children move through exploratory language, the words, "for learning" are introduced. This is in recognition of the shift primary students make in using oral language as a means for more formal school learning. The following eight phases of language development describe this progression (Education Department of Western Australia, 1994a, 1994b).

Beginning language. As children enter the world, they immediately begin learning language. Children at this phase use cries, coos, and other sounds to make their needs and wants known. Over time, they produce single words and then two word combinations, such as *car go* or *daddy up*. As they begin to understand language, children in this phase also understand simple questions and directions and enjoy language games and songs (such as *I'm a Little Teapot*).

Early language. At the early language phase, children begin to experiment with sound through rhymes and repetition, begin to use prepositions, often confuse pronouns, and start to read environmental print. They are still very egocentric and focused on their own life and experiences, producing questions such as *I go to the store?* At this phase, children very much enjoy imaginative play, retelling events and stories, and love to ask question after question.

Exploratory language. Later in their development, children use language to contribution to conversations, engage others, and predict future events. They have developed a good sense of grammar, although they still make overgeneralizations with tenses and plurals, such as *goed* and *mouses*. Their questioning becomes more focused and they often utilize a "who, what, where, when, why, and how" format. Parents everywhere recall the insistence of the toddler demanding to know *Why is the sky blue?*, *Where do fish sleep at night?*, and on and on! At this phase, children become more reflective in their thinking and their resulting use of language.

Emergent language for learning. Many children entering school are somewhere near this phase of oral language development. At this phase, students know when spoken sentences are grammatically correct and can adapt their speech and writing to ensure that tenses and verbs agree. In terms of speech, students begin to develop a sense of tone, volume, pace, intonation, and gestures to complement the content they wish to present. Further, they are expanding their vocabulary and use words for different purposes. They also understand that they can use language to persuade, inform, and reason with their peers, teachers, and parents. Words like *because* figure prominently in the emergent language user's vocabulary as they seek to persuade, inform, and reason!

Consolidated language for learning. By this phase, students in the primary grades can communicate effectively, offer advice and their own opinion, and interpret messages for different layers of meaning. They are developing the ability to make inferences and judgments based on the information provided. Further, they have become skilled at using slang with their peers and switching to more formal registers with adults.

For songs that children like, visit www.childrensmusic.org or www.songsforteaching.com.

Extended language for learning. Building on the skills acquired in the consolidated language for learning phase, primary and intermediate students subsequently develop an ability to summarize information effectively and efficiently, use language to form hypotheses, and engage in constructive criticism. In addition, students at this phase can use language in novel ways to engage their audiences as well as use language to create mental images for their listeners.

Proficient language use for learning. Once proficient, intermediate grade students learn to adjust their language to include or exclude individuals from the conversation by adding or deleting details, word choice, and paraphrasing. They also have developed a sense of main idea and can easily take notes during spoken conversations and lectures. Finally, they can use language to reflect on their own ideology or position on an issue.

Advanced language use for learning. The final phase identified in the First Steps Framework includes the development of a very sophisticated understanding of the power of language to cause emotional reactions. Advanced language users in intermediate and middle school grades can analyze spoken messages for cultural relevance, values, attitudes, and assumptions. They can also interpret the speaker's tone to make inferences. Speakers at the advanced language use phase have the ability to immediately modify their content and style based on verbal and nonverbal feedback they receive from the audience (Education Department of Western Australia, 1994a, 1994b).

As you read about the developmental phases of oral language development, were you struck by the similarities to the reading and writing skills and strategies we teach throughout the elementary and middle school years? Look again at the literacy strategies referenced in these school-age phases in Figure 6.1. These strategies typically associated with reading and writing have their basis in oral language development.

As students develop increasingly more advanced language, they expand their range of formality used in conversations. This range, called language registers, is influenced by many social factors.

Figure 6.1   Relationship Between Literacy Learning and Oral Language Development

Language Phase	Grade Span	Literacy Strategies
Emergent	Entering school	Expand vocabulary; use language to persuade, inform, reason
Consolidated	Primary	Offer opinions; interpret messages for meaning; make inferences and judgments
Extended	Primary/intermediate	Summarize; form hypotheses; engage in criticism; craft mental images
Proficient	Intermediate	Word choice; paraphrasing; take notes; reflect on ideology or position
Advanced	Intermediate/middle	Analyze for cultural relevance, values, attitudes, and assumptions; modify content and style to suit audience

What Are Language Registers?

There are a number of factors related to the formality of speech, including the setting, age of the listeners, or background knowledge of the listeners. Sociolinguists—people who study the ways in which language is used socially—describe this phenomenon as **language registers.** Sociolinguists note that language registers are one of the ways in which social relationships reveal themselves in language. "The concept of register is typically concerned with variations in language conditioned by uses rather than users and involves consideration of the situation or context of use, the purpose, subject-matter, and content of the message, and the relationship between the participants" (Romaine, 1994, p. 20). The more registers a speaker possesses, the more able they are to communicate effectively in a variety of settings. There are five generally agreed upon language registers, including (Payne, 1995):

Fixed or frozen. Fixed speech is reserved for traditions in which the language does not change. Examples of fixed speech include the Pledge of Allegiance, Shakespeare plays, and civil ceremonies such as weddings.

Formal. At the formal level, speech is expected to be presented in complete sentences with specific word usage. Formal language is the standard for work, school, and business and is more often seen in writing than in speaking. However, public speeches and presentations are expected to be delivered in a formal language register.

Consultative. The third level of language, consultative, is a formal register used in conversations. Less appropriate for writing, students often use consultative language in their interactions in the classroom.

Casual. This is the language that is used in conversation with friends. In casual speech, word choice is general and conversation is dependent upon non-verbal assists, significant background knowledge, and shared information.

Intimate. This is the language used by very close friends and lovers. Intimate speech is private and often requires a significant amount of shared history, knowledge, and experience.

Payne (1995) argues that students often do not understand the match between the language register and the setting. She strongly advocates that teachers provide students instruction in language registers. This requires that teachers scaffold students use of language and do not try to eliminate registers or dialects that students use in different settings. In other words, teaching students about language registers should be an additive model of education—one that encourages students to maintain their heritage language, dialect, and/or accent *and* provides them access to standard English (Brock, Boyd, & Moore, 2003).

Students use a variety of language registers for a variety of purposes. Regardless of your students' developmental levels, there are specific functions and interaction skills children develop to use language effectively and efficiently.

Respecting students' varied use of language creates trust in the classroom.

What Interaction Skills Do Speakers Use?

Speakers of all ages must develop interaction skills in order to be understood by listeners. In addition, interactions need to be respectful and efficient in purpose. These interaction skills permeate conversations in and out of school and begin to develop long before a child enters the classroom. Although these skills transcend the classroom, increasingly sophisticated use influences the use of other literacies as well (Pinnell & Jaggar, 2003, pp. 889–892):

- *Conversational discourse.* This means speakers understand the ways in which conversations occur, including turn-taking, listening and responding, and maintaining interest.

- *Sensitivity to audience.* Understanding that language changes depending on who is listening is also important. Children learn that they change their speech and language registers depending on the social context, background knowledge of the listeners, age of the listeners, and the expectations for the setting. Speech registers involve the level of formality in presenting information. For example, we use different registers to explain directions to a toddler and a teenager.

- *Arguing, persuading, and controlling others.* Another function of language is to make your perspective known and to attempt to influence the thinking of others. Persuasion is an important skill and is often the focus of writing instruction. This function is also important as students develop skills in conflict resolution.

- *Making requests and asking for information.* Over time, children learn how to ask for things and information with direct statements. They also develop their skills in using questions to gain what they want.

- *Informing.* Some of the time, people use language to inform others. Effectively providing information requires skills in organizing thinking and sharing information in a way that allows the listener or reader to follow the logic and flow of ideas.

- *Imagining.* This function encourages children to assume different characters and roles as they engage in play. As they do so, they become skilled in using descriptive language to share their thoughts. Interestingly, the development of imagining is related to understanding narrative stories and story grammar (Galda, 1984).

- *Telling stories and narrative discourse.* To tell a story, students must learn the conventions of story grammar and the idea that all stories have specific parts. In stories and narrative discourse, children learn to sustain longer monologues and to focus on their audience and the audience's interest. Importantly, stories provide students an opportunity to reflect on and present their own language, ethnicity, culture, religion, and experience with the world.

  Story grammar was explained in chapter 1

- *Inquiry.* As Vygotsky (1986) noted, learning requires that students use inquiry and "inner speech" as they solve problems, acquire new information, and modify what they already know. Inquiry, as a process, allows children to continuously make sense and understand their world.

These types of interactions are used throughout the day both in and out of school, and some, such as informing and inquiring, are used frequently during the school day. In the classroom, these interactions are most commonly conducted in the formal and consultative registers. This talk between and among students and the teacher is referred to as **classroom discourse.** Oral language development occurs in part when teachers foster meaningful classroom discourse through purposeful instruction.

CLASSROOM DISCOURSE IN THE LANGUAGE ARTS WORKSHOP

Arguably the most important teaching tool at a teacher's disposal is talk. Teachers rely on talk, both their own and their students', to drive instruction. It should therefore come as no surprise that classroom teachers deliver most of the information during the day orally. The oral language demands of school are intense. There are, however, good and not so good ways to use speaking and listening in the classroom. In particular, the questioning habits of teachers can increase or suppress classroom discourse.

What Are Effective Questioning Habits?

Evidence Based

Reading researchers report from their classroom observations at the elementary level that the majority of questions that are used in classroom discourse on a daily basis are teacher-generated, explicit, and required only one correct answer (Armbruster et al.,1991; Block, 2001). An important series of studies on the questioning habits of teachers was conducted by Cazden (1986, 1988). Like others before her, she found that classroom instruction is dominated by a particular cycle of questioning known as IRE: **Initiate, Respond, and Evaluate** (Dillon, 1988; Mehan, 1979). The IRE pattern of questioning is familiar to all—the teacher initiates a question, students respond, and then the teacher evaluates the quality and accuracy of the responses. Here's an example of IRE:

> *Teacher:* Why did the plants with both water and sun grow the best? (Initiate)
>
> *Student:* They used photosynthesis. (Response)
>
> *Teacher:* Good. (Evaluate) Why else? (Initiate)

Here's the difficulty with that question—the student could have also answered that water contains nutrients needed by the plant, that plants can convert sunlight into chemical forms of energy, or a host of other answers. The question is based on recall and consists of a teacher-directed query that excludes any discussion or debate among students. A classroom where IRE is the dominant form of discourse quickly becomes a passive learning environment dependent on the teacher for any kind of discussion. The danger, of course, in the overuse of an IRE pattern of questioning is that the teacher alone becomes the mediator of who will speak and who will not (Mehan, 1979). The students learn that the only questions worth considering are those formulated by the teacher. Ironically, the teachers in Cazden's study (1988) reported that they wanted a student-centered, constructivist classroom, yet clung to IRE as their dominant instructional method for inquiry. If you doubt the pervasiveness of this questioning pattern, then eavesdrop on kindergartners "playing school." Invariably, the five-year-old "teacher" will engage in this questioning pattern with his or her "students." If only all teaching behaviors were this easy to teach!

> If you want to gain insight into how your students perceive you as a teacher, invite them to teach for a day!

Factors impacting classroom discourse. Of course, fostering meaningful classroom discourse can be challenging. Many teachers have had the experience of posing a question to a class, only to be greeted with silence. *What's wrong with them?* the teacher thinks. *Don't they know any of this? Haven't they been listening?* This is usually immediately followed by *What's wrong with me? Am I that ineffective as a teacher?* None of these are probably true. Instead, a mixture of complex factors may be at play.

They include:

- *Academic factors.* Lack of prior knowledge, lack of understanding of current content of study
- *Language factors.* Difficulty in utilizing academic language to answer the question posed, or lack of understanding of the question itself
- *Intrinsic factors.* The student may be shy, uncomfortable speaking in front of the group, uncomfortable with his or her language skills, or unmotivated to participate in the activity
- *Extrinsic factors.* Fear of the perceptions of specific members of the class, or the class as a whole

Evidence Based

Peggy Orenstein presents an inside look at the role of gender in schools in her book *Schoolgirls.*

As you can see, this adds up to a mélange of reasons why the same handful of students seem to answer your questions. This is borne out in research as well. According to several studies collected in classrooms of various ages, boys are up to eight times more likely to call out an answer than girls (Brophy, 1985; Sadker & Sadker, 1986) and therefore gain more of the teacher's attention in comparison (Holden, 1993). Moreover, teachers need to be mindful of more than just the types of questions asked. There is evidence that teachers call on boys to talk in class significantly more often than girls (Sadker & Sadker, 1995).

Courtney Cazden (2001) suggests that all teachers ask themselves two questions about classroom discourse:

- How do patterns of talk in classrooms affect the equality of students' educational opportunities and outcomes?
- How is discourse used as a support for deeper student learning?

Focusing on these questions as you establish your classroom will ensure that students are engaged in meaningful ways and that you achieve both excellence and equity as you develop the skills students need to be successful. However, changes to questioning habits alone will not automatically foster more meaningful classroom discourse. Students also need to be taught how to communicate effectively in the classroom in order to support their own learning through creative and critical thinking. This is called accountable talk.

What Is Accountable Talk?

Accountable talk is one of nine Principles of Learning. For more information, see www. instituteforlearning. org

Recall some of the classrooms in which you have participated. Were you held accountable for what you thought and said? Were you allowed to sit quietly and not participate in any way in the class activities and lessons? If so, how much did you learn? "The shy, quiet and reserved child may seem like a model of good behavior—but that child may be cause for concern, not celebration. *All* children need opportunities to talk *a lot* to develop word knowledge and language skills" (National Center on Education and the Economy, 2001, p. 12).

Accountable talk is the practice of fostering classroom discourse about learning through partner conversations and whole group discussions. This term was developed and researched by Lauren Resnick and her colleagues at the Institute for Learning, University of Pittsburgh, to describe high levels of engagement in creative and critical thinking among learners. Although the term seems to suggest that it is about speaking, listening is essential to accountable talk because the discourse springs from careful listening to the conversation. A focus on accountable talk provides teachers and students with expectations for their conversations and discussions. The basic principles of accountable talk include:

- Accountability that discussions are on the topic
- Accountability to use accurate information
- Accountability to think deeply about what is being discussed

Although not easy to achieve, an excellent indicator of accountable talk is when discussion in the classroom ceases to be brokered by the teacher and becomes a series of interchanges among students. When this occurs, the teacher no longer has to be the originator of all the questions (recall IRE) because students are asking and responding to the inquiries and comments of classmates.

Indicators of accountable talk. Accountable talk is developed through modeling the kinds of questions and follow-up probes used in meaningful classroom discourse. The purpose of these follow-ups is to encourage creative and critical thinking. Following up student responses with an additional probe is an excellent means for modeling how meaningful exchanges can occur. The Institute for Learning, University of Pittsburgh, has identified specific indicators of accountable talk required of teachers and students. We've included an example in italics after each to illustrate.

- Press for clarification and explanation: *Can you tell me more about that?*
- Require justification of proposals and challenges: *What facts support your idea?*
- Recognize and challenge misconception: *I don't agree because _____.*
- Demand evidence for claims and arguments: *Can you give me an example?*
- Interpret and use each other's statements: *Tino's idea reminded me of _____.*

Teaching accountable talk. Accountable talk is used throughout the language arts workshop. Focus lessons and guided instruction are ideal times to provide instruction on listening carefully to one another in order to participate in meaningful discussion. Accordingly, accountable talk is fostered through multiple opportunities to interact with a partner. For instance, a focus lesson might begin with each student identifying a classmate for partner talk. Throughout the lesson, the teacher pauses and instructs students to "turn to a partner and . . ." followed by a discussion prompt. While students discuss the prompt with one another, the teacher moves about, listening for accountable talk and interjecting when necessary to coach higher quality conversations.

Accountable talk is an integral element of the language arts workshop because conversations, discussions, and dialogues are critical to the learning process. Therefore, it is necessary for the teacher to create a climate and culture in which students are respected when they speak. In addition, the learning environment must be one in which asking questions and challenging ideas is valued.

For more information on establishing a respectful classroom climate, see *Because We Can Change the World: A Practical Guide To Building Cooperative, Inclusive Classroom Communities* by Mara Sapon-Shevin.

Resources for Identifying Oral Language Skills

Visit the state department of education website to view the standards for your state.

There are several sources that have articulated the speaking and listening skills that students should develop as they progress through school. It is likely that your state has specific speaking and listening standards established for students in grades K–12. In addition, the New Standards Project of the National Center on Education and the Economy and the University of Pittsburgh published *Speaking and Listening For Preschool Through Third Grade* (2001). In this resource, they present the habits students should develop, the kinds of talk and genres students need to know, as well as the language use and conventions expected at each grade level.

The National Communication Association (NCA) also developed standards for speaking and listening. In addition, they note the relationship between visual and media literacy and language development. Thus, of their 20 standards, five are devoted to media literacy. You will note from Figure 6.2 that these standards are focused on all students in grades K–12 and not only on elementary children. In addition, *Creating Competent Communicators* (Cooper & Morreale, 2003a, 2003b) provides teachers with a host of ideas and activities for meeting these standards.

SPEAKING AND LISTENING IN THE LANGUAGE ARTS WORKSHOP

The phases of instruction in the language arts workshop are ideal for developing the speaking and listening skills of students. The emphasis is on offering a variety of strategies for using language to foster creative and critical thinking. Students also have numerous opportunities to talk with partners to develop the skills of accountable talk.

Focus Lessons

Focus lessons provide a time when the teacher can model, coach, and scaffold instruction for oral language development. When using these strategies, remember to pause from time to time to tell students about the language you are using. This makes the purpose of instruction more explicit to students.

Transportable teaching strategies are effective across content areas and grade levels.

Think-Pair-Share. One of the most transportable teaching strategies is *Think-Pair-Share* (Lyman, 1981). Think-Pair-Share introduces an intermediate stage between when the question is asked and the answer is delivered and serves as an important strategy for developing accountable talk (Resnick, 1995). After asking the question, the teacher invites students to think about the possible answers. When a short amount of time has elapsed (30 seconds or so), the teacher then instructs them to turn to a partner and discuss their answers. After allowing a few moments to discuss, the teacher then invites students to offer answers. Invariably, more hands go up because they have had some time to consider their answer, listen to someone else, and refine their response. In addition, the answers are likely to be rich and detailed because of this intermediate step. A classroom poster for Think-Pair-Share can be found in Figure 6.3.

There is another compelling reason for using Think-Pair-Share and it has to do with oral language and engagement. For the reasons cited above, some students are reluctant to participate in large group discussion. Some of those students may remain silent during the whole class conversation. However, when Think-Pair-Share is utilized, *every student participates*. Thirty students answer, not just one, because they have responded to another classmate.

A variation of Think-Pair-Share is *Read-Write-Pair-Share*. The difference lies in what students do before discussing their ideas with a partner. Students first read a

Figure 6.2 NCA's Standards for Speaking, Listening, and Media Literacy in K–12 Education

Fundamentals of Effective Communication

Competent communicators demonstrate knowledge and understanding of. . .

1. The relationships among the components of the communication process
2. The influence of the individual, relationship, and situation on communication
3. The role of communication in the development and maintenance of personal relationships
4. The role of communication in creating meaning, influencing thought, and making decisions

Competent communicators demonstrate the ability to. . .

5. Demonstrate sensitivity to diversity when communicating
6. Enhance relationships and resolve conflict using appropriate and effective communication strategies
7. Evaluate communication styles, strategies, and content based on their aesthetic and functional worth
8. Show sensitivity to the ethical issues associated with communication in a democratic society

Speaking

Competent speakers demonstrate. . .

9. Knowledge and understanding of the speaking process
10. The ability to adapt communication strategies appropriately and effectively according to the needs of the situation and setting
11. The ability to use language that clarifies, persuades, and/or inspires while respecting differences in listeners' backgrounds
12. The ability to manage or overcome communication anxiety

Listening

Competent listeners demonstrate. . .

13. Knowledge and understanding of the listening process
14. The ability to use appropriate and effective listening skills for a given communication situation and setting
15. The ability to identify and manage barriers to listening

Media Literacy

Media literate communicators demonstrate. . .

16. Knowledge and understanding of the ways people use media in their personal and public lives
17. Knowledge and understanding of the complex relationships among audiences and media content
18. Knowledge and understanding that media content is produced within social and cultural contexts
19. Knowledge and understanding of the commercial nature of media
20. The ability to use media to communicate to specific audiences

Source: From *NCA's Standards for Speaking, Listening, and Media Literacy in K-12 Education.* Retrieved from http://www.natcom.org/Instruction/new_page_1.htm. Used by permission of the National Communication Association.

Figure 6.3 Think-Pair-Share

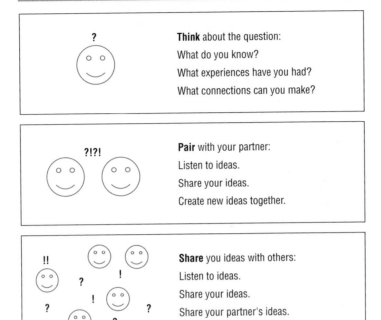

Think about the question:
What do you know?
What experiences have you had?
What connections can you make?

Pair with your partner:
Listen to ideas.
Share your ideas.
Create new ideas together.

Share you ideas with others:
Listen to ideas.
Share your ideas.
Share your partner's ideas.
Create new ideas together.

question that has been posted on the board or a brief piece of text, then write a response. After a few minutes of writing, pairs of students discuss what they have written. Finally, the entire class is invited to share their ideas as well as their partner's.

Additional information about storytelling in the classroom, including listening rubrics and self-assessment tools can be found at www.storyarts.org

Storytelling. Many teachers are also excellent storytellers who weave words together in imaginative ways and capture the minds of their students. We know that storytelling is an art and we believe that it is an art that can be learned. The benefits of storytelling are numerous. Not only do students develop their listening skills, they also learn new words or words in interesting contexts and are reinforced in their understanding of story grammar. Rubright (1996), Wajnryb and Ur (2003), and Weissman (2002) all provide guidance for teachers who wish to learn more about storytelling. In general, quality storytelling requires attention to voice, pace, dialects, facial expressions, sound effects, and audience participation. Guidelines for quality storytelling can be found in Figure 6.4.

In addition to teachers as storytellers, Whaley (2002) notes that storytelling is also an excellent way to engage students in speaking in front of their peers because it fosters narrative discourse, an important interaction skill. Collins and Cooper (1997) provide teachers with ideas to help students develop their storytelling, and thus oral language, skills. In Mr. Meza's fifth-grade class, one literature circle group finished reading *Esperanza Rising* (Ryan, 2002) and requested that they retell the book to the class using drama and storytelling. James served as the narrator to advance the plot of the book while Keshia, Juan, Mariah, and Jessica acted out key scenes. The entire

Figure 6.4 Effective Storytelling Performance Skills

When telling a story, an effective storyteller demonstrates the following traits observable by others:

Voice Mechanics

Speaks with an appropriate volume for the audience to hear
Employs clear enunciation
Uses non-monotonous, vocal expression to clarify the meaning of the text

Face/Body/Gesture

Expressively uses non-verbal communication to clarify the meaning of the text

Focus

Concentration is clear
Eye contact with audience is engaging
Maintains a charismatic presence in space (stage presence)

Characterization

If dialogue is employed, characters are believable to listener; storyteller's natural voice is differentiated from character voices

Use of Space

Storyteller seems comfortable, relaxed and confident in front of listeners
Storyteller maintains clear spatial relationships for characters and narrator

Pacing

Story is presented efficiently and keeps listeners' interest throughout

Source: http://www.storyarts.org/classroom/usestories/storyrubric.html#skills Heather Forest, Story Arts, P.O. Box 354, Huntington, NY 11743, 631-271-2511, heather@storyarts.org

production was student-initiated and student-directed with planning occurring over the course of two workshops. Using a loose script they created, their classmates were treated to a reenactment of scenes that included a house fire, a train journey, and a labor strike.

Shared writing. We have discussed Language Experience Approach at length in the chapter on guided instruction (Ashton-Warner, 1963). In LEA, the teacher engages a student in conversation about a book or experience and invites the child to orally compose a message. The teacher writes down everything the child says, reinforcing speech to print connections. These writings then become reading material for the student during subsequent instruction.

Chapter 3.

A version of LEA for use with groups is called *shared writing* (McKenzie, 1985). As in LEA, the speech of children is written down on chart paper for all to see. However, in shared writing the teacher takes a more active role in shaping the composition of the message as the group is helped toward consensus on the text. Because LEA and shared writing result in a written product, it is easy to overlook the role of oral language development in this activity. However, much of the value of shared writing lies in the oral composition, as students alternately offer ideas, listen to others, and use their words to persuade. You will recall from earlier in this chapter the importance of these interaction skills. In shared writing, it is important not to rush through the oral composition in an effort to get the text written down on the page.

Daily News. A popular version of shared writing is Daily News. This may be done inside of the language arts workshop, as in a focus lesson, or during the morning circle routine of the classroom. In either case, students are asked about an event that will be occurring that day, such as an assembly or visitor to the classroom, or another noteworthy incident that may have happened in the community. After discussing the event, selecting and refining the message, and developing word choices, the agreed message is written on the chart or board along with the date. Alternatively, you can use an 18″ × 24″ tablet labeled "Daily News" and make it available for collaborative reading. These collections are popular with the students, who enjoy seeing a chronicle of their school year develop over time.

Developing K-W-L language charts. One of the most widely used instructional activities used by classroom teachers is the K-W-L chart. In a survey of teachers, a significant portion of them named K-W-L as a tool used frequently in their classroom (Spor & Schneider, 1999). K-W-L is a peg mnemonic for What do you **k**now? What do you **w**ant to know? and What have you **l**earned? (Ogle, 1986). The K-W-L chart is developed through discussion with the class at the beginning and end of a book or unit of study. Before the reading or topic of study, the class discusses the first question (What do we know?) to activate background knowledge about a subject. Development of K-W-L charts is highly regarded in part because it mirrors an approach to research that begins with reviewing what is known, developing questions to guide the study, then evaluating what has been learned (Ogle, 1986), making this approach useful for developing creative and critical thinking skills.

A peg mnemonic is an arrangement of letters used as a memory device. See chapter 8 for more information.

In a second-grade classroom about to begin literature circles on spiders, the class listed all the things they knew about spiders. The teacher's role was to elicit their comments through a series of questions prepared in advance.

- Have you ever seen a spider?
- What do they look like?
- Where do they live?
- What do they eat?
- What about poisonous spiders?

Some teachers feel more comfortable entitling this portion "What do we think we know?" in order to allow for incorrect statements.

Once students have thoroughly discussed their background knowledge about the topic, the conversation moved to the next level: *What do we want to know?* During this phase, the teacher's role is now to assist the class in formulating questions. This portion of the K-W-L is critical because it encourages students to anticipate information they are likely to encounter during the reading, as well as in fostering inquiry as an interaction skill.

Figure 6.5   Spider Book Titles Read in Literature Circles

Berger, M. (2003). *Spinning spiders*. New York: HarperTrophy.

Cole, J. (1995). *Spider's lunch: All about garden spiders*. New York: Grosset & Dunlap.

Gibbons, G. (1994). *Spiders*. New York: Holiday House.

Glaser, L. (1999). *Spectacular spiders*. Riverside, NJ: Millbrook.

Reinhart, M. (2003). *Young naturalist's handbook: Insect-lo-pedia*. New York: Hyperion.

Robinson, F. (1996). *Hello spider!* New York: Scott, Foresman.

Winer, Y. (1998). *Spiders spin webs*. Watertown, MA: Charlesbridge.

Figure 6.6   KWL Chart on Spiders from Second Grade

Know?	Want to know?	Learned?
Spiders are scary	What do spiders eat?	Most spiders are harmless to people
Have 8 legs	What if you get bit by a poisonous spider?	They are useful because they control insects
Make spider webs	What kinds of spiders live here?	Some spiders eat small animals
They bite	How many spiders are there in the world?	Not all spiders make webs (trapdoor spider)
Eat bugs		Tarantulas are not very poisonous
Tarantulas are poisonous		Black widow spiders are more poisonous
Some are hairy		
Live in the garden		
"Charlotte's Web"		

Students then worked in literature circles to read the spider books. They used the K-W-L language chart they created to confirm or disconfirm their beliefs and predictions about the topic. A list of the spider books read by this class appears in Figure 6.5.

The last column, *What have we learned?* is intended to solicit answers to the questions developed during the "W" portion of the activity. Of course, it is possible that not all questions will be answered during the subsequent reading; these can be used to extend the experience later for further study through a process called K-W-L Plus (Carr & Ogle, 1987). The "plus" portion represents a fourth question: *What do we want to know next?* Figure 6.6 contains a completed K-W-L chart on spiders from the second-grade classroom.

Oral language development is a key component in developing a K-W-L chart on a topic. Student participation can be enhanced by using a think-pair-share approach to foster student engagement. As well, students participating in K-W-L benefit from opportunities to formulate and refine questions and craft answers that are accurate and succinct.

Guided Instruction

During guided instruction, the teacher works with students in a small group to give attention to a particular skill or strategy. Guided instruction is an excellent time for

Spiders, written and illustrated by Gail Gibbons. Used with the permission of Holiday House.

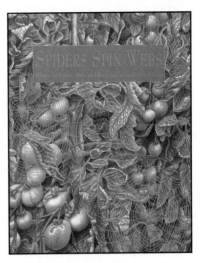

Spiders Spin Webs, written by Yvonne Winer and illustrated by Karen Lloyd-Jones. Used with permission by Charlesbridge Publishing, Inc.

oral language development because students have many opportunities to use speaking and listening skills.

Oral cloze method. Have you wondered why some teachers seem to pause before a key word in a statement? For example, a first grade teacher says, "The punctuation mark we use to end a sentence is called a _____." The students complete the statement with the word *period.* This "fill in the blank" technique is called an *oral cloze method.* By posing such questions (and they really are questions, despite their declarative appearance), teachers are able to accomplish several goals:

A similar cloze method in reading is discussed in chapter 10 on comprehension.

- Check for understanding
- Increase engagement through active participation
- Rehearse vocabulary and concept knowledge:

Oral cloze is useful as a classroom management technique.

Unlike many of the other strategies in this chapter, oral cloze should not be the focus of your lesson. Rather, it is a simple technique for increasing response rates among students while giving them an opportunity to practice academic language. Students who are English language learners can benefit from this technique, especially if they are uncomfortable with their pronunciation of unfamiliar words. Like Think-Pair-Share, this is a transportable teaching strategy that is useful in all content areas. It is transportable across the language arts workshop as well, especially during focus lessons.

Evidence Based

Discussion webs. Discussion in small group instructional arrangements has great value across several dimensions. Gambrell identified these elements in a review of the research on small group discussions (1996, pp. 30–31):

- Promotes higher level thinking and problem-solving (Almasi, 1995; Villaume & Hopkins, 1995)

- Improves communication skills (Fisher, 1968; Goatley & Raphael, 1992)
- Increases understanding of text (Morrow & Smith, 1990; Palinscar & Brown, 1984)

As with large group discussions conducted during focus lessons, small group discussions can benefit from structures that give students an opportunity to formulate opinions, consider alternative views, and reach conclusions. An excellent technique for accomplishing all of these goals is the *discussion web* (Alvermann, 1991), used by Mr. Alvarez in the opening scenario at the beginning of this chapter. A discussion web converges on a central question and is conducted in three distinct stages similar to the think-pair-share approach. First, students write both pro and con responses to the question. The group then discusses their responses with one another. Next, they read the assigned piece, looking for evidence defending both positions. Once again, the group discusses both sides of the issue, this time using the text to support the positions. The discussion web promotes accountable talk because participants are required to furnish evidence and challenge misconceptions (Resnick, 1995). After the discussion, they return to the discussion web to note any points they missed. Students now have an excellent tool to write a persuasive essay for either position particularly because effective persuasive essays require that the writer acknowledge the other side of the issue. A discussion web form can be found in Figure 6.7.

ReQuest. *ReQuest* is an instructional procedure for fostering comprehension through developing questions about a reading (Manzo, 1969). ReQuest is typically done be-

Figure 6.7 Discussion Web

Central Question:

Yes		No
	Before Reading	
	After Reading	
	After Discussion	

tween a teacher and a group of students, although it was initially intended to be completed with an individual student. The steps for ReQuest are simple to follow:

1. Select a text for reading and assign roles as questioner and responder. The students and teacher read silently and formulate possible questions for the first section of the reading.
2. The responder closes the book while the questioner asks a question about the passage.
3. The responder answers the question and then checks the passage for accuracy.
4. Select the next passage and change roles. After several rotations, the teacher invites predictions about the rest of the reading. The students continue to read to the end of the text.

Task cards can assist students in remembering each of the steps. These can be seen in Figure 6.8. The ReQuest procedure requires students to listen carefully to one another and use the interaction skills of inquiring and informing.

Collaborative Learning

The collaborative phase of the workshop is a time when students work together to support the learning of one another. The use of accountable talk is critical to activities conducted during this time.

Books clubs and literature circles. We have discussed the nature and purpose of the collaborative reading groups in chapter 4 on collaborative learning. Remember that these peer-led reading groups meet over the course of several weeks to discuss a single text (Daniels, 2002). Young and inexperienced students benefit from guidelines for how the literature circle should function. Older students respond well to the

Figure 6.8 ReQuest Task Cards

Questioner Task Card

1. Read the first passage silently. Pay attention to the information it contains.
2. Think of questions to ask. Try to use your own words, not exact phrases from the passage.
3. Keep your book open while you ask your question. Listen to the answer, then check to see if it is accurate. If it is not, ask another question to help the person arrive at the correct answer.

Respondent Task Card

1. Read the first passage silently. Pay attention to the information it contains.
2. Think of questions you might be asked. Check the passage you just read for possible answers.
3. Close your book and answer each question you are asked. You can ask the questioner to rephrase or clarify a question you do not understand.
4. When finished, change roles. Repeat 2–3 times.

Source: Fisher, D., & Frey, N. (2004). *Improving adolescent literacy: Strategies at work.* Upper Saddle River, NJ: Merrill/Prentice Hall.

assignment of specific roles within the group. The most common ones include (Daniels, 2002):

- Discussion director
- Vocabulary enricher
- Passage picker
- Real-life connector
- Illustrator

Accountable talk is an important aspect of an effective literature circle. Students should use their roles to guide their discussion using the expectations associated with accountable talk, including supplying evidence, using the statements of others, and asking follow-up questions to clarify understanding (Resnick, 1995). Figure 6.9 shows a poster for use by literature circle participants to remind them how to use accountable talk in their discussion.

In addition to the roles assumed by each member of the group, the composition of students must be considered as well. Will these groups be homogeneous or heterogeneous in nature? According to what elements? It is not uncommon to form groups based on reading ability; this is perhaps the most popular way. However, there are other factors that influence the success of group interactions. You will recall from earlier in this chapter that academic, language, intrinsic, and extrinsic factors can negatively impact whole class discussions. The same is true for peer discussions in literature circles. Wiencek and O'Flahavan (1994) suggest considering the relative abilities of each student in using three skill sets when creating literature circles and book clubs.

Information on grouping students was presented in chapter 1.

Figure 6.9 Poster to Promote Accountable Talk During Literature Circles

Remember to. . .	Sounds like. . .
Ask questions when you don't understand a statement.	• Can you tell me more? • Would you say that again? • Can you give another example so I can understand?
Give a reason why your idea is a good one.	• This reminds me of _____ because _____. • I believe this is true because _____.
Ask for evidence when something sounds incorrect.	• I'm not sure that's right. Can you tell me why you think it is true? • Can you show me a place in the book that illustrates that idea?
Give evidence to support your statements.	• Read a passage from the book that illustrates your idea. • Bring other information sources to support your idea.
Use idea from others to add to your own.	• I agree with _____ because _____. • _____'s idea reminds me of _____.

Source: Adapted from Resnick, L. (1995). From aptitude to effort: A new foundation for our schools. *Daedalus, 124*(4), 55–62.

Independent = accuracy of 95% or above and 90% comprehension; instructional is 90%–94% in accuracy and 75% comprehension; frustration is 89% or below in accuracy.

- *Social ability*. Is the student very quiet during group discussions? Are they very vocal and often the leader?

- *Interpretive ability*. Do they comprehend text and share their ideas with others? Do they have difficulty locating evidence to support their assertions?

- *Reading ability*. Will this text be at the student's independent, instructional, or frustration level?

The researchers suggest rating each child on a scale of 1–3 for each dimension and composing groups of 5–6 students with a mixed range of abilities for these skills (Wiencek & O'Flahavan, 1994). In this way, oral language development can be enhanced through the use of accountable talk with peers.

Jigsaw. Book clubs and literature circles promote discussion of a single text, but at other times students need to analyze multiple texts at the same time. When a group of readers is presented with information from several texts, they are more likely to make connections between those readings, called *intertextuality* (Bloome & Egan-Robertson, 1993). However, it can be difficult to organize multiple readings for use in a discussion. One instructional arrangement for doing so is a *jigsaw* (Aronson, 1978).

The readings used in a jigsaw may be chosen because they each offer similar perspectives of the same concept or event (*complementary*), or because they present very different views (*conflicting*) (Hartman & Allison, 1996). A third arrangement divides a concept or idea into smaller elements

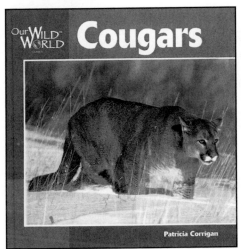

From COUGARS by Patricia Corrigan, of the Our Wild World series. Copyright 2001 by NorthWord Books for Young Readers. Reprinted by permission of NorthWord Books for Young Readers.

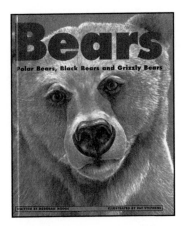

Cover from *Bears* written by Deborah Hodge and illustrated by Pat Stephens is used by permission of Kids Can Press Ltd., Toronto. Cover illustration © 1996 Pat Stephens.

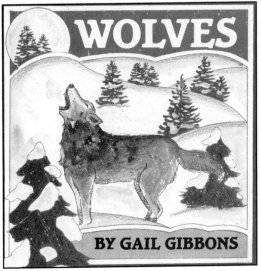

Wolves, written and illustrated by Gail Gibbons. Used with the permission of Holiday House.

Figure 6.10   Text Sets for Jigsaw

Type	Purpose
Complementary Example: California Gold Rush	Texts focus on single concept: Chambers, C. E. (1998). *California gold rush.* New York: Troll. Kalman, B. (1999). *The gold rush.* New York: Crabtree. Krensky, S. (1996). *Strike it rich!* New York: Scott, Foresman. Schanzer, R. (1999). *Gold fever!* Washington, DC: National Geographic.
Conflicting Example: Vietnam War	Texts focus on divergent perspectives of a concept: Bunting, E. (1992). *The wall.* New York: Clarion. Whelan, G. (1993). *Goodbye Vietnam.* New York: Yearling. Quang, N. H. (1986). *The land I lost: A boy in Vietnam.* New York: HarperTrophy. White, E. E. (2002). *The journal of Patrick Seamus Flaherty: U.S. Marine Corps, Khe Sanh, Vietnam,* 1968. New York: Scholastic.
Divided Example: Predators of North America	Concept is divided among texts: Berger, M. (2002). *Snap! A book about alligators and crocodiles.* New York: Cartwheel. Corrigan, P. (2001). *Cougars: Our wild world.* Chanhassen, MN: NorthWord. Gibbons, G. (1995). *Wolves!* New York: Holiday House. Hodge, D. (1999). *Bears: Polar bears, black bears, and grizzly bears.* Tonawanda, NY: Kids Can Press.

so that the topic is only fully understood after all the readings have been discussed (Aronson, 1978). Examples of these types of text sets appears in Figure 6.10.

The jigsaw is accomplished through two types of groups—the home group and the expert group. First, members of a home group divide the task of reading multiple texts among themselves. Each reader is responsible for identifying the important elements of the text to report to the home group. Students then meet in an expert group of students reading the same text to discuss the reading and take notes for use in the home group. Finally, students reconvene in their home group to learn and share information from each of the readings. A procedural map for jigsaw is illustrated in Figure 6.11.

Table topics. One of the ways to ensure that students can practice organizing their thinking and presenting their ideas orally is the use of *table topics.* As students arrive at a center dedicated to table topics, they each select a slip of paper from a container. Sample table topics include:

- What's best on pizza?
- Who should be class president and why?
- Why does England have a Queen?
- What does it mean to be a friend?

Once they have randomly selected their table topics, students take a few minutes to make notes and organize their thinking. The person who has the paper with the

Figure 6.11   Jigsaw

Phase One: Home Groups

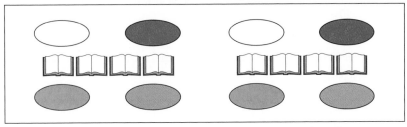

Students meet in home groups to divide the readings among themselves.

Phase Two: Expert Groups

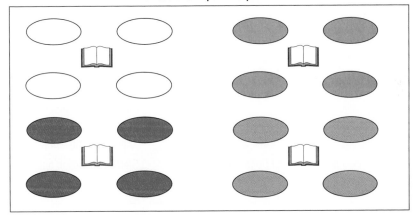

Students meet in expert groups to discuss one of the readings.

Phase Three: Home Groups

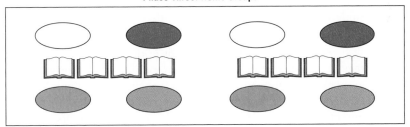

Students reconvene in home groups to discuss all of the readings.

Number the topics so that students can operate independently at this center and not need to ask you when they should talk.

lowest number presents first. Remaining topics are presented in numerical order. Someone in the group sets the timer and the first person presents. Students know that they are to state their opinion or idea first, then provide two to four supporting details, facts, or points, and then summarize or close. When the presentation is complete, other students in the group provide feedback. Again, a timer is used to ensure that each person in the group has an opportunity to share. The students know that this is not a time to disagree—that arguing over a position or opinion is not the point

Figure 6.12   Speaking Checklist for Extemporaneous Presentations

Directions: Listen closely to each speaker and check the box that best describes his or her performances.

Name of speaker: _____

Name of listener: _____

Topic: _____

Eye contact	❑ Doesn't look at audience	❑ Sometimes looks at audience	❑ Looks at audience frequently
Volume	❑ Speaks too softly to be heard	❑ Sometimes hard to hear	❑ Easy to hear
Voice quality	❑ Voice is flat	❑ Voice and words don't always match	❑ Uses voice effectively to make points
Content	❑ Content is inaccurate	❑ Makes points, but does not support with facts	❑ Uses facts to support points
Structure	❑ Confusing or lacks structure	❑ States main points but does not follow all of them; topics wander	❑ States main points at the beginning and follows them
Interest	❑ Does not use a story or fact to promote interest	❑ Uses one story or fact to promote interest	❑ Uses stories or facts to promote interest
Conclusion	❑ Does not use a conclusion	❑ States conclusion but leaves out some main points	❑ Conclusion summarizes main points

of this center. Rather, they focus on the speaking performance of the presenter and provide compliments and constructive criticism. In addition, they must listen carefully in order to provide specific feedback. The checklist in Figure 6.12 is useful for students to record their thoughts as the speaker presents.

Oral composition before writing. Emergent and early writers, while often eager to write, may not take as much time as they should to plan their writing. Brainstorming ideas and creating concept maps can be two useful strategies to encourage planning, although for the youngest writers this can sometimes be cognitively demanding. We encourage the use of peers to plan through *oral composition*. During collaborative writing, students meet with a peer to tell a story they are planning to write. The classmate listens to the story, then retells in his or her own words. The writer listens to the retelling to make sure the message was clear. At this point, the listener can ask clarifying questions and make suggestions. The intent of oral composition is to foster creative and critical thinking and give students opportunities to engage in narrative discourse. We keep a small poster to remind students about the steps for oral composition. It can be viewed in Figure 6.13.

Group retellings. Students often find themselves reading the same material in order to complete a project or assignment. However, not all students in a group will com-

| Figure 6.13 | Oral Composition Poster |

Oral Composition

	Writer's Job		Listener's Job
☺	Greet your partner.	☺	Greet your partner.
💬	Tell your story to the listener. Try to tell it the way you want to write it.	👂	Listen carefully and do not interrupt.
👂	Listen carefully and do not interrupt.	💬	Retell the writer's story as best as you can.
👂	Ask your partner if there were any parts they did not understand. Listen carefully to the answers and do not interrupt.	💬	Answer your partner's questions. Tell your partner about the parts you liked.
☺	Thank your partner for listening to your story.	☺	Thank your partner for sharing their story.
✏️	Use what you learned from your partner in your writing.		

prehend the text equally. This is particularly true in heterogeneously constructed groups of students possessing a range of reading abilities. We encourage our students to use a *group retelling* when they are reading an assignment together. Group retelling is the student practice of reading a portion of the assignment, then stopping to retell to a partner what has been read (Wood & Jones, 1998). In this way, students can check each others's understanding, clarify difficult concepts, and ask questions. We suggest introducing group retelling as a focus lesson, modeling the type of language used in a retelling. As students practice, the teacher can circulate and listen in on student retellings to provide assistance to individuals.

Tableau. As students move into the middle grades they often become reluctant to perform in front of the class. For many, the potential for embarrassing themselves in front of peers outweighs any displeasure the teacher may show about their nonparticipation. An alternative to public performance is the tableau. Ironically, this is a silent activity that involves a group of students striking a group pose to dramatize a scene from a book. For example, students reading *Lord of the Flies* (Golding, 1954) can recreate the scene where the boys create rules for their life on the island, including the rule that the person who holds the conch shell gets to talk. The group reads the scene and discusses how it might look. They use simple props and the position of their bodies to illustrate the scene for the class while a narrator explains the tableau. The oral language development, of course, comes from the conversations within the group to plan the scene.

Independent Learning

How do you use oral language during independent learning? Remember that "independent" doesn't mean "isolated"—instead, it refers to time when students use the skills and strategies they have been learning to create original experiences. Therefore, this phase of the language arts workshop allows students to apply their listening and speaking skills in ways that are less structured than the collaborative learning activities.

See chapter 5 for a review of author's chair.

Author's chair. The *author's chair* is time during the language arts workshop when writers share their work with others. Like other public performances, this is an opportunity for students to read and discuss their writing with classmates. Even emergent and early writers can share their work and take pride in their accomplishments. The author's chair itself is different from the others in the room (it may be a rocking chair, an ottoman, or other unique piece) and is placed in an area that allows for a small audience. Older students who may be more reticent about such public displays enjoy the *literacy lounge*, a more intimate arrangement of groups of students who read their work to one another while sharing hot chocolate or other treats. These experiences give students an opportunity to use conversational discourse while sharing their writing.

Extemporaneous speaking. Many of us may recall a type of debate team competition called *extemporaneous speaking*. While we borrow the term, it is not performed as a competitive event in the language arts workshop. Instead, we are borrowing the format of extemporaneous speaking:

- Three topics are drawn out of a jar and the speaker chooses one to focus on.
- The speaker is given 15 minutes to prepare talking points on the topic.
- The speaker speaks for three minutes on the topic using their notes.

Topics should be general in nature and developmentally appropriate. For example, first-grade topics might include a favorite vacation, a book they recommend for a younger child, or the best kind of pet. Students in Ms. Allen's fifth-grade class use extemporaneous speaking as a time to discuss current events of interest. The topic itself is less important than the routine of speaking in front of others. We recommend creating a classroom job of Featured Speaker along with others like the Door Holder, Line Leader, and Materials Manager.

During independent time in the language arts workshop, the featured speaker makes notes about what he or she wants to say, using many of the principles of accountable talk to prepare his or her talk. Older students can write these on 3 × 5 cards while younger students can use a form like the one in Figure 6.14. Later, they address the class by rereading their topic and speaking from their notes.

BIG IDEAS ABOUT ORAL LANGUAGE DEVELOPMENT

Like other aspects of literacy, oral language is a developmental process that is enhanced with intentional instruction. In the language arts workshop, this means that students have many opportunities to talk with each other, to use academic language to understand concepts, and to speak to groups on more formal topics. Oral language development is tied to reading and writing as well and is an integral part of the process of becoming literate.

 ## INTEGRATING THE STANDARDS

Create lesson plans that meet your state's standards by visiting our Companion Website at www.prenhall.com/frey. There you'll find lessons created to meet the NCTE/IRA

Figure 6.14 Extemporaneous Notes

What is the topic?
What do I know about it?
Make a personal connection
Give an example
State the topic again
Thank the audience

Standards. Adapt them to meet the standards of your own state through links to your state's standards, and keep them in the online portfolio. You can collect lesson plans for each chapter in an online portfolio, providing you with invaluable tools to meet your state's standards when you head into your own classroom.

CHECK YOUR UNDERSTANDING

1. What are the relationships between speaking, listening, reading, and writing?
2. What interaction skills do students use?
3. What are effective questioning habits?
4. What is accountable talk?

CLASSROOM CONNECTIONS

1. Discuss the speaking and listening skills of your students with your classroom teacher. How are students assessed for oral language development? What are the skills your teacher believes are most important?
2. Review your state's grade level standards for speaking and listening.

3. With your teacher's permission, tape a conversation with two students with differing abilities in oral language. What kinds of instruction would be useful for each child?

4. Compare the language registers used by your students in: the lunchroom, a collaborative learning group, and when speaking in front of the class.

References

Almasi, J. F. (1995). The nature of fourth graders' sociocognitive conflicts in peer-led and teacher-led discussions of literature. *Reading Research Quarterly, 30,* 314–351.

Alvermann, D. E. (1991). The discussion web: A graphic aid for learning across the curriculum. *The Reading Teacher, 45,* 92–99.

Armbruster, B., Anderson, T., Armstrong, J., Wise, M., Janisch, C., & Meyer, L. (1991). Reading and questioning in content areas. *Journal of Reading Behavior, 23,* 35–59.

Aronson, E. (1978). *The jigsaw classroom.* Beverly Hills, CA: Sage.

Ashton-Warner, S. (1963). *Teacher.* New York: Simon & Schuster.

Block, S. (2001). Ask me a question: How teachers use inquiry in a classroom. *American School Board Journal, 188*(5), 43–45.

Bloome, D., & Egan-Robertson, A. (1993). The social construction of intertextuality in classroom reading and writing lessons. *Reading Research Quarterly, 28,* 305–333.

Brock, C. H., Boyd, F. B., & Moore, J. A. (2003). Variation in language and the use of language across contexts: Implications for literacy learning. In J. Flood, D. Lapp, J. R. Squire, & J. M. Jensen (Eds.), *Handbook of research on teaching the English language arts* (2nd ed., pp. 446–458). Mahwah, NJ: Lawrence Erlbaum Associates.

Brophy, J. (1985). Interactions of male and female students with male and female teachers. In L. C. Wilkinson & C. B. Marrett (Eds.), *Gender influences in classroom interaction* (pp. 115–142). Orlando, FL: Academic Press.

Burgess, S. R. (2002). The influence of speech perception, oral language ability, the home literacy environment, and pre-reading knowledge on the growth of phonological sensitivity: A one-year longitudinal investigation. *Reading and Writing: An Interdisciplinary Journal, 15,* 709–737.

Carr, E., & Ogle, D. (1987). K-W-L plus: A strategy for comprehension and summarization. *Journal of Reading, 30,* 626–631.

Cazden, C. B. (1986). Classroom discourse. In M. Wittrock (Ed.), *Handbook of research on teaching* (3rd ed., pp. 432–462). New York: Macmillan.

Cazden, C. B. (1988). *Classroom discourse: The language of teaching and learning.* Portsmouth, NH: Heinemann.

Cazden, C. B. (2001). *Classroom discourse: The language of teaching and learning* (2nd ed.). Portsmouth, NH: Heinemann.

Collins, R., & Cooper, P. J. (1997). *The power of story: Teaching through storytelling* (2nd ed.). Boston: Allyn & Bacon.

Cooper, D. H., Roth, F. P., Speece, D. L., & Schatschneider, C. (2002). The contribution of oral language skills to the development of phonological awareness. *Applied Psycholinguistics, 23,* 399–416.

Cooper, P., & Morreale, S. (Eds.). (2003a). *Creating competent communicators: Activities for teaching speaking, listening, and media literacy in K–6 classrooms.* Scottsdale, AZ: Holcomb Hathaway Publishers.

Cooper, P., & Morreale, S. (Eds.). (2003b). *Creating competent communicators: Activities for teaching speaking, listening, and media literacy in 7–12 classrooms*. Scottsdale, AZ: Holcomb Hathaway Publishers.

Daniels, H. (2002). *Literature circles: Voice and choice in book clubs and reading groups* (2nd ed.). York, ME: Stenhouse.

Devine, T. G. (1978). Listening: What do we know after fifty years of research and theorizing? *Journal of Reading, 21*, 269–304.

Dillon, J. T. (1988). *Questioning and teaching: A manual of practice*. New York: Teachers College Press.

Education Department of Western Australia. (1994a). *Oral language developmental continuum*. Melbourne, Australia: Longman.

Education Department of Western Australia. (1994b). *Oral language resource book*. Melbourne, Australia: Longman.

Fearn, L., & Farnan, N. (2001). *Interactions: Teaching writing and the language arts*. Boston: Houghton Mifflin.

Fisher, D., & Frey, N. (2004). *Improving adolescent literacy: Strategies at work*. Upper Saddle River, NJ: Merrill/Prentice Hall. Used with permission.

Fisher, F. L. (1968). The influence of reading and discussion on the attitudes of fifth graders toward Indians. *Journal of Educational Research, 62*, 130–134.

Fisher, K. (2003). If we can talk about it, we can write about it; If we can write about it, we can read about it. *Michigan Reading Journal, 35*(2), 6–12.

Forest, H. (n.d.) *A storytelling skills rubric*. Retrieved from http://www.storyarts.org/classroom/usestories/storyrubric.html skills.

Galda, L. (1984). Narrative competence: Play, storytelling, and story comprehension. In A. D. Pellegrini & T. Yawkey (Eds.), *The development of oral and written language in social contexts* (pp. 105–117). Norwood, NJ: Ablex.

Gambrell, L. B. (1996). What research reveals about discussion. In L. B. Gambrell & J. F. Almasi (Eds.), *Lively discussions! Fostering engaged readings* (pp. 25–38). Newark, DE: International Reading Association.

Goatley, V. J., & Raphael, T. E. (1992). Non-traditional learners' written and dialogic response to literature. In C. K. Kinzer & D. J. Leu (Eds.), *Literacy research, theory, and practice: Views from many perspectives* (pp. 313–322). Chicago, IL: National Reading Conference.

Guilford, J. P. (1959). Traits of creativity. In H. H. Anderson (Ed.), *Creativity and its cultivation* (pp. 142–161). New York: Harper.

Harste, J., & Short, K. G. (1988). *Creating classrooms for authors: The reading-writing connection*. Portsmouth, NH: Heinemann.

Hartman, D. K., & Allison, J. (1996). Promoting inquiry-oriented discussions using multiple texts. In L. B. Gambrell & J. F. Almasi (Eds.), *Lively discussions! Fostering engaged readings* (pp. 106–133). Newark, DE: International Reading Association.

Holden, C. (1993). Giving girls a chance: Patterns of talk in co-operative group work. *Gender and Education, 5*, 179–189.

Lyman, F. T. (1981). The responsive classroom discussion: The inclusion of all students. In A. Anderson (Ed.), *Mainstreaming digest* (pp. 109–113). College Park: University of Maryland Press.

Manzo, A. V. (1969). The ReQuest procedure. *Journal of Reading, 11*, 123–126.

McKenzie, M. G. (1985). Shared writing: Apprenticeship in writing. *Language Matters, 1–2,* 1–5.

Mehan, H. (1979). *Learning lessons.* Cambridge, MA: Harvard University Press.

Morrow, L. M., & Smith, J. K. (1990). The effects of group size on interactive storybook reading. *Reading Research Quarterly, 25,* 213–231.

National Center on Education and the Economy. (2001). *Speaking and listening for preschool through third grade.* Washington, DC: New Standards.

National Communication Association (n.d.). *NCA's standards for speaking, listening, and media literacy in K–12 education.* Retrieved December 9, 2004, from www.natcom.org/Instruction.new_page_1.htm.

Ogle, D. M. (1986). K-W-L: A teaching model that develops active reading of expository text. *The Reading Teacher, 39,* 564–570.

Ong, W. J. (1989). *Orality and literacy: The technologizing of the word.* New York: Routledge.

Orenstein, P. (1994). *Schoolgirls: Young women, self-esteem, and the confidence gap.* New York: Doubleday.

Ouaknin, M. A. (1999). *Mysteries of the alphabet.* New York: Abbeville.

Palinscar, A. S., & Brown, A. L. (1984). Reciprocal teaching of comprehension-fostering and comprehension-monitoring activities. *Cognition and Instruction, 12,* 117–175.

Paul, R., Binker., A., Jensen, K., & Kreklau, H. (1990). *Critical thinking handbook: A guide for remodeling lesson plans in language arts, social studies and science.* Rohnert Park, CA: Foundations for Critical Thinking.

Payne, R. K., (1995). *A framework for understanding and working with students and adults from poverty.* Baytown, TX: RFT Publishing.

Pinnell, G. S., & Jaggar, A. M. (2003). Oral language: Speaking and listening in elementary classrooms. In J. Flood, D. Lapp, J. R. Squire, & J. M. Jensen (Eds.), *Handbook of research on teaching the English language arts* (2nd ed., pp. 881–913). Mahwah, NJ: Lawrence Erlbaum Associates.

Resnick, L. (1995). From aptitude to effort: A new foundation for our schools. *Daedalus, 124*(4), 55–62.

Romaine, S. (1994). *Language in society: An introduction to sociolinguistics.* New York: Oxford University Press.

Ross, R. (1964). A look at listeners. *The Elementary School Journal, 64,* 369–372.

Rubright, L. (1996). *Beyond the beanstalk: Interdisciplinary learning through storytelling.* Portsmouth, NH: Heinemann.

Sadker, M., & Sadker, D. (1986). Sexism in the classroom: From grade school to graduate school. *Phi Delta Kappan, 67,* 512–515.

Sadker, M., & Sadker, D. (1995). *Failing at fairness: How America's schools cheat girls.* New York: Scribner.

Sapon-Shevin, M. (1999). *Because we can change the world: A practical guide to building cooperative, inclusive classroom communities.* Boston: Allyn & Bacon.

Spor, M. W., & Schneider, B. K. (1999). Content reading strategies: What teachers know, use, and want to learn. *Reading Research and Instruction, 38,* 221–231.

Villaume, S. K., & Hopkins, L. (1995). A transactional and sociocultural view of response in a fourth-grade literature discussion group. *Reading Research and Instruction, 34,* 190–203.

Vygotsky, L. S. (1986). *Thought and language* (A. Kozulin, Ed.). Cambridge, MA: MIT Press.

Wajnryb, R., & Ur, P. (2003). *Stories: Narrative activities for the language classroom.* Cambridge: Cambridge University Press.

Weissman, A. (2002). *Do tell! Storytelling for you and students.* Worthington, OH: Linworth Publishing.

Whaley, C. (2002). Meeting the diverse needs of children through storytelling. Supporting language learning. *Young Children, 57*(2), 31–34.

Wiencek, J., & O'Flahavan, J. F. (1994). From teacher-led to peer discussion groups about literature: Suggestions for making the shift. *Language Arts, 71,* 488–498.

Wood, K. D., & Jones, J. (1998). Flexible grouping and group retellings include struggling learners in classroom communities. *Preventing School Failure, 43,* 37–38.

Children's Literature Cited

Berger, M. (2002). *Snap! A book about alligators and crocodiles.* New York: Cartwheel.

Berger, M. (2003). *Spinning spiders.* New York: HarperTrophy.

Bunting, E. (1992). *The wall.* New York: Clarion.

Chambers, C. E. (1998). *California gold rush.* New York: Troll.

Cole, J. (1995). *Spider's lunch: All about garden spiders.* New York: Grosset & Dunlap.

Corrigan, P. (2001). *Cougars: Our wild world.* Chanhassen, MN: NorthWord.

Gibbons, G. (1994). *Spiders.* New York: Holiday House.

Gibbons, G. (1995). *Wolves!* New York: Holiday House.

Glaser, L. (1999). *Spectacular spiders.* Riverside, NJ: Millbrook.

Golding, W. (1954). *Lord of the flies.* New York: Perigee.

Hodge, D. (1999). *Bears: Polar bears, black bears, and grizzly bears.* Tonawanda, NY: Kids Can Press.

Kalman, B. (1999). *The gold rush.* New York: Crabtree.

Krensky, S. (1996). *Strike it rich!* New York: Scott, Foresman.

Reinhart, M. (2003). *Young naturalist's handbook: Insect-lo-pedia.* New York: Hyperion.

Robinson, F. (1996). *Hello spider!* New York: Scott, Foresman.

Ryan, P. M. (2002). *Esperanza rising.* New York: Scholastic.

Schlosser, E. (2002). *Fast food nation: The dark side of the all-American meal.* New York: HarperCollins.

Schanzer, R. (1999). *Gold fever!* Washington, DC: National Geographic.

Quang, N. H. (1986). *The land I lost: A boy in Vietnam.* New York: HarperTrophy.

Whelan, G. (1993). *Goodbye Vietnam.* New York: Yearling.

White, E. E. (2002). *The journal of Patrick Seamus Flaherty: U.S. Marine Corps, Khe Sanh, Vietnam, 1968.* New York: Scholastic.

Winer, Y. (1998). *Spiders spin webs.* Watertown, MA: Charlesbridge.

7

Teaching Spelling and Word Study in the Language Arts Workshop

BIG IDEAS ABOUT SPELLING AND WORD STUDY

Students benefit from spelling instruction that is purposeful and follows a gradual release of responsibility model. Like other aspects of literacy acquisition, students move through developmental phases as they learn the sounds, patterns, and structures of the language. Teachers in the language arts workshop provide engaging spelling instruction and activities to develop each student's growing ability to spell the words they need for written communication.

Questions to Consider

When you have finished reading this chapter, you should be able to answer these questions:

- Why should time be devoted to spelling instruction in the language arts workshop?
- How do students learn to spell? What is the natural development of spelling?
- Which words should be taught in a spelling curriculum?
- What instructional activities support spelling acquisition?

Key Vocabulary

Speech-to-print connection

Graphs

Emergent stage

Letter Name stage

Within Word Pattern

Syllable Juncture

Derivational Constancy

VCE

Homophones

Synonyms

Antonyms

Affixes

Etymology

Homographs

Latin and Greek root words

Prefix

Suffix

Acquisition

Retention

Automaticity

Elkonin boxes

Letter boxes

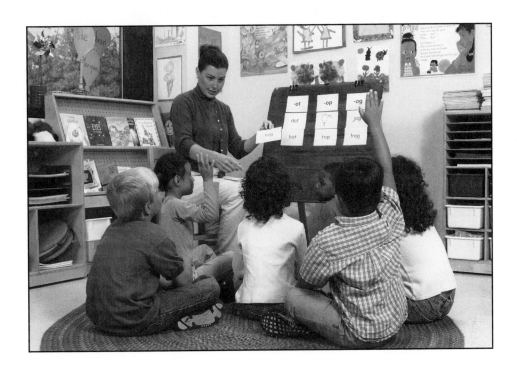

A LOOK INSIDE

While Ms. Allen confers with individual students, others are working independently in this fifth-grade classroom. The students in Lupita's group are writing in their spelling journals. Miriam is practicing the class focus words by using a simple study technique called "*Look-Cover-Say-Write-Check.*" Leo is using his *Have-a-Go notes* to figure out the correct spelling for *suggest,* puzzled about whether it has one *g* or two. He writes it both ways and settles on the latter, then continues with his writing. Meanwhile, Steve and Tino are working through a *word sort,* trying to create categories for the list of words they are learning this week. Lupita is contemplating which of the independent spelling activities she will do next. (The list, laminated and attached to each folder, can be seen in Figure 7.1.) She has just completed her "*Words to Learn*" list where she has identified the "tricky parts" of each word. At that moment, Ms. Allen checks in on the group to see how they are progressing. "I've got a new word for *Stump the Teacher,*" says Lupita with a twinkle in her eye. "Great!" says Ms. Allen. "Bring it on—I'm ready!"

The students in this classroom are engaged in spelling and no one seems to be writing each word ten times or copying definitions out of the dictionary. Yet their spelling scores have risen all year, thanks to this teacher's developmental approach to spelling. These and many other spelling activities will be discussed throughout this chapter.

Figure 7.1   Fifth-Grade Spelling Folder

Independent Spelling Notebook Activities

▶ **Word Sorts**–study your words very carefully, decide how you want to sort them

▶
Look   Cover   Say   Write   Check

▶ **Word Relationships**–add a **prefix** (re, un, dis) or **suffix** (ing, ed, s, er) of both to create relationships

> Example: count, recount, discount, counting, counted, countable, countless

▶ **Spellamadoodle**–create a design using your spelling words three times

▶ **Find a synonym** (a word that has a similiar meaning) for your spelling words

▶ **Find an antonym** (a word that is the opposite) for your spelling words

▶ **Itty Bitty**–find smaller words in your spelling words

> Caterpillar: cat, rat, pill, later, liar

▶ **Rhyme Time**–find words that rhyme with your spelling words

> Example: might, flight, sight

▶ **ABC Order**–put your spelling words in alphabetical order

▶ **Spelling Riddles**

> I have 7 letters.
> I rhyme with might.   Answer: delight
> I begin with the letter d.
> I have two syllables.

▶ **Crazy Crossword**

> where   cat
>   a   trace
>   p   a   a
>   place   i   team
>   y   n

SPELLING AND WORD STUDY IN THE LANGUAGE ARTS WORKSHOP

Students in the language arts workshop use words to read and write about the world. Their ability to use words well means that there is purposeful instruction in spelling and word study. Word study is the term used to describe a host of practices, including phonics, vocabulary, and spelling (Harris & Hodges, 1995). In this chapter, we will focus on spelling instruction as a key component of word study.

Focusing on Spelling

Why should students learn to spell? Don't you know someone who is a successful adult who regularly says, "I can't spell to save my life."? Why do we, as teachers, focus instructional time on a skill that may not be useful for adults? We were asked these questions when an Internet posting started circulating. It read, in part:

> Aoccdrnig to a rscheearch at an Elingsh uinervtisy, it deosn't mttaer in waht oredr the ltteers in a wrod are, the olny iprmoetnt tihng is taht the frist and lsat ltteer is at the rghit pclae. The rset can be in a toatl mses and you can sitll raed it wouthit any porbelms. Tihs is bcuseae we do not raed ervey lteter by istlef but the wrod as a wlohe.

Most people had little difficulty in reading this posting. We maintain that this is because most readers have a fairly well-developed sense of English spelling and can move the letters around to make the writing make sense. We also note that poor spellers or emerging readers and writers have more difficulty with this passage because of their under-developed spelling, and thus reading, ability.

Why Should Students Learn to Spell?

We imagine that your answer included something about the importance of making oneself understood in written communication. If so, then you understand that we do not teach spelling so that students can simply spell. Very few students want to spell just to excel in the local spelling bee. Instead, we focus on spelling so that students can read and write. Spelling is an important skill in the language arts workshop because it offers a means for successful expression of thoughts and ideas (Schlagal, 2002). Imagine students beginning their independent writing and not having any words at their disposal. Frustrating for the student, right? Beyond that, the language arts workshop becomes a waste of time that is also frustrating for the teacher.

Fearn and Farnan (2001) make an interesting point about this. They suggest that there is a difference in spelling needs depending on which side of the table the paper is on. In their example, when a student is writing, he or she only needs enough skill in spelling to be able to read the piece and edit it. However, this is not the case when, as Fearn and Farnan note, the paper crosses the table. When the reader, and not the writer, has the paper, there is an expectation that the words will be spelled correctly. Readers tend to notice errors in spelling and this can be very distracting for them (Thibodeau, 2002). In the worst-case scenario, the poor spelling makes the text unintelligible for the reader.

From *Albert's Alphabet* by Leslie Tryon, © 1994 by Simon & Schuster. Used by permission of Simon & Schuster.

What Is the Speech-to-Print Connection?

Phonemes are the smallest units of sounds in a language. There are about 80 phonemes represented in the world's languages.

It is a common misconception that entry into school represents an introduction to language. To the contrary, children entering school have been drenched by the sounds of language since their birth. During the first five years of life they have learned to sort out the 44 phonemes of the English language in order to make sense of the jumble of sounds coming at them.

For many children, kindergarten does represent an introduction to the formal operations of the language. During the primary years, they will learn the **speech-to-print connection** that lies at the heart of reading and writing. Stated simply, these students will become skilled at recognizing how spoken words can be represented through **graphs** (symbols). Understanding the speech-to-print connection comprises three elements:

- *Phonemic awareness*—The ability to manipulate sounds, for instance, segmenting the sounds in *cat* and converting it into /c/ /a/ /t/
- *Letter knowledge*—Recognizing the names and shapes of the letters of the alphabet
- *Sound/symbol relationships*—Matching the sounds of the language to the letters and letter combinations

Each of these elements is essential to literacy development. The first, phonemic awareness, has been found to be a strong predictor in learning to read (Wagner, Torgensen, & Rashotte, 1994) and spell (Nation & Hulme, 1977). Among first-graders, letter knowledge was identified as the critical variable in spelling acquisition (Foorman, Francis, Novy, & Liberman, 1991). As well, instruction in sound-symbol relationships, especially regular spelling patterns, is necessary for spelling development (Snow, Burns, & Griffin, 1998). Knowledge of these and other elements of language development are at the heart of sound early literacy instruction (Moats, 2000). In addition to understanding the role of language in spelling, it is also necessary to recognize the developmental phases children move through.

Evidence Based

How Do Students Learn to Spell— What Is the Natural Development of Spelling?

The easy answer to this question is that students learn to spell when their teachers (and parents) teach them how to spell. The more complex answer to this question requires an explanation of spelling development. Over the past several decades, researchers have examined the spelling patterns children use (Henderson, 1990). Ganske (2000) provides an overview of each of the stages of spelling development: **Emergent, Letter Name, Within Word Pattern, Syllable Juncture,** and **Derivational Constancy.** We'll examine each of these stages in greater depth and provide examples of student writing that demonstrate each stage. The Developmental Screening Assessment for determining student levels will be explored further in chapter 11 on assessment (Ganske, 2000).

Emergent. Figure 7.2 contains student work samples at Stage I: Emergent. You will note that children at this stage of development have recognized that print conveys a message, but that they are not yet reading. They use scribbles, wavy lines, symbols that resemble letters, and random letters on the page. Children in Stage I often engage in writing-like activities and use drawings as part of their writing. At this stage, there is no correlation between the letter a child writes and the sound it was intended to represent (Bear, Invernizzi, Templeton, & Johnston, 2004).

Figure 7.2 Stage I: Emergent

Spelling Word	Emergent Speller's Representation
dog	OSX
Mom	IS2S
cat	DC WO

Figure 7.3 Stage II: Letter Name

Spelling Word	Letter Name Speller's Representation
dog	dG
Mom	MM
cat	kt

The instructional implications for students at this stage include a focus on phonemic awareness (Adams, Foorman, Lundberg, & Beeler, 1998), read alouds (Yopp, 1995), and sound play activities such as singing, chanting, and rhyming words (Fisher, McDonald, & Strickland, 2001; Yopp & Yopp, 1997). In addition, as students develop their awareness of and skills in phonemic awareness, they need instruction in the concept of the word and concepts about print (Clay, 2000). For example, a teacher may point to individual words as they read. This builds one-to-one correspondence between the spoken and printed word. At this stage, children enjoy multiple rereadings of a single text. This also allows them to predict the story and memorize the words for their own "read" of the book. Finally, late in this stage, students need instruction in the letter knowledge and sound-symbol correlations. They also begin to memorize the spelling of specific words, such as their name, *mom, dad,* and other common words that they hear and use. Teachers often use word sorts based on the first letter of a word for students at this stage. This means that students sort words on cards based on common characteristics of sound or meaning. These are discussed in more detail later in this chapter.

> Knowledge of the way print works on the page and in books is referred to as concept about print.

Letter Name. Figure 7.3 contains student work samples at Stage II: Letter Name. You will note that students at this stage have started to master the sound-symbol relationships and the concept of a word. The name of this stage came from the evidence that students used the names of letters and their emerging understanding of the alphabetic principle to spell (Bear, Invernizzi, Templeton, & Johnston, 2004; Read, 1975). This leads to rather unconventional spelling of words, such as KSL for castle and PLES for police.

As you observe readers at this stage, you will likely note that they will read aloud slowly. This provides the novice reader time to figure out words they do not know and to use any picture or context clues to help with the words (Ganske, 2000). As you notice writers at this stage, you will likely notice that they are very purposeful in their writing. They often write each letter deliberately and continually sound out the word to identify the next letter (Sipe, 1998).

Figure 7.4 Stage III: Within Word Pattern

Spelling Word	Letter Name Speller's Representation
dog	dog
Mom	Mom
cat	cat
clock	clok
goat	gote
enough	enuf

See chapter 3

The instructional implications for students at this stage include read alouds and independent readings of predictable texts and texts that have repetition, rhyme, rhythm, or any other features that help the new reader expect words (Ganske, 2000). Again, teachers focus on the speech-to-print connection and provide explicit phonics instruction, often during the guided reading portion of the language arts workshop. Commonly, students need instruction on initial and final consonants, initial blends and digraphs, short vowels, and final blends and digraphs. Teachers also provide focus lessons, often via interactive writing, on concepts about print and common spelling patterns as well as word sorts on word families and common spelling patterns.

Information on interactive writing was presented in chapter 2.

Within Word Pattern. Figure 7.4 contains student work samples at Stage III: Within Word Pattern. You will note that many of the common sight vocabulary words have been mastered and are spelled correctly. You will also notice that students at this stage can read increasingly difficult texts, including chapter books, because of their knowledge of letter sounds and short vowel patterns (Bear, Invernizzi, Templeton, & Johnston, 2004). Students at this stage are not relying on individual sounds to spell words, but rather can chunk words and use familiar word families and patterns to make either correct or closer approximations to conventional spelling (Ganske, 2000). In terms of both reading and writing, students are quicker. They also read longer texts and write longer papers. As budding writers, they begin to consider their audience and establish a purpose for their writing.

See information on using word walls later in this chapter

The instructional implications for students at this stage include an increased focus on the word wall, individual spelling dictionaries, and systematic spelling instruction with self-corrected tests. An instructional shift to "what students use but confuse" (Bear, Invernizzi, Templeton, & Johnston, 2004, p. 16) is important. Commonly this shift includes **VCE** patterns (such as *make, drive*), r-controlled vowel patterns (such as *girl, hurt*), complex consonant patterns (such as *fight, knee*), and abstract vowel patterns that are not clearly long or short (such as *plow, boil*) (Ganske, 2000). In addition, students need to focus on **homophones** (*dear/deer, their/there/they're*), **synonyms** (*bucket/pail, present/gift*), and **antonyms** (*high/low, empty/full*) as described in Figure 7.5. These are often taught via whole class games such as Jeopardy™, word wall bingo, Concentration, and in cloze activities. In cloze activities, a word is removed from a sentence, producing a "fill-in-the-blank" action. Again, word sorts are useful as students sort words based on these characteristics.

VCE stands for "vowel-consonant-silent *e*."

Other cloze activities can be found in chapter 11 on assessment.

Figure 7.5   Dictionary of Language Terms

Language term	Definition	Examples
Homophone* (or homonym**)	Words that sound alike but are spelled differently and have different meanings	road/rode allowed/aloud our/hour
Synonym	Words that have similar meanings	rock/stone house/home sad/unhappy
Antonym	Words that are opposite one another in meaning	smooth/rough sunny/cloudy hot/cold

*Homophones are words of the same language that are pronounced alike even if they differ in spelling, meaning, or origin, such as "pair" and "pear." Homophones may also be spelled alike, as in "bear" (the animal) and "bear" (to carry). But this list consists only of homophones that are not spelled alike.

**Homonym is a somewhat looser term than homophone, sometimes referring to all homophones and only homophones, and sometimes referring to the subset of homophones that are spelled alike.

Figure 7.6   Level IV: Syllable Juncture

Spelling Word	Letter Name Speller's Representation
table	tabel
confusion	confushun
cotton	coton
coming	comming
dollar	doller

Syllable Juncture. Figure 7.6 contains student work samples at Level IV: Syllable Juncture. You will note that students at this stage are skillful readers and writers. They spell most common words correctly and have a growing oral vocabulary. Literacy has increased in value for them as they explore various topics, genres, and ideas. Content areas such as social studies, art, music, science, physical education, and math provide students with access to new information as well as a challenge to read and write in increasingly complex ways. Students at this stage "write to persuade, explain, describe, summarize, and question, using such forms as letters, essays, and various types of response logs to convey their ideas" (Ganske, 2000, p. 17).

The instructional implications for students at this stage include a focus on words in which the -ed or -ing ending requires an /e/ to be dropped and the final consonant to be doubled (such as *taping* or *tapping*), doubling the consonant at a syllable juncture (such as *shopping* or *cattle*), and focus on stressed and unstressed syllables (such as *trample* or *hockey*) (Bear, Invernizzi, Templeton, & Johnston, 2004; Ganske, 2000). This is often accomplished when teachers meet with individual students during language arts workshop conferences, during self-corrected spelling tests, and a specific instructional focus on **affixes** (prefix, suffix, and roots).

More information on affixes will be presented later in the chapter.

Figure 7.7   Level V: Derivational Constancy

Spelling Word	Letter Name Speller's Representation
consensus	concensus
noticeable	noticable
guarantee	garantee
memento	momento
privilege	priviledge

Derivational Constancy. Figure 7.7 contains student work samples at Level V: Derivational Constancy. This final stage of spelling development typically begins in middle school and continues through adulthood. You will note that students at this stage rarely spell words incorrectly and that they are beginning to learn that words with similar meanings share common spelling patterns (such as *demonstrate, demonstration, demonstrable*). Students at this stage learn about the history of the language as well as the **etymology** (word origins).

The instructional implications for students at this stage allow the teacher to teach students to scrutinize words for their histories. Importantly, the teacher will often learn a lot about words as his or her students engage in this level of word study. Students should be encouraged to keep word journals and to capture the related etymology for the word in these journals. Often students like to record the first known use of the word, related words, and a typical sentence in which the word is used. As Bear, Invernizzi, Templeton, and Johnston suggest, the teacher can initiate the word study with a simple question, "Did you find any interesting words in your reading?" (2004, p. 20). In addition, Ganske (2000) suggests that teachers focus on silent and sounded consonants (such as *hasten* and *haste*), affixes, and vowel changes (such as *democracy* to *democratic*).

What Doesn't Work for a Spelling Curriculum?

As Templeton noted, "most classroom teachers may not be explicitly aware of the nature of English spelling and the different types of information that the system represents; nor may they be comfortable with how best to facilitate the development of this knowledge in students" (2003a, p. 738). As a result, there are at least three common approaches to spelling instruction that are ineffective, or even harmful, to the development of spellers who can use words correctly in their reading and writing.

Neglect. It's almost embarrassing to write about, but ignoring spelling instruction will not provide students the support they need to spell as they write or to read independently. Unfortunately, it is still too common for teachers to believe that spelling will just develop naturally as students read. Simply reading and absorbing patterns, as Bosman and Van Orden note, "is not the most effective way to learn to spell" (1997, p. 188). Perfetti was more explicit in his writing: "practice at spelling should help reading more than practice at reading helps spelling" (1997, p. 31). As Zutell (1994) notes, students need explicit instruction in spelling. Thus it should be clear that the language arts workshop cannot be productive if spelling is neglected or ignored.

The Monday-to-Friday routine. Giving students a list of words on Monday, asking them to practice the words at home during the week, and then testing their knowledge on

Friday is also an insufficient route to spelling. While we know that this is a common route, the evidence for this approach is lacking (Templeton, 2003a). In contrast with this tradition of "giving the words then the test," teachers in the language arts workshop focus instruction on the weekly spelling words on a regular basis. Students correct their own tests, not just on Friday, but every day (Fearn & Farnan, 2001).

Evidence Based

Writing the words ten times (or 100 times for that matter). Writing words as a list is also an ineffective way to improve the spelling performance (Ganske, 2000). We all know students who write each letter in a column ten times until the word appears ten times. Not only is this ineffective, but it wastes time—time that students could use to learn how to spell.

Isn't English Too Irregular to Learn Easily?

English is known to be a confusing language—just recall the opening e-mail posting to consider the difficulty. However, English is more consistent than most people realize (Templeton, 2003a). As Bear, Invernizzi, Templeton, and Johnston (2004) note, English requires an understanding of three systems to spell correctly: alphabet, pattern, and meaning. First, regarding alphabet, English is based, at least in part, on the sound-symbol relationship. Students have to learn to read to voice the sounds from left to right matching sounds to symbols as appropriate. However, we all know that this approach will only work for a portion of the words in English. The word *flight*, for example, requires more than alphabetic knowledge to read correctly.

The second system that has to be mastered to spell correctly in English is the pattern. This layer requires that readers extend beyond a single letter to understand the sound that should be produced. One pattern that guides our understanding is the CVCe, found in words such as *bake, flake,* and *make*. Learning the pattern provides the reader with a transportable skill for decoding and encoding.

CONSONANT-VOWEL-CONSONANT-SILENT *e*

Unfortunately, the alphabet and patterns are not all that are required. English also relies on meaning for some spellings (Templeton, 2003b). This third layer provides readers a clue for words with sounds that do not necessarily match their spelling. For example, *clinic* and *clinician* or *physics* and *physicist* rely on the meaning level for spelling while the individual words are pronounced differently. This is also evidenced in **homographs,** which are words that are spelled alike but differ in meaning and sometimes sound. Consider the following:

- Sally will *present* the *present* to the birthday girl.
- The state now *permits permits* for fishing and hunting.
- "I *object!*" shouted the prosecutor when the *object* was shown to the jury.

Taking into account these three systems that operate in English, teachers must focus their instruction accordingly. Early in a students' spelling career, the focus will remain on the alphabet. As students become more sophisticated in their spelling development, teachers add the patterns and meaning levels. Obviously, these systems have implications not only for instruction, but also for the choice of words that comprise the spelling curriculum.

Which Words Should Be Taught in a Spelling Curriculum?

The issue of spelling lists has plagued teachers and researchers for years. As Henderson noted, "Those who set out to remember every letter of every word will never make it. Those who try to spell by sound alone will be defeated. Those who learn how to 'walk through' words with sensible expectations, noting sound, pattern, and meaning relationships, will know what to remember, and they will learn to spell English" (1990, p. 70).

Shane Templeton in his review of published research on spelling instruction, noted that sole reliance on high-frequency words or on commonly misspelled words does not provide the student with an understanding of the "logical and negotiable patterns" found in English (2003a, p. 745). In other words, while these types of word lists are useful as part of the spelling curriculum, they are not sufficient.

Evidence Based

Similarly, Fearn and Farnan suggest that spelling words come from lists that are organized such that students understand patterns. As they note, "spelling from lists of words might seem archaic" (2001, p. 415). However, the research evidence on spelling suggests that presenting words in context is less effective and more time consuming than presenting words from widely accepted lists (Beckham-Hungler & Williams, 2003; Templeton & Morris, 1999). So what kinds of words should be featured in spelling curricula? We will look at five kinds of words to use. The proportion of words from each of these categories will vary depending on your students' developmental spelling levels, but all should be featured to varying degrees through grades 1–8:

- Word patterns
- Latin and Greek root words
- Affixes
- High frequency words
- Commonly misspelled words

Word patterns. As you can imagine, there are a number of word lists that have been reviewed as appropriate for specific grade levels. We have used the everyday spelling list in our classrooms (www.everydayspelling.com/spellinglist). These words were selected based on common misspellings of students at each grade level. Appendix 7.1 contains the first lesson for each of the grade levels as presented in this curriculum.

The onset is comprised of the consonants up to the first vowel; the rime is made up of the vowel and subsequent letters.

You'll note that, consistent with the developmental level of the spellers, the words move from onset and rime patterns, to common spelling patterns, to more difficult words. You'll also note that some serious thought went into the organization of the words, which are clustered into patterns that help students understand the patterns of the language (Templeton, 2003a).

It is important to be aware that presenting words in an organized list does not mean that teachers should not add additional words. We do suggest that students learn Latin and Greek root words, affixes, high-frequency words, and commonly misspelled words. We also believe that some spelling words should be selected from the content they are learning. These words can, and should, be incorporated into the lists you use to teach students to spell (Ganske, 2000).

Latin and Greek root words. The English language derives words from languages all over the world—*luau* from Hawaiian, *bazaar* from Persian, *shampoo* from Hindi. Other words like *blog* enter our language because they represent a new concept. However, most of the words in the English language are derivatives of the Latin and Greek languages. Teaching some of the more common Latin and Greek root words gives students a transportable set of strategies to use as they spell new words. For exam-

A *blog* is an Internet web log for posting comments and information.

The role of derivations in vocabulary is discussed in chapter 8.

ple, when a student knows that *port* means "to carry," he can use that information to figure out both the spelling and meaning of *airport, portable,* and *import.* A list of common Latin and Greek root words can be found in Appendix 7.2.

Affixes. Prefixes, which come before the root word, and **suffixes,** which come after, are together referred to as affixes. These units of meaning modify the root word to further refine the exact definition. For example, in the word *disruption, dis-* is the prefix and *-tion* is the suffix. These basic affixes are highly transportable within the language. In fact, five basic suffixes make up more than 50% of the prefixes used, while four suffixes make up 65% of the suffixes used (Cunningham, 2002). By teaching these affixes alone within a spelling curriculum, students can utilize these to spell thousands of words. A list of these and other common affixes can be found in Figure 7.8.

High-frequency words. Approximately 50%–75% of all words used in schoolbooks, library books, newspapers, and magazines are in the Dolch Basic Sight Vocabulary of 220 words (Dolch, 1936). Many of these words cannot be sounded out because they do not follow decoding rules. Appendix 7.3 contains a listing of all of the words and the approximate age/grade at which students can recognize the words. It is important to note that the age/grade notation is based on a student's ability to sight *read* the word, not write it. We believe that these words are appropriate spelling words across the elementary school curriculum as students must automatically recognize these words if they are to read and write fluently. The Dolch list has been revised and updated several times (Johns, 1981), but the original list remains the most commonly taught.

Commonly misspelled words. Another word list was compiled by Cramer and Cipielewski (1995). This list is fairly unique in that it focuses on the words that are most commonly misspelled by students in grades 1—8. The list can be found in Appendix 7.4. You will likely notice that there is an overlap between the Dolch word list and the most commonly misspelled words.

Did you know that *misspelled* is a commonly misspelled word?

How Will They Remember All These Words?

As you likely recall from your own school days, cramming for a spelling test does not result in long-term retention of the words. Students cannot simply pass through

Figure 7.8 Common Affixes

Prefixes	Re- Dis- Un- In-/Im-	De- A-/An- Pro-
Suffixes	-s/-es -ed -ing -en -ly -er/-or	-tion/-sion -able/-ible -al -ness -er/-est -ful/-less

the spelling lists and be expected to remember the words when the time comes to use them. Fearn and Farnan (2001) identify a 3-phase process required for students to authentically learn how to spell: **acquisition, retention,** and **automaticity.** Let's take each of these in turn and examine their application.

Acquisition. This first component of spelling concerns students learning to spell words correctly. As Fearn and Farnan (2001) note, students must pay attention to the words they can and cannot spell. One way to focus students' attention is through a self-corrected spelling test. However, these tests should not occur only on Friday after students have "studied" the words for a week. Students should participate in regular testing situations and receive immediate feedback via self-corrections.

See chapters 3 and 5 for more information on guided instruction and conferences.

In addition to self-corrected spelling tests, students learn to spell words during guided reading and conferencing times. Teachers can focus students' attention to words as they find them in reading assignments and as they work on successive versions of their writing. A short small group or individualized session focused on spelling in which the student is really paying attention can pay big dividends in learning. It is important to remember, however, that these times should be used to focus on spelling words that are part of a system and not isolated words. As we have noted before, there are simply too many words to learn if we expect students to learn them all one at a time!

Retention. Once students have learned a set of words in a given lesson, there is a risking that they will be forgotten. Retention requires remembering the spelling of words once they have been acquired. As Fearn and Farnan note, "Learning depends not only on attention, but also on the ability to hold information in active memory long enough for it to be recorded in long-term memory" (2001, p. 431). One way that teachers can provide students some practice with retention is to include some "old favorites" on the self-corrected spelling lists. This provides students an opportunity to draw words from memory. Teachers can also use word activities and games that

See word pyramids as an example of a word recall activity.

provide students with an opportunity to use the words they have learned. Finally, teachers ensure that students have multiple opportunities to write during the language arts workshop. This provides young writers with authentic opportunities to use, and spell, words in contexts in which they need them.

Automaticity. Interestingly, accurate spelling on a test does not mean the student can use it in his or her writing. In a study of their second-grade students, Beckham-Hungler and Williams discovered that the children consistently misspelled words in their writing that they had successfully spelled on pretests. They speculated that "the cognitive demands of the pretest situation were much less than the demands of journal writing" (2003, p. 304).

Successful spelling in connected writing signals **automaticity.** This means that students can spell, or write, a chosen word automatically and without thinking about it. This is especially important during writing. If a writer has to stop continually to think about how words are spelled, he or she will not be able to focus on the ideas to be written. Writers need a host of words to draw from as they write. Understanding the developmental nature of spelling, a teacher would not expect a first grader to automatically spell *playground*. The student will likely slow down when he or she comes to that word. However, the teacher can and should expect the student to have a number of words flow automatically, and without conscious effort, from the student's fingers.

The development of automaticity, is not a given. Students need practice to move words from acquisition and retention to automaticity. One way to practice is with the use of given word sentences (Fearn & Farnan, 2001). For example, the teacher may ask the students to "write a sentence with our spelling word *grateful* in the third position of the sentence. In addition, daily timed Power Writing (Fearn & Farnan, 2001) provides students with the opportunity to use the words they know in novel ways. Power Writing, which is discussed in detail in chapter 9 on fluency, invites students to write in 1-minute cycles to increase their writing output. With this type of regular practice, students move many more words from acquisition and retention to automaticity, and thus become stronger writers and readers.

You may recall from our discussion in chapter 3 that we sometimes extend given word sentences into longer pieces of generative writing (Fisher & Frey, 2003).

APPROACHES TO TEACHING SPELLING AND WORD STUDY IN THE LANGUAGE ARTS WORKSHOP

As with other areas of instruction, spelling instruction and practice occurs in each component of the language arts workshop. You'll recall that each day the teacher provides the whole class with focus lessons and then moves to guided instruction, collaborative learning events, and finally independent practice. Importantly, each component of the language arts workshop provides the teacher an opportunity to provide students with different types of spelling instruction.

Focus Lessons The focus lesson portion of the language arts workshop offers students time when the teacher models, coaches, and scaffolds instruction on a skill or strategy. Spelling and word study focus lessons emphasize opportunities for students to use strategies to use their growing understanding of the patterns and structures to solve words.

Practicing words. One of the most basic learning strategies taught is the use of rehearsal as a method for learning new material. As adults, many of us have learned how to do this either through instruction in study skills (if we were lucky) or by trial and error (more likely). Teachers often conduct a focus lesson in September on how to learn new material using a simple 5-step plan:

- *Look* at the word and repeat the letters.
- *Cover* the word.
- *Say* the letters again.
- *Write* the word.
- *Check* to see if you spelled it correctly.

Because this is such a fundamental method of rehearsal, we introduce a poster at the same time for students to refer to when they are studying.

Word walls. Having a word wall in the language arts classroom should be a given because they are so valuable for teaching aspects of spelling and word study. Every classroom should be a print-rich environment in which students can use the environmental print in their reading and writing. However, simply having a word wall is not adequate. Students must be taught to use the word wall. It is recommended that

Figure 7.9 Kindergarten Word Wall

5 to 10 minutes every day be devoted to word wall activities (Cunningham, Hall, & Sigmon, 1999). The words are added to the wall gradually—only five or so a week. The idea is to spend time teaching those words well. Word walls for younger children are often arranged alphabetically or by rime patterns. A photograph of a kindergarten word wall is in Figure 7.9. Word walls for older students are often arranged thematically based on the specific units of study, such as westward expansion, the human body, or the water cycle. In some classrooms there are multiple word walls—some for the words necessary to learn the content of science, math, social studies, music, and so on, and some for the specific spelling words that students are learning.

As part of the focus lesson, a teacher may ask students to find words with specific spelling patterns on the word wall. In a primary-grade classroom, the teacher may say a word from the spelling list and ask a student to go to the wall and point out the word. One of our favorites is a version of the "I Spy" game. In a first-grade classroom the teacher announces, "I spy with my little eye a word that contains a th-consonant digraph." Students then scan the word wall to find a word that fits. Subsequent clues help them narrow the possible words down to *there, with, them, the,* and *think.* When the teacher adds the hint that it is a word to describe what they do in school, they all shout, "Think!" Cunningham, Hall, and Sigmon (1999) have other suggestions for using the word wall:

- *On the Back*—The teacher recites five sentences featuring word wall words and the students write down the words they hear.

- *Add an Ending*—Students create new words to write by adding a suffix to word wall words.

- *Chant, Clap, Cheer, Write, Check*—In unison, the children chant, clap, and cheer the spelling of each of the five focus words, then write the words on paper and check against the word wall for accuracy.

One way that teachers use their word wall is through a weekly word wall bingo game. Students are provided with blank bingo forms and are instructed to write words from the word wall into any of the squares they want. The teacher then calls words until one of the students earns a bingo!

Another class-wide use of the word wall is known as non-negotiable words. In every piece of student writing, the teacher expects all of the word wall words to be spelled correctly. When students submit papers with word wall words spelled incorrectly, the teacher returns the paper and asks the student to find the word wall word that is not correct.

Spelling tests with self-correction. The most significant way to ensure that students learn to spell is through self-corrected tests—tests that the students correct themselves to focus on where they are making mistakes (Henderson, 1990; Templeton, 2003a). We agree with Fearn and Farnan (2001) in that once per week is not sufficient to provide students the practice they need in noticing where they make mistakes. We maintain that students need regular, if not daily, spelling tests to learn to spell well.

The self-corrected spelling instruction and test might occur something like this. On Monday, Ms. Allen asks students to participate in a spelling test. She reads them a list of 10 words. Once she has read the list through two times, she asks students to correct their papers as she reads the words and spells each one. For example, she says, "arrest, ah rest, a-r-r-e-s-t." Students circle any missing letters, added letters, or transposed letters.

She then asks students to give themselves a letter grade for *each* word (A is no errors, B is one error, and so on). When they finish this first round, she asks her students to turn their papers over and she presents the same list again in a different order. Following the same procedure, she provides her students with time to self-correct and circle the places on the word where they make mistakes. Students then record these words in the Words to Learn section of their journal where they write notes to themselves about the "tricky parts." A copy of the Words to Learn log can be seen in Figure 7.10.

By Wednesday, over half the class has all the words correct and they no longer need to participate in the spelling tests. They track their own progress on the Words to Learn log. By Friday, nearly every student in her class can spell the entire list correctly. The key to learning to spell this way is successive approximations (Fearn & Farnan, 2001). In other words, students are participating in an instructional event in which they are not immediately told that they have "failed the spelling test, again," but rather can see their grades slowly improve as they pay attention to the places in the word that they make mistakes.

Guided Instruction

During the guided instruction portion of the language arts workshop, students meet with the teacher to participate in small group learning. Students assume more responsibility and the teacher provides coaching as needed while the learner uses newly learned literacy skills and strategies.

Elkonin boxes. During guided reading instruction, students sometimes need more direct experiences to process the sounds in words. One method for pairing manipulatives with phonemic awareness instruction is called **Elkonin boxes** (Elkonin, 1963). Elkonin boxes are represented as empty squares for each phoneme in a word. Several

Another name for this strategy is *sound boxes.*

Figure 7.10 Words to Learn Log

Look	Cover	Say	Spell (thing)	Write (thing)	Check			TESTS	

Word	Tricky Part / Key Feature	1	2	3	4
1 Way	Tricky part for me is "a".				
2 these ✓	The "s" is tricky.				
3 might ✓	The tricky part is "gh".				
4 float ✓	The "a" is tricky.				
5 close ✓	The "os" is tricky.				
6 tried ✓	The "i" is tricky.				
7 pricey ✓	The "i" is tricky.				
1 April					
2 Hello ✓	It sounded like "w".				
3 white ✓	The tricky part is "hi".				
4 silent ✓	The tricky part is "i".				
5 future ✓	The tricky part is the "u".				
6 even ✓	The tricky part is "e".				

manipulatives (unifix cubes, bingo chips, or pennies) are given to the student along with a mat like the one seen in Figure 7.11. The teacher says each word slowly while the student pushes a chip into a box for each sound they hear. Therefore, the word *dog* would need three boxes, as would the word *fish* (/sh/ is one phoneme).

Letter boxes. Reading Recovery teachers use a variation of Elkonin boxes called **letter boxes.** When a student becomes stuck on a word during guided writing, the teacher draws a corresponding number of boxes for each letter on a separate sheet of paper. The teacher then prompts the student to write all the sounds they hear in the word they are attempting to spell. Depending on the student's knowledge of spelling, the teacher may supply letters the student is unlikely to figure out on their own. For example, Ms. King used letter boxes to assist Andre, a kindergartener, in

Figure 7.10   Words to Learn Log *(continued)*

			TESTS			
Look Cover Say Spell (thing) Write (thing) Check						
Word	Tricky Part / Key Feature	1	2	3	4
1 once	The "n" is the tricky part.				
2 another	The "a" is the tricky part.				
3 does	The "oe" is the tricky part.				
4 began	The "e" is the tricky part.				
5 until	The "u" is the tricky part.				
6 which	The "h" doesn't have sound.				
1 everything	The "e" is tricky.				
2 early	The "a" is tricky.				
3 appeared	The double "p" is tricky.				
4 wrapped	The "w" is tricky.				
5 wrapping	The double "p" is tricky.				
6 Earth	The "ar" is tricky.				
7 lived	The "ed" is tricky.				

figuring out how to spell *bike*. Since she knew it was unlikely that Andre would know about silent *e,* she drew four boxes and wrote the letter *e* in the last box. She then prompted him to first make and then write each letter in the boxes. In less than 1 minute, Andre had arrived at the correct spelling and was back to writing his sentence. We have duplicated Ms. King and Andre's letter boxes in Figure 7.12.

Magnetic letters, Magna Doodles, and Have-a-Go notes. How many times have you written a tricky word on a slip of paper to see if it looks right? That's because spelling utilizes both visual and auditory memory. During guided instruction, teachers use magnetic letters and Magna Doodles with young spellers to encourage experimentation. When they come to a word they are unsure how to spell, we make these manipulatives available so they freely move the letters around until they arrive at a satisfactory spelling. There

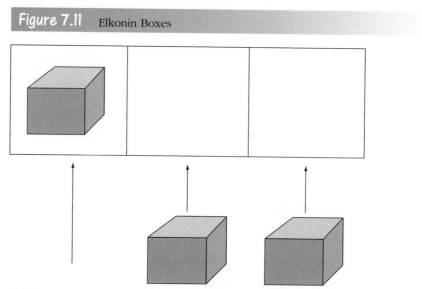

Figure 7.11   Elkonin Boxes

A child pushes three cubes into the boxes to represent the sounds in fish (/f/ /i/ /sh/).

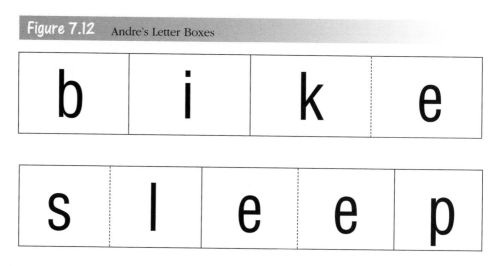

Figure 7.12   Andre's Letter Boxes

is an advantage for the teacher as well. Because students are working on a larger scale, the teacher can observe the problem-solving processes they are using.

Have-a-Go notes can be introduced in spelling journals to students as they move into the letter name stage of spelling (Routman, 1991). These notes feature several columns for students to attempt spelling. While the teacher coaches ("Write all the sounds you hear"), the child makes two tries at the word. If the child does not arrive at the correct spelling, the teacher writes the correct spelling in the third column for the student to use in his or her writing. We also put a check mark next to the correct spelling so that they can consult their notes at other times. While we initially use magnetic letters, Magna Doodles, and Have-a-Go notes during guided instruction, we make these tools available for use during collaborative and inde-

Figure 7.13   Have-a-Go Notes

Have-a-Go	Have-a-Go	Correct Spelling
bist sekind were ✔	best ✔ sekond	second ✔

pendent time as well in order to promote generalization. A version of Have-a-Go notes is in Figure 7.13.

Personal spelling lists. As we explained earlier, many of the words on a student's list of spelling words will have been selected because they possess characteristics consistent with the learner's developmental level (i.e., word families, word derivations). However, even students in the same stage of spelling have individual needs and interests that should be incorporated into the spelling curriculum. Therefore, each week, students should have a personal list of words they are studying. This personal list augments the primary list and can consist of anywhere from one to five additional words. There are several means for selecting these words with students. We've outlined a few below:

- *Words misspelled by the student.* Self-editing is an important skill for students to develop. Have students edit one to two pieces per week, underlining each word they believe they have misspelled. The words chosen for their personal spelling list are the misspelled ones they *did not* underline.

- *Challenge words.* Most students are fascinated by unusual words. Let them choose up to five challenge words that interest them. Encourage them to use dictionaries, thesauri, and their narrative and expository readings to find novel words.

- *BOLO (Be On the Lookout) words.* Ask students to keep track of words they encounter that are difficult for them to spell. They should "be on the lookout" throughout the school day and at home for words they find difficult. When they encounter such a word, they should note it on the BOLO list. This list becomes a source of potential personal spelling words. We've included a copy of the BOLO list in Figure 7.14.

- *Stump the Teacher.* This has proven to be a perennial favorite in classrooms, regardless of grade level. This is a standing challenge to students to bring a word that might "stump the teacher." There is a catch, though—the student must be able to spell and define the word and use it in a sentence. We keep a chart of the words that have been brought to the class along with the results.

Figure 7.14   BOLO Spelling List

BOLO Personal Spelling List

"Be On the Lookout for Tricky Words"

BOLO Word	Date Found	Date Added to Personal Spelling List

Collaborative Learning

When students collaborate with peers, they utilize literacy skills and strategies to read and write. These paired and small group activities are designed to get students talking about what they know and why they know it. In addition, they are able to assist one another when a learning activity is more challenging.

Making words. Students in letter-name and within word pattern stages of spelling development are ideal candidates for Making Words, "an activity in which children are individually given some letters and use these letters to make words" (Cunningham & Hall, 1994, p. 1). The letters for each lesson come from a "secret word" that has been chosen in advance. The letters are on small slips of paper and rest in a folded tent to hold the letters, much like a Scrabble display. Students make a succession of words, beginning with two-letter words, then three-, and so on. With each word that is made, all students arrange their letters to spell the word. Eventually, they rearrange the letters until they have discovered the secret word. Finally, words can be sorted according to word families (rimes), beginning letters (onsets), or conceptually (for meaning). A list of common rimes, based on the work of Wylie and Durrell (1970), is featured in Appendix 7.5.

The Making Words instructional materials feature lessons and blackline masters for hundreds of lessons.

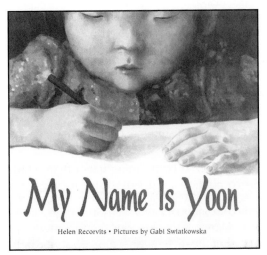

My Name Is Yoon

Helen Recorvits • Pictures by Gabi Swiatkowska

Korean-born Yoon dislikes her name in English and tries to find ways to feel more comfortable in her new school and new country.

Illustrations © 2003 by Gabi Swiatkowska from MY NAME IS YOON by Helen Recorvits. Used with permission of Farrar, Straus and Giroux.

This instructional strategy is typically introduced during the shared activity time in the language arts workshop, however, we have chosen to feature it under the collaborative learning portion because of its potential as a student-directed center. Once students have mastered the routine of this activity through shared experiences, Making Words lessons, letters, and tents can be placed in the word center for repeated enjoyment. Students take turns directing the activity. An example of a word tent appears in Figure 7.15.

Word sorts for spelling patterns. Sorting words is a useful activity for students to practice the spelling patterns of many words. Sorts typically feature words or pictures on individual cards and a mat for keeping the cards organized. There are two kinds of sort cards:

- *Sound sorts* build phonemic awareness and feature pictures of common objects possessing the same initial, medial, or final sounds. For example, cards containing pictures of a sun, pan, panda, saw, and

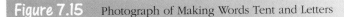

Figure 7.15   Photograph of Making Words Tent and Letters

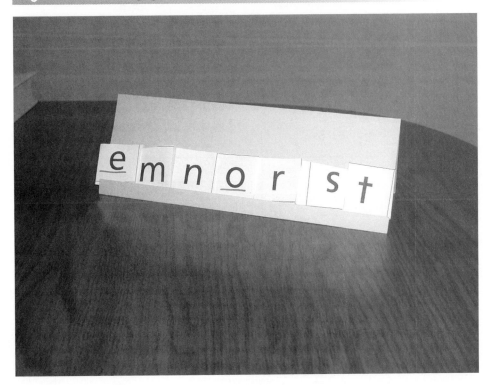

pig can be sorted into words that begin with the sound of /s/ and those that begin with the sound of /p/.

- *Word sorts* feature printed words instead of pictures.

Students can sort these pictures or words using one of three conditions:

- *Closed sorts* are sorts that are accompanied by stated categories. Students sort the cards based on these categories. A closed sort is featured in Figure 7.16.
- *Open sorts* come without stated categories. The students must examine all the cards to construct their own categories.
- *Conceptual sorts* use cards that are categorized by meaning rather than word structure. Conceptual sorts to build vocabulary are discussed in chapter 8.

Using reference materials. Students often bemoan dictionary work and the drudgery of looking up words and writing definitions. Many of us have our own memories of endless lists and an enormous dictionary. Using the dictionary to look up a word you don't know how to spell is notoriously ineffective, especially because you need to know how to spell the word in order to use the dictionary! We advocate making many interesting dictionaries and reference materials available to students while they read and write. In addition to age-appropriate traditional dictionaries, classroom reference materials should include:

- Rhyming dictionaries for poetry writing
- Visual dictionaries
- Student thesauri
- Thematic word walls with content area words (science, mathematics, social studies, etc.)
- Language charts of affixes, synonyms, and antonyms

Figure 7.16   Closed Sort

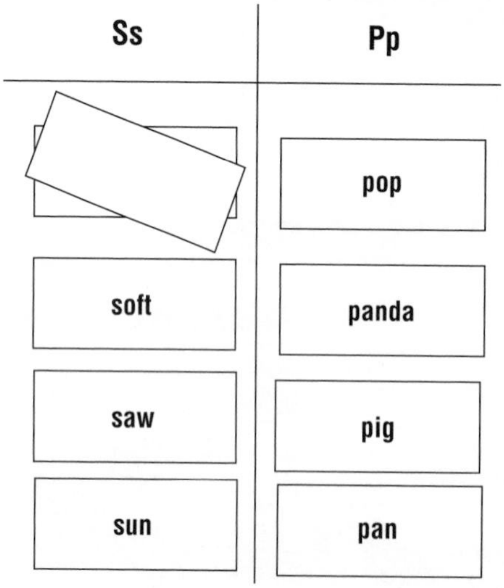

Itty-Bitty. In addition to making words, students can break spelling words into smaller words. Similar to the making words activity, Itty-Bitty (Young, 2001) provides students with practice recalling words they had previously learned. For example, if the fifth grade spelling word is spinach, students can make lists of the one-letter, two-letter, three-letter, four-letter, five-letter, and six-letter words that can be made from their spelling word. From the word spinach, students could make I, in, an, is, pin, nip, hip, spin, chip, pinch, chips, and many others.

> Itty-Bitty aids in long-term retention of words.

Independent Learning

Students engage in independent learning activities to consolidate their understanding of literacy skills and strategies. Spelling journals and other games are useful during the independent learning phase of the workshop.

Spelling journals. We have saved spelling journals for discussion during the independent phase of the language arts workshop, but in truth they are used throughout the day. Spelling journals are maintained by students in order to organize their spelling work. A diagram of a spelling journal can be found in Figure 7.17. A typical spelling journal can take the form of a folder, binder, or notebook and contains the following items:

- Words to Learn list
- Personal spelling list
- Have-a-Go notes

Figure 7.17 Spelling Journal

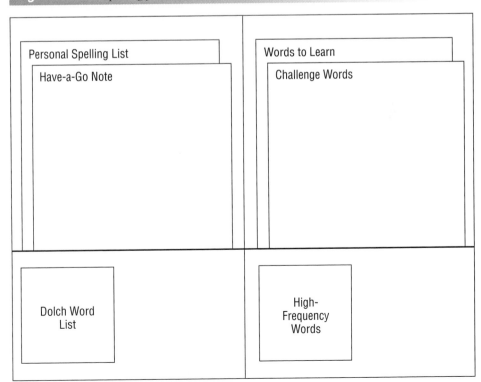

- Challenge words list
- Stump the Teacher list
- Alphabet cards (for younger students)
- High-frequency or Dolch words list
- Notes taken during spelling focus lessons
- Independent spelling activities

The scenario at the beginning of this chapter featured student work in a spelling journal. It is also important to note that these journals are not in full use during the first week of school. Each of these components, from Have-a-Go notes to interest lists are taught first in the shared portion of the workshop, then further extended through guided and collaborative activities. Only after the first month are spelling journals being fully utilized in the classroom.

Personal dictionaries. These are closely related to the personal spelling lists and are used extensively in K–2 classrooms. As students acquire words for their personal list, they add them to a small journal (4 × 6) of 26 pages. Each page represents a letter of the alphabet. Students add words to the pages along with a definition in their own words and are encouraged to use their dictionaries when writing.

Word games. Games are an excellent method for creating opportunities for rehearsal and practice. Because they are engaging they also are chosen frequently by students. These include board games like Scrabble®, Concentration, and Boggle. In addition, there are other easy word game activities that students can do independently:

- *Spellamadoodle.* This is a fun activity whose only purpose is to invite students to focus on the spelling of a word for a few minutes (Rees,

Figure 7.18   Word Pyramid

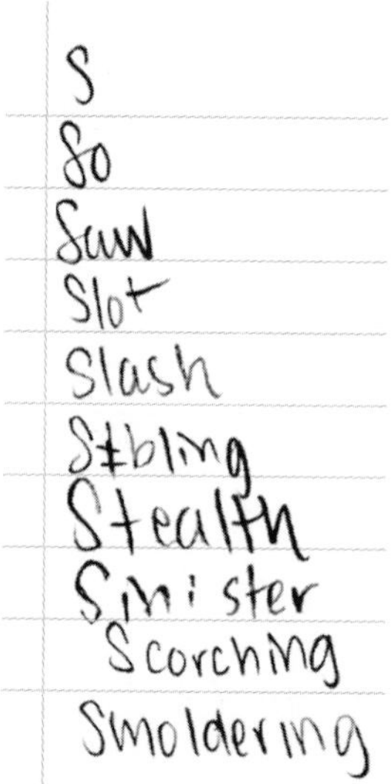

S
So
Saw
Slot
Slash
Stbling
Stealth
Sinister
Scorching
Smoldering

Kovalevs, & Dewsbury, 1997). Students create designs using spelling words in order to convey the meaning as well as the letters.

- *Word pyramids.* Students begin with one letter and then write a two-letter word that begins with the same letter. This is followed by a three-letter word, then four-letter word, and so on. The goal is to build a pyramid of words that extends to 10 letters or beyond. When they can go no further, they write a sentence for each word in the pyramid (Fearn & Farnan, 2001). An eighth grader's word pyramid is in Figure 7.18.

- *Endless words.* Beginning with a three- or four- letter word, the student creates a list by changing only one letter at a time to create new words. For example, a sequence might look like this:

> pat rat sat Sam Pam tam Tim tin tan tap. . .

The goal is to make the longest list!

> This is also a great class game when you have five minutes to fill before going to lunch!

BIG IDEAS ABOUT SPELLING AND WORD STUDY

In sum, spelling instruction matters (Graham, Harris, & Chorzempa, 2002). We cannot assume that students will learn to spell, and thus read and write, without instruction. Like other aspects of literacy, students progress developmentally through stages of acquisition. Therefore, it is important for teachers to know where their students are developmentally and understand what instructional activities provide their learners with opportunities for growth. Active learning occurs when students use manipulatives, sorts, and other interactive processes. Student interest is also essential and therefore children should have input on the words they learn as well.

 ## INTEGRATING THE STANDARDS

Create lesson plans that meet your state's standards by visiting our Companion Website at www.prenhall.com/frey. There you'll find lessons created to meet the NCTE/IRA Standards. Adapt them to meet the standards of your own state through links to your state's standards, and keep them in the online portfolio. You can collect lesson plans for each chapter in an online portfolio, providing you with invaluable tools to meet your state's standards when you head into your own classroom.

CHECK YOUR UNDERSTANDING

1. Why should time be devoted to spelling instruction in the language arts workshop?
2. How do students learn to spell? What is the natural development of spelling?
3. Which words should be taught in a spelling curriculum?
4. What instructional activities support spelling acquisition?

CLASSROOM CONNECTIONS

1. Choose two students to assess. Use the Developmental Spelling Assessment (Ganske, 2000) in chapter 11 to determine their stage of spelling and develop an instructional plan.

2. Take note of the reference materials (dictionaries, thesauri) available in the classroom. Write down the titles of the ones you like best for later use in your own classroom.

References

Adams, M., Forman, B., Lundberg, I., & Beeler, T. (1998). *Phonemic awareness in young children*. Baltimore, MD: Paul H. Brookes.

Bear, D. R., Invernizzi, M., Templeton, S., & Johnston, F. (2004). *Words their way: Word study for phonics, vocabulary, and spelling instruction* (3rd ed.). Upper Saddle River, NJ: Merrill/Prentice Hall.

Beckham-Hungler, D., & Williams, C. (2003). Teaching words that students misspell: Spelling instruction and young children's writing. *Language Arts, 80,* 299–309.

Blachowicz, C., & Fisher, P. J. (2002). *Teaching vocabulary in all classrooms* (2nd ed.). Upper Saddle River, NJ: Merrill/Prentice Hall.

Bosman, A. T., & Van Orden, G. C. (1997). Why spelling is more difficult than reading. In C. A. Perfetti & L. Rieben (Eds.), *Learning to spell: Research, theory, and practice across languages* (pp. 173–194). Mahwah, NJ: Lawrence Erlbaum Associates.

Clay, M. M. (2000). *Concepts about print: What have children learned about the way we print language?* Portsmouth, NH: Heinemann.

Cramer, R. L., & Cipielewski, J. F. (1995). *Spelling research and information: An overview of current research and practices.* Glenview, IL: Scott, Foresman and Company.

Cunningham, P. M. (2002). *Prefixes and suffixes: Systematic sequential phonics and spelling.* Greensboro, NC: Carson-Dellosa.

Cunningham, P. M., & Hall, D. P. (1994). *Making words: Multilevel, hands-on, developmentally appropriate spelling and phonics activities.* Torrance, CA: Good Apple.

Cunningham, P. M., Hall, D. P., & Sigmon, C. M. (1999). *The teacher's guide to the four blocks: A multimethod, multilevel framework for grades 1–3.* Greensboro, NC: Carson-Dellosa.

Dolch, E. W. (1936). A basic sight vocabulary. *The Elementary School Principal, 36,* 456–460.

Elkonin, D. B. (1963). The psychology of mastery of elements of reading. In B. Simon & J. Simon (Eds.), *Educational psychology in the USSR* (pp. 165–179). London: Routledge and Kegan Paul.

Fearn, L., & Farnan, N. (2001). *Interactions: Teaching writing and the language arts.* Boston: Houghton Mifflin.

Fisher, D., & Frey, N. (2003). Writing instruction for struggling adolescent readers: A gradual release model. *Journal of Adolescent and Adult Literacy, 46,* 396–405.

Fisher, D., McDonald, N., & Strickland, J. (2001). Early literacy development: A sound practice. *General Music Today, 14*(3), 15–20.

Foorman, B. R., Francis, D. J., Novy, D. M., & Liberman, D. (1991). How letter-sound instruction mediates progress in first-grade reading and spelling. *Journal of Educational Psychology, 83,* 456–469.

Ganske, K. (2000). *Word journeys: Assessment-guided phonics, spelling, and vocabulary instruction.* New York: Guilford Press.

Graham, S., Harris, K. R., & Chorzempa, B. F. (2002). Contribution of spelling instruction to the spelling, writing, and reading of poor spellers. *Journal of Educational Psychology, 94,* 669–686.

Harris, T. L., & Hodges, R. E. (1995). *The literacy dictionary: The vocabulary of reading and writing.* Newark, DE: International Reading Association.

Henderson, E. H. (1990). *Teaching spelling* (2nd ed.). Boston: Houghton Mifflin.

Johns, J. L. (1981). The development of the revised Dolch list. *Illinois School Research and Development, 17,* 15–24.

Moats, L. C. (2000). *Speech to print: Language essentials for teachers.* Baltimore, MD: Paul H. Brookes.

Nation, K., & Hulme, C. (1997). Phonemic segmentation, not onset-rime segmentation, predicts early reading and spelling skills. *Reading Research Quarterly, 32,* 154–167.

Perfetti, C. A. (1997). The psycholinguistics of spelling and reading. In C. A. Perfetti & L. Rieben (Eds.), *Learning to spell: Research, theory, and practice across languages* (pp. 21–38). Mahwah, NJ: Lawrence Erlbaum Associates.

Read, C. (1975). *Children's categorizations of speech sounds in English* (Research Report No. 17). Urbana, IL: National Council of Teachers of English.

Rees, D., Kovalevs, K., & Dewsbury, A. (1997). *Spelling resource book.* Portsmouth, NH: Heinemann.

Routman, R. (1991). *Invitations: Changing as teachers and learners K–12.* Portsmouth, NH: Heinemann.

Schlagal, B. (2002). Classroom spelling instruction: History, research, and practice. *Reading Research and Instruction, 42,* 44–57.

Sipe, L. R. (1998). Transitions to the conventional: An examination of a first grader's composing process. *Journal of Literacy Research, 30,* 357–388.

Snow, C., Burns, M., & Griffin, P. (1998). *Preventing reading difficulties in young children.* Washington, DC: National Academy Press.

Templeton, S. (2003a). Spelling. In J. Flood, D. Lapp, J. R. Squire, & J. M. Jensen (Eds.), *Handbook of research on teaching the English language arts* (2nd ed.). (pp. 738–751). Mahwah, NJ: Lawrence Erlbaum Associates.

Templeton, S. (2003b). The spelling/meaning connection. *Voices from the Middle, 10*(3), 56–57.

Templeton, S., & Morris, D. (1999). Questions teachers ask about spelling. *Reading Research Quarterly, 34,* 102–112.

Thibodeau, G. (2002). Spellbound: Commitment to correctness. *Voices from the Middle, 9*(3), 19–22.

Wagner, R. K., Torgensen, J. K., & Rashotte, C. A. (1994). Development of reading-related phonological processing abilities: New evidence of bidirectional causality from a latent longitudinal study. *Developmental Psychology, 30,* 73–87.

Wylie, R. E., & Durrell, D. D. (1970). Teaching vowels through phonograms. *Elementary English, 47,* 787–791.

Yopp, H. (1995). Read aloud books for developing phonemic awareness in young children. *The Reading Teacher, 45,* 696–703.

Yopp, H. K., & Yopp, R. H. (1997). *Oo-pples and boo-noo-noos: Songs and activities for phonemic awareness.* Orlando, FL: Harcourt.

Young, L. (2001). *An individualized approach for teaching spelling.* Unpublished Master's Thesis, San Diego State University, San Diego, California.

Zutell, J. (1994). Spelling instruction. In A. Purves, L. Papas, & S. Jordan (Eds.), *Encyclopedia of English studies and language arts* (Vol.2) (pp. 1098–1100). New York: Scholastic.

Appendix 7.1   Spelling Lists by Grade Level

GRADE 1	GRADE 2	GRADE 3
(Words with Short a)	**(Words with c, k, and ck)**	**(Words with dr, sc, ft, nk)**
at	can	dry
bat	could	dream
cat	kind	drink
an	like	score
man	book	soft
ran	sick	left
	second	think
(Everyday words)	woke	dragon
and	took	drum
am	back	scared
	pack	scarf
	kick	gift
		thank
	(Challenge words)	bank
	bacon	
	attic	**(Challenge words)**
	stuck	drawer
		scanner
		aircraft
		prank

GRADE 4	GRADE 5	GRADE 6
(Words with thr, scr, str, squ)	**(Words with sk, sp, st)**	**(Getting letters in correct order)**
throat	skinny	poetry
through	task	beautiful
screen	risk	thirteen
scratch	spider	tongue
scream	wasp	pieces
strange	crisp	neighborhood
street	stopped	thousand
strike	style	through
square	arrest	unusual
squeeze	suggest	building
threat	skeleton	license
thrown	skunk	remodel
thrill	brisk	grateful
scrub	spilled	enemy
skyscraper	spinach	instrument
strawberry	grasp	perform
strength	stumble	prefer
squeal	statue	judged
squirm	boast	adjusted
squirt	adjust	soldier
(Challenge words)	**(Challenge words)**	**(Challenge words)**
arthritis	snakeskin	preliminary
description	inspire	tremendous
instrument	respect	mediocre
astronaut	frostbite	perception
squeezable	obstacle	neutrality

GRADE 7	GRADE 8
(Getting letters in correct order)	**(One consonant or two?)**
comple*tely*	embarrassment
bel*ie*ve	unnecessary
w*ei*rdest	occasionally
b*ei*ge	trespass
thr*ough*	dismissed
thi*rt*ieth	challenge
exper*i*ment	forbidden
pe*rf*ume	accompany
do*es*n't	immediately
de*cis*ion	exaggerate
poli*tely*	possessive
f*ie*rce	aggressive
br*ie*fcase	accessory
sl*ei*gh	compassionate
l*ieu*tenant	cancellation
man*euv*er	commemorate
recr*uit*	moccasin
bisc*uit*	accumulate
g*aug*e	dilemma
p*re*serve	appropriate
(Challenge words)	**(Challenge words)**
uny*ie*lding	preoccupation
beg*ui*ling	saccharin
b*eau*teous	insufficient
p*re*cipitation	constellation
p*re*ferably	commiserate

Appendix 7.2   Common Latin and Greek Root Words

Root	Meaning	Examples
aer	air	Aerial, aeronautical
aster/astr	star	Astronomical, asterisk
auto	self	Automatic, autograph
bio	life	Biography, biology
chron	time	Chronicle, synchronous
derm	skin	Epidermis, pachyderm
fac, fact	to make; to do	Factory, facsimile
fer	to carry	Transfer, ferry
gram	written	Grammar, diagram
graph	to write	Biography, graphic
hydr	water	Hydrant, hydroponics
logo	reason	Logic, epilogue
meter	measure	Metric, thermometer
micro	small	Microscope, microwave
mono	one	Monastery, monotonous
par	get ready	Prepare, repair
port	to carry	Airport, export
phon	sound	Telephone, phonics
photo	light	Photograph, photosynthesis
stat	to stand	Status, station
tech	art; skill	Technology, technical
therm	heat	Thermometer, thermal
vid, vis	to see	Video, vision

Sources: Bear, D. R., Invernizzi, M., Templeton, S., & Johnston, F. (2004). Greek word roots (p. 274). *Words their way: Word study for phonics, vocabulary, and spelling instruction* (3rd ed.). Upper Saddle River, NJ: Merrill/Prentice Hall. Blachowicz, C., & Fisher, P. J. (2002). The most common Latin words in the vocabulary of children (p. 196). *Teaching vocabulary in all classrooms* (2nd ed.). Upper Saddle River, NJ: Merrill/Prentice Hall.

Appendix 7.3   Dolch Sight Vocabulary Words

Preprimer	Primer	First	Second	Third
a	all	after	always	about
and	am	again	around	better
away	are	an	because	bring
big	at	any	been	carry
blue	ate	as	before	clean
can	be	ask	best	cut
come	black	by	both	done
down	brown	could	buy	draw
find	but	every	call	drink
for	came	fly	cold	eight
funny	did	from	does	fall
go	do	give	don't	far
help	eat	going	fast	full
here	four	had	first	got
i	get	has	five	grow
in	good	her	found	hold
is	have	him	gave	hat
it	he	his	goes	if
little	into	how	green	keep
look	like	jump	its	kind
make	must	just	made	laugh
me	new	know	many	light
my	no	let	off	long
not	now	live	or	much
one	on	may	pull	myself
play	our	at	read	never
red	out	old	right	only
run	please	once	sing	own
said	pretty	open	sit	pick
see	ran	over	sleep	seven
the	ride	put	tell	shall
three	saw	round	their	show
to	say	some	these	six
two	she	stop	those	small
up	so	take	upon	start
we	soon	thank	us	ten
where	that	them	use	today
yellow	there	then	very	together
you	they	think	wash	try
	this	walk	which	
	too	warm	why	
	under	were	wish	
	want	when	work	
	was		would	
	well		write	
	went		your	
	what			
	white			
	who			
	will			
	with			
	yes			

Appendix 7.4   Commonly Misspelled Words, Grades 1–8

1. too	26. didn't	51. like	76. about
2. a lot	27. people	52. whole	77. first
3. because	28. until	53. another	78. happened
4. there	29. with	54. believe	79. Mom
5. their	30. different	55. I'm	80. especially
6. that's	31. outside	56. thought	81. school
7. they	32. we're	57. let's	82. getting
8. it's	33. through	58. before	83. started
9. when	34. upon	59. beautiful	84. was
10. favorite	35. probably	60. Everything	85. which
11. went	36. don't	61. very	86. stopped
12. Christmas	37. sometimes	62. into	87. two
13. were	38. off	63. caught	88. Dad
14. our	39. everybody	64. one	89. took
15. they're	40. heard	65. Easter	90. friend's
16. said	41. always	66. what	91. presents
17. know	42. I	67. there's	92. are
18. you're	43. something	68. little	93. morning
19. friend	44. would	69. doesn't	94. could
20. friends	45. want	70. usually	95. around
21. really	46. and	71. clothes	96. buy
22. finally	47. Halloween	72. scared	97. maybe
23. where	48. house	73. everyone	98. family
24. again	49. once	74. have	99. pretty
25. then	50. to	75. swimming	100. tried

Source: Table "100 Most Frequently Misspelled Words from Research in Action" by Ronald L. Cramer and James F. Cipielewski from *Spelling Research & Information: An Overview of Current Research and Practices.* Copyright © 1995 by Scott, Foresman and Company. Used by permission of Pearson Education, Inc.

Appendix 7.5   Common Rimes and Words to Use with Them

These 37 rimes can make more than 500 words.

-ack back, pack, stack	-aw raw, saw, thaw	-ink rink, sink, think
-ail pail, mail, snail	-ay day, say, play	-ip lip, nip, slip
-ain rain, stain, drain	-eat heat, meat, bleat	-ir fir, sir, stir
-ake rake, snake, bake	-ell sell, tell, smell	-ock rock, sock, stock
-ale pale, bale, whale	-est best, rest, chest	-oke joke, poke, smoke
-all fall, tall, small	-ice rice, nice, spice	-op hop, top, stop
-ame name, fame, flame	-ick pick, sick, trick	-or or, for
-an can, man, than	-ide ride, side, glide	-ore core, more, chore
-ank rank, spank, thank	-ight light, might, fright	-uck duck, tuck, struck
-ap cap, tap, trap	-ill fill, mill, grill	-ug hug, tug, slug
-ash mash, sash, smash	-in fin, pin, grin	-ump hump, lump, slump
-at cat, mat, scat	-ine fine, mine, shrine	-unk dunk, junk, trunk
-ate *gate, late, crate*	-ing *wing, sing, fling*	

Vocabulary Development in the Language Arts Workshop

BIG IDEAS ABOUT VOCABULARY DEVELOPMENT

Teaching vocabulary words in isolation is an inefficient way to facilitate word knowledge because there are simply too many words to teach. We know that students learn a number of words through reading and using their knowledge of how words are structured. However, many teachers and educational researchers have expressed dissatisfaction with only selecting words from classroom readings because of the hodge-podge nature of the word selection. Unlike spelling, the research is less clear on word choice for vocabulary instruction. Instructional practices have shifted toward culling vocabulary words from narrative and informational reading selections using a set of criteria. Accordingly, we advocate for a balance between words from their readings and words that students should know at a given grade level.

Questions to Consider

When you have finished reading this chapter, you should be able to answer these questions:

- How do students acquire vocabulary knowledge?

- How should vocabulary be chosen?

- What are the objectives of vocabulary instruction?

- What instructional strategies are useful throughout the phases of the language arts workshop?

Key Vocabulary

General vocabulary

Specialized vocabulary

Technical vocabulary

Concepts

Labels

Vocabulary self-awareness

Semantic Feature Analysis

List-group-label

Vocab-o-grams

Mnemonics

Shades of meaning

Concept ladders

A–Z charts

Semantic maps

Word maps

Concept word sorts

Open sorts

Closed sorts

Quiz-me cards

Vocabulary role play

Vocabulary cards

Individualized word lists

Vocabulary self-selection strategy

Scavenger hunt

Realia

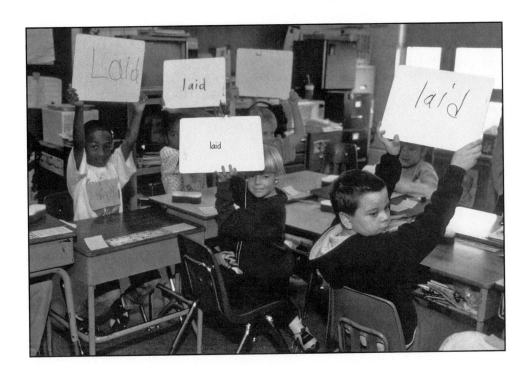

⇛→♦←⇝

A LOOK INSIDE

See chapter 4 for more information on literature circles.

Fourth graders Jacob, Sujit, Theresa, Miguel, and Tanja have just begun a new book in their literature circle, *Bud, Not Buddy* (Curtis, 1999). During their last meeting, they agreed to read chapters 1 and 2 and assigned literature circle roles. Tanja had agreed to be the Vocabulary Enricher for this meeting (Daniels, 2002). Miguel opens the discussion by stating, "I don't know about the rest of you, but some of the words in the first two chapters were hard. Well, not hard like I had never heard them before, but hard because I didn't know what they were talking about. Did anyone else have that trouble?"

The others nod in agreement and Miguel continues. "Like right on page 2, the woman says 'I know you don't understand what it means, but there's a depression going on all over this country.' I wasn't sure what depression was."

Tanja, the History Connector, looked excited. "I found it in our social studies book, all about the Great Depression. It was in the 1930s and lots of people in the country were poor."

"That makes sense, because look at the next sentence—'People can't find jobs and these are very, very difficult times for everyone'" (Curtis, 1999, p. 2).

At this point, Ms. Pearman, who had stopped by the group to observe, offered to clarify. She went on to explain about the Great Depression and the type of life many people led during this period. "You'll see a lot of vocabulary in this book that sounds old-fashioned because the story is set 70 years ago. This will be a good feature for the Vocabulary Enricher to pay attention to in this book."

Miguel brightens at this. "I found a whole bunch, but I just didn't know how to define them. Like *doggone* and *shucks*. No one talks like that anymore."

Ms. Pearman responds. "Exactly, Miguel. Some of the words used by an author are kind of strange and we have to use context clues to figure out what they mean because they're really not dictionary words. As the Vocabulary Enricher, you'll have to decide what words are important and what are just curious. *The Great Depression* is really important in this book and it's a concept word. *Doggone* isn't—it's a label word. Good readers pay attention to the words they need to investigate and recognize the words they don't need to spend too much time with."

Theresa, who had been listening quietly to the exchange, joined the conversation. "The Great Depression was during the 1930s, right?" There was a long silence as the others considered this. A little sheepishly, she added, "Um, when were you born?"

VOCABULARY DEVELOPMENT

Loquacious means "full of excessive talk."

See chapter 7 for information on spelling.

Word families are groups of words related by a common root or pattern, such as *sign*, *significant*, and *signify*.

In addition to vocabulary, comprehension is also influenced by prior knowledge, fluency, text difficulty, and interest, among other things.

How Do Students Acquire Vocabulary Knowledge?

"She is so *loquacious* that she often gives away secrets." Do you know what the highlighted word means? Have you heard it and have a vague sense of the meaning? Do you need to know the word to understand the sentence? If you were given a multiple-choice list consisting of the following: a) honest; b) lackadaisical; c) talkative; d) rude, would you get it right?

What, then, does it mean to know a word? It is not as simple as being able to spell the word, although that is an important skill. To know a word, do you have to pass a multiple-choice test? That is an easy and convenient way to suggest that someone knows a word—or is a good test-taker or has enough sense of words and how they work to make an educated guess (Graves, 1986). Alternatively, does a student know a word when he or she can use it in authentic writing events?

The vocabulary demands on children skyrocket during the school years, ballooning to an estimated 88,500 word families by the time a student is in high school (Nagy & Anderson, 1984). Given the number of word families, it is estimated that students are exposed to over 500,000 words while they are in grades 3–9. While these academic language demands are high, it is estimated that everyday speech consists of only 5,000–7,000 words (Klein, 1988). Thus the difference between the number of words a student uses commonly as he or she speaks and the number of words needed to be successful in school is huge. This difference in word knowledge is problematic because of its impact on content learning and reading comprehension (Flood, Lapp, & Fisher, 2003). In fact, knowledge of vocabulary is a strong predictor of how well a reader will comprehend a text (Biemiller, 2003; Spearitt, 1972).

Unlike spelling, there is evidence that students do acquire vocabulary knowledge from reading and listening to texts being read to them (Anderson, 1996; Krashen, 1989). In fact, research suggests that students' vocabularies increase at a rate of approximately 3,000 words per year (Nagy & Anderson, 1984). This occurs despite the

Evidence Based

evidence that teachers often do not teach vocabulary (Durkin, 1978–1979) and that textbooks often lack an intensive vocabulary learning focus (Jenkins & Dixon, 1983). What, then, accounts for this development? It appears that vocabulary acquisition is enhanced by experiences with analyzing the context in which the word occurs, and in knowing about the structure of words.

Context. Some researchers suggest that students learn words because of the contexts in which they see them (Nagy, Herman, & Anderson, 1985). Context clues are the signals authors use to explain a word meaning. There are several types of contextual clues readers use to understand a word. We have provided examples of the five types described by Baumann, Edwards, Boland, Olejnik, & Kame'enui (2003). The vocabulary word is in bold and the contextual clue is italicized:

- *Definition:* Philosophy was important to the ancient Greeks. Philosophy means the *beliefs, ideas, and values of the arts and sciences.*
- *Synonym:* Socrates was accused of teaching his students to rebel against the government. Officials said Socrates encouraged students to *fight against* the rulers of Athens.
- *Antonym:* Aristotle came from an impoverished background, unlike the *rich* philosopher Plato.
- *Example:* The government of city-states such as *Athens* and *Sparta* did not always welcome philosophers, especially if the ideas might threaten the government.
- *General:* Aristotle studied politics to explain *how people were governed,* and *how rulers were chosen.*

As many have noted, there are just too many words in English to systematically teach them all and students seem to learn a lot from natural contexts. However, others have expressed concern about allowing context to be the teacher as "not all contexts are created equal" (Beck, McKeown, & McCaslin, 1983). In other words, the contextual clues imbedded in a given text may be good, bad, or indifferent. Therefore, these researchers and others (Schatz & Baldwin, 1986) have argued that relying solely on natural contexts to teach students the vocabulary they need to be successful is risky at best and counterproductive at worst, misleading readers with weak definitions and loose associations. Students must also be able to use their knowledge of the structure of words.

Review chapter 7 for a discussion of affixes and roots.

Structure. In addition to context, students use structure to figure out new words, including prefixes, suffixes, and root words. When students understand common prefixes like *re-, dis-,* and *un-,* as well as suffixes such as *-s/-es, -ing,* and *-er/-or,* they can use this knowledge when they encounter a new word. Roots of words are also helpful in understanding the meaning of a new word. For instance, when students are able to recognize the root in the word *emperor,* they can make a good prediction about related words such as *empire* and *imperious.*

Students can acquire new vocabulary by using contextual clues and knowledge of the structures of words to determine the meaning of unfamiliar words. These strategies are especially important for readers, as they should be intentional about using context and structure when encountering new words in a passage. When students use contextual and structural knowledge to solve unfamiliar words, they are able to learn new vocabulary independently. However, learners also benefit from intentional instruction of specific vocabulary that is essential to understanding the concepts and topics being taught. Choosing the words to be taught requires an understanding of the types of vocabulary used by students.

What Types of Vocabulary Should Students Learn?

Teachers must be aware of all three types of vocabulary in order to avoid teaching only the technical terms associated with a specific content.

Vacca and Vacca (2001) suggest that there are three types of vocabulary to consider—**general, specialized,** and **technical.** General vocabulary consists primarily of words used in everyday language, usually with widely agreed upon meanings. Examples of general vocabulary words include *frightened, timid,* and *apprehensive.* The meaning of these three words tends to be consistent across contexts, and the appearance of any one of these words would signal the reader that the subject of these adjectives would be *worrisome* indeed!

Some teachers rely on a selection from the "500 Most Used Words List" (Harwell, 2001) of words commonly used in speaking and writing (see appendix 8.1). This list represents general vocabulary for elementary students. In addition, this list is useful for English language learners who are new to the language.

In contrast, specialized vocabulary is flexible and transportable across curricular disciplines—these words hold multiple meanings in different content areas. For example, the word *prime* has a common meaning—of high quality—as well as a more specialized definition in mathematics, where *prime* is a number that can only be divided by itself and 1.

Finally, there are technical vocabulary words that are specific to only one field of study. *Senate* in social studies, *photosynthesis* in science, and *pi* in mathematics are all examples of technical vocabulary because they have only one meaning and are associated with only one content area. This means that these words can be more difficult to teach because there is little association with previously known word meanings. In addition, these technical vocabulary words tend to be "dense" in meaning; that is, the level of knowledge necessary to fully understand the word is directly related to the content itself. For example, knowing the meaning of photosynthesis is directly related to a learner's understanding of how plants transform light into energy. Technical vocabulary, in particular, tends to be vexing for teachers because the fallback system for learning is often rote memorization. In the absence of instruction, students are handed a long list of words to learn, usually by writing definitions and sentences using the words. The problem is that the sheer number of vocabulary words in a novel or book can be overwhelming. It is useful to use some guidelines for choosing which words will be taught, whether they are general, specialized, or technical vocabulary.

How Should Vocabulary Words Be Chosen?

As you have already realized, it would be an impossible task to provide direct instruction for each vocabulary word a student might encounter. Therefore, it is essential to have a method for selecting the words that *will* be taught. It is not uncommon for teachers to use a more haphazard approach such as choosing all the "big words" or those that are unusual. However, this is particularly inefficient for ensuring that students are focusing on critical vocabulary. Therefore we offer these questions for considering vocabulary words to teach. They can also be seen in the chart in Figure 8.1.

Conceptual value. Does the word represent an important concept that is needed in order to understand the reading? For example, *Great Depression* was important for the

Figure 8.1   Considerations for Selecting Vocabulary Words

Considerations for Selecting Vocabulary to Teach	Questions to Ask
Representative	Is the concept represented by the word critical to understanding the piece?
Repeatability	Will the word be used again during the school year?
Transportable	Will the word be used in other subject areas?
Contextual Analysis	Can students use context clues to determine meaning?
Structural Analysis	Can students use structural analysis to determine meaning?
Cognitive Load	Have I identified too many words?

fifth-grade students in the opening scenario to more fully appreciate the hardships Bud faced traveling across America in the 1930s. An important consideration in choosing vocabulary relates to the usefulness of the word. Some words are **concepts,** while others are **labels.** Given that students need to acquire a tremendous volume of vocabulary words each year, it seems careless to squander valuable instructional time on words that function only as labels in a particular reading.

For example, in Lois Lowry's story *The Giver* (1994), a boy is faced with the challenge of confronting truth in his "perfect" community. The word *utopia* is a concept word, for it is central to the understanding of a society with no illness or poverty. On the other hand, the word *tunic* is a label describing the type of clothing worn by the characters. *Utopia* is well worth the instructional effort for students to think deeply about the complexities represented by this one word; *tunic* is a word that can be inferred through context clues and is not essential to comprehension. Students also benefit from instruction on the differences between concept and label words because it can prevent them getting bogged down in minutia at the expense of big ideas. Ms. Pearman's conversation at the beginning of this chapter concerning *doggone* illustrates this point.

> Context clues are hints about word meaning derived from phrases and sentences immediately around the word in question.

Repeatability. Is the word going to be used throughout the school year? Some words are worth teaching because they are useful and will be used often. For instance, it is worth taking the time to instruct students on the meaning of *confer* because it will be used throughout the year in the language arts workshop.

Transportability. Some words should be selected because they will appear in many subjects or content areas. Teaching students the word *immigration* as it appears in *Letters from Rifka* (Hesse, 1999) is useful because students will also be using this word in social studies.

Contextual analysis. If students can use context clues to determine the word meaning then direct instruction is not necessary. In *The Tale of Despereaux* (DiCamillo, 2003, p. 39), readers can use context clues to determine both the meaning of *rodent* and the perceptions of them in the following sentences.

"Mice are rodents," said the king. He adjusted his crown. "They are related to. . . rats. You know our own dark history with rats."

Structural analysis. Words that contain affixes and Latin or Greek root words students are familiar with can be analyzed through structural analysis. For example, the word *magnification* may not need to be included in the list of vocabulary words if students understand the meaning of *magnify* and recognize that the suffix *-tion* is used to change verbs into nouns.

Cognitive load. While there is debate about the number of vocabulary words that should be introduced to students at a given time, most agree that the number should reflect the developmental level of the students and the length of the reading. In a brief reading, 2–3 words is often sufficient for emergent and early readers, while transitional readers can utilize 5 or so. Most agree that no more than 10 should be introduced at any time.

We support the assertion made by Stahl (1988), that teachers must create a balance between learning words in context and systematic, explicit instruction of words selected for teaching. Our experience suggests that students will learn a great number of words from well-chosen texts *and* from the selection of words for intentional instruction.

In sum, teachers can select words both from lists of words that are commonly used, as well as from their readings. Regardless, the criteria for word selection should focus on the transportability and generalizability of the words across situations, curricula, and meaning. Another important consideration for selecting vocabulary for teaching is based on student need. As with other aspects of the language arts workshop, the role of the student is essential in teaching vocabulary.

What Is the Students' Role in Learning Vocabulary?

Teaching vocabulary is further complicated by the varying word knowledge levels of individual students. Even when the core reading is held in common, students bring a range of word understanding to the text. Rather than apply a "one size fits all" approach to vocabulary instruction, it is wise to assess students before the reading. This awareness is valuable for the student as well because it highlights their understanding of what they know, as well as what they still need to learn in order to comprehend the reading. One method for accomplishing this is through *Vocabulary Self-Awareness* (Goodman, 2001). Words are introduced at the beginning of the reading or unit, and students complete a self-assessment of their knowledge of the words. An excerpt of a third-grade student's vocabulary chart for *High Tide in Hawaii* (Osborne, 2003) can be found in Figure 8.2.

Learners use the vocabulary self-awareness chart to rate each vocabulary word according to his or her understanding, including an example and a definition. If they are very comfortable with the word, they give themselves a "+" (plus sign). If they think they know, but are unsure, they note the word with a "✓" (check mark). If the word is new to them, they place a "−" (minus sign) next to the word. Over the course of the reading or unit, students add new information to the chart. The goal is to replace all the check marks and minus signs with a plus sign. Because students continually revisit their vocabulary charts to revise their entries, they have multiple opportunities to practice and extend their growing understanding of the terms. A version of a vocabulary awareness chart for younger children appears in Figure 8.3.

Vocabulary development is recursive. In order for a term to become part of a student's vocabulary, they need opportunities to revisit it.

Figure 8.2 Vocabulary Self-Awareness Chart

Word	+	✓	−	Example	Definition
Tidal wave		✓			A really big wave
volcano	+			Mt. St. Helen	A mountain that explodes
tsunami			−		
paradise		✓			A very beautiful place
Put a "+" next to a word if you can write an example and definition of the word. Put a "✓" next to a word if you can write only a definition or an example, but not both. Put a "−" next to words that are new to you.					

Source: Goodman, L. (2001). A tool for learning: Vocabulary self-awareness. In C. Blanchfield (Ed.), *Creative vocabulary: Strategies for teaching vocabulary in grades K–12* (p. 46). Fresno, CA: San Joaquin Valley Writing Project. Used with permission.

Figure 8.3 Vocabulary Self-Awareness Chart for Younger Students

Word	✔	👂	?	Here's what it means	Here's an example

✔ means I can write about it

👂 means I have heard it before

? means it is new to me

What Are the Objectives of Vocabulary Instruction?

Baumann, Kame'enui, and Ash (2003) suggest that any comprehensive vocabulary curriculum will have at least the following three objectives. These objectives are important as they transfer responsibility for learning to the students as well as providing an instructional role for the teacher. Following each goal, we provide a sample of activities to meet the goal. Additional instruction activities for teaching vocabulary can be found toward the end of this chapter.

Evidence Based

> *Objective 1: Teach students to learn words independently* (Baumann, Kame'enui, & Ash, 2003, p. 778). There are a number of ways that students can learn words independently, including independent reading, listening to read

alouds and shared readings, listening to books on tape, writing plays, poems, and other texts, using dictionaries and thesauri, and allowing students to explore words that interest them.

Objective 2: Teach students the meanings of specific words (Baumann, Kame'enui, & Ash, 2003, p. 778). Independent learning of vocabulary will only extend a student's vocabulary so far. Students also need instruction. This instruction can involve pre-teaching vocabulary for upcoming texts, focusing on affixes, synonyms, homonyms, and antonyms through rote memorization or mnemonics, and teaching labels for words.

> A mnemonic is a device to aid in remembering.

Objective 3: Help students to develop an appreciation for words and to experience enjoyment and satisfaction in their use (Baumann, Kame'enui, & Ash, 2003, p. 778). In other words, make vocabulary learning fun. Students need to see their teachers interested in words, they must be allowed to play with words and their meanings, and they should be encouraged to use their expanding vocabulary in school and non-school situations. We recommend using books like *Miss Alaineous: A Vocabulary Disaster* (Frasier, 2000) and *Word Wizard* (Falwell, 1998).

What Are the Components of Effective Vocabulary Instruction?

While considerable debate remains about what it means to know a word, how vocabulary should be taught, and which words to teach, Baumann, Kame'enui, and Ash (2003) identified 10 suggestions for guiding decisions about vocabulary instruction. Their top 10 included:

1. Establish vocabulary learning goals for your students.

2. Include goals that provide for teacher-initiated vocabulary learning as well as ones that strive for student independence in vocabulary learning (Fisher, Blachowicz, & Smith, 1991).

3. Include instruction in both specific-word and transferable and generalizable strategies. Research by Baumann, Edwards, Boland, Olejnik, & Kame'enui with fifth-graders found that "brief, explicit, teacher-led lessons on text-relevant vocabulary enhanced student learning and recall of words" (2003, p. 481).

4. Select instructional strategies and procedures that are carefully aligned with your goals (Baker, Simmons, & Kame'enui, 1998).

5. Provide struggling readers a systematic and sustained program of vocabulary instruction that teaches them more important words and efficient strategies in less time (Baker, Simmons, & Kame'enui, 1998; Kame'enui & Simmons, 1990; Stanovich, 1986).

6. Select assessment tasks and formats that are consistent with your instructional strategies and desired outcomes.

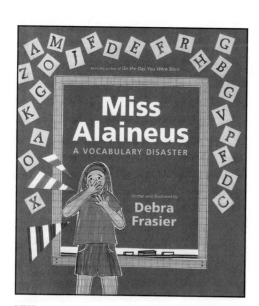

MISS ALAINEUS: A VOCABULARY DISASTER, written and illustrated by Debra Frasier. Originally published by Harcourt, Inc. in 2000. Copyright © 2000 by Debra Frasier. Reprinted by permission.

7. Consider the cost and benefits of instruction (Graves & Prenn, 1986) in terms of student and teacher time and effort when matching instructional methods to goals.

8. Select the most effective and efficient strategy or strategies for each instructional objective.

9. Do not limit yourself to a narrow set of vocabulary instructional techniques. Select suitable strategies from a range of empirically validated instructional procedures that are compatible with your instructional objectives. Bromley (2002, p. 8) sums up the available research and suggests that "strategies that are effective are those that include some repetition of definitions and the use of context—that actively engage students in meaningful learning."

10. Continually evaluate your vocabulary learning objectives and the procedures and techniques you have chosen to address each (Baumann, Kame'enui, & Ash, 2003, p. 777).

Blachowicz and Fisher (2000) identified four principles for effective vocabulary instruction. These authors note that while their principles apply to all learning, their experience has shown that these conditions are vital for vocabulary acquisition and retention. They advise that students should

1. Be actively involved in word learning.

2. Make personal connections.

3. Be immersed in vocabulary.

4. Consolidate meaning through multiple information sources.

The way that you define what it is to know a word will lead to some specific instructional plans. Learners need to have practice using their new vocabulary in their reading, writing, speaking, and listening. Importantly, they need to experience many types of vocabulary activities in order to build their contextual and structural understandings of words, and to develop a deeper understanding of the concepts represented by a term.

APPROACHES TO TEACHING VOCABULARY IN THE LANGUAGE ARTS WORKSHOP

Now that you've selected your words and are convinced that you should teach vocabulary, we will shift our conversation to "how" to teach words and their meanings. It is important to pause here and make an especially important comment—students satiate on vocabulary instruction. In other words, they become bored and less focused when vocabulary instruction becomes routine. While you may believe that most types of routines can become boring for students, we submit that this is especially true in terms of vocabulary instruction. Please take note and rotate your vocabulary instruction on a regular basis. Brassell and Flood (2004) provide at least 25 strategies teachers can use to teach vocabulary. We've organized these vocabulary instructional strategies in terms of the components of the language arts workshop in which they are commonly taught. As with most strategies, they can be adapted and used in other components of the workshop.

Focus Lessons   This phase of the language arts workshop provides an opportunity to lead discussion about vocabulary as it relates to the concepts being taught. The discussions used

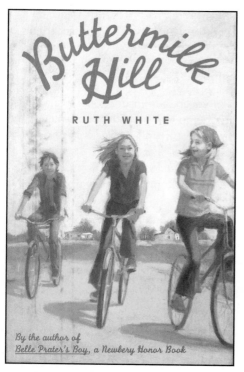

Piper's growing interest in vocabulary and talent for poetry help her find a voice to say the things that are hardest.

Jacket art © 2004 by Nancy Carpenter from BUTTERMILK HILL by Ruth White. Used with the permission of Farrar, Straus and Giroux.

SFA draws on what we know about visual display of information.

to create the charts for semantic feature analysis, list-group-label, and vocab-o-grams introduce vocabulary while fostering predictions about the words they expect to encounter in their reading.

Semantic feature analysis. A popular instructional strategy for categorizing terms by characteristics is **semantic feature analysis** (Anders & Bos, 1986). This procedure, also known as SFA, assists students in assigning characteristics, or features, in a grid pattern. Vocabulary terms comprise the rows, and the features make up the columns. Students place a "+" in each cell to indicate a relationship between the term and the feature, and a "−" when it is not a characteristic. Typically, students complete the grid in conjunction with a piece of assigned text. For example, students in a third-grade class analyzed terms related to natural disasters. The teacher created the grid in Figure 8.4 for students as they read *More Freaky Facts About Natural Disasters* (Duey & Barnes, 2001) and *Super Storms* (Simon, 2001). They completed the grid as they discovered answers to the conceptual relationships.

Many teachers attribute the power of SFA to its visual arrangement, particulary because it mimics the way the brain organizes information (Pittleman, Heimlich, Berglund, & French, 1991). Arnie, a student in this classroom, seemed to confirm this observation when he said, "It's like we made a map of the storms!"

List-group-label. Taba (1967) suggested that students could be taught to think about the ways that words could belong in categories. **List-group-label** is an instructional technique to encourage students to first make predictions about the vocabulary they expect to encounter during a reading then categorize those predictions into an organized frame. By doing this, students create more detailed predictions. After the reading, they revisit the chart to add information and make corrections. Moss (2003) advises using the following steps to conduct a successful List-group-label lesson:

1. Select an informational text.

2. Before reading the text, invite students to list vocabulary words they know about a topic. Record their ideas on the board.

3. Once the list has been created, discuss how the words and phrases can be grouped.

4. Develop labels for each of the groups they have created. Arrange in a grid and write the words and phrases again under the appropriate categories.

5. Read the text.

6. After the reading, add new words and phrases to the existing categories. New categories can be created as well.

Figure 8.4 Semantic Feature Analysis Example

Vocabulary word / Feature	Occurs in or near oceans	Occurs in mountains	Occurs in plains	Warning system
hurricane	+	–	–	+
Tidal wave	+	–	–	+
mudslide	–	+	–	–
tornado	–	–	+	+
earthquake	+	+	+	–
Wild fire	–	+	+	–

Figure 8.5 List-Group-Label After Reading

Who was he?	Where did he live?	Why was he famous?	How did he help the American Revolution?
patriot	A long time ago	Rode a horse	He told when the British were coming
colonist	Boston, MA	There's a poem about him	**He rode to Lexington and Concord to warn minutemen**
silversmith	American colonies	Lanterns in a church told him the message	
father		**He helped the minutemen win the first fight of the war**	

Before reading *And Then What Happened, Paul Revere?* (Fritz, 1996), students in Ms. Jimenez's fifth-grade class made these predictions, which were then organized into the following chart in Figure 8.5. After they read the book, they added other facts to the same chart. The information they added after the reading are in the shaded boxes.

Vocab-o-grams. **Vocab-o-grams,** also called predict-o-grams, are used to make predictions about vocabulary use in narrative text (Blachowicz & Fisher, 2002; Brassell & Flood, 2004). The teacher first lists vocabulary words from a reading and then students make predictions about how the word will be used in association with a story element. Any words the students cannot assign to a category go in the mystery word box. The teacher facilitates discussion of the rationale for why a particular word might be associated with an element of the story. For example, the word *castle* is

Figure 8.6   Vocab-O-Gram

Vocab-O-Gram
Story Title:

New Vocabulary Words	
Setting	Which words tell you about when and where the story took place?
Characters	Which words tell you about the characters in the story?
Problem/Goal	Which words describe the problem or goal?
Action	Which words tell you what might happen?
Resolution	Which words tell you how the story might end?
What question(s) do you have?	
Mystery Words	

Source: Brassell, D., & Flood, J. (2004). *Vocabulary strategies every teacher needs to know.* San Diego, CA: Academic Professional Development. Used with permission.

likely to be associated with setting while the word *finicky* probably refers to a character. After assigning the vocabulary words, but before reading, each student writes a question they expect to have answered in the reading. A form for vocab-o-grams appears in Figure 8.6.

Vocabulary mnemonics. Mnemonics are devices used to aid memory. The term is derived from the Greek word *mnemonikos,* meaning *mindful.* These are useful for remembering meanings, strings of terms, and even spelling. There are several different types of mnemonics:

- *Peg mnemonics.* These are perhaps the most familiar to most of us and are useful for recalling a list of terms. For example, many of us learned the name of the Great Lakes by using the peg mnemonic of HOMES, which stands for Huron, Ontario, Michigan, Erie, and Superior.

- *Visual mnemonics.* An effective means for remembering the meaning of words is to associate them with a visual representation. When students create vocabulary cards (later in this chapter) they are constructing their own visual mnemonics to remember a term. See Figure 8.7 for a visual mnemonic an eighth grader drew to remember the word *narcissism.* A helpful teacher resource for visual mnemonics is *Vocabulary Cartoons* (Burchers, Burchers, & Burchers, 1998).

Figure 8.7   *Student Example Using Visual Mnemonics*

- *Physical mnemonics.* This technique involves physical movement as an element in aiding memory. The technique of Total Physical Response (TPR) utilizes physical mnemonics to help English language learners acquire new language (Asher, 1969). We like to activate physical mnemonics with our students through Guess My Word, a simplified version of Charades. A teacher displays a vocabulary word the class is learning to all but one student. The class uses gestures and movement to represent the word in order to help the student name the correct word. It is important to remember that the words used in Guess My Word have been previously introduced and are identified in advance by category or known list.

What mnemonics do you use to remember things?

Guided Instruction

The guided instruction phase of the workshop provides an opportunity for the teacher to work in small groups with students on the vocabulary they are learning. Often, the vocabulary lesson serves as an introduction to a reading or writing activity. As with the strategies presented in the focus lesson section, these instructional activities can be used in other phases of the workshop. The intent of the shades of meaning and concept ladder activities is to encourage students to consider the relationship of words to one another. The A–Z chart invites students to catalog terms related to the topic of study.

Figure 8.8   Shades of Meaning Paint Chip

Shades of meaning. Relationships between words can be particularly challenging when discussing synonyms. The difference between *annoyance* and *harassment* is a fine but distinct one. This ability to discern between this gradient of meaning is a skill tested on the Scholastic Aptitude Test and other achievement exams. The difference between the right word and the almost right word can impact the ability of the student to use precise language. The "**shades of meaning**" can be taught in an imaginative way using paint chip cards from the local hardware store (Blanchfield, 2001). Students attach a paint chip card containing shades of color to notebook paper to illustrate a string of synonyms. Definitions are written to the right of the paint chip card on which the word has been written. For example, Mariana created the card in Figure 8.8 to illustrate shades of meaning around *happy*.

Many paint or hardware stores will provide the paint chips to you for free.

Concept ladders. **Concept ladders** are developed for vocabulary words that represent a concept by associating it with the characteristics of the concept (Gillet & Temple, 1986; Upton, 1973). In this way, students learn to associate words with one another rather than viewing them as a string of unrelated terms. The teacher identifies the focus word then guides students in developing their understanding of the concept by "climbing up the ladder" to identify these attributes:

- What is it a kind of?
- What is it a part of?

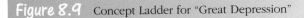

Figure 8.9   Concept Ladder for "Great Depression"

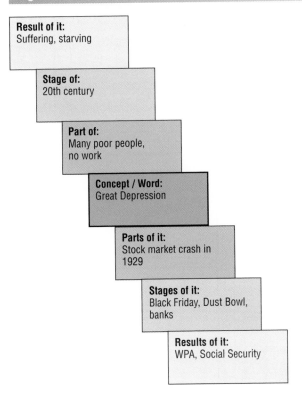

- What is it a stage of?
- What is it a product or result of? (Brassell & Flood, p. 12)

They then "climb down" the ladder to develop examples of the focus word:

- What are kinds of it?
- What are parts of it?
- What are stages of it?
- What are products or results of it? (Brassell & Flood, p. 12)

A concept ladder for the focus word *Great Depression* appears in Figure 8.9.

A–Z charts. **A–Z charts** are another means for encouraging student monitoring of their own learning (Allen, 2000). This simple chart like the one seen in Figure 8.10 contains alphabetically arranged blocks for students to record all the words they know in association with a particular topic. The teacher then collects them to assess how many terms the students already know and therefore do not need to be taught. These A–Z charts can be used again after a few lessons have been taught so that students might add to the list. Ask students to draw a line under the last word written in the box so they know what they've added. Again, the charts should be collected to find out how their learning is progressing. This process can be repeated again near the

Figure 8.10   A–Z Chart

A–B	C–D	E–F
G–H	**I–J**	**K–L**
M–N	**O–P**	**Q–R**
S–T	**U–V**	**WXYZ**

Source: From *Yellow Brick Roads: Shared and Guided Paths to Independent Reading* by Janet Allen, copyright © 2000. Used with permission of Stenhouse Publishers.

end of the unit of study. By giving students opportunities to add to their list, they are able to witness evidence of their own learning. For example, when Mr. Lee introduced *Profiles in Courage* (Kennedy, 1956) to his eighth graders, he began by inviting them to complete a class A–Z chart of terms they associated with courage. Initially they included words like *heroic* and *brave.* As they read the chapters on Sam Houston and John Quincy Adams, they expanded their repertoire to include *fearlessness, facing hardship, integrity, tenacity,* and *persistence.*

Collaborative Learning

The activities featured in the collaborative learning phase of the language arts workshop provide students with a chance to talk about words with a peer. These strategies should be introduced first during a focus lesson or guided instruction to ensure

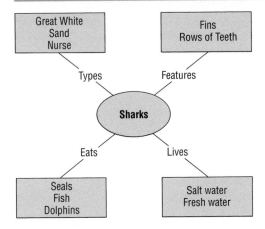

Figure 8.11   Semantic Map from Second Grade

that students know how to complete the task. The interaction with peers is intended to create a sense of fun around words, an important objective in vocabulary instruction. As with the other vocabulary activities, the maps and sorts discussed in this section can be used throughout the workshop, depending on your students' needs.

Semantic maps and word maps. Arguably the most popular method for teaching vocabulary through association is the use of **semantic mapping** (Heimlich & Pittleman, 1986). Semantic maps are recognizable because they feature the focus word in the center of a web connected by lines that are labeled to show relationships. Students first brainstorm what they know about a word then sort the ideas into attributes or categories. Many teachers use prepared semantic map forms when their students are first learning to construct these webs but gradually shift to student-created maps once they are comfortable with it. Semantic webs are also useful as a method to organize ideas for writing. Inspiration® and Kidspiration® software can be used by students to create semantic maps on the computer. A second-grade example of a semantic map for the word *sharks* can be seen in Figure 8.11.

Word maps are very similar to semantic maps and feature specific categories for describing the concepts that underlie the focus word. These categories are worded in the form of questions:

- What is it?
- What is it like?
- What are some examples?

Moss (2003) recommends these for grades 3 and up, either before or after the reading. A version of a word map appears in Figure 8.12.

Open and closed concept word sorts. **Concept word sorts** are another means for encouraging students to create classification systems based on word meaning (Bear, Invernizzi, Templeton, & Johnston, 2004). We have previously described word sorts to build phonics knowledge through the use of word families. This instructional technique can also be used to develop vocabulary through the creation of categories to group words.

Teacher Tip

Teachers can create semantic maps and other graphic organizers at http://teachers.teach-nology.com/web_tools/graphic_org/

Figure 8.12   Word Map

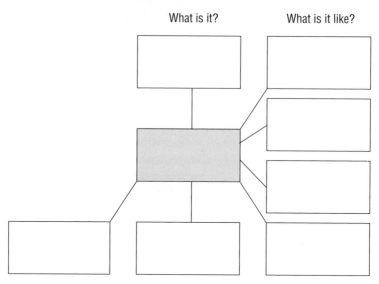

What is it?   What is it like?

What are some examples?

Like word maps and semantic maps, we recommend using sorts during the collaborative phase of the language arts workshop because of the conversations that happen between learners. Sorts can either be **closed** (categories are furnished by the teacher) or **open** (students develop their own categories). Because concept word sorts, especially open ones, are rarely identical among students, conversation about their understandings of word meaning occur naturally.

Like word sorts for phonics development, concept word sorts typically feature words on slips of paper or index cards (recommended for younger students). Younger students find it easier to sort words using a mat made of construction paper or tag board to create a defined field for placing the word cards. For example, a group of first-grade students sorted the vocabulary words in Figure 8.13 using a closed sorting system provided by their teacher. You'll notice that there are a number of correct variations possible with these categories of the seasons:

The next example is an open sort from the same first-grade classroom. One group labeled their categories as *breakfast, lunch, dinner,* and *snacks* and sorted accordingly (see Figure 8.14). At the same time, another collaborative group with the same words created two categories: *we're allowed to have* and *we're not allowed to have!*

Quiz-me cards. Rehearsal of new words is essential for integrating the word into the student's permanent vocabulary. Some of this rehearsal can come from practicing words with peers, as with **quiz-me cards.** Students create these cards on 3″ × 5″ cards. As vocabulary is introduced, a word is written on the card, along with the definition. On the back of each card is space for five signatures. A hole is punched in the corner and the cards are strung on a binder ring. A sample of the quiz-me cards can be seen in Figure 8.15. Students are required to collect five signatures from peers for

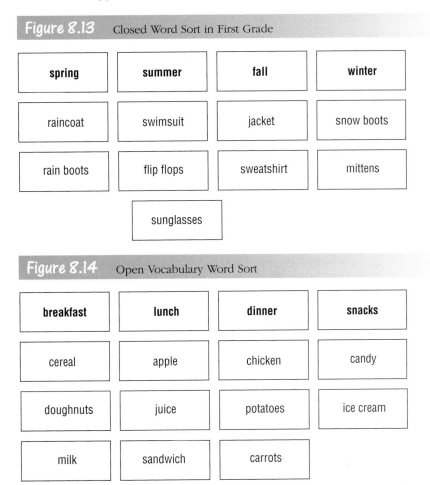

Figure 8.13   Closed Word Sort in First Grade

spring	summer	fall	winter
raincoat	swimsuit	jacket	snow boots
rain boots	flip flops	sweatshirt	mittens
	sunglasses		

Figure 8.14   Open Vocabulary Word Sort

breakfast	lunch	dinner	snacks
cereal	apple	chicken	candy
doughnuts	juice	potatoes	ice cream
milk	sandwich	carrots	

each word. They are instructed to approach a classmate and then request their assistance. The peer quizzes the student on each word, then signs the back of each correct response. In addition to creating a purposeful repetition and rehearsal, it also serves as a way for students to interact with one another as they practice social exchanges. These quiz-me cards can be used effectively outside the classroom as well. Another version is to require adult signatures. Students must approach an adult, explain the assignment and ask for their assistance. This can be particularly valuable for middle school students who are adjusting to a larger school and new routines.

> Activities like quiz-me cards can encourage students to initiate conversations with adults outside of the classroom.

Vocabulary role play. Earlier we discussed the role of physical mnemonics in learning vocabulary through an activity called Guess My Word. Another example of **vocabulary role play** is the practice of "acting out" vocabulary which extends from Total Physical Response, a method of language instruction used with students who are English language learners (Asher, 1969) and those who are deaf (Marlatt, 1995). Students engaged in vocabulary role play use words, gestures, and drama to enact vocabulary they are learning. Because they are involving kinesthetic, visual, and auditory modes of learning, they are able to more fully experience each word, aiding in memory and recall.

> Kinesthetic learning refers to the use of movement.

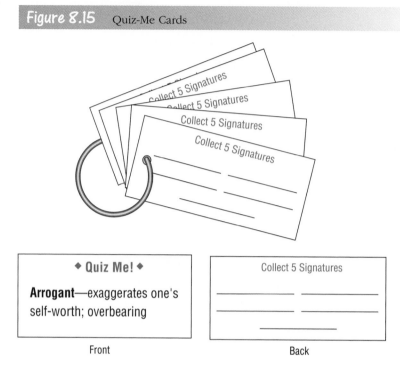

Figure 8.15   Quiz-Me Cards

Front

◆ **Quiz Me!** ◆

Arrogant—exaggerates one's self-worth; overbearing

Back

Collect 5 Signatures

Source: Adapted from Fisher, D., & Frey, N. (2003). *Improving adolescent literacy: Strategies at work.* Upper Saddle River, NJ: Merrill/Prentice Hall.

In a fourth-grade classroom, collaborative groups of students created short plays featuring assigned vocabulary words and later performed them for one another. Michelle, Aubrey, Scott, and Marcellus were assigned the words *North Pole, South Pole, latitude, longitude, equator,* and *prime meridian.* The four students wrote an imaginative conversation featuring an increasingly exasperated pirate captain trying to explain to a new pirate about how they navigate the ship to stage surprise attacks on unsuspecting towns. (We suspect they were inspired by the movie *Pirates of the Caribbean!*)

Independent Learning

The independent phase of the language arts workshop provides learners with an opportunity to extend their understanding of terms in unique ways. Like the other activities, they are modeled first in a focus lesson and students receive further practice in the guided and collaborative phases. The strategies profiled here, especially vocabulary cards and the self-selection strategy, are intended to give students an opportunity to practice learning words independently. Others, such as the scavenger hunt, allow students to use mnemonic devices to learn new terms.

Vocabulary cards. To create **vocabulary cards,** students are given a set of 4" × 6" index cards and instructed to divide each into quadrants (see Figure 8.16). Depending on the content and focus, specific terms are selected. The example used to illustrate visual mnemonics earlier in this chapter is a vocabulary card. For example, a sixth-grade teacher selected terms related to the Latin root word *manu-* meaning "to

Figure 8.16	Vocabulary Cards in Sixth Grade

Template

Vocabulary word	Definition in student's own words
Graphic or picture	Sentence using word

Example

manufacture	make a large amount of things on an assembly line
	Car factories manufacture autos.

make." Students created their vocabulary word cards for *manufacture, manuscript,* and *manual.* The target word is written in the top left quadrant, and the definition, after class instruction, is recorded in the student's own words in the upper right quadrant of the card. An antonym or something that the word does not mean is written in the lower right quadrant and an illustration or graphic symbol representing the term is drawn in the lower left quadrant.

Constructing vocabulary cards serves several uses (Bromley, 2002). First, when placed on a binder ring the cards become an easily accessible reference for the student. The time involved in creating each card also provides an opportunity for the student to spend an extended period of time concentrating on the meaning, use, and representation of the term, thereby increasing the likelihood that the term will become a part of their permanent vocabulary.

Individualized word lists. Another popular method for expanding written vocabulary is through specialized word lists, thesauri, and dictionaries. Many teachers have experienced the overuse of terms like "said" in their students' writing. This may occur because students have not explored the ways writers convey the way a message is spoken by a character to illuminate the action. **Individualized word lists** can focus on a particular aspect of the language. For example, teachers can adopt the "said" word list to assist students in using more descriptive terms in place of "said." Called "'Said' is Dead" (Peterson, 1996), students are provided with a list of words to help

Figure 8.17   Expanded Vocabulary Word List

"Said" Is Dead	
Enrich your dialogue writing with more descriptive terms like these:	
added	
advised	mumbled
allowed	objected
barked	parroted
babbled	pronounced
begged	protested
blurted	quipped
cajoled	reported
complained	scolded
confessed	scoffed
confided	simpered
demanded	snapped
dithered	swore
droned	stuttered
gasped	taunted
groaned	teased
howled	wailed
interrupted	whimpered
jeered	yammered
moaned	yelled

Source: Peterson, A. (1996). *The writers workout book: 113 stretches toward better prose.* Berkeley, CA: National Writing Project. Reprinted with permission.

The Internet has provided another important source of information on words and phrases. Teachers often bookmark websites like *http://www.rhymezone.com* for resources on rhyme schemes, *www.grammarbook.com* for help with punctuation and grammar, and *www.dictionary.com* for an all-purpose site for word definitions.

them use more interesting terms like *confided, quipped,* and *scoffed* in place of "said" when writing dialogue (see Figure 8.17). Similarly, students may also have a wealth of reference materials available to them to support their word choices. Student thesauri are useful for budding writers struggling to find the perfect word, but other specialized materials like a slang thesaurus, rhyming dictionary, and books of quotations are also popular with students.

Vocabulary self-selection strategy. An important part of vocabulary development is instilling a love for words. One example of this is the Stump the Teacher strategy we profiled earlier in this book, where students seek out words to challenge the teacher. Another version is the **vocabulary self-selection strategy** (Blachowicz & Fisher,

Figure 8.18   Kindergarten Vocabulary Scavenger Hunt

Fruits and Vegetables	
apple	orange
blueberry	pear
broccoli	peas
corn	tomato
cucumber	watermelon

2002; Haggard, 1986). Students identify words they believe are important for the class to learn during the independent phase of the language arts workshop. During class discussion, they share how they located the word (for example, heard on television or read in the newspaper) and why they believe it is important. The class then decides which words they will study during the coming week.

When developing VSS with younger students, we read the book *Donavan's Word Jar* (DeGross, 1994). This story of a boy who is fascinated with words resonates with emergent and early readers. Like Donavan, they are encouraged to write down words they enjoy to be added to the class word jar. Words are shared with the class for selection for further study.

Scavenger hunts and realia. Like vocabulary self-selection, **scavenger hunts** challenge students to locate representations of new vocabulary (Brassell & Flood, 2004; Vaughn, Crawley, & Mountain, 1979). Students are given a list of words, both new and familiar, that are related conceptually. They have one week to find either visual examples (i.e., magazine clippings), **realia** (the object itself), or evidence of the use of the word in something other than their textbooks. For instance, kindergarteners can be given a list of vocabulary words like the ones in Figure 8.18. While many are familiar words, others will be new to most of them.

Vocabulary self-awareness. We discussed vocabulary self-awareness earlier in the chapter in relation to the student's role in learning vocabulary. These self-awareness charts can be completed by students during the focus lessons or guided phases of the language arts workshop as they read or write. In addition to those prepared in advance by the teacher, such as those seen earlier, we encourage students to create their own vocabulary self-awareness charts during their reading. Good readers notice when they have encountered a less than familiar term. Students can keep a blank log of words they run across in their reading for use during conferences with the teacher.

BIG IDEAS ABOUT TEACHING VOCABULARY

Learning words is an important part of the language arts workshop. Scott, Jamieson-Noel, and Asselin (2003) maintain that:

✓ Word knowledge is complex: Knowing a word is more than knowing how to spell it or knowing the definition.

✓ Word learning is incremental: Word knowledge develops in small steps.

✓ Words are heterogeneous: Words are different and require different learning strategies.

✓ Definitions, context, and word parts all supply important information about a word, but each of these components has limitations in use.

Therefore, vocabulary instruction is multifaceted and includes word derivations, word associations, and word appreciation. Techniques include sorts, metacognitive strategies like self-awareness, predictions, and list-group-label, and exposure to narrative and expository literature that fosters vocabulary development.

INTEGRATING THE STANDARDS

Create lesson plans that meet your state's standards by visiting our Companion Website at www.prenhall.com/frey. There you'll find lessons created to meet the NCTE/IRA Standards. Adapt them to meet the standards of your own state through links to your state's standards, and keep them in the online portfolio. You can collect lesson plans for each chapter in an online portfolio, providing you with invaluable tools to meet your state's standards when you head into your own classroom.

CHECK YOUR UNDERSTANDING

1. How do students acquire vocabulary knowledge?

2. How should vocabulary be chosen?

3. What are the objectives of vocabulary instruction?

4. What instructional strategies are useful throughout the phases of the language arts workshop?

CLASSROOM CONNECTIONS

1. Ask your teacher how he or she selects vocabulary for study in the classroom. What is the role of word lists, words culled from readings, and words related through structure or concept?

2. Examine the teacher editions of the content textbooks your students are using for examples of vocabulary development. How many are similar to the ones discussed in this chapter? Note examples that differ from the ones in this chapter.

3. Gather samples of graphic organizers and other forms for vocabulary development used in your classroom. Create a file labeled "Vocabulary Development" and save them for use in your own classroom.

4. Use an Internet search engine to locate websites on Greek and Latin root words. Bookmark the ones you like best.

References

Allen, J. (2000). *Yellow brick roads: Shared and guided paths to independent reading 4–12* (p. 266). York, ME: Stenhouse.

Anders, P. L., & Bos, C. S. (1986). Semantic feature analysis: An interactive strategy for vocabulary development and text comprehension. *Journal of Reading, 29,* 610–616.

Anderson, R. C. (1996). Research foundations to support wide reading. In V. Greaney (Ed.), *Promoting reading in developing countries* (pp. 55–77). Newark, DE: International Reading Association.

Asher, J. J. (1969). The total physical response approach to second language learning. *Modern Language Journal, 53*(1), 3–17.

Baker, S. K., Simmons, D. C., & Kame'enui, E. J. (1998). Vocabulary acquisition: Instructional and curricular basics and implications. In D. C. Simmons & E. J. Kame'enui (Eds.), *What reading research tells us about children with diverse learning needs* (pp. 219–238). Mahwah, NJ: Lawrence Erlbaum Associates.

Baumann, J. F., Edwards, E. C., Boland, E. M., Olejnik, S., & Kame'enui, E. J. (2003). Vocabulary tricks: Effects of instruction in morphology and context on fifth-grade students' ability to derive and infer word meanings. *American Educational Research Journal, 40,* 447–494.

Baumann, J. F., Kame'enui, E. J., & Ash, G. E. (2003). Research on vocabulary instruction: Voltaire redux. In J. Flood, D. Lapp, J. M. Jensen, & J. R. Squire (Eds.), *Handbook of research on teaching the English language arts* (2nd ed., pp. 752–785). Mahwah, NJ: Lawrence Erlbaum Associates.

Bear, D. R., Invernizzi, M., Templeton, S., & Johnston, F. (2004). *Words their way: Word study for phonics, vocabulary, and spelling instruction* (3rd ed.). Upper Saddle River, NJ: Merrill/Prentice Hall.

Beck, I. L., McKeown, M. G., & McCaslin, E. S. (1983). Vocabulary development: All contexts are not created equal. *Elementary School Journal, 83,* 177–181.

Biemiller, A. (2003). Vocabulary: Needed if more children are to read well. *Reading Psychology, 24,* 323–335.

Blachowicz, C. L. Z., & Fisher, P. J. (2000). Vocabulary instruction. In M. L. Kamil, P. B. Mosenthal, P. D. Pearson, & R. Barr (Eds.), *Handbook of reading research* (Vol. III, pp. 503–523). Mahwah, NJ: Lawrence Erlbaum Associates.

Blachowicz, C., & Fisher, P. J. (2002). *Teaching vocabulary in all classrooms* (2nd ed.). Upper Saddle River, NJ: Merrill/Prentice Hall.

Blanchfield, C. (Ed.). (2001). *Creative vocabulary: Strategies for teaching vocabulary in grades K–12.* Fresno, CA: San Joaquin Valley Writing Project.

Brassell, D., & Flood, J. (2004). *Vocabulary strategies every teacher needs to know.* San Diego, CA: Academic Professional Development.

Bromley, K. (2002). *Stretching students' vocabulary: Best practices for building the rich vocabulary students need to achieve in reading, writing, and the content areas.* New York: Scholastic.

Burchers, S., Burchers, M., & Burchers, B. (1998). *Vocabulary cartoons: Elementary edition.* Punta Gorda, FL: New Monics.

Daniels, H. (2002). *Literature circles: Voice and choice in book clubs and reading groups* (2nd ed.). York, ME: Stenhouse.

Durkin, D. D. (1978-1979). What classroom observations reveal about reading comprehension instruction. *Reading Research Quarterly, 14,* 481–533.

Fisher, P. J. L., Blachowicz, C. L. Z., & Smith, J. C. (1991). Vocabulary learning in literature discussion groups. In J. Zutell & S. McCormick (Eds.), *Learner factors/teacher factors:*

Issues in literacy research and instruction: Fortieth yearbook of the National Reading Conference (pp. 201–217). Chicago: National Reading Conference.

Flood, J., Lapp, D., & Fisher, D. (2003). Reading comprehension instruction. In J. Flood, D. Lapp, J. M. Jensen, & J. R. Squire (Eds.), *Handbook of research on teaching the English language arts* (2nd ed., pp. 931–941). Mahwah, NJ: Lawrence Erlbaum Associates.

Gillet, J. W., & Temple, C. (1986). *Understanding reading problems: Assessment and instruction.* Boston: Little, Brown, & Co.

Goodman, L. (2001). A tool for learning: Vocabulary self-awareness. In C. Blanchfield (Ed.), *Creative vocabulary: Strategies for teaching vocabulary in grades K–12.* Fresno, CA: San Joaquin Valley Writing Project.

Graves, M. F. (1986). Vocabulary learning and instruction. In E. Z. Rothkopf (Ed.), *Review of research in education* (Vol. 13, pp. 49–89). Washington, DC: American Educational Research Association.

Graves, M. F., & Prenn, M. C. (1986). Costs and benefits of various methods of teaching vocabulary. *Journal of Reading, 29,* 596–602.

Haggard, M. R. (1986). The vocabulary self-collection strategy: An active approach to word learning. In E. K. Dishner, T. W. Bean, J. E. Readence, & D. W. Moore (Eds.), *Reading in the content areas: Improving classroom instruction* (pp. 179–183). Dubuque, IA: Kendall/Hunt.

Harwell, J. M. (2001). *Complete learning disabilities handbook: Ready-to-use strategies and activities for teaching students with learning disabilities* (2nd ed.). Paramus, NJ: Center for Applied Research in Education.

Heimlich, J. E., & Pittleman, S. D. (1986). *Semantic mapping: Classroom applications.* Newark, DE: International Reading Association.

Jenkins, J. R., & Dixon, R. (1983). Learning vocabulary. *Contemporary Educational Psychology, 8,* 237–260.

Kame'enui, E. J., & Simmons, D. (1990). *Designing instructional strategies for the prevention of academic learning problems.* Upper Saddle River, NJ: Merrill/Prentice Hall.

Klein, M. L. (1988). *Teaching reading comprehension and vocabulary: A guide for teachers.* Upper Saddle River, NJ: Prentice Hall.

Krashen, S. (1989). We acquire vocabulary and spelling by reading: Additional evidence for the input hypothesis. *The Modern Language Journal, 73,* 440–464.

Marlatt, E. A. (1995). Language through total physical response. *Perspectives in Education and Deafness, 13*(4), 18–20.

Moss, B. (2003). *25 strategies for guiding readers through informational texts.* San Diego, CA: Academic Professional Development.

Nagy, W. E., & Anderson, R. C. (1984). How many words are there in printed school English? *Reading Research Quarterly, 19,* 304–330.

Nagy, W. E., Herman, P. A., & Anderson, R. C. (1985). Learning words from context. *Reading Research Quarterly, 20,* 233–253.

Peterson, A. (1996). *The writer's workout book: 113 stretches toward better prose*. Berkeley, CA: National Writing Project.

Pittleman, S. D., Heimlich, J. E., Berglund, R. L., & French, M. P. (1991). *Semantic feature analysis: Classroom applications*. Newark, DE: International Reading Association.

Schatz, E. K., & Baldwin, R. S. (1986). Context clues are unreliable predictors of word meanings. *Reading Research Quarterly, 21,* 439–453.

Scott, J., Jamieson-Noel, D., & Asselin, M. (2003). Vocabulary instruction throughout the school day in 23 Canadian upper-elementary classrooms. *The Elementary School Journal, 103,* 269–286.

Spearitt, D. (1972). Identification of subskills of reading comprehension by maximum likelihood factor analysis. *Reading Research Quarterly, 8,* 92–111.

Stahl, S. A. (1988). Review of the nature of vocabulary acquisition. *Journal of Reading Behavior, 20,* 89–95.

Stanovich, K. E. (1986). Matthew effects in reading: Some consequences of individual differences in the acquisition of literacy. *Reading Research Quarterly, 21,* 360–407.

Taba, H. (1967). *Teacher's handbook for elementary social studies*. Reading, MA: Addison-Wesley.

Upton, A. (1973). *Design for thinking: A first book of semantics*. Palo Alto, CA: Pacific.

Vacca, R. T., & Vacca, J. L. (2001). *Content area reading: Literacy and learning across the curriculum* (7th ed.). Boston: Allyn & Bacon.

Vaughn, S., Crawley, S., & Mountain, L. A. (1979). A multiple-modality approach to word study: Vocabulary scavenger hunts. *The Reading Teacher, 32,* 434–437.

Children's Literature Cited

Curtis, C. P. (1999). *Bud, not Buddy*. New York: Scholastic.

DeGross, M. (1994). *Donavan's word jar*. New York: HarperCollins.

Di Camillo, K. (2003). *The tale of Despereaux: Being a story of a mouse, a princess, some soup, and a spool of thread*. Cambridge, MA: Candlewick Press.

Duey, K., & Barnes, M. B. (2001). *More freaky facts about natural disasters*. New York: Aladdin.

Falwell, C. (1998). *Word wizard*. New York: Houghton Mifflin.

Frasier, D. (2000). *Miss Alaineous: A vocabulary disaster*. San Diego: Harcourt.

Fritz, J. (1996). *And then what happened, Paul Revere?* New York: Scholastic.

Hesse, K. (1999). *Letters from Rifka*. New York: Scholastic.

Kennedy, J. F. (1956). *Profiles in courage*. New York: HarperCollins.

Lowry, L. (1994). *The giver*. New York: Laurel Leaf.

Osborne, M. P. (2003). *High tide in Hawaii*. New York: Random House.

Simon, S. (2002). *Super storms*. New York: Sea Star.

Appendix 8.1 500 Most Used Words List

A
Able
About
Above
Across
Afraid
After
Again
Against
Air
All
Almost
Also
Always
Am
And
Angry
Animal
Another
Answer
Any
Are
Around
As
Ask
At
Ate
Away

B
Baby
Back
Bad
Ball
Be
Beautiful
Because
Bed
Been
Before
Began
Begin
Being
Believe
Below
Best
Better
Between
Big
Bird
Black
Blue
Book
Both

Box
Boy
Bread
Bring
Brother
Brought
Brown
Build
Built
Busy
But
Buy
By

C
Call
Came
Can
Car
Carry
Cat
Catch
Caught
Cent
Chase
Child
Children
City
Clean
Climb
Close
Clothes
Cold
Color
Come
Cook
Corner
Could
Country
Cow
Cried
Cry
Cut

D
Daddy
Dance
Dark
Day
Deep
Did
Didn't
Different
Dig

Dinner
Dirty
Do
Does
Dog
Doing
Done
Don't
Door
Down
Draw
Dress
Drink
Drive
Drop
During

E
Each
Early
Easy
Eat
Eight
Enough
Even
Ever
Every
Eye

F
Face
Fall
Family
Far
Farm
Fast
Father
Feed
Feel
Feet
Felt
Few
Finally
Find
Finish
Fire
First
Fish
Five
Flew
Fly
Follow
Food
For

Found
Four
Friend
From
Friday
Front
Fruit
Full
Funny

G
Game
Garden
Gave
Get
Girl
Give
Glad
Go
Goes
Going
Good
Got
Grass
Great
Green
Grew
Ground
Grow
Guess

H
Had
Hand
Happen
Happy
Has
Hat
Have
He
Head
Hear
Heard
Help
Her
Here
Herself
Hide
High
Hill
Him
Himself
His
Hold

Home
Hope
Hot
Hour
House
How
Huge
Hundred
Hungry
Hunt
Hurry
Hurt

I
Ice
Idea
If
Important
In
Is
It

J
Join
Jump
Just

K
Keep
Kept
Kick
Kind
Kitchen
Kitten
Knew
Know

L
Land
Large
Last
Late
Laugh
Learn
Leave
Left
Let
Letter
Life
Light
Like
Listen
Little
Live
Long
Look

Lose
Loud
Love
Lunch

M
Made
Make
Man
Many
May
Me
Mean
Men
Met
Might
Mile
Milk
Mine
Monday
Money
More
Morning
Most
Mother
Mountain
Mr.
Mrs.
Music
Must
My

N
Name
Near
Neck
Need
Neighbor
Never
New
Next
Nice
Night
Nine
No
Noise
North
Not
Nothing
Now
Number

O
Ocean
Of
Off

Office
Often
Old
On
Once
One
Only
Open
Or
Orange
Other
Our
Out
Over
Own

P
Page
Paint
Paper
Park
Part
Party
Pass
Penny
People
Pick
Picnic
Picture
Piece
Plant
Play
Please
Point
Pony
Pretty
Print
Prize
Problem
Proud
Pull
Puppy
Push
Put

Q
Question
Quick
Quiet
Quit
Quite

R
Rabbit
Rain
Ran

Reach
Read
Real
Red
Remember
Rid
Right
River
Room
Round
Run

S
Sad
Said
Same
Sat
Saturday
Saw
School
Second
See
Seem
Send
Sentence
Seven
Several
She
Short
Should
Show
Side
Since
Sing
Sister
Six
Sleep
Slowly
Small
Snow
So
Some
Soon
South
Space
Stand
Start
Stay
Stop
Store
Story
Street
Such
Suddenly
Swim

T
Take
Talk
Teach
Tell
Ten
Than
Thank
That
The
Their
Them
Then
There
These
They
Thing
Think
Third
This
Those
Thought
Three
Through
Thursday

Time
To
Today
Together
Told
Tomorrow
Too
Took
Toward
Town
Toy
Travel
Tree
Tried
Truck
True
Tuesday
Turn
Two

U
Under
Until
Up
Upon

Us
Use
Usually

V
Very
Visit
Voice

W
Wait
Walk
Want
Was
Wash
Watch
Water
We
Wednesday
Week
Well
Went
Were
West
What

When
Which
While
White
Who
Why
Will
With
Woman
Word
Work
World
Would
Write

Y
Yard
Year
Yellow
Yes
Yesterday
You
Young
Your

Source: Harwell, J. M. (2001). *Complete learning disabilities handbook: Ready-to-use strategies and activities for teaching students with learning disabilities* (2nd ed.). Paramus, NJ: Center for Applied Research in Education. Used with permission.

CHAPTER

Building Reading and Writing Fluency in the Language Arts Workshop

BIG IDEAS ABOUT FLUENCY

Fluency is the ability to read and write smoothly, accurately, and at a rate that does not interfere with the clarity of the message. Reading fluency is increased primarily through repetition, primarily repeated readings of familiar text. Instruction in writing fluency is focused on timed writing and practice at word choice to convey the message concisely. Fluency in reading and writing contributes to motivation and interest, especially as it relates to a feeling of competency.

Questions to Consider

When you have finished reading this chapter, you should be able to answer these questions:

- What is flow?
- What is reading fluency?
- What is writing fluency?
- What activities contribute to reading and writing fluency?

Key Vocabulary

Reading fluency
Writing fluency
Flow
Rate
Prosody

Accuracy
Automaticity
Read alouds
Power Writing
Dictoglos
Predictable books
Neurological Impress Model
Choral reading
Repeated reading
Readers Theatre
Beat the Clock
Paired reading
Independent reading
Freewriting

A LOOK INSIDE

In honor of the 100th anniversary of the Wright brothers' first flight, Ms. DeGuzman's seventh-grade students have been reading a number of fiction and nonfiction texts on aviation. During the past few weeks, they have analyzed the picture book *Amelia and Eleanor Go for a Ride* (Ryan, 1999) during shared reading and read excerpts during guided reading from *Wings of Madness* (Hoffman, 2003) about Brazilian aviator Albert Santos-Dumont.

A small group of students is busy creating an original performance of a notable event in aviation history—Lindbergh's crossing of the Atlantic in 1927. Ms. DeGuzman has bookmarked a website for their use in developing a Reader's Theatre script of the flight. Reader's Theatre is a fluency-building reading strategy that results in a performance, much like a radio play. Ms. DeGuzman has used the resources featured on Eyewitness to History (www.eyewitnesstohistory.com), a website specializing in first-person accounts, to bring historical events to life. Caroline, Evan, Ting, Paul, and Maria have read Lindbergh's recollections of this event ("Lindbergh Flies the Atlantic, 1927," 1999) on this website and even listened to a recording of a speech delivered by Lindbergh after the flight (www.eyewitnesstohistory.com/Lindbergh.htm). Using direct quotes from Lindbergh's own account, they created a

Figure 9.1   Readers Theatre Script for Lindbergh's First Flight

Lindbergh Flies the Atlantic, 1927

Narrator #1—Caroline
Narrator #2—Paul
Lindbergh—Ting and Evan

Trivia master—Maria
Crowd—all

Narrator #1: At 7:52 a.m., May 20, 1927 Charles Lindbergh gunned the engine of the "Spirit of St Louis" and aimed her down the dirt runway of Roosevelt Field, Long Island. Heavily laden with fuel, the plane bounced down the muddy field, gradually became airborne and barely cleared the telephone wires at the field's edge.

Narrator #2: The crowd of 500 thought they had witnessed a miracle.

Crowd: It's a miracle!

Lindbergh: The field was a little soft due to the rain during the night and the plane gathered speed very slowly. After passing the halfway mark, however, it was apparent that I would be able to clear the obstructions at the end. I passed over a tractor by about fifteen feet and a telephone line by about twenty, with a fair reserve of flying speed.

Narrator #2: Thirty-three and one-half hours and 3,500 miles later he landed in Paris, the first to fly the Atlantic alone.

Crowd: Alone? It's madness! It can't be done!

Trivia Master: The *Spirit of Saint Louis* was built in San Diego to Lindbergh's specifications for $10,585. Before making his transatlantic flight. Lindbergh flew it from its factory in San Diego to Long Island. Stopping only in St. Louis, he made the flight in 21 hours and 20 minutes—a new coast-to-coast record.

Crowd: Across the country in less than a day? It's a miracle!

Narrator #1: Lindbergh continued his flight over Cape Cod and Nova Scotia and headed for the open Atlantic as darkness fell.

Lindbergh: There was no moon and it was very dark. The tops of some of the storm clouds were several thousand feet above me and at one time, when I attempted to fly through one of the larger clouds, sleet started to collect on the plane and I was forced to turn around and get back into clear air immediately and then fly around any clouds which I could not get over.

Trivia Master: Lindbergh designed the *Spirit of St. Louis* without a front window. This provided more room for fuel but forced him to use the plane's side windows to view the world around him.

Crowd: No front window? It's madness!

Narrator #2: Lindbergh continued his course, at times skimming only 10 feet above the waves as he tried to find a way around the fog and maintain his course. The appearance of fishing boats below alerted him that he was nearing land.

Lindbergh: The first indication of my approach to the European Coast was a small fishing boat which I first noticed a few miles ahead and slightly to the south of my course. There were several of these fishing boats grouped within a few miles of each other. I flew over the first boat without seeing any signs of life. As I circled over the second, however, a man's face appeared, looking out of the cabin window.

Man on fishing boat: Is that an airplane up there? It's a miracle!

Lindbergh: When I saw this fisherman I decided to try to get him to point towards land. When the plane passed within a few feet of the boat I shouted, "Which way is Ireland?"

Man on fishing boat: He doesn't know the way to Ireland? It's madness!

Lindbergh: Less than an hour later a rugged and semi-mountainous coastline appeared to the northeast. I was flying less than two hundred feet from the water when I sighted it. I located Cape Valencia and Dingle Bay, then resumed my compass course towards Paris.

Narrator #1: Lindbergh flew over Ireland and then England at an altitude of about 1500 feet as he headed towards France. The weather cleared and flying conditions became almost perfect.

Lindbergh: I first saw the lights of Paris a little before 10 p.m., or 5 p.m., New York time, and a few minutes later I was circling the Eiffel Tower at an altitude of about four thousand feet.

Narrator #2: Lindbergh then set out to find the field at le Bourget, where he was supposed to land.

Lindbergh: The lights of Le Bourget were plainly visible, but appeared to be very close to Paris. I spiraled down closer to the lights. Presently I could make out long lines of hangars, and the roads appeared to be jammed with cars.

Trivia Master: There were 100,000 people waiting for Lindbergh to land!

Crowd: It's madness! We must see it for ourselves!

Lindbergh: I flew low over the field once, then circled around into the wind and landed.

Crowd: It's a miracle! We have seen it for ourselves!

Source: Adapted from "Lindbergh Flies the Atlantic, 1927." (1999). *EyeWitness to history*. Retrieved December 17, 2003 from www.eyewitnesstohistory.com/lindbergh.htm. Used with permission.

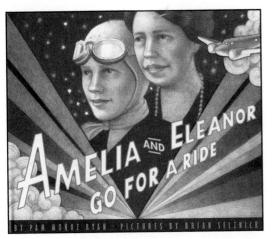

From AMELIA AND ELEANOR GO FOR A RIDE by Pam
Muñoz Ryan, illustrated by Brian Selznick. Copyright © 1998
by Scholastic Inc. Reprinted by permission of Scholastic Inc.

Readers Theatre script by dividing the reading into
parts. The script they wrote appears in Figure 9.1.

After finalizing the script, they rehearsed their parts
for several days during the collaborative phase of the
language arts workshop. Because they are familiar
with Readers Theatre, they know that they do not
need to memorize the script because they will use
them during the performance. Instead, they are busy
perfecting their timing and phrasing, using what Ms.
DeGuzman calls their "radio voices." When the day arrives, they perform for the class to rounds of applause.

FLUENCY IN READING AND WRITING

Fluency—to be fluent—has many connotations in education. One focuses on the
skills in learning language, as in she is a fluent speaker. Another focuses on learning additional languages, as in "she is newly fluent in Spanish." However, the one
we will focus on in this chapter concerns the rate and accuracy at which students'
process text. We are concerned with both reading fluency and writing fluency in the
language arts workshop. **Reading fluency** focuses on the rate and accuracy at
which students read while **writing fluency** focuses on the rate and accuracy at
which they write. We'd like to consider the concept of *flow*. We believe that the theory of flow explains why a focus on fluency is so important.

**Flow—What Is
That?**

If you like sports, you know what it means to be "in the zone." Athletes "in the zone"
report feeling that time is suspended and that their movements are fluid. Similarly,
some people report "getting lost" in a book or good movie. Mihalyi Csikszentmihalyi
(1990) (pronounced "chick-SENT-me-high") has studied this phenomenon and called
it **flow.** He believes that flow is an optimal experience for humans.

In simple terms, Csikszentmihalyi's research suggests that people are generally
unhappy doing nothing, happy doing things, and on the whole know very little
about what makes them happy. However, the people are fully engaged by a task
they are doing, they "get lost" in the activity, or "get in the zone." He calls the state
of getting lost in the activity, "flow." According to Csikszentmihalyi (1997) there are
a number of characteristics of flow. These include:

- *Complete involvement, focus, concentration*—due either to innate curiosity or
  as the result of training
- *A sense of ecstasy*—of being outside everyday reality
- *A great inner clarity*—knowing what needs to be done and how well it is going

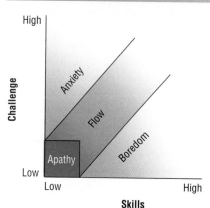

Figure 9.2   Flow as a Relationship Between Challenge and Skills

- *Knowledge that the activity is doable*—that one's skills are adequate, and that the task does not create anxiety or boredom
- *A sense of serenity*—no worries about self, feeling of growing beyond the boundaries of ego—afterwards feeling of transcending ego in ways not thought possible
- *Timeliness*—thorough focus on the present, no notice of time passing
- *Intrinsic motivation*—whatever produces "flow" becomes its own reward

As you can imagine, a goal of teachers is to keep students in flow for as much of the school day as possible. However, as Figure 9.2 indicates, there are times that students may not be in a state of flow. As Csikszentmihalyi (1997, 2000) notes, humans cannot be in flow all of the time—it is an optimal state, not necessarily a common state of being. When the challenge is relatively high and skills are relatively low, students become anxious. Importantly, when the challenge is relatively low and skills are relatively high, students become bored. When both are low, a profound sense of apathy is apparent.

Flow and motivation. Beyond the obvious implication that a challenging task is balanced by the learner's skills, Csikszentmihalyi notes that motivation is important because of its relationship to learning. In other words, we often learn more efficiently and effectively when we are motivated to do so. A challenge is that flow requires significant intrinsic motivation. Look again at the list of characteristics of flow—each is something that is generated from within the learner. This contrasts with extrinsic motivation such as rewards, grades, and praise, which typically come from an outside source like the teacher. He believes that one way to intensify intrinsic motivation is to make students aware of how much fun learning can be.

Flow and fluency. We believe that flow in the language arts workshop is influenced, in part, by fluency in reading and writing. Not being able to read smoothly and accurately is frustrating, causes anxiety, and results in poor comprehension. The message, as processed by the brain, becomes halting, choppy, and disjointed. A similar phenomenon occurs with disfluent writing. When ideas are coming faster that one can write, students become frustrated. If they do not have good command of spelling and vocabulary, they oversimplify their sentences with low-level words and ideas, or give up altogether on their creative writing. Alternatively, smooth and accurate reading allows the reader to concentrate on the meaning of the message, an important contributor to motivation and interest. Likewise, the ability to compose a message without having to stop after every word to recall spelling or syntax allows the writer to concentrate on more sophisticated writing behaviors, such as planning, composing, and revising to create the best message. Without a doubt, fluency in reading and writing are important components of the language arts workshop because they contribute to the learner's ability to fully engage with the literacy activity.

What Is the Importance of Reading Fluency?

"Reading fluency is the ability to read quickly and accurately, with appropriate and meaningful expression" (Rasinski, 2003a, p. 16). In other words, reading fast is not the true goal of fluency. Readers must understand what they are reading and add expressiveness to their oral reading. Comparing fluency with music, Worthy and Broaddus (2001/2002) note that fluency "consists not only of rate, accuracy, and automaticity, but also of phrasing, smoothness, and expressiveness. Fluency gives language its musical quality, its rhythm and flow, and makes reading sound effortless" (p. 334). More simply stated, "we know it when we hear it!" (Archer, Gleason, & Vachon, 2003, p. 96).

Defining reading fluency. Let's define some of those terms that were just mentioned. **Rate** is the speed at which the learner reads. If the reader's rate is too slow (less than 50 words per minute) it will interfere with comprehension because the reading becomes choppy and disconnected from other ideas in the sentences and paragraphs (Burns, Tucker, Hauser, Thelen, Holmes, & White, 2002). If it is too fast, especially in oral reading, it may also interfere with comprehension as the reader rushes too quickly past the details that make the passage meaningful (Dyson & Haselgrove, 2000). Reading too fast may also indicate that the learner lacks **prosody,** the ability to adjust tone, pitch, and rate to read with expression appropriate to the meaning of the words (Martinez, Roser, & Strecker, 1998–1999). After all, a reader can only use expression when the meaning of the message is understood. Finally, **accuracy** refers to the ability to read the words correctly. Remember that the relative accuracy of a reader reflects text difficulty. **Automaticity** is the ability to recognize words with a minimum of attention, allowing the reader to direct most of his or her attention to matters of comprehension (LaBerge & Samuels, 1974). Not surprisingly, automaticity is closely associated with decoding and spelling.

Text difficulty:
Independent =
95–100%;
Instructional =
90–94%; Frustration
= 89% or below. See
chapter 3 for a review.

Reading fluency, decoding, and comprehension. Expanding on this connection, Rasinski (2003a, 2003b) suggests that fluency is the bridge between decoding and comprehension. As you discovered in previous chapters, students learn to decode words by matching sounds and symbols. This ability is related to their oral language development and early phonemic awareness. You also noted that children do not only use decoding to read. Some English words are difficult to decode and are learned as sight words.

Evidence Based

See chapters 6, 7, and 8 for more information on these ideas.

Figure 9.3 Norms for Reading Fluency (in words correct per minute)

SILENT		ORAL	FALL	WINTER	SPRING
Grade	WPM[1]	Grade	WCPM[2]	WCPM[2]	WCPM[2]
1	-	1	-	-	60
2	86	2	53	78	94
3	116	3	79	93	114
4	155	4	99	112	118
5	177	5	105	118	128
6	206	6	115	132	145
7	215	7	147	158	167
8	237	8	156	167	171

[1] Words Per Minute
[2] Words Correct Per Minute

Source: From Albert J. Harris and Edward R. Sipay, *How to Increase Reading Ability: A Guide to Development and Remedial Methods,* 9e. Published by Allyn and Bacon, Boston, MA. Copyright © 1990 by Pearson Education. Adapted by permission of the publisher.

> Children are taught sight words to be visually recognized, not sounded out.

As we noted in the chapter on spelling, readers use patterns and meaning to understand the printed page. We also know that skilled readers group words into phrases (Archer, Gleason, & Vachon, 2003).

Fluent oral readers should be able to read orally with speed, accuracy, and appropriate expression (National Institute of Child Health and Human Development. 2000; Rasinski, 2003b). The National Reading Panel report cautions, "if text is read in a laborious and inefficient manner, it will be difficult for the child to remember what has been read and to relate the ideas expressed in the text to his or her background knowledge" (National Institute of Child Health and Human Development, 2000, n.p.). The ability to remember what has been read and relate it to background information is critical for reading comprehension.

Fluency in oral and silent reading. In addition to fluent oral reading, students must also be fluent in silent reading. While much less attention has been given to this area, the goal of reading is that students read independently for both enjoyment and information. Again, they must read fast enough to make sense of the information and accurately enough to gain information.

> Notice that oral and silent rates differ.

As Rasinski (2000) notes, slow, inefficient, and disfluent reading should be taken seriously. These readers will likely have reading difficulties for their entire school experience if nothing is done. Therefore it is useful to attend to both silent and oral fluency rates throughout the academic year to monitor progress. Figure 9.3 offers a chart of silent and oral fluency rates by grade level.

In addition to assessing individual fluency rates, it can be useful to map the fluency development of the entire class. One means for doing so is to construct a class summary of the fluency rates of every member of the class (Barr, Blachowicz, Katz,

Figure 9.4 Class Summary for Fluency

Teacher: _____				Grade:_____				
WCPM	date	date	date	date	**WCPM**	date	date	date	date
185					100				
180					95				
175					90				
170					85				
165					80				
160					75				
155					70				
150					65				
145					60				
140					55				
135					50				
130					45				
125					40				
120					35				
115					30				
110					25				
105					20				

& Kaufman, 2002). A form for doing so appears in Figure 9.4. This form allows you to enter the names of students reading at rates from 20–185 words correct per minute (WCPM). In addition, you can use this form for grouping students for fluency instruction.

What Is the Importance of Writing Fluency?

Writing fluency has received significantly less research attention compared with reading fluency. However, it stands to reason that not writing quickly enough would be frustrating for students. Imagine having all kinds of ideas in your head, but having them leave you before you can record them! Similarly, poor writing volume results in few words to edit. After all, if a student only generates a few dozen words after 15 minutes of writing, he or she will not have much to edit and revise. Most importantly, a focus on writing fluency requires that students get to the business of writing and not procrastinate. We've all watched a student staring off into space after being asked to respond in writing to a prompt. When asked, this student will respond, "I'm thinking" or "I'm not sure what to write." A focus on writing fluency provides students with the skills to record their thoughts, supplies them with ideas to edit and revise, and addresses the frequent delays associated with writing performance.

While there are a number of theories about writing and how writers write, Hayes and Flower (1980) maintain that all writers use three components and that these components are interactive and recursive: "*planning* what to say, *translating* those plans into written text, and *reviewing* those written texts or plans" (McCutchen, Covill, Hoyne, & Mildes, 1994, p. 256). We maintain that a focus on writing fluency requires attention to each of these three components.

Fluency and planning the message. First, during planning students must develop the skills to rapidly organize their thinking and develop a scheme for their ideas. Naturally there are a number of strategies that focus on this component, including brainstorming ideas, partner talks, thinking and searching through texts, and developing concept maps (e.g., Hyerle, 1995–1996; Whittaker & Salend, 1991). In a study of fourth- and fifth-grade students, those who receive intentional instruction in planning activities produce higher quality writing than those who received only process writing instruction (Troia & Graham, 2002).

Fluency and translating the message. Second, as students translate their plans into text, they must have developed the motor skills for extended writing tasks, they must have the stamina to write for extended periods, and they must be able to make connections between what they've written and what they're thinking. Predictably, there are specific instructional strategies to help students develop this component, including quick writes (Daniels & Bizar, 1998), freewrites (Elbow, 1981), timed writings (Kasper-Ferguson & Moxley, 2002), Power Writing (Fearn & Farnan, 2001), and dictoglos (Wajnryb, 1990).

Fluency and reviewing the message. Finally, in terms of reviewing, students need to be able to read what they've written and revise accordingly. Again, it's important to note that writing is recursive and interactive—writers revise as they write and think as they revise and so on. As you probably expected, there are a number of instructional strategies useful in helping students revise their work including teacher and peer conferences and rubrics. Once again, intentional instruction in revision has been shown to produce longer and more sophisticated essays (De La Paz & Graham, 2002). Muschla (1993) suggests that all students be taught a simple plan for revision:

Conferencing is discussed in chapter 5.

Evidence Based

1. Read the piece silently and then aloud. Reading it aloud can highlight the flow and rhythm of the words.
2. Consider the whole piece first. What are its strengths? What parts do you like best? What are its weaknesses? How can the weaknesses be improved? What can be added? What can be eliminated?
3. Next, focus on the paragraphs. Are they well organized? Does each have a main idea supported by details? Do the paragraphs follow each other logically? Are the transitions between them smooth?
4. Now consider the sentences. Do they follow logically? Are they clear?
5. Focus on the words and phrases. Which should be changed? What are examples of clutter? (pp. 62–63)

Evidence Based

Unfortunately, there is no expected writing fluency rate that can provide teachers guidance with determining how many words per minute students should be able to write. In a study of fourth graders who received intentional writing instruction in fluency, the class average increased from 10 words per minute to 25 words per minute (Kasper-Ferguson & Moxley, 2002). The fastest writer in the study began in October writing an average of 20 words per minute and could sustain 59 words per minute in May. Importantly, these researchers noted, "ceiling effects in writing did not appear" (p. 249). In other words, students continued to make progress, and given enough time, there was no telling how many words per minute they could have written.

Fluency and writing maturity. As with reading, writing fluency is not only about writing more words. As students become more fluent writers, they also become more sophisticated writers. Bayliss and Walker (1990) and Bayliss (1994) have identified signs of maturing writing fluency, including:

- Providing details
- Elaborating on the subject
- Varying sentence patterns
- Deepening and unfolding the presentation
- Sustaining focus

The sentences in this paragraph are examples of elaboration.

As writers become more fluent, they are able to use these devices to produce more sophisticated pieces of writing. When a writer adds detail, the reader can visualize the setting and characters. Elaboration on a subject helps the reader to more fully understand what the writer is discussing. As well, a mature writer can deepen and unfold a presentation by building on concepts in a logical manner. Finally, a good writer does not wander from topic to topic. Taken together, these characteristics form a good definition of good writing.

Writing fluency is important in the language arts workshop because it contributes to more sophisticated expression of ideas. Reading fluency contributes to more sophisticated understanding of ideas. Neither reading or writing fluency exist in isolation, but rather are influenced by a learner's understanding of phonemic awareness, phonics, comprehension, and vocabulary. However, fluency serves as an important bridge between these processes. Instruction in reading and writing fluency contribute to improving literacy skills of students.

APPROACHES TO IMPROVING READING AND WRITING FLUENCY IN THE LANGUAGE ARTS WORKSHOP

Like other skills and strategies, fluency activities in the language arts workshop are first introduced in focus lessons, where the teacher models, coaches, and scaffolds instruction. A gradual release of responsibility model helps students become increasingly independent in using the strategies.

Focus Lessons

Reading and writing fluency focus lessons are typically brief in nature (often 3–10 minutes). The focus lesson is an ideal time to use read alouds for modeling prosody and expression in oral reading. The intent of the read aloud is not to engage in prolonged readings of large pieces of text; rather, it is designed to read short, meaningful pieces of text. Similarly, Power Writing provides students with timed writing practice to develop stamina and fluency in writing volume.

Read alouds. The practice of reading aloud in public dates to the dawn of written language. Throughout history, town criers shared local news, religious orders proclaimed scriptures, and *lectors* read classical works and newspapers to Cuban cigar factory workers, paid for by the laborers themselves (Manguel, 1996). Even in widely literate societies, the act of being read to continues to enthrall. Audio book industry reports indicate that demand for audio books rose 75% between 1995 and 1999, and estimates suggest that one audio book is sold for every ten print books sold (Block, 1999).

While **read alouds** have been shown to be effective for young children's literacy development, they can also be used to motivate older, reluctant readers (Beckman, 1986; Erickson, 1996). In a study of 1700 adolescents, Herrold, Stanchfield, and Serabian (1989) found positive changes in attitude toward reading among students who were read to by their teacher on a daily basis. Likewise, a survey of 1765 middle school students conducted more than a decade later reported that 62% of the participants identified teacher read alouds as a favorite literacy activity (Ivey & Broaddus, 2001). Students themselves have reported that a preferred instructional practice is having teachers read aloud portions of text to introduce new readings and promote interest (Worthy, 2002). It appears that the read-aloud event is appreciated by students as an opportunity to share the teacher's enthusiasm and interest in the topic. Most importantly, it is one of the key ways that students can hear fluent reading and have fluency modeled for them.

> These items also serve as indicators of effective instructional practice for administrative observations.

There are several elements to consider in planning and delivering read alouds to students (Fisher, Flood, Lapp, & Frey, 2004). A self-assessment rubric of these elements appears in Figure 9.5.

- *Select readings appropriate to content, students' emotional and social development, and interests.* Read alouds can be especially useful for activating background knowledge and connecting to student experiences. The read aloud should be brief and focused, with most going no longer than 10 minutes or so. Remember, the emphasis is on quality, not quantity.

- *Practice the selection.* You wouldn't go on stage without rehearsing, would you? Think of the read aloud as a performance. Rehearsal allows you to make decisions about inflection, rate, and pitch.

- *Model fluent oral reading.* In addition to exposure to content information, a read aloud also serves as a place for students to hear fluent oral reading. Reading acquisition for students with reading difficulties, as well as some English language learners, can be inhibited by their own disfluent reading.

- *Engage students and hook them into listening to the text.* Creating anticipation for the reading, as the teacher did in the *Midnight Ride of Paul Revere* scenario, can activate student interest and increase meaning. When appropriate, pair read alouds with other supporting materials such as props, diagrams, manipulatives, or illustrations.

- *Stop periodically to ask questions.* Talk within the text enhances student understanding. Plan questions for critical thinking in advance and write it on a Post-it® note to remind you. Don't rely only on "constrained questions" (Beck & McKeown, 2001) that can be answered in a few words. For example, "What do you believe was the author's purpose for writing this story?" allows for a

Figure 9.5   Read Aloud Rubric for Self-Assessment

	Successfully implemented	Moderately successful	Just getting started	Not evident
Text chosen appropriate for students' interests and level				
Selection has been previewed and practiced				
Clear purpose established				
Teacher provides a fluent reading model				
Students are engaged in listening				
Teacher stops periodically and questions thoughtfully to enhance focus (literal, interpretive, and evaluative)				
Students engaged in discussion				
Connections to reading and writing				
Comments:				

Source: Fisher, D., & Frey, N. (2004). *Improving adolescent literacy: Strategies at work.* Upper Saddle River, NJ: Merrill/Prentice Hall.

more detailed response than "Where did the story take place?" Create inferential questions that invite connections beyond the text as well.

- *Engage students in book discussions.* This is related to the questioning that is done during the reading. Choose read alouds that foster further discussion once the reading is complete. Perhaps you may ask students to predict why you chose this particular reading, or how it relates to the current topic of study.
- *Make explicit connections to students' independent reading and writing.* A read aloud should relate directly to the content—otherwise, it might have limited applicability in the curriculum. As well, the read aloud should also connect to other literacy experiences. For instance, the end of a read aloud event might signal an ideal time to invite students to write a response. Questions raised through the discussion following the reading might also prompt further research and outside reading by students.

Power Writing. **Power Writing** is the term used to describe brief, timed writing events that build fluency (Fearn, 1980). Fearn and Farnan describe it as "a structured free-write where the objective is quantity alone" (2001, p. 501). Typically, this exercise is performed daily in three rounds of timed writes, each 1 minute in length. Students are given a word or phrase to use somewhere in their writing and are reminded to "write as much as you can, as well as you can" in their writer's notebooks (Fearn & Farnan, 2001, p. 196). At the end of 1 minute, they count the number of words they have written and note the total in the margin. This cycle is repeated two more times using different words or phrases. After the last cycle, students are asked to reread what they have written and circle words they believe they may have misspelled. This allows the teacher to evaluate students' self-monitoring of their spelling. Each student then records the highest number for the day on a graph they keep in their writer's notebook.

The purpose of tracking progress is not to establish a competitive atmosphere; these graphs are kept in the writer's notebook and are viewed only by the teacher and student. These simple charts can be constructed on graph paper or reproduced using the form in Figure 9.6. The words per minute are recorded on the vertical axis

Figure 9.6   Power Writing Chart

My Power Writing Progress

Name: _____ Date: _____ to _____

↓ Words per minute

→
Date

and should begin with a number that is just below the writer's current range of words. For instance, if a writer currently averages 32 words per minute, the first square might begin with 25.

To introduce the Power Writing, offer a prompt related to a topic that is meaningful to the students. For emergent readers, this may be simply writing all the words they know. For older writers, offer a prompt of a single familiar word and ask them to use it in their writing. How the word is used is less important than the fact that it gets them to put something down on paper. A timer is used to signal students when to begin and end, then instruct them to count the number of words they have written. Students graph their results on their personal Power Writing chart. Beginning writers can do this exercise once or twice, while older writers should regularly perform three rotations of Power Writing, entering the highest number only.

Students completing three sessions of Power Writing are likely to observe another unexpected benefit. Typically, performance increases between the first and third rotation. Like physical exercise, the repetitions result in increased fluidity of writing. By assessing their own progress, students internalize their own motivation as they seek to improve on their last effort. This is especially important for struggling writers, who commonly complain that they "don't know what to write about." If they are stuck, they should be instructed to write the prompt word repeatedly until an idea forms.

Dictoglos. Taking dictation involves a number of skills, especially the ability to rapidly convert speech into print. The **dictoglos** procedure challenges students to do so through repeated readings of a brief text passage that is meaningful in its content (Wajnryb, 1990). While the procedure is simple and straightforward, it provides students much needed practice in listening, writing fluency, and partner conversations. Herrell (2000) describes it in five steps.

1. Select a relevant text and read it aloud while students listen.
2. Now read the passage two more times, instructing students to note important words and phrases.
3. Pair students to recreate as much of the text as they can. The goal is to write a passage that closely matches the original.
4. Students now meet in groups of four to further refine their passage, writing it as closely as they can to the original.
5. Representatives from each group read their passage. Display the original text on the overhead so the class can compare.

We recommend choosing text that is within the students' instructional or independent range so they are more likely to be successful. In addition, consider the length of the passage as it relates to the students' developmental levels. Use passages of 20 words or so with younger writers. Older students can recreate passages of 50 words or more.

Guided Instruction

During guided instruction, students use carefully chosen books to increase their reading fluency through repeated practice of familiar text. Repetition has been found to build reading fluency because of the practice that comes with the focus on familiar readings (National Institute of Child Health and Human Development, 2000).

Writing fluency is increased through practice emphasizing careful word choice to convey the message.

Reading predictable books for fluency. Emergent and early readers are engaged in a substantial amount of literacy acquisition in the first years of school. They are learning the sounds of the language, the letters associated with them, and the way print works on the printed page. It is easy in Kindergarten and first grade to concentrate on the parts of the language at the expense of the whole. While children are learning letters they should also be learning about the meaning of the words used to illustrate those letters at the same time. Another unintended by-product of letter- and word-level instruction is that it can inadvertently breed disfluent reading through choppy, interrupted readings. Even the earliest readers should receive purposeful instruction on oral fluency.

See chapter 7 for a review of this discussion.

One way to increase oral fluency is through the use of **predictable books.** Predictable books feature text that utilizes rhyme and rhythm, repetitive words and phrases, story structures and illustrations that encourage young readers to predict and anticipate what will happen next. Predictable books may be based on a song (*Chicken Soup with Rice,* Sendak, 1962) or feature a catchy chant such as "Tikki tikki tembo-no sa rembo-chari bari ruchi-pip peri pembo" (Mosel, 1968, p. 2). Even the most emergent readers will catch on to the lively phrasing of such infectious texts. Repeated reading of these and other favorites encourages young readers to "make it sound like talking." A list of predictable books appears in Figure 9.7.

Figure 9.7   Predictable Books

Predictable Books for K–1
Ahlberg, J., & Ahlberg, A. (1979). *Each peach pear plum.* New York: Viking.
Brown, M. W. (1991). *The runaway bunny.* New York: HarperFestival.
Christelow, E. (1988). *Five little monkeys jumping on the bed.* New York: Clarion.
Fox, M. (1993). *Time for bed.* San Diego: Harcourt Brace.
Galdone, P. (1998). *The three billy goats gruff.* New York: Houghton Mifflin.
Guarino, D. (1991). *Is your mama a llama?* New York: Scholastic.
Keats, E. J. (1999). *Over in the meadow.* New York: Puffin.
Martin, B., Jr. & Archambault, J. (1983), *Brown bear, brown bear, what do you see?* New York: Holt.
Mosel, A. (1968). *Tikki tikki tembo.* New York: Holt.
Numeroff, L. J. (1985). *If you give a mouse a cookie.* New York: Laura Geringer.
Sendak, M. (1962). *Chicken soup with rice.* New York: Harper and Row.
Siebert, Diane. (1999). *Train song.* New York: HarperCollins.
Suess, Dr. (1960). *One fish, two fish, red fish, blue fish.* New York: Random House.

Neurological Impress Model. In 1966, Heckelman developed a process of "imprinting" words into children's minds called the **Neurological Impress Model** or NIM. As he noted, this is an economical and time-saving method for helping students become fluent readers. In general, the teacher and student sit side-by-side (also known as "at the elbow"), reading the same instructional-level text. Together, the teacher and student read aloud. The teacher directs his or her voice directly into the reader's ear. The student follows along, reading at the normal reading rate of the teacher. The teacher does not stop to correct oral reading mistakes. Instead, the teacher focuses on having the student duplicate the appropriate reading rate. In the beginning, it may be necessary for the student to repeat sentences and/or paragraphs several times to perform at normal speed. Over time, the student reads faster, as does the teacher.

Evidence Based

The research evidence for NIM is fairly specific (e.g., Gibbs & Proctor, 1977; Heckelman, 1986; Henk, 1983). Students typically require a total of 12 hours of instruction and need to participate in NIM on a regular basis, several times each week, until they can read fluently.

Choral reading. Choral reading is a time-honored tradition in many elementary classrooms. In **choral reading**, the class reads aloud simultaneously. This should not be confused with round robin reading, the particularly ineffective practice of single children taking turns reading aloud (Optiz & Rasinski, 1998). The emphasis in choral reading is on the performance and expression used to accurately convey the meaning of the text. The teacher is the first to read the text aloud so students can focus first on meaning. Only then are children invited to join in the choral reading.

One of the advantages of choral reading is the sense of community created through the practice. Therefore, Rasinski (2003b) encourages the use of texts with community meaning, such as the Pledge of Allegiance, favorite songs and poems, and other spirited texts. In teaching choral reading, consider these points:

- Choose texts that are lively and engaging to read. Poems, predictable books like the ones in Figure 9.7, and song lyrics are ideal.

- Make sure the text is accessible to all, both in terms of difficulty and in visual display. Students may have their own copy, or the text can be displayed on an overhead or chart.

Inferencing is the ability to "read between the lines" — an important comprehension strategy.

- Be sure to model what the passage should sound like before students try it. Discuss why you are using particular expression, tone, pitch, or volume to model inferencing.

- Choose text for choral readings that can be revisited over the course of the week. Remember that with fluency, repetition is the key (Optiz & Rasinski, 1998).

Evidence Based

Repeated readings. Mastropieri, Leinart, and Scruggs (1999) suggest that **repeated readings** are a useful way to improve reading fluency, especially when combined with peer tutoring, computer-guided practice, and previewing of texts. Smith (2000) noted that rereading was one of the strategies that adults use to understand the text. In addition to improving fluency, repeated readings also aid comprehension and retention of information (Millis & King, 2001) as well as enjoyment (Faust & Glenzer, 2000). The National Reading Panel identified repeated readings as a notable strategy for improving reading fluency (National Institute of Child Health and Human Development, 2000). As we have noted before, fluency and comprehension are significantly related to one another. Of course there are a number of ways to facilitate students in rereading the same text. As you have guessed, this does not occur naturally. Most of us do not like to reread things a second or third time unless there is a specific purpose that has been established.

McDonald and Fisher (1999), for example, created a performance expectation in their teaching of poetry. Groups of students were to memorize and then perform poems. The format of the presentations required three repetitions of the poem. First the poem was said using expression, intonation, and vocal qualities. Second, the poem was said with expression and a movement sequence was added. Third, the movement sequence was performed without words so that students would voice the words in their heads. Establishing expectations such as these provides students an authentic reason to reread the text. The performance also provides students with practice in building fluency.

Word limiters. After Theodor Geisel (Dr. Suess) had published several successful books, his editor Bennett Cerf challenged him to write a book that only utilized the 220 Dolch sight words. *The Cat in the Hat* (1957) was the result. Unfazed, Cerf challenged him to do the same with only 50 words. Three years later, *Green Eggs and Ham* (1960) was published and became the best-selling Suess book of all time. Never underestimate what a few carefully chosen words can do.

While it may seem counter to our focus on fluency, the word limiter strategy requires that students limit the number of words they can use in a sentence (Fearn & Farnan, 2001). We see it as a fluency activity with specific limits. Students must produce sentences that comply with the guidelines provided. They really have to focus on the words they select and the ways in which they construct sentences. Of course, they have to do this in a specific amount of time.

For example, Mr. Vandenberg knows that his students write quickly. They get to work immediately when he provides them a prompt. However, he has noticed that their sentences are sloppy and contain imprecise language. Mr. Vandenberg uses word limiters to maintain the focus on production while requiring increasing planning and thought. For example, during a guided instruction lesson focus on the book *Esperanza Rising* (Ryan, 2000), Mr. Vandenberg asked the students seated at the table with him to quickly write a sentence to explain Esperanza's reaction to learning that her family had become poor. He instructed students in the group to write a sentence that contained no more and not less than 14 words. This limitation to the sentence required that students produce a longer than usual sentence for them and provided them an opportunity to choose words that would convey their understanding.

Collaborative Learning

The collaborative learning phase of the language arts workshop provides students with an opportunity to practice their reading and writing fluency with a partner. Repeated reading strategies like Readers Theatre are fun and motivating, an important aspect of flow.

Readers Theatre. Probably the most common recommendation for improving reading fluency is Readers Theatre (Blau, 2001; Rasinski, 2003b; Martinez, Roser, & Strecker,1998–1999;Worthy & Broaddus, 2001/2002). **Readers Theatre** is a choral reading strategy that that uses scripts of poems, plays, and children's literature to create a performance piece. Unlike traditional school plays, the performers do not use costumes, staging, lighting, or even gestures. Instead, they use their voices to convey the appropriate meaning of the text. As well, they do not memorize their parts; they use the script to read. The opening scenario describing Lindbergh's first transatlantic flight is an example of Readers Theatre.

Readers Theatre is considered a fluency-building activity because students engage in repeated readings while perfecting their parts. Struggling readers in particular may resist reading anything more than once, but the accountability of performance in front of peers can eliminate such hesitancies (Tyler & Chard, 2000). Poems, picture books, and other text can be easily adapted for use as Readers Theatre scripts (for example, the script in Figure 9.1). There are a number of books and Internet resources available as well. Some of these are listed in Figure 9.8.

Martinez, Roser, and Strecker (1998/1999) propose a 5-day instructional plan for managing multiple Readers Theatre groups during collaborative learning. On the first day, the teacher introduces the stories that will be performed to the entire class during shared reading, discussing meaning, building background knowledge, and teaching vocabulary. Groups of students are then assigned to perform the script later in the week. On each of the subsequent days, the group rereads the script, discusses roles, and rehearses. Finally, the group performs for the class. A summary of the 5-day instructional plan appears in Figure 9.9.

Figure 9.8 Readers Theatre Resources

Barchers, S. I. (2000). *Multicultural folktales: Readers theatre for elementary students.* Portsmouth, NH: Teacher Ideas Press.

Fleischman, P. (1988). *Joyful noise: Poems for two voices.* New York: Harper & Row.

Fleischman, P. (1989). *I am phoenix: Poems for two voices.* New York: HarperTrophy.

Fleischman, P. (2000). *Big talk: Poems for four voices.* Cambridge, MA: Candlewick.

Fredricks, A. D. (2000). *Silly salamanders and other slightly stupid stuff for readers theatre.* Portsmouth, NH: Teacher Ideas Press.

Pappas, T. (1991). *Math talk: Mathematical ideas in poems for two voices.* San Carlos, CA: Wide World Publishing Tetra.

White, M. R. (1996). *Mel White's readers theatre anthology.* Colorado Springs, CO: Meriwether.

Aaron Shepard's World of Story – www.aaronshep.com

Lisa Blau's Script of the Month – http://www.lisablau.com/scriptomonth.html

Lois Walker's Take Part Read Aloud Story Scripts: www.loiswalker.com/catalog

Figure 9.9 Five-Day Instructional Plan for Readers Theatre

Day 1	Teacher: • Models fluency by reading aloud the stories on which the week's scripts are based. • Offers a focus lesson that presents explicit explanation of some aspect of fluency. • Discusses each of the stories. • Distributes scripts for students to read independently.
Day 2	Students: • Gather in collaborative groups using scripts with parts highlighted. • Read the script several times, taking a different part with each reading. Teacher: • Circulates and coaches, providing feedback.
Day 3	Procedures the same as day 2. • During final 5 minutes, students within each group negotiate and assign roles. • Students are encouraged to practice their part at home.
Day 4	Students: • Read and reread their parts with their collaborative group. • During final 10 minutes, group makes character labels and decides where each member will stand during the performance.
Day 5	Collaborative groups perform, reading before the audience.

Source: Adapted from Martinez, M., Roser, N. L., & Strecker, S. (1998/1999). "I never thought I could be a star": A Readers Theatre ticket to fluency. *The Reading Teacher, 52,* 326–334. Copyright © 1998/1999 by the International Reading Association.

Paired reading. Students can also work in collaborative groups to reread texts (Koskinen & Blum, 1986). In this model, called **paired reading,** students choose passages and read their selected passages to a partner. The reading is shared three different times with feedback from the peer solicited each time. Peers can be taught about the feedback they are expected to provide during guided instruction and then continue to use repeated paired readings during collaborative learning. Using this procedure, students have the opportunity to read texts aloud, receive feedback on their reading, and improve their reading fluency.

Using songs as texts. An increasing number of songs are now available in book form to promote fluency. Students can follow along and sing songs using the book. When a published book is unavailable, lyrics can often be found on the Internet. Whether using books or web-based song lyrics, check carefully for accuracy by comparing it to the recording. For young students especially, it can be confusing to hear a song that follows a pattern different from the book. We have listed some popular book titles featuring song lyrics in Figure 9.10.

See www.lyrics.com for song lyrics.

Beat the Clock. Another reading fluency activity students can practice together is called **Beat the Clock**. This is ideal as a center activity and requires a minimum amount of set up. In Beat the Clock, students read a selection several times while timing themselves. The only materials needed are selected passages from books, poems, newspaper articles, and other reading materials and a digital timer. We like to store passages

Figure 9.10 Song Lyrics for Fluency Building

Books Based on Songs
Barnwell, Y. (1998). *No mirrors in my nana's house.* San Diego: Harcourt.
Bates, K. L. (2001). *America the beautiful.* New York: Atheneum.
Berlin, I. (2002). *God bless America.* New York: HarperCollins.
Carpenter, M. C. (1998). *Halley came to Jackson.* New York: HarperCollins.
Denver, J. (2003). *Sunshine on my shoulders.* Nevada City, NV: Dawn.
Gollub, M. (2000). *The jazz fly.* Santa Rosa, CA: Tortuga Press.
Goodman, S. (2003). *The train they call the City of New Orleans.* New York: Putnam.
Guthrie, W. (1998). *This land is your land.* New York: Megan Tingley.
Heyward, D. (1999). *Summertime:* From Porgy and Bess. New York: Simon & Schuster.
Rodgers, R. (2001). *My favorite things.* New York: HarperCollins.
Rodgers, R., & Wells, R. (2002). *Getting to know you! Rodgers and Hammerstein favorites.* New York: HarperCollins.
Spier, P. (1992). *The star-spangled banner.* New York: Yearling.
Thiele, B., & Weiss, G. D. (1995). *What a wonderful world.* New York: Atheneum.

Figure 9.11 Beat the Clock Directions

	**Beat the Clock!**
1.	Choose a reading from the file with your partner.
2.	Read the passage silently so you understand what it is about.
3.	Ask your partner about any words you do not know. Help them with words they don't know.
4.	Set the timer to 0:00. Push "start" when you are ready.
5.	Read the entire passage aloud. Push "stop" on the timer when you finish. Write your time down.
6.	Have your partner read the same passage using the timer.
7.	Each partner should read the passage two more times. Can you beat the clock?

in a hanging file labeled by genre or topic so students can select according to interest. A set of instructions for completing Beat the Clock is included in Figure 9.11.

Collaborative Power Writing. Once students have become comfortable with the format of Power Writing, they can take responsibility for the task themselves. Writing partners can generate prompts for each other or use writing prompt cards prepared in advance by the teacher. One student monitors the timer (egg timers are inexpensive and durable) and reads the prompt to their partner or members of the group (depending on the size). If done as partners, after the first three rotations, students reverse roles. After graphing their best response, they read each other's writing. If done in a small group, one member reads the first prompt and manages the timer. Another member does the second, another the third, and so on until each member of the group has at least three entries. The remainder of this collaborative writing session is used to expand one of the prompts to a longer piece of writing. Students may each select one of their own or agree to use a single entry to expand together.

Independent Learning

As with other skills and strategies taught in the language arts workshop, the independent phase is time for students to incorporate these skills for new learning. These activities emphasize exploration as students expand their understanding of their own learning.

Reading into recorder. This oral fluency exercise, like many of the others discussed in this chapter, is predicated on the value of repeated readings. Many children like to hear the sound of their voice on a tape recording, and reading into a tape recorder capitalizes on this motivation. The student selects a brief reading (50–100 words) and records his or her voice while reading aloud. After stopping the recorder, the student reads the same passage three more times aloud. For the fifth reading, the student records himself again and then plays the entire tape back. Students are often astounded at how the quality of their oral reading has improved.

Independent reading. Although it may seem like an oversimplification, fluency in any skill, whether it is reading or writing or making free throws, requires time to practice those skills. There is an oft-repeated story about basketball player Michael Jordan, who holds the NBA record for the most free throws made in a game (20), and his penchant for daily practice. Similarly, even good readers benefit from daily practice through the act of reading. Many teachers use Sustained Silent Reading every day in their classroom so that students have time to read material of their own choosing. In addition, students spend time every day reading assigned material during **independent reading**. Independent reading and SSR increase reading volume, the overall amount of reading a student engages. In turn, reading volume is correlated to reading achievement (Stanovich, 1986). Thus, the language arts workshop should provide students time to engage in regular independent reading and writing.

SSR and independent reading are explained in more detail in chapter 5.

Journal writing. From the time children enter school they are becoming writers. We believe that every student should have a place to keep his or her writing. This is often accomplished through the use of a writing journal. Although organization of the writer's notebook varies by teacher, grade level, and purpose, most are arranged chronologically. Therefore, the various writing exercises done during shared, guided, and collaborative writing are likely to be in there. We recommend devoting a section of the notebook to fluency exercises like Power Writing. During independent writing, we sometimes invite students to review past Power Writing work in the journal and select one to expand into a more finished piece. Students frequently discover the kernel for a good idea lurking in the notebook.

Writer's notebooks are discussed in chapters 2, 3, 4, and 5.

Students also need time to write for their own purposes and should be encouraged to write for their own motivation. We return to the concept we began this chapter with—flow. Elbow (1981) describes a process called **freewriting** as a method for opening creative pathways. For 10 minutes a day, students write independently on a topic of their own choice. During this time, no editing takes place. The sole purpose is to get words down on paper. This differs slightly from Power Writing in that it is not viewed as a competition against the clock but rather a way of accessing ideas. When stuck, writers are instructed to write anything—even squiggles—until the words come again. Freewriting can be of value for students to tap into their understanding of the world and themselves. It's not a matter of simply brainstorming, then drafting, followed neatly by editing, revision, and publication. It's much messier than that and occasionally (if we are very lucky) reaches a state of flow. Writing researcher Donald Graves wrote:

> The writing process is anything a writer does for the time the idea came until the piece is completed or abandoned. There is no particular order. So it's not effective to teach writing process in a lock-step, rigid manner. What a good writing teacher does is help students see where writing comes from; in a chance remark or an article that really burns you up. I still hold by my original statement: if kids don't write more than three days a week they're dead, and it's very hard to become a writer. If you provide frequent occasions for writing then the students start to think about writing when they're not doing it. I call it a constant state of composition. (Graves, quoted in Nagin, 2003, p. 23)

BIG IDEAS ABOUT FLUENCY

Reading fluency focuses on the rate at which students read while writing fluency focuses on the rate at which they write. Reading fluency is influenced by rate, prosody, accuracy, and especially automaticity, the ability to instantly recognize certain words. Fluency in writing is associated with the notions of flow and stamina. Both of these are developed through intentional instruction of strategies in the language arts workshop. Reading fluency is developed primarily through opportunities for repetition like Readers Theatre, partner reading, and predictable texts. Writing fluency is developed through timed writings and freewrites that promote both volume and creativity.

INTEGRATING THE STANDARDS

Create lesson plans that meet your state's standards by visiting our Companion Website at www.prenhall.com/frey. There you'll find lessons created to meet the NCTE/IRA Standards. Adapt them to meet the standards of your own state through links to your state's standards, and keep them in the online portfolio. You can collect lesson plans for each chapter in an online portfolio, providing you with invaluable tools to meet your state's standards when you head into your own classroom.

CHECK YOUR UNDERSTANDING

1. What is flow?
2. What is reading fluency?
3. What is writing fluency?
4. What activities contribute to reading and writing fluency?

CLASSROOM CONNECTIONS

1. Discuss reading and writing fluency with your teacher. What does he or she believe are the students' fluency challenges and strengths?

2. Select a passage and read it silently three times for 1 minute. Count the number of words you read each time. Did it increase?

3. Engage in freewriting for 10 minutes on any topic you like. What did you notice?

References

Archer, A. L., Gleason, M. M., & Vachon, V. L. (2003). Decoding and fluency: Foundation skills for struggling older readers. *Learning Disability Quarterly, 26*(2), 89–101.

Barr, R., Blachowicz, C. L. Z., Katz, C., & Kaufman, B. (2002). *Reading diagnosis for teachers: An instructional approach.* Boston: Allyn & Bacon.

Bayliss, V. A. (1994). Fluency in children's writing. *Reading Horizons, 34,* 247–256.

Bayliss, V. A., & Walker, N. L. (1990). *Bayliss/Walker scales: Holistic writing evaluation, grades 1–6.* Springfield, MO: Southwest Missouri State University.

Beck, I. L., & McKeown, M. G. (2001). Text talk: Capturing the benefits of read-aloud experiences for young children. *The Reading Teacher, 55,* 10–35.

Beckman, J. (1986). Turning reluctant readers into lifetime readers. *English Journal, 73,* 84–86.

Blau, L. (2001). 5 surefire strategies for developing reading fluency. *Instructor, 110*(7), 28–30.

Block, D. G. (1999, November 11). Spoken word still a stronghold. *TapeDisc Business: The International Business Magazine for Media Manufacturers.* Retrieved April 13, 2002, from http://www.tapediscbusiness.com/tdb_nov99/11spoken.htm

Burns, M. K., Tucker, J. A., Hauser, A., Thelen, R. L., Holmes, K. J., & White, K. (2002). Minimum reading fluency rate necessary for comprehension: A potential criterion for curriculum-based assessments. *Assessment for Effective Intervention 28*(1), 1–7.

Csikszentmihalyi, M. (1990). *Flow = The psychology of optimal experience.* New York: Harper and Row.

Csikszentmihalyi, M. (1997). *Finding flow: The psychology of engagement with everyday life.* New York: BasicBooks.

Csikszentmihalyi, M. (2000). *Beyond boredom and anxiety: Experiencing flow in work and play.* San Francisco: Jossey-Bass Publishers.

Daniels, H., & Bizar, M. (1998). *Methods that matter: Six structures for best practice classrooms.* York: ME: Stenhouse.

De La Paz, S., & Graham, S. (2002). Explicitly teaching strategies, skills, and knowledge: Writing instruction in middle school classrooms. *Journal of Educational Psychology, 94,* 687–698.

Dyson, M., & Haselgrove, M. (2000). The effects of reading speed and reading patterns on the understanding of text read from screen. *Journal of Research in Reading, 23,* 210–223.

Elbow, P. (1981). *Writing with power: Techniques for mastering the writing process.* New York: Oxford University Press.

Erickson, B. (1996). Read-alouds reluctant readers relish. *Journal of Adolescent & Adult Literacy, 40,* 212–214.

Faust, M. A., & Glenzer, N. (2000). "I could read those parts over and over": Eighth graders rereading to enhance enjoyment and learning with literature. *Journal of Adolescent & Adult Literacy, 44,* 234–239.

Fearn, L. (1980). *Teaching for thinking.* San Diego: Kabyn.

Fearn, L., & Farnan, N. (2001). *Interactions: Teaching writing and the language arts.* Boston: Houghton Mifflin.

Fisher, D., Flood, J., Lapp, D., & Frey, N. (2004). Interactive read alouds: Is there a common set of implementation practices? *The Reading Teacher, 58,* 8–17.

Fisher, D., & Frey, N. (2004). *Improving adolescent literacy: Strategies at work.* Upper Saddle River, NJ: Merrill/Prentice Hall. Used with permission.

Gibbs, V., & Proctor, S. (1977). Reading together: An experiment with the Neurological-Impress Method. *Contemporary Education, 48,* 156–157.

Hayes, J. B., & Flower, L. S. (1980). Writing as problem solving. *Visible Language, 14,* 388–399.

Heckelman, R. G. (1966). Report on Neurological Impress Method. *Academic Therapy, 1,* 235–239.

Heckelman, R. G. (1986). N.I.M. revisited. *Academic Therapy, 21,* 411–420.

Henk, W. A. (1983). Adapting the NIM to improve comprehension. *Academic Therapy, 19,* 97–101.

Herrell, A. L. (2000). *Fifty strategies for teaching English language learners.* Upper Saddle River, NJ: Merrill/Prentice Hall.

Herrold, W. G., Jr., Stanchfield, J., & Serabian, A. J. (1989). Comparison of the effect of a middle school, literature-based listening program on male and female attitudes toward reading. *Educational Research Quarterly, 13*(4), 43–46.

Hyerle, D. (1995–1996). Thinking maps: Seeing is understanding. *Educational Leadership, 53*(4), 85–89.

Ivey, G., & Broaddus, K. (2001). "Just plain reading": A survey of what makes students want to read in middle school classrooms. *Reading Research Quarterly, 36,* 350–377.

Kasper-Ferguson, S., & Moxley, R. (2002). Developing a writing package with student graphing of fluency. *Education and Treatment of Children, 25,* 249–267.

Katstra, J., Tollefson, N., & Gilbert, E. (1987). The effects of peer evaluation on attitude toward writing and writing fluency of ninth-grade students. *The Journal of Educational Research, 80,* 168–172.

Koskinen, P. S., & Blum, I. H. (1986). Paired repeated reading: A classroom strategy for developing fluent reading. *The Reading Teacher, 40,* 70–75.

LaBerge, D., & Samuels, S. J. (1974). Toward a theory of automatic information processing in reading. *Cognitive Psychology, 6,* 293–323.

Manguel, A. (1996). *A history of reading.* New York: Penguin.

Martinez, M., Roser, N. L., & Strecker, S. K. (1998–1999). "I never thought I could be a star": A reader's theatre ticket to fluency. *The Reading Teacher, 52,* 326–334.

Mastropieri, M. A., Leinart, A., & Scruggs, T. E. (1999). Strategies to increase reading fluency. *Intervention in School and Clinic, 34,* 278–283.

McCutchen, D., Covill, A., Hoyne, S. H., & Mildes, K. (1994). Individual differences in writing: Implications of translating fluency. *Journal of Educational Psychology, 86,* 256–266.

McDonald, N., & Fisher, D. (1999). Living haiku: Scenes of sound in motion. In S. Totten, C. Johnson, L. R. Morrow, & T. Sills-Briegel (Eds.), *Practicing what we preach: Preparing middle level educators* (pp. 273–275). New York: Falmer.

Millis, K. K., & King, A. (2001). Rereading strategically: The influences of comprehension ability and a prior reading on the memory for expository text. *Reading Psychology, 22,* 41–65.

Muschla, G. R. (1993). *Writing workshop survival kit.* Paramus, NJ: The Center for Applied Research in Education.

Nagin, C. (2003). *Because writing matters: Improving student writing in our schools.* San Francisco: Jossey-Bass.

National Institute of Child Health and Human Development. (2000). *Report of the National Reading Panel. Teaching children to read: An evidence-based assessment of the scientific research literature on reading and its implications for reading instruction* (NIH Publication No. 00–4769). Washington, DC: U.S. Government Printing Office.

Optiz, M. F., & Rasinski, T. V. (1998). *Good-bye round robin: 25 effective oral reading strategies.* Portsmouth, NH: Heinemann.

Rasinski, T. V. (2000). Speed does matter in reading. *The Reading Teacher, 54,* 146–151.

Rasinski, T. V. (2003a). Fluency is fundamental. *Instructor, 113*(4), 16–20.

Rasinski, T. V. (2003b). *The fluent reader: Oral reading strategies for building word recognition, fluency, and comprehension.* New York: Scholastic.

Smith, M. C. (2000). The real-world reading practices of adults. *Journal of Literacy Research, 32,* 25–52.

Stanovich, K. E. (1986). Matthew effects in reading: Some consequences of individual differences in the acquisition of literacy. *Reading Research Quarterly, 21,* 360–406.

Troia, G. A., & Graham, S. (2002). The effectiveness of a highly explicit, teacher-directed strategy instruction routine: Changing the writing performance of students with learning disabilities. *Journal of Learning Disabilities, 35,* 290–305.

Tyler, B., & Chard, D. J. (2000). Using Readers Theatre to foster fluency in struggling reader: A twist on the repeated reading strategy. *Reading and Writing Quarterly, 16,* 163–168.

Wajnryb, R. (1990). *Grammar dictation.* Oxford, England: Oxford University Press.

Whittaker, C. R., & Salend, S. J. (1991). Collaborative peer writing groups. *Journal of Reading, Writing, and Learning Disabilities International, 7,* 125–136.

Worthy, J. (2002). What makes intermediate-grade students want to read? *The Reading Teacher, 55,* 568–569.

Worthy, J., & Broaddus, K. (2001/2002). Fluency beyond the primary grades: From group performance to silent, independent reading. *The Reading Teacher, 55,* 334–343.

Children's Literature Cited

Ahlberg, J., & Ahlberg, A. (1979). *Each peach pear plum.* New York: Viking.

Brown, M. W. (1991). *The runaway bunny.* New York: HarperFestival.

Christelow, E. (1988). *Five little monkeys jumping on the bed.* New York: Clarion.

Fox, M. (1993). *Time for bed.* San Diego: Harcourt Brace.

Galdone, P. (1998). *The three billy goats gruff.* New York: Houghton Mifflin.

Guarino, D. (1991). *Is your mama a llama?* New York: Scholastic.

Hoffman, P. (2003). *Wings of madness: Alberto Santos-Dumont and the invention of flight.* New York: Theia.

Keats, E. J. (1999). *Over in the meadow.* New York: Puffin.

"Lindbergh Flies the Atlantic, 1927." (1999). *EyeWitness to history*. Retrieved December 17, 2003 from www.eyewitnesstohistory.com/lindbergh.htm.

Martin, B., Jr. & Archambault, J. (1983). *Brown bear, brown bear, what do you see?* New York: Holt.

Mosel, A. (1968). *Tikki tikki tembo*. New York: Holt.

Numeroff, L. J. (1985). *If you give a mouse a cookie*. New York: Laura Geringer.

Ryan, P. M. (1999). *Amelia and Eleanor go for a ride*. New York: Scholastic.

Ryan, P. M. (2000). *Esperanza rising*. New York: Scholastic.

Sendak, M. (1962). *Chicken soup with rice*. New York: Harper and Row.

Siebert, D. (1999). *Train song*. New York: HarperCollins.

Suess, D. (1957). *The cat in the hat*. New York: Random House.

Suess, D. (1960). *Green eggs and ham*. New York: Random House.

Suess, D. (1960). *One fish, two fish, red fish, blue fish*. New York: Random House.

CHAPTER

10

Comprehension Strategy Instruction in the Language Arts Workshop

BIG IDEAS ABOUT COMPREHENSION

Comprehension is the ultimate goal of literacy instruction. When comprehension is deficient, the reader is unable to make meaning of the text. For this reason, comprehension instruction begins in Kindergarten and continues throughout the school years. Comprehension instruction involves teaching students how to use strategies to plan and monitoring their understanding of what is being read.

Questions to Consider

When you have finished reading this chapter, you should be able to answer these questions:

- What is the research on comprehension?
- What do good readers do?
- What should good teachers do?
- How is reading comprehension developed?
- Can I focus on comprehension when students don't yet know how to read?
- What instructional activities support comprehension?

Key Vocabulary

Comprehension

Bloom's taxonomy

Text structures

Signal words

Cross-age tutoring

Think aloud

Writing to learn

Question ring

Anticipation guide

Question-Answer Relationship (QAR)

Writing models

Generating Interaction Between Schemata and Text (GIST)

Reciprocal teaching

Retellings

Role-Audience-Format-Topic (RAFT)

A LOOK INSIDE

The lights are out in Ms. Butler's fourth-grade classroom. Every eye is glued to the screen on which she has projected a website explaining the history of chocolate. Ms. Butler reads the information aloud, pausing periodically to share her thinking about the text. At one point, she pauses and says, "I see huge vats of chocolate melting and some guy standing there stirring the chocolate. I can just smell the sweetness of the chocolate as it melts." These words are not in the text. Ms. Butler is adding her own visualizations, something she knows that good readers do as they read.

As she finishes the shared reading having focused on the role chocolate has played in civilization and on visualization as a comprehension strategy, one group of students joins her at the guided reading table. All of the other students are engaged in their collaborative learning centers. Ms. Butler knows that the students in this first group have difficulty with visualizing the text. She has selected an excerpt of *Charlie and the Chocolate Factory* by Roald Dahl (1964) to read with them. She knows that many of the students in this group have either read this book or will read this book after this lesson. However, that isn't her focus with them. The part of the book she has selected finds the group inside the chocolate factory looking at the chocolate river. She reads the passage to the group and asks each student to visualize as she reads. When she has finished, she asks for students to volunteer to share "the pictures in your minds."

Arturo volunteers to speak first and says, "I was looking down into the river, but I couldn't see anything because the chocolate was too thick." Sarah says, "the smell, ohh, that smell. I just can't stand it! It's too sweet. Who could eat that much chocolate?" Bryan adds, "I can feel it between my toes. It's almost like mud, but thicker. I try to splash the river with my feet, but the chocolate is so thick that it just moves around."

Ms. Butler reads other passages about chocolate that she has identified from the book. Again, students share their visualizations. After about 20 minutes, she is satisfied with their visualizations and excuses the members of this group to the collaborative learning activities and invites another group of students to the table.

COMPREHENSION INSTRUCTION

There is arguably no more important aspect of reading instruction than **comprehension** because understanding what is written is the "gold standard" of reading. Reading comprehension is an active process of making meaning of written text (Block, Gambrell, & Pressley, 2002). Comprehending readers make personal connections, draw conclusions, make inferences, and formulate questions as they read. Without it, reading is reduced to word calling, with students merely identifying the words without grasping the meaning. From the beginning of Kindergarten, effective reading instruction focuses on some aspect of comprehension. Previous chapters in this book have discussed some of these aspects, including understanding of the genres of text, fluency, word study, and vocabulary. Perhaps because reading comprehension is so multi-faceted, it has been the focus of much research over the past 150 years.

For a glossary of terms, see appendix 10.1.

What Is the Research on Comprehension?

The term *comprehension* was first introduced by J. Russell Webb in 1856 in his Normal Readers series of student textbooks (Smith, 1965). Over the years, the debate has shifted attention to meaning making during oral reading (Mathews, 1966), to teaching subskills of reading comprehension in order to answer text-based questions (Davis, 1944), to the current focus on comprehension instruction during guided and independent practice (Flood, Lapp, & Fisher, 2003). Although the focus of reading comprehension has evolved, these and many other researchers share a common goal—to promote understanding of what is read (Block & Pressley, 2002). Two major areas have emerged in reading comprehension research. The first highlights what good readers do. The second area of research examines what teachers can do to promote reading comprehension.

The study of reading is the oldest type of educational research.

Evidence Based

What do good readers do? Perhaps the best way to understand what good readers do is to let students speak for themselves. The National Assessment of Educational Progress (NAEP) is an assessment of students in public schools that is given in each of the states in the U.S. to survey the achievement of fourth, eighth, and twelfth graders. Data from the sample of students who participated in NAEP were analyzed. One of the research questions focused on what good readers do as they read. The idea was that by understanding good readers, teachers could intentionally teach

The NAEP is sometimes called "the nation's report card."

these components to average or struggling readers and thus create better readers all around. According to the NAEP (1998) data:

1. Good readers have positive habits and attitudes about reading.
2. Good readers are fluent enough to focus on the meaning of what they read.
3. Good readers use what they know to understand what they read.
4. Good readers form an understanding of what they read by extending, elaborating, and critically evaluating the meaning of the text.
5. Good readers use a variety of effective strategies to enhance and monitor their understanding of text.
6. Good readers can read a variety of texts and can read for a variety of purposes. (p. 9)

Clearly each of these six factors associated with good reading are all related to comprehension. These six factors received additional support in 2001 when the RAND Reading Study Group, an educational think tank, verified the factors identified by NAEP and emphasized their importance.

Because reading comprehension ultimately happens in the mind of the reader, it cannot be reduced to a finite set of skills (e.g., "this week I'll teach fluency, and next week I'll teach motivation"). Rather, it must be promoted through thoughtful and purposeful instruction. Like other aspects of reading, what constitutes good comprehension instruction has been at times controversial.

What should good teachers do? Similar to the debates between phonics and whole language instruction, comprehension instruction has been the focus of much attention. A 1987 article by Carver is illustrative of the debate. In it, he argued that reading comprehension should not be taught because the evidence was weak, nonexistent, or directly counter to the data. Carver further stated, "It makes more sense to regard comprehension skills as study skills in disguise, and teaching them to unskilled readers is a questionable practice" (p. 125). Alternatively, Haller, Child, and Walberg's (1988) research synthesis suggested that there was sufficient evidence to maintain a focus on comprehension instruction. Pearson and Hamm have suggested that the debate about reading comprehension continues because we "only ever see its residue, its wake, its artifacts" because it is dependent on the reader's ability to tell us what he or she understands (2003, p. 5). In other words, the only ways we can determine whether a reader has understood the text is to formulate questions or create a task and then have them respond orally or in writing.

More recently, balanced approaches to reading comprehension instruction have been introduced into the professional literature to ensure that teachers provide both skills and literature-based instruction. In this vein, Duke and Pearson (2002) recommend that teachers focus on the following components to ensure a *balanced* approach to comprehension instruction:

Evidence Based

- A great deal of time spent actually reading
- Experience reading real texts for real reasons
- Experience reading at least the range of text genres that we wish students to comprehend

- An environment rich in vocabulary and concept development, through reading, experience, and, above all, discussion of words and their meanings
- Substantial facility in the accurate and automatic decoding of words
- Lots of time spent writing texts for others to comprehend
- An environment rich in high-quality talk about text (pp. 207–208)

Like the recommendations made by NAEP and the RAND Reading Study Group on what good readers do, the Duke and Pearson recommendations are clearly discernable in the language arts workshop. Using this workshop approach, teachers have the time and structure to ensure that comprehension instruction is balanced.

How Is Reading Comprehension Developed?

While reading comprehension is not necessarily "taught" in the sense that it occurs in the mind of the reader, purposeful instruction still plays a key role. As we stated earlier, reading comprehension does not simply happen through lots of reading; it is developed through activities designed to teach students about what good readers do. In particular, you will recall from the NAEP and RAND studies that good readers are purposeful in reading and that they use strategies to extend their understanding. Three approaches are essential in developing reading comprehension: building metacognitive awareness by teaching students what to do before, during, and after the reading; developing students' ability to formulate questions as they read; and providing intentional instruction in using strategies to support their comprehension.

Building metacognition to develop reading comprehension. You will recall from earlier chapters that metacognition is often described as thinking about one's thinking; it is also being aware of what one knows and does not know. For instance, readers use metacognitive skills in reading when they:

- Develop a plan of action
- Maintain/monitor the plan
- Evaluate the plan (Kujawa & Huske, 1995)

As we described at the beginning of this chapter, reading comprehension is an active process undertaken by the reader. Therefore, the reader approaches a reading with a plan, uses the plan, and then checks to see if the plan worked. This metacognitive awareness can be modeled through shared reading instruction using questions before, during, and after the reading (Kujawa & Huske, 1995).

- *Before the reading—developing the plan.* Before beginning a reading, discuss questions like the following:
  - What is the purpose for the reading?
  - What do I already know about this topic?
  - How long do I think it will take for me to read it?

- *During the reading—monitoring the plan.* While reading, pause occasionally to ask these questions:
  - Do I understand what I'm reading?
  - If not, what can I do to help myself?

◇ Do I need to change my pace?

◇ What are the important ideas?

- *After the reading—evaluating the plan.* Once the reading is finished, revisit the plan by asking questions such as:

  ◇ How did I do?

  ◇ Did the reading meet my expectations?

  ◇ Did I understand?

  ◇ Do I need to revisit any part of the text?

These metacognitive strategies are typically first modeled by the teacher during read alouds and shared readings. By interjecting these questions throughout the reading, students learn that reading is meant to be a purposeful activity. Questions can take other forms as well. Another method for reading comprehension instruction is to use a taxonomy of knowledge to develop questions for reading.

Using Bloom's taxonomy to develop reading comprehension. In 1956, Benjamin Bloom, an educational psychologist at the University of Chicago, published a series of handbooks on the domains of learning—psychomotor, affective, and cognitive. The handbook devoted to the cognitive domain outlined a classification system that described six levels of competence. This classification system, referred to commonly as **Bloom's taxonomy,** has become a cornerstone in the description of questions used in the classroom and on tests (Bloom, 1956). Bloom described these competencies; we've included a sample question to illustrate each one from the children's story *Goldilocks and the Three Bears:*

- *Level 1—Knowledge:* States facts, terms, and definitions

  ◇ *Sample question:* Recall the items used by Goldilocks in the three bears' house.

- *Level 2—Comprehension:* Change the information to compare to another form

  ◇ *Sample question:* Explain why Goldilocks liked Baby Bear's chair best.

- *Level 3—Application:* Solve a new problem using information

  ◇ *Sample question:* Describe what Goldilocks would use if she came into your house.

- *Level 4—Analysis:* Identifies components and infers causes or motives

  ◇ *Sample question:* Compare the story to reality. What incidents could not have happened?

- *Level 5—Synthesis:* Create a new product using information in a novel way

  ◇ *Sample question:* Propose how the story would be different if it were "Goldilocks and the Three Fishes."

- *Level 6—Evaluation:* Make judgments and defend opinions

  ◇ *Sample question:* Judge whether Goldilocks was good or bad and be prepared to defend your position.

Evidence Based

Today's standardized tests not only assess basic skills, they increasingly demand test takers utilize more sophisticated strategies like predicting, inferring, and synthesizing information.

Teacher Tip

The questions got more difficult, didn't they? This is where the terminology of higher- and lower-order questions comes from. Knowledge and comprehension questions are sometimes referred to as literal questions because they require the student to draw upon memorization or location of facts. In other words, the answers to these types of questions are usually located verbatim in a text. They are also the easiest questions to compose and test. Guszak (1967) estimated that 70% of the questions asked in a typical classroom are knowledge or comprehension questions. That means that only 30% of the queries required students to apply knowledge in unique ways, or to construct understanding by assembling disparate information. It is the imbalance between literal and non-literal questions that is problematic, not the questions themselves. Brophy and Good (1986) noted that students who have experience with lower-order questions do well on tests of basic skills because these tests mirror this type of question.

Bloom's taxonomy is useful in considering what you want students to know and understand about a reading. When developing questions or tasks related to a reading, consider the range of comprehension. It is more than just identifying the facts of the reading; comprehension involves making connections, using prior knowledge, and evaluating the text. These levels of reading comprehension are further developed through intentional instruction of strategies used by good readers.

To focus attention on the various levels of questioning, groups of students in Ms. Oxenhandler's sixth-grade class write questions using Bloom's taxonomy. The questions are based on the focus lesson for the day and each level in the taxonomy must be represented by at least one question. In their collaborative learning centers, students construct questions that Ms. O can use the following day to test their knowledge. Ms. O knows that students learn a great deal when they can construct questions based on the information they are learning (Chin, Brown, & Bruce, 2002). As Gillespie (1990–1991) noted, student-generated questions ensure that reading is an active process and compel students to pay attention to what they are reading.

Using strategies to develop reading comprehension. Studies of effective readers have greatly influenced our understanding of the active processes of reading comprehension. In particular, the work of Paris, Wasik, and Turner describes the use of reading comprehension strategies as "a prime characteristic of expert readers," in contrast to novice readers and older struggling readers who "often focus on decoding single words, fail to adjust their reading for different texts or purposes, and seldom look ahead or back in text to monitor and improve comprehension" (1991, p. 609). Tovani further describes the use of strategies as "an intentional plan that readers use to help themselves make sense of their reading" (2000, p. 5).

Our understanding of reading has greatly expanded in the last decades as research has increasingly focused on how readers actively use strategies to make sense of their reading. The National Reading Panel (National Institute of Child Health and Human Development, 2000) report reviewed 205 text comprehension studies and recommended the following:

- *Comprehension monitoring* to encourage readers to be aware of when they understand and do not understand

- *Cooperative learning* opportunities so students can work on strategies together

- *Graphic organizers and story maps* to create visual representations of text
- *Question answering and question generation* to answer the teacher's questions and create their own
- *Story structure* instruction to aid in retelling and recall
- *Summarization* instruction to describe themes and main ideas (p. 15)

Good readers weave their strategies throughout their reading; they do not merely follow a step-by-step process to make meaning. For example, a reader may begin by make predictions based on the title ("I think this will be about . . . ") and activate his or her background knowledge ("I already know about . . . "). However, the reader continues to predict and use background knowledge throughout the reading, especially as new information is introduced. At times, he or she makes personal connections to the text ("This reminds me of . . . "). In addition, the reader monitors understanding, always on the lookout for confusing passages ("That last paragraph didn't make sense . . . "). Of course, he or she must go beyond recognition and use "fix up" strategies to get back on track ("I need to reread that section . . . ").

Appendix 10.1 contains a glossary of these, and many other, comprehension-related terms.

Instruction in the use of reading strategies is effective in teaching students how to approach reading as a purposeful and active process. However, you may be wondering about when it is appropriate to begin teaching about the use of comprehension strategies.

Can I Focus on Comprehension when Students Don't Yet Know How to Read?

Juel, Biancarosa, Coker & Deffes (2003) call this "anchored word study."

As you may have predicted, our answer is an unqualified yes! Let us explain why. You may have heard the saying, "learning to read and reading to learn," to describe the difference between the literacy goals for young children and older students. We are cautious about this dichotomy. While there is certainly more emphasis for young children to learn to read, they are also making meaning as they do so. For example, as a student learns the word *boat,* the teacher is also providing examples and definitions. Similarly, as students learn to decode sentences such as "hop on pop" from the Dr. Seuss book, they are also using the pictures to understand what that means.

Fostering comprehension for young readers. One of the most commonly used techniques for fostering reading comprehension is retelling the story. Toddlers delight in retelling familiar stories, sometimes using the pictures of the book to support recall of the details and important plot twists. Effective primary teachers build upon this practice by encouraging students to recall and retell the story. Not only does this establish good metacognitive practices in the mind of the young reader, it also provides the teacher with an assessment of the child's understanding (Alvermann, Swafford, & Montero, 2003).

Story structure, or story grammar, was presented in chapter 1.

Graphic organizers are one useful way to help students understand the structure of the story. Figure 10.1 is an example of a template for charting the plot of the story. These can be constructed as language charts by the teacher during shared reading experiences. In this way, the teacher models how the plot can be described. In addition, Figure 10.2 is useful for discussing story grammar, or the common elements of story like character, setting, plot, problem, and resolution. Figure 10.3 is another way of creating a graphic organizer based on narrative text, this time focused on the rising and falling action in the story. Again, even emergent readers can identify these elements through modeling, scaffolding, and instruction. Students can then use these

Figure 10.1 Charting Story Plot—Beginning, Middle, and End

Title of Story:

Author:

Illustrator:

These things happen at the beginning of the story:

1.

2.

3.

This is what happens at the middle of the story:

1.

2.

3.

This is what happens at the end of the story:

1.

2.

3.

Figure 10.2 Story Grammar

Title: _____ Author: _____

Story Grammar

CHARACTERS Who are the important characters?

SETTING Where does the story take place?

PLOT What are the important events that take place?

PROBLEM What problem does the main character face?

SOLUTION How is the problem solved?

THEME What is the "big idea" in the story?

graphic organizers to recall and retell the stories they have read. These are also useful for older, struggling readers who have not mastered these skills.

As you know by now, students will read both informational and narrative texts. While the graphic organizers described above are useful for students as they explore fiction and narrative texts, students also need to develop a sense of the common text structures used in informational or non-narrative texts.

Figure 10.3   Plot Graph for Rising and Falling Action

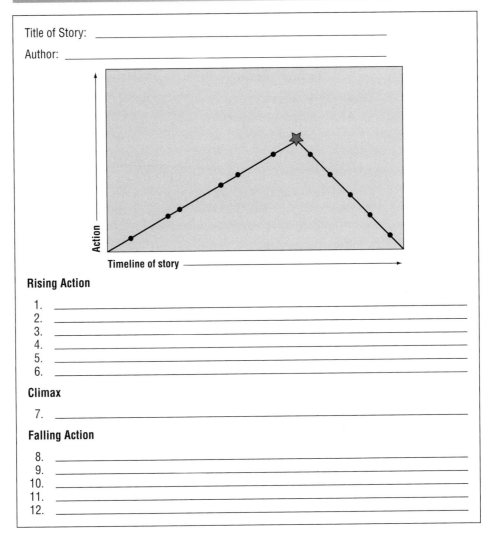

Title of Story: _____

Author: _____

Rising Action

1. _____
2. _____
3. _____
4. _____
5. _____
6. _____

Climax

7. _____

Falling Action

8. _____
9. _____
10. _____
11. _____
12. _____

Which Expository Text Structures Do Students Need to Know?

There are a number of common **text structures.** Teachers know that texts differ greatly across subject areas. For instance, mathematics textbooks are organized differently than social studies texts. As students become more sophisticated users of informational texts, they will begin to recognize these text structures. Of course, they will require instruction to name them and use them in their writing.

We believe that students should be explicitly taught the structures and styles used in their content area textbooks and informational trade books. We have seen students approach expository text as if it is narrative, looking for the familiar story grammar of character, setting, plot, and the like. Unfortunately, knowledge of narrative structures is unlikely to be of much help in a social studies textbook or a trade book about frogs. However, explicit instruction in the types of structures found in these books and the signal words associated with each structure will sustain and improve their comprehension.

The most common types of text structures are:

1. Description/exemplification (concept/definition)
2. Compare/contrast
3. Cause/effect
4. Problem/solution
5. Sequential

These text structures can often be identified by their use of **signal words**—words or phrases used in the text to alert the reader to how the information is being organized. Good readers use knowledge of structure and signal words more effectively than struggling readers (Kletzien, 1992). Figure 10.4 shows the relationship between types of informational texts and the signal words most closely associated with them.

Description/exemplification. This type of text describes people, places, or phenomena. Nearly all informational books have passages that are descriptive. Signal words for exemplification text structures include descriptive adjectives, adverbs, and phrases. For instance, the mummy isn't merely old, it is "wrapped in discolored linen bandages wound tightly around the entire body, lying undisturbed for thousands of years deep in the cool, dark mudbrick pyramid."

Compare/contrast. Text structures that compare and contrast use descriptive language, but also explain how two or more people, places, or phenomena are similar or different. Like exemplification, most textbooks contain some compare/contrast passages as well. Signal words like *although, yet, while, however, same/different, like/unlike* and other words that show opposites are likely to appear. "<u>Although</u> the first mummies were probably accidental, mummification became an art in ancient Egypt. <u>While</u> members of the noble classes were mummified, poor people usually were not."

Cause and effect. These text structures, which show the causal relationships between phenomena, can be deceptively similar to compare/contrast, but their signal words give them away. Words like *since, because, as a result,* and *if . . . then* statements are frequently seen in these passages. "<u>Because</u> the Incas lived in the high Andes, they created ice mummies that were preserved in the thin, frigid mountain air."

Problem/solution. Another text structure is *problem/solution*. Seen frequently in mathematics textbooks, they contain signal words like *questions, answer, thus, accordingly,* and *decide*. A challenge of problem/solution is that it is more subtle than some of the others, and may develop over the course of several sentences or paragraphs. "Theft and the desert climate have taken their toll on Egyptian mummies. <u>Accordingly</u>, the government has taken steps to preserve the remaining mummies by installing climate controlled displays and sophisticated security devices."

Signal words are also helpful to students who are taking standardized tests.

Sequential/temporal. More easy to detect is our final text structure, the *sequential* or *temporal* (time-based) passage. These signal words jump out of the text for most readers and include words like *first, next, last, before, afterwards, another,* and *finally*. (If you were paying attention to the structure of this sequential paragraph, you

Figure 10.4   Signal Words in Expository Texts

Text structure	Purpose	Signal words
Exemplification	Describes people, places, or phenomena	Descriptive adjectives, adverbs, and phrases For example For instance
Compare and contrast	Explains how two or more people, places, or phenomena are alike or different	Although Compared to However In comparison Like/unlike Same/different Similar to Whereas While Yet
Cause and effect	Shows causal relationships	As a result Because If . . . then In order to Since So So that Therefore
Problem and solution	Describes problems and solutions	Accordingly Answer Decide Question Problem Thus
Temporal or sequential	Chronological order	Afterwards Another Before Finally First In addition Last Next Second Then Third

knew we were coming to the end by the use of the word *finally*.) "The <u>first</u> step in the mummification process was to remove all the internal organs. <u>Next</u>, the embalmer drained the body of fluids. <u>Finally</u>, the body was wrapped in linens."

Knowledge about text structures supports reading comprehension of informational books.

Fostering Comprehension with Older Struggling Readers

Chris Tovani describes her life as a struggling reader (2000):

> Ever since I could read words, I've wanted to know what else a person had to do in order to make sense of the text. I didn't have a problem decoding. I had a problem understanding. I faked comprehension for years . . . I thought I was just born a bad reader. (p. 2)

Tovani's students told her they made sure to choose books they figured their teachers had not read.

Unfortunately, there are many students in our classrooms who "fake read"—using coping strategies like copying the back cover of a novel to complete a book report.

While some students like Tovani's may escape detection because they are able to compensate with other strengths, others are quickly noticeable in their lack of reading ability. Unfortunately, many of these students receive a double dose of phonics instruction at the expense of comprehension. There is evidence that teachers spend very little time on comprehension instruction with older students who cannot read the words easily (Ivey, 1999a). Johnston and Allington (1991) noted that students who struggle to read receive very little instruction on meaning and comprehension and the majority of their instructional time is consumed with understanding and decoding print. That is ironic considering the number of studies demonstrating that poor readers often have deficits in semantic, or meaning knowledge (Stanovich, Nathan, & Zolman, 1988; Vellutino & Scanlon, 1987).

Evidence Based

We concur with Ivey (2002) that this is a big mistake. Students of all ages and reading skills need instruction in understanding and meaning making. As Ivey notes, teachers sometimes "wrongly assume that struggling readers who have limited ability to read the words are incapable of thinking about text in complex ways" (2002, p. 235). In fact, there is evidence that students who have difficulty decoding do have complex questions about texts and want to participate in conversations about the texts (e.g., Ivey, 1999b). The key is to provide them opportunities to do so.

Ivey (2002) developed a set of recommendations for teachers who teach older students who have difficulty decoding texts. These include:

Read alouds build background knowledge, an important component of comprehension.

- *Read alouds.* As we have discussed throughout this book, read alouds are an especially important aspect of reading instruction. Hearing books read aloud provides students with opportunities to focus on the content and to engage in complex conversations about the text.

You can also find high-interest/low-vocabulary books at http://members.rogers.com/hip-books.

- *High-interest, easy texts.* There are a growing number of books written on topics that older students like, but with words and structures that are easier to read. School librarians are an excellent source of these books as they keep current on new titles and their corresponding reading level.

- *Repeated readings.* We have also discussed the importance of rereading texts. As we noted in chapter 9, there are a number of ways to encourage students to reread, including partner activities and performance events.

- *Cross-age tutoring.* An effective approach to encourage students to focus on decoding, word knowledge, and comprehension simultaneously is by establishing **cross-age tutoring** programs in which the older struggling students are assigned to read to younger students (Jacobson, Thrope, Fisher, Lapp, Frey, & Flood, 2001). Results suggest that the major beneficiary of cross-age peer tutoring is the older reader, who is able to refine and extend his or her comprehension of the text through the act of teaching and explaining it to the younger reader.

- *Teacher modeling.* As we have discussed throughout this book, teachers must model the strategies, activities, and critical and creative thinking that they would like to see from their students. This is most often done during the focus lesson in the language arts workshop, but is reinforced during the guided instruction.

APPROACHES TO TEACHING COMPREHENSION IN THE LANGUAGE ARTS WORKSHOP

There are dozens of comprehension strategies that teachers use to teach students to become independent readers. Again, many of these strategies are flexible and can be used at different times in the language arts workshop (See also appendix 10.1). We present them here as we have seen them commonly used and make note, as appropriate, of their use at other times in the workshop.

Focus Lessons

The focus lesson is an ideal time to introduce the use of new comprehension strategies to your students. As they become more proficient at using a strategy, they are able to apply it in other phases of the workshop. One of our favorite instructional strategies for modeling comprehension is the think aloud.

Think alouds. As fluent, strong readers, we use a number of mental processes that are invisible to our students. The goal of the **think aloud** is to make these processes visible and recognizable for our students. As Wilhelm notes, "teachers model their thinking by voicing all the things they are noticing, doing, seeing, feeling, and asking as they process the text" (2001, p. 26). In other words, the idea is that the teacher explicitly or intentionally models the strategies that good readers use as they read.

See chapter 2 for more information on shared reading.

The procedure is fairly simple once the teacher has selected a text and specific strategies to model. As we noted in the chapter on focus lessons, the teacher reads the text aloud while students follow along. This can be done by projecting the text with an overhead projector or by providing each student with a copy of the text. At specific, pre-determined points, the teacher shares his or her thinking about the text. Typically, the thinking is strategy-based and may involve asking questions of the author or about the text, predicting what may happen next, summarizing what is already known about the text, visualizing the scene or event, analyzing the behavior of the character, to name a few. Common think aloud strategies, based on the work of Harvey and Goudvis (2000), are described in Figure 10.5.

These strategies are also used in guided instruction as well as shared reading. For example, Pressley, El-Dinary, Gaskins, Schuder, Bergman, Almasi, and Brown (1992) observed a second-grade teacher use a think aloud based on *Where the Wild Things Are* by Maurice Sendak (1963). You'll notice the teachers' use of both visualization and prediction strategies:

That night Max wore this wolf suit and made mischief of one kind and another . . .
Boy, I can really visualize Max. He's in this monster suit and he is chasing after his

Figure 10.5   Common Think Aloud Topics

Strategy	Type	Example
Making connections	Text-to-self connections	This reminds me of a time when I . . .
	Text-to-text connections	I'm thinking about another book we read . . .
	Text-to-world connections	Something like this happened in our city when . . .
Questioning	Making predictions	What will happen next?
	Gaining information	Where can I find more information about . . .?
	Monitoring comprehension	Did I understand that paragraph?
Visualizing	Activate prior knowledge	I can just feel the warm sun on my face, like when I go to the beach.
	Understand dimensions of time and space	That means Wilbur is now about five months old.
Inferring	Cover, title, illustrations	The picture on the cover is of a boy holding a pen. What does that have to do with the title, *Frindle*?
	Plot and themes	The author keeps using words like *friendship* and *loyalty*. I think I am seeing a pattern.
	Historical concepts	I can tell from the date that these characters were poor because the story took place during the Great Depression.
Determining importance	Text structures	This book begins with a table of contents. That's where I can find all the topics in the book.
	Finding specific information	I can use the index to find the answer to my question about lizards.
	Sifting topics from important details	The phrase "three important reasons" means I need to search for three things.
	Forming opinions	The writer of this letter is a dancer. I can expect that he will argue for increased spending on the arts.
Synthesizing	Retelling	So far in this story . . .
	Making notes	I'm going write that word down because I am not sure I know what it means.
	Making comparisons	The author has told me that the differences between moths and butterflies are . . .
	Forming personal responses	The reason I like this poem is because . . .

Source: From *Strategies That Work: Teaching Comprehension to Enhance Understanding* by Stephanie Harvey and Anne Goudvis, copyright © 2000, with permission of Stenhouse Publishers.

dog with a fork in his hand. I think he is really starting to act crazy. I wonder what made Max act like that . . . Hm-m-m . . . I bet he was getting a little bored and wanted to go on an adventure. I think that is my prediction.

In a fifth-grade classroom, we observed Ms. Fleck use a think aloud to make her thinking of the opening paragraph of *Old Yeller* (Gibson, 1956) explicit for students. The first paragraph of the book reads:

> We called him Old Yeller. The name had a sort of double meaning. One part meant that his short hair was dingy yellow, a color we called "yeller" in those days. The other meant that when he opened his head, the sound he let out came closer to being a yell than a bark. (p. 1)

Ms. Fleck's think aloud demonstrated the way in which a reader activates his or her prior knowledge, summarizes information, and predicts future events in the text. She said to the class, "Oh, I had a dog like that. He used to make the most awful sound when he tried to bark. We never thought to call him "yeller," but wow, what a sound he could make! I like the way the author tells us how this dog was named—he got his name from the color of his fur *and* because of the sounds he makes. I think that is a great way to pick a name for a dog. I bet both of those things—his color and his bark—will be important as we read the story. The author is probably telling us this to get us ready for really important things in the pages to come."

Students can also be taught to think aloud as they read. This is useful during independent learning and conferring as teachers assess students' use of strategies. Think alouds can also be used in collaborative learning situations as heterogeneous groups of students learn from one another. For example, Oster (2001) taught her seventh graders to think aloud and was able to assess their understanding of texts and use of strategies as they read John Steinbeck's *The Pearl* (1945).

Writing to learn. **Writing to learn** differs from other types of writing because it is not a process writing piece that will go through multiple refinements toward an intended final product. Instead, it is meant to be a catalyst for further learning—an opportunity for students to recall, clarify, and question what they know and what they still wonder about. Writing to learn also provides teachers an opportunity to find out what students understand about the information they are studying.

> Writing to learn pieces do not go through revisions.

Writing to learn "involves getting students to think about and to find the words to explain what they are learning, how they understand that learning, and what their own processes of learning involve" (Mitchell, 1996, p. 93). As Jenkinson explains, "writing should be a process in which writers discover what they know and do not know about their topics, their language, themselves, and their ability to communicate with specific audiences" (1988, p. 714).

> Prior knowledge refers to schemas a student has already created. These are influenced by experiences, topic knowledge, and cultural perspectives.

For example, following a shared reading of a newspaper article on Hepatitis A, Mr. Green asked his eighth-grade students to respond to the following writing to learn prompt: "explain to your younger brother or sister why hand washing is important." Responding to this prompt requires that the student consider their prior knowledge about germs, the cognitive development of their younger siblings, what they have read or listened to about the topic, and how to best convey this information in writing.

A writing to learn question can be open ended—"What did you think was confusing about this topic?"—to fairly specific—"Discuss the role of photosynthesis in plant life." The range of writing to learn opportunities can include (Andrews, 1997; Fisher, 2001; Fisher & Frey, 2004; Mitchell, 1996):

- *Admit slips*—upon entering the classroom, students write on an assigned topic such as "Will Marty tell his parents he has hidden Shiloh?"
- *Crystal ball*—students describe what they think class will be about, what will happen next in the novel they are reading, etc.
- *Found poems*—students reread an assigned text and find key phrases that "speak" to them, then arrange these into a poem structure without adding any of their own words
- *Awards*—students recommend someone or something for an award that the teacher has created such as "the best artist of the century, living or dead"
- *Cinquains*—a five-line poem in which the first line is the topic (a noun), the second line is description of the topic in two words, the third line is three *–ing* words, the fourth line is a description of the topic in four words, and the final line is a synonym of the topic word from line one
- *Yesterday's news*—students summarize the information presented the day before, either from a film, discussion, or reading
- *"What if" scenarios*—students respond to prompts in which information is changed from what they know and they predict outcomes (for example, students may be asked to respond to "What would be different if Shiloh were a cat?")
- *Take a stand*—students discuss their opinions about a controversial topic such as "school uniforms—yes or no?"
- *Letters*—students write letters to others, including elected officials, family members, friends, people who made a difference, etc. (for example, students may respond to the prompt, "write a letter to Dr. Martin Luther King informing him of the progress we have made on racism since his death")
- *Exit slips*—used as a closure activity at the end of the period, students write on an assigned prompt such as "The three best things I learned today are . . . "

The critical element that all of these writing to learn events have in common is that students do not correct or rewrite their pieces. Instead, each becomes a starting point for learning and each provides the teacher with a glimpse inside the student's head to determine what they understand.

Questioning ring. Questioning is one of the most common ways in which teachers assess students' comprehension (e.g., Durkin, 1978–1979). Research evidence suggests that students think about texts in the way that they are questioned about the text by their teachers, peers, and parents (Anderson & Biddle, 1975; Hansen, 1981). That is, if students are only asked factual questions about their reading, then they begin to focus on facts as they read. Similarly, if they are asked more complex thinking questions or questions that require analysis of the text, they will read for this type of information.

Evidence Based

Teachers use a number of strategies to ensure that they are asking a range of types of questions during their focus lessons and read alouds. One common strategy is to write questions on sticky notes and place them in the text for their use before, during or after the reading.

Teacher Tip

Another strategy is to use a **question ring.** As teachers, many of us rely on a small range of questions to ask our students as we read with them. These "old favorites" are often overused and focus on recall of facts (e.g., "what was the boy's name?"). We like to use a question ring to help us formulate better questions of our students. Typically this involves a series of questions that the teacher has printed on 3″ × 5″ cards. The cards are hole-punched in the top left corner and attached with a binder ring. As the teacher reads, he or she uses the cards as a prompt to ask a range of questions. We like to loop the question ring right over an index finger while we conduct a read aloud or shared reading because it helps us remember to ask good questions. This strategy ensures that we balance our questioning between information, facts, inferences, and predictions. A list of sample questions used in a questioning ring can be found in Figure 10.6.

Anticipation guides. An **anticipation guide** is a teacher-prepared list of statements based on a specific text. The purpose is to activate prior knowledge, encourage predictions, and stimulate curiosity about a topic (Head & Readence, 1986). These guides are useful for promoting class discussion as well, because they can spark debate and foster the inevitable need to consult other sources of information.

Teacher Tip

Heather Fields used an anticipation to introduce her seventh-grade students to their study of Islam. Ms. Fields prepared an anticipation guide like the one in Figure 10.7 to encourage her students to begin thinking about the content. At the end of the unit, after the class has read about, watched videos, conducted Internet searches, and carefully examined Islam, they will return to the anticipation guide and re-answer the questions. As you can see from the sample, the use of anticipation guides activates prior knowledge, focuses attention to specific topics within a unit of study, and provides students an opportunity to check their understanding and learning at the end of the unit.

The steps to creating a guide are fairly simple (Head & Readence, 1986):

1. *Identify the major concepts.* What are the main ideas in the passage or unit of study? Keep it to two or three so the guide won't be too long.

2. *Consider your students' prior knowledge?* What are they most likely to hold misconceptions about?

3. *Write five or ten statements pertaining to the reading.* Don't make them all factual—be sure to create open-ended statements as well. Look again to your major concepts to make sure you are creating statements that relate to larger concepts rather than isolated facts.

Guided Instruction

The guided instruction portion of the language arts workshop is time when the teacher meets with a small group of students to offer intentional instruction on comprehension strategies. Because questioning is so important to building comprehension, guided instruction is an excellent opportunity to reinforce strategies first introduced in a focus lesson.

Evidence Based

Question-Answer Relationship. The **Question-Answer Relationship (QAR)** strategy describes four types of questions: *Right There, Think and Search, Author and You,* and *On Your Own* (Raphael, 1982, 1984, 1986). It is based on the three categories of question classification described by Pearson and Johnson (1978): *text explicit* (the answer is directly quoted in the text); *text implicit* (the answer must be implied from several

Figure 10.6   Questions Used in a Question Ring

The Story

What happened in the story?
How can you tell this story is make-believe?
What happened first, next. . . last?
Were you able to predict the ending?
What other way might the story have ended?
What will probably happen next?
What might have happened if a certain action had not taken place?
What was the most important part of the story?
Under a heading (such as People, Animals, Places, Things) list important words.

Setting

Where did the story take place?
What was the place like?
Could there be a place like this?
Do you know of a place like this?
When did the story take place? (past, present, future)
Which part of the story best describes the setting?
What words does the author use to describe the setting?

Informational Books

What is the book about?
Who is the author?
What was your favorite part?
Was the book easy to read? Why? Why not?
What else would you like to know?
Did you use the Table of Contents?
Does the book make you want to learn more about this topic?
What did you find out that you didn't know before?
Did the book have pictures, charts, maps, graphs, tables, or photos?
Did the author tell you enough?
What were some "topic" words the author used?

Author

What do you know about the author?
Why do you think the author wrote the book?
What is the author trying to tell you in the book?
What does this book tell us about the author?
What sorts of things does your author like to dislike? (People, places, behaviors, feelings)
What did the author have to know about to write this book?

Characters

Who are the main characters in the story?
(Choose one character) Why is this character important in the story?
Do you know anyone like the characters?
Do any of the characters change?
Why did they behave as they did?
How are the characters different/alike?
Are people really like these characters?
Was the behavior of a particular character right or wrong?
What lesson did the character learn in the story?

(continued)

Figure 10.6   Questions Used in a Question Ring *(continued)*

Basic Questions

Was there anything you liked about this book?
What especially caught your attention?
What would you have liked more of?
Was there anything you disliked?
Were there parts that bored you?
Was there anything that puzzled you?
Was there anything you thought strange?
Was there anything that completely surprised you?

General Questions

When you first saw the book, what kind of book did you think it was going to be?
What made you think this?
Now you've read it, is it as you expected?
Have you read other books like the one you've just finished?
How is it the same or different?
While you were reading, or now when you think about it, were there words or phrases or other things to do with the language that you liked? Or didn't?
Have you noticed anything special about the way language is used in this book?
When people speak, they often use some words or phrases or talk in a way that you recognize as theirs.
If the writer asked you what could be improved in the book, what would you say?
If you had written this book, how would you have made it better?
Has anything that happens in this book ever happened to you?
What parts in the book seem to you to be the most true-to-life?
Did the book make you think differently about your own similar experience?
When you were reading, did you "see" the story happening in your imagination?
Which details—which passages—helped you "see" it best?
Which passages stay in your mind most vividly?
How many different stories can you find within the main story?
What will you tell your friends about this book?
We've listened to each other's thoughts and heard all sorts of things that each of us has noticed. Are you surprised by anything someone else said?
Has anyone said anything that has changed your mind about this book?
Or helped you to understand it better?
Tell me about the things people said that struck you the most.

Special Questions

How long did it take the story to happen?
Did we find out about the story in the order in which the events actually happened?
Do you always tell a story in sequential order? Why? Why not?
Where did the story happen?
Could it just as well have been set anywhere?
Did you think about the setting as you were reading?
Are there passages in the book that are especially about the place where the story is set?
Which character interested you the most?
Is that character the most important in the story?
Or is it really about someone else?
Was there a character who you did not like?
Did any of the characters remind you of people you know or characters from other books?
Who was narrating the story?

(continued)

Figure 10.6   Questions Used in a Question Ring *(continued)*

Do we know?

Is the story told in first person or third person?

What does the person telling the story think about the characters?

Do you think he/she likes them?

Think of yourself as a spectator. With whose eyes did you see the story?

Did you only see what one character in the story saw, or sometimes did you see the story through another character? (Were you inside the head of one character or a number of characters?)

When you were reading the story did you feel it was happening now?

Or did you feel it had happened in the past and was being remembered?

What in the writing made you feel this way?

Did you feel as though you were an observer, watching what was happening but not a part of the action?

If you were an observer, where were you watching from? (beside characters, above them looking down on the action)

Can you tell me places in the book where you felt that way?

Figure 10.7   Anticipation Guide for Islam Unit

Name: _____   Date: _____

Anticipation Guide for "Islam: Empire of Faith"

Directions: Read each statement and write a "+" for true statements and a "o" for false statements.

Statement	Before viewing	After viewing
Baghdad is the holy city of the Muslim faith.		
The pilgrimage of the Muslim faithful is called the Hajj.		
The Middle East is a natural land bridge between east and west.		
The center of the Middle East is the city of Mecca.		
Merchants were the most influential people in Baghdad.		
The center of scholarship was the House of Wisdom.		
Arabic numerals are still in use today.		
The growth of the Middle East can be traced to the Renaissance in Europe.		
Muslim scholars used the scientific process first described by the ancient Greeks.		
Muslim physicians invented hospitals.		
Development of the science of optics first began in the Islamic world.		
Discoveries about optics led to the later invention of the camera.		
Paper was first used in Egypt.		

Figure 10.8 Question-Answer Relationship Poster

In the text . . . RIGHT THERE	In the text . . . THINK AND SEARCH
When was the Declaration signed?	*What are some of Thomas Jefferson's notable accomplishments?*
The Declaration of Independence was adopted on <u>July 4, 1776.</u>	*The Declaration of Independence* was adopted on July 4, 1776. John Hancock signed first, and <u>Thomas Jefferson, the author,</u> signed as a delegate of Virginia. He later became the <u>third president</u> of the United States.
Answers to Right There questions are in the text. The words in the question usually matches a sentence in the text.	Answers to Think and Search questions are in the text. The answer is compiled through segments of several sentences.
In your head . . . AUTHOR AND YOU	In your head . . . ON YOUR OWN
What influence did participation in the development of the Declaration have on the signers?	*If you were a delegate of the Second Continental Congress, would you sign?*
Answers to Author and You questions in the text. You need to consider both what the author has told you and what you already know about the answer.	Answers to On Your Own questions are not in the text. You need to consider your personal experiences and how they relate to the topic.

Source: Fisher, D., & Frey, N. (2004). *Improving adolescent literacy: Strategies at work.* Upper Saddle River, NJ: Merrill/Prentice Hall.

> Posting comprehension tools like QAR in the classroom assists students in applying the strategy after the initial instruction has been completed.

passages in the book); and *script implicit* (requires both the text and prior knowledge and experiences). A classroom poster on Question-Answer Relationships appears in Figure 10.8.

QAR requires teachers to model the different levels of questions that are associated with a text. QAR should not be confused with Bloom's taxonomy of questions (Bloom, 1956) because QAR "does not classify questions in isolation but rather by considering the reader's background knowledge and the text" (McIntosh & Draper, 1996, p. 154). In addition to serving as a tool for teachers to develop questions, it is also a framework for students to apply in answering questions. QAR is a student-centered approach to questioning because it "clarifies how students can approach the task of reading texts and answering questions" (Raphael, 1986, p. 517). A comparison chart illustrating the relationship between these concepts of text questioning can be found in Figure 10.9.

Students use QAR to generate their own questions about a text. For example, students can write "right there" and "think and search" questions for one another to check on their understanding of the facts of the passage. This inquiry interaction promotes more personal involvement than using only teacher-generated questions. As

Figure 10.9   Question-Answer Relationship Comparison Chart

QAR Strategy	Category	Description
Right There	*Text explicit*	The question is asked using words from the text and the answer is directly stated in the reading.
Think and Search	*Text implicit*	The questions are derived from the text and require the reader to look for the answer in several places and to combine the information.
Author and You	*Script- and text implicit*	The question has the language of the text but in order to answer it the reader must use what he/she understands about the topic. The answer cannot be found directly in the text, but the text can provide some information for formulating an answer. The information is implied and the reader infers what the author meant by examining clues in the text.
On My Own	*Script implicit*	The question elicits an answer to come from the reader's own prior knowledge and experiences. The text may or may not be needed to answer the question.

Source: Fisher, D., & Frey, N. (2004). *Improving adolescent literacy: Strategies at work.* Upper Saddle River, NJ: Merrill/Prentice Hall.

When students can connect text with their own experiences or other texts, they are able to understand and remember information efficiently.

well, "author and you" and "on your own" questions invite the reader to integrate personal experiences and prior knowledge into their responses. These inferential and evaluative questions require the reader to make connections between text, self, and world (Keene & Zimmerman, 1997). As they generate "author and you" and "on your own" questions, the reader deduces, infers, connects, and evaluates (Leu & Kinzer, 1995; Raphael, 1982, 1986).

The instructional power of QAR lies in the explicit instruction of identifying what type of question is being asked, and therefore what resources are required to answer the question. Raphael (1984) notes that less effective readers are often puzzled by where to locate answers to questions based on a reading. Some students rely only on the text, sometimes fruitlessly searching for an answer that is just not there. Conversely, other students rarely return to the text for any answers, believing that they can only depend on information they can recall from memory. By teaching the relationship between questions and answers, students can apply the framework to answer more efficiently and accurately.

The QAR framework can typically be taught in one lesson—often in a whole class focus lesson. We advise the teacher to read aloud a small segment of text and ask a question about what was read. The teacher reflects aloud on the selection and answers the question. What is critical is to identify the level of the question and the source of the answer. When students learn to classify questions and locate answers, they learn to recognize that the reading process is influenced by both the reader and the text. Eventually, students are ready to formulate original questions in response to text.

Teacher Tip

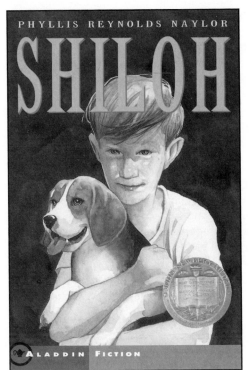

From *Shiloh* by Phyllis Reynolds Naylor, cover illustration by Barry Moser, © 2000 by Simon & Schuster. Used by permission of Simon & Schuster.

The use of QAR, applying the strategy in real time as students read, can be reinforced during guided instruction. For example, after a group of Ms. Allen's fifth-grade students read a chapter of *Hatchet* (Paulsen, 1987), the students asked one another a series of questions about the chapter they had just finished. When asked a question, the respondent first indicated which type of question it was and then provided the answer. At one point in the conversation, Maggie asked Joe, "could this really happen? Could a boy live alone after a plane crash?" Joe responded, "I think this is an "author and you" question because the author really does not tell you if this could happen and I have to think about this in my own brain and there are clues in the book. But, I think it could happen. Kids know things and they can live. Brian knows a lot because he learned things from his father and from his teachers. So, I think it really could happen."

Writing models. Using an already existing piece of writing and making changes to it provides another opportunity for students and teachers to work together on comprehension. Fisher and Frey (2003) note that **writing models** provide students with a framework to support their individual creations.

There are a number of ways to use writing models in the language arts workshop. For example, during a guided instruction lesson, Ms. Alvarez read from the book *Somewhere Today: A Book of Peace* (Thomas, 1998). Each page presents readers with a photograph and a sentence that starts with "somewhere today . . . " As she finished the book, Ms. Alvarez asked each member in the group to write a few sentences that started with the words "somewhere today" and focused on peace. This allowed her to assess her students' understanding of the book, their comprehension of the purpose of the selection, as well as their developing writing skills. Some of the sentences students wrote included:

- Somewhere today my grandma is writing a letter to my dad in the Navy.
- Somewhere today a teacher helps someone read.
- Somewhere today a guy turned in his gun to the police.

The frame for the "I am poem" can be found in chapter 3.

In addition to using children's literature as a writing model, there are writing frames that provide scaffolding. Many of these were discussed in chapter 3 as well. You probably remember one such frame called the "I am poem" (Fisher & Frey, 2003).

When a group of fourth graders were reading *Shiloh* (Naylor, 1991), they used the "I am poem" to analyze the characters in the book. One of the students, Justin, included the following lines in his poem:

I am Marty.
I wonder if Shiloh will ever be mine.
I hear Judd calling, calling, calling for his dog.
I want to keep Shiloh safe—am I strong enough?

In addition to these writing models, you will recall that teachers can create paragraph frames for students to use in their writing. These frames are teacher-developed and allow the teacher to determine if students understand the content as well as grammar structures required to complete the task. At each place where there is an ellipse (a series of three periods), students add as many words as they want to make the paragraph work. For example; a paragraph frame could read, "I was walking through the halls when . . . When I looked up . . . Then I heard . . . I was so scared. I nearly . . . And then, finally, . . . " This paragraph frame was used with students to introduce the genre of mysteries. There are simply hundreds, if not thousands, of paragraph frames you can create that are based on your lesson or unit of study.

Strategy-focused group work. With some groups of students, you'll want to follow up on specific comprehension strategies you used during the focus lesson. For example, if you have used predictions as part of your think aloud, some students will need additional instruction to be able to use that strategy. It is important to note that instruction should not just cycle through a number of strategies as students need to learn to deploy many strategies for comprehending simultaneously (Pinnell & Fountas, 2003). However, it is worthwhile to reinforce specific strategies on a regular basis during guided instruction. Some of the strategies you'll want to focus on are presented in appendix 10.1.

As you noticed, the teacher in the opening vignette for this chapter focused on the use of a specific comprehension strategy (visualizing) to concentrate on during both her focus lesson as well as during her guided instruction. In this way, students receive regular instruction in thinking about texts and learn to use these strategies in real time in their independent reading.

Collaborative Learning

The collaborative learning phase of the language arts workshop provides students with time to use comprehension strategies with other students. You may recall that the National Reading Panel identified cooperative learning as a critical feature of research-based comprehension instruction.

GIST. Generating Interactions Between Schemata and Text, or **GIST** (Cunningham, 1982), is a strategy designed to help students create summaries of texts. Summary writing serves a number of purposes. In addition to being a skill for writing, learning how to summarize information fosters comprehension (National Institute of Child Health and Human Development, 2000; Oded & Walters, 2001; Radmacher & Latosi-Sawin, 1995).

Frey, Fisher, and Hernandez (2003) used GIST to teach students to summarize information and improve their comprehension of informational texts. A GIST lesson begins with selecting a brief informational text (200–300 words) that has been chunked into major passages. We like to section the reading at the end of paragraphs or before the next heading. These passages are sectioned with a line that reads "STOP." The marked text is distributed to students and read in its entirety so that the piece is understood. The first passage is then read again. This time the teacher leads students in a discussion about the important points presented in the passage, recording students' ideas on the board or a language chart. The goal is to formulate these ideas into one sentence. The procedure is repeated for each passage, generating a one-sentence summary for each section. At the end, the sentences are read in sequence

Figure 10.10   Steps for Direct Instruction of GIST

1.	Distribute copies of a short text (1–1½; pages). Each text should be divided into four or five sections that represent logical summarizing points, indicated by a line and the word "STOP" in the margins.
2.	Explain GIST: students read a portion of a text, stop, and write a sentence that summarizes the "gist" of the passage. At the end of the text, students will have written four or five sentences, or a concise summary of the text.
3.	Introduce the text to be read, build prior knowledge and discuss key vocabulary. Read aloud the entire text then reread the first passage of the text while students read along silently.
4.	Lead class discussion about important facts from the first passage, writing their ideas on the board.
5.	Lead class discussion about how to formulate ideas into a sentence, allowing students to share ideas and negotiating these ideas to craft an accurate and precise sentence.
6.	Write the agreed upon sentence on the board, numbering it #1. Students write the sentence in their journals.
7.	Read aloud the second passage, following same sequence above, and numbering agreed upon sentence #2. Repeat cycle until text is finished.
8.	Discuss how the class has condensed a page of text into a limited number of sentences. Reread the series of sentences to check for meaning. Make any changes necessary so that it serves as a concise written summary.

Source: Frey, N., Fisher, D., & Hernandez, T. (2003). "What's the GIST?" Summary writing for struggling adolescent writers. *Voices from the Middle, 11*(2), 43–49. Used with permission.

to check for agreement about the accuracy of the summary. The steps for providing instruction for GIST are summarized in Figure 10.10.

Reciprocal teaching. If teachers wish to move instruction from delivery to discovery, **reciprocal teaching** is an essential strategy for consideration (Palincsar & Brown, 1984). As an approach that allows students to directly assist with the discovery of material and the subsequent construction of meaning, the strategy is ideally suited for the teacher intent on putting learning in the hands of the learner (Little & Richards, 2000). As an engaging, student-centered process, reciprocal teaching appeals to students (Oczkus, 2003).

Evidence Based

In addition to being a captivating strategy, reciprocal teaching is an important (and highly effective) strategy for students who are at risk in the traditional classroom either through disaffection or even oppositional attitudes to direct instruction (e.g., Carter, 1997; Palincsar & Herrenkohl, 2002). In fact, a review of 16 studies on reciprocal teaching suggests that this strategy increases standardized test scores for all students (Rosenshine & Meister, 1994). Reciprocal teaching has also been an effective strategy for students who struggle to read (Alfassi, 1998). Finally, reciprocal teaching is a powerful strategy for consideration in the multi-cultural classroom, as diverse viewpoints are considered and made part of the discovery of the text (King & Parent Johnson, 1999; Palincsar & Herrenkohl, 2002).

Students can use these skills individually and in concert in many aspects of the academic day.

Evidence Based

More information about reciprocal teaching was presented in chapter 4.

This is a good opportunity to teach about questioning.

Reciprocal teaching can be defined as a strategy in which students use *predicting, questioning, clarifying,* and *summarizing* to help or teach each other in the understanding of a text (Palincsar & Brown, 1984). While there are many variations of reciprocal teaching, each is centered upon these four comprehension skills requiring students to monitor their progress as they read the text. Fluent readers use these same behaviors to support their comprehension. Many believe that the effectiveness of reciprocal teaching comes from the metacognition required of the reader. "Without good metacognitive abilities, readers have little facility to understand what they read simply because, for them, the process of constructing meaning will not take place" (Carter, 1997, p. 65).

Each of the four components of reciprocal teaching is based on current knowledge of comprehension instruction (Flood, Lapp, & Fisher, 2003; Harvey & Goudvis, 2000; Keene & Zimmermann, 1997). When students predict, they use their background (or prior) knowledge and make an educated guess about the text and its resolution. In addition, predicting provides students with a purpose for reading the text as well as a motivator (to see if their predictions are correct). A discussion tool students can use in their reciprocal teaching groups was presented in chapter 4.

The second phase of reciprocal teaching, questioning, ensures that students are focusing on the main ideas of the text. "This, in essence, is a time for students to test what the other students know about the reading" (Little & Richards, 2000, p. 191). In other words, students use their skills in determining main ideas and form those ideas into questions. Students are encouraged to vary the types of questions they ask and not limit their questioning to literal information. A side benefit of the questioning phase of reciprocal teaching is that students learn the difference between questions that provide them access to information and those that do not. As Keene and Zimmerman note, "proficient readers use questions to focus their attention on important components of the text; they understand that they can pose questions critically" (1997, p. 119).

Once students have used their predicting and questioning skills, they are encouraged to clarify their understanding of the text with their peers. Clarifying encourages students to monitor their own comprehension—a strategy that good readers use regularly (Flood, Lapp, & Fisher, 2003). In addition, clarifying allows students to ask all kinds of questions about things they may not have understood including vocabulary words, references to unknown events, or connections the text has to other texts or the world (Harvey & Goudvis, 2000).

Finally, students are asked to summarize the information they have just read and talked about. This final phase is based on the idea that comprehension is increased when readings are discussed and written about (Daniels, 1994; Palincsar, 1987). Teachers (and group members) also use summarization to assess comprehension. Teachers often ask themselves, "Did the group get the main idea of the reading passage?" Group members often ask each other to share key points and then discuss those points until they can form a summary in their own words.

Once students learn the steps involved with reciprocal teaching, it is a meaningful way for groups of students to read texts together. Most teachers teach the whole class the process of reciprocal teaching in the beginning of the school year and then move this procedure to collaborative learning centers. If students forget one of the processes, they can refer to the posters that are hung in the classroom (see chapter 4).

Independent Learning

The goal of all reading instruction, especially comprehension instruction is for students to independently use the skills and strategies that they have developed throughout the language arts workshop. With an intentional focus on comprehension instruction, you will notice students choosing to read when provided an opportunity. This is the ultimate goal and you should have a profound sense of accomplishment when your students read and write with understanding. As such, there are not a large number of strategies to use in the independent phase of the language arts workshop in terms of comprehension instruction. Rather, teachers mostly monitor reading and writing for understanding. Two examples are retellings and RAFTs.

Retellings. **Retellings** are an excellent way to assess students' comprehension. In the language arts workshop, retellings are often done during independent reading and writing when teachers confer with students. Scholl (1997) notes that retellings are an excellent way to engage students in book conversations while assessing and teaching comprehension.

For example, Mr. Espinosa invites Anthony to his desk and asks that he bring the book he is reading. Anthony joins Mr. Espinosa for a conference about the book *Monster* (Myers, 1999). Anthony, an eighth grader, relates Steve's (the main character) experience in the courtroom and in prison as he is tried as an accomplice to murder. As Mr. Espinosa confers with Anthony, he is sure that this student not only understands the book but is also comparing the character's life to his own. Mr. Espinosa takes a few extra minutes to talk about violence and the consequences of violence with Anthony, and then invites another student to the table for her conference.

See chapter 3.

RAFT. You will recall from chapter 3 that **RAFT** (Santa & Havens, 1995) is a writing frame that invites students to take perspectives in their writing. The ability to assume a character's perspective requires that the reader understand the motives, traits, and behaviors of the individual or subject. RAFT stands for:

R = **role** (who is the writer, what is role of the writer?)

A = **audience** (to whom are you writing?)

F = **format** (what format should the writing be in?)

T = **topic** (what are you writing about?)

RAFTs are often used in the language arts workshop in a focus lesson to teach students perspective writing. Once students are familiar with the RAFT format, teachers can assign groups of students different components and then invite group conversations about the topic at hand. For example, students may enter the room to find the following written on the board:

	Last name A–M	**Last name N–Z**
R	King George	colonists
A	colonists	King George
F	Informational letter	Protest letter
T	Why the taxes?	Why the taxes?

RAFTs also provide students with a unique opportunity to engage in independent reading and writing comprehension in the language arts workshop. During independent time, students can select a picture book from a special bin in the classroom designated as such. Inside the front cover, students will find the RAFT. Their task is to independently read the picture book and then respond to the RAFT. A set of sample RAFTs can be found in Figure 10.11. As an example, a student in Mr. Tomay's class selected the book *From Cocoa Bean to Chocolate* (Nelson, 2003). Inside the book, Calvin found the following RAFT.

R   Digestive System

A   Chocolate

F   Love letter

T   Why I need you

Calvin, using the content information he learned in science, responded by writing the following:

Dear Chocolate,

I like how you get into my mouth and how my teeth can bite you into little, yummy pieces. I can't resist you! I also like it when you work with my saliva and break down into even smaller, yummy pieces. When I eat too much of you, my morals hurt. My esophagus works to push you down. I can't taste you anymore when you pass into my stomach and then intestines. I really needed because you help my small intestine by giving me the milk so my bones can grow stronger. Soon I'll be saying good-bye to you as you leave my system. I just say, "Can I have some more?" I can't live without you.

Sincerely,

Calvin

Figure 10.11   Sample RAFT Prompts

CASEY AT THE BAT (Thayer and Bing, 2000)

R	Sports reporter
A	Mudville fans
F	Newspaper article
T	Mudville loses

A PICTURE BOOK OF HARRIET TUBMAN (Adler, 1993)

R	Slave catcher
A	The public
F	Wanted poster
T	"Moses"

FROM SLAVE SHIP TO FREEDOM ROAD (Lester, 1998)

R	Author
A	Reader
F	Position statement
T	Would you risk going to jail for someone you didn't know?

THE STAR-SPANGLED BANNER (Spier, 1973)

R	American soldier in charge of flag
A	His family
F	A letter
T	Last night at Ft. McHenry

As you can see, Calvin had to mobilize his reading comprehension strategies to read and understand the text he selected. He also had to demonstrate his understanding in writing, organizing his writing to ensure that readers could understand his perspective.

BIG IDEAS ABOUT COMPREHENSION

Comprehension in reading is considered to be the ultimate goal of reading instruction. Students are never too young to benefit from comprehension instruction, which should be integrated into all aspects of the language arts workshop. Good readers are recognizable for their comprehension skills, which continue to develop through wide reading, self-monitoring of understanding, fluency, and positive attitudes toward reading. Intentional instruction for comprehension includes think alouds that model how a reader monitors comprehension. In addition, instruction in the questions and their relationships to answers enhances comprehension. Other questioning strategies like reciprocal teaching mirror the internal comprehension strategies utilized by good readers.

INTEGRATING THE STANDARDS

Create lesson plans that meet your state's standards by visiting our Companion Website at www.prenhall.com/frey. There you'll find lessons created to meet the NCTE/IRA Standards. Adapt them to meet the standards of your own state through links to your state's standards, and keep them in the online portfolio. You can collect lesson plans for each chapter in an online portfolio, providing you with invaluable tools to meet your state's standards when you head into your own classroom.

CHECK YOUR UNDERSTANDING

1. What is the research on comprehension?
2. What do good readers do?
3. What should good teachers do?
4. How is reading comprehension developed?
5. Can I focus on comprehension when students don't yet know how to read?
6. What instructional activities support comprehension?

CLASSROOM CONNECTIONS

1. Discuss comprehension instruction with your teacher. What does he or she believe are the students' challenges and strengths in this area?
2. Select a passage and determine which comprehension skills or processes you used to make meaning. How could you teach those skills or processes to students?
3. Develop a lesson plan in which you explicitly teach a comprehension strategy. Begin with a focus lesson, then plan for guided, collaborative, and independent learning.

References

Alfassi, M. (1998). Reading for meaning: The efficacy of reciprocal teaching in fostering reading comprehension in high school students in remedial reading classes. *American Educational Research Journal, 35,* 309–332.

Alvermann, D. E., Swafford, J., & Montero, M. K. (2003). *Content area literacy instruction for the elementary grades.* Boston: Pearson Allyn & Bacon.

Anderson, R. C., & Biddle, W. B. (1975). On asking people questions about what they are reading. In G. H. Bower (Ed.), *The psychology of learning and motivation* (Vol. 9, pp. 9–129). New York: Academic Press.

Andrews, S. E. (1997). Writing to learn in content area reading class. *Journal of Adolescent & Adult Literacy, 41,* 141–142.

Block, C. C., Gambrell, L. B., & Pressley, M. (2002). *Improving comprehension instruction: Rethinking research, theory, and classroom practice.* San Francisco, Jossey-Bass.

Block, C. C., & Pressley, M. (2002). *Comprehension instruction: Research-based best practices.* New York: Guilford.

Bloom, B. S. (1956). *Taxonomy of educational objectives: The classification of educational goals: Handbook I, cognitive domain.* New York: Longman.

Brophy, J., & Good, T. (1986). Teacher behavior and student achievement. In M. Wittrock (Ed.), *The handbook of research on teaching* (3rd ed., pp. 328–375). New York: Macmillan.

Carter, C. J. (1997). Why reciprocal teaching? *Educational Leadership, 54*(6), 64–68.

Carver, R. (1987). Should reading comprehension skills be taught? In J. E. Readence & R. S. Baldwin (Eds.), *Research on literacy: The Yearbook of the National Reading Conference* (Vol. 36). Rochester, NY: National Reading Conference.

Chin, C., Brown, D. E., & Bruce, B. C. (2002). Student-generated questions: A meaningful aspect of learning in science. *International Journal of Science Education, 24,* 521–549.

Cunningham, J. W. (1982). Generating interactions between schemata and text. In J. A. Niles & L. A. Harris (Eds.), *New inquiries in reading research and instruction* (pp. 42–47). Rochester, NY: National Reading Conference.

Daniels, H. (1994). *Literature circles: Voice and choice in the student-centered classroom.* York, ME: Stenhouse.

Davis, F. B. (1944). Fundamental factors of comprehension. *Reading Psychometrika, 9,* 185–197.

Duke, N. K., & Pearson, P. D. (2002). Effective practices for developing reading comprehension. In A. E. Farstrup & S. J. Samuels (Eds.), *What research has to say about reading instruction* (3rd ed., pp. 205–242). Newark, DE: International Reading Association.

Durkin, D. (1978–1979). What classroom observations reveal about reading comprehension instruction. *Reading Research Quarterly, 15,* 481–533.

Fisher, D. (2001). "We're moving on up": Creating a schoolwide literacy effort in an urban high school. *Journal of Adolescent & Adult Literacy, 45,* 92–101.

Fisher, D., & Frey, N. (2003). Writing instruction for struggling adolescent readers: A gradual release model. *Journal of Adolescent & Adult Literacy, 46,* 396–405.

Fisher, D., & Frey, N. (2004). *Improving adolescent literacy: Strategies at work.* Upper Saddle River, NJ: Merrill/Prentice Hall.

Flood, J., Lapp, D., & Fisher, D. (2003). Reading comprehension instruction. In J. Flood, D. Lapp, J. R. Squire, & J. M. Jensen (Eds.), *Handbook of research on teaching the English language arts* (2nd ed.) (pp. 931–941). Mahwah, NJ: Lawrence Erlbaum Associates.

Frey, N., Fisher, D., & Hernandez, T. (2003). "What's the GIST?" Summary writing for struggling adolescent writers. *Voices from the Middle, 11*(2), 43–49.

Gillespie, C. (1990–1991). Questions about student-generated questions. *Journal of Reading, 34,* 250–257.

Guszak, F. J. (1967). Teacher questioning and reading. *The Reading Teacher, 21,* 227–234.

Haller, E. P., Child, D. A., & Walberg, H. J. (1988). Can comprehension be taught? A quantitative synthesis of "metacognitive" studies. *Educational Researcher, 17,* 5–8.

Hansen, J. (1981). The effects of inference training and practice on young children's reading comprehension. *Reading Research Quarterly, 16,* 391–417.

Harvey, S., & Goudvis, A. (2000). *Strategies that work: Teaching comprehension to enhance understanding.* York, ME: Stenhouse.

Head, M. H., & Readence, J. E. (1986). Anticipation guides: Meaning through prediction. In E. K. Dishner, T. W. Bean, J. E. Readence, & D. W. Moore (Eds.), *Reading in the content areas* (2nd ed., pp. 229–234). Dubuque, IA: Kendall-Hunt.

Ivey, G. (1999a). Reflections on teaching struggling middle school readers. *Journal of Adolescent & Adult Literacy, 42,* 372–381.

Ivey, G. (1999b). A multicase study in the middle school: Complexities among young adolescent readers. *Reading Research Quarterly, 34,* 172–192.

Ivey, G. (2002). Building comprehension when they're still learning to read the words. In C. C. Block & M. Pressley (Eds.), *Comprehension instruction: Research-based best practices* (pp. 234–246). New York: Guilford.

Jacobson, J., Thrope, L., Fisher, D., Lapp, D., Frey, N., & Flood, J. (2001). Cross-age tutoring: A literacy improvement approach for struggling adolescent readers. *Journal of Adolescent & Adult Literacy, 44,* 528–536.

Jenkinson, E. B. (1988). Learning to write/writing to learn. *Phi Delta Kappan, 69,* 712–717.

Johnston, P., & Allington, R. L. (1991). Remediation. In R. Barr, M. L. Kamil, P. M. Mosenthal, & P. D. Pearson (Eds.), *Handbook of reading research* (Vol. 2, pp. 984–1012). Mahwah, NJ: Lawrence Erlbaum Associates.

Juel, C., Biancarosa, G., Coker, D., & Deffes, R. (2003). Walking with Rosie: A cautionary tale of early reading instruction. *Educational Leadership, 60*(7), 12–18.

Keene, E. O., & Zimmermann, S. (1997). *Mosaic of thought: Teaching comprehension in a reader's workshop.* Portsmouth, NH: Heinemann.

King, C. M., & Parent Johnson, L. M. (1999). Constructing meaning via reciprocal teaching. *Reading Research and Instruction, 38,* 169–186.

Kletzien, S. B. (1992). Proficient and less proficient comprehenders' strategy use for different top-level structures. *Journal of Reading Behavior, 24,* 191–215.

Kujawa, S., & Huske, L. (1995). *The strategic teaching and reading project guidebook* (Rev. ed.) Oakbrook, IL: North Central Regional Education Laboratory.

Leu, D. J., & Kinzer, C. K. (1995). *Effective reading instruction K–8* (3rd ed.). Upper Saddle River, NJ: Merrill/Prentice Hall.

Little, Q., & Richards, R. T. (2000). Teaching learners—learners teaching: Using reciprocal teaching to improve comprehension strategies in challenged readers. *Reading Improvement, 37,* 190–194.

Mathews, M. (1966). *Teaching to read: Historically considered.* Chicago: University of Chicago Press.

McIntosh, M. E., & Draper, R. J. (1996). Using the question-answer relationship strategy to improve students' reading of mathematics texts. *Clearing House, 69,* 154–162.

Mitchell, D. (1996). Writing to learn across the curriculum and the English teacher. *English Journal, 85,* 93–97.

National Assessment of Educational Progress (NAEP). (1998). *Reading framework for the National Assessment of Educational Progress: 1992–1998.* Washington, DC: U.S. Department of Education, Office of Educational Research and Improvement.

National Institute of Child Health and Human Development. (2000). *Report of the National Reading Panel. Teaching children to read: An evidence-based assessment of the scientific research literature on reading and its implications for reading instruction.* Washington, DC: U.S. Government Printing Office.

Oczkus, L. D. (2003). *Reciprocal teaching at work: Strategies for improving reading comprehension.* Newark, DE: International Reading Association.

Oded, B., & Walters, J. (2001). Deeper processing for better EFL reading comprehension. *System, 29,* 357–370.

Oster, L. (2001). Using the think-aloud for reading instruction. *The Reading Teacher, 55,* 64–69.

Palincsar, A. S. (1987). Reciprocal teaching: Can student discussion boost comprehension? *Instructor, 96*(5), 56–58, 60.

Palincsar, A. S., & Brown, A. L. (1984). Reciprocal teaching of comprehension-fostering and comprehension-monitoring activities. *Cognition and Instruction, 1,* 117–175.

Palincsar, A. S., & Herrenkohl, L. R. (2002). Designing collaborative learning contexts. *Theory Into Practice, 41*(1), 26–32.

Paris, S. G., Wasik, B. A., & Turner, J. C. (1991). The development of strategic readers. In R. Barr, M. L. Kamil, P. Mosenthal, & P. D. Pearson (Eds.), *Handbook of Reading Research* (Vol. 2, pp. 609–640). New York: Erlbaum.

Pearson, P. D., & Hamm, D. (2003). Reading comprehension assessment: One very resilient phenomenon. Retrieved August 9, 2004 from www.ciera.org/library/presos/2003/pearson/irarca.pdf

Pearson, P. D., & Johnson, D. D. (1978). *Teaching reading comprehension.* New York: Holt Rinehart, and Winston.

Pinnell, G. S., & Fountas, I. C. (2003). Teaching comprehension. *The California Reader, 36*(4), 7–14.

Pressley, M., El-Dinary, P. B., Gaskins, I., Schuder, T., Bergman, J. L., Almasi, J., & Brown, R. (1992). Beyond direct explanation: Transactional instruction of reading comprehension strategies. *The Elementary School Journal, 92,* 513–555.

Radmacher, S. A., & Latosi-Sawin, E. (1995). Summary writing: A tool to improve student comprehension and writing in psychology. *Teaching of Psychology, 22,* 113–115.

Raphael, T. E. (1982). Teaching children question-answering strategies. *The Reading Teacher, 36,* 186–191.

Raphael, T. E. (1984). Teaching learners about sources of information for answering questions. *Journal of Reading, 27,* 303–311.

Raphael, T. E. (1986). Teaching children question-answering relationships, revisited. *The Reading Teacher, 39,* 516–522.

RAND Reading Study Group. (2001). *Reading for understanding: Toward an R & D program in reading comprehension.* Technical report for the Office of Educational Research and Improvement.

Rosenshine, B., & Meister, C. (1994). Reciprocal teaching: A review of research. *Review of Educational Research, 64,* 479–530.

Santa, C., & Havens, L. (1995). *Creating independence through student-owned strategies: Project CRISS.* Dubuque, IA: Kendall-Hunt.

Scholl, J. (1997). Reading, (w)riting, and retelling the three r's for the twenty-first century. *Ohio Reading Teacher, 31*(2), 35–38.

Smith, N. B. (1965). *American reading instruction.* Newark, DE: International Reading Association.

Stanovich, K. E., Nathan, R. G., & Zolman, J. E. (1988). The developmental lag hypothesis in reading: Longitudinal and matched reading-level comparisons. *Child Development, 59,* 71–86.

Tovani, C. (2000). *I read it, but I don't get it: Comprehension strategies for adolescent readers.* York, ME: Stenhouse.

Vellutino, F. R., & Scanlon, D. M. (1987). Linguistic coding and reading ability. In S. Rosenberg (Ed.), *Advances in applied psycholinguistics* (Vol. 2, pp. 1–69). New York: Cambridge University Press.

Wilhelm, J. D. (2001). Think-alouds boost reading comprehension. *Instructor, 111*(4), 26–28.

Children's Literature Cited

Adler, D. A. (1993). *A picture book of Harriet Tubman.* New York: Holiday House.

Dahl, R. (1964). *Charlie and the chocolate factory.* New York: Viking Penguin.

Gibson, F. (1956). *Old yeller.* New York: HarperCollins.

Lester, J. (1998). *From slave ship to freedom road.* New York: Dial Books.

Myers, W. D. (1999). *Monster.* New York: HarperCollins.

Naylor, P. R. (1991). *Shiloh.* New York: Atheneum.

Nelson, R. (2003). *From cocoa bean to chocolate.* Minneapolis, MN: Lerner Publications.

Paulsen, G. (1987). *Hatchet.* New York: Viking Penguin.

Sendak, M. (1963). *Where the wild things are.* New York: Harper & Row.

Spier, P. (1973). *The star-spangled banner.* New York: Doubleday.

Steinbeck, J. (1945). *The pearl.* New York: Penguin Books.

Thayer, E. L., & Bing, C. (2000). *Casey at the bat: A ballad of the Republic sung in the year 1888.* New York: Handprint.

Thomas, S. M. (1998). *Somewhere today: A book of peace.* Morton Grove, IL: Albert Whitman.

Appendix 10.1   Reading Comprehension Glossary of Terms

Cause and effect—text structure used to explain the reasons and results of an event or phenomenon. Signal words for cause include *because, when, if, cause,* and *reason.* Words like *then, so, which, effect,* and *result* signal an effect.

Compare and contrast—text structure used to explain how two people, events, or phenomenon are alike and different. Some comparison signal words are *same, at the same time, like,* and *still.* Contrast signal words include *some, others, different, however, rather, yet, but,* and *or.*

Connecting—linking information in the text to personal experiences, prior knowledge, or other texts. This is commonly taught using three categories (Zimmerman & Keene, 1997):

- ❑ *Text to self*—personal connections
- ❑ *Text to text*—connections to other books, films, etc.
- ❑ *Text to world*—connections to events in the past or present

Determinining importance—a comprehension strategy used by readers to differentiate between essential information and interesting (but less important) details.

Evaluating—the reader makes judgments about the information being read, including its credibility, usefulness to the reader's purpose, and quality.

Inferencing—the ability to "read between the lines" to extract information not directly stated in the text. Inferencing is linked to a student's knowledge of vocabulary, content, context, recognition of clues in the text, and experiences.

Monitoring and clarifying—an ongoing process used by the reader to ensure that what is being read is also being understood. When the reader recognizes that something is unclear, he or she uses a variety of clarifying strategies, including rereading, asking questions, and seeking information from another source.

Predicting—the reader uses his or her understanding of language, content, and context to anticipate what will be read next. Prediction occurs continually during reading but is most commonly taught as a pre-reading strategy.

Problem/solution—text structure used to explain a challenge and the measures taken to address the challenge. Signal words for a problem include *trouble, challenge, puzzle, difficulty, problem, question,* or *doubt.* Authors use signal words for a solution like *answer, discovery, improve, solution, overcome, resolve, response,* or *reply.*

Question-Answer Relationships (QAR)—relationships developed to help readers understand where information can be located. There are four types of questions in two categories.

1) *In the Text*—these answers are "book" questions because they are drawn directly from the text. These are sometimes referred to as *text explicit* questions:

- ❑ *Right There*—the answer is located in a single sentence in the text.
- ❑ *Think and Search*—the answer is in the text but is spread across several sentences or paragraphs.

2) *In Your Head*—these answers are "brain" questions because the reader must generate some or all of the answers. These are sometimes called *text implicit* questions:

- ❑ *Author and You*—the reader combines information from the text with other experiences and prior knowledge to answer the question.
- ❑ *On Your Own*—the answer is not in the text and is based on your experiences and prior knowledge.

Questioning—a strategy used by readers to question the text and themselves. These self-generated questions keep the reader interested and are used to seek information. Specific types of questioning includes QAR, QtA, and ReQuest.

Questioning the Author (QtA)—an instructional activity that invites readers to formulate questions for the author of the text. The intent of this strategy is to foster critical literacy by personalizing the reading experience as readers consider where the information in the textbook came from and what the author's intent, voice, and perspectives might be.

Synthesizing—the reader combines new information with background knowledge to create original ideas.

Summarizing—the ability to condense a longer piece of text into a shorter statement. Summarizing occurs throughout a reading, not just at the end.

Temporal sequence—a text structure used to describe a series of events using a chronology. Signal words and phrases include *first, second, last, finally, next, then, since, soon, previously, before, after, meanwhile, at the same time,* and *at last.* Days of the week, dates, and times are also used to show a temporal sequence.

Visualizing—a comprehension strategy used by the reader to create mental images of what is being read.

Using Assessments to Guide Instruction in the Language Arts Workshop

BIG IDEAS ABOUT ASSESSMENT

Assessment in the language arts workshop is not done in order to rank students in comparison to one another because this fails both the child and the teacher. Teacher-based assessments "are valuable when they:

- Form the basis for instructional decisions
- Provide information about the progress of an individual
- Lead to an examination of the conditions under which a child is operating (West Australia Department of Education, 1994, p. 121)

Like the instruction delivered in the language arts workshop, the assessments are selected based on a developmental view of literacy. The tasks assessed are meaningful and constructed within each child's zone of proximal development.

Questions to Consider

- How do I select an assessment?
- How do formal and informal assessments differ from each other?
- What are the major types of informal assessments?

Key Vocabulary

Formal assessments

Norm-referenced

Criterion-referenced

Informal assessments

Observations

Portfolios

Inventories

Rubrics

Conferences

Self-assessments

Surveys

Informal reading inventories

Holistic assessment

—————————————————————— ❧❦❧ ——————————————————————

A LOOK INSIDE

Although it is only August, Ms. Allen is already gathering assessment data about her new fifth graders. A week before school began she mailed each of them a letter with the following message:

> Have you ever wondered how your family came to live in this country? Have you wondered why it's hot in the summer and cold in winter? Welcome back to school! We're going to be studying lots of interesting things this year. When you come to school next Monday, be ready to discuss this question: how do we know what we know?

When her students arrive on the first day of school, Ms. Allen will lead the first discussion of the year on the topic of knowledge. During this time, she will make notes about her students' oral language skills, one of the first assessments she completes every year. In a few weeks when she knows them better, she will complete a Student Oral Language Observation Matrix (SOLOM) for each of her students, all of whom are English Language Learners. Like all good teachers, her most powerful assessment tool is her ability to observe her students and make instructional decisions based on her observations.

Ms. Allen views the first six weeks of school as a critical time to establish her language arts workshop. During this period she will use several surveys to find out more about her students, especially the Elementary Reading Attitude Survey (McKenna & Kear, 1990) and the Writing Attitude Survey (Kear, Coffman, McKenna, & Ambrosio, 2000). "At this age, attitude is everything," she continues, "but I also want to know what they think about themselves as learners. These surveys give me some insight into that." During the first week, she'll administer a series of timed writings to assess their writing fluency and a Developmental Spelling Analysis (Ganske, 2000) to establish groups for guided spelling instruction.

The assessment she is most excited about is a new one for her this year. "I'm really emphasizing metacognition this year—I want them to 'know how they know.' That's why I started our school year with the discussion about knowledge." She will be administering the Metacomprehension Strategies Index (Schmitt, 1990) to assess their use of comprehension strategies in reading. Much of her instruction for the year will be influenced by the results of this assessment, which will guide her teaching about strategies like previewing, predicting, inferencing, summarizing, and using background knowledge. "That's the way readers 'know how they know'—by consciously using strategies to help themselves. Isn't this going to be a great year?"

ASSESSMENT IN THE LANGUAGE ARTS WORKSHOP

Why do teachers assess students? Think about this for a minute. Is it because they want to find out what students do not know? Or is it because assessments and testing are part of the official behaviors of teachers? Or maybe it's because teachers don't know where to begin instruction without good assessment information. Lapp, Fisher, Flood, and Cabello (2001) suggest that teachers assess students for at least four reasons, including:

- *Diagnosing individual student needs* (e.g., assessing developmental status, monitoring and communicating student progress, certifying competency, determining needs)
- *Informing instruction* (e.g., evaluating instruction, modifying instructional strategies, identifying instructional needs)
- *Evaluating programs*
- *Providing accountability information* (p. 7)

There are entire books written on diagnosing individual student needs. For example, James Shanker and Eldon Ekwall focus on this aspect of assessment in their book *Locating and Correcting Reading Difficulties* (2002). They note the various ways that teachers and reading specialists can use assessment information to determine a specific student's literacy development and what can be done about it.

That is not, however, the focus of this book. As a language arts educator, you will make numerous decisions about instruction that matter in very significant ways. This chapter provides you with some tools to make instructional decisions so that you can utilize the principles of the language arts workshop: a developmental view of literacy, a gradual release of responsibility, and meaningful experiences that allow a learner to work in his or her zone of proximal development. We believe that in-

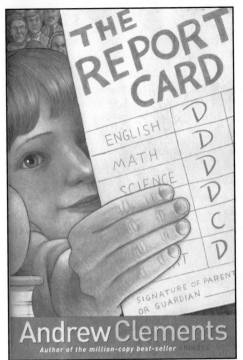

From *The Report Card* by Andrew Clements, cover illustration by Brian Selznick, © 2004 by Simon & Schuster. Used by permission of Simon & Schuster.

structional decisions within the language arts workshop must be based on the assessment information that teachers maintain on their students.

Over the years, we've come to realize that assessments are the link between teaching and learning. This concept lies at the heart of the language arts workshop because the workshop is based on learner-centered instruction. This means the teacher doesn't merely march lock-step through the content of a standards-based curriculum, but rather balances the content with the needs of the learner. These needs are identified through ongoing assessment that is linked to subsequent instruction. In this model, assessment and instruction are considered to be recursive because they repeat as students learn new content. In learner-centered classrooms, teachers first assess to establish what children know and do not know, then plan instruction based on this information. Next, they deliver the instruction they have designed and observe how learners respond. Based on these observations, educators reflect on the results and assess again to determine what needs to be taught next. A diagram representing this concept can be seen in Figure 11.1.

This model may sound as if it would take a lot of time to complete; in fact, effective teachers perform many of these

Figure 11.1   Relationship Between Assessment and Instruction

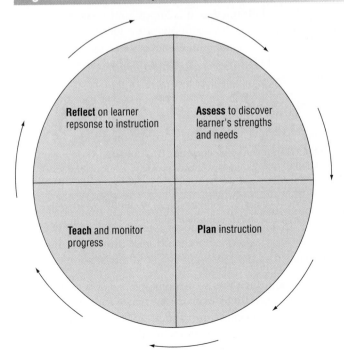

complex tasks rapidly. In well-organized classrooms, assessment happens throughout the day as teachers use questioning, discussions, and assignments to measure progress. In addition, teachers administer assessments to monitor progress and formulate future instruction. In this chapter we will concentrate on illustrating assessment events that occur within the language arts workshop and inform future teaching. The first step is selecting the correct assessments.

How Do I Select an Assessment?

The usefulness of every assessment is dependent on a proper fit between purpose and type of assessment used. It is important to remember that every assessment is useful and not useful *at the same time.* Any given assessment is useful in the hands of a conscientious educator who understands the limitations of the tool being used. Any given assessment is useless if it is interpreted to show something it was not intended to show. You would be very suspicious of a doctor who ordered a chest X-ray when you were seeking help for a sprained ankle. There is nothing inherently wrong with a chest X-ray, it is simply the wrong test for the task. In the same regard, the type of reading or writing assessment selected must match its intended use. Guillaume (2004) offers these considerations for selecting an assessment. Each assessment needs to be:

- Tied to your stance on learning
- Driven by learning goals
- Systematic
- Tied to instruction
- Inclusive of the learner
- Integrated into a manageable system (p. 131)

Tied to your stance on learning. Every teacher brings a philosophy of education and a view of literacy to his or her practice. It is important to recognize how assessment choices fit into that perspective. For example, an educator who possesses a viewpoint of learning as a developmental phenomenon will be interested in assessment instruments that reflect benchmarks of developmental phases of learning. Teachers with a skills-based orientation will find skills measures to be usefull.

Driven by learning goals. Assessments used in the language arts workshop should be consistent with state content standards for the grade level. Currently, 49 of the 50 states have content standards (Iowa is the exception), and these standards can be found on most state department of education websites.

Systematic. Teachers select assessments that can be administered and analyzed in a systematic way at both the individual and class levels. Good assessments should possess data recording protocols that make it easy for the teacher to interpret the information at a later date. In addition, the teacher must determine how often they will be administered. Finally, each assessment should measure what it purports to measure (valid) and yield results that are consistent across administrations and assessors (reliable).

Tied to instruction. Although this seems apparent, it is worth stating again. Assessments should be linked directly to instruction, either to determine what should be taught next (pre-testing) or to check for understanding of skills or strategies that have just been taught (post-testing). Assessments that are not connected to instruction are likely to be frustrating for students because they appear purposeless, and inadequate for teachers because they do not provide relevant information.

Inclusive of the learner. Assessments in the language arts workshop are intended to be completed in conjunction with the needs of the learner. Most of the assessments in this chapter are not completed in isolation by students, who then return the completed test to the teacher. Instead, these assessments are designed to capture the work of children in the act of learning. Whether through listening to a student reading text (running records and Informal Reading Inventories) or using a rubric to discuss a student's writing (holistic writing assessment), these tools are intended to involve the learner in their own measures of progress. A position statement issued by the International Reading Association suggests that "children have a right to reading assessment that identifies their strengths as well as their needs and involves them in making decisions about their own learning" (IRA, 2000, p. 7).

Integrated into a manageable system. No teacher can devote all his or her time to collecting and analyzing assessment data. The demands of assessment on the time available can become overwhelming and even crowd out equally valuable instructional time. Therefore, it is in the interests of the teacher to understand what each assessment does, then select the one that best fits the needs of the students, teacher, and curriculum. Having a collection of good, all-purpose assessments is preferable to administering overlapping assessments that do little to shed new light on a student's progress. Many of the instruments used in the language arts workshop are called informal assessments, although some are formal assessments.

The complete version of this position statement can be viewed at http://www.reading.org/positions/MADMMID.html

What Is the Difference Between Formal and Informal Assessments?

Figure 11.2 provides an overview of the various types of assessments that teachers give. Some of these assessments are **formal,** meaning that they have been developed to be administered to students using a prescribed format concerning time, directions, and level of assistance. Most often, these assessments are given in conditions that do not reflect the ways in which students learned the tested skills. Most

Figure 11.2   Formal Assessments

Formal Assessments		
Type	**Purpose**	**Administration**
Standardized Norm-referenced	Yields a student's academic performance ranking compared to a normed sample of students	• Schedule determined by state and local agencies; often yearly • Tests are usually timed and have strict protocols
Standardized Criterion-referenced	Measures a student's performance compared to a set of academic skills or objectives. Scores are reported as the proportion of correct answers	• Tests may be timed or untimed • May be administered annually or more frequently

Source: Adapted from Fisher, D., & Frey, N. (2004). *Improving adolescent literacy: Strategies at work.* Upper Saddle River, NJ: Merrill/Prentice Hall.

formal assessments include a lengthy testing protocol and student test booklets for collecting data. Protocols are the detailed directions for administering the text. Examples of formal assessments include the National Assessment of Educational Progress (NAEP), given in all 50 states, as well as achievement tests like the Stanford Achievement Test (SAT-9) and Terra Nova (CAT/6). These assessments are **norm-referenced** using thousands of students in order to compare each individual's achievement to other students. Other standardized assessments are **criterion-referenced,** meaning that they measure a student's achievement against those skills expected to have been learned at a particular age or grade level. Examples of criterion-referenced formal assessments include the Stanford Diagnostic Reading Test (SDRT) and the Gates-MacGinitie Reading Test (GMRT).

The scoring of most formal assessments is completed by the test publisher and the results are then reported back to the school and district, often several months later. Many of these formal assessments are used to measure school and district progress toward various state and national accountability targets.

Others assessments are **informal,** meaning that they are administered and interpreted by the same person, usually the classroom teacher. Because administration and interpretation happen in close succession, these instruments are often more useful for making immediate instructional decisions. In order to make these assessments easy for you to view and duplicate, we have created a compendium of assessments located at the end of this book.

Types of Informal Assessments

There are a number of types of informal assessments commonly used in elementary and middle school classrooms. They include observations, portfolios, inventories, rubrics, conferences, self-assessments, and surveys. A summary of informal assessments is featured in Figure 11.3.

Observations. **Observations** are perhaps the assessment tool most commonly used by teachers and identified by them as the most useful (West, 1998). There are several advantages to the use of observation as a tool for assessment (Frey & Hiebert, 2003):

- It focuses on student work in authentic learning situations.
- It mitigates some of the problems associated with formal testing, especially learner stress, because it occurs in the daily learning environment.
- The teacher is able to obtain and analyze the information immediately, allowing for flexibility in instructional plans.

Teacher Tip

Observational notes can be difficult to collect if you don't have a system. We suggest you begin by identifying specific students you want to observe during a particular day. If you select two to three students per day for targeted observation, you can collect notes on all of your students in 10 days. Having said that, we also know that opportunities for observation sometimes arise serendipitously. The trouble arises when you make a note of something then lose the note! In order to handle that problem, we create a clipboard of index cards, one for each student, at the beginning of the year. Each card contains pertinent information about the student. The cards are taped individually to the clipboard in a slightly overlapping fashion so that each card can be lifted. The student's name is written at the bottom edge of the card so it can

Figure 11.3 Informal Assessments

Informal Assessments		
Type	**Purpose**	**Administration**
Observation	Gathers information about a student's academic, behavioral or social skills used in an authentic setting	Teacher records observational data in anecdotal notes, journals, or daily logs
Portfolio	Provides evidence of a student's academic growth through the collection of work samples	Student and teacher select representative samples of student work for display in a binder or other organizer
Inventory	Documents students use of specified skills during a single observation	A commercially or teacher-produced form of observable behaviors is completed by the teacher
Conference	Involves the student in direct feedback to the teacher in a one-to-one discussion	Often scheduled by the teacher at regular intervals to gauge progress on more complex academic behaviors such as reading comprehension
Self-assessment	Allows the student to engage in reflective learning and think about learning	Students assess their own academic performance using an age-appropriate checklist of indicators
Survey	Collects student feedback about their interests, prior knowledge, or motivation about a topic	Student completes a commercially or teacher-produced survey of items

Source: Adapted from Fisher, D., & Frey, N. (2004). *Improving adolescent literacy: Strategies at work.* Upper Saddle River, NJ: Merrill/Prentice Hall.

be seen at all times. Anytime we jot a note on a Post-It about a student, we can place it on their card for later organization and filing. See Figure 11.4 for a diagram of this organizational system.

While the act of reflective teaching is defined by a recursive cycle of teaching, observing, and reflecting, it is not realistic to think that any teacher could (or would even want to) record every observation. However, a simple observation form like the one in compendium 1 can assist a busy teacher in documenting meaningful observation data.

Portfolios. The term **portfolio** in language arts is used to describe a collection of student work that represents progress made over time (Tierney, Clark, Wiser, Simpson, Herter, & Fenner, 1998). Like an artist's portfolio, they are constructed by the learner in partnership with the teacher. Students are often invited to select a range of work, not just the most exemplary pieces, in order to represent their learning. The assembled portfolio is then used as a conference tool between parent, teacher, and student.

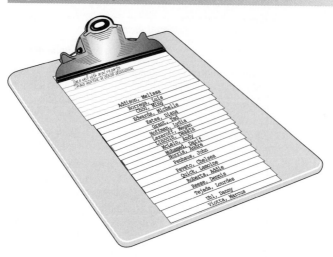

Figure 11.4   Clipboard for Classroom Observations

Wilcox (1997, p. 35) suggests that a portfolio of student work be organized around the following topics:

Review chapter 4 for discussion of these practices.

- *Reading artifacts* like reading journals, book reviews and literature circle journals.
- *Thinking artifacts* that demonstrate the learner's process of understanding. Examples include notes, concept maps, and self-assessments.
- *Writing artifacts* like finished pieces and works in progress.

Review chapter 4 for more on these artifacts.

- *Interacting artifacts* that reflect work accomplished with peers. These might include peer conferences and dialogue journals.

Review chapter 6 for information about oral language development

- *Demonstrating artifacts* that represent public performance by the student, including oral reports, demonstrations, and author's chair.

Inventories. An inventory of a store lists the items contained within the store. Likewise, language arts inventories are lists of observable behaviors that can be easily identified and recorded by the teacher. These inventories most often come in the form of a checklist for easy transcription. An inventory can be commercially prepared, or may be constructed by the teacher. A checklist of observable behaviors is especially useful when meeting with parents to discuss their child's progress. An example of an inventory for young readers can be found in compendium 2.

Rubrics. Students often have difficulty predicting precisely what the teacher wants to see in an assignment or project. This is due in part to the difficulty teachers sometimes have in defining what they want. **Rubrics** are designed to clear up such confusion. These scoring guides are distributed and discussed in advance so that students are clear on what is expected. Rubrics are usually designed by the teacher, although many design rubrics with the class in order to prompt discussion about the characteristics of a good performance. An all-purpose rubric suitable for development with students appears in compendium 3.

A helpful website for developing and storing your rubrics can be found at http://www.rubistar.4teachers.org.

Conferences. As you read in chapter 5, teachers in the language arts workshop meet individually with students during the independent phase of instruction to discuss literacy learning. These **conferences** are valuable because they are an opportunity to collect informal assessment information about a student. The information gathered during a conference on a child's reading and writing provides authentic assessment data for use in planning future instruction.

Self-assessments. As we have discussed on several occasions throughout this book, the ability to **self-assess** is an essential skill for developing metacognitive awareness. You will recall that metacognitive awareness is the ability of a learner to describe how he or she best learns. In addition, it refers to a learner's ability to develop a plan for learning, then monitor and evaluate that plan (Kujawa & Huske, 1995). For example, a student of ours wrote, "I just wanted to let you know some of the skills I would like to work on. One of them is 'inference' or 'reading between the lines.' For example, I am very bad at answering questions in someone else's shoes such as 'What would this author say. . .', or 'Why was this piece written'." One of the ways students develop metacognitive awareness is through the use of self-assessments. An example of a self-assessment for intermediate and middle grade students in collaborative groups appears in compendium 4.

Surveys. Assessment tools such as **surveys** can be an efficient way for a teacher to collect information about a large number of students in a short period of time. Surveys can be constructed on any topic and can measure student background knowledge or interest. Information collected from surveys can then be compiled to make instructional decisions. A reading survey for the beginning of the school year can be found in compendium 5.

An effective teacher in the language arts workshop uses a variety of assessments, including observations, portfolios of student work, inventories, rubrics, conferences, and self-assessments to monitor the progress of students and plan future instruction. Using a variety of assessment instruments, both formal and informal, provides the student with opportunities to more fully demonstrate his or her strengths in reading and writing and reveal areas of continued need. As with instruction, assessment should also be learner-centered.

ASSESSING READING IN THE LANGUAGE ARTS WORKSHOP

Reading assessment is essential in the language arts workshop because it provides the teacher with information needed to plan instruction and reflect on the effectiveness of a lesson or unit of instruction. Like instruction, reading assessments are utilized with a developmental model of literacy in mind.

Assessing Emergent and Early Readers

Teachers of emergent and early readers use a cadre of assessments that profile a child's growing sense of sounds, letters, words, and stories. As you have seen in previous chapters, these early literacy skills should not be viewed as a linear progression but rather as braided strands forming an increasingly stronger cord of language (Rumelhart, 1994). Therefore, even the most emergent reader is assessed in many aspects of literacy learning. These aspects of learning all contribute to reading comprehension, the ability to understand what is read.

Reading comprehension is divided into two important parts: language comprehension and decoding. If a child has difficulty with either language comprehension (understanding spoken language) or decoding (transforming written words into language), they will have difficulty reading.

Language comprehension. The ability to process the spoken language is key to early reading development. Closely related to language comprehension are these skills:

- *Background knowledge*—the amount of information a child has about a topic, usually gained through experience and exposure
- *Linguistic knowledge*—an understanding of the rules that govern language; these fundamentals of linguistics are called:
  - ◊ *Phonology*—the ability to discern the phonemes (individual units of sound) in a language. The English language has 46 phonemes; other languages differ (Salus & Flood, 2002)
  - ◊ *Syntax*—the grammatical rules of the language
  - ◊ *Semantics*—the meaning of the words and concepts represented

Decoding. Decoding is the ability to translate the squiggly black shapes on the page (for this is what print looks like to young children) to letters and combinations of letters representing sounds. Like language comprehension, there are a number of elements of knowledge that must consolidate in order for a reader to successfully decode. These are called:

> Spelling is the opposite of decoding and is called encoding.

- *Cipher knowledge*—the relationship between how the word sounds and how it is spelled in phonetically regular words like *cat* and *book*
- *Lexical knowledge*—the ability to decode phonetically irregular words like *laugh* and *write*. Both cipher and lexical knowledge are in turn influenced by four sets of skills:
  - ◊ *Letter knowledge*—recognition of the shapes and names of each of the 26 letters in the English language
  - ◊ *Alphabetic principle*—understanding that letters and combinations of letters in words are associated with the sounds (phonemes) of spoken language
  - ◊ *Phonemic awareness*—the ability to manipulate the sounds of the language; rhyming is one type of phoneme awareness
  - ◊ *Concepts about print*—understanding the way print works on the page (for example, knowing that the words are read from left to right is one element of concepts about print)

> A database of K–2 reading assessments can be found at http://www.sedl.org/reading/rad.

These fundamental emergent and early reading skills are necessary for students to master and therefore become the focus of assessment in the language arts workshop. The first category, language comprehension, is assessed using inventories that invite students to demonstrate their knowledge of phonemes and use language to explain stories.

Language Comprehension Assessments

A large portion of instructional time for emergent and early readers is devoted to language comprehension—fostering each child's ability to process and produce spoken language in order to develop fundamental reading comprehension skills.

Yopp-Singer Test of Phoneme Segmentation. The Yopp-Singer test (Yopp, 1995) is a 22-item assessment of a child's ability to repeat the phonemes of one-syllable words. This assessment is administered individually and takes no more than 10 minutes to complete. Phonemic awareness is considered to be a predictor of later reading success (Nation & Hulme, 1997). A copy of the test and administration directions can be found in compendium 6.

Retellings. The purpose of assessing language comprehension is to determine whether a child can process language when the burden of reading a text is removed. One of the easiest ways to do this is to read a short book to a student then invite them to retell the story. A narrative story retelling rubric can be found in compendium 7 and one for informational texts can be found in compendium 8. As students begin to read, they can also retell the story based on their reading comprehension.

Did he or she understand the story? What about characters and setting? Prompting students to retell the story they have just listened to can provide insight into how much the reader understands the text. To assess a story retelling, make notes about the level of detail and breadth of knowledge about the key parts of the story. The retelling can include prompts or questions to promote further detail.

It should be noted that retelling should be used cautiously. Retelling can devolve into a test of memory rather than understanding; for this reason we usually encourage students to return to the text to support their retelling. As well, successful retellings should not be seen as the ultimate measure of comprehension. As teachers, we want readers to respond on a personal level to the book. This means that they formulate opinions, make connections to themselves and the world, and analyze the text. Rather, retellings should be viewed as a basic measure of a student's understanding of the text.

Decoding Assessments

Just as children need to be able to understand sounds and meaning of the spoken language around them, they also need to accurately and efficiently process the printed word. This decoding processing is an essential component for reading. As described earlier, decoding is made up of several dimensions, including letter and alphabetic knowledge, and an understanding of how print works. There are several useful tools that collectively assess these aspects of decoding.

Letter identification. One of the most basic skills needed for decoding is the ability to recognize both lowercase and uppercase letters. This assessment is typically administered individually to students who look at a student form (compendium 9) and identify the letter or the sound of the letter. A recording sheet to accompany the assessment is in compendium 10. It should be noted that this assessment may be administered in more than one sitting.

Sight words. There are many words we want young readers to decode using their knowledge of alphabetic principles; other words are more efficiently learned using recognition skills. Called sight words, these represent some of the most frequently used words in the English language and are taught from Kindergarten to third grade. Edward Dolch identified a list of 220 of the most commonly used words, now called the Dolch sight word list (Dolch, 1948). Some of these words are irregular in letter-sound correspondence and are therefore more easily learned by sight (*the, one*).

Others are phonetically regular but so frequently used that they can be processed more quickly when learned through sight recognition (*I, a, for*). These five lists appear in compendiums 11–15.

Phonics. Phonics is the term used to describe the relationship between sounds and symbols (letters). It differs from phonemic awareness, which only focuses on the ability to distinguish sounds. These sound-symbol relationships are essential for students to effectively and efficiently decode. The first step is letter identification and the next is the ability to chunk clusters of letters together to read more fluently. In the primary grades, rimes are taught to assist students in rapidly expanding their knowledge of many words. A rime is the cluster of letters in a one-syllable word following the beginning consonant or consonants, called the onset. A rime always begins with a vowel. For example, in the word *sink*, /s/ is the onset and /ink/ is the rime. Some additional examples can be found in Figure 11.5.

These rimes are an efficient way to teach a large bank of words to young readers. Wylie and Durrell (1970) estimated that the 37 most common rimes could be used to make more than 500 words. Because these rimes can form clusters of words, they are sometimes called word families. A list of these word families appears in compendium 16.

Rimes are one aspect of phonics knowledge that can be assessed in the language arts workshop. There are a variety of other phonics assessments that are too extensive for this book. We recommend using a phonics battery to assess students; for instance, the CORE Phonics Survey (CORE, 1999). This collection of assessment instruments was initially compiled for California schools and is widely available from districts across the state. It has since been published for the national market.

Concepts about print. As young readers master the alphabetic code, they also learn how print works on the page. In particular, they learn that books have an expected format that includes a front and back cover and a title with the author's name. They learn about book handling skills like turning pages and orienting the book so that the print is not upside down. These students also discover that print must be read from left to right across the page, progressing line by line from top to bottom. This collection of skills is called concepts about print (Clay, 1979). Mastery of concepts about print represent important benchmarks in a child's reading development. A checklist of concepts about print appears in compendium 17.

Figure 11.5 Samples of Onsets and Rimes

Word	Onset	Rime
pan	p-	-an
rake	r-	-ake
stick	st-	-ick
string	str-	-ing

Assessing Reading of Meaningful Text

These strategies, collectively called the cueing system, are discussed in chapter 3 on guided reading.

Many of the assessments discussed in the previous section on assessing decoding are designed to record progress at the letter or word level. However, it is equally important that we assess even the youngest readers as they read meaningful text—books, stories, and poems. Remember that as with instruction, these assessments should not be viewed as a hierarchy. In the language arts workshop, emergent and early readers are taught language comprehension, decoding, and reading comprehension strategies from the beginning. Therefore, these aspects of literacy development are assessed from the start of school. By creating a permanent record of a child's oral reading, we can analyze their growing understanding of the phonological, syntactic, semantic and pragmatic strategies they are using to comprehend text.

Evidence Based

Running record. A simple means for transcribing these oral reading behaviors is through the use of a running record (Clay, 1979). This recording system was influenced by the research on miscue analysis (Goodman & Burke, 1972). The purpose for collecting running records of oral reading behavior is to make instructional decisions regarding the level of text used by the teacher and student. In addition, analysis gives the teacher insight into the types of strategies that a child is using as he or she reads.

Running records can be viewed as a coded form of notations to describe an emergent or early reader's oral reading performance and are typically used on readings of less than 100 words. They are then analyzed for miscues, or errors a child makes in an attempt to solve the problems posed by the text. In this stance toward literacy, miscues are viewed as a window into the reader's command of problem-solving strategies related to the cueing system (Goodman & Burke, 1972). The types of miscues recorded include:

- *Substitutions*—replacing one word for another; for instance reading "horse" when the print says "house"
- *Omissions*—skipping a word in a sentence
- *Insertions*—adding a word that is not in print to a sentence
- *Appeals*—student asks the teacher for help, either verbally or nonverbally
- *Teacher told*—teacher furnishes word for student. This may or may not be proceeded by an appeal for help
- *Self-correction*—student makes a miscue and then fixes it independently
- *Reruns*—student rereads a word, phrase, or the entire sentence

A consistent coding system is essential for running records to be understood and interpreted later. A coding system based on the word of Clay (1979) and Goodman and Burke (1972) appears in compendium 18. A few basic guidelines make coding running records easy to learn with a little practice.

1. Only the coding is recorded. The title of the text is identified at the top of the running record form so that it can be consulted later if needed. However, the only words of the text that are written are those involved in a miscue.
2. The correct word in the text always appears below the line; the miscue appears above the line.

3. Multiple codes can be used to record an event. For instance, when a reader asks for help (*appeal*) and then is told the correct word (*teacher told*), both miscues are recorded as *ATT*.

4. A running record is intended as a means of noting the performance of a child reading aloud. It can be difficult to capture every nuance of the oral reading. Don't worry—the goal is to get down as much as you can. If you feel you have missed something important, make a note of it in the observation box at the bottom of the running record form.

Teacher Tip

We recommend placing a copy of the coding system inside a clear sheet protector for easy reference while you collect running records. A blank form for recording running records can be viewed in compendium 19.

At a later time, the running record is analyzed and scored in order to make instructional decisions. A scoring sheet for capturing results of an oral reading event can be found in compendium 20. A series of calculations are made after first tallying the total number of words in the book. Next, total miscues are counted and recorded. Note that self-corrections and reruns are not counted as miscues (although an error within a rerun is). The number of self-corrections is also written down because growth in self-corrections is seen as an advance in the reader's use of problem-solving strategies. The number of miscues is subtracted from the total number of words to yield a score. For example, if a child read a book with a total of 34 words in it and made 2 miscues, the score is 32. The score is then divided by the total number of words in order to calculate a percentage. In this example, the student reads at an instructional accuracy rate of 94%, indicating that the text level is suitable for guided reading.

Independent, instructional, and frustration levels of text are discussed at length in chapter 3 on guided reading.

Once calculated, the teacher can then review the results of the running record and make decisions about future instruction. Instructional questions for consideration include:

- Would the student benefit from easier or more difficult text?
- Does the student need more instruction in vocabulary?
- Does the student need more instruction at the letter or word level?
- Does the student need more instruction in the syntax of the language?
- Is the student using early reading strategies, including making predictions, monitoring understanding, and applying problem-solving strategies to decode unknown words?

The assessments profiled thus far represent a broad crosssection of the types of instruments available for teachers of emergent and early readers. As students progress in their literacy development, the types of assessments needed change as well.

Assessing Transitional and Self-Extending Readers

As with primary teachers, educators of older readers require assessment tools that provide a portrait of the student's strengths and areas of need. You will recall from the discussion of developmental phases of reading in chapter 1 that students at the transitional and self-extending levels of reading differed significantly from their younger counterparts. In particular, they possess more background knowledge and prior experience and are more sophisticated in their ability to access this during their reading. These readers also have more stamina for reading and can read longer, more complex passages of text. Because they have read more widely, they can make connections between texts. Some of the tools discussed in the previous section are also useful in grade 3–8 classrooms. For instance, the retelling rubrics are not bound by age or developmental reading level. However, most assessment instruments used in intermediate and middle grade classrooms are designed to focus on the areas of word recognition, comprehension, fluency, and reading attitude.

Assessing Word Recognition

Prefixes and suffixes together are called affixes.

The task of untangling an unfamiliar word to convert it into a meaningful unit of sound is a complex one. As you know from your reading in chapter 8 on vocabulary, readers use their knowledge of letter identification, word families, affixes, and word derivations when they encounter an unknown word. We've discussed assessment of letter identification, sight words, and word families in the previous section. In grades 3–8, it is not uncommon to encounter a student who does not have a strong foundation in early decoding skills. Another means of assessing a student's ability to decode unfamiliar words is to use the Nonword Reading Test (Snowling, Stackhouse, & Rack, 1986). This assessment, which appears in compendium 21, measures a student's ability to apply decoding strategies to nonwords. Student performance on this assessment can alert the teacher to difficulties a student may be experiencing with decoding one- and two-syllable nonwords.

Assessing Reading Comprehension

More information on the regional laboratory for your state can be found at http://www.relnetwork.org.

Reading comprehension is embedded in many of the other aspects of literacy already discussed. A student's knowledge of how letters and words work is woven into the ability to formulate those words into meaningful sentences and paragraphs. All of this is influenced by the reader's background knowledge and experiences. Therefore, assessment of reading comprehension is influenced by a student's command of all these elements of reading.

The Northwest Regional Laboratory (NWREL, 2001) describes six traits of effective readers. NWREL is one of ten federally funded information networks across the nation that serve as clearinghouses for resources and research for teachers, parents, administrators, and policy makers. They describe good readers as being able to use:

- Decoding conventions to read new or unfamiliar words
- Comprehension strategies to determine meaning
- Context to determine setting or time period
- Synthesis of information to make connections
- Interpretations to formulate opinions
- Evaluation to support those opinions

As you know from chapter 10 on comprehension, these traits form the heart of reading comprehension strategies for transitional and self-extending readers. Therefore, the assessments used by teachers of these students focus on these aspects of reading. This is accomplished through informal reading inventories, cloze procedures, metacomprehension assessments, attitude surveys, and self-assessments.

Informal reading inventory. One of the most popular ways of assessing reading comprehension of transitional and self-extending readers is through the use of a criterion-referenced assessment called an **informal reading inventory,** or IRI. An informal reading inventory uses a series of graded level passages to measure a student's

Figure 11.6   Informal Reading Inventories

IRI	Grades	Special Features
Basic Reading Inventory (Johns)	K–8	Graded word lists CD-ROM for administration guidance
Burns/Roe Informal Reading Inventory (Burns & Roe)	K–12	Graded word lists Silent and oral reading measures Expository and narrative passages
Classroom Assessment of Reading Processes (Swearingen & Allen)	1–6	Expository and narrative passages
Critical Reading Inventory (Applegate, Quinn, & Applegate)	K–12	Evaluates critical literacy skills Expository and narrative passages Includes case study examples
Flynt-Cooter Reading Inventory for the Classroom (Flynt, Cooter, & Flynt)	K–12	Uses sentences for passage selection Expository and narrative passages
Qualitative Reading Inventory (Leslie & Caldwell)	K–8	Questions for prior knowledge Graded word lists Expository and narrative passages
Stieglitz Informal Reading Inventory (Stieglitz)	K–6	Graded word lists Writing assessments Phonemic awareness assessments Expository and narrative passages

accuracy, as well as their ability to answer literal and inferential questions after the reading is completed. The most popular ones are commercially prepared narrative and expository passages of 100–150 words. The student first reads the passage silently, then aloud. During the oral reading, miscues are coded using a system similar to the one used with running records. However, the words of the passage are already provided on the form so that only coding of miscues is necessary. Questions after the reading probe the reader's understanding of the text. Each IRI comes with an extensive set of directions for administering and scoring the reading. Figure 11.6 features a list of some of the most widely available IRIs in schools. Two others, the Developmental Reading Assessment (Beavers, 1997) and the Analytic Reading Inventory (Woods & Moe, 1999) are further discussed in the section on criterion-referenced tests.

Cloze procedure. The cloze procedure is an assessment used to gauge a reader's comprehension by omitting every fifth word from a passage. The reader fills in the missing words using context clues and syntactic strategies to complete the passage accurately. The words the student supplies must match exactly to be considered accurate. Although some will argue that synonyms should be counted as an accurate response, research on this scoring procedure has found that too many variables are introduced when synonyms are allowed (Henk & Selders, 1984).

Synonyms are words that are similar in both meaning and syntax.

A cloze passage and assessment can be easily prepared by a teacher. Simply type in a grade level passage using word processing software, then highlight and delete every fifth word in the passage. Be sure to paste the deleted words onto another document to create an answer sheet. Ideally, a cloze passage should contain 250 words, leaving 50 omitted words for the student to supply. The first and last sentence of the cloze passage are left intact to support the reader's comprehension. The number of correct responses are counted and multiplied by two to yield a percentage rate. The completed cloze is scored as follows:

- 57–100% accuracy: independent level of reading
- 44–56% accuracy: instructional level of reading
- 43% or below: frustration level of reading

A teacher-constructed cloze passage for use in an eighth-grade classroom has been adapted from *The Head Bone's Connected to the Neck Bone: The Weird, Wacky, and Wonderful X-Ray* (McClafferty, 2001). The passage and answer sheet appear in compendiums 22 and 23.

Metacomprehension Strategies Index. Another measure of reading comprehension is the Metacomprehension Strategies Index, a 25-item questionnaire that asks students about their use of comprehension strategies during the reading (Schmitt, 1990). This strategy can be administered either individually to students in an interview format, or to the entire group as an independent task. Many teachers like to preview this assessment by first telling students about the purpose (to find out about the way they use strategies in their reading), then giving them a short independent reading. Students are invited to pay attention to how they read and understand. After the reading, they complete the MSI. Compendium 24 features the entire MSI.

Scoring of the MSI is straightforward, with an answer key and categorization chart included in compendium 25. Responses are regrouped into six categories:

- *Predicting and verifying*—good readers make predictions about a reading, then check and adjust their predictions as they read
- *Previewing*—good readers scan the text to foster predictions
- *Purpose setting*—good readers understand the purpose for reading (gain knowledge, etc.)
- *Self-questioning*—good readers generate questions as they read and search for answers to these questions
- *Drawing from background knowledge*—good readers use prior experiences and knowledge to understand the text
- *Summarizing and applying fix-up strategies*—good readers summarize as they read and know what to do when they are having difficulty understanding what they are reading

Assessing Reading Attitude

Motivation and interest in reading play an important part in reading acquisition. After all, if a reader is not interested in reading, this is likely to inhibit their exposure to texts and thereby limit time spent practicing the strategies needed to comprehend text. A decline in attitudes toward reading occurs throughout the elementary years,

Evidence Based

precisely at the time when reading as a vehicle for learning content begins to rise (Kush & Watkins, 1996). The impact of negative reading attitude persists into adulthood, where those who perceive reading negatively continue to engage in less reading than their peers who enjoy reading (Smith, 1990).

Elementary Reading Attitude Survey. A useful instrument for assessing attitude toward reading is the Elementary Reading Attitude Survey (McKenna & Kear, 1990). This 20-item survey for students in grades 1–6 can be administered to the entire group or conducted as an interview with individual students. The original survey used four "Garfield" cartoon figures of the cat exhibiting expressions that range from very happy to quite displeased. Students circle the appropriate character in response to questions like "How do you feel about reading for fun at home?" and "How do you feel about reading your school books?" Scoring is completed for two aspects—recreational and academic—and a table of normed results collected on over 18,000 students across the country can measure individual scores against expected ones. A copy of the survey and scoring sheet with new graphics appears in compendium 26.

Motivation to Read Profile. Older students may not find the cartoon figures used on the Elementary Reading Attitude Survey to be appropriate or interesting. The Motivation to Read Profile (MRP) serves as a useful alternative (Gambrell, Palmer, Codling, & Mazzoni, 1996, p. 521). Designed for students in grades 2–6, this assessment consists of two parts—a survey of 20 items on self-concept and perceived value of reading, and a follow-up conversational interview on motivation. A question from the survey appears below:

11. I worry about what other kids think about my reading
- ☐ every day
- ☐ almost every day
- ☐ once in a while
- ☐ never

The authors suggest using the conversational interview after the survey has been scored so that the teacher can tailor the discussion. This interview can also be used as a conferencing tool to promote further dialogue about the student's perceptions about reading. Questions from the interview portion include "What do you think you have to learn to be a better reader?" and "What are some things that get you really excited about reading books?" (p. 524).

Self-Assessment in Reading

Closely related to reading attitude and motivation is the concept of self-assessment. We spoke extensively in chapter 1 about the role of metacognition in student learning. While strategies for students to learn how to support their own understanding of the text are explicitly taught in the language arts workshop, this is not the same as knowing it has been learned. Self-assessments can assist students in becoming more aware of how they solve problems during reading.

Using a self-assessment tool can draw the learner's attention to these aspects of reading. NWREL has developed a simple self-assessment for students in grades 3–12 using the six traits of effective readers discussed at the beginning of this section. Like the Elementary Reading Attitude Survey, it uses a range of "smiley face" graphics to represent student responses. This self-assessment appears in compendium 27.

Informal reading assessments form the basis for instructional decisions in the language arts workshop. However, norm-referenced standardized assessments also provide important information to teachers and schools. Their use by educators as a way to make curricular decisions to provide effective instruction is increasing.

Norm-Referenced Standardized Reading Assessments

While these are used less frequently in the language arts classroom, they are an important part of the repertoire of assessments. Many schools and districts use standardized reading assessments as part of their accountability plans and interpretation of the results can be useful in planning. Detailed directions for administration and interpretation can be found in the test administrator's manual that accompanies the tests.

Gates-MacGinitie Reading Test (MacGinitie, MacGinitie, Maria, & Dreyer, 2000). This group-administered test measures students' performance on a range of subskills for reading, including vocabulary, reading comprehension, and sentence context. A version for younger readers tests concepts about print, phonemic awareness, and letter knowledge. The assessment is useful for teachers to determine the range of readers in their class as well as progress made during the school year.

Stanford Diagnostic Reading Test (Karlsen & Gardner, 1995). This group-administered test has forms available for students in first grade and above and measures phonics, reading and listening vocabulary, and reading comprehension. Again, this assessment provides teachers with information about the range of readers in their classroom and is useful in forming guided reading groups, for example.

Criterion-Referenced Standardized Reading Assessments

In addition to norm-referenced tests, schools frequently use criterion-referenced assessments to make programmatic and instructional decisions. All of these criterion-referenced assessments yield information about an individual's performance compared to expected grade or developmental level competencies.

Observation Survey of Early Literacy Achievement (Clay, 2002). This extensive individually administered series of six assessments for K–3 students has heavily influenced early literacy assessment approaches. Indeed, several of the informal assessments discussed earlier in this chapter originated with the work of Clay on the *OS*. The six subtests are:

- *Text reading.* A coded notation system for recording and analyzing a child's oral reading behavior. This is similar, though more extensive at the level of analysis, to the running record discussed earlier.
- *Concepts about print.* Assesses a child's book handling skills and understanding of print conventions.
- *Letter identification.* Measures a child's knowledge of the names and sounds of the uppercase and lowercase alphabet.
- *Ohio word test.* Three lists of 20 words are available to assess a student's knowledge of sight words and other common one-syllable words.

- *Writing vocabulary.* The child is invited to write all the words they know for up to 10 minutes.

- *Hearing and recording sounds in words.* A sentence is dictated to the child, who writes each word to the best of their ability. Scoring occurs by counting the number of sounds recorded.

Each of these six subtests is administered and analyzed both within and across subtests. Detailed information about a child's performance can be gained in areas of strength and need. It should be noted that while several of these assessments may appear similar to informal assessments in this chapter, the information yielded through administration and analysis of the *Observation Survey* is far more extensive. For this reason, the *OS* is a popular choice among primary teachers for use with struggling readers. It is also the assessment of choice for Reading Recovery teachers, who are specially trained to provide intensive support to struggling first-grade readers.

We have placed the *Observation Survey* in the list of criterion-referenced assessments because it yields information about a child's literacy development in comparison to expected levels. However, it can also be seen as a norm-referenced instrument for first graders because of the tables that rank performance according to stanines.

> You can obtain more information about the Reading Recovery Council of North America at http://www.readingrecovery.org.

> Stanines are a way of reporting standardized test scores to reflect a range of scores from 1 to 9.

Developmental Reading Assessment (Beavers, 1997). This assessment uses graded level reading passages to evaluate students' use of semantic, syntactic, and phonological systems to decode connected text. It is individually administered by a teacher who introduces a benchmark book following a scripted prompt. The child reads aloud and the teacher completes a coded record of the oral reading behavior using codes similar to the ones used on running records. A rubric for story retelling is completed after the child has finished reading.

Analytic Reading Inventory (Woods & Moe, 1999). This individually administered test is appropriate for grades 4 and up and is used to describe three reading elements: listening comprehension, oral reading and silent reading. Like the DRA, it is administered using benchmark reading passages.

Critical Reading Inventory (Applegate, Quinn, & Applegate, 2004). The CRI represents a new generation of criterion-referenced informal reading inventories because of its emphasis on the critical literacy skills of the reader to make connections, analyze, and evaluate.

WRITING ASSESSMENTS IN THE LANGUAGE ARTS WORKSHOP

Like the reading assessments used daily by classroom teachers, writing assessments in the language arts workshop are given in order to make instructional decisions about individual learners. These decisions may include grouping, introduction of new skills, reteaching, or demonstrating mastery.

Effective writing assessment requires examination of multiple aspects of writing. Some assessments target particular subskills of writing like spelling and fluency. Other assessments look at the overall quality of the writing using a holistic rubric to articulate how well the student is progressing in becoming a more competent writer.

In this section, we will look at useful tools for assessing spelling and fluency then examine holistic scoring of writing. Finally, we will return to the notion of attitude and motivation in writing.

Assessing Spelling

Expressive language includes writing and speaking; receptive language includes listening, reading, and viewing.

See chapter 7 for more information on spelling instruction.

Interactive writing is discussed in detail in chapter 2.

We've spoken at length about the role of decoding in early literacy development. At the same time, children learn how to encode or spell the words they are reading. Remember our discussion in chapter 1 on the differences between expressive and receptive language. Typically, receptive language exceeds expressive language. Therefore, students are likely to be able to read more words than they can write. This does not mean that spelling should be ignored until students are reading—to the contrary, spelling instruction begins in Kindergarten. At the most emergent levels, this takes the form of interactive writing instruction, an instructional practice of collaborative writing between student and teacher.

The perspective on the teaching of spelling has changed considerably as well. Spelling is now seen, like reading and writing, as a developmental process. Therefore, students are assessed and taught developmentally. These developmental stages have been described by Henderson (1990) as follows:

- *Emergent*—uses little or no sound-letter associations
- *Letter name*—spelling by sound
- *Within word pattern*—uses familiar patterns to spell one-syllable words
- *Syllable juncture*—uses syllables, double consonants to arrive at spellings
- *Derivational constancy*—uses word origins to spell new words

The table in Figure 11.7 demonstrates how spelling changes over time as the speller advances through these stages.

It is useful to assess students at the beginning of the year to determine what developmental spelling stage they are currently working in. This can be accomplished

Figure 11.7 Stages of Spelling Development

	EMERGENT *Pre-phonetic*	EMERGENT *Semi-phonetic*	LETTER NAME	WITHIN WORD PATTERN	SYLLABLE JUNCTURE	DERIVATIONAL CONSTANCY
AGES:	1–7	1–7	4–9	6–12	8–12	10+
GRADES:	Pre-K to Mid-1	Pre-K to Mid-1	1–2	2–4	3–8	5–8+
PAN	BƎIGT	N	PAN	PAN	PAN	PAN
STEM	132TB	CM	SAM	STEM	STEM	STEM
BIKE	ERL88I	K	BIK	BIEK	BIKE	BIKE
CHART	ABGE	HT	CRT	CHRAT	CHART	CHART
DOTTED	ƎA23	DD	DIDT	DOTID	DOTED	DOTTED
DRIZZLE	IABTT	Z	JREZL	DRIZUL	DRIZZEL	DRIZZLE
CRITICIZE	BBEGBA	K	CRETSIZ	CRITUSIZE	CRITASIZE	CRITISIZE
MAJORITY	8BGRE	M	MGRT	MUJORTEA	MEJORATY	MEJORITY

Source: Ganske, K. (1999). The developmental spelling analysis: A measure of orthographic knowledge. *Educational Assessment, 6*(1), 41–70. Used with permission.

through the use of the Developmental Spelling Analysis Screening Inventory featured in Compendium 28 (Ganske, 2000). This screening inventory is administered only once to determine a student's developmental spelling level; subsequent assessment is accomplished through the use of other tools of analysis such as those discussed in the chapter on spelling.

Administration and scoring of the screening inventory can be completed quickly. The inventory is divided into four sets of five words. The first set is administered and subsequent sets are used only if the student gets at least two correct answers in a set. When a child gets only one or none of the words correct, the assessment ends. Each correct spelling earns one point and the total number of correct answers is compared to the chart in Compendium 29 to determine the student's developmental spelling level (Ganske, 2000).

Assessing Writing Fluency

Accurate spelling contributes to the overall quality of writing. As well, writers need to write smoothly and quickly in order to compose meaningful text. This aspect of writing is referred to as fluency and it is assessed through timed writing sessions. There are not set benchmarks for writing fluency expectations by grade level, and of course a writer's fluency is impacted by a number of factors, including topic, background knowledge, and motivation. However, timed writing samples should be collected each grading period to track student progress as they become more proficient and fluent writers. This can be easily accomplished by administering a 5-minute timed writing prompt. These writing prompts should be general in nature so that background knowledge does not confound performance. Useful prompts for collected timed writing samples include:

See chapter 9 on fluency for a Power Writing chart to record individual progress.

- Describe a time when you were surprised.
- Tell about a time when you tasted a new food.
- If you could travel to any place in the world, where would it be and why?

Students are encouraged to write as much as they can and as well as they can and to write continuously for the entire period. At the end of 5 minutes, the papers are collected and analyzed to yield three measures of student success. First, the overall number of words are counted. You'll save time if you teach your students how to do this before handing their paper in. All words are counted whether they are spelled correctly or not and numbers, regardless of digits, count as one word. Next, the piece is read and each error in spelling, punctuation, or grammar is underlined, yielding a total number of errors. Finally, the overall number of sentences is counted. Based on these numbers, the average number of errors per sentence, mean sentence length, and total number of words can be recorded (Fearn & Farnan, 2001). This quantitative measure can serve as a way of reporting the overall fluency of each student. A classroom log of writing fluency can be found in compendium 30.

Teacher Tip

Assessing Writing Holistically

In addition to assessing the mechanics of writing related to spelling and fluency, there are also times when we want to evaluate the writing as a whole. This requires that we use an instrument that addresses both the content of the piece and the extent to which the writer conveyed the message with clarity and accuracy (Lapp, Fisher, Flood, & Cabello, 2001). This type of writing evaluation is referred to as a

holistic assessment. The term holistic comes from the study of holism, a theory utilized in biology, anthropology, and physics that the universe can only be correctly viewed as systems of whole organisms, not the sum of its parts. In the same fashion, holistic writing assessments measure the merits of the piece across several indicators. Most commonly, this is accomplished through the use of a rubric. Holistic writing rubrics are not confined to informal classroom assessments; indeed, they are widely used for large-scale state writing assessments at the elementary, middle, and high school levels. Be sure to check your state's Department of Education website to view the holistic writing rubric used. These rubrics can be useful in gauging your students' progress on state accountability measures.

Teacher-constructed writing rubrics. Rubrics are typically constructed by first determining what the key features should be, then writing descriptors across a continuum of achievement from exemplary to inadequate. An example of a teacher-constructed rubric for friendly letters using the Rubistar website can be found in compendium 31.

Rubistar is a web-based rubric generator at www.rubistar.4teachers.org.

Six+1Trait® assessment. Another excellent source for writing rubrics is the Northwest Regional Laboratory's (2001) Six+1Trait writing assessment. This system for evaluating student writing defines seven elements for consideration:

These writing rubrics can be found at http://www.nwrel.org/assessment/.

- *Ideas*—clearly developed, accurate, and interesting
- *Organization*—uses an opening, orders ideas coherently, and ends effectively
- *Voice*—writes with a point of view to a specific audience
- *Word choice*—accurate and engaging language
- *Sentence fluency*—sentence variety, flow, and clarity
- *Conventions*—spelling, punctuation, capitalization, and indenting observed
- *Presentation*—format, handwriting, and neatness

These elements are evaluated across a continuum of performance from one to five. Learning to score writing using the rubrics takes practice, and the website features student papers from every grade level for teachers to develop their assessment skills. This practice allows you to calibrate your evaluations to more fully understand the nuances between ratings for each of the elements. As well, there is a Six-Traits Assessment for beginning writers in grades Kindergarten through second grade available at the same website.

Assessing Writing Attitude and Motivation

Evidence Based

As with reading, the role of attitude and motivation in writing can greatly affect student performance (Spaulding, 1992). Consistent with the research on reading attitudes, student perceptions of writing decline through the elementary and middle school years (Knudson, 1991). Therefore, a primary purpose for assessing attitude toward writing is to make adjustments to writing instructional practice that speak to student engagement.

Writing Attitude Survey. A survey similar to the Elementary Reading Attitude Survey (McKenna & Kear, 1990) is the Writing Attitude Survey (Kear, Coffman, McKenna, &

Ambrosio, 2000). The 54 items on the survey use a cartoon character format for gauging student responses to questions like "How would you feel telling in writing why something happened?" (p. 16), and "How would you feel if your classmates read something you wrote?" (p. 21). Normed tables are available for grades 1–12, thereby giving teachers a comparison against same-aged peers. The Writing Attitude Survey can be found in compendium 32.

Writer Self-Perception Scale. Closely related to the concept of attitude is the way students perceive their level of competency. The Writer Self-Perception Scale was developed to measure a student's beliefs about their competency. This 38-item assessment asks students to respond on a scale of one to five (from strongly agree to strongly disagree) to statements like, "Other kids think I'm a good writer" and "My writing has improved" (Bottomley, Henk, & Melnick, 1997–1998). Scores are reported on several constructs, including their beliefs about their progress, their perceptions of themselves within the social context of the class, and their psychological state. The authors of the WSPS recommend that it be used in fourth-, fifth-, and sixth-grade classrooms.

ORAL LANGUAGE ASSESSMENT IN THE LANGUAGE ARTS WORKSHOP

The role of language in literacy cannot be underestimated. It is how children interact with one another, how they convey information, and how they learn. These components are of particular interest in the language arts workshop because oral language is a primary vehicle for learning. We will begin by examining some tools for gauging discussions and presentations to the class. Then we will turn our attention to assessment of language skills of English language learners.

Review chapter 6 for detailed information about oral language development.

Assessing Discussions

It is impossible to sort out language from learning because the use of language, both written and oral, is integral to learning. As with reading and writing, it is important to capture each student's progress in oral language development in order to plan instruction and report on progress. Student discussions are an ideal time to record and evaluate oral language development.

Speaking checklist. From the time children enter school, they speak in front of others. For young children, this often comes in the form of daily classroom news discussions or sharing time. As children enter elementary school, they participate in impromptu and formal presentations to the class. All of these require speaking skills to make one understood to others. Since students in the language arts workshop speak regularly to the class, this offers an ideal time to assess their speaking skills. A speaking checklist like the one found in compendium 33 offers teachers an easy way to document growth over the course of the school year. This checklist is even more useful when coupled with the self-assessment checklist in compendium 34. Use the speaking checklist and the self-assessment together on the same day. These two completed forms offer an ideal set of tools when conferring with the student.

Teacher Tip

Assessing Presentations

In addition to speaking during discussions and other classroom exchanges, students also offer more formal presentations. In the language arts workshop, this often comes in the form of book talks and author's chair presentations of original writing.

These events provide another opportunity to assess how well the student is progressing in their formal public speaking. The checklist in compendium 35 is one such instrument for capturing these performances.

Assessing English Language Development

Many classrooms in America have students who speak a heritage language other than English. These students are learning both the content of their curriculum as well as the language needed to master that content. Students who are English language learners are using their new language and experimenting with vocabulary, grammar, and social language throughout the day. The routines of language acquisition demand different skills of the speaker. For instance, the requirements of talking with classmates on the playground are very different than delivering a formal report in front of the class. Student comfort in one setting does not automatically mean a similar degree of comfort in another. So how can English language development be assessed?

One of the best ways to assess language development is holistically. That is to say, by observing the student in a variety of daily interactions that require informal social language as well as academic language. Like many other assessments you have already seen in this chapter, a rubric is a useful tool for this type of assessment. One such assessment, the Student Oral Language Observation Matrix (SOLOM), is widely used in classrooms and districts throughout the country.

Student Oral Language Observation Matrix. The SOLOM was developed for the California Department of Education as a means for articulating the progress of the state's English language learners. The administration of the SOLOM allows a teacher to observe the interaction between oral language proficiency termed Basic Interpersonal Communication Skills (BICS) and the Cognitive Academic Language Skills (CALP) required for proficiency in reading and writing (Cummins & Swain, 1986). This type of analysis informs teachers about how students' strengths and weaknesses in oral English interact in the four skills of language arts: listening, speaking, reading and writing. The SOLOM is designed to assess authentic oral language used for real, day-to-day classroom purposes and activities. In addition, language assessment allows a teacher to closely observe students' development of different features of language proficiency in a holistic fashion. This information is useful in planning appropriate instruction for second language readers and writers. A copy of the SOLOM appears in compendium 36.

Administering the SOLOM. To obtain an accurate measure, you should observe the student in several different authentic classroom activities in which he or she is interacting with classmates, such as cooperative group tasks. Each observation should last for a minimum of 5 minutes. On each occasion, mark the rankings on the matrix according to your impressions of the child's use of English.

You may wish to audio record one or more of your sessions to review and confirm your impressions or to look for certain patterns of errors or usage. Rate the child's language use on a scale from 1 to 5 on each of these traits: comprehension, fluency, vocabulary, pronunciation, and grammar. Cross-check your ratings from the different contexts in which you observed the child for consistencies or variations that may indicate different levels of proficiency according to language function or purpose.

Scoring the SOLOM. The SOLOM yields ratings for four phases of English language proficiency.

- Phase 1 = 5–11
- Phase 2 = 12–18
- Phase 3 = 19–24
- Phase 4 = 25 (English proficiency)

Questions to consider when planning instruction. One of the primary purposes of the SOLOM is to plan future instruction based on assessment results. Questions to inform planning include:

- Did the child's level of overall fluency allow him/her to participate fully in academic activities or was his or her participation impaired?
- Did you note a marked difference between the child's performance in social settings within the classroom versus his or her performance on academic tasks?
- Was the child's command of vocabulary adequate for him or her to gain "comprehensible input" from academic instruction?
- Did the child's pronunciation and/or grammar usage impede others' abilities to comprehend the child? If so, did this occur occasionally or frequently?
- What modifications in instruction and/or interpersonal communications did you observe for this child? Would you recommend different or additional accommodations based on this analysis?

Not surprisingly, all of these reading, writing, and oral language assessments can add up to an enormous amount of paper. Even more frustrating, if not organized properly the assessments collected by a teacher may go unused because they cannot be located. Therefore, organization of materials is as important as the assessment protocols you use.

Organizing Assessment Materials

Organization of assessment items really involves two aspects: the materials you need to conduct the assessments, and where to store the assessments once they have been given and analyzed.

Assembling materials for assessments. Each assessment requires its own unique materials, so be sure to read the directions completely before you administer the assessment. When first using an unfamiliar assessment, consider practicing with a more skilled reader or writer and save assessing students who are struggling until after you've gotten some practice. You may want to store assessment materials in one location so you'll be able to find items immediately. We suggest that you pack a medium-sized plastic storage tub with handles and lid with the following items:

- Clipboard for writing notes
- Post-it notes
- Extra pens and pencils
- Blank paper, lined and unlined
- An expanding file envelope with blank copies of assessments

Be sure to save a master copy of each assessment you use in a file cabinet. It can be frustrating to discover you have consumed the last copy of your favorite assessment!

Storing student assessments. Once an assessment has been completed and analyzed, the challenge is how to store them for future use. While these can be filed a number of different ways, including in a file cabinet or in a binder, we advise using a plastic crate with hanging files in them. Label each hanging file in alphabetical order by student, then place manila files in each one. We use a filing system that reflects the aspects of literacy we are teaching, so we keep a folder for each K–2 student using the following categories:

- Phonological Awareness
- Phonics
- Oral reading
- Fluency
- Vocabulary
- Comprehension
- Writing

Teachers of older students will find other organization systems more useful. Students in grades 3–8 are likely to have assessment information collected by their teachers in these categories:

- Fluency
- Comprehension
- Vocabulary
- Writing
- Motivation and attitude

Of course, every teacher customizes his or her filing system to fit the needs of the classroom. What's really important is that there is a system in place to organize materials and store collected assessment data.

ANALYZING ASSESSMENTS IN THE LANGUAGE ARTS WORKSHOP

This entire chapter has focused on the many kinds of assessment instruments available to classroom teachers to plan instruction, monitor growth, and evaluate learning. However, as we stated at the beginning, no one assessment is ideal for every situation. As the teacher, you will need to determine what kinds of information you need about your students, which instruments can give you the information you are seeking, and what kind of time you have available to administer and analyze. Therefore, we believe that the assessments themselves need to be analyzed to see which best fit your purposes. Every time you consider a new assessment, we encourage you to ask yourself these questions:

- *What does this assessment really measure?* Don't be fooled by the title of the assessment. Look closely at the task demands to make sure that other skills like reading, writing, or language ability don't confound results.

- *What will the results tell me? What will the results not tell me?* Make sure that the information yielded by an assessment is necessary and is not duplicated by another. Also, be clear about what other assessments might be needed to give a more complete picture of a learner.

- *What expenditure of my time and effort will be required to administer and analyze the assessment?* The time you have available is finite. Some assessments are time-consuming to administer but yield rich results that make them worthwhile. Others are quick but may deliver little in the way of useable information. Plan your assessment calendar like you do your curricular one to ensure you are using your time (and your students') wisely.

- *How can this assessment figure into my grading and reporting?* Not every assessment is suitable for grading but many are useful for reporting purposes. Consider how the assessments you use can also be helpful in parent conferences and student conferences.

- *How does this help my instruction?* There's a proverb from New Zealand that says, "You don't fatten sheep by weighing them." We are concerned about the increase in the amount of testing that is occurring in schools in the name of accountability. Instructional time is increasingly being whittled away in order to do more testing. This chapter has focused on classroom assessments that translate to instructional decisions. When chosen wisely and analyzed with care, these assessments ultimately save instructional time by allowing the teacher to be more precise in choosing what to teach, what to reteach, and when the student can move on to new content.

Having said that, it is useful to examine the ways in which teachers can and do use assessment information to guide their instruction. We will now turn our focus to the use of assessments in a Kindergarten and fourth-grade classroom.

Case Study #1: Using Assessments to Inform Instruction in Kindergarten

Craig Wilsie, a Kindergarten teacher who was concerned about one of his students, used a variety of assessments to plan his instruction. Over the first few months of the school year, Mr. Wilsie collected a variety of assessments and continually revised his instruction. Let's review what Mr. Wilsie knew about this student and what he did about it. This case study is relayed from Mr. Wilsie's point of view and perspective based on all that he learned.

Luis Mario is a young kindergartener, having just turned 5 years old on November 9, 2002. He is a very slight boy. The first couple of weeks he needed help getting his belt on or off when using the restroom. He walked very slowly in line; if there was a gap in line, more often than not it was Luis Mario. When he speaks, it is very softly with the sound of little bits of extra air escaping from the corners of his mouth. His mother noted that he started pre-school the previous year, but was removed because he refused to participate or even speak. His mother reported, "He would actually turn his entire body away from the teacher and ignore her." Accordingly, I took extra steps to make sure he was involved and connected to the class. He is intermittently interested in what's going on in class, but still somewhat daydreamy.

The initial assessment revealed that Luis Mario could identify three capital letters, no lowercase letters, and that he could write three out of the four letters in his first name. Curiously enough, he didn't recognize two letters he was able to write. This seemingly is a trend in Luis Mario's learning. He has pockets of knowledge, but not necessarily all connected. For example, he has one-to-one correspondence, but doesn't recognize that letters make words.

Luis Mario seemed overly concerned about my whereabouts when I was absent and the class had a sub. Over the first couple of months, I also learned that I can be a distraction for him as well. When his guided reading group worked with me, often he would lose his concentration. The pages he would be unable to get through with me at the table, he would zoom through after the lesson.

The CORE assessment tools and my observations were most helpful as I determined instruction goals for Luis Mario. During the first few guided reading sessions, it is most apparent what strengths and needs Luis Mario has. Originally based on his assessment data, Luis Mario was in a reading group that consisted of several students who struggled with Kindergarten literacy concepts. Even though he demonstrated one-to-one correspondence and left to right orientation, he was in this group primarily because he had very little letter-sound identification and correspondence. He soon mastered this and moved to other groups.

Assessments. A number of assessments have guided the instructional plans for Luis Mario over the year, including a teacher-created intake survey, the CORE assessment, and the Yopp-Singer Test of Phonemic Segmentation. From the "first week of school" assessment that focused on letter knowledge and letter-sound correspondence, Luis Mario had very poor letter-sound identification. After about a month's worth of reciting the alphabet daily, as well as focusing on a single letter weekly, and doing a variety of seatwork involving classmate's names, Luis Mario was assessed with the CORE assessment. By that time, he had developed these skills and was ready for more advanced instruction.

The Yopp-Singer proved to be too difficult for Luis Mario in September and he scored zero. He was able to get a few beginning letter sounds but seemed confused by the task. He was unable to stretch out the letter sounds of any of the words. Stretching out all the sounds was difficult for Luis Mario, which clearly was an area that would require focused instruction.

On the Concepts about Print from the *Observation Survey* (Clay, 2002) and the Show Me Book (combination reading and writing assessment), Luis Mario demonstrated good book handling skills, one-to-one correspondence, left to right and return sweep. However, he could not distinguish between one letter and two, or between letters and words.

See chapter 2.

See chapter 3 for more information.

See chapter 5 for more information.

Based on the assessment data and my many observations of him during writing activities, I decided that I should focus on letter-sound identification and writing with Luis Mario. I knew that his writing needs would be addressed during the class focus lessons using interactive writing. I also decided that I would focus on letter-sound identification during small group reading instruction. A sample lesson for one of the guided reading sessions follows. As a follow-up, I created a lesson using an alphabet book. This lesson was part of the individualized time I have with students during independent reading and writing. The alphabet book lesson plan (individual) follows the letter lesson plan (small group) below.

Spotlight on Instruction

Letter Lesson Plan Based on Assessment Information

Learning Objectives:
Students will use their knowledge of the letters in their names to practice the individual sounds of those letters, to reinforce their understanding of lowercase and capital letters and to further develop their understanding that letters make up words.

Content Standards:

Concepts About Print

1.5   Distinguish letters from words.

1.6   Recognize and name all uppercase and lowercase letters in the alphabet.

Decoding and Word Recognition

1.14   Match all consonant and short-vowel sounds to appropriate letters.

Anticipatory Set
Teacher will use alphabet flash cards to quiz students and get them thinking about the sounds that letters make. The students who answer correctly will be handed the card and be asked to point out a lowercase or capital letter.

Instruction
Worksheets with each student's name on it will be distributed. Pointing out each student's name, the teacher will explain that each name is made up of letters and that the letters in our names make different sounds. Using photos of each student, the teacher will ask each student what letter their name starts with. Then each student will be asked what sound the letter makes. Students will be directed to paste the photo under the first letter of their name. The teacher will explain that they will be matching cutout letters with the letters in their name and then pasting them underneath. The teacher will model this using his name—WILSIE. Students will be asked which letters they need for their name (i.e., "Who needs the letter A").

Guided / Independent Practice
Students will paste letters corresponding to the letters in their names. Teacher will guide their work and provide feedback accordingly.

Assessment & Closure
Teacher will invite students to read each letter in their name, followed by the sound each letter makes. Each student will write his or her name underneath the pasted cutouts.

Spotlight on Instruction

Alphabet Book Lesson Plan Based on Assessment Information

Learning Objectives:
Mario will use his knowledge of an object in a picture to practice the individual sounds of the beginning letters and to reinforce his understanding of lowercase and capital letters.

Content Standards:

Concepts About Print
1.5   Recognize and name all uppercase and lowercase letters in the alphabet.

Decoding and Word Recognition
1.14 Match all consonant and short-vowel sounds to appropriate letters.

Penmanship
1.4   Write uppercase and lowercase letters of the alphabet independently, attending to the form and proper spacing of the letters.

Anticipatory Set
The teacher will use the worksheets with student's names spelled out with alphabet flash cards (created during Letter Lesson). He will have Luis Mario read the names to get him thinking about letter sounds.

Instruction
Five letters will be selected by Luis Mario to concentrate on. The teacher will write the capital letter on index cards and place them in front of Luis Mario. The idea is to have letters that he knows the sounds of, and a couple of letters that he is still learning. Mario is then shown different pictures to identify. Once he identifies (or is told) what the picture is, he is asked to determine which letter the object begins with. There will be several pictures for Luis Mario to identify, and the most recognizable to him will be the most beneficial to use for this lesson. The reason for this is that the pictures are to be pasted to index cards and made into a book that Luis Mario will be able to keep and practice with.

Guided / Independent Practice
Luis Mario will identify the object, determine what letter sound the word begins with, and match the object to the letter. He should have at least three objects per letter. The teacher will guide his work as needed. Once the book contains at least three pictures per letter, Luis Mario is asked to write the lowercase letter on the back side of the card.

Assessment & Closure
Once Luis Mario has three pictures per letter, all the pictures, letters and letter sounds will be reviewed.

Case Study #2: Using Assessments to Inform Instruction in Fourth Grade

See chapter 5.

Ms. Natalie Thompson, a fourth-grade teacher, regularly collects assessment information. To ensure that each of the 34 students in her class receive appropriate instruction, she maintains a portfolio for each student. Students add their favorite pieces to their portfolios, as does Ms. Thompson. She also keeps track of her observations, formal and informal assessments, and her checklists in each portfolio. She often uses her conferring time during independent activities as a time to collect and record assessment information. Steve is a bilingual (Spanish and English) student identified as gifted. However, he has various needs in oral language, reading, and writing as he continues to learn the English language. She further describes Steve as "extremely shy—I need to help him open up, make friends, and feel more comfortable taking risks."

Steve is an intelligent fourth grader who is capable of higher-level thinking and always tries his best. He knows how to use his resources when he is stuck, which is a major strength as students approach middle school. He uses the teacher's assistance as his last resort to finding an answer to a question, which sets an excellent example for the other students. He is highly motivated and maintains a positive repertoire in the classroom. His peers respect him and welcome him into social groups in the classroom. Although he has many strengths and positive aspects, Steve has needs stemming from his oral language development and vocabulary. Because his English proficiency is not yet in the early intermediate stage, Steve needs specific help in order to improve his oral language development. Steve also needs help in reading and writing although writing is his strongest area in language arts. Ms. Thompson believes his writing is his strongest area because he knows how to use resources such as dictionaries, his "Words I Learn to Read" card (kept in his writing folder), the word wall, and other resources based on a particular lesson or unit. He is focused and motivated to learn and be successful and his "learner" attitude allows him to be successful.

Assessments. Ms. Thompson used both informal and formal assessments to plan her instruction. For example, she administered the DRA (Beavers, 1997) toward the beginning of the school year and used this information in planning her groups for guided reading and writing. She also used the SOLOM to determine Steve's oral language development. The results suggested that Steve needs to focus on vocabulary and pronunciation. In analyzing the various situations in which SOLOM data were collected, it was clear that Steve needs practice with the English language in smaller settings so that he feels comfortable making mistakes.

Ms. Thompson also collected a timed writing sample. From her analysis of this data, she knows that Steve's writing is much more developed than his reading and speaking. She also noted that he still needs help with spelling, paragraph development, and vocabulary enhancement. It is clear that Steve has complex thoughts and wants to express his higher level thinking, but he has trouble communicating exactly what he wants to say.

In addition to these more formal assessments, Ms. Thompson uses data collected informally during focus lessons and guided reading sessions. For example, Ms. Thompson noted that during guided reading, Steve read quietly and was somewhat reserved. He participated by choice, but rarely contributed orally to the discussion. When Ms. Thompson used a retelling inventory, she wrote that Steve had sufficient comprehension skills, but could not provide many story details.

Ms. Thompson also remarked that examining a student's homework or independent practice component of a lesson is a great way to see if a student is understanding the material. As she said, "Homework is a wonderful assessment tool because the students are required to apply recently learned concepts to a new contextual environment. If students can apply their newly learned concepts to an independent homework assignment in a different environment in which they learned it, they have mastered the concept(s). This takes skill and is an effective assessment tool for teachers."

Developing Lessons Based on Assessment Information

Toward the beginning of the year, Ms. Thompson focused on a making words activity for the students in the small group where Steve was assigned. Based on her assessment information, Ms. Thompson knew that Steve sometimes had trouble making the sounds of letters correctly and needed to improve his spelling. Her anecdotal notes indicate that Steve "was pretty successful at this activity because he found the pattern in the word families. Steve found the letter-sound patterns almost immediately while some students struggled making the words correctly." Because Steve caught on rapidly, Ms. Thompson moved Steve to another guided reading group and focused on transferring his learning to writing in content areas.

In terms of focus lessons with the whole class, Ms. Thompson knew that her students loved games and competition with their classmates. She also knew that her students needed to learn homophone pairs and increase their knowledge of words, their spelling, and their understanding of the words' meanings. As a result, she modified the game Pictionary and called it, Homophone Pictionary. She noted that when it was Steve's turn to draw a picture, he felt no shame or embarrassment because he wanted to win for his teammates. When his teammates drew pictures, Steve was actively participating and using his oral language skills to participate in the game. Steve left all his previous insecurities aside for this game because he was so engaged.

Because Steve also needed vocabulary development, Ms. Thompson decided to make this the focus of her conferring time. She created a lesson using a child's thesaurus to increase Steve's vocabulary to "five-dollar words" rather than just "dollar words." The use of the thesaurus was helpful for Steve when the students were writing Cinquain Poems during their week at the zoo. Her analysis of his homework and independent work revealed that rather than using simple words like he did in his Haiku poems, Steve used more complex vocabulary in his Cinquain because he looked up the words he wanted to use in a thesaurus to find other words that meant the same thing.

BIG IDEAS ABOUT ASSESSMENT

The principles of the language arts workshop apply to assessment and interpretation. The goal is for each learner to engage in meaningful tasks within his or her zone of proximal development. Using a gradual release of responsibility model, students are carefully instructed and assessed. The purpose of these assessments is to plan future instruction and reflect on past teaching effectiveness. The cycle of assessment and instruction is therefore recursive as teachers continually assess, plan, teach, and reflect.

INTEGRATING THE STANDARDS_____

Create lesson plans that meet your state's standards by visiting our Companion Website at www.prenhall.com/frey. There you'll find lessons created to meet the NCTE/IRA Standards. Adapt them to meet the standards of your own state through links to your state's standards, and keep them in the online portfolio. You can collect lesson plans for each chapter in an online portfolio, providing you with invaluable tools to meet your state's standards when you head into your own classroom.

CHECK YOUR UNDERSTANDING_____

1. How do I select an assessment?
2. How do formal and informal assessments differ from each other?
3. What are the major types of informal assessments?

References

Clay, M. M. (1979). *Preventing reading difficulties in young children*. Portsmouth, NH: Heinemann.

Cummins, J., & Swain, M. (1986). *Bilingualism in education: Aspects of theory, research, and practice*. New York: Longman.

Dolch, E. W. (1948). *Problems in reading*. Champaign, IL: Garrard.

Fearn, L., & Farnan, N. (2001). *Interactions: Teaching writing and the language arts*. Boston: Houghton Mifflin.

Fisher, D., & Frey, N. (2004). *Improving adolescent literacy: Strategies at work*. Upper Saddle River, NJ: Merrill/Prentice Hall.

Frey, N., & Hiebert, E. H. (2003). Teacher-based assessment of literacy learning. In J. Flood, D. Lapp, J. R. Squire, & J. M. Jensen (Eds.), *Handbook of research on teaching the English language arts* (2nd ed., pp. 608–618). Mahwah, NJ: Erlbaum.

Gansk, K. (1999). The developmental spelling analysis: A measure of orthographic knowledge. *Educational Assessment, 6*(1), 41–70.

Gansk, K. (2000). *Word journeys: Assessment-guided phonics, spelling, and vocabulary instruction*. New York: Guilford.

Goodman, Y. M., & Burke, C. L. (1972). *Reading miscue inventory manual: Procedure for diagnosis and evaluation*. New York: Macmillan.

Guillaume, A. M. (2004). *K–12 classroom teaching: A primer for new professionals* (2nd ed.). Upper Saddle River, NJ: Merrill/Prentice Hall.

Henderson, E. H. (1990). *Teaching spelling* (2nd ed.). Boston: Houghton Mifflin.

Henk, W. A., & Selders, M. L. (1984). Test of synonymic scoring of cloze passages. *The Reading Teacher, 38,* 282–287.

International Reading Association. (2000). *Making a difference means making it different: Honoring children's rights to excellent reading instruction*. Newark, DE: Author.

Knudson, R. E. (1991). Development and use of a writing attitude survey in grades 4 and 8. *Psychological Reports, 68,* 807–816.

Kush, J. C. & Watkins, M. W. (1996). Long-term stability of children's attitudes toward reading. *Journal of Educational Research, 89,* 315–319.

Lapp, D., Fisher, D., Flood, J., & Cabello, A. (2001). An integrated approach to the teaching and assessment of language arts. In S. R. Hurley & J. V. Tinajero (Eds.), *Literacy assessment of second language learners* (pp. 1–26). Needham Heights, MA: Allyn & Bacon.

McClafferty, C. K. (2001). *The head bone's connected to the neck bone: The weird, wacky, and wonderful X-ray.* New York: Farrar, Straus & Giroux.

Nation, K., & Hulme, C. (1997). Phonemic segmentation, not onset-rime segmentation, predicts early reading and spelling skills. *Reading Research Quarterly, 32,* 154–167.

Rumelhart, D. E. (1994). Toward an interactive model of reading. In R. B. Ruddell, M. R. Ruddell, & H. Singer (Eds.), *Theoretical processes of reading* (4th ed., pp. 864–894). Newark, DE: International Reading Association.

Salus, P. H., & Flood, J. (2002). *Language: A user's guide: What we say and why.* San Diego, CA: Academic Professional Development.

Shanker, J. L., & Ekwall, E. E. (2002). *Locating and correcting reading difficulties* (8th ed.). Upper Saddle River, NJ: Merrill/Prentice Hall.

Smith, C. M. (1990). The relationship of adults' reading attitude to actual reading behavior. *Reading Improvement, 27,* 116–121.

Snowling, M. J., Stackhouse, J., & Rock, J. P. (1986). Phonological dyslexia and dysgraphia: A developmental analysis. *Cognitive Neuropsychology, 3,* 309–339.

Spaulding, C. L. (1992). The motivation to read and write. In J. W. Irwin & M. A. Doyle (Eds.), *Reading/writing connections: Learning from research* (pp. 177–201). Newark, DE: International Reading Association.

Tierney, R. J., Clark, C., Wiser, B., Simpson, C. S., Herter, R. J., & Fenner, L. (1998). Portfolios: Assumptions, tensions, and possibilities. *Reading Research Quarterly, 33,* 474–486.

West Australia Department of Education. (1994). *First steps reading resource book.* Portsmouth, NH: Heinemann.

West, K. R. (1998). Noticing and responding to learners: Literacy evaluation and instruction in the primary grades. *The Reading Teacher, 51,* 550–559.

Wilcox, B. (1997). Writing portfolios: Active vs. passive. *English Journal, 86,*(6), 34–35.

Wylie, R. E., & Durrell, D. D. (1970). Teaching vowels through phonograms. *Elementary English, 47,* 787–791.

Assessments Cited

Applegate, M. D., Quinn, K. B., & Applegate, A. J. (2004). *Critical reading inventory: Assessing students' reading and thinking.* Upper Saddle River, NJ: Prentice Hall.

Beavers, J. (1997). *Developmental reading assessment.* Parsippany, NJ: Celebration Press.

Bottomley, D. M., Henk, W. A., & Melnick, S. A. (1997–1998). Assessing children's views about themselves as writers using the writer self-perception scale. *The Reading Teacher, 51,* 286–296.

Burns, P. C., & Roe, B. D. (2001). *Burns/Roe informal reading inventory: Preprimer to twelfth grade* (6th ed.). Boston: Houghton Mifflin.

California Department of Education. (2000). *Student oral language observation matrix (SOLOM).* Sacramento, CA: Author.

Clay, M. M. (2002). *An observation survey of early literacy achievement* (2nd ed.). Portsmouth, NH: Heinemann.

CORE. (1999). *CORE assessing reading: Multiple measures for kindergarten through eighth grade*. Novato, CA: Arena.

Flynt, E. S., Cooter, R. B., Jr., & Flynt, D. S. (1998). *Flynt-Cooter reading inventory for the classroom*. Upper Saddle River, NJ: Merrill/Prentice Hall.

Gambrell, L. B., Palmer, B. M., Codling, R. M., & Mazzoni, S. A. (1996). Assessing motivation to read. *The Reading Teacher, 49,* 518–533.

Johns, J. L. (2001). *Basic reading inventory* (8th ed.). Dubuque, IA: Kendall-Hunt.

Karlsen, B., & Gardner, E. (1995). *Stanford Diagnostic Reading Test: 4th edition*. San Antonio, TX: Psychological.

Kear, D. J., Coffman, G. A., McKenna, M. C., & Ambrosio, A. L. (2000). Measuring attitude toward writing: A new tool for teachers. *The Reading Teacher, 54,* 10–23.

Kujawa, S., & Huske, L. (1995). *The strategic teaching and reading project guidebook*. Oakbrook, IL: North Central Regional Education Laboratory.

Leslie, L. D., & Caldwell, J. (2001). *Qualitative reading inventory* (3rd ed.). Upper Saddle River, NJ: Merrill/Prentice Hall.

MacGinitie, W. H., MacGinitie, R., Maria, K., & Dreyer, L. (2000). *Gates-MacGinitie reading tests* (4th ed.). Itasca, IL: Riverside.

McKenna, M. C., & Kear, D. (1990). Measuring attitude toward reading: A new tool for teachers. *The Reading Teacher, 43,* 626–639.

Northwest Regional Laboratory. (2001). Reading scoring guides. Retrieved November 13, 2003 from http://www.nwrel.org/assessment/scoring

Northwest Regional Laboratory. (2001). 6 + 1 trait writing. Retrieved November 27, 2003 from http://www.nwrel.org/assessment/about.asp?odelay=1&d=1

Schmitt, M. B. (1990). A questionnaire to measure children's awareness of strategic reading processes. *The Reading Teacher, 43,* 454–461.

Stieglitz, E. L. (2002). *The Stieglitz informal reading inventory* (3rd ed.). Boston: Allyn & Bacon.

Swearingen, R., & Allen, D. (2000). *Classroom assessment of reading processes* (2nd ed.). Boston: Houghton Mifflin.

Woods, M. L., & Moe, A. (1999). *Analytic reading inventory:* (6th ed.). Upper Saddle River, NJ: Merrill/Prentice Hall.

Yopp, H. K. (1995). A test for assessing phonemic awareness in young children. *The Reading Teacher, 49,* 20–29.

Compendium of Assessments

Name: _____   **Date:** _____

Time: From _____ **to** _____

Student observing working:

☐ independently
☐ collaboratively with _____
☐ guided instruction with _____

Task observed:

_____

Sequence of events observed:

_____

Notes and reflections:

_____

Abbreviations

S₁ — student being observed
T — teacher
S₂–S₆ — other students working with observed student

Compendium 2 Storybook Reading Inventory

Broad Categories	Date	Book Title
Attending to pictures, not forming stories	_____	_____
	_____	_____
	_____	_____
Attending to pictures, forming oral stories	_____	_____
	_____	_____
	_____	_____
Attending to pictures, reading and storytelling mixed	_____	_____
	_____	_____
	_____	_____
Attending to pictures, forming written stories	_____	_____
	_____	_____
	_____	_____
Attending to pictures and print.	_____	_____
	_____	_____
	_____	_____
	_____	_____

Source: Adapted from Vukelich, C. (1997). Assessing young children's literacy: Documenting growth and informing practice. *The Reading Teacher, 50,* 430–434. Copyright © 1997 by the International Reading Association.

Compendium 3 Basic Rubric

What Makes a Good Cheeseburger?

The Basics: bun, patty, cheese
Enhancements: lettuce, tomatoes, bacon, ketchup, mustard, pickles—you name it!
Appearance: Smooth bun, stacked up in an even column, no ingredients hanging out
Mistakes to Avoid: Don't overcook or undercook, don't drop on the floor

Now Let's Use the Cheeseburger to Develop a Rubric for _____

	What Does It Look Like?	Evidence
The Basics		
Enhancements		
Appearance		
Mistakes to avoid		

Compendium 4   Self-Assessment of Group Work

Name: _____   Date: _____

Project: _____   Members of my group:

_____

_____

_____

Please rank yourself based on your contributions to the group. Circle the one that best describes your work.

5 = always   4 = almost always   3 = sometimes   2 = once or twice   1 = never

I completed my tasks on time.	5	4	3	2	1
I contributed ideas to the group.	5	4	3	2	1
I listened respectfully to the ideas of others.	5	4	3	2	1
I used other people's ideas in my work for the project.	5	4	3	2	1
When I was stuck, I sought help from my group.	5	4	3	2	1

Additional comments:

Compendium 5   Reading Interest Survey

Name: _____   **Date:** _____

Please circle the answer that is best for *you*.

Reading Survey Questions

1. I like to choose my own books to read.

    Always   *Sometimes*   *Never*

2. I can usually find a good book to read.

    Yes   *No*

3. I like to read chapter books.

    Yes   *Not yet*

4. I read at home.

    Every day   *Every few days*   *Not if I can help it*

5. At home I like to read

    In bed   *On the floor*   *In a comfortable chair*

6. The kinds of books I like to read include:

    ____ chapter books   ____ nonfiction
    ____ books with pictures   ____ animal stories
    ____ joke and riddle books   ____ mysteries
    ____ sports books   ____ funny stories

    Other _____

7. Books and authors I have read:

    _____

Directions for Administering

1. Have one test sheet for each child in the class.
2. Assess children individually in a quiet place.
3. Keep the assessment playful and game-like.
4. Explain the game to the child exactly as the directions specify.
5. Model for the child what he or she needs to do with each of the practice words. Have them break apart each word with you.

Children are given the following directions upon administration of the test:

> Today we're gong to play a word game. I'm going to say a word and I want you to break the word apart. You are going to say the word slowly, and then tell me each sound in the word in order. For example, if I say "old," you should say "oooo-llll-d." (The teacher says the sound, not the letters.) Let's try a few words together.

The practice items are *ride, go,* and *man.* The teacher should help the child with each sample item—segmenting the item for the child if necessary and encouraging the child to repeat the segmented words. Then the child is given the 22 item test. If the child responds correctly, the teacher says, "That's right." If the child gives an incorrect response, he or she is corrected. The teacher provides the appropriate response. The teacher circles the numbers of all correct answers.

If the child breaks a word apart incorrectly, the teacher gives the correct answer:

	Child says	You say
Uses onset and rime	/d/ - /og/	/d-/o-/g/
Repeats word	dog	/d-/o-/g/
Stretches word out	d - o - g	/d-/o-/g/
Spells letters in word	"d - "o" - "g"	/d-/o-/g/
Says first and last sounds	/d/ - /g/	/d-/o-/g/
Says another word	bark	/d-/o-/g/
Says a sentence	I don't know	/d-/o-/g/

The child's score is the number of items correctly segmented into all constituent phonemes. No partial credit is given. For instance, if a child says "/c/-/at/" instead of "/c/-/a/-/t/," the response may be noted on the blank line following the items but is considered incorrect for purposes of scoring. Correct responses are only those that involve articulation of each phoneme in the target word.

A blend contains two or three phonemes in each of these and each should be articulated separately. Hence, item 7 on the test, *grew,* has three phonemes /g/-/r/ew/. Digraphs such in item 5, *she,* and the /th/ in item 15, *three,* are single phonemes. Item 5, therefore has two phonemes and item 15 has three phonemes. If a child responds with letter names instead of sound, the response is coded as incorrect, and the type of error is noted on the test.

Students who obtain high scores (segmenting all or nearly all of the item correctly) may be considered phonemically aware. Students who correctly segment some items are displaying emerging phonemic awareness. Students who are able to segment only a few items or none lack appropriate levels of phonemic awareness. Without intervention, those students scoring low on the test are likely to experience difficulty with reading and spelling.

(continued)

Source: Yopp, H. K. (1995). A test for assessing phonemic awareness in young children. *The Reading Teacher, 49,* 20–29. Used with permission.

Student Test Sheet

Yopp-Singer Test of Phoneme Segmentation

Student's name _____ Date _____

Score (number correct) _____

Directions: Today we're going to play a word game. I'm going to say a word and I want you to break the word apart. You are going to tell me each sound in the word in order. For example, say "old," you should say /o/-/l/-/d/." (Administrator: Be sure to say the sounds, not the letters in the word.) Let's try a few together.

Practice items: (Assist the child in segmenting these items as necessary.)
          ride   go   man

Test items: (Circle those items that the student correctly segments; incorrect responses may be recorded on the blank line following the item.)

1. dog _____	12. lay _____
2. keep _____	13. race _____
3. fine _____	14. zoo _____
4. no _____	15. three _____
5. she _____	16. job _____
6. wave _____	17. in _____
7. grew _____	18. ice _____
8. that _____	19. at _____
9. red _____	20. top _____
10. me _____	21. by _____
11. sat _____	22. do _____

Return to the Test Directions

The author, Hallie Kay Yopp, California State University, Fullerton, grants permission for this test to be reproduced. The author acknowledges the contribution of the late Harry Singer to the development of this test.

Compendium 7 Narrative Story Retelling Rubric

Narrative Retelling Rubric

Name: _____ Date: _____

Title of book: _____

Who read the story? ☐ **Teacher** ☐ **Student**

	Proficient—3	Adequate—2	Needs Attention—1
Character	Main and supporting characters and their characteristics identified. Examples given to describe characters.	Most main and supporting characters identified. Characteristics are less descriptive.	Overlooked characters essential to the story. Few or no examples or descriptions of characteristics offered.
Setting	Setting is identified and described in detail using vivid vocabulary.	Setting is identified and description is accurate. Some detail included.	Setting is either not identified or identified incorrectly.
Problem	Central problem of the story is identified. Character motivations or potential solutions included.	Central problem is identified. Character motivations or potential solutions are not included.	Central problem is not identified or is incorrectly identified.
Solution	Solution is identified. Retelling features connections to characteristics of characters. Student relates this to story's moral or theme.	Solution is identified but retelling does not include connection to moral or theme.	Solution is not identified or is incorrectly identified.
Plot	Sequence of story is told in correct order.	Sequence of story is told in nearly correct order, with 1–2 events out of sequence.	Sequence of story has 3 or more errors.

Script retelling in the box below, then score quality of the retelling.

	Character: ☐
	Setting: ☐
	Problem: ☐
	Solution: ☐
	Plot: ☐
	TOTAL: ☐

Compendium 8   Informational Text Retelling Rubric

Informational Text Retelling Rubric

Name: _____   Date: _____

Title of book: _____

Who read the story?   ☐ Teacher   ☐ Student

	Proficient—3	Adequate—2	Needs Attention—1
Main ideas	Main ideas are identified. Examples are given to illustrate these ideas.	Most main ideas identified. Examples are less descriptive.	Overlooked main ideas essential to the text. Few or no examples or descriptions of main ideas offered.
Supporting details	Supporting details are clearly connected to the main ideas.	Supporting details are identified but are not told in association with main ideas.	Few or no supporting details offered.
Sequence	Sequence of retelling is accurate and reflects the order used by the author.	Sequence is similar to order in book, with some instances of "double back" during retelling.	Sequence is difficult to discern.
Accuracy	Facts are relayed accurately.	Retelling is mostly accurate, with few errors.	Retelling is inaccurate.
Inferences	Student makes connections within text (e.g., meaning of title; usefulness of information).	Student makes few associations between pieces of information in text.	Student makes no associations within text.

Script retelling in the box below, then score quality of the retelling.

	Main ideas: ☐
	Details: ☐
	Sequence: ☐
	Accuracy: ☐
	Inferences: ☐
	TOTAL: ☐

Compendium 9   Student Form for Letter Identification

O	W	E	X
S	A	G	D
H	K	P	J
C	N	U	V
Y	R	B	I
Q	L	F	M
Z	T		
o	w	e	x
s	a	g	d
h	k	p	j
c	n	u	v
y	r	b	i
q	l	f	m
z	t	a	g

Compendium 10   Teacher Recording Form for Letter Identification

Name: _____   **Date:** _____

Teacher: _____

LETTER	*CORRECT*	*INCORRECT*	LETTER	*CORRECT*	*INCORRECT*
O			o		
W			w		
E			e		
X			x		
S			s		
A			a		
G			g		
D			d		
H			h		
K			k		
P			p		
J			j		
C			c		
N			n		
U			u		
V			v		
Y			y		
R			r		
B			b		
I			i		
Q			q		
L			l		
F			f		
M			m		
Z			z		
T			t		
			a		
			g		
Total uppercase	/26	/26	**Total lowercase**	/28	/28

Code for scoring: Correct = ✓
Incorrect = record student response

Compendium 11   Dolch Sight Word Assessment—Preprimer

Name: _____   **Teacher:** _____

Directions: Present the student each Dolch sight word on an index card. Highlight or circle each correct response using the color code at the bottom of the page.

Dolch Sight Words: Preprimer

a	funny	look	see
and	go	make	the
away	help	me	three
big	hers	my	to
blue	I	not	two
can	in	one	up
come	is	play	we
down	it	red	yellow
find	jump	run	you
for	little	said	

Coding for sight words:
1st administration: red   (Date:)
2nd administration: blue   (Date:)
3rd administration: green   (Date:)
4th administration: yellow   (Date:)

Compendium 12   Dolch Sight Word Assessment—Primer

Name: _____   **Teacher:** _____

Directions: Present the student each Dolch sight word on an index card. Highlight or circle each correct response using the color code at the bottom of the page.

Dolch Sight Words: Primer

all	four	out	this
am	get	please	too
are	good	pretty	under
at	has	ran	want
ate	he	ride	was
be	into	saw	well
black	like	say	went
brown	must	she	what
but	new	so	white
came	no	soon	who
did	now	that	will
do	on	there	with
eat	our	they	yes

Coding for sight words:
1st administration: red   (Date:)
2nd administration: blue   (Date:)
3rd administration: green   (Date:)
4th administration: yellow   (Date:)

Compendium 13 Dolch Sight Word Assessment—First Grade

Name: _____ **Teacher:** _____

Directions: Present the student each Dolch sight word on an index card. Highlight or circle each correct response using the color code at the bottom of the page.

Dolch Sight Words: First Grade

after	from	let	some
again	give	live	stop
an	going	may	take
any	had	of	thank
as	has	old	them
ask	her	once	then
by	him	open	think
could	how	over	walk
every	just	put	where
fly	know	round	when

Coding for sight words:
1st administration: red   (Date:)
2nd administration: blue   (Date:)
3rd administration: green   (Date:)
4th administration: yellow   (Date:)

Compendium 14 Dolch Sight Word Assessment—Second Grade

Name: _____   **Teacher:** _____

Directions: Present the student each Dolch sight word on an index card. Highlight or circle each correct response using the color code at the bottom of the page.

Dolch Sight Words: Second Grade

always	fast	pull	use
around	first	read	very
because	five	right	wash
been	found	sing	which
before	gave	sit	why
best	goes	sleep	wish
both	green	tell	work
buy	its	their	would
call	made	these	write
cold	many	those	your
does	off	upon	
don't	or	us	

Coding for sight words:
1st administration: red   (Date:)
2nd administration: blue   (Date:)
3rd administration: green   (Date:)
4th administration: yellow   (Date:)

Compendium 15   Dolch Sight Word Assessment—Third Grade

Name: _____   **Teacher:** _____

Directions: Present the student each Dolch sight word on an index card. Highlight or circle each correct response using the color code at the bottom of the page.

Dolch Sight Words: Third Grade

about	fall	kind	seven
better	far	laugh	shall
bring	full	light	show
carry	got	long	six
clean	grow	much	small
cut	hold	myself	start
done	hot	never	ten
draw	hurt	only	today
drink	if	own	together
eight	keep	pick	try
			warm

Coding for sight words:

1st administration: red	(Date:)
2nd administration: blue	(Date:)
3rd administration: green	(Date:)
4th administration: yellow	(Date:)

Compendium 16 Frequently Used Rimes

Frequently Used Rimes in English

-ack	-aw	-ink
-ail	-ay	-ip
-ain	-eat	-ir
-ake	-ell	-ock
-ale	-est	-oke
-all	-ice	-op
-ame	-ick	-or
-an	-ide	-ore
-ank	-ight	-uck
-ap	-ill	-ug
-ash	-in	-ump
-at	-ine	-unk
-ate	-ing	

Compendium 17   Early Concepts of Print Checklist

Name: _____   **Teacher:** _____

Grade Level: _____

Directions: Choose a picture book with large print and a variety of punctuation marks. Tell the child you will read the story but you will need some help. Note responses to the prompts in the right column.

Concepts About Print Prompts

Front of book	Hand book to child upside down. **"Show me the front cover of the book."**	
Title and Author	**"This book is called _____ and it is written by _____. Show me where that's written."**	
Turns pages	**"Show me how to open the book."**	
Locates print	Turn to first page of story. **"I'm going to read this to you. Show me where to begin reading."** Correct response is pointing to a word on first page.	
Directionality on page	**"Show me which way to read the words."** Correct response indicates left to right.	
Return sweep	On a page with more than one line of print: **"Which way do I go when I get to the end of the first line?"**	
1:1 correspondence	**"Point to the words while I read."**	
Beginning and end of story	**"Show me the beginning of the story."** **"Show me the end of the story."**	
Period	Point to a period at the end of a sentence. **"What does this mean?"**	
Question mark	Point to a question mark at the end of a sentence. **"What does this mean?"**	
Directionality within words	Point to a word with at least three letters. **"Show me the first letter in the word."** **"Show me the last letter in the word."**	

Notes:

Compendium 18   Coding Sheet for Running Records

RESPONSES AND MISCUES	EXPLANATION	CODING	EXAMPLE
Correct	Calls words correctly	✓	✓ ✓ ✓ ✓ ✓ ✓ The house is blue and white.
Substitution	Calls one word for another	horse ───── house	**horse** ✓ **house** ✓ ✓ ✓ The house is blue and white.
Omission	Skips a word	-- ───── house	-- ───── ✓ **house** ✓ ✓ ✓ The house is blue and white.
Insertion	Adds a word	_big_	✓ **big** ✓ ✓ ✓ ✓ The house is blue and white.
Appeal	Asks for help	A ───── house	**A** ✓ **house** ✓ ✓ ✓ The house is blue and white.
Teacher told	Teacher tells word	TT ───── house	**TT** ✓ **house** ✓ ✓ ✓ The house is blue and white.
Rerun	Student repeats words, phrases, or entire sentence	← RR ───── The house	**RR** ✓ ✓ ✓ ✓ ✓ ✓ The house is blue and white.
Self-correction	Reader corrects error on own	horse SC ───── house	✓ **horse SC** ✓ ✓ ✓ **house** The house is blue and white.

Compendium 19 Blank Running Record Form

Name: _____   **Date:** _____

Title of book: _____   **Book Level:** _____

Page	Miscues

Notes:

Compendium 20   Collecting Data for Running Record

Running Record Scoring Sheet

Name: _____   **Date:** _____

Title of book: _____   **Book Level:** _____

CALCULATION	RESULT
Total words in book	
Total miscues*	
Total self-corrections	
Total words – miscues = score	
Score ÷ total words = percentage	
Text difficulty for this reader	☐ independent ☐ instructional ☐ frustration

*Do not count self-corrections and reruns as miscues. Count miscues of proper nouns (e.g., names, places) only once.

TEXT DIFFICULTY	PERCENTAGE	INSTRUCTIONAL USE
Independent	95–100% accuracy	Independent and reading
Instructional	90–94% accuracy	Guided reading
Frustration	89% or less accuracy	Shared reading and read alouds

Compendium 21 The Nonword Reading Test

Name: _____   Date: _____

Directions: Print these words individually on cards and present them in random order for the child to read aloud. Record all reading responses. Either a regular or irregular pronunciation is acceptable, i.e., *jint* can be correctly read as rhyming with *lint* or *pint*.

One Syllable		Two Syllable
plood	nowl	louble
aund	swad	hausage
wolt	chove	soser
jint	duede	pettuce
hign	sworf	kolice
pove	jase	skeady
wamp	freath	dever
cread	warg	biter
slove	choiy	islank
fongue		polonel
		narine
		kiscuit

For 7 year olds, a score below 3 falls significantly below the norm.

For 10 year olds, a score below 26 on one-syllable words and 7 on two-syllable words falls significantly below the norm.

Source: Snowling, M. J., Stackhouse, J., & Rack, J. P. (1986). Phonological dyslexia and dysgraphia: A developmental analysis. *Cognitive Neuropsychology, 3,* 309–339. Used with permission of Psychology Press. http://www.psypress.co.uk/journals.asp

Compendium 22   Sample Cloze Procedure—Student Form

Cloze Passage

Directions: Every fifth word has been deleted from this passage. Read the passage and write the words on a separate sheet of paper that best fit both the meaning and the structure of the sentence. You may read the passage more than once.

The Early Use of X-rays
By Carla Killough McClafferty

In the early days, even the major hospitals of the world considered X-rays to be experimental and not very important. No one was sure __1__ the use of X-rays __2__ some doctors' practices would __3__ a lasting part of __4__ patients' treatment or a __5__ fad. Because of this __6__ the location of the __7__ room was not a __8__ for hospitals. They placed __9__ room in any nook __10__ cranny they could find. __11__ it would be in __12__ closetlike room in the __13__ or under a staircase, __14__ even a section of __15__ waiting room that had __16__ partitioned off.

The X-ray __17__ didn't care how cramped __18__ stuffy the rooms were. __19__ were just happy to __20__ the chance to experiment. __21__ available space in their __22__ room was filled with __23__ glass X-ray tubes. They __24__ have electric lights and __25__ sockets in every room __26__ we have today. The __27__ came from a coil __28__ the room that was __29__ to the X-ray tube. __30__ wires that connected them __31__ ran around the room, __32__ up the wall, and __33__ from the gaslight fixtures __34__ the ceiling.

When these __35__ X-ray rooms were ready __36__ the first patient, they __37__ not only cluttered but __38__ looked frightening. Dr. Mihran __39__ , considered to be an __40__ on the subject of __41__ , wrote a textbook published __42__ 1907 titled *Roetgen Rays __43__ Electro-Therapeutics.* In it he __44__ how the X-ray operator __45__ prepare the patient for __46__ examination: "Those that are timid __47__ be previously instructed to __48__ noises, flashes, etc., necessarily __49__ during the examination."

Occasionally, __50__ an X-ray taken could be an electrifying experience. In his book Dr. Kassabian told about a case when "the machine emitted great sparks and once or twice gave the patient a shock."

Source: McClafferty, C. K. (2001). *The head bone's connected to the neck bone: The weird, wacky, and wonderful X-ray* (pp. 33–34). New York: Farrar, Straus & Giroux.

Compendium 23   Sample Cloze Procedure Answer Key

1. if
2. in
3. be
4. their
5. passing
6. uncertainty
7. X-ray
8. priority
9. the
10. or
11. Sometimes
12. a
13. basement

14. maybe
15. the
16. been
17. pioneers
18. or
19. They
20. get
21. Every
22. tiny
23. extra
24. didn't
25. wall
26. as

27. electricity
28. in
29. connected
30. The
31. sometimes
32. and
33. hung
34. on
35. pint-sized
36. for
37. were
38. sometimes
39. Kassabian

40. expert
41. X-rays
42. in
43. *and*
44. described
45. should
46. the
47. should
48. ignore
49. occurring
50. having

Name: _____ Date: _____

Metacomprehension Strategy Index

Directions: Think about what kinds of things you can do to help you understand a story better before, during, and after you read it. Read each of the lists of four statements and decide which one of them would help you the most. Circle the letter of the statement you choose.

I. In each set of four, choose the one statement, which tells a good thing to do to help you understand a story better *before* you read it.

1. Before I begin reading, it's a good idea to:
   A. See how many pages are in the story.
   B. Look up all of the big words in the dictionary.
   C. Make some guesses about what I think will happen in the story.
   D. Think about what has happened so far in the story.

2. Before I begin reading, it's a good idea to:
   A. Look at the pictures to see what the story is about.
   B. Decide how long it will take me to read the story.
   C. Sound out the words I don't know.
   D. Check to see if the story is making sense.

3. Before I begin reading, it's a good idea to:
   A. Ask someone to read the story to me.
   B. Read the title to see what the story is about.
   C. Check to see if most of the words have long or short vowels in them.
   D. Check to see if the pictures are in order and make sense.

4. Before I begin reading, it's a good idea to:
   A. Check to see that no pages are missing.
   B. Make a list of words I'm not sure about.
   C. Use the title and pictures to help me make guesses about what will happen in the story.
   D. Read the last sentence so I will know how the story ends.

5. Before I begin reading, it's a good idea to:
   A. Decide on why I am going to read the story.
   B. Use the difficult words to help me make guesses about what will happen in the story.
   C. Reread some parts to see if I can figure out what is happening if things aren't making sense.
   D. Ask for help with the difficult words.

6. Before I begin reading, it's a good idea to:
   A. Retell all of the main points that have happened so far.
   B. Ask myself questions that I would like to have answered in the story.
   C. Think about the meaning of the words, which have more than one meaning.
   D. Look through the story to find all of the words with three or more syllables.

7. Before I begin reading, it's a good idea to:
   A. Check to see if I have read this story before.
   B. Use my questions and guesses as a reason for reading the story.
   C. Make sure I can pronounce all of the words before I start.
   D. Think of a better title for the story.

8. Before I begin reading, it's a good idea to:
   A. Think of what I already know about the things I see in the pictures.
   B. See how many pages are in the story.
   C. Choose the best part of the story to read again.
   D. Read the story aloud to someone.

9. Before I begin reading, it's a good idea to:
   A. Practice reading the story out loud.
   B. Retell all of the main points to make sure I can remember the story.
   C. Think of what the people in the story might be like.
   D. Decide if I have enough time to read the story.

10. Before I begin reading, it's a good idea to:
    A. Check to see if I am understanding the story so far.
    B. Check to see if the words have more than one meaning.
    C. Think about where the story might be taking place.
    D. List all of the important details.

II. In each set of four, choose the one statement, which tells a good thing to do to help you understand a story better *while* you are reading it.

11. While I am reading, it's a good idea to:
    A. Read the story very slowly so that I will not miss any important parts.
    B. Read the title to see what the story is about.
    C. Check to see if the pictures have anything missing.
    D. Check to see if the story is making sense by seeing if I can tell what's happened so far.

12. While I am reading, it's a good idea to:
    A. Stop to retell the main points to see if I am understanding what has happened so far.
    B. Read the story quickly so that I can find out what happened.
    C. Read only the beginning and the end of the story to find out what it is about.
    D. Skip the parts that are too difficult for me.

(continued)

13. While I am reading, it's a good idea to:
    A. Look all of the big words up in the dictionary.
    B. Put the book away and find another one if things aren't making sense.
    C. Keep thinking about the title and the pictures to help me decide what is going to happen next.
    D. Keep track of how many pages I have left to read.

14. While I am reading, it's a good idea to:
    A. Keep track of how long it is taking me to read the story.
    B. Check to see if I can answer any of the questions I asked before I started reading.
    C. Read the title to see what the story is going to be about.
    D. Add the missing details to the pictures.

15. While I am reading, it's a good idea to:
    A. Have someone read the story aloud to me.
    B. Keep track of how many pages I have read.
    C. List the story's main character.
    D. Check to see if my guesses are right or wrong.

16. While I am reading, it's a good idea to:
    A. Check to see that the characters are real.
    B. Make a lot of guesses about what is going to happen next.
    C. Not look at the pictures because they might confuse me.
    D. Read the story aloud to someone.

17. While I am reading, it's a good idea to:
    A. Try to answer the questions I asked myself.
    B. Try not to confuse what I already know with what I am reading about.
    C. Read the story silently.
    D. Check to see if I am saying the new vocabulary words correctly.

18. While I am reading, it is a good idea to:
    A. Try to see if my guesses are going to be right or wrong.
    B. Reread to be sure I haven't missed any of the words.
    C. Decide on why I am reading the story.
    D. List what happened first, second, third, and so on.

19. While I am reading, it is a good idea to:
    A. See if I can recognize the new vocabulary words.
    B. Be careful not to skip any parts of the story.
    C. Check to see how many of the words I already know.
    D. Keep thinking of what I already know about the things and ideas in the story to help me decide what is going to happen.

20. While I am reading, it's a good idea to:
    A. Reread some parts or read ahead to see if I can figure out what is happening if things aren't making sense.
    B. Take my time reading so that I can be sure I understand what is happening.
    C. Change the ending so that it makes sense.
    D. Check to see if there are enough pictures to help make the story ideas clear.

III. **In each set of four, choose the one statement, which tells a good thing to do to help you understand a story better *after* you have read it.**

21. After I've read a story it's a good idea to:
    A. Count how many pages I read with no mistakes.
    B. Check to see if there were enough pictures to go with the story to make it interesting.
    C. Check to see if I met my purpose for reading the story.
    D. Underline the causes and effects.

22. After I've read a story it's a good idea to:
    A. Underline the main idea.
    B. Retell the main points of the whole story so that I can check to see if I understood it.
    C. Read the story again to be sure I said all of the words right.
    D. Practice reading the story aloud.

23. After I've read a story it's a good idea to:
    A. Read the title and look over the story to see what it is about.
    B. Check to see if I skipped any of the vocabulary words.
    C. Think about what made me make good or bad predictions.
    D. Make a guess about what will happen next in the story.

24. After I've read a story it's a good idea to:
    A. Look up all of the big words in the dictionary.
    B. Read the best parts aloud.
    C. Have someone read the story aloud to me.
    D. Think about how the story was like things I already knew about before I started reading.

25. After I've read a story it's a good idea to:
    A. Think about how I would have acted if I were the main character in the story.
    B. Practice reading the story silently for practice of good reading.
    C. Look over the story title and pictures to see what will happen.
    D. Make a list of the things I understood the most.

Source: Schmitt, M. C. (March 1990). A questionnaire to measure children's awareness of strategic reading processes. *The Reading Teacher, 43,* 454–461.

Compendium 25 Metacomprehension Strategies Index Answer Key

Interpreting Results of the Metacomprehension Strategies Index

The MSI (Schmitt, 1990) is a measure of a student's use of strategies with narrative text. It may be read to the student, or administered silently. The wording of the items can be substituted to reflect expository text. For example, you can replace the wording of #2 to read,

Before I begin reading, it's a good idea to:
  a. Look at the illustrations to see what the chapter will be about.
  b. Decide how long it will take for me to read the chapter.
  c. Sound out the words I don't know.
  d. Check to see if the information is making sense.

Answer Key: These answers represent the best answers; items may include strategies that are somewhat useful but not as efficient for the situation described.

1. C	6. B	11. D	16. B	21. C
2. A	7. B	12. A	17. A	22. B
3. B	8. A	13. C	18. A	23. C
4. C	9. C	14. B	19. D	24. D
5. A	10. C	15. D	20. A	25. A

Interpreting: The following item analysis is organized to more fully describe the types of metacomprehension strategies tested.

Strategies	Items
Predicting and Verifying Predicting and verifying the content of a story promotes active comprehension by giving readers a purpose to read (i.e., to verify predictions). Evaluating predictions and generating new ones as necessary enhances the constructive nature of the reading process.	1, 4, 13, 15, 16, 18, 23
Previewing Previewing the text facilitates comprehension by activating background knowledge and providing information for making predictions.	2, 3
Purpose Setting Reading with a purpose promotes active, strategic reading.	5, 7, 21
Self-questioning Generating questions to be answered promotes active comprehension by giving readers a purpose for reading (i.e., to answer the questions).	6, 14, 17
Drawing from Background Knowledge Activating and incorporating information from background knowledge contributes to comprehension by helping readers make inferences and generate predictions.	8, 9, 10, 19, 24, 25
Summarizing and Applying Fix-up Strategies Summarizing the content at various points in the story serves as a form of comprehension monitoring. Rereading or suspending judgment and reading on when comprehension breaks down represents strategic reading.	11, 12, 20, 22

Source: Adapted from Schmitt, M. C. (1990). A questionnaire to measure children's awareness of strategic reading processes. *The Reading Teacher, 43,* 454–461. Used with permission.

Elementary Reading Attitude Survey

Directions for use

The Elementary Reading Attitude Survey provides a quick indication of student attitudes toward reading. It consists of 20 items and can be administered to an entire classroom in about 10 minutes. Each item presents a brief, simply-worded statement about reading, followed by four pictures of Garfield. Each pose is designed to depict a different emotional state, ranging from very positive to very negative.

Administration

Begin by telling students that you wish to find out how they feel about reading. Emphasize that this is NOT a test and that there are no "right" answers. Encourage sincerity.

Distribute the survey forms and, if you wish to monitor the attitudes of specific students, ask them to write their names in the space at the top. Hold up a copy of the survey so that the students can see the first page. Point to the picture of Garfield at the far left of the first item. Ask the students to look at this same picture on their own survey form. Discuss with them the mood Garfield seems to be in (very happy). Then move to the next picture and again discuss Garfield's mood (this time, a *little* happy). In the same way, move to the third and fourth pictures and talk about Garfield's moods—a little upset and very upset. It is helpful to point out the position of Garfield's *mouth,* especially in the middle two figures.

Explain that together you will read some statements about reading and that the students should think about how they feel about each statement. They should then circle the picture of Garfield that is closest to their own feelings. (Emphasize that the students should respond according to their own feelings, not as Garfield might respond!) Read each item aloud slowly and distinctly; then read it a second time while students are thinking. Be sure to read the item number and to remind students of page numbers when new pages are reached.

Scoring

To score the survey, count four points for each leftmost (happiest) Garfield circled, three for each slightly smiling Garfield, two for each mildly upset Garfield, and one point for each very upset (rightmost) Garfield. Three scores for each student can be obtained: the total for the first 10 items, the total for the second 10, and a composite total. The first half of the survey relates to attitude toward recreational reading; the second half relates to attitude toward academic aspects of reading.

Interpretation

You can interpret the scores in two ways. One is to note informally where the score falls in regard to the four nodes of the scale. A total score of 50, for example, would fall about midway on the scale, between the slightly happy and slightly upset figures, therefore indicating a relatively indifferent overall attitude toward reading. The other approach is more formal. It involves converting the raw scores into percentile ranks by means of Table 1. Be sure to use the norms for the right grade level and to note the column headings (Rec = recreational reading, Aca = academic reading, Tot = total score). If you wish to determine the average percentile rank for your class, average the raw scores first; then use the table to locate the percentile rank corresponding to the raw score mean. Percentile ranks cannot be averaged directly.

Source: McKenna, M. C., & Kear, D. (1990). Measuring attitude toward reading: A new tool for teachers. *The Reading Teacher,* *43,* 626–639. Used with permission.

(continued)

Elementary Reading Attitude Survey

School_____ Grade _____ Name _____

1. How do you feel when you read a book on a rainy Saturday?

2. How do you feel when you read a book in school during free time?

3. How do you feel about reading for fun at home?

4. How do you feel about getting a book for a present?

(continued)

5. How do you feel about spending free time reading?

6. How do you feel about starting a new book?

7. How do you feel about reading during summer vacation?

8. How do you feel about reading instead of playing?

(continued)

9. How do you feel about going to a bookstore?

10. How do you feel about reading different kinds of books?

11. How do you feel when the teacher asks you questions about what you read?

12. How do you feel about doing reading workbook pages and worksheets?

(continued)

13. How do you feel about reading in school?

14. How do you feel about reading your school books?

15. How do you feel about learning from a book?

16. How do you feel when its time for reading class?

(continued)

17. How do you feel about the stories you read in reading class?

18. How do you feel when you read out loud in class?

19. How do you feel about using a dictionary?

20. How do you feel about taking a reading test?

(continued)

APPENDIX
Technical Aspects of the Elementary Reading Attitude Survey

The norming project

To create norms for the interpretation of scores, a large-scale study was conducted in late January, 1989, at which time the survey was administered to 18,138 students in Grades 1-6. A number of steps were taken to achieve a sample that was sufficiently stratified (i.e., reflective of the American population) to allow confident generalizations. Children were drawn from 95 school districts in 38 U.S. states. The number of girls exceeded by only 5 the number of boys. Ethnic distribution of the sample was also close to that of the U.S. population (*Statistical abstract of the United States,* 1989). The proportion of Blacks (8.5%) was within 3% of the national proportion, while the proportion of Hispanics (8.2%) was within 2%.

Percentile ranks at each grade to both subscales and the full scale was presented in Table 1. These data can be used to compare individual students' scores with the national sample and they can be interpreted like achievement-test percentile ranks.

Table 1
Mid-year percentile ranks by grade and scale

Raw Scr	Grade 1 Rec	Aca	Tot	Grade 2 Rec	Aca	Tot	Grade 3 Rec	Aca	Tot	Grade 4 Rec	Aca	Tot	Grade 5 Rec	Aca	Tot	Grade 6 Rec	Aca	Tot
80			99			99			99			99			99			99
79			95			96			98			99			99			99
78			93			95			97			98			99			99
77			92			94			97			98			99			99
76			90			93			96			97			98			99
75			88			92			95			96			98			99
74			86			90			94			95			97			99
73			84			88			92			94			97			98
72			82			86			91			93			96			98
71			80			84			89			91			95			97
70			78			82			88			89			94			96
69			75			79			84			88			92			95
68			72			77			81			86			91			93
67			69			74			79			83			89			92
66			66			71			76			80			87			90
65			62			69			73			78			84			88
64			59			66			70			75			82			86
63			55			63			67			72			79			84
62			52			60			64			69			76			82
61			49			57			61			66			72			79
60			46			54			58			62			70			74
59			43			51			55			59			67			73
58			40			47			51			56			64			69
57			37			45			48			53			61			66
56			34			41			44			48			57			62
55			31			38			41			45			53			58
54			28			35			38			41			50			55
53			25			32			34			38			46			52
52			22			29			31			35			42			48
51			20			28			28			32			39			44
50			18			23			25			28			36			40
49			15			20			23			26			33			37
48			13			18			20			23			29			33
47			12			15			17			20			26			30
46			10			13			15			18			23			27
45			8			11			13			16			20			25
44			7			9			11			13			17			22
43			6			8			9			12			15			20
42			5			7			8			10			13			17
41			5			6			7			9			12			15
40	99	99	4	99	99	5	99	99	6	99	99	7	99	99	10	99	99	13
39	92	91	3	94	94	4	96	97	5	97	98	6	98	99	9	99	99	12
38	89	88	3	92	92	2	94	95	4	95	97	5	96	98	8	97	99	10

(continued)

Score																		
37	86	85	2	88	89	2	90	93	3	92	95	4	94	98	7	95	98	8
36	81	79	2	84	85	2	87	91	2	88	93	3	91	96	6	92	98	7
35	77	75	1	79	81	1	81	88	2	84	90	3	87	95	4	88	97	6
34	72	69	1	74	78	1	78	83	2	78	87	2	82	93	4	83	95	5
33	66	63	1	88	73	1	69	79	1	72	83	2	77	90	3	78	93	4
32	58	58	1	62	67	1	63	74	1	66	78	1	71	86	3	74	91	3
31	52	53	1	56	62	1	57	69	0	60	75	1	65	82	2	69	87	2
30	44	49	1	50	57	0	51	63	0	54	70	1	59	77	1	62	82	2
29	38	44	0	44	51	0	45	58	0	47	64	1	50	71	1	58	78	1
28	32	38	0	37	48	0	38	52	0	41	58	1	48	66	1	51	73	1
27	26	34	0	31	41	0	33	47	0	38	52	1	42	60	1	48	67	1
26	21	30	0	25	37	0	28	41	0	29	48	0	35	54	0	39	60	1
25	17	25	0	20	32	0	21	38	0	23	40	0	30	49	0	34	54	0
24	12	21	9	15	27	0	17	31	0	19	35	0	25	42	0	28	48	0
23	9	18	0	11	23	0	13	24	0	14	29	0	20	37	0	24	42	0
22	7	14	0	8	18	0	9	22	0	11	25	0	16	31	0	19	38	0
21	5	11	0	6	15	0	6	18	0	9	20	0	13	26	0	15	30	0
20	4	9	0	4	11	0	5	14	0	8	16	0	10	21	0	12	24	0
19	2	7		2	8		3	11		5	13		7	17		10	20	
18	2	6		2	6		2	8		3	8		6	13		8	13	
17	1	4		1	5		1	5		2	7		4	9		8	11	
16	1	3		1	3		1	4		2	5		3	8		4	8	
15	0	2		0	2		0	3		1	3		2	4		3	6	
14	0	2		0	1		0	1		1	2		1	2		1	3	
13	0	1		0	1		0	1		0	1		1	2		1	2	
12	0	1		0	0		0	0		0	1		0	1		0	1	
11	0	0		0	0		0	0		0	0		0	0		0	0	
10	0	0		0	0		0	0		0	0		0	0		0	0	

Reliability

Cronbach's alpha, a statistic developed primarily to measure the internal consistency of attitude scales (Cronbach, 1951), was calculated at each grade level for both subscales and for the composite score. These coefficients ranged from .74 to .89 and are presented in Table 2.

It is interesting that with only two exceptions, coefficients were .80 or higher. These were for the recreational subscale at Grades 1 and 2. It is possible that the stability of young children's attitudes toward leisure reading grows with their decoding ability and familiarity with reading as a pastime.

Table 2
Descriptive statistics and internal consistency measures

Grade	N	Recreational Subscale				Academic Subscale				Full Scale (Total)			
		M	SD	S_2M	Alpha[a]	M	SD	S_2M	Alpha	M	SD	S_2M	Alpha
1	2.518	31.0	5.7	2.9	.74	30.1	8.8	3.0	.01	61.0	11.6	4.1	.87
2	2.974	30.3	5.7	2.7	.78	28.8	6.7	2.9	.01	59.1	11.4	3.9	.88
3	3.151	30.0	5.6	2.5	.80	27.8	6.4	2.8	.01	57.8	10.9	3.8	.86
4	3.679	29.5	5.8	2.4	.83	26.9	6.3	2.6	.03	56.5	11.0	3.6	.89
5	3.374	28.5	6.1	2.3	.86	25.6	6.0	2.5	.02	54.1	10.8	3.6	.89
6	2.442	27.9	6.2	2.2	.87	24.7	5.8	2.5	.01	52.8	10.5	3.5	.89
All	18.136	29.5	5.9	2.5	.82	27.3	6.6	2.7	.03	56.8	11.3	3.7	.89

[a]Cronbach's alpha. (Cronbach, 1851).

(continued)

Elementary Reading Attitude Survey
Scoring Sheet

Student Name _____

Teacher _____

Grade _____ Administration Date _____

```
┌─────────────────────────────────────────┐
│             Scoring Guide                │
│                                          │
│   4 points      Happiest Garfield        │
│   3 points      Slightly smiling Garfield│
│   2 points      Mildly upset Garfield    │
│   1 point       Very upset Garfield      │
└─────────────────────────────────────────┘
```

Recreational Reading	Academic Reading
1. _____	11. _____
2. _____	12. _____
3. _____	13. _____
4. _____	14. _____
5. _____	15. _____
6. _____	16. _____
7. _____	17. _____
8. _____	18. _____
9. _____	19. _____
10. _____	20. _____

Raw score: _____   _____

Full scale raw score (Recreational + Academic): _____

Percentile ranks   Recreational   ┌──────────┐
                                        │   │
                        Academic   ├──────────┤
                                        │   │
                        Full scale   ├──────────┤
                                        │   │
                                        └──────────┘

Compendium 27   Self-Assessment for Traits of Effective Readers

Comprehension

1. I make predictions before I read.

| Always | Sometimes | Never | ? Unsure |

2. I understand the message—the text makes sense to me.

| Always | Sometimes | Never | ? Unsure |

3. I know when I am having trouble understanding the text.

| Always | Sometimes | Never | ? Unsure |

4. I know the main idea of the text.

| Always | Sometimes | Never | ? Unsure |

5. I know the main characters.

| Always | Sometimes | Never | ? Unsure |

6. I can retell the beginning, middle and end of the text.

| Always | Sometimes | Never | ? Unsure |

(continued)

Source: Northwest Regional Laboratory. (2001). *Reading scoring guides.* Retrieved November 13, 2003 from http://www.nwrel.org/assessment/scoring. Used with permission.

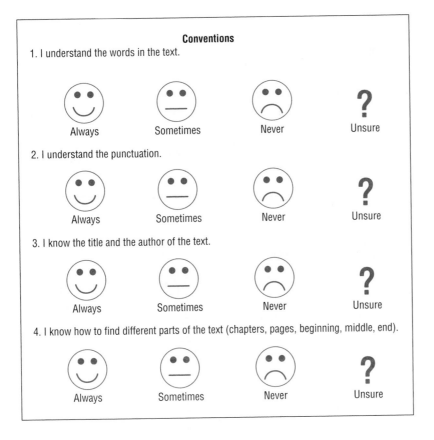

Conventions

1. I understand the words in the text.

Always   Sometimes   Never   Unsure

2. I understand the punctuation.

Always   Sometimes   Never   Unsure

3. I know the title and the author of the text.

Always   Sometimes   Never   Unsure

4. I know how to find different parts of the text (chapters, pages, beginning, middle, end).

Always   Sometimes   Never   Unsure

(continued)

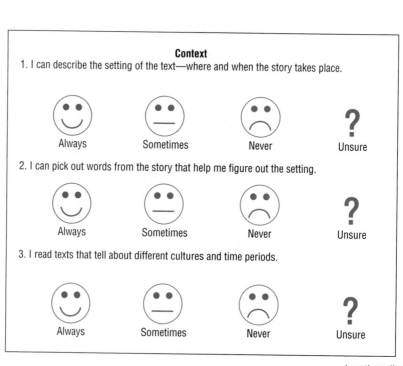

Interpretation

1. I notice when something is left out of the text or it doesn't make sense.

   Always   Sometimes   Never   Unsure

2. I can pick out clues from the reading to help me make an interpretation.

   Always   Sometimes   Never   Unsure

3. I know how to make an interpretation by telling what I think the author means or what happended in the story and why.

   Always   Sometimes   Never   Unsure

Context

1. I can describe the setting of the text—where and when the story takes place.

   Always   Sometimes   Never   Unsure

2. I can pick out words from the story that help me figure out the setting.

   Always   Sometimes   Never   Unsure

3. I read texts that tell about different cultures and time periods.

   Always   Sometimes   Never   Unsure

(continued)

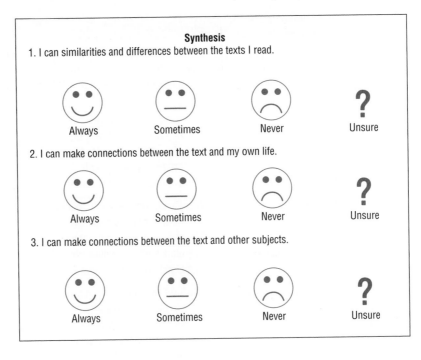

Synthesis

1. I can similarities and differences between the texts I read.

| Always | Sometimes | Never | Unsure |

2. I can make connections between the text and my own life.

| Always | Sometimes | Never | Unsure |

3. I can make connections between the text and other subjects.

| Always | Sometimes | Never | Unsure |

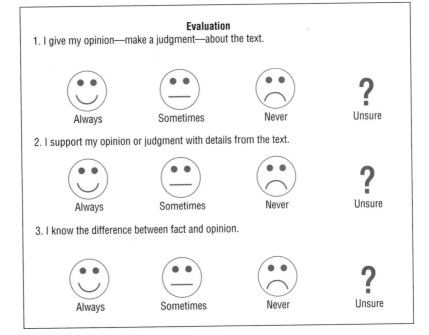

Evaluation

1. I give my opinion—make a judgment—about the text.

| Always | Sometimes | Never | Unsure |

2. I support my opinion or judgment with details from the text.

| Always | Sometimes | Never | Unsure |

3. I know the difference between fact and opinion.

| Always | Sometimes | Never | Unsure |

Compendium 28 Developmental Spelling Analysis Screening Inventory

Directions: I am going to say some words that I want you to spell for me. Some of the words will be easy to spell, and some will be more difficult. When you don't know how to spell a word, just do the best you can. Each time, I will say the word, then use it in a sentence, and then I will say the word again.

1.	hen	The hen sat on her eggs.
2.	wish	The boy made a wish and blew out the candles.
3.	trap	A spider web is a trap for flies.
4.	jump	A kangaroo can jump high.
5.	brave	A brave dog scared the robbers.
6.	smile	A smile shows that you're happy.
7.	grain	One kind of grain is called wheat.
8.	crawl	The baby can crawl but not walk.
9.	clerk	The clerk sold some shoes to me.
10.	clutch	The clutch in the car needs fixing.
11.	palace	The king and queen live in a palace.
12.	observe	I like to observe birds at the feeder.
13.	shuffle	Please shuffle the cards before you deal.
14.	exciting	The adventure story I'm reading is very exciting.
15.	treason	The man was found guilty of treason.
16.	column	His picture was in the first column of the newspaper.
17.	variety	A grocery store has a wide variety of foods.
18.	extension	The workers need an extension ladder to reach the roof.
19.	competition	There was much competition between the two businesses.
20.	illiterate	An illiterate person is one who cannot read.

Stop when the child has spelled 0 or 1 word correctly out of any set of five.

Source: Ganske, K. (2000). *Word journeys: Assessment-guided phonics, spelling, and vocabulary instruction.* New York: Guilford. Used with permission.

Compendium 29	Developmental Spelling Analysis Screening Inventory Prediction Chart

Inventory Score	Predicted Stage(s)
20	DC
19	DC
18	DC
17	DC
16	SJ/DC
15	SJ/DC
14	SJ
13	SJ
12	SJ
11	WW/SJ
10	WW/SJ
9	WW
8	WW
7	WW
6	LN/WW
5	LN/WW
4	LN
3	LN
2	LN
1	LN*
0	LN*

*Children who achieve a score of 0 or 1 may or may not be letter name spellers.

Source: Ganske, K. (2000). *Word journeys: Assessment-guided phonics, spelling, and vocabulary instruction*. New York: Guilford. Used with permission.

Compendium 30 Class Record of Writing Fluency

DATE																
NAME	TW	TS	EPS	MSL	TW	TS	EPS	MSL	TW	TS	EPS	MSL	TW	TS	EPS	MSL

TW = total words written
TS = total sentences written
EPS = average number of errors per sentence (TS ÷ # of errors)
MSL = mean sentence length (TW ÷ TS)

Compendium 31 Holistic Writing Rubric for Friendly Letter

Letter-Writing: Friendly Letter

Student's Name: _____

CATEGORY	4	3	2	1
Greeting and Closing	No mistakes	1–2 mistakes	3 or more mistakes	No greeting or closing
Format	Has all the elements of a friendly letter.	Has almost all the elements of a friendly letter.	Has several of the elements of a friendly letter.	Has few of the elements of a friendly letter.
Ideas	It was easy to figure out what the letter was about.	It was mostly easy to figure out what the letter was about.	Has to read it more than once to figure out what the letter was about.	It was hard to figure out what the letter was about.
Grammar & spelling (conventions)	No spelling or grammar mistakes.	1–2 mistakes in grammar or spelling.	3–4 mistakes in grammar or spelling.	4 mistakes in grammar or spelling.
Capitalization and Punctuation	No mistakes in capitalization and punctuation.	1–2 errors in capitalization and punctuation.	3–4 errors in capitalization and punctuation.	More than 4 errors in capitalization and punctuation.

Compendium 32 Writing Attitude Survey

Writing Attitude Survey

Name _____ School _____ Grade _____

1. How would you feel writing a letter to the author of a book you read?

2. How would you feel if you wrote about something you have heard or seen?

3. How would you feel writing a letter to a store asking about something you might buy there?

4. How would you feel telling in writing why something happened?

(continued)

Source: Kear, D. J., Coffman, G. A., McKenna, M. C., & Ambrosio, A. L. (2000). Measuring attitude toward writing: A new tool for teachers. *The Reading Teacher, 54,* 10–23. Used with permission.

5. How would you feel writing to someone to change their opinion?

6. How would you feel keeping a diary?

7. How would you feel writing poetry for fun?

8. How would you feel writing a letter stating your opinion about a topic?

9. How would you feel if you were an author who writes books?

(continued)

10. How would you feel if you had a job as a writer for a newspaper or magazine?

11. How would you feel about becoming an even better writer than you already are?

12. How would you feel about writing a story instead of doing homework?

13. How would you feel about writing a story instead of watching TV?

14. How would you feel writing about something you did in science?

(continued)

15. How would you feel writing about something you did in social studies?

16. How would you feel if you could write more in school?

17. How would you feel about writing down the important things your teacher says about a new topic?

18. How would you feel writing a long story or report at school?

19. How would you feel writing answers to questions in science or social studies?

(continued)

20. How would you feel if your teacher asked you to go back and change some of your writing?

21. How would you feel if your classmates talked to you about making your writing better?

22. How would you feel writing an advertisement for something people can buy?

23. How would you feel keeping a journal for class?

24. How would you feel writing about things that have happened in your life?

(continued)

25. How would you feel writing about something from another person's point of view?

26. How would you feel about checking your writing to make sure the words you have written are spelled correctly?

27. How would you feel if your classmates read something you wrote?

28. How would you feel if you didn't write as much in school?

(continued)

Writing Attitude Survey
Directions for Use

The Writing Attitude Survey provides a quick indication of student attitudes toward writing. It consists of 28 items and can be administered to an entire classroom in about 20 minutes. Each item presents a brief, simply worded statement about writing, followed by four pictures of Garfield. Each pose is designed to depict a different emotional state, ranging from very positive to very negative.

Administration

Begin by telling students that you wish to find out how they feel about writing. Emphasize that this is not a test and that there are no right answers. Encourage sincerity.

Distribute the survey forms and, if you wish to monitor the attitudes of specific students, ask them to write their names in the space at the top. Hold up a copy of the survey so that the students can see the first page. Point to the picture of Garfield at the far left of the first item. Ask the students to look at this same picture on their own survey form. Discuss with them the mood Garfield seems to be in (very happy). Then move to the next picture and again discuss Garfield's mood (this time, somewhat happy). In the same way, move to the third and fourth pictures and talk about Garfield's moods—somewhat upset and very upset.

Explain that the survey contains some statements about writing and that the students should think about how they feel about each statement. They should then circle the picture of Garfield that is closest to their own feelings. (Emphasize that the students should respond according to their own feelings, not as Garfield might respond!) In the first and second grades, read each item aloud slowly and distinctly, then read it a second time while students are thinking. Be sure to read the item number and to remind students of page numbers when new pages are reached.

In grades 3 and above, monitor students while they are completing this survey. It is not necessary for the teacher to read the items aloud to students, unless the teacher feels it is necessary for newer or struggling readers.

Teachers should review the items prior to the administration of the survey to identify any words students may need defined to eliminate misunderstanding during completion of the instrument.

Scoring

To score the survey, count four points for each leftmost (very happy) Garfield circles, three points for the next Garfield to the right (somewhat happy), two points for the next Garfield to the right (somewhat upset), and one point for the rightmost Garfield (very upset). The individual scores for each question should be totaled to reach a raw score.

Interpretation

The scores should first be recorded on the scoring sheet. The scores can be interpreted in two ways. An informal approach would be to look at where the raw score falls related to the total possible points of 112. If the raw score is approximately 70, the score would fall midway between the somewhat happy and somewhat upset Garfields, indicating the student has an indifferent attitude toward writing. The formal approach involves converting the raw score to a percentile rank by using Table 1. The raw score should be found on the left-hand side of the table and matched to the percentile rank in the appropriate grade-level column.

**Writing Attitude Survey
Scoring Sheet**

Student's name _____
Teacher _____
Grade _____
Administration date _____

	Scoring Guide
4 points	Very happy Garfield
3 points	Somewhat happy Garfield
2 points	Somewhat upset Garfield
1 point	Very upset Garfield

Item scores:

1.	_____	15.	_____
2.	_____	16.	_____
3.	_____	17.	_____
4.	_____	18.	_____
5.	_____	19.	_____
6.	_____	20.	_____
7.	_____	21.	_____
8.	_____	22.	_____
9.	_____	23.	_____
10.	_____	24.	_____
11.	_____	25.	_____
12.	_____	26.	_____
13.	_____	27.	_____
14.	_____	28.	_____

Full scale raw score: _____
Percentile rank: _____

Compendium 33 Speaking Checklist

Speaking Checklist

Name: _____

When _____ speaks in a group, he/she:

	Sept.	Dec.	Mar.	June
sticks to the topic.				
builds support for the subject.				
speaks clearly.				
takes turns and waits to talk.				
talks so others in the group can hear.				
speaks smoothly.				
uses courteous language.				
presents in an organized and interesting way.				
supports the topical thesis.				
answers questions effectively.				
is comfortable speaking publicly.				
maintains listeners' interest.				
volunteers to answer in class.				
speaks only to those who share the same native language.				

A = always, S = sometimes, N = never

My Speaking Checklist (Self-Assessment)

Name: _____

Please read each sentence. Answer by writing YES or NO in the box.

	Sept.	Dec.	Mar.	June
I stick to the topic.				
I build support for the subject.				
I speak clearly.				
I take turns and wait for my turn to talk.				
I talk so others in the group can hear me.				
I speak smoothly.				
I keep the interest of listeners.				
I listen to what others say.				
My talk is organized and interesting.				
I talk so everyone can hear me.				
I use courteous language.				
I answer questions about my talk.				
I am comfortable speaking publicly.				
I enjoy oral presentations.				
I like to talk with all of the other class members.				

Source: From Sandra Hurley & Josefina Tinajero, *Literacy Assessment of Second Language Learners*. Published by Allyn and Bacon, Boston, MA. Copyright © 2001 by Pearson Education. Reprinted by permission of the publisher.

Compendium 34 Speaking Self-Assessment Checklist

Student Assessment Record

How am I doing on the following tasks?

Color the one most like you.

		Super	Just OK	Needing practice
Talking in English	I am	😊	😐	☹️
Talking in Spanish	I am	😊	😐	☹️
Writing in English	I am	😊	😐	☹️
Writing in Spanish	I am	😊	😐	☹️
Reading in English	I am	😊	😐	☹️
Reading in Spanish	I am	😊	😐	☹️

Date: ___

Name: ___

Color the one most like you.

		Super	Just OK	Needing practice
Talking in English	I am	😊	😐	☹️
Talking in Spanish	I am	😊	😐	☹️
Writing in English	I am	😊	😐	☹️
Writing in Spanish	I am	😊	😐	☹️
Reading in English	I am	😊	😐	☹️
Reading in Spanish	I am	😊	😐	☹️

Date: ___

Name: ___

Source: From Sandra Hurley & Josefina Tinajero, *Literacy Assessment of Second Language Learners*. Published by Allyn and Bacon, Boston, MA. Copyright © 2001 by Pearson Education. Reprinted by permission of the publisher.

Compendium 35   Oral Presentation Checklist

Name: _____   Date: _____

Topic: _____   Time: _____

Criteria	Assessment			
States name	3	2	1	0
States purpose for presentation	3	2	1	0
Makes eye contact with audience	3	2	1	0
Uses gestures to support talk	3	2	1	0
Voice can be heard by participants	3	2	1	0
Pacing is appropriate for topic	3	2	1	0
Uses grammatically correct language	3	2	1	0
Uses appropriate vocabulary for topic	3	2	1	0
Adheres to time limit	3	2	1	0

3 – exceeds standards
2 – meets standards
1 – below standards
0 – not evidenced

Total Points: ☐

Student Name: _____ Grade: _____ Age: _____ Language: _____

	1	2	3	4	5	Scores
Comprehension	Cannot be said to understand even simple conversation.	Has great difficulty following what is said. Comprehends only social conversation spoken slowly with frequent repetitions.	Understands most of what is said at slower-than-normal speed with repetitions.	Understands nearly everything at normal speed, although occasionally repetition may be necessary.	Understands everyday conversations and normal classroom discussions without difficulty.	
Fluency	Speech is so halting and fragmentary as to make conversation virtually impossible.	Usually hesitant; often forced into silence by language limitations.	Speech in everyday conversation somewhat limited because of inadequate vocabulary.	Speech in everyday conversation and classroom discussion is generally fluent, with occasional lapses while student searches for the correct manner of expression.	Speech in everyday conversation and classroom discussion is fluent and effortless, approximating that of a native speaker.	
Vocabulary	Vocabulary limitations so extreme as to make conversation virtually impossible.	Misuse of words and very limited vocabulary make comprehension quite difficult.	Frequently uses the wrong words; conversation somewhat limited because of inadequate vocabulary.	Occasionally uses inappropriate terms and/or must rephrase ideas because of lexical inadequacies.	Use of vocabulary and idioms approximates that of a native speaker.	
Pronunciation	Pronunciation problems so severe as to make speech virtually unintelligible.	Very hard to understand because of pronunciation problems. Must frequently repeat in order to be understood.	Pronunciation problems necessitate concentration on the part of the listener and occasionally lead to misunderstanding.	Always intelligible, though one is conscious of a definite accent and occasional inappropriate intonation patterns.	Pronunciation and intonation approximates that of a native speaker.	
Grammar	Errors in grammar and word order so severe as to make speech virtually unintelligible.	Grammar and word errors make comprehension difficult. Must often rephrase and/or restrict self to basic patterns.	Makes frequent errors and word order which occasionally obscure meaning.	Occasionally makes grammatical and/or word order errors which do not obscure meaning.	Grammatical usage and word order approximate that of a native speaker.	
Stages of Language Development	Pre-Production Score: 20%	Early Production Score 24–40%	Speech Emergence Score: 44–60%	Intermediate Score: 64–80%	Advanced Native-like Fluency Score: 84–100%	TOTAL ____ × 4 = ____ %

Book Choices by Grade Level

KINDERGARTEN

Briggs, Raymond	The Snowman
Burningham, John	Mr. Gumpy's Outing
Carle, Eric	The Very Quiet Cricket
Delacre, Lulu	Arroz Con Leche
Eastman, P. D.	Are You My Mother?
Fox, Mem	Time for Bed
Galdone, Paul	The Little Ren Hen
Gibbons, Gail	Farming
Haskins, Jim	Count Your Way Through Mexico
Henkes, Kevin	Owen
Hoban, Russell	Bedtime for Frances
Hoberman, MaryAnn	A House is a House for Me
Hutchins, Pat	Titch
Keats, Ezra Jack	Goggles
Kovalski, MaryAnn	The Wheels on the Bus
Lionni, Leo	Alexander and the Wind-up Mouse
McPhail, David	The Bear's Toothache
Minarik, Else	Little Bear
Piper, Watty	The Little Engine That Could
Rey, H. A.	Curious George
Rockwell, Anne	Fire Engines
Rylant, Cynthia	Birthday Presents
Seuss, Dr.	The Cat in the Hat
Shaw, Charles	It Looked like Spilt Milk
Williams, Vera B.	A Chair for My Mother
Wood, Audrey	Quick as a Cricket
Zolotow, Charlotte	I Know a Lady

FIRST GRADE

Aliki	Digging up Dinosaurs
Anno, Mitsumasa	All in A Day
Arnold, Tedd	Green Wilma
Baker, Barbara	Digby and Kate and the Beautiful Day
Brown, Mark	Arthur's Eyes
Carle, Eric	The Grouchy Ladybug

Chaucer, Geoffrey	Chanticleer and the Fox
Cronin, Doreen	Click, Clack, Moo: Cows That Type
De Brunhoff, Jean	The Story of Babar
De Paola, Tomie	Nana Upstairs and Nana Downstairs
Dooley, Nora	Everybody Cooks Rice
Feelings, Muriel	Moja means One: Swahili Counting Book
Fox, Mem	Tough Boris
Freeman, Don	A Pocket for Corduroy
Gag, Wanda	Millions of Cats
Gerstein, M.	The Absolutely Awful Alphabet
Henkes, Kevin	Chrysanthemum
Hoban, Russell	Bread and Jam for Frances
Hoff, Sid	Captain Cat
Keats, Ezra Jack	Whistle for Willie
Krauss, Ruth	The Carrot Seed
Leonni, Leo	Swimmy
Lobel, Anita & Arnold	On Market Street
Lobel, Arnold	Frog and Toad Together
Mayer, Mercer	Just for You
McMillan, Bruce	Mouse Views: What the Class Pet Saw
Paulsen, Gary	The Tortilla Factory
Polacco, Patricia	Thunder Cake
Sendak, Maurice	Chicken Soup With Rice
Seuss, Dr.	Green Eggs and Ham
Simont, Marc	The Stray Dog
Sloat, Teri	There Was an Old Lady Who Swallowed a Trout!
Tresselt, Alvin	The Mitten

SECOND GRADE

Adler, David	A Picture Book of Martin Luther King Jr.
Aliki	Corn is Maize
Allard, Harry	Miss Nelson is Missing
Anderson, Laurie Halse	The Big Cheese of Third Street
Bemelmans, Ludwig	Madeline
Byars, Betsy	My Brother, Ant
Bunting, Eve	The Wednesday Surprise
Creech, Sharon	A Fine, Fine School
De Paola, Tomie	Now One Foot, Now the Other
Dorros, Arthur	Abuela
Friedman, Ina	How My Parents Learned to Eat
Howe, James	Horace and Morris But Mostly Dolores
Leaf, Munro	The Story of Ferdinand
Lobel, Arnold	Frog and Toad All Year
Lovell, Patty	Stand Tall, Molly Lou Melon
Lomas Garza, Carmen	Family Pictures (Cuadros de Familia)
Lyon, George	Come a Tide
Marshall, James	George and Martha

Morris, Ann	Bread, Bread, Bread
Noble, Trinka H.	The Day Jimmy's Boa Ate the Wash
Parish, Peggy	Amelia Bedelia
Pilkey, Dav	The Paperboy
Potter, Beatrix	The Tale of Peter Rabbit
Ringgold, Faith	Dinner at Aunt Connie's House
Seuss, Dr.	And To Think I Saw It on Mulberry Street
Sharmat, Marjorie	Nate The Great
Stadler, John	The Cats of Mrs. Calamari
Steig, William	Sylvester and the Magic Pebble
Van Allsburg, Chris	Two Bad Ants
Viorst, Judith	Alexander, Who Used To Be Rich Last Sunday
Wiesner, David	The Three Pigs
Young, Ed	Lon Po Po

THIRD GRADE

Aardema, Verna	Why Mosquitoes Buzz in People's Ears
Ada, Alma Flor	Dear Peter Rabbit
Andersen, Hans Christian	The Emperor's New Clothes
Arnold, Tedd	Parts
Base, Graeme	The Eleventh Hour: A Curious Mystery
Baylor, Byrd	I'm in Charge of Celebrations
Blume, Judy	Freckle Juice
Cherry, Lynne	A River Ran Wild
Cleary, Beverly	Ramona and her Father
Cole, Jonna	The Magic School Bus
Dahl, Roald	The Magic Finger
Danziger, Pauka	Amber Brown Goes Fourth
Duffey, Betsy	How to be Cool in the Third Grade
Giff, Patricia Reilly	Kidnap at the Catfish Cafe
Grimes, Nikki	Meet Danitra Brown
Kuskin, Karla	The Philharmonic Gets Dressed
Macaulay, David	Black and White
McDonald, Megan	Judy Moody
Milne, A.A.	Winnie the Pooh
Ringgold, Faith	Tar Beach
Rylant, Cynthia	The Relatives Came
San Souci, Robert	N.C. Wyeth's Pilgrims
Seuss, Dr.	The 500 Hats of Bartholomew Cubbins
Siebert, Diane	Heartland
Soto, Gary	The Skirt
Steptoe, John	Mufaro's Beautiful Daughters
Surat, Michele	Angel Child, Dragon Child
Turkle, Brinton	Thy Friend, Obadiah
Warner, Gertrude Chandler	The Boxcar Children
White, E.B.	Stuart Little
Wiesner, David	Tuesday

FOURTH GRADE

Blume, Judy	Tales of a Fourth Grade Nothing
Clements, Andrew	Frindle
Creech, Sharon	Granny Torrelli Makes Soup
Creech, Sharon	Love That Dog
DiCamillo, Kate	Because of Winn-Dixie
Fleischman, Sid	By the Great Horn Spoon
Gardiner, John	Stone Fox
Horvath, Polly	The Trolls
Howe, Deborah	Bunnicula: A Rabbit-tale of Mystery
Ibbotson, Eva	Island of the Aunts
King-Smith, Dick	Harriet's Hare
Konigsburg, E. L.	The View From Saturday
Korman, Gordon	The Sixth Grade Nickname Game
Lowry, Lois	See You Around, Sam!
MacLachlan, Patricia	Sarah, Plain and Tall
O'Dell, Scott	Island of the Blue Dolphins
Rylant, Cynthia	The Van Gogh Café
Sachar, Louis	Sideways Stories from Wayside School
Smith, Doris	A Taste of Blackberries
Spinelli, Jerry	Maniac Magee
White, E. B.	Charlotte's Web
Wilder, Laura Ingalls	Little House on the Prairie

FIFTH GRADE

Blackwood, Gary	The Shakespeare Stealer
Bunting, Eve	Spying on Mrs. Muller
Byars, Betsy	McMummy
Dahl, Roald	Danny, the Champion of the World
Farley, Walter	The Black Stallion
Fitzhugh, Louise	Harriet the Spy
Fritz, Jean	The Double Life of Pocahontas
Giblin, James Cross	George Washington: A Picture Book Biography
Henry, Marguerite	Misty of Chincoteague
Jones, D	Wild Robert
Kellogg, Steven	Paul Bunyan
King-Smith, Dick	Three Terrible Trins
Konigsburg, E.L.	From the Mixed Up Files of Mrs. Basil E. Frankweiler
Lindgren, Astrid	Pippi Longstocking
Lord, Bette	In the Year of the Boar and Jackie Robinson
Morgenstern, S.	A Book of Coupons
Nixon, Joan Lowry	If You Were A Writer
Paulsen, Gary	Hatchet
Polacco, Patricia	The Keeping Quilt
Porter, Connie	Meet Addy
Pullman, Philip	I Was a Rat!

Say, Allen	El Chino
Scieszka, Jon	The Math Curse
Singer, Isaac.B	Zlateh the Goat
Snicket, Lemony	A Series of Unfortunate Events
Speare, Elizabeth	The Witch of Blackbird Pond
Staples, S.	The Green Dog: A Mostly True Story
Van Allsburg, Chris	The Wreck of the Zephyr

SIXTH GRADE

Almond, David	Skellig
Babitt, Natalie	Tuck Everlasting
Billingsley, Franny	The Folk Keeper
Burnett, Frances H.	The Secret Garden
Cameron, Ann	Colibri
Clements, Andrew	The Landry News: A Brand New School Story
Coman, Carolyn	What Jamie Saw
Creech, Sharon	Chasing Redbird
Gaiman, Neil	Coraline
Gantos, Jack	Joey Pigza Swallowed the Key
Juster, Norton	The Phantom Tollbooth
Kipling, Rudyard	The Jungle Book
Konigsburg, E. L.	Silent to the Bone
Lowry, Lois	Number the Stars
Montgomery, Lucy	Anne of Green Gables
McCaughrean, G	The Kite Rider: A Novel
North, Sterling	Rascal
Park, Linda Sue	A Single Shard
Patterson, Katherine	Bridge to Terabithia
Platt, Richard	Castle Diary: The Journal of Tobias Burgess
Price, Leontyne	Aida
Pullman, Philip	Clockwork
Rylant, Cynthia	Missing May
Sachar, Louis	Holes
Swell, Ana	Black Beauty
Sperry, Armstrong	Call It Courage
Spinelli, Jerry	Crash
Taylor, Mildred	Roll of Thunder, Hear My Cry

SEVENTH GRADE

Alexander, Lloyd	The Book of Three
Alvarez, Julia	Before We Were Free
Clements, Andrew	Things Not Seen
Cooper, Susan	The Dark is Rising
Cushman, Karen	Catherine, Called Birdy
De Angeli, Marguerite	The Door in the Wall
Deans, Sis	Racing the Past

Dickens, Charles	A Christmas Carol
Fisher, Leonard Everett	Johann Gutenberg
Hamilton, Virginia	Cousins
Ho, Minfong	Rice without Rain
Jimenez, Francisco	Breaking Through
Lazo, Caroline	The Terra Cotta Army of Emperor Qin
Mcdonald, Fiona	Ancient Japan: What Life was Like for the Ancient Japanese
Mikaelsen, Ben	Petey
Myers, Walter Dean	Scorpions
Paulsen, Gary	The Crossing
Pitts, Paul	Racing the Sun
Rawlings, Marjorie	The Yearling
Stevenson, Robert Louis	Treasure Island
Tolkein, J. R. R.	The Hobbit
Wieniewski, David	Sundiata: Lion King of Mali

EIGHTH GRADE

Alcott, Louisa May	Little Women
Bruchac, Joseph	Sacajawea
Carbone, Elisa	Stealing Freedom
Couloumbis, Audrey	Getting Near to Baby
Delacrue, Lulu	Salsa Stories
Edmonds, Walter	Drums Along the Mohawk
Forbes, Esther	Johnny Tremain
Feelings, Tom	Middle Passage: White Ships/Black Cargo
Filipovic, Zlata	Zlata's Diary
Flake, Sharon	The Skin I'm In
Frank, Anne	Anne Frank: Diary of a Young Girl
Grimes, Nikki	Talkin' About Bessie: The Story of Aviator Elizabeth Coleman
Haddix, Margaret	Among the Hidden
Hesse, Karen	Out of the Dust
Johnson, Angela	Heaven
Kennedy, John F.	Profiles in Courage
Lasky, Kathryn	A Time for Courage
London, Jack	Call of the Wild
Na, An	A Step from Heaven
Patterson, Katherine	The Master Puppeteer
Paulsen, Gary	Nightjohn
Steinbeck, John	The Red Pony
Trueman, Terry	Stuck in Neutral
Yolen, Jane	The Devil's Arithmetic

2

Children and Young Adult Titles by Genre

Find these titles and thousands more on the children's literature database attached to the text.

HISTORICAL FICTION

Primary Grades

Bunting, E. (1990). *The wall*. New York: Clarion.

Byars, B. (1992). *Hooray for the Golly sisters!* New York: HarperTrophy.

Coerr, E. (1989). *The Josefina story quilt*. New York: HarperTrophy.

Hopkinson, D. (1995). *Sweet Clara and the freedom quilt*. New York: Dragonfly.

Marcellino, F. (1999) *I, crocodile*. New York: HarperCollins.

McKissack, P. (2001). *Goin' someplace special*. New York: Atheneum.

Polacco, P. (2000). *The butterfly*. New York: Philomel.

Scieszka, J. (1991). *Knights of the kitchen table*. New York: Penguin.

Scieszka, J. (1996). *Tut tut*. New York: Penguin.

Tunnell, M. (1997). *Mailing May*. New York: Greenwillow.

Intermediate Grades

Avi. (1997). *The true confessions of Charlotte Doyle*. New York: HarperTrophy.

Creech, S. (2004). *Walk two moons*. New York: HarperTrophy.

Curtis, C. P. (2002). *Bud, not Buddy*. New York: Yearling.

Cushman, K. (2000). *Matilda bone*. New York: Clarion.

Fleischman, S. (1998). *Bandit's moon*. New York: Greenwillow.

Grutman, J. H. (1994). *The ledgerbook of Thomas Blue Eagle*. New York: Lickle.

Holm, J. (1999). *Our only May Amelia*. New York: HarperCollins.

Osborne, M. (2000). *Adaline falling star*. New York: Scholastic.

Patterson, K. (1994). *Lyddie*. New York: Puffin.

Paulsen, G. (1995). *The rifle*. San Diego: Harcourt Brace.

Peck, R. (1998). *A long way from Chicago*. New York: Puffin.

Peck, R. (2000). *A year down yonder*. New York: Dial.

Ryan, P. M. (2000). *Esperanza rising*. New York: Scholastic.

Middle School

Anderson, L. (2000). *Fever, 1793*. New York: Simon & Schuster.

Avi. (2002). *Crispin: The cross of lead*. New York: Hyperion.

Collier, J. L. (1989). *My brother Sam is dead*. New York: Scholastic.

Fuqua, J. (2002). *Darby*. Cambridge: Candlewick Press.

Hesse, Karen. (2003). *Witness*. New York: Scholastic.

Meyer, L. A. (2002). *Bloody Jack: Being an account of the curious adventures of Mary "Jacky" Faber, ship's boy*. San Diego: Harcourt.

Polacco, P. (1994). *Pink and Say*. New York: Philomel.

Staples, S. F. (1989). *Shabanu: Daughter of the wind*. New York: Knopf.

Taylor, M. (2001). *The land*. New York: Penguin.

REALISTIC FICTION

Primary Grades

Di Paola, T. (1990). *Oliver Button is a sissy*. Orlando, FL: Voyager.

Fox, M. (1989). *Wilfred Gordon McDonald Partridge*. New York: Scott, Foresman.

Hutchins, P. (1989). *The doorbell rang*. New York: Greenwillow.

Rosa-Casanova, S. (1997). *Mama Provi and the pot of rice*. New York: Anthenum.

Shannon, D. (1999). *No, David!* New York: Scholastic.

Whitcomb, M. E. (1998). *Odd velvet*. San Francisco: Chronicle.

Intermediate Grades

Alexander, L. (1997). *The fortune-tellers*. New York: Puffin.

Clements, A. (1996). *Frindle*. New York: Aladdin.

Clements, A. (2000). *The janitor's boy*. New York: Simon & Schuster.

DiCamillo, K. (2000). *Because of Winn-Dixie*. Cambridge, MA: Candlewick.

Fletcher, R. (1998). *Flying solo*. New York: Clarion.

Garland, S. (1997). *The lotus seed*. San Diego: Harcourt Brace.

Gorman, C. (1999). *Dork in disguise*. New York: HarperCollins.

Horvath, P. (2001). *Everything on a waffle*. New York: Farrar, Straus & Giroux.

Spinelli, J. (2000). *Maniac Magee*. New York: Little, Brown.

Woodson, J. (2001). *The other side*. New York: Putnam.

Middle School

Bauer, J. (2000). *Hope was here*. New York: Putnam.

Bauer, J. (2004). *Stand tall*. New York: Putnam.

Flake, S. G. (1998). *The skin I'm in*. New York: Jump at the Sun.

Hiaasen, C. (2002). *Hoot*. New York: Knopf.

Horvath, P. (2003). *The canning season*. New York: Farrar, Straus & Giroux.

Martin, A. (2002). *A corner of the universe*. New York: Scholastic.

Mikaelsen, B. (2001). *Touching Spirit Bear*. New York: HarperCollins.

Mosher, R. (2001). *Zazoo*. New York: Clarion.

Spinelli, J. (1997). *Crash*. New York: Knopf.

Spinelli, J. (2000). *Stargirl*. New York: Knopf.

Tolan, S. (2002). *Surviving the Applewhites*. New York: HarperCollins.

Van Draanen, W. (2001). *Flipped*. New York: Knopf.

Walter, V. (1998). *Making up megaboy*. New York: DK Publishing.

Whelan, G. (2000). *Homeless bird*. New York: HarperCollins.

Woodson, J. (2000). *Miracle's boys*. New York: Putnam.

FANTASY

Primary Grades

DePaola, T. (1979). *Stega nona*. New York: Aladdin.

Falconer, I. (2002). *Olivia saves the circus*. New York: Atheneum.

Feiffer, J. (1999). *Bark, George*. New York: HarperCollins.

Ryan, P. M. (2001). *Mice and beans*. New York: Scholastic.

Steig, W. (1998). *Pete's a Pizza*. New York: HarperCollins.

Teague, M. (2002) *Dear Mrs. Larue: Letters from obedience school*. New York: Scholastic.

Thomas, S. (2002). *Good night, good knight*. New York: Dutton.

Intermediate grades

Dahl, R. (1961). *James and the giant peach*. New York: Penguin.

Dahl, R. (1964). *Charlie and the chocolate factory*. New York: Knopf.

DiCamillo, K. (2003). *The tale of Despereaux: Being the story of a mouse, a princess, some soup, and a spool of thread*. Cambridge, MA: Candlewick.

Fleischman, P. (1996). *Dateline: Troy*. Cambridge, MA: Candlewick.

Fleischman, P. (1999). *Weslandia*. Cambridge, MA: Candlewick.

Rowling, J. K. (2003). *Harry Potter and the order of the phoenix*. New York: Scholastic.

Spinelli, J. (1997). *The library card*. New York: Scholastic.

Middle School

Dickinson, P. (2003). *The ropemaker*. New York: Delacorte.

DuPrau, J. (2003). *The city of Ember*. New York: Random House.

Farmer, N. (2004). *The house of the scorpion*. New York: Simon & Schuster.

Haddix, M. (1998). *Among the hidden*. New York: Simon & Schuster.

Jacques, B. (1986). *Redwall*. New York: Philomel.

Lewis, C. S. (1951). *The lion, the witch, and the wardrobe*. New York: HarperCollins.

Philbrick, R. (2000). *The last book in the universe*. New York: Blue Sky.

Sanvoisin, E. (1998). *The ink drinker*. New York: Delacorte.

POETRY
Primary Grades

Alarcón, F. X. (1997). *Laughing tomatoes and other spring poems*. San Francisco: Children's Book Press.

Prelutsky, J. (1993). *The dragons are singing tonight*. New York: Greenwillow.

Prelutsky, J. (2000). *The Random House book of poetry for children*. New York: Random House.

Scheer, J. (1964). *Rain makes applesauce*. New York: Holiday House.

Stevenson, J. (1998). *Popcorn: Poems*. New York: Greenwillow.

Updike, J. (1999). *A child's calendar: Poems*. New York: Holiday House.

Intermediate Grades

Fleischman, P. (1992). *Joyful noise: Poems for two voices*. New York: HarperCollins.

Janeczko, P. (2001). *A poke in the I: A collection of concrete poems*. Cambridge, MA: Candlewick.

Janeczko, P. (2001). *Dirty laundry pile: Poems in different voices*. New York: HarperCollins.

Mak, K. (2002). *My Chinatown: One year in poems*. New York: HarperCollins.

Thayer, E. L., & Bing, C. (2000). *Casey at the bat: A ballad of the republic sung in the year 1888*. New York: Handprint.

Woodson, J. (2003). *Locomotion*. New York: Putnam.

Middle School

Florian, D. (1999). *Insectlopedia*. San Diego: Harcourt Brace.

Gordon, R. (Ed.). (1995). *Pierced by a ray of sun: Poems about the times we feel alone*. New York: HarperCollins.

Hesse, K. (1997). *Out of the dust*. New York: Scholastic.

Hirsch, R. (2002). *FEG: Ridiculous stupid poems for intelligent children*. Boston: Little, Brown.

Janeczko, P. (Ed.). (1990). *The place my words are looking for: What poets say about and through their work*. New York: Simon & Schuster.

Nye, N. S. (2002). *19 varieties of gazelle: Poems of the Middle East*. New York: Greenwillow.

BIOGRAPHY AND AUTOBIOGRAPHY
Primary Grades

De Paola, T. (1999). *26 Fairmount Avenue*. New York: Putnam.

Gerstein, M. (2003). *The man who walked between the towers*. Brookfield, CN: Roaring Brook.

Krull, K. (2000). *Wilma unlimited: How Wilma Rudolph became the world's fastest woman*. Orlando, FL: Voyager.

Krull, K. (2003). *Harvesting Hope: The Story of Cesar Chavez*. San Diego: Harcourt.

Lasky, K. (2000). *A vision of beauty: The story of Sarah Breedlove Walker*. Cambridge, MA: Candlewick.

St. George, J. (2000). *So you want to be president*. New York: Philomel.

Wilder, L. I. (1973). *Little house on the prairie*. New York: HarperTrophy.

Intermediate Grades

Bridges, R. (1999). *Through my eyes*. New York: Scholastic.

Coerr, E. (1993). *Sadako and the thousand paper cranes*. New York: Puffin.

Krull, K. (1995). *Lives of the artists: Masterpieces, messes (and what the neighbors thought)*. San Diego: Harcourt.

Mochizuki, K. (1997). *Passage to freedom: The Sugihara story*. New York: Lee & Low.

Paulsen, G. (1998). *My life in dog years*. New York: Bantam Doubleday Dell.

Sis, P. (1996). *Starry messenger: A book depicting the life of a famous scientist, mathematician, astronomer, philosopher, physicist, Galileo Galilei.* New York: Farrar, Straus & Giroux.

Middle School

Gantos, J. (2002). *Hole in my life.* New York: Farrar, Straus & Giroux.

Jimenez, F. (1997). *The circuit: Stories from the life of a migrant child.* Albuquerque, NM: University of New Mexico.

Kerley, B. (2001). *The dinosaurs of Waterhouse Hawkins: An illuminating history of Mr. Waterhouse Hawkins, artist and lecturer.* New York: Scholastic.

Partridge, E. (2002). *This land was made for you and me: The life and songs of Woody Guthrie.* New York: Viking.

Rembert, W. (2003). *Don't hold me back: My life and art.* New York: Cricket/Marcato.

Stanley, D. (2002). *Saladin: Noble prince of Islam.* New York: HarperCollins.

Tyuchiya, Y. (1988). *Faithful elephants: A true story of animals, people, and war.* Boston: Houghton Mifflin.

EXPOSITORY AND INFORMATIONAL TEXT
Primary Grades

Andrews-Goebel, N. (2002). The pot that Juan built. New York: Lee & Low.

Cowley, J. (1999). *Red-eyed tree frog.* New York: Scholastic.

Gibbons, G. (1994). *The planets.* New York: Holiday House.

Micucci, C. (1997). *Life and times of the peanut.* Boston: Houghton Mifflin.

Weitzman, J. P., & Glasser, R. P. (1998). *You can't take a balloon into the Metropolitan museum.* New York: Dial.

Weitzman, J. P., & Glasser, R. P. (2000). *You can't take a balloon into the National Gallery.* New York: Dial.

Intermediate Grades

Aliki. (1986). *Corn is maize: The gift of the Indians.* New York: HarperCollins.

Ancona, G. (1993). *Pablo remembers: The day of the dead.* New York: Lothrop, Lee, & Shepard.

Christelow, E. (1999). *What do illustrators do?* New York: Clarion.

Deem, J. (1998). *Bodies from the bog.* Boston: Houghton Mifflin.

Jenkins, S. (1999). *Top of the world: Climbing Mount Everest.* Boston: Houghton Mifflin.

Knight, M. B. (1999). *Talking walls.* Gardiner, ME: Tilbury House.

Simon, S. (1998). *Muscles: Our muscular system.* New York: William Morrow.

Yin. (2001). *Coolies.* New York: Philomel.

Middle School

Fleischman, J. (2002). *Phineas Gage: A gruesome but true story about brain science.* New York: Houghton Mifflin.

Fradin, D. (2002). *The signers: The 56 Stories behind the Declaration of Independence.* New York: Walker.

Murphy, J. (2003). *An American plague: The true and terrifying story of the yellow fever epidemic of 1793.* New York: Clarion.

Pringle, L. (1997). *An extraordinary life: The story of a monarch butterfly.* New York: Orchard.

Wick, W. (1997). *A drop of water: A book of science and wonder.* New York: Scholastic.

SHORT STORIES
Primary Grades

Lionni, L. (1985). *Frederick's fables: A Leo Lionni treasury of favorites.* New York: Knopf.

Rylant, C. (1997). *Poppleton.* New York: Scholastic.

Intermediate Grades

Huynh, Q. N. (1982). *Land I lost: Adventures of a boy in Vietnam.* New York: HarperCollins.

Krull, K. (1997). *Lives of the athletes: Thrills, spills (and what the neighbors thought).* San Diego: Harcourt Brace.

Marshall, J. (1991). *Rats on the roof and other stories.* New York: Dial.

Sachar, L. (1998). *Sideways stories from wayside school*. New York: HarperTrophy.

Yolen, J. (Ed.). (1995). *The haunted house: A collection of original stories*. New York: HarperCollins.

Middle School

Armstrong, J. (Ed.). (2002) *Shattered: Stories of children and war*. New York: Knopf.

Blume, J. (Ed.). (1999). *Places I never meant to be: Original stories by censored writers*. New York: Simon & Schuster.

Carlson, L. (Ed.). (1996). *American eyes: New Asian-American short stories for young adults*. New York: Ballantine.

Cart, M. (Ed.). (1999). *Tomorrowland: 10 stories about the future*. New York: Scholastic.

Hague, M. (Ed.). (1995). *The book of dragons*. New York: William Morrow.

Hurwitz, J. (Ed.). (1997). *Birthday surprises: Ten great stories to unwrap*. New York: Beech Tree.

Myers, W. (2001). *145th Street: Short stories*. New York: Delacorte.

FOLKTALES
Primary Grades

Diakité, B. W. (1997). *The hunterman and the crocodile: A West African folktale*. New York: Scholastic.

Martin, F. (2000). *Clever tortoise: A traditional African tale*. Cambridge, MA: Candlewick.

McDermott, G. (1977). *Arrow to the sun: A Pueblo Indian tale*. New York: Puffin.

McDermott, G. (1987). *Anansi the spider: A tale from the Ashanti*. New York: Henry Holt.

McDermott, G. (2000). *Musicians of the sun*. New York: Aladdin.

Montes, M. (2000). *Juan Bobo goes to work*. New York: HarperCollins.

Sierra, J. (2001). *Tasty baby belly buttons*. New York: Knopf.

Wiesner, D. (2001). *The three pigs*. New York: Clarion.

Yep, L. (2002). *The khan's daughter: a Mongolian folktale*. New York: Scholastic.

Intermediate Grades

Demi. (1997). *One grain of rice: A mathematical folktale*. New York: Scholastic.

Hamilton, V. (1997). *A ring of tricksters: Animal tales from America, the West Indies, and Africa*. New York: Blue Sky.

Keats, E. J. (1965). *John Henry: An American legend*. New York: Pantheon.

Manna, A. (1997). *Mr. Semolina-Semolinus: A Greek folktale*. New York: Atheneum.

Martin, R. (1998). *The rough-face girl*. New York: Puffin.

San Souci, R. D. (1989). *Talking eggs: A folktale from the American south*. New York: Dial.

Scieszka, J. (1996). *The true story of the three little pigs*. New York: Puffin.

Yolen, J. (1998). *King long shanks*. San Diego: Harcourt Brace.

Middle School

Gerson, M. (2001). *Fiesta femenina: Celebrating women in Mexican folktale*. New York: Barefoot.

Jaffe, N., & Zeitlin, S. (1998). *The cow of no color: Riddle stories and justice tales from around the world*. New York: Holt.

Lunge-Larsen, L. (1999). *Troll with no heart in his body and other tales of trolls from Norway*. Boston, MA: Houghton Mifflin.

McKinley, R. (1997). *Rose daughter*. New York: Greenwillow.

San Souci, R. (1995). *The faithful friend*. New York: Simon & Schuster.

Wisniewski, D. (1996). *Golem*. New York: Clarion.

APPENDIX

3

Literary Devices for Narrative Texts

To understand the narrative structure used in fiction, students must acquire a keen sense of the **literary devices** that authors use as they write. All authors use literary devices to describe, compare, and teach. It is the expert use of literary devices that makes some writing truly artistic. In addition to identifying these devices in their readings, a goal of instruction on literary devices is that it is used in student writing as well.

It should be noted that many literary devices are used in informational text as well; however, they are frequently taught first using narrative text structures. A number of common literary devices are described below in alphabetical order. There are, of course, may other literary devices that authors use to weave their stories. Literary devices are common to the English language arts standards. Consult your state standards documents to determine when specific devices should be taught.

Allegory. An allegory is a story that is used to teach something. Usually the stories are long and require analysis to find the allegory or intention. For example, the parables in the Bible and Aesop's fables are allegories.

Alliteration. Alliteration occurs when the author uses the same letter or sound to start each word in a string. For example, *Andrea anxiously awaited arrangement.* Alliteration is used frequently in books for emergent readers in part to foster phonemic awareness.

Allusion. An allusion is a reference to a well-known person, myth, historical event, biblical story, et cetera as in "She's just like Narcissus" or "It's as bad as the sinking of the Titanic."

Flashback. A flashback pauses the action to comment or portray a scene that took place earlier. For example, during a scene in which a person walks through a dark alley, the author pauses to relate a story about another time the character was scared.

Foreshadowing. Foreshadowing is a hint of things to come—usually, but not always, an unpleasant event.

Hyperbole. Hyperbole is an exaggerated comment or line used for effect and not meant to be taken literally. For example, when faced with a long line at the Department of Motor Vehicles, Andrew said, "It will take an eternity to be allowed to drive."

Imagery. Imagery involves language that evokes one or all of the five senses: seeing, hearing, tasting, smelling, touching as in "her lips taste of honey and dew" or "walking through the halls, amid the crashing sound of lockers closing and the smell of yesterday's coffee, I saw the radiant teacher."

Irony and satire. Irony and satire use sophisticated humor in relaying a message, often saying what something is when the opposite or reverse could be true. Authors use irony to say one thing when they mean another. For example, James is looking at the shark bite out of his surfboard and says, "Finally, I've got a short board." Satire focuses more on mockery or wit to attack or ridicule something.

Metaphor. In contrast with similes, metaphors make a direct statement and do not use "like" or "as" to make the comparison. Metaphors simply make a comparison in which one thing is said to be another. For example, "the dog's fur was electric, standing on end in fear."

Personification. When authors give animals, ideas, or actions the qualities of humans, we call it personification. This is common in Disney films as well as with children's authors. Personification is also used for more abstract ideas such as "Hate has you trapped in her arms."

Point of view. Stories are often told from a specific point of view. In first person, the story is told from the perspective of the narrator and we readers cannot know or witness anything the narrator does not tell us. In second person, the narrator speaks directly to the reader, as in "you will likely know by now that Andre is a bad guy." Finally, in third person, the narrator is omniscient (all-knowing) and can convey different perspectives at different times.

Simile.   A simile is a statement in which two things are compared and said to be *like* or *as* another. For example, "Like a rain-filled cloud, Anna cried and cried when she learned of her lost fortune."

Symbolism.   When an object or action that means something more than its literal meaning is used we note the symbolism. For example, when an author introduces a black crow into the text, readers are prepared for death. This compares with the sighting of a white dove, which conveys peace or life to readers.

Tone and mood.   The attitude an author takes toward a subject or character such as hateful, serious, humorous, sarcastic, solemn, or objective. It conveys the tone or mood. The author can use dialogue, settings, or descriptions to set a tone or mood.

The use and understanding of literary devices allows students to understand texts and share conversations with their peers about texts using common terms. Further, as students understand increasingly complex literary devices and read them in texts, they will begin to use these devices in their writing thus making their writing come alive.

Index

Ryan Library, Iona College
New Rochelle, N. Y.